A LIFE OF JUNG

A LIFE OF JUNG

Ronald Hayman

BLOOMSBURY

First published 1999

Copyright © 1999 by Ronald Hayman

Bloomsbury Publishing Plc, 38 Soho Square, W1V 5DF

The moral right of the author has been asserted

A CIP catalogue record for this book is available from the British Library

ISBN 0 7475 4575 8

10 9 8 7 6 5 4 3 2 1

Typeset by Hewer Text Ltd, Edinburgh
Printed in Great Britain by Clays Ltd, St Ives Plc

FOR BERYL

Contents

Acknowledgements

Each time I finish a biography, I feel I've incurred a large overdraft of gratitude to people who have helped me – friends, acquaintances and many who were strangers when I approached them or they approached me. I've been incredulous at the generosity of those who have taken time and trouble to help, and I'm glad to be living in a country where overdrafts are permitted.

My two biggest debts are to Anthony Storr and another expert on Jung – I've promised not to name him – who both read a complete draft of this book and made invaluable comments.

I'm also indebted to the indefatigable Andrew Burniston, who read parts of it, put his knowledge of comparative religion at my disposal and kept surprising me with photocopies of articles I'd otherwise have missed.

In Britain I've received both conversational stimulus and practical help from Wilfred Beaver, Ean Begg, Paul Bishop, Beverley Cohen, Ann Colcord, Michael Fordham, Vera van der Heyde, Steven Karcher, Roger Payne, Catherine Peters, Laurens van der Post, Andrew Samuels, Ann Shearer, Molly Tuby, and Lewis Wolpert. I was grateful to be allowed to use the libraries of the Society for Analytical Psychology and the Analytical Psychology Club.

I've also received substantial help from my publishers, Bloomsbury. David Reynolds did more than edit the book and Ingrid von Essen did more than copy-edit it: both made significant structural contributions, while Helena Drakakis and Walter Scott have been unfailingly cooperative.

In Switzerland I had enjoyable conversations with two of Jung's grandsons, Peter Jung and Ulrich Hoerni, who showed me round the tower at Bollingen, and with Mario Jacoby. I'm grateful to both Rudolf Ritsema and Crista Robinson for being so welcoming and so informative when I visited the Eranos Centre at Moscia, Ascona; to the exceptionally helpful librarians Ella Stillman at the Jung Institute in Küsnacht and Gudrun Seel at the Psychology Club in Zurich. At the Burghölzli, Herr Moessli was kind and helpful, showing me the hospital, the museum and material from the archive. And I'd like to thank Pro Helvetia, the Arts Council of Switzerland, for its generous contribution to the expenses I incurred in Switzerland.

At the Francis Countway Medical Library in Boston, Molly Craig was welcoming and helpful. In New York at the C. G. Jung Center I profited from conversations with Michelle McKee, David Ward and Steven O'Neill, as well as from their help in pointing me towards books, archive material and videos.

Though I have given page references to the English-language editions of Jung's collected works and his letters, the reader will notice that the translation in the passages I quote is different. Sometimes, for the sake of accuracy, I have retranslated Jung's German, sometimes I have revised an existing translation. With *Memories, Dreams, Reflections* I give page references to both the German text and the translation, which is often unfaithful to it.

Chronology

1794 Carl Gustav Jung, paternal grandfather, born (died 1864)
1799 Samuel Preiswerk, maternal grandfather, born (died 1871)
1805 Augusta Faber, maternal grandmother, born (died 1862)
1842 Johann Paul Achilles Jung born
1848 Emilie Preiswerk born

Chapter 2
1873 Paul Jung, their first child, born and dies in infancy
1875
26 Jul Carl Gustav Jung born in Kesswil, by Lake Constance
Dec family moves to Laufen, near Schaffhausen
1879 family moves to Klein-Hüningen
  Paul Jung appointed chaplain to Friedmatt mental hospital
1882
30 Mar Emma Rauschenbach born in Schaffhausen
1884 Gertrud Jung born

Chapter 3
1886 Jung starts at the Gymnasium in Basel
1887 off school for six months after accident
1889 holiday at Entylebuch, near Lucerne
1890 his father prepares him for confirmation

Chapter 4
1895
18 Apr CGJ starts medical studies at Basel University
18 May joins Zofingia fraternity
Jun organises first seances in his home. The medium is his cousin, Helly Preiswerk
autumn his father falls ill and
1896
28 Jan dies
spring the family moves to Binningen

Chapter 5
Nov CGJ gives his first Zofingia lecture
1897
winter elected chairman of Zofingia

1898
winter   course in psychiatry under Professor Wille
1899   stops attending seances
summer   does a second psychiatry course under Professor Wille
Jul   final exam
1900
Jul   takes state exam to graduate from the university
         period of service in the infantry
27 Nov   receives diploma from university

Chapter 6
10 Dec   starts work as assistant doctor at Burghölzli Lunatic Asylum, Zurich
1901
25 Jan   reads paper at meeting about Freud's *On Dreams*
         CGJ's boss, Bleuler, inaugurates research into word association
         CGJ works at thesis 'On the Psychology and Pathology of So-Called
         Occult Phenomena'
spring   starts work with Riklin on word – association tests
summer   during his annual military service, CGJ is commissioned as an officer
         in the medical corps
1902
Jun–Aug works on hysterical woman in prison
17 Jul   awarded doctorate
         thesis published

Chapter 7
         goes to Paris and attends lectures by Pierre Janet
         new involvement with Helly and with a Jewish girl
1903
Jan   first visit to London
14 Feb   marries Emma Rauschenbach
1904   becomes senior doctor (clinical director) at Burghölzli

Chapter 8
17 Aug   Sabina Spielrein arrives at the Burghölzli as a patient
Dec   CGJ completes his analysis of her
26 Dec   his first child, Agathe, born
1905   publishes 'The Reaction-Time Ratio in the Association
         Experiment' as *Habilitationsschrift* (to qualify as an unpaid lecturer in
         psychiatry at Zurich University)
Apr   appointed senior doctor at the Burghölzli
1 Jun   Sabina Spielrein discharged
Jun   CGJ appointed director of new outpatient clinic
21 Oct   inaugural lecture at Zurich University

Chapter 9
1906   CGJ's sister Trudi arrives at the Burghölzli, where she
         works as a nurse till 1908

1 Apr	Freud writes to thank him for sending a copy of *Diagnostic Association Studies*
27 May	defends Freud against attack by Gustav Aschaffenburg at conference in Baden-Baden
2 Jun	second daughter, Gret, born
summer	completes *On the Psychology of Dementia Praecox*
23 Oct	CGJ writes to Freud about Sabina Spielrein
1907	
Jan–Feb	Ludwig Binswanger uses CGJ as subject in association test
2 Mar	CGJ and Emma visit Freud in Vienna with Binswanger
summer	CGJ takes Emma to Geneva and Paris, where he visits Pierre Janet
Sep	delivers paper on hysteria to conference in Amsterdam and speaks about Freud
Oct	CGJ writes to Freud about an early homosexual experience

Chapter 10

Dec	*The Psychology of Dementia Praecox* published
1908	Trudi starts doing secretarial work for her brother
late Jan	bout of influenza from which he is slow to recover
early Apr	convalescent holiday on the Lago Maggiore
27 Apr	congress of International Psychoanalytic Association in Salzburg Decision taken to publish a yearbook with CGJ as editor
6 May	Freud commits Otto Gross to confinement in the Burghölzli
17 Jun	Gross escapes
Jun	CGJ begins intimate relationship with Sabina
Aug	she leaves for Russia
1–15 Sep	CGJ on holiday
17–22 Sep	Freud stays in CGJ's flat
Oct	military service; Sabina returns to Zurich for autumn term
1 Dec	Franz born
1909	Trudi moves in with their mother in Küsnacht
mid-Jan	Sabina's mother receives anonymous letter about relationship CGJ gives notice but agrees to go on working till March
late Feb	first half volume of yearbook *Jahrbuch für psychoanalytische und psychopathologische Forschung* published
26 Feb	Sabina attacks CGJ
7 Mar	he leaves his job at the Burghölzli
25–30 Mar	CGJ and Emma see Freud in Vienna
early Apr	CGJ and Emma in Italy on a cycling holiday

Chapter 11

25 May	he moves into the Küsnacht house without Emma and the children
30 May	Sabina starts writing to Freud
12 Jun	Emma and children move in
late Jul	CGJ in Munich. Visits Kraepelin's clinic
20 Aug	CGJ meets Freud and Ferenczi in Bremen
21–29 Aug	they sail to New York
7–11 Sep	they lecture at Clark University, Massachusetts

11 Sep   CGJ and Freud receive honorary doctorates
21–29 Sep   they sail back to Bremen

Chapter 12
Oct   CGJ's voracious reading of mythology begins
Nov   he and Freud plan review section in yearbook
Dec   Freud is obsessed with the idea of a nuclear complex in neurosis
1910
Jan   affair with Maria Moltzer begins; CGJ psychoanalyses Emma
12 Jan–16 Feb   six public lectures in Zurich on mental disturbances in children
9 Mar   CGJ sails for the US to see Medill McCormick, and returns for
30–31 Mar   International Psychoanalytic Association holds its second congress in
            Nuremberg. CGJ appointed as president for two years
Apr   arrival of Antonia Wolff as patient at Burghölzli
16 May   CGJ lectures on symbolism at Herisau
from 24 Jul at least two weeks boating holiday on Lake Constance

Chapter 13
late Aug   two weeks of military service
early Sep   visit to London for a consultation
Sep   Sabina returns to Zurich and he helps with her dissertation
27 Sep   fourth child, Marianne, born
Oct   CGJ goes to Italy with Dr Wolf Stockmayer but
16 Oct   returns to Zurich before he had planned to
early Nov   CGJ resumes affair with Sabina

Chapter 14
25–26 Dec   Freud meets Bleuler and then CGJ in Munich
1911
16–19 Jan   Sabina takes her finals, and
11 Feb   leaves for Munich
mid-Feb   CGJ sends off Part One of *Transformations and Symbols of the Libido* to
            the printer
28 Mar   Honegger kills himself
mid-Aug   Part One of *Transformations and Symbols* published in yearbook
16–20 Sep   Freud in Küsnacht
21–22 Sep   International Psychoanalytic Association holds its third congress in
            Weimar
            Emma starts writing to Freud

Chapter 15
1912
winter   Sabina marries Dr Paul Scheftel
Feb   CGJ finishes final chapter in *Transformations and Symbols*
Apr   holiday in Italy
mid-Apr   Sabina sees Freud, who will start analysing her in the autumn
late May   Freud visits Binswanger in Kreuzlingen without seeing CGJ
summer   CGJ writes nine lectures to deliver in the USA

Sep–Oct	CGJ lectures at Fordham University, New York; spends three days in St Elizabeth's Hospital, Washington, DC; lectures in Baltimore, New York and Chicago, where he meets Edith Rockefeller McCormick
22 Nov	lectures in Zurich on 'The Psychology of the Negro'
24 Nov	conference in Munich; Freud has fainting fit
late Dec	*Transformations and Symbols* published

Chapter 16

1913

3 Jan	Freud breaks off their correspondence
Mar	CGJ sails to the USA to see Edith Rockefeller
Apr	returns to Zurich with her and her son Fowler
Aug	goes to London and lectures at international medical conference
7–8 Sep	International Psychoanalytic Association holds its fourth congress in Munich
Oct	CGJ has vision of catastrophe on train to Schaffhausen

Chapter 17

29 Oct	resigns as editor of the yearbook
Nov–Dec	apocalyptic dreams and visions
12 Dec	turning point in breakdown – feeling of letting himself fall

Chapter 18

1914

14 Mar	fifth child, Helene, born
Apr	resigns as university lecturer
20 Apr	resigns as president of International Psychoanalytic Association
Apr–Jul	recurrent dream about spread of ice wave over Europe
mid-Jul	yearbook published, containing Freud's attack on CGJ
end of Jul	CGJ lectures in Aberdeen
3 Aug	Germany declares war on France
end of Aug	CGJ returns to Zurich

1915

summer	holiday with Emma, Toni and Harold McCormick

1916

26 Feb	inaugural meeting of Psychological Club
16 Apr	CGJ invites Maeder, Riklin, Toni, Maria Moltzer, Herbert Oczeret and Dr C. Schneiter to attend regular fortnightly meetings
13 May	these meetings begin
summer	CGJ writes *Septem Sermones ad Mortuos*

Chapter 19

summer	meets Hermann Hesse
autumn	Psychological Club holds first banquet in new building CGJ writes 'The Transcendent Function' and 'The Structure of the Unconscious'
Oct	writes 'Adaptation, Individuation, Collectivity'
1917	appointed commandant of a camp for British internees at Château d'Oex

Chapter 20
1918
11 Nov   armistice ends war
1919   works on *Psychological Types*
late Jun   leaves for England
4 Jul   reads a paper to the Society for Psychical Research on 'Psychological Foundations of Belief in Spirits'
11 or 12 Jul   addresses the Royal Society of Medicine 'On the Problem of Psychogenesis in Mental Disease'
Jul   reads paper on 'Instinct and the Unconscious' at Bedford College

Chapter 21
1920
15 Mar   leaves with Hermann Sigg on trip to North Africa
Apr   they return to Zurich
summer   visits England and conducts a seminar at Sennen Cove, Cornwall
1921   *Psychological Types* published
Jan   Hermann Hesse arrives in Zurich and starts analysis with CGJ
May or Jun   Hesse breaks off analysis
1922   CGJ meets Richard Wilhelm at Darmstadt School of Wisdom
May   lectures 'On the Relation of Analytical Psychology to Poetry'
Sep   CGJ, Emma and Toni Wolff resign from the Psychological Club

Chapter 22
1923
Feb   death of CGJ's mother
    he begins building the tower at Bollingen
Jul   seminar on 'The Technique of Analysis' at Polzeath, Cornwall
1924
spring   the tower is completed

Chapter 23
Dec   CGJ sails for New York from Bremen
24 Dec   With Fowler McCormick and George Porter, he leaves for Chicago
1925   Martha Boddinghaus marries Hermann Sigg, who dies later in the year
    Trudi Jung stops doing secretarial work for her brother, and Emma takes over some of the work.
1 Jan   CGJ, Fowler McCormick and Porter visit the Grand Canyon
5 Jan   they arrive in Taos
9 Jan   they visit New Orleans and Washington
24 Feb   Medill McCormick kills himself
Mar   Harry Murray arrives in Zurich
23 Mar–6 Jul   CGJ gives seminars in English on analytical psychology
Apr   lives in the tower for three weeks preparing new edition of 'On the Psychology of the Unconscious'
10–13 May   gives three lectures in London for the New Education Fellowship
June   seances with Bleuler, Schrenck-Notzing and Rudi Schneider

late July to
7 Aug   seminar in Swanage on dreams and symbolism
Aug   CGJ meets H. G. Wells; visits exhibition at Wembley
Sep   starts analysing Christiana Morgan
15 Oct   leaves for Africa with Peter Baynes and George Beckwith
12 Nov   they arrive in Mombasa

Chapter 24
1926
winter   the American designer Robert Edmond Jones arrives in Zurich
Apr   CGJ returns to Zurich
June   Christiana Morgan and her husband arrive in Küsnacht
1927
24 Feb   George Porter shoots himself, leaving $20,000 to CGJ

Chapter 25
1928   CGJ starts studying alchemy
22 Feb   lectures to Kulturbund in Vienna
20–22 Apr   General Medical Society for Psychotherapy holds congress in
             Baden-Baden
Oct   Conference of the Association for Intellectual Collaboration in
             Prague
7 Nov   CGJ resumes seminars in English at the Psychological Club, starting a
             series on dream analysis
1929
Jan   Barbara Hannah arrives in Zurich
12 Apr   General Medical Society for Psychotherapy holds congress in Bad
             Nauheim
             CGJ writes commentary on *The Secret of the Golden Flower*
June   lectures on Paracelsus in the house where he was born – at
             Einsiedeln
1930   Appointed vice president of the General Medical Society for
             Psychotherapy

Chapter 26
Feb   club's carnival ball
25 Jun   final seminar on dream analysis
Jul   meets Horace Walpole
Oct   gives seminar in German on Christiana's visions
30 Oct   starts series of seminars in English on Christiana's visions at the club

Chapter 27
1931   Marianne starts doing secretarial work for her father
31 Apr   International Medical Congress for Psychotherapy in Dresden
1932
Apr   Marie-Jeanne Schmid become CGJ's secretary
3–8 Oct   the Indologist J. W. Hauer gives seminars on Kundalini yoga
12 Oct – 2 Nov   CGJ gives seminars on Kundalini yoga

1933

Feb lectures in Cologne and Essen on 'The Meaning of Psychology for Modern Man'

Mar holiday in Egypt and Palestine

6 Apr Ernst Kretschmer resigns as president of General Medical Society for psychotherapy. CGJ reorganises it as the International General Medical Society for Psychotherapy, and is elected its president

10–13 May its statutes are ratified during its congress at Bad Nauheim

26 Jun interview on Berlin radio; first of five seminars on dreams

Aug CGJ speaks on individuation at Eranos Conference

15 Sep German branch of the society founded with Matthias Göring as president

7–8 Oct Swiss Academy of Medical Science meeting at Prangins

20 Oct CGJ starts lecturing on Modern Psychology at the Federal Polytechnic

Oct or Nov meets Wolfgang Pauli

Chapter 28

1934

27 Feb Dr G. Bally attacks CGJ in the *Neue Zürcher Zeitung*

13 and 14 Mar CGJ replies in the *Neue Zürcher Zeitung*

21 Mar last seminar on Christiana's visions

2 May starts a new series of seminars on Nietzsche's *Zarathustra*

10–13 May presides at congress of the International General Medical Society for Psychotherapy in Bad Nauheim

Aug Eranos lecture on the archetypes

Sep James Joyce asks CGJ to treat his daughter Lucrezia

Chapter 29

1935 CGJ becomes titular professor at the Federal Polytechnic, Zurich

27–30 Mar presides at congress of the International General Medical Society for Psychotherapy in Bad Nauheim

12 Jul completes his course on Modern Psychology at the Polytechnic

Aug Eranos lecture on 'Dream Symbols in the Individuation Process'

30 Sep to 4 Oct five Tavistock lectures in London

Chapter 30

1936

Mar publishes article on 'Wotan' in the *Neue Schweizer Rundschau*

Aug Eranos lecture on alchemy

Sep participates in Harvard's Tercentenary Conference

winter starts a series of seminars on children's dreams at the Polytechnic

1937

1–7 Jan speaks at a conference on spiritual leadership in Königsfeld

spring completes his series of seminars at the Polytechnic

28 May Psychotherapy Conference in Bern

Aug Eranos lecture on 'The Visions of Zosimos'

2–4 Oct   congress of the International General Medical Society in Copenhagen
Oct   gives Terry Lectures at Yale on 'Psychology and Religion'
Dec   leaves for India with Fowler McCormick

Chapter 31
Mar   German troops march into Austria
May   CGJ founds Teaching Institute for Psychotherapy at Zurich University
29 Jul - 2 Aug   chairs congress of International General Medical Society in Oxford and receives honorary degree (DSc) from university
Aug   Eranos lecture on the mother archetype
28 Oct   starts lecturing on Eastern texts at the Polytechnic
1939
15 Feb   gives last seminar on Nietzsche
4 Apr   lecture in London for Royal Society of Medicine
5 Apr   lecture on 'The Symbolic Life' to the Guild of Pastoral Psychology
Jun   gives his last lecture on Eastern texts at the Polytechnic and starts lecturing on Loyola's spiritual exercises
Jul   CGJ offers to resign as president of the International General Medical Society. Stays on, but appoints Göring as co-editor of *Zentralblatt*
Aug   Eranos lecture on rebirth; CGJ meets Paul and Mary Mellon
3 Sep   war declared
23 Sep   Freud dies; CGJ writes obituary

Chapter 32
1940
8 Mar   gives his last lecture on Loyola at the Polytechnic
Apr   holiday in Ascona with the Mellons
spring   moves into a boarding house in Saanen, near Gstaad
June   France surrenders; CGJ returns to Küsnacht
summer   resigns as president of International General Medical Society
Aug   Eranos lecture on the Trinity
8 Nov   starts lecturing on alchemy at the Polytechnic
1941
17 May   lectures at the club on the symbolism of the Mass
11 Jul   CGJ gives his last lecture at the Polytechnic
19 Jul   fourth annual meeting of Swiss Academy of Medical Science's Psychotherapy Committee
Aug   CGJ retires from the Polytechnic
gives Eranos lecture on 'Transformation Symbolism in the Mass'
7 Sep and 5 Oct   lectures at Basel and Einsiedeln on Paracelsus
7 Dec   Japanese attack on Pearl Harbor provokes USA into joining war
1942
Aug   CGJ gives two Eranos lectures on 'The Spirit Mercurius'; retires

from lecturing at the Polytechnic, but accepts a chair in Medical Psychology at Basel University

26 Sep   Psychology Conference in Zurich

1943

Nov   Herbert Read visits him to discuss translation of collected works

Chapter 33

1944

11 Feb   CGJ breaks his fibula by falling

21 Feb   suffers a heart attack

Jul   discharged from hospital

Dec   quota imposed on number of Jewish members in club

1945

Apr   doctors say CGJ is fit to resume work

7 May   Germany surrenders

late Jul or
early Aug   correspondence with Father Victor White begins

6 and 9 Aug   two atomic bombs dropped on Japan

Aug   CGJ gives Eranos lecture on 'The Psychology of the Spirit'

Chapter 34

1946   CGJ publishes *Essays on Contemporary Events*

20 March   contract signed by Kegan Paul and Bollingen Press for co-publication of collected works

Aug   CGJ gives Eranos lecture on 'The Spirit of Psychology'

25 Aug   signs the contract at Eranos

Nov   CGJ has another heart attack

1948

24 Apr   C. G. Jung Institute opened

Aug   CGJ gives Eranos lecture 'On the Self'

early Sep   Victor White stays at Bollingen

1949

Feb   Ezra Pound awarded Bollingen Foundation's first poetry prize

Chapter 35

Oct   Emma hospitalised after fracturing her shoulder in a fall

1950

Nov   Pope promulgates dogma about Virgin's bodily ascension

1951

spring   CGJ writes *Answer to Job* while suffering from liver trouble
Victor White stays at Bollingen

Chapter 36

Aug   Eranos lecture 'On synchronicity'

1952

May   CGJ replies in *Merkur* to criticism from Martin Buber

July   Victor White stays in Bollingen

Sep   Una Thomas takes over as CGJ's secretary

1953

19 Mar   Toni Wolff dies

Jun   *Psychology and Alchemy* published as the first volume of CGJ's *Collected Works*

1954

autumn   Victor White sent to California

1955

April   Victor White's review of *Answer to Job* appears in *Blackfriars*

May   CGJ breaks off their correspondence for four years

autumn   Aniela Jaffé takes over as CGJ's secretary

27 Nov   Emma dies

Chapter 37

1957   final additions to the tower

Aniela Jaffé works with him on *Memories, Dreams, Reflections*

1958   CGJ writes on flying saucers

Apr   completes work on the first three chapters of *Memories, Dreams, Reflections*

1959

Jan   Starts writing 'Late Thoughts', a new final chapter

Chapter 38

Oct   interviewed by John Freeman on BBC television

1960

May   Victor White dies

Sep   CGJ taken ill while on motoring trip with Fowler McCormick and Ruth Bailey

1961

spring   stays at Bollingen

6 Jun   dies

Part One

Glimpses of God

One

Bursting Out

'This man is as natural as any peasant, and yet he has also the most remarkable mind I have ever met.' In descriptions of Jung, the words *peasant* and *natural* keep recurring. 'The first impression was one of great reassurance,' testified an analyst, 'because he seemed so completely natural, and he had a kind of peasant-like instinct with a highly cultivated mind. He was always marvelous at getting people to be very much themselves.' The same analyst, Joseph Henderson, called him 'a sort of humanist in the old Renaissance style . . . the most deeply rooted man I ever met'.

He seemed to be fully in touch with his own identity. Una Thomas, his secretary in the early fifties, said: 'He was always himself – quite the hardest thing anyone can be . . . He lived himself more than anyone I could imagine.' Relishing his talent for being himself, he displayed both the self and the relish. Instead of disappearing, as Freud did by putting patients on a couch and sitting behind them, Jung enjoyed confrontation. When lecturing he 'constantly took off his glasses and then put them on again; he sought eye contact with his audience and found it indispensable.'

The combination of charisma, simplicity and directness empowered him to create a sense of contact in face-to-face encounters, lectures and even television programmes. At the age of eighty-four, he appeared in the BBC series *Face to Face*. Throughout the interview (which survives on video) Jung is animated, forceful, friendly. The eyes twinkle over gold-rimmed glasses, the voice is reassuring, the accent charming, the smile engaging. He is affable, authoritative, relaxed. His informality and spontaneity make him look like a paragon of honesty and openness. A cleaner who had never heard of him asked Laurens van der Post: 'Did you see that wonderful show on television last night?'

Henderson has described his behaviour with patients:

During most interviews he paced back and forth, gesturing as he talked, and he talked of everything that came to his mind, whether about a human problem, a dream, a personal reminiscence, an allegorical story or a joke. Yet he could become quiet, serious and extremely personal, sitting down almost too close for comfort and delivering a pointed interpretation of one's miserable personal problem so its bitter truth would really sink in.

In lectures, as in conversations, he was, as one of his patients noticed,

particularly adept at presenting his ideas in such a way that they would not be rejected out-of-hand by people representing other disciplines. I heard him present his basic theory about the collective unconscious in two different ways to two different groups. The first was that this area of the unconscious represented an anatomical construct which produced images and symbols as the thyroid produces thyroxin or the kidneys, urine . . . The other explanation postulates that there is indeed a vast area 'out there' and that these symbols exist somehow outside the individual, and happen to him.

Jung thought of the collective unconscious as a force that could intervene correctively in private relationships and public affairs. 'It doesn't matter to me in the slightest whether God and the unconscious are ultimately identical or not.' What the religious man calls God, he said, is what the scientific intellect calls the collective unconscious. For him, the terms *collective unconscious* and *psyche* were interchangeable: since it is 'antecedent to man and is a *sine qua non* of his psychic life, I allow myself to call this "psyche" (or whatever it may be) "divine" in contradistinction to "human" '. In a 1945 letter to a priest, he said: 'Man's vital energy or libido is the divine pneuma all right, and it was this conviction which it was my secret purpose to bring into the vicinity of my colleagues' understanding.' But when addressing scientists, 'you cannot start with a religious creed . . . If I were talking to peasants I certainly would talk about God, since I know that they know of what I am talking.'

He often made statements like these in letters to friends and clergymen, but in work for publication he was more cautious. Wanting to be regarded as a scientist, he hated to be called a 'mystic'. He insisted he was an empiricist, concerned only with facts that could be checked. 'What matters to me is what can be verified by experience . . . Anything I cannot demonstrate in the realm of human experience I let alone, and if someone should assert that he knows more about it, I ask him to furnish me with the necessary proofs.' He never tired of reiterating this in lectures, essays, books and letters. In 1933 he claimed to be 'utterly incapable of coming up with a mixture of theology and science'.

'About God himself,' he wrote on 8 February 1941, 'I have asserted nothing because according to my premise nothing whatever can be asserted about God himself. All such assertions refer to the psychology of the God-image.' And writing to Victor White in October 1945, he insisted: 'I have nothing to say about the nature of God.' But in a letter of September 1944, he wrote: 'As a Christian, of course, I take my stand on the Christian truth.'

Hanging on the wall behind his desk was a photograph covered with a cloth he kept permanently drawn, like a curtain. The photograph was of the Turin Shroud. The imprint of Christ's face had been left on the shroud, according to Catholic tradition, after Joseph of Arimathea had wrapped his body in it. The features gave Jung the impression of an extraordinarily powerful personality. 'Its stern and august countenance has confirmed my formerly vague expectations.'

Was Jung trying to keep his psychological work separate from his religious beliefs? One way to answer this question is to make another attempt at telling the story of his life. Since he died in 1961, a great many attempts have been made, but it is hard to take the proper measure of Jung. What he said of Paracelsus could be said of him: 'We cannot possibly be fair to him: since we can only underestimate or overestimate him, we remain permanently dissatisfied with our efforts to understand even one aspect of his multitudinous nature.' As Henderson said, Jung could 'never be put in a frame . . . He always burst out of it, destroying the frame at the same time.'

Two

A Cannibal Jesus

A child of the nineteenth century, Jung grew up in rural Switzerland, where Christianity and superstition were intertwined. At the Franciscan monastery in Rapperswil, a village close to Lake Zurich, one of the monks had a reputation for curing sick animals. The neighbourhood was predominantly Protestant, but it was said that parsons no longer had any magic, and when cows yielded little milk, farmers wrote down the names of the 'bewitched' animals and went with a five-franc piece to the monastery, or to the witch doctor in the hills.

He was a peasant who could produce testimonials and letters of appreciation from grateful patients. His most prized possession was a book he had been given by a monk – a book of spells for making magic in the name of such pagan gods as Venus and Baldur. He had a reputation for curing animals and 'calming' humans by driving the devil out. He was said to have captured six hundred devils and imprisoned them in an old quarry with a magic circle around it. Monks at the nearby monastery of Einsiedeln had given him an ancient book on black magic and incantations about witches.

In the 1950s, according to Jung, magic and medicine men had followers in all the Swiss villages, and archaic customs were preserved. In the Lotschental, a valley in the Bernese Alps, 'things you read about in Paracelsus still exist,' he said in 1942. 'I've met sorcerers, spell-casters. Did you know that there are some places in Bern or St Gall where they make pacts with the devil and sign them with blood?'

As a child, he had no doubt his mother was in touch with spirits. She mumbled 'as if talking to herself, though what she said was meant for me and it usually went straight to the centre of my being, so that I was usually lost for words'. It was she who taught him the prayer he had to recite before she kissed him good night. In it he asked Lord Jesus to spread out his wings and *einnehmen* the *Küchlein* Satan wanted to devour. In Swiss German both words have a double meaning – *einnehmen* can mean take possession of or eat, while *Küchlein* can mean little chicken or little cake. She had unintentionally taught Carl to believe in a cannibal Jesus.

Paul Achilles Jung was a parson in the Swiss Reformed Church. At Göttingen University he had studied Oriental languages and written a dissertation on the Arabic version of the Song of Songs. Scholarly and sensitive, this commentary shows he was more sophisticated than his son makes him out to be. *Memories, Dreams, Reflections* depicts him as a well-meaning but ineffectual man who tried to perpetuate the glory he had achieved at university by preserving such undergraduate habits as smoking a long pipe. The dissertation was submitted to the university for a doctorate in philosophy, and, as Joel Ryce-Menuhin has written, it shows him to be 'a true monotheist with a much broader range of comprehension of the sources of Semitic religions than Jungians have realised. I believe this atmosphere, in the household of a Swiss Protestant minister, would have been unique in the Switzerland in which C. G. Jung grew up.' The family lived in a series of country parsonages. Paul Jung was thirty-one and his wife Emilie twenty-five when she gave birth to a baby in August 1873. Named Paul, he lived only a few days, and nearly two years passed before Carl Gustav was born on 26 July 1875 at Kesswil, a village on the shores of Lake Constance.

The parish there had been given to the parson after he completed his theological studies, and, since clergymen are cantonal officials, his duties included keeping records and statistics. He may have felt frustrated and depressed by a working routine that gave him little opportunity to flex his intellectual muscles or fulfil his creative potential. Carl was less than five months old when they moved to Laufen, near Schaffhausen, where they stayed for four years.

Paul Jung took charge of the impressive church, which is still there. Laufen is by the Rhine Falls, the most powerful waterfall in Europe. The river plunges from a height of seventy feet, and the flow averages 25,000 cubic feet a second. To Carl, the roar of water was threatening. The river is five hundred feet wide here, and when crossing the bridge to the neighbouring village, Neuhausen, he learned to be careful. Once he slipped and almost fell through the railings, but the maid caught him. He never forgot the vicarage, which stood by itself, not far from the castle (which is now a restaurant), and never forgot the garden, the laundry house, the church, the low brick house belonging to the sexton, or the cemetery.

Though the village was small, it seemed to him that funerals were frequent. Digging a deep hole, the sexton heaped up earth on both sides, ready for the long black-draped box escorted by grim-faced mourners in black clothes, tall hats and shiny boots. The parson's voice rang out as the

box was ceremoniously buried. What was going on? Carl was told 'that
"Lord Jesus" sometimes "took people to himself", and this was the same as
burying them in the ground'.

The death of baby Paul left its mark on the way Carl's parents treated him.
A mother who loses her first baby is anxious about the second, and so is the
father. The anxiety may decrease if they have a third baby who survives, but
for nine years, Carl was an only child.

Eight of his uncles were parsons – two of his father's brothers and six of his
mother's. Dressed in black frock coats and shiny boots, they looked as if their
duty was to patrol the frontier between life and death.

Picking up scraps of knowledge from overheard theological discussions,
Carl often failed to make sense of them. The name *Jesus* was like the name
Jesuit. Jesuits were banned from Switzerland. Why? Perhaps they were
dangerous. Jesus was not banned, though he was obviously dangerous. One
hot day, when Carl was three, he was alone in front of the vicarage, playing
in the sand. Coming down the road that led to the wood on the hilltop was a
man in a broad hat and a long black dress that reached to his feet. Perhaps he
was a Jesuit disguised as a woman. Carl hid in the attic, and for several days
he was too scared to go out of doors.

He often had nightmares. In one, birds were sitting on telegraph wires
that grew fatter. He never forgot a night when he was 'restless, feverish,
sleepless. My father picks me up in his arms, walks up and down the room
singing his old student songs. I remember one I specially liked, which always
comforted me . . . Today I still remember my father's voice singing for me
in the silence of the night.'

Comfort was often needed and often unavailable. His parents were
sleeping in separate rooms, and, overpowered by an atmosphere that seemed
to be growing thicker, he could not distinguish between reality and illusion.

> Frightening influences came from the door of Mother's room. At night
> Mother was uncanny and mysterious. One night I saw a rather luminous,
> indefinite figure stepping from her door, and its head came off its neck and
> floated in front of it in the air like a little moon. A new head appeared
> immediately, but it came off too. This process was repeated six or seven
> times.

Some of Paul Jung's parishioners liked him much better than his wife. One
woman said he was kind-hearted, quiet, unassuming, good at preaching to
peasants, generally liked and respected, while his wife was fat, ugly, bossy
and haughty. According to other sources, his colleagues found him boring,
while a friend of Jung's remembered his mother as wise and courageous.

Almost uneducated, she was stronger and more dynamic than her husband, but permanently in conflict with herself.

Like her son, she was the victim of an oppressive childhood. She had been brought up to believe the living were surrounded by the spirits of the dead. Her father was Samuel Preiswerk, *Antistes* of Basel. To explain the word *Antistes* Jung later told patients: 'You would have called him the Bishop of Basel,' and added: 'From everything I heard of him, his Old Testament name Samuel must have suited him very well.' Assuming Hebrew to be the language spoken in heaven, Samuel Preiswerk devoted his life to studying it.

After his first wife died, he kept a chair for her in his study, where she was said to visit him every week. This upset his second wife, Augusta – Jung's grandmother – but did not make her question his sanity. Superstition and madness often overlap: many obsessional ideas are like improvised super-stitions. From the age of twenty, she had believed herself to be in touch with the spirit world. The turning point had been a mental crisis. After she had been comatose for thirty-six hours, a red-hot poker was applied like a branding iron to her head, and she came to, babbling prophetically. The pattern continued throughout her life: she went into trances and brought back what seemed to be information from the dead.

The Preiswerk family had a predilection for the paranormal. Four of Jung's uncles were said to have second sight, and Jung later described his Old Testament grandfather as 'very intelligent, a clergyman who often had waking hallucinations (mostly visions, often whole dramatic sequences with dialogue)'.

Though Carl never met his grandfather, the dead were never entirely absent from the world he grew up in. During his mother's childhood, when she sat by her father to stop ghosts from passing behind his back while he worked on his sermons, she could have no doubt about their reality. Would she be sitting there if they never disturbed him? And Carl, each time he visited a spinster aunt, thought he could see Samuel Preiswerk move. Hanging on her wall was a picture of the *Antistes* wearing full regalia and standing on the terrace of his house. At the bottom of the steps that led down from it was a footpath to the cathedral, and, kneeling on a chair to look at the picture, Carl never believed his aunt when she said: 'But my dear, he's not walking, he's still standing there.'

According to the Community Register in Basel, the baby born in July 1875 was given the names Karl Gustav, but he soon took to spelling his first name Carl, after his paternal grandfather, Carl Gustav Jung, who was rumoured to be an illegitimate son of Goethe. Though he sometimes claimed to be embarrassed by this rumour – for which there turned out to be no foundation – he took it seriously and, as a student, boasted about being Goethe's great-grandson.

Son of a German physician, the first Carl Gustav Jung had studied natural sciences and medicine in Heidelberg, where he kept a pig and amused the citizens by treating it like a dog, even taking it out for walks. By the age of twenty-four he was lecturing on chemistry in the Royal Prussian School of War in Berlin, and working at a hospital as surgical assistant to an ophthalmologist. After emigrating to France, he met Alexander von Humboldt, the naturalist and geographer, whose recommendation secured him the job of reorganising the medical faculty at the university in Basel. Settling there, he became one of the city's foremost personalities. He was appointed rector of the university, where he tried to inaugurate a chair of psychiatry. He was also Grand Master of the Swiss Freemasons. Married twice, he had as many children as Samuel Preiswerk – thirteen.

Carl was only four when his father was transferred to Klein-Hüningen, a parish on the shores of the Rhine, close to Basel. Since 1908, when it was incorporated into the city's canton, Klein-Hüningen has been an industrialised suburb, but in 1879 it was a patriarchal village populated with peasants and surrounded by woods, fields and rivulets. The family lived in a big presbytery, complete with stables and a garden. It had belonged to a patrician family, but the Jungs could not afford a patrician lifestyle. There was a mental hospital in Klein-Hüningen, the Friedmatt, and, alongside his parochial duties, the parson worked there as chaplain.

Books played a major role in Jung's life, even before he could read. His first contact with them was through his mother. He loved the *Orbis Pictus*, an illustrated children's book about Hinduism and other religions. He was fascinated by pictures of Brahma, Vishnu and Shiva. But though his mother exerted the strongest influence on his childhood, most of the references to her in *Memories, Dreams, Reflections* are negative. He loved her 'animal warmth' and the food she gave him, but he does not appear to have remembered moments of close physical contact. Having lost her first baby, she may have felt so overanxious when handling her second that she failed to make him feel relaxed in her arms.

When she had to spend a few months in the mental ward of a Basel hospital, a young maid looked after him, and this girl made an indelible physical impression. 'I still know how she picked me up, and I lay my head on her shoulder. She had black hair and an olive complexion and was quite different from my mother. I remember the hairline, the throat with the strongly pigmented skin and the ear.'

The memory of being picked up by his father seems to date from the same period in 1878 when his mother was absent. Carl, who was two or three, suffered from general eczema, which persisted for a long time. It may have been due partly to emotional stress, and in retrospect he blamed it on a temporary separation between his parents. He later diagnosed his mother's illness as neurotic hysteria. As a child he attributed it to disappointment that her husband had never fulfilled the promise he had shown as a student. In a sentence that was cut from *Memories, Dreams, Reflections*, Jung said she did not recover her health till after his death.

Jung never forgave her for her absence. 'From that time onwards, I was always distrustful immediately the word *love* was mentioned. For a long time, the feeling I associated with women was natural unreliability. *Father* I associated with reliability and – powerlessness. That is the handicap I started with.' His mother later said he had been a melancholy child, and while this disposition could have developed when he was two or three, it would not have persisted without being fomented by subsequent experiences. He may have been projecting other memories backwards when he blamed her absence for his difficulties both with the word *love* and with the emotion.

Having been thrown back so painfully on his own resources, he found it safer to confine himself to them voluntarily. This affected his relationships with other children. When he was five, a boy of the same age was brought to play with him in the parsonage. 'But there was nothing to be done. Carl was sitting in the middle of the room, playing with a little bowling game, and he did not pay the slightest attention to me . . . I had never seen such an anti-social monster.'

Though written fifty-five years after the event, this confirms Jung's memories. 'I played alone, and in my own way. Unfortunately I cannot remember what I did, only that I did not want to be disturbed. I was profoundly immersed in my games, and could not bear to be observed or criticised.' Without being observed, a child stands little chance of integrating what seem like separate bits of his own existence.

Jung says he was only three or four when he had a dream that was to preoccupy him throughout his life.

In a meadow he found a dark, rectangular, stone-lined hole containing a stone stairway. Further down, a round doorway was masked by a heavy green curtain. Behind it was a small square chamber with an arched ceiling. On the flagstoned floor, a red carpet led to a golden throne on a platform. From the throne to the ceiling stretched something like a tree trunk. Made of bare skin and flesh, it had a rounded head with no face, no hair, and an immobile central eye. At any moment the thing might start crawling towards him. 'Yes, take a good look at him,' said his mother's voice. 'That's the man-eater.' The word he says she used – *Menschenfresser* – would also have been the word for an ogre in a fairy tale, but in the mouth of his mother, the word would have suggested Jesus.

Jung gives its dimensions as twelve to fifteen feet in height and between eighteen inches and two feet in thickness, but the measurements are more likely to derive from reconstruction than from the dream of such a young child. When reporting on dreams, he usually fails to differentiate between the original experience and the accretion of detail that is inevitable when dreams are remembered and reconstructed.

It was not until much later, he says, that he identified the fleshy thing on the throne as a phallus, and later still as a *ritual* phallus. He also suggests it may have been 'a subterranean god'. At the age of three or four he knew nothing about phallic rituals or underground gods, but when he was interpreting dreams, he assumed that images could pop up from anywhere in the collective unconscious, and he used the word *amplification* for his technique of interpreting. By mentioning whatever comes into his mind, the interpreter tries to make connections with 'universal imagery', and when writing about himself, Jung often projects mature ideas backwards into childhood, moving away from the original experience, while depersonalising and mythifying personal or sexual material. If Freud was overeager to explain religious feelings in terms of sexuality, Jung was overeager to translate sexuality into religion.

Though his mother had been a character in the dream, he did not tell her about it. She would have assigned it to the world she dismissed so contemptuously when she spoke about 'heathens'. Nor did he discuss it with anyone else. He portrays himself as taking great pride from childhood onwards in secretiveness:

> In the same way that the member of a secret society is bound by oath to follow a different route from that of the undifferentiated collectivity, the individual on his lonely path also needs a secret which for one reason or another he is not allowed or not able to share . . . The need for a secret of this kind is in many cases so great that it leads to thoughts and actions for which the individual can no longer accept responsibility. What often lies behind it is neither wilfullness nor arrogance but a dire necessity which is inexplicable to the individual himself.

Reluctance to talk about shameful dreams may soon have been conflated with the difficulty of talking about masturbation. In a nineteenth-century Swiss parsonage, parents would have been intolerant towards a boy's natural curiosity about his own body. Jung may have repressed memories of threats about how he would be punished – during this life and the next – if he masturbated. Later, discussing the lovelife of students, he refers to female but never to male masturbation, and he says nothing in *Memories, Dreams, Reflections* about his sexual secrets, though it is hard to believe these contributed nothing to his faith in the value of silence.

His secretiveness went hand in hand with his isolation: each exacerbated the other. His fear of intimacy intensified both his self-hatred and his narcissism. His dreams and fantasies intensified his conviction that he was 'either outlawed or elect, cursed or blessed'. But he gives no substantial reason in *Memories, Dreams, Reflections* for feeling outlawed or cursed.

In his 1912 book *Transformations and Symbols of the Unconscious*, he writes about schizophrenic tendencies in children of three or four. The normal child, he says, strives to conquer the world and leave the mother behind.

> But the dementia praecox patient (or schizophrenic) strives to leave the world behind and regain the subjectivity of childhood. In dementia praecox the up-to-date world-picture is rejected in favour of an archaic world-picture. When a child evades the task of adapting himself to reality . . . the recent adaptation will be replaced by archaic modes of adaptation.

He does not explain why some children are unable to confront reality, but his own modes of adaptation at that age seem to have been archaic. Instead of developing a sunny spontaneity and stepping forward confidently into an easy-going relationship with other people, he retreated into an alternative space, a world of secrets, fantasies and private rituals.

He admits that the psychic life of the child is a problem to parents, teachers and doctors, 'but when normal, the child has no real problems of its own. It is only when a human being has grown up that he can have doubts about himself and be at variance with himself.' Jung's childhood was far from normal. Reviewing *Memories, Dreams, Reflections* in 1963, the pediatrician and psychiatrist D. W. Winnicott argued that psychotic illness must have set in by the age of four, and that Carl's personality was split as he defended himself. But he had a strong will to recovery, and arrived at an understanding of his psychosis. His secretiveness was part of his defence system, and it was characteristic that he neither confided in anyone about his dream of the outsize penis nor connected it with his own sexuality.

Many psychiatrists dissent from Winnicott's verdict, but one who agrees with it is the analytical psychologist Michael Fordham – one of the editors Jung chose for the English edition of his collected works. After reading a draft of the first three chapters in *Memories, Dreams, Reflections*, he told Jung 'he had been a schizophrenic child, with strong obsessional defences, and that had he been brought to me I should have said that the prognosis was good, but that I should have recommended analysis. He did not contest my blunt statement.' In January 1995, meeting Dr Fordham shortly before he died, I asked how the draft had differed from the published version. He said Jung's mother had emerged as a hysteric, and the childhood as more disturbed.

Carl was about six when he attacked a boy of his own age, the well-dressed son of a neighbour. On Sundays the boy and his two sisters wore patent-leather shoes, white frills and white gloves. Even on weekdays they were clean and well dressed. Carl, who usually had dirty hands, holes in his shoes and tattered trousers, was told he ought to behave more like those nice children. The revenge he took conforms to a pattern that often develops, according to Winnicott, from internalising a bad relationship between parents. Afterwards, Carl's mother told him off, but later, playing with his bricks behind the old spinet, he heard her muttering to herself, and finally she spoke out loud: 'Of course, a litter like that should never have been kept.' Glad she was on his side, he knew she would not want to be more explicit.

His father was teaching him Latin, and he started going to the village school, which he attended till he was nine. Corporal punishment was used to drill the alphabet into the pupils. 'We were eight boys sitting on a bench, and the teacher had a whip of three willow wands, just long enough to touch all the backs at once. He said, "This is A" (bang), "This is B" (bang) . . . It was not very painful, because when he beat on eight backs at the same time, you just cringed and did not feel it very much.' The intention was to make the letters unforgettable by causing suffering and anger.

Having learned to read by the age of five, Carl could easily keep ahead of his seven classmates – all peasant children – but he did not enjoy playing with them. 'I joined in their fun or got them to join in escapades which at home would never, so it seemed, have occurred to me.' He felt ill at ease with other people and with objects. 'It was as if I sensed and feared a splitting in my self.'

He protected himself by devising quasi-magical rituals that involved playing with fire. The old stone walls in the garden were pocked with crevices like miniature caves. In one of these he lit a fire, intending never to let it go out. He allowed other children to help him collect wood, but not to put it on the flames. They could make fires in other crevices, but his 'had an unmistakable flavour of sanctity'. Symbolically it was his inner self. 'For a long time this was my favourite game.' When psychotics have no oppor-tunity to play with fire, they often talk about it. According to R. D. Laing, 'Fire may be the uncertain flickering of the individual's own inner aliveness. It may be the destructive alien power which will devastate him.'

In his seventh and eighth years Carl enjoyed playing with building blocks and making towers, which he destroyed with earthquakes. He also played a solitary game with a big stone that jutted out from the slope by the wall. He sat on it for hours, pretending it was as aware of him as he was of it. 'Then the question arose: "Am I the one who is sitting on the stone, or am I the stone *he* is sitting on?" ' And he adopted a small stone that was oblong and blackish. After painting it to divide it into two halves, he carried it around in his trouser pocket.

The disorientation seems to have begun when vague fears of extinction grew into a more specific fear of suffocation, and anxiety dreams began to coincide with physical symptoms. Sometimes he saw a tiny ball in the distance; and as it came nearer, it grew into something monstrous and suffocating. By the age of seven he had contracted pseudo-croup, a respiratory infection which involved strained, noisy breathing, a harsh cough and fits of choking. More common in younger children, it got its name because croup was often associated with diphtheria. During one nocturnal attack, Carl had to stand at the foot of his bed with his head bent back while his father held him under the arms. 'Above me I saw a bright blue circle the size of the full moon, and in it were moving golden figures which I took to be angels. Each time it occurred, this vision allayed the fear of suffocation, but this returned in my dreams . . . the spiritual atmosphere was becoming unbreathable.' Fear of suffocation sometimes convinced him that the quality of the air was changing.

He became more dependent on secret rituals. He enjoyed carving wood, and when he was nine, he took a ruler, cut about two inches off the end, and created a small figure with a top hat, a frock coat and boots. He blackened all these with ink, giving the manikin something in common with the clergymen in the family. Like a younger child dressing a teddy bear or a doll, he made it a little black woollen coat and a little bed. The ruler had belonged in a yellow varnished pencil case. This became the home of the manikin, who was put into it with the coat, bedding and the painted stone, which now became *his* stone.

The attic at the top of the parsonage was out of bounds because the floorboards were worm-eaten and rotten. Defying the ban, Carl clambered up one of the beams to hide the pencil case in a space under the roof. 'It made me feel safe and released from the painful feeling of being at odds with myself. In every difficult situation, when I had done something wrong, or my sensitivity had been wounded, or I was oppressed by my father's irritability or my mother's poor health, I thought about my manikin.'

Unlike the fire and the stones, it did not represent his secret self. If it had, he would not have made it look like a clergyman. Its function was more like that of the teddy bear, the doll or the piece of soft material that so often becomes indispensable to a much younger child. Winnicott uses the term 'transitional object' for 'the first not-me object' that can be possessed and manipulated. Fordham, too, regards the manikin as a transitional object.

Though Carl's sister Gertrud was born during 1884, he does not mention this as one of the vexations that made him need the manikin. His parents had failed to prepare him for what was going to happen, and, always resentful when his mother took to her bed, he had noticed neither that she was resting more than usual nor that her stomach was swelling.

When he saw the baby, his feelings were negative. His excited father took him into the bedroom where his mother held out 'a little creature that looked extremely disappointing: a red crumpled face like an old man's, the eyes closed, probably blind, like a puppy. The thing had on its back some single red-blond hairs, which they showed me – had it been intended to grow into a monkey?' His parents said the baby had been brought by a stork, but at nine Carl was not naive enough to be taken in. What about litters of puppies and kittens? Did the stork fly backwards and forwards to deliver them separately? And how could a stork carry a baby calf? Once again his parents were trying to deceive him; once again his mother had done something furtive. His vague feelings of distrust intensified. 'Later suspect reactions from my mother confirmed my suspicion that something rather regrettable was connected with the birth.'

Each of his rituals led to another. Keeping the manikin in a safe hiding place, he needed to communicate with it. He invented a private language and, while at school, wrote messages on small scrolls of paper. Stealing up to the attic, he left the messages in the pencil box, and the accumulation of little scrolls was like a miniature library.

Three

Such a Wicked Thought

Carl was eleven when he was sent to the Gymnasium in Basel. Each morning he had a thirty-minute walk from Klein-Hüningen, mainly along the banks of the Rhine. After a rustic childhood, he was seeing the city every day – steep, narrow streets full of busy shops, expensive-looking horse-drawn carriages, people in streets and cafés with impressive clothes and coiffures, the bustling fish market, the great sandstone cathedral with its two Gothic towers, the pinnacled belfry and the frescoes on the façade of the town hall, the esplanade set above the Rhine, the old port, elaborate advertisements promoting fashions and forthcoming performances in theatres and concert halls.

Basel had a strong tradition of Protestant culture. With a population of about fifty thousand, the city was small enough for people to recognise each other. Carl knew he was being pointed out as the grandson of Carl Gustav Jung, and in the streets he often saw the famous Jakob Burckhardt, the sixty-seven-year-old cultural historian, and another writer, Johann Jakob Bachofen, a strikingly whiskery septuagenarian.

Hearing his classmates talk about pocket money, seaside holidays and weekends in the Alps, Carl realised how low his family ranked in the hierarchy of wealth, power and style. Becoming self-conscious about threadbare sleeves and holes in his shoes, he became more critical of his parents. Uneasy when people looked at him, he was embarrassed by his mother's habit of shouting after him as he left the house. Had he washed his hands? Did he have a handkerchief? 'Don't forget to wipe your nose.'

He comforted himself by praying – not to Lord Jesus, but to God. God was a mystery. Jesus had a beard and wore brightly coloured robes, but nobody knew what God looked like. Divinity classes were boring, and so were maths classes. Unlike animals, flowers and fossils, digits and algebraic symbols were insipid, and it was pointless to say *a* equals *b*. How could they be the same? And how could parallel lines meet at infinity? Carl passed muster in maths only by using his photographic memory to recall algebraic symbols he had seen on the blackboard.

Some teachers might have helped if he had admitted to the uneasiness he felt with abstract concepts, but he had trained himself to be secretive. Devouring books he chose at random in his father's library, he absorbed ideas and facts unconnected with what was being taught at school. Casually, he was giving himself an education his teachers would have condemned as anarchic, and without knowing about it, they seemed to disapprove of him. In spite of his talent for drawing and carving, he was forbidden to attend art classes, but the worst ordeal was gymnastics. He hated being told how to move.

He was twelve when, in the summer of 1887, the pattern of his religious thinking was changed by a dream or daydream. We do not know which it was, but in it, God was shitting. (I use the word Jung wanted to use – not the euphemism editorially imposed in *Memories, Dreams, Reflections*.) He describes a sunny afternoon in Basel, where, walking from school to the cathedral square, he struggles to ward off a thought that might be punished with eternal damnation. In the daydream version, which occupies four pages of *Memories, Dreams, Reflections*, the struggle continues overnight. The dream version – in which, being asleep, he has no chance to resist – appears in the book *C. G. Jung* by his English friend Edward Bennet. (Jung read this in typescript, and made manuscript corrections, which were incorporated.) In both versions, God is pictured squatting on a golden throne and dropping a massive turd which shatters the dome of the cathedral.

Why had such a wicked thought come into Carl's mind? The family devoted a great deal of time to reading the Bible, and the image may have been inspired by the passage at the end of Exodus about God's refusal to show Moses his face. 'Behold, there is a place by me, and thou shalt stand upon a rock: and it shall come to pass, while my glory passeth by, that I will put thee in a cleft of the rock, and will cover thee with my hand while I pass by: and I will take away mine hand, and thou shalt see my back parts: but my face shall not be seen.'

Like Moses, Jung believed God had revealed himself – intimately. 'I have not done this to myself, or wanted it . . . Where do such things come from? . . . God had put me into this situation, and then left me to my own devices . . . I had no doubt that God had devised this decisive test for me, and that everything depended on understanding him correctly.' There is nothing odd about this juvenile fantasy of being singled out for direct contact with God. What is odd is that it should survive so long. The octogenarian Jung still believed that in assigning the thought to him, God had been selecting him for a special relationship. But the belief may originally have been no more than a consolation prize Carl awarded himself. What he would have preferred was a loving relationship with two parents who loved each other. But this was a secret he kept even from himself.

The other main event of 1887 was an accident that interrupted his education. At midday, after morning school finished, he usually walked most of the way home with a classmate. Waiting for him in the cathedral square, he was pushed violently by another boy, lost his balance and just before his head hit the kerb, it occurred to him that he might now have an excuse for staying away from school. This half-formed idea may have made him hit his head harder than necessary. Dazed, he stayed on the ground, partly to revenge himself on the boy who had pushed him. He was picked up and taken to the nearby home of two spinster aunts.

On the morning he was sent back to school, he fainted, and each time he was made to do homework or go to school, he repeated what had been partly a strategem. It was believed until the early sixties that children never suffered from depression, but there is no better word for his condition during his six months of absence from school. He was daydreaming, playing solitary games in the woods, drawing battle scenes, trying to make an imaginative connection with trees, water, marshland, stones, animals, and with books in his father's library.

During his months at home, he saw more than usual of his sister, Trudi. *Memories, Dreams, Reflections* says almost nothing about her, and he had forgotten that he was nine years her senior. In the autobiographical material he wrote and dictated, he kept referring to a six-year age gap. Their relationship was never close, and, as a child, she was sickly and delicate, clinging to her mother in a way that irritated him. He decided she was born to be a spinster. Nothing would ever become of her, he said, if his mother went on bringing her up like that.

But he had always admired Trudi, he said, and he kept praising her posture. In his original typescript for the first three chapters, he calls her a 'born lady', and says she died one, but this sentence is cut, as is a passage comparing her with Goethe's sister Cornelia, who also suffered from hives or nettle rash, also remained single, also spent most of her life at home. From childhood, Trudi lived in a world of fantasy, and instead of writing her own name in her books, used an aristocratic alias. Their paternal grandfather had a younger sister who spent her life in an institution for aristocratic ladies, and it seemed to Jung that Goethe, his grandfather and he had the same kind of sister. After Trudi's death he sometimes dreamed about her and sometimes saw her as his anima, or a personification of his unconscious.

After the accident, Jung knew it was up to him whether he took a long time to recover. Having loosened his attachment to external reality, he felt uncomfortable. His parents should have been able to make him feel connected with other people, but his main relationship was with himself, and it felt as if he was running away. Separated from his classmates, he had resumed the solitude of his childhood, and he was consolidating his habit of secretiveness.

The fantasy of the divine turd was important to him, but can it have been quite as important as he makes out? He says: 'My whole youth can be understood in terms of the secret . . . and today I am still isolated, because I know things and have to hint at things other people do not know and mostly do not want to know.' Millions of boys have wondered whether God and Jesus use a lavatory, but the problem is unlikely to shape their subsequent relationship with the world.

Did Jung have another big secret alongside the two dreams, the manikin game and the (unspecified) sexuality of a solitary schoolboy? Lewis Mumford has suggested that the dream about the big penis may have been much later than Jung tells us. Both this dream and the need to stay away from school may have been connected with a homosexual experience.

This is not mentioned in *Memories, Dreams, Reflections*. He had been married for four and a half years when he wrote to Freud about a traumatic experience in boyhood. It may have had a more blighting effect on his emotionality than his mother's prolonged absence, but (as if to hold it at arm's length) Jung deals with it in a single cryptic sentence: 'When I was a boy, I submitted to a man I once venerated.' In the published translation of the letters, this is given as 'I suffered a sexual assault from', but '*Ich bin unterlegen*', as Erik Erikson points out, 'literally means "laid under", that is, I submitted'.

We may never know what happened or how old Jung was at the time. If we are to believe Jolande Jacobi, who worked under him later, the incident did not occur until he was eighteen. But by then he was too big and too strong to submit involuntarily to a sexual assault, and since I have found no corroboration for this, it seems possible the incident occurred earlier. In her book *Die Hiobsbotschaft C. G. Jungs*, Renate Hofer argues that of all his secrets, this is the one he found most burdensome, and he was thinking of it when he wrote that he was in God's hands and had been created to carry out his will.

A dream he later recorded may refer to the incident. In the dream, a man was desperately trying to get behind him and jump on his back. He knew nothing about the man, except that he had taken something Jung had said and tried to twist it into 'a rather grotesque travesty of my meaning'. Jung does not say whether it was a recurring dream or when he had it, but he says it baffled him for a time. Finally, in a 1961 essay, he interprets it in terms of a saying, '*Du kannst mir auf dem Buckel steigen*', which literally means 'You can climb on my back' or, figuratively, 'I don't care what you say.' Was he elucidating the dream or obfuscating it?

Although the penis dream, the fantasy about a shitting God and the manikin game were crucial to his imaginative world, he never talked about them. After the abortive attempt to confide in Freud about the homosexual episode, he remained equally silent about that. The dream remained a secret till he was in his sixty-sixth year, and he never confided in his wife about the fantasy or the manikin game till late in their marriage.

During his protracted absence from school, his parents consulted several doctors. One prescribed a holiday in Winterthur, eighteen miles northwest of Zurich, where he stayed with relations and spent time at the railway station, watching trains. Another doctor suspected epilepsy. One day the boy overheard what his father was saying to a friend. No one could diagnose what was wrong. 'It would be terrible if he's incurable. I've lost the little I had, and what will happen if he can't earn a living?'

This made Carl decide to recover. Galvanised into activity, he sat down to work at his Latin grammar, and soon found himself opening books every day.

Sent back to school a few weeks later, he felt ashamed of having stayed away so long. Swinging to the opposite extreme, he imposed a draconian regime on himself. 'I regularly got up at five to study, and before going to school I often worked from three in the morning till seven.'

His self-confidence had improved, but he was building on unsteady foundations, as he found when he challenged the authority of a school-friend's father – a man who owned a factory, two houses and several horses. One of the houses was by Lake Lucerne, where the family had a boat-house and a rowing boat. When Carl and his friend were allowed to take it out on the lake, they were told to be careful. Knowing how to row a *Waidling* (a boat of the gondola type), Carl started out confidently, standing on the stern seat and using an oar to push off. His friend's father whistled them back, and Carl was severely told off.

Though he had disobeyed orders, he inwardly rejected the man's right to criticise him. He had begun to think he consisted of two people; and the incident exacerbated the delusion. One day in Klein-Hüningen, when an ancient green carriage from the Black Forest drove past, he felt inexplicably elated, as if he had driven in similar carriages during the eighteenth century, and had somehow been cheated of experiences that were his due. In an aunt's house, seeing a terracotta statuette of two eighteenth-century Basel personalities, he felt sure he had once worn those buckled shoes.

Later on – not writing about himself – he said childhood fantasies of belonging to a different family indicated an emotional rejection of the parents. As he suggested in a 1912 lecture, a neurotic child will do better if taken away from the damaging family atmosphere, even without medical treatment. Carl had no treatment and stayed in the damaging atmosphere.

He had two simultaneous lives. The twelve-year-old boy had to obey his seniors and come to terms with his incompetence in algebra; but in his fantasy, he was an important man in the eighteenth century, wearing buckled shoes and a powdered wig, driving about in a coach.

He went back to the idea that had presented itself when he was told off for standing up in the boat. He consisted of two people. As a schoolboy he was inferior to classmates who worked harder, paid more attention to teachers, washed more often and dressed more neatly. But his other personality – he called it Number Two – had the wisdom of a mature man. Sceptical and mistrustful, he preserved his detachment from other people, but not from nature. Carl's lifeline depended on his system of splitting himself.

Number Two had power and authority, but Number One was too shy to let him display them. His schoolfriends were mostly insecure, simple boys. In most subjects he could have come top of the class, but, uneasy when he aroused envy, he contrived to come second. He went on reading widely, and whenever he was sent to fetch books from the university library, he prolonged his absence to sample them. But, as before, most of his reading was unconnected with schoolwork.

He alienated both teachers and classmates by cultivating his independence. Big for his age and strong, he could defend himself when attacked. One day, seven boys ambushed him. Grabbing one of them by the arms, Carl used his legs as a weapon against the others, swinging him round and knocking several of them over. When he was punished, he thought – not unreasonably – that this was unfair.

He insists that 'play and counterplay between Personalities Number One and Number Two, which persisted throughout my life, has nothing to do with "dissociation" [*Spaltung*] in the ordinary medical sense.' A different view is suggested by R. D. Laing's description of schizoid behaviour in his 1960 book *The Divided Self*. Scared that other people want to destroy or corrupt the core of his identity, the schizoid puts one of his two selves at risk in order to shelter the other, more valuable self. This one, which seems to be 'his own', 'inner', 'true' and 'real', enters the condition that Kierkegaard called 'containment'. Shut up within itself, it seems disembodied and uninvolved in the activities of the false self.

No psychosis develops when the individual trusts himself to interrelate freely with other people, but the psychotic feels safe only when interacting with phantoms, images or other parts of the self. Even if many of Laing's ideas have since been discredited, it would still be hard to improve on his account of division in the self.

Desire for solitude often interpenetrates with a need for omnipotence. The individual who feels unsafe when interacting with other people rationalises his isolation by condemning them as vulgar, commonplace, trivial. He may pine for immersion in the hurly-burly, but relaxed relationships are feasible only when both parties are sure of their own ground. The unbalanced individual who has suffered since infancy from chronic fears of annihilation will make only ineffectual attempts to form friendships. The moment he feels threatened, he withdraws, telling himself to remain elusive and uncommitted. Otherwise something might be taken, like a hostage, by people who could damage his inner self. To love or be loved is to make it vulnerable, but narcissism is not necessarily involved in the schizoid position. The intrapersonal relationship approximates to the condition of interpersonal relationships. He feels as if he is plural.

From the age of eleven, Carl was expected to sympathise when his mother confided in him, stating and probably overstating the case against her husband, revealing to the boy anxieties she concealed from his father. She made alarming allegations, only to change the story next time she told it. Carl was baffled by her duality. 'In the daytime she was a loving mother, but at night she seemed weird. Then she was like a visionary who was at the same time a strange beast, like a priestess in a bear's cave. Archaic and ruthless. Ruthless as truth and nature. Then she was the embodiment of what I've called the "natural mind".' He used this English phrase for the thinking that owes nothing to education but wells up from the earth like a natural spring.

Sometimes he emulated her primitive directness, abrogating intellectual control over what he said. Cultivating his intuitive powers, he tried to develop clairvoyance. Frightening though she often was, she seemed more honest than her husband, who aligned himself with Protestant orthodoxy. 'I was sure this was the wrong way to approach God, for I knew from experience that this grace was accorded only to those who unreservedly fulfilled His will.' Clergymen might think they knew how to please God, but 'could anyone who claimed to know his will have foreseen what He made me do?' Carl's faith in his own direct relationship with God was inversely proportional to his faith in his father's religious teaching. The pastor, in Carl's view, was stable and reliable as a parent, but not as a theologian.

In all this time, the only girls Carl played with were his cousins. His godfather was his mother's elder brother Rudolf, a locksmith – the fifth of Samuel Preiswerk's thirteen children. Between 1866 and 1889, Rudolf's wife, Celestine, gave birth to fifteen children. The seventh, Luise (Luggy), was Carl's favourite cousin. Tall, slim, lively and intelligent, she had regular features, an attractive body, bright eyes and beautifully arched eyebrows. She often did housework for her aunt Emilie, and Jung described her as his first love. But he never told her he was in love with her.

In the summer Carl's father regularly took a solitary holiday in Sachseln, by Lake Sarnen, sixteen miles from Lucerne, leaving his children at home with their mother. In adult life Jung would take a great many holidays, having had so few in his boyhood. He was given one when he was fourteen, because he was ailing, with no appetite. The doctor recommended a cure at Entlebuch, west of Lucerne, and he was to be quartered in the house of a Catholic priest. Before leaving, he bought himself an English jockey cap and a bamboo cane.

He spent his nights at the priest's house and his days under the supervision of an old country doctor who ran a sanatorium for convalescents. One of Carl's table companions, a chemist, taught him to play croquet, and they went on outings together. One day they visited a distillery and, drinking from too many of the glasses set out for visitors, Jung got drunk for the first time. In the swaying streets he kept his balance by catching hold of lampposts and supporting himself against walls, but the euphoria promised that adult life would be full of pleasant surprises.

On his last day in Entlebuch, his father arrived, and they went to Lucerne, where they boarded a steamship and travelled about seventeen miles to a village called Vitznau. What Jung remembered was not the time they spent together but moments of self-sufficiency – wearing a stiff black hat, carrying the cane and sipping coffee at a table under a striped awning on the terrace of a palatial lakeside hotel, eating croissants with butter and jam, and planning a steamship outing across the lake, which was surrounded by glacier-covered mountains.

Making only intermittent efforts to be companionable, the pastor treated his son to a ride on the funicular railway that ran up to the peak of the nearest mountain, the Rigi. Pressing a ticket into the boy's hand, he explained that one was all he could afford. Breathing mountain air and enjoying the spectacular view, Carl told himself he was in the real world – God's world – where there were no teachers, no classmates and no homework. But since there were precipices on every side, it was important to observe the rules. He kept carefully to the paths.

The pastor had not given up hope of improving his relationship with his son, who had to be prepared for confirmation at fifteen. Though the job could have been delegated to one of the other clergymen in the family, the pastor decided to do it himself. He may have been hoping they would confide in each other, but everything he said bored his son. Reading the catechism, Carl found some of it incomprehensible and some of it sentimental. Having never understood what the Trinity was, he was looking forward to hearing an explanation, but when they came to it, his father said: 'We'd now be coming to the Trinity, but we'll skip that because I don't understand anything about it.' Suggesting that his father lacked both intelligence and intellectual courage, Jung's account of this incident is hard to reconcile with the sophistication of the dissertation on the Song of Songs.

The godfather at the confirmation was a wheelwright who was usually to be seen in his shop, bending over his lathe. Dressed in a frock coat and top hat, he looked awkward. Wearing his robes, Paul Achilles Jung was waiting behind the altar. Loaves from the local baker had been cut into small pieces. Wine was poured from a pewter jug into a pewter cup. After eating bread, the pastor swallowed some wine and passed the cup to one of the old men, who all seemed uninvolved. Carl had registered an atmosphere just like this at scores of baptisms, weddings and funerals. Finally he swallowed insipid bread and sour wine. Walking home, he knew nothing had changed, except that he had a new black suit with a longish jacket which split into two wings over the seat of his trousers.

Browsing through his father's theological books for information about God, he found nothing helpful, but when his mother recommended *Faust*, he at last discovered a writer who took the devil seriously, though Goethe should not have let his hero gamble his soul away so frivolously. He deserved to be damned, and Mephistopheles should not have been tricked out of the soul he had won. The ending made evil seem innocuous. But the development of Jung's ideas was influenced by Goethe, who had studied the medieval alchemists and believed, as they did, that there were hidden harmonies and interrelationships in all matter.

Carl's alienation from classmates, teachers and formal education deepened when he was accused of plagiarism. Usually he took little trouble over essays and got average marks. When he, for once, exerted himself, the teacher thought he had been copying from a book. Without being sure whether his isolation was the consequence of repulsive traits he could not see, he withdrew even further into himself. It was after this he acquired the nickname 'Abraham the Patriarch', which he resented, 'but in the background I felt it somehow suited me'.

The inner split deepened. Beside 'the old man who belonged to the centuries', the Number One personality faded into nonexistence, and when it reasserted itself, the old man seemed like a dream. Increasingly isolated,

Carl blamed his rustic origins. Mistrustful of these city-dwellers, he looked compassionately into 'the sad, abandoned eyes of cows, and the resignation in horses' eyes'. Trees must be 'a direct representation of life's incomprehensible meaning'. Taking lonely walks in the woods, and still feeling an affinity with stone, he was certain the same divine nature was common to dead and living matter.

He met few teenage girls apart from his Preiswerk cousins. One significant-seeming encounter occurred one summer when, at fifteen or sixteen, he was invited to visit his father while he was taking his usual holiday without his wife in Sachseln, where he knew the Catholic priest. Carl was encouraged to visit the nearby hermitage of Flüeli, which contained the relics of a fifteenth-century German mystic, St Nicholas of Cusa. The hermitage was above a valley, and strolling up the hill, Carl saw a pretty peasant girl in the local costume. She smiled, and they walked down the hill together.

Shyly he told her he was there on holiday. They were walking together, he thought, as naturally as if they belonged together, but she was clearly a Catholic, and he did not admit his father was a Protestant clergyman. Nor did he try to talk about Schopenhauer or Goethe – only about the weather and the view. He went on thinking about her afterwards, knowing he would never see her again.

Of the girls he met in the next few years, none displaced this memory, but he became more assertive and more determined to solve the mysteries. What did life mean? Reading philosophy systematically, he found the ideas of Pythagoras, Heraclitus, Empedocles and Plato 'beautiful and academic, like a gallery of paintings, but somewhat remote'. Meister Eckhart's mysticism was attractive, but Carl did not feel at home with Aquinas or Hegel. Schopenhauer was exciting: instead of enthusing about human goodness and divine benevolence, he confronted the cruelty of nature and the blindness of the world-creating Will.

Philosophical reading increased Carl's self-confidence. 'I became conspicuously more accessible and more communicative. I discovered that poverty was no handicap and was by no means the main reason for my sufferings: the sons of the rich were not in a stronger position than boys who were badly off and badly dressed . . . I made more and better friends than I had before.'

During the protracted period of schizoid solitude, his imaginative world centred on faith in his direct experience of divine grace, which survived alongside ideas deriving from his extensive reading. Schelling's equation of Nature with Spirit and von Hartmann's insistence that reality is knowable made less impact than Goethe, Nietzsche, Schopenhauer and Kant, but he was deeply affected by the German tradition of Romantic idealism, which reinforced his antipathy to materialism and scientific rationalism. For him the word *psyche* was synonymous with the word *Seele*, for which the closest English approximation is *soul*. But Freud, in his seminal 1900 book *The Interpretation of Dreams*, defined the psyche by analogy with the optical apparatus. For him, the mind was an apparatus with the function of transmitting and transforming a specific energy.

The more Carl was inspired by the Romantics and his private religion, the further he retreated from contact with other people. By referring to books that had never been discussed in class, he impressed neither classmates nor new acquaintances, who were mistrustful of allusions to Kant and Schopenhauer. 'Some people thought I was a boaster or that I was talking through my hat.' His instinct was to stay aloof, but he was thrown into contact with classmates by events in the school calendar, and during the spring of 1894, according to his school report, he got into trouble for behaving badly and disrupting an outing.

Instead of cultivating the internal split, he tried to heal it, but it reasserted itself whenever he thought about his future career. Personality Number One was attracted to the prospect of studying objective realities in zoology, palaeontology or geology; Number Two to the opportunities of focusing on spiritual problems in Graeco-Roman, Egyptian or prehistoric archaeology. Thinking he would make a good theologian, one of his maternal uncles – pastor at the church of St Alban in Basel – regularly invited him to lunch on Thursdays. Much of the conversation centred on theological doctrine and biblical accounts of miracles. Nietzsche was never mentioned; Burckhardt was regarded as a freethinker, and Kant as a heretic. Though he felt unrelaxed, Carl found the conversation more stimulating than his attempts to discuss these issues with his father, who told him not to think, just to believe.

He rarely went to church, and the pastor did not grumble. Carl went on reading a great deal, especially during the holidays. He subscribed to a scientific periodical and collected not only fossils and samples of minerals but bones – mammoth bones from a gravel pit in the Rhineland plain, and human bones from a mass grave outside Hüningen, dating from 1811. He looked forward to studying at a university, but the only affordable one would be Basel, where there was no course in archaeology.

'The boy is interested in everything under the sun,' said the worried pastor, 'but doesn't know what he wants.' Nor could he afford to remain undecided much longer: he had to register for a faculty. Two dreams influenced his decision. In one he was in a dark wood by the Rhine. Coming to a burial mound and starting to dig, he found bones of prehistoric animals. There was a wood in the other dream. Thick undergrowth surrounded a circular pool with clear, deep water and a round animal in it, a shimmering, opalescent radiolarian. 'These two dreams overwhelmingly made up my mind in favour of natural science.' Radiolaria are a species of marine planktonic protozoa with numerous fingerlike protrusions of the cell surface. He may have read about them in Bachofen.

If he studied zoology, he would end up as a teacher. What about medicine? The pastor applied to the authorities for a scholarship, which was granted, rather to his son's surprise, for Number Two dictated his view of Number One, who was 'flawed with a series of defects, such as sporadic laziness, cowardice, depression, inept enthusiasm for ideas and things valued by nobody, imaginary friendships, narrowness, prejudice, stupidity (mathematics!), deficient understanding of other people, lack of clarity and philosophical confusion, neither a Christian nor anything else'.

Faust meant more to him than any of the Gospels, and Faust himself seemed to have an affinity with Number Two. But then Carl dreamed about holding a tiny light while running away from a gigantic dark figure, which meant − or so he persuaded himself − that his consciousness, the bearer of light, was lodged in Number One, while Number Two followed it like a shadow. Taking the dream to be a message from something more intelligent than he was, he began to identify more with Number One. Though Number Two might be more intelligent and have something to do with the creation of dreams, it no longer felt like part of himself.

In his eighteenth year Carl renewed his efforts to communicate with his father, who was becoming increasingly bad-tempered. During outbursts of rage he was unapproachable, and when he prayed, he sounded 'desperate about his faith'. As the only one who knew the truth about God's nature, Carl wanted his father to benefit from the revelation he had been granted, but the pastor seemed exasperated when, instead of talking openly, Carl asked intellectual questions.

Obviously, the pastor was a victim. First the church had ensnared him into the habit of theological thinking, which gave him no chance to make direct contact with God. Then it had abandoned him. It was obvious that he had lost his faith − once Carl heard him praying for it to be given back to him. Carl somehow arrived at the conclusion that his father had allowed himself to be infected by the materialism of the asylum doctors who believed the soul to be a secretion of the brain. Then, instead of helping him, the church had abandoned him.

God was right to be fed up with theology and the church that had been founded on it, but why did he let them go on misleading people? Clearly, He was at fault. 'It would have been ridiculous to blame men for allowing such things to go on.' But the pastor was not entirely innocent. Turning a blind eye to God's shortcomings, he was floundering in his failing faith instead of engaging actively with humanity's spiritual problems. The son would have to take over the duties his father was neglecting.

By the summer of 1895, it was clear that Paul Jung, who was in his early fifties, was seriously ill. His symptoms included the sensation of having stones in his abdomen, but the doctor could find nothing wrong.

This was not the only crisis in his son's life. It would have been out of character for Jung to write confessionally about any of his early sexual experiences. Even if he had not been the victim of a homosexual attack, he would have looked back with embarrassment on the 'obscene fantasies' and schoolboy chatter that poured 'like a torrent of dirty water' over delicate feelings. Boys still have childish souls alongside the adult sexuality that 'fills them with brutal desires and needs; few escape the painful problem of masturbation'. Like skin erupting with acne, the psyche is unbalanced. Their 'psychological puberty' can last till they are in their mid-twenties. Sexuality, which is still 'purely animal', is often fixed at 'too low a level' by experiences with 'the most inferior women' or with men – homosexual affairs are 'much more frequent than is usually acknowledged'.

Four

The Geology of the Person

Glad to have left the Gymnasium, Jung sometimes claimed in later life that he had never been bored, except at school. Not quite twenty when he was admitted on 18 April 1895 into the medical school at Basel University, he was expecting anatomy and physiology to provide an explanation of what life meant.

His syllabus would include organic and inorganic chemistry, physics, optics, mechanics and electricity, but most of his time would be given to zoology and biology. The professor, Friedrich Zschokke, had taken over the department two years earlier at the age of thirty-two, and had made the course on 'comparative anatomy' into one on comparative zoology. Zschokke believed the overall evolution of humanity was reiterated in the anatomy of each individual. He spoke about 'the geology of the person', maintaining that everything in the human body can be traced down the evolutionary ladder. Convinced that warm-blooded animals had souls, and that plants, so long as they were growing, expressed the thoughts of God's world, Jung responded positively to this idea, which has since been discredited.

It was popularised a few years later in *The Riddles of the Universe* by Ernst Haeckel, a biologist who argued that 'ontogenesis recapitulates phylogenesis', meaning that the lifelong development of the individual human body goes through the same stages as the evolution of the human race. In 1899 Haeckel had proposed a 'phylogenetic psychology' focused on 'the phylogeny of the soul'. If the development of human thought could be shown to parallel biological evolution, the new science of psychology would illuminate the history of humanity.

A quarter of a century later, ethology taught us to take environment into account, alongside heredity, in the study of animal behaviour, but Jung persisted in believing what Zschokke had taught. As the next incumbent in the chair, Adolf Portmann, puts it, 'Jung did not look at the reptile, a lizard say, in a concrete way, in terms of the behaviour that ethology has shown us. He looked at the lizard as a stage in the hierarchical evolution of our nervous system.'

Jung quickly proved himself to be a good student. He was appointed junior assistant in anatomy, and was soon afterwards put in charge of the course on histology, which is concerned with the minute structure of tissues. But what fascinated him most was 'the morphological view in its widest sense'. Morphology deals with structures governing the form of animals and plants.

He was familiar with 'neo–vitalist' theories – those which contradicted Darwinian materialism. They were later formulated in such books as Eugen Bleuler's 1921 *Naturgeschichte der Seele* (*Natural History of the Soul*). By 1895 such formulae as 'struggle for life' and 'survival of the fittest' were already under attack, and Darwin was being accused of simplifying the relationship between organism and environment. But Zschokke, who accepted evolution as a fact, was not primarily concerned with either theories or explanations. Confronted with the mysteries of evolution, he alternated between empiricism and reverence, as did Jung, who held what Portmann calls 'a hidden creed about life', and there was nothing in Zschokke's teaching to unsettle it. The professor concentrated on the forms of animals, looking at structures and apparent correspondences between them.

In May 1895, a month after the beginning of his first term, Jung joined a colour-wearing fraternity, Zofingia. The regalia approximated to military uniform, incorporating a peaked cap, a sash over a tuniclike jacket, breeches and boots that came almost to the knee. As old as the oldest German fraternities, Zofingia had maintained its Swiss independence, and while members were free to join any political party except the anarchists, their motto was: 'For Fatherland, friendship and letters.'

At social gatherings, mixing jocularity with formality, members delivered speeches on a variety of topics, including federal banks, folk songs and freshmen. Becoming more self-confident, Jung made friends inside and outside the fraternity. One of its main activities was drinking in a pub called the Breo, and his nickname, 'Barrel', derived from his size and the amount of beer he could accommodate.

The impression he made on his fellow students was at odds with the one he thought he was making. 'He seemed infallible, often overwhelmingly self-confident,' writes Gustav Steiner. 'None of us Zofingians would have suspected he saw himself as being – in his own way – lonely and somehow misunderstood or isolated . . . He lived in a world that was known only to him . . . He went his own way, had fits of anger, was convinced the teachers did not like him, while he mistrusted them.' Unlike Albert Oeri, who was quietly helpful to other students, Jung seemed deeply immersed in his own problems. Albert Oeri was the boy who had found Jung unapproachable at the age of five.

It was natural that Jung gravitated towards spiritualism. His cousins had talked about strange goings-on in the family, and the vogue for seances, which had started in the USA during the 1840s, had spread to Europe during the 1850s. Nor would psychology and spiritualism have seemed uncon- nected. One mainstream approach to the unconscious was through the activities of mediums. Some of the most eminent thinkers and doctors – William James, Théodore Flournoy, Frederick Myers – became involved in parapsychology.

Staying for a few days in the Schaffhausen home of a friend, Jung picked up a book on spiritualism in the library of the boy's father. According to *Memories, Dreams, Reflections*, this was at the end of his second term, but he told his friend E. A. Bennet it was in 1896 or 1897. The book was by a theologian, whose accounts of manifestations whetted Jung's appetite for spiritualist literature. He devoured seven books by Emanuel Swedenborg, the eighteenth-century Swedish scientist who was in his fifties when a religious crisis convinced him that dreams offer direct access to an otherwise invisible world from which angels and demons exert influence on everyday reality.

The book that most influenced Jung had come out in 1829 – Justinus Kerner's *The Visionary of Prevorst* (*Die Seherin von Prevorst*). Kerner had worked as district physician in Weinsberg, near Heilbronn. Prevorst is a Württemberg village, where a gamekeeper's daughter had been having visions and premonitions. Friederike Hauffe had admired a preacher whose funeral coincided with her engagement to the man her parents were forcing on her, and after the wedding, she believed herself to be in bed with the preacher's corpse. Becoming seriously ill, she did not respond to medication, but her condition improved when Kerner mesmerised her. She then began to lead a 'bodiless life', going into trances and talking about the spiritual world, not in her usual Swabian dialect but in High German.

She also foretold the future, and offered advice to visitors. One of these was the theologian David Straus, whose *Life of Jesus* challenged the Gospel accounts. 'Her conversation with blessed spirits or about them,' he wrote, 'was conducted so truthfully that we could have no doubt we were really in the presence of a prophetess in touch with a higher world.' Sometimes she spoke in what she called mankind's original language. In her trances she prescribed medication that was effective both against her own ailments and those of other people.

The term *mesmerise* comes from the name of an eighteenth-century Austrian physician, Franz Anton Mesmer, who is sometimes said to have discovered hypnosis and used it to induce trances, thinking it involved magnetism. He seems to have thought animal magnetism was a force or 'fluid' that could form an imbalance in the human body or in the atmosphere, and he tried to channel magnetism from his own body into that of the patient. Jung was quick to master the art of making 'magnetic passes'.

In 1886, Hippolyte Bernheim, professor of internal medicine at the university of Nancy, published a textbook, *Suggestive Therapeutics*. Unlike Jean-Martin Charcot, the pioneer of neurology who took hypnosis to be a pathological condition, Bernheim regarded it merely as a heightened state of suggestibility, and recommended its therapeutic use. For a time the terms *psychotherapy* and *hypnotism* were synonymous. It was not difficult to acquire the technique, and Jung probably learned from reading the book and watching hypnotists in action.

He enjoyed having temporary control over people who had been in control of him. His mother scoffed at the idea of mesmerism, but, offering to show her how it worked, he asked her to hold her arm up. When she did, he told her she would be unable to lower it. She said this was nonsense, and finding it was true, insisted she was holding her arm up because she wanted to. She was sitting in a chair, and when he straightened one of her legs, she sat there with her arm raised and her leg stuck out till he told her to move them.

In 1895, though he was seeing a good deal of his Preiswerk cousins, Jung was still immersed in isolation and the feeling of uncleanness, which were compounded by his secretiveness. He oscillated between self-hatred and narcissism: he had never outgrown the conviction of being 'either outlawed or elect, cursed or blessed'. Most of his fellow students formed relationships with girls, but though he was to go through a long period of trying to find a father substitute, he was already building the foundations for his theory that the psyche's most important relationship is with itself, that the path to spiritual maturity is through integration of the self.

His first practical experiences of spiritualism involved his cousins. When he organised a series of seances, it was with his mother's encouragement, or, as he put it, the encouragement of her Number Two personality. She came to the seances, but the parson, lying in bed in the same house, was kept in ignorance about them. Though Luggy did not believe in spirits, she came with her sister Helly (Helene), who was thirteen and a half, and Helly's best friend, Emmy Zinnstag. Helly was absent-minded, delicate and pale, with dark, penetrating eyes, a brittle, nervous temperament, and a clever, alert-seeming face. Sometimes she was timid, sometimes boisterous to the point of indecency.

A Preiswerk with the same predilection as her aunt Emilie for the paranormal, Helly must have seemed like a younger version of her. They were using a round walnut table that had belonged to Samuel Preiswerk, and when it moved, tapping sounds came both from it and from the walls. Spirits were indicating their presence.

Helly went into a trance, turned pale, sank to the floor, drew several deep breaths and began to talk in the person of Samuel Preiswerk. Imitating him and speaking in High German instead of her usual Swiss dialect, she sounded older and more mature. When she rose to her feet, she moved more gracefully, and her voice suddenly sounded like a man's.

He said he was speaking from heaven, and she was flying through icy heights over the North Pole. He loved her more than anyone else, and knew all her thoughts, but could answer no questions about her. They should pray for her elder sister Bertha, who had given birth to 'a little nigger'. She had been forgiven, but the family would not be forgiven unless they forgave her and prayed for her. They should repent and love each other. Though she had never met her grandfather, who died in 1871, she had heard about his familiarity with spirits and his weekly meetings with his dead wife, but it is hard to explain how she could reproduce his voice and his mannerisms well enough to convince the others that he was speaking through her.

Bertha, who had been living with a half-caste in Brazil and already had a two-year-old child, gave birth to a baby on the same day as the seance – if Jung's subsequent calculations were accurate. Helly, who afterwards seemed exhausted, said she had been present at the baby's birth in Brazil.

Now that Jung's appetite had been whetted, he was keen to hold a second seance, and he prepared for it by marking slips of paper with letters and numbers. These were arranged in a circle on the table around an upturned tumbler, and they all sat with two fingers on the glass. It was twilight when the seance began, and as it got darker, Helly jumped to her feet, fell on her knees and asked the others whether they could see that star. Agitated and frightened, she called for a light and complained of feeling ill, not knowing what was wrong with her. She calmed down when the lamp arrived.

Again, when the table moved, tapping sounds were heard. The others did what Helly told them to do as the glass began shuttling across the table, spelling out words, sometimes backwards. Samuel Preiswerk started to speak, but he was interrupted by the first Carl Gustav Jung. The two grandfathers had disliked each other, someone said, but later on, according to Helly, they were arm in arm, and they jointly promised to look after the surviving members of the family.

From semiconsciousness Helly sank back into a trance before she talked about another sister, Dini (Celestine), who was pregnant. She was going to lose her child. Her dead grandfather could not help her. But she would be forgiven. Regaining consciousness, Helly seemed to know nothing about what she had said. She asked where she had been.

She said nothing about losing the baby to Dini, who said a black demon had been standing by her bed during the night, wanting to take her baby away, but, trying to protect her, a white angel struggled with the demon. In reality, she had been infected by her syphilitic husband, and at the end of August the baby was born prematurely, dead.

When a third seance was held at the end of July, Helly again reacted to the gathering darkness. She lay back on the sofa and closed her eyes, breathing deeply. For a while she lay motionless with her eyes closed, and then, shifting into a half-sitting posture, spoke in an altered voice. Sometimes Samuel Preiswerk or one of the other dead relations seemed to speak through her; at other times she seemed to remain herself. Jung cross-questioned the spirits, and tapped on the table in a rhythm Helly took up and developed.

But Luggy was worrying about her young sister, who often seemed to be in danger: her soul, she said, was attached to her body only by a thin thread. She was preparing for her confirmation in the spring of 1897, and it was clear to Luggy that she was under too much strain. It would be better to hold no more seances till she had been confirmed.

The strain on Helly was due partly to her feelings for Jung. Four years younger than he was, she was passionately in love with him, and jealous of her better-looking sister Luggy. Helly's confused emotions heightened the urgency of her visions and fantasies. Retreating from reality, she surrendered her imagination to hallucinations, identifying desperately with figures from the family's past – especially with the grandfather she had in common with Jung.

Luggy can be seen in a family photograph taken during 1891. At seventeen she has a well-developed hourglass figure. According to a book by their niece, Helly's 'somnambulism' was designed to draw his attention away from . . . Luggy. Whenever she became prophetic or fell into a trance, his attention returned to her.' But he took Luggy to a Zofingia carnival ball, where she wore national costume and spoke in an inland dialect. Thinking she was a genuine peasant, fraternity members congratulated Jung on his conquest.

The pastor knew nothing about the seances that were being held in his parsonage. He had once been a member of Zofingia, and he accompanied his son on a fraternity outing to a wine-growing village in the Markgrafen, where he amused everyone by delivering a whimsical speech over the wine.

Given an unexpected glimpse into the high-spirited, hopeful young man his father had once been, Jung could suddenly empathise. As a student, Paul Jung must have been as excitable and as greedy for knowledge as his son was now.

This was their last happy outing. In the autumn of 1895, the pastor took to his bed. In the last months of his life, the man who had once been so strong and erect said his son had to carry him around like a heap of bones in an anatomy class.

Arriving home on 28 January 1896, Jung asked how his father was. Still the same, said his mother, very weak. The invalid asked a question, and indicating with her eyes that he was delirious, she relayed it to their son: had he passed the state examination? He pretended he had done very well. With a sigh of relief, the pastor closed his eyes.

She went out of the room, and not long afterwards, Jung heard a rattling noise in his father's throat. Later, he described 'the staring eyes of the dying, with their inattentive, thoughtful, faraway look'. Jung went to his mother, who was knitting by the window. Unable to say his father was dead, he told her he was dying. She went in to look at him. 'How quickly it's all gone by,' she said. The comment she made later – 'He died at the right time for you' – seemed to come from her Number Two personality. In six months Jung would come of age: his father's presence in the house would have been an obstacle.

Soon after the funeral, Jung, now head of the family, moved into his father's room, and, from now on, it was he who handed his mother her weekly housekeeping money. Within six or seven weeks he had a recurring dream about the dead man, who said he had made a good recovery and was coming home from his holiday. Jung felt guilty both about believing him to be dead and occupying his room.

They were in trouble financially. In the spring of 1896, taking her son and the sister he so rarely mentions, the widow moved in with her eldest sister, Augusta, and her husband, who was confined to a wheelchair and had a speech defect. They lived in a big house called the Bottminger Mill. Built on two floors with a huge sloping roof, it was close to a railway track in Binningen, a suburb on the other side of Basel, to the southeast. The house, which was surrounded by a big, overgrown garden, was said to be haunted. Twenty years older than Emilie, Augusta had been fifty-eight when she married a lame widower. They stayed on ground level, while the three newcomers occupied the upper floor.

Some of the family tried to pressure Jung into giving up his studies to take a clerical job, but his mother's brother Edward gave them money. Jung was earning a small salary from his job as a junior assistant at the university, and he supplemented it by helping his aunt and uncle to sell their collection of antiques, piece by piece. They gave him a percentage on each article he sold, but he was still short of money. Presented with a box of cigars, he rationed himself to one a week, making it last for a year.

On Saturday afternoons, Luggy, Helly and their older sister Emmy came to the mill to see their cousins and go out for a walk or play games, but seances had been prohibited by Jung's uncle Samuel Gotlob – guardian to both him and Helly, following the death of their fathers. Like the pastor, Rudolf Preiswerk died in his early fifties. Instead of holding seances, the youngsters did their best to tame the wild garden.

Hoping to convert Luggy, Jung gave her spiritualistic books, and often walked home with her, which took over an hour. They frequently continued their conversation about spiritualism in the presence of Helly and her elder sister Mathilde, who believed throughout her life that she was in touch with 'the other side'. Emmy and Dini were interested in spirits, too, but their mother, Celestine, thought spiritualism was ungodly. One day, finding Luggy reading an occult book Jung had lent her, she threw it into the fire.

One morning when the twenty-one-year-old Jung was going to see his friend in Schaffhausen, his mother told him to look up the Rauschenbach family, who lived in a house that was named after its rose garden, the *Haus zum Rosengarten*. In Laufen the pastor had often taken his son on walks with a family called Schenck. The daughter, Berta, had married the owner of a factory that made watches and machines. Jung, who had been four when his family moved from Laufen, remembered her as a pretty girl with fair hair and blue eyes. Calling at their house, he saw their elder daughter, Emma, a girl of fourteen, on the staircase. They did not speak, but, convinced he had just seen his future wife, he confided this to a friend, who laughed.

He later had this to say about 'falling in love at first sight'. 'The archetype is a force. It has an autonomy and it can suddenly seize you . . . You see, you have a certain image in yourself without knowing it, of woman, of *the* woman. You see that girl, or at least a good imitation of your type and instantly you get a seizure and you are gone.'

Walking home from the Breo meant going through the woods, and at night Jung carried a revolver – he had not wholly overcome the nocturnal terrors of his childhood. Outside the bar, he always tried to involve Albert Oeri or one of his other friends in a conversation, 'and so, without noticing it, one would find oneself accompanying him to his front door. Along the route he would interrupt himself with such remarks as: "This is where Dr Götz was murdered." Saying goodnight, he would offer his revolver for the trip back.'

Once, after an all-night drinking session, Jung was sufficiently alert on the way home to pick a bouquet of wild flowers for his mother. Oeri describes him as 'very merry' and always ready for confrontations with 'the League of Virtue', as he called the more puritanic students. 'He was seldom drunk but was noisy when he was. He did not think much of college dances, flirting with housemaids and suchlike gallantries. He said it was totally pointless to hop around a dance floor with some woman until you were drenched in sweat.'

At first he took no part in the weekly discussions. In his fourth term he joined in, but did not deliver his first lecture till November 1896. Instead of being handicapped by what remained of the split in his personality, he made it into a joke, depicting his Number One self from the viewpoint of Number Two. He must have been born in an evil hour, he said. Behaving with the impropriety his black heart inspired, he had acquired a reputation for being rude, uncivil, insolent, cheeky and unmannerly. Desperately though he needed the audience's indulgence, he did not know how to present his 'repellent person and repellent speech'. Perhaps the committee would prefer to have him shipped back to hell. He could only plead for acceptance in human society and instruction in the art of appearing well bred.

Titled 'The Borders of Exact Science', his lecture was an impassioned protest against scientific empiricism. In 1872 the German physiologist Emil Heinrich DuBois-Reymond, who had pioneered the study of electrical activity in nerve and muscle fibres, made a famous attempt to define the frontier between what can be discovered scientifically and what we can never expect to know. He was certain we will never be able to analyse what mind is, or what matter is. When Jung challenged him, he was not merely displaying the provocative panache of a student debater, he was revealing the preoccupations that would determine his development.

Scientists often venture into metaphysics, Jung argued. How else can they assume the ether exists? Light cannot pass through a vacuum, but it travels through a medium that seems immaterial, though it has properties perceptible to our senses. Going on to question the theory of universal gravitation, he wrote in his draft: 'We have arrived at the frontier of something which simply leaves science behind.' But, not wanting to be too provocative, he cut this sentence when he read the paper.

Complaining about careerism and greed for money, he may have reminded himself of his father's sermons. It annoyed him that educated people were squandering time so frivolously, but he cut some of the angrier passages, including 'Man's discriminating intellect is functioning on a level that would disgust a pig.' But he did not conceal his scorn for dinner parties at which people chatted about plays, concerts and art galleries, about the news on Turkey's oppression of the Armenians, or about X-rays, which had been discovered the previous year. Thinking partly of the local bourgeoisie and partly of his father's decline into mental stagnation, he asked: 'Do not we have a sacred duty to protect the youthful seed of awakening knowledge from the fatal frost of indifference?'

It puzzled him that other people were not going all out to discover the purpose of life. 'Whenever we look for the real *reason*, we reach the great void, an area of the vaguest hypotheses. Our flimsy intelligence simply stops functioning at the point where the true explanation starts.' Throughout his long career, Jung's priorities remained substantially unchanged, and he revealed them when he exhorted his audience to 'abandon the safe path that has been laid out for us by esteemed scientists and acclaimed philosophers, to make our own independent sorties into the realm of the unfathomable, to pursue nocturnal shadows and bang on doors which DuBois-Reymond has locked permanently with his little key saying *Ignorabimus*. (We shall not know.)'

Jung had plentiful opportunities to air his views on science and contemporary society – in the fraternity, in religious discussions with theology students and at home with his father's former vicar. There was a vogue for the teachings of August Ritschl, a theologian who had died in 1889. According to him, the impact of Christ's coming was passed down through the centuries in the same way that a train can be driven by an engine in the rear. Jung preferred to think that Jesus had been replaced after his death by the Holy Ghost.

Five

Magnetic Passes

Helly was fifteen in November 1896, the month of Jung's lecture to the Zofingia society. Her birthday present from him was a copy of Justinus Kerner's *The Visionary of Prevorst*. The seances resumed before Christmas, but they were different now, partly because, as he had expected, the book influenced her, and partly because she had lost her father.

The seances still had a sexual undertone – the precocious Helly found new ways of competing with Luggy for Jung's attention – and they now had strong religious overtones. Having started in the parsonage while the pastor was terminally ill, they continued after death had acquired a new meaning for both Jung and the girls. Sitting apprehensively around the table with fingers on the upturned glass, excited and surprised at their own daring as they quizzed the dead, the young mourners were consoling themselves with a ritual that reaffirmed their faith in the survival of the soul.

Helly was becoming less childish. The seances had helped to mature her, and Jung had succeeded in convincing her it was possible to remember former incarnations. She then convinced herself she had been a princess during the Renaissance, and had married Luigi Sforza. The girls' brother Willi, who was two years younger than Luggy and five years older than Helly, tried in vain to stop them from taking Jung so seriously.

Dramatising her previous incarnations, Helly introduced more spirits into the improvisations. The most important spirit she called Ivenes. Though she had never met any Jews, Helly confidently declared Ivenes to be Jewish, and described her as almost entirely liberated from her body, which was that of a black-haired woman, distinctively Jewish in type, wearing white clothes and a turban. Like Swedenborg, who was her brother, she said, and like her sister, Florence Cook, the medium used by Sir William Crookes, but unlike any other spirit, Ivenes had lived at least once in every two centuries. In the nineteenth she had been Friederike Hauffe, the clairvoyante of Prevorst. At the end of the eighteenth, she had been seduced by Goethe and borne him a son. It was to punish her for this sin that she had been afflicted with all Friederike Hauffe's ailments. She had been a martyr during Nero's persecution of the Christians, had been burned as a witch in the Middle Ages, and had given birth to earlier incarnations of both Samuel Preiswerk and the first C. G. Jung. For a girl of fifteen devising a plot that had to go on developing like a serial, Helly was prodigiously ambitious.

It is not surprising that she seemed exhausted at the end of each seance. She lay back on the sofa, eyes half closed, eyeballs turned upwards. She had seen all sorts of things, she claimed, but refused to discuss them. She appeared to have forgotten the conversations she had relayed in her trance. Sometimes she asked who had been present and what had been said. Often she seemed surprised or indignant when she was told. She grumbled about the spirits: next time she would tell Ivenes not to allow them anywhere near her.

Jung was playing a prominent role in the series of dramas. By conversing with the spirits, he was encouraging Helly to continue her performance and to believe in it. No less than an actress, a medium can imagine her way into almost total identification with the character. As he said later, describing the seances in his doctoral thesis, the unconscious personality that builds itself up 'owes its existence simply to suggestive questions that strike an answering chord in the medium's own disposition'.

For the first four of his five years as a medical student, Jung spent a lot of time and energy on asking questions as if he believed (or half believed) he was talking to spirits. How much sincerity was there in his performance? *Memories, Dreams, Reflections* says the seances were 'the great experience that transcended the whole of my early philosophy and enabled me to arrive at a psychological viewpoint'.

He may also have been struggling, as Helly matured, to fend off awareness of not being indifferent to her fixation on him. Trying to woo him through Ivenes, she was using symbolical language when she spoke about unseen forces of attraction in the darkness. Sometimes Ivenes visited a space between the stars which contained innumerable spirit worlds, and she elaborated a system of world forces in the Beyond. On one side was light, and on the other were the powers of attraction. Later she drew a circular diagram to illustrate tensions between three systems of force. Her account of these spirit worlds may have been inspired by what Jung had told her about Kant's concepts of attraction and repulsion between cosmic forces.

In the thesis he gives detailed accounts of three seances. In one Helly lay back on the sofa as if sleeping lightly, and spoke softly in what sounded like a mixture of French and Latin. Her face was pale and her hands felt cold. Afterwards, told she had been talking in her sleep, she seemed annoyed. In the next seance she took on the identity of a gossip who spoke with a north German accent and gave his name as Ulrich von Gerbenstein. While Helly was in Japan, he said, he was looking after her body. He may have seemed more effeminate than she wanted him to. When she appeared to wake up, she was in a bad temper. In the third seance she twice threw herself on her knees to pray.

Other dead characters presented themselves through her. Speaking in Swiss dialect, a young man addressed one of the women at the seance, saying he had always admired her when he was alive. Many of Helly's dead relatives seemed similar to her grandfather. Though she introduced varied names for the spirits, most of them were either schoolgirlish, like Ulrich von Gerbenstein, or solemnly pious, like her version of Samuel Preiswerk and the sanctimonious clerical uncle who had confirmed her.

None of Ivenes's far-fetched statements stopped Jung from judging her to be more mature than Helly. More intelligent, more self-confident, more modest and reserved, she struck him as preferable in every way. Her world-weariness and her longing for the Beyond seemed almost saintly, though she obviously owed her mournful resignation to her prototype, Friederike Hauffe. But Helly was not just mimicking. She poured her soul into Ivenes, exerting herself to create an ideal of goodness, while impersonating the woman she wanted to become – poised, gracious, self-confident, powerful, sagacious, virtuous.

Other changes in her performance patently derived from the book. She started to 'magnetise' herself at the end of each trance, saying she wanted to stave off the headaches that ensued. She combined regular passes with strange circles and figures of eight executed with both arms. She also claimed to have been doing what Friederike Hauffe had done – preaching to black spirits who lived under the Earth's surface. She provided information about star-dwellers, who had no souls, and about Mars, which had canals all over it. There were no bridges, but everyone travelled in flying machines. No wars broke out on the stars, because there were no differences of opinion. Human space travellers were not allowed to land, and star-dwellers had to stay at least seventy-five feet away from the Earth's surface. If they broke this rule, they had to take human form, which was how Napoleon Bonaparte arrived on the Earth.

In 1897, after Basel had been selected as host city for the first international Zionist conference, Helly announced that her grandfather had entrusted her with the mission of converting the Jews to Christianity and leading them to Palestine. Though he had been in favour of giving them a homeland, he would not, in reality, have wanted them to convert. What is surprising, though, is not that Helly made mistakes but that she made so few.

Did Jung suspect her of moving spirits like chess pieces in the game she was playing to involve him emotionally and to manoeuvre the family into forgiving Bertha and Dini? After the death of her baby, Dini became convinced she had been bewitched by her mother-in-law and that this woman was the reincarnation of a seventeenth-century poisoner, Madame Voisin. Dini appealed for help to Helly, who came back from one of the seances looking so exhausted that her mother blamed Jung and forbade her to go on with them. Ashamed, Helly took to her bed and refused to eat. Her mother arranged for her to become an apprentice dressmaker in Basel, but the plan was abandoned.

At first Jung felt sure she was not faking, though all the spirits who spoke through her seemed fairly immature. If she was acting, she was astonishingly accomplished. While the somnambulistic ego was speaking, nothing could distract her, but when the automatic personalities took over, they could be interrupted at any moment. Whenever he felt sceptical, he told himself his young cousin could neither be so imaginative nor so talented.

At other times she did not seem quick-witted. She often came to the parsonage, and sometimes, in a shop or a street, she lapsed into what he called automatisms. An animated conversation would abruptly peter out as she slipped into a distracted state. Looking dreamily out of half-closed eyes, she talked nonsensically and monotonously till she snapped back into alertness. Questioned about the lapse, she would be evasive, saying she had felt giddy or had a headache. Later she might blame the spirits. Did they think she was there just for their benefit? It seemed to her that they could waft her body to distant places, draining her strength.

She complained of having visions in bed while falling asleep. Abruptly the room lit up, she said, and, wrapped in veil-like robes, shining white figures detached themselves from the brightness. Later she might see them in broad daylight, but only fleetingly. Usually the visions were blissful; occasionally frightening or demonic. Once in a dark hallway a copper-red face glared at her.

If Jung accepted the tenets of spiritualism, he would have answers to such questions as whether the psyche is identical with the soul and what divides the living from the dead. Did part of his father still exist? Was Helly really in touch with both his grandfathers? Though his attitude to Jesus had never been that of a normal Christian, his habits of thinking had evolved in a clerical environment, and spiritualism seemed preferable to materialism. He tried to reconcile science with spiritualism while rejecting orthodox Christianity.

The seances were to continue, with interruptions, for four and a half years, and in spite of all her disadvantages in the rivalry with her older, bigger, more attractive sister, Helly made a deep and lasting impression on him. Later, as a young doctor, he talked about her to a patient who became his lover, Sabina Spielrein, and one day, when he showed her his diary, telling her to open it at random, she found a passage in which Helly

> appeared to Dr Jung one night in a white garment . . . she was supposed to be very pretty and intelligent. This girl was deeply rooted in him, and she was my prototype . . . Later on he would sometimes turn reflective when I said something to him; such and such a woman had spoken in just this way. And it was always this girl!

It may have been *The Visionary of Prevorst* that gave him the idea of hypnotising her. Thanks to Kerner's 'magnetic' passes, Friederike Hauffe had suffered less; and it gave Jung more control over what happened if he could help Helly into trances. Sometimes Ivenes visited a space between the stars which contained innumerable spirit worlds, and she talked about a moonlit valley destined for generations still unborn. Spirits never needed to converse, she said. They could read each other's thoughts.

Trying to reconcile science with spiritualism while rejecting both ortho-dox Christianity and materialism, Jung read Schopenhauer's comments on spiritualism. 'Anyone who nowadays doubts the facts of animal magnetism,' he had written, 'and the clairvoyance it confers must be regarded not as sceptical but as ignorant.' Schopenhauer believed in a 'dream organ' that functioned during both sleep and consciousness, introducing into the world of phenomena impressions rooted in *noumena*. 'The dream organ of two people can be involved in the same activity, wherein a ghost . . . takes on the appearance of a body.' This organ would be at work during trances, and to induce them by hypnotism would be to invite intimacy between the dream organs of the hypnotist and the medium.

Kant had been more ambivalent about spirits, and in May 1897, when Jung gave his second lecture to the fraternity, two months before his twenty-second birthday, he misled his audience, as he had misled himself, about the meaning of Kant's 1766 essay *Dreams of a Spirit-Seer*, which debates whether the psyche could be independent of space and time – a question that will always be crucial to Jung's thinking.

In 1756 when Swedenborg was in Göteborg, he talked to friends about a big fire that had broken out 250 miles away, close to his house in Stockholm. He told them when the flames were extinguished, and his telepathic knowledge was subsequently validated. Kant, who wrote to him but received no answer, admitted he was 'inclined to endorse the existence of immaterial beings in the universe', but the inclination depended on 'the specific bent of the human mind', which is prejudiced. We weigh evidence in scales that are inaccurate: 'the lever inscribed "Future hopes" has the mechanical advantage'.

Jung's lecture contains seven quotations from Kant's essay, and, taken out of context, they seem to affirm belief in spirits, and to support Jung's argument that 'We must fight crass sensualism with the weapons of transcendental truth . . . Religions are created by men who have given practical demonstrations of the reality of mystery and the "extrasensory sphere".' If consciousness is, as Schopenhauer held, 'the object of a transcendental idea', the transcendental subject could legitimately be called 'soul'. Going on to define soul as 'an intelligence independent of space and time', Jung said he was providing 'empirical evidence substantiating our definition of the soul'. One day, he predicted, materialism would be blamed 'for the fact that everyone and everything is deteriorating'. Now, in 1897, the universities should sponsor research into psychic phenomena.

Committing himself to ideas that aroused scepticism, he was nervous of making himself as unpopular as he had been at school; but his audience was impressed. Holding it under his spell, he obviously enjoyed the power he wielded, even if he underestimated it. In the debate after his second lecture, he clashed with Oeri, who spoke up for a theology student Jung attacked for defending the leading theologians of the day. But in the election for the new chairman of the society, Oeri proposed Jung as a candidate. He had a popular rival, and the issue had to be put to the vote four times before Jung was declared the winner. He would take office at the beginning of the winter term. But when *Memories, Dreams, Reflections* was published, fellow students found that the book presented a man quite different from the Jung they remembered. As a student he must have been 'living in a world that was known only to him'.

In private conversation, too, he was impressive. Few of his fellow students took his belief in spiritualism seriously, but he argued cogently that it was possible to research scientifically into metaphysics. 'Students of natural sciences and mathematics supported him, but theology students remained silent.'

Once he tried to convert a young theology student to spiritualism. After a long evening of drinking, they walked through the woods together. Jung talked so forcefully about ghosts and demons that his frightened companion suddenly ran back to the city. Writing afterwards to one of his friends, he said Jung now despised him, and showed it.

There can be no doubt that Jung enouraged Helly to believe the dead were speaking through her. In some ways he was handicapped by conflict between his scientific ambitions and his interest in spiritualism, but in other ways he was helped. The tension sharpened his scientific curiosity about the psyche. As a medical student, he found it puzzling that so little was known about it, though philosophers said that without it there could be neither knowledge nor insight. When he read books by Swedenborg and other spiritualists, he accepted that what was being described was 'the objective behaviour of the soul'.

It was William James who established the American branch of the Society for Psychical Research, and many reputable scientists committed themselves to spiritualism – Sir William Crookes, for instance, in London. But it was only in private that Jung would talk enthusiastically about his convictions. 'It was really splendid to let oneself be lectured as one sat in his room with him. His dear little dachshund would gaze at me so intelligently, as if he could understand each word, and Jung told me how piteously the sensitive animal whimpered whenever occult forces were at work.'

The title he chose for his next lecture to the Zofingia Society was 'Thoughts on Christianity'. What was needed, he said, was an uncompromising rejection of modern rationalism. He denounced theologians who tried to explain away all the mysteries of religion and to deny the possibility of intimate communication with God. If Christianity was to have any substance, he said, they 'must accept once again the whole metaphysical and conceptual universe of the early Christians'. Christianity 'represents nothing less than a break with the entire world'. You cannot believe in the possibility of mystic union with God without renouncing 'any chance of distinguishing between reality and hallucination'.

This is consistent with a statement he made thirty-eight years later:

> My chief curiosity was always the question: What does the human mind, inasmuch as it is a natural involuntary functioning, produce if left to itself? Such a problem, of course, is only possible after a complete renunciation of all traditional truth, no matter how true it may be. Whatever my statements are, they are always based upon experiences, and whatever I say is never intended to contradict or to defend an existing truth. Its sole purpose is to express what I believe I have seen.

This is reminiscent of Rudolf Steiner's claim: 'I will never say anything about spiritual matters that I do not know from direct spiritual experience. This is my guiding star, and this has enabled me to see through every illusion.' Like Steiner, Jung had followers eager to be guided by the same star. 'I consider it my task and duty,' said Jung, 'to educate my patients and pupils to the point where they can accept the direct demand that is made on them from within.' But most of them needed him to tell them what was being demanded.

Though he claimed it was only because he enjoyed arguing that he so often became involved in arguments with students of theology, he was obviously interested in theological problems, and there were many early indications of the splitting that will characterise his work as a psychologist. However keen he was to be regarded as an empiricist, he could not ignore his own beliefs.

The lectures he attended ran parallel with the seances he attended, and he learned from both. Through Ivenes, Helly told gossipy stories about members of the family, dead and alive, while other messages derived from her presumptions about what was going on in Jung's mind. Jealous of a woman who seemed to have replaced Luggy as her chief rival for Jung's affection – a widow whose husband had died of tuberculosis – Helly produced a lot of gossip intended to discredit her. According to one dead witness, the husband had been poisoned with a fluid that attracted tubercle bacilli: wicked spirits had taught his wife how to use it. Most of Helly's stories were designed to be unverifiable. Her self-confidence was extra-ordinary for someone so young, and she made clever use of details she had picked up from family conversations.

One person who envied her was Trudi, her junior by three years. After trying so hard to engage the attention of the brother who was so much older and bigger and cleverer, and after having so much less success than Helly, Trudi, who was fourteen in the summer of 1898, made a serious bid for his attention.

One afternoon when Helly had come to tea, Trudi suddenly went into a trance. They put her on a sofa, and Jung felt her pulse, which was faint. Her breathing was shallow, and she was very pale. Speaking in a deep voice, she addressed her brother as if she were their father. He should have no fear of death. He had been spared – another was atoning for him. She was talking about their cousin Fritzi, who had been drowned in the river together with two friends during June 1898, when their boat overturned. But Trudi was less impressive than Helly, who was content to remain a spectator. They put Trudi to bed, and Helly went home.

Jung was in his fourth year at medical school, but his thirst for knowledge was still unslaked. He could accept everything Helly said about her spiritual journeys through a universe in which countless concentric worlds related to each other, but he was still impatient for answers to the fundamental questions about the meaning of life. During the winter term of 1898–9 he took a course in psychiatry, but found the lecturer, Professor Wille, uninspiring, and in Jung's fourth Zofingia lecture, which he delivered that term, he attacked his teachers.

If the university was a microcosm of Swiss society, fraternity members were like parishioners who had to be reminded they could not save their souls by earning money. In the Middle Ages, he said, men had enjoyed a closer bond with nature, and life had centred on inwardness. The comforts of modern life encouraged superficiality, while secularisation made everyone like everyone else. Commercial success would not bring happiness. No one had ever made enough money not to feel greedy for more, and, as Schopenhauer had said, behind our existence lies something that becomes accessible only when we have put the world aside.

Science could be satisfying only if imbued with faith and wisdom. 'Every authentic philosophy, as the full expression of metaphysical desire, is religion.' Jung was lecturing over a hundred years ago, when science, philosophy and religion seemed to interpenetrate more than they do in the post-Einsteinian ethos. How could the Earth, he asked, have conceived life if it had not been fitted out like a bride by the forces of creation? Hartmann must have been right to argue that the principle which generated the material world was divergence into a polarised dualism, and Jung thought he could demonstrate in a single lecture the roots of dualism in both organic nature and the principles of physics.

His destiny, he believed, was to penetrate the secret meaning of nature. What he meant by 'causal instinct' was the drive that compelled him to investigate causes. The strongest component in his individuality, he thought, was insatiable curiosity. This led him back to religion. Neither denying the external world in favour of inner reality, nor affirming it on the basis of mere phenomena, he would go on penetrating from the known into the unknowable. Characterising Kant's *noumena* as unknowable, he was moving towards his own later idea of the archetype – something that is unknowable but serves as an unconscious structure, a concept-forming principle.

In January 1899 Jung gave his last lecture to the fraternity. Still believing in revelation, he held that knowledge of good and evil should come from direct understanding of God's will. Hartmann had questioned whether ethics could be divorced from metaphysics, arguing that without metaphysical ideas, worship becomes meaningless, while ethics wither into abstraction. Jung agreed. The time had come for an uncompromising rejection of rationalism.

At first Helly had been in no doubt about the reality of the spirits, but now she was either losing faith in them or finding it hard to avoid repeating herself. More and more time was wasted on the superficial chit-chat of Ulrich von Gerbenstein, while Ivenes became more tentative, less mature, and Helly, not wanting to lose her power over her audience, resorted to trickery. After smuggling objects into the room under her clothes, she produced them as if they had suddenly materialised, but she was less accomplished as a conjuror than as an actress, and when Jung brought some student friends to a seance, they were not taken in.

Humiliated by her failure to deceive them, Helly refused to attend the seances Jung organised in the autumn of 1898, and Trudi was given another chance. But she failed to impress her brother, and he stopped the seances. 'He was not specially interested in his sister's dreams,' comments Stefanie Zumstein-Preiswerk. Jung writes about Helly's puberty as bringing phys-iological changes, new unconscious feelings, romantic ideas, exalted reli-giosity and mysticism, together with a desire for independence. It also sharpened her desire for him. In 1899, when the last seance was held, she was nearly eighteen. The four and a half years – formative in both her life and Jung's – must have spanned many changes in their feelings for each other. We shall never know how much agony she suffered, or what happened when she appeared in his room, dressed in a white robe. Drafting *Memories, Dreams, Reflections*, he wrote that he finally broke off his relationship with her, but this phrase was cut by his family, who perhaps, as Alan Elms suggests, 'felt particularly sensitive about what sort of relationship it may have been'.

At about this time, Jung tells us, there were some inexplicable explosions at the mill, but he gives contradictory accounts of them, and it is hard to be sure what – if anything – really happened. According to a letter he wrote in the thirties, the first explosion involved a breadknife, and he was in the garden when there was a noise like a pistol shot. 'The knife was in a basket beside a loaf of bread and the basket was in a locked drawer of the sideboard . . . the knife had exploded into four parts and was still lying scattered inside the sideboard.' A few days later he heard another noise like a pistol shot in an adjoining room and found that a round table had split.

According to *Memories, Dreams, Reflections*, the first explosion involved the round table, which had belonged to his paternal grandfather, and about two weeks later he came home to find his mother, his sister and the maid puzzled by a noise they had just heard from the sideboard. He opened it to find the breadknife had fractured into four pieces.

Helly's niece, Stephanie Zumstein-Preiswerk, says the round table was the one that had been used in the seances and had belonged to Jung's other grandfather. His mother was in no doubt that a message was being sent to them, telling them to resume the seances. Perhaps Samuel Preiswerk had been trying to tell them something after Fritzi drowned, and they had not understood. Jung agreed that the explosions must have something to do with Helly's powers as a medium. But in *Memories, Dreams, Reflections* he says the explosions occurred after the last seance.

In the letter, which was to J. B. Rhine, the author of *Extra-Sensory Perception*, Jung says the explosions occurred before the seances began and were possibly 'connected with an acquaintance I had just made in these days . . . a young woman with marked mediumistic tendencies . . . She hadn't come anywhere near my house then . . . but she told me she had vividly thought of these seances just in those days when the explosions occurred.' He sent Rhine a photograph of a breadknife with three breaks in the blade. He admired Rhine's work, which makes it even harder to explain why he should deviate so far from the facts about Helly.

In July, on the day before he took the state examination to graduate from the university, Jung wrote in his diary: 'Today is a specially solemn day . . . I'm in a state of calm expectation, my soul on fire with suspense.' On the evening after the exam he went to the theatre for the first time in his life. He was twenty-five.

Since the death of his father, his mother had been living on 2200 francs a month. Jung had been outside Switzerland only once, when he walked over eighty miles to Belfort, near Mulhouse in France, and spent sixty francs on a two-week holiday, paying fifty centimes to spend the night in a barn, sleeping on the hay. His second holiday abroad was during the first ten days of September 1900, when he went to Munich.

On graduating he was offered a job by Friedrich von Müller, head of the medical clinic, who was giving up his position to practise in Munich, where he needed an assistant. The opportunity would have been irresistible if Jung had not been so attracted to psychiatry. It was regarded as an inferior branch of medicine, but he took a second course with Professor Wille in the summer of 1889, and read the standard textbook on psychiatry, Richard von Krafft-Ebing's *Lehrbuch der Psychiatrie*, which describes neuroses as 'diseases of the personality'. This, says Jung, was what convinced him that his only possible future was as a psychiatrist. 'Here was the field of experience common to biological and spiritual facts, which I had sought everywhere and had not found. Here, finally, was the place where nature would collide with spirit.'

It has been suggested that what really motivated his decision to study the subject was uncertainty about hereditary mental illness in his family. After the two courses with Wille and after reading Krafft-Ebing, he may have looked back more critically – and more anxiously – on the split between his mother's two personalities and on the split between his own. Knowing that a doctor had diagnosed his fainting fits as 'degenerative' and epileptic, he may have thought psychiatry would improve his chances of saving himself from madness.

In his 1935 Tavistock lectures he made a half-joking reference to 'the reason why men with somewhat unbalanced minds often like to be alienists. It is humanly understandable because it gives you a tremendous satisfaction when you are not quite sure of yourself to be able to say "Oh the others are much worse." '

Six

Lunatic Asylum

In Switzerland at the turn of the century, the only training for a psychiatrist was experience in what was still called a lunatic asylum. The Burghölzli, which was not only an asylum but also the psychiatric clinic of Zurich University, became famous when its director was Auguste Forel – psychiatrist, neurologist, entomologist and social reformer. Retiring from the Burghölzli in 1899 at the age of fifty-one, he handed over to a former pupil, the forty-three-year-old Eugen Bleuler. At this time there were only four doctors to look after 340 inmates.

For fourteen years Jung's life had centred on Basel. He left partly to distance himself from his mother and the relations who still treated him like a boy. Before he could accept the job Bleuler offered, he had to complete his military service. After serving in the infantry at Aarau, he was discharged in time to start work on 10 December 1900. Tradition, education and culture all counted for more in Basel than in Zurich, which struck him as being like a village. Looking back in old age on his arrival there, he called it 'Switzerland's most materialistic city'. He felt isolated: 'There was nobody ready-made for my needs. I then shaped some for me.'

The Burghölzli was a big, austere building on a hill above the lake, but it had been built so that patients would have no view of the water – in case it inspired suicidal ideas. Except in the doctors' quarters, there was no upholstered furniture, only hard wooden benches. Doctors and assistants had to live in, like Bleuler, and to work almost as hard as he did. They completed their first round of the wards in time to report on patients at the staff meeting, which started at eight thirty. Two or three times a week it was followed by another meeting at ten to discuss new patients. Doctors and assistants made another round in the evening between five and seven. They typed out their notes on case histories, and the working day rarely ended before ten in the evening, when the hospital doors were closed for the night. Senior doctors had keys, but juniors and assistants had to borrow one if they wanted to come in later.

For the first six months, Jung rarely went outside the hospital. He was always reading, either in his room or in the library. Owning only one pair of trousers and a couple of shirts, he would have had difficulties if he had wanted an active social life, but he did not. More energetic and more ambitious than his colleagues, he was struggling to fill the gaps in his knowledge of clinical practice. In six months he worked his way through fifty volumes of the *Allgemeine Zeitschrift für Psychiatrie*.

The other doctors assumed he was either psychotic or melancholic. The only friendship he formed was with a brain surgeon, Muralt, and this ended when Muralt married a woman who objected to his spending time with another man.

Though Forel had believed in emotional contact with patients, his doctors were mostly Germans who did not understand the Swiss dialect spoken by most of the patients. When doctors wrote that a patient remained silent or spoke unintelligibly, they were reporting mainly on a linguistic barrier that did not exist for either Jung or Bleuler, who had been born of farming stock in Zollikon on the outskirts of Zurich. He studied in Paris and ran the large mental hospital in Rheinau, a converted Benedictine monastery on an island near the Rhine Falls. A straightforward, humane man, he pioneered the approach later used by Jung and later still by R. D. Laing. Rejecting the idea that the babble of schizophrenics was meaningless, he listened to it carefully. Bleuler believed in spending time with patients, chatting, empathising, and giving them tasks that would show them they could cope with practical problems. He worked hard, visiting wards at least four times a day, and usually completing his first round by six in the morning.

Jung described him as 'a man to whom all outward forms of recognition are anathema. He is motivated by a truly Christian desire not to stand in the way of other people, and has a youthful eagerness to learn such as only an extremely clever and intelligent man possesses at his age.' His main limitation was diffidence: he found it hard to make contact with other people. He was still a bachelor when he habituated himself to living in the hospital and spending most of his day with patients. After marrying a social worker twelve years his junior, Hedwig Waser, who shared the belief in temperance he had in common with Forel, he lived in the hospital with her in a self-contained flat.

One of the doctors, Alphonse Maeder, described the Burghölzli as 'a kind of factory where everyone worked hard for low wages'. No alcohol was allowed on the premises, but Bleuler was no authoritarian. If doctors or assistants made mistakes, they were not taken to task, and he often came to drink coffee in their room after lunch, discussing new developments in medicine and surgery, not so much to test their knowledge as to keep abreast of it.

Deprived of contact with the outside world and of emotional fulfilment, patients gave themselves in fantasy and delusion what they lacked in reality. Hysterics, obsessional neurotics and schizophrenics all deteriorated, un-helped by the drugs that would later become available. Self-abasement was carried further than Jung had believed possible. He saw patients eating excrement, drinking urine and masturbating almost incessantly. One killed himself in this way. An educated young catatonic alternated between sticking his finger into his mouth and into his anus. Others smeared themselves with excrement. One woman flaunted herself at Jung by daubing faeces all over her body: 'Do I please you so?' But he warded off depression by livening things up as much as he could, organising dances and an annual costume ball at which patients could dress up and dance with doctors.

He also had to deal with outpatients, including a six-year-old girl who accused her foster father of molesting her. During her first session she 'spontaneously hallucinated "a sausage that would get fatter". When I asked where she saw the sausage, she promptly answered: "On the Herr Dok-tor." '

Sexual and physical anarchy existed alongside the chaos of delusions. In schizophrenia, as Jung put it, 'every single thing is projected outwards'. Delusional ideas were mostly a mixture of wish-fulfilment with the sense of being injured or persecuted – a feeling sometimes compensated by mega-lomania. In the fantasies of female patients, doctors were regularly cast as romantic heroes or villainous seducers, and delusions of grandeur were common. 'I, the Grand Duke of Mephisto, shall have you treated with blood vengeance for orang-outang representation.' 'I have long since established the monopoly. I am triple owner of the world.' 'I am double polytechnic irreplaceable. That is the highest, all highest – the highest of dressmaking.' 'I created the highest mountain peak, the Finsteraarhorn.' 'Naples and I must look after the world with noodles.'

Nearly a quarter of the inmates had irreparable brain damage, while schizophrenia accounted for 70 to 80 per cent of the chronic cases. Ensnared in conversation, a doctor might think he was being helpful, or that he would eventually be able to modulate into rational discourse. Instead he often became the victim of verbal aggression. Patients alternated between polite subservience and abuse prompted by envy of the doctors' power and freedom. One morning Jung was greeted: 'Here comes one of the troupe of dogs and monkeys who thinks he's a messiah.'

In patients he could observe in exaggerated form 'all the phenonomena present only fleetingly in normal people'. Walking round the wards with him, a visiting friend said: 'It's just like Zurich in miniature. A quintessence of the population. It's as if all the types you meet every day in the street had been collected here in their classical purity.'

Going into wards, sometimes alone, sometimes with Bleuler and a retinue of assistants and nurses, Jung found little could be done. Twice a day he visited a bed-ridden catatonic who had not spoken for years. Except by reflex actions, catatonics never responded to stimuli, and Jung called them ' "reflex-machines" – they remain sitting or lying in some favourite position until roused to reflex action'.

Bleuler was helpful and encouraging. At first, Jung emulated him. Visiting the hospital, Albert Oeri found the former Barrel had 'followed his master, Bleuler, on the path to total abstinence'. Meeting patients who were standing about or lying on their beds, Oeri chatted with one until another tried to punch him. Unable to stop laughing, Jung said this man sometimes hit people very hard if they came too close.

But Jung's admiration for Bleuler was short-lived. By Basel standards he was uncultured, and Jung later described him as a cross between a peasant and a schoolteacher. He is rarely mentioned in the interviews Jung gave, or in *Memories, Dreams, Reflections*, which accuses Burghölzli doctors of classifying symptoms and categorising patients without listening to them. In fact, they were under orders to see patients twice a day and write down everything they said, whether it seemed to make sense or not.

For twelve months Jung had little leisure. Doing compulsory military service in Basel, he took an officer's training course and was given the rank of lieutenant. Back at the hospital, in addition to his ordinary duties as an assistant to Bleuler, he had to complete a thesis in order to qualify as a doctor.

An evening meeting was held once a month to discuss psychological literature. Bleuler would ask one of the doctors or assistants to read a new book or article and report on it to his colleagues, who would then ask questions or make comments. At the end of the evening Bleuler would sum up. In 1896, while at Rheinau, he had reviewed *Studies on Hysteria* by Sigmund Freud and Joseph Breuer. 'Introducing a completely new view of the workings of the psyche,' he had written, 'the book is one of the most important additions of recent years in the field of normal or pathological psychology.'

Bleuler now asked Jung to review Freud's *On Dreams* (*Über den Traum*) at the next meeting. The book made an impact on Jung. In his 1939 obituary of Freud, he calls *The Interpretation of Dreams* (*Die Traumdeutung*) 'probably the boldest attempt ever been made to master the riddles of the unconscious psyche on the apparently firm ground of empiricism'. But in 1900, according to *Memories, Dreams, Reflections*, he gave the book only a cursory reading 'because I did not yet grasp it. At twenty-five I lacked the experience to appreciate Freud's theories. Such experience did not come till later. In 1903 I once again took up *The Interpretation of Dreams* and discovered how it all linked up with my own ideas.' But in August 1957, in a filmed interview with Richard Evans, he admitted: 'I studied the book very attentively . . . I thought "This is a masterpiece – full of future." I had no ideas then of my own; I was just beginning.'

What he had to review was not the complete *Interpretation of Dreams* but a summary that appeared early in 1901 as part of a serial publication. Dated 25 January 1901, Jung's paper was found among his posthumous writings. Presenting it six weeks after his arrival at the Burghölzli, he acknowledges that analysis of dreams has shed new light on what prompts them and on their connection with waking life.

Freud regarded *The Interpretation of Dreams* as the basis for what he achieved, but it failed to establish his reputation. In 1899, for the first edition, six-hundred copies were printed, but it took eight years to sell them. Nineteen years older than Jung, he was in his forty-fourth year at the turn of the century, but had never had a professorial appointment. The book was rooted in the self-analysis he started in 1897. His approach was based on the 'free association' he had evolved as an alternative to hypnosis. Comfortable, relaxed, unconcerned to impress anyone, the analysand, like the dreamer, lets his mind drift at random between childhood and recent experiences, between anxieties and desires, ideas and feelings. The analyst learns not only from what is said but from silences, hesitations, transitions, changes of tempo, volume and direction.

Maintaining that memories and fantasies from early childhood surface in the hallucinations that constitute dreams, Freud distinguishes between their manifest content (what the dreamer remembers) and their latent content (underlying wishes and fears). What Freud calls 'dreamwork' consists of bringing the latent content to the surface. The object is to sidestep dream censorship – the sleeping equivalent to repressions that protect us from being disturbed by fantasies and wishes which originate in early life. This is why we forget both early childhood experiences and dreams.

In 1900, after reading *On Dreams* carefully enough to write an eight-page report, Jung worked on the complete *Interpretation of Dreams* and on the earlier *Studies on Hysteria* by Freud and Joseph Breuer, which had been published in 1895. He made references to both books in footnotes to his doctoral thesis, which was ready by the middle of 1902.

Before Freud, psychiatrists had attributed most neurotic symptoms to lack of integration, and the word *dissociation* was used for what looked like disconnection between the personality and thoughts, actions, dreams, delusions and compulsions that seemed to be out of character. Breuer had introduced the term *hypnoid* to describe a state like the one produced by hypnosis: consciousness appears to be taken over by something tangential to the subject's mental life. Groups of split-off associations rise to the surface, only to vanish when normal consciousness returns. Breuer and Freud had been writing about hysteria, but Jung may have been reminded of the trances he had induced by hypnotising Helly.

Finding Freud's writing could illuminate mysteries he had to face in the wards, he saw that repression was a factor in psychosis, as in neurosis, and that delusions could be analysed like dreams.

Two years earlier, there could have been no question of writing a doctoral thesis on seances, but in 1900 the professor of psychology at the University of Geneva, Théodore Flournoy, brought out his book *From India to Planet Mars*. For five years he had been studying the case of a department-store saleswoman who worked as a medium under the name Helen Smith. In her trance state she described three previous existences: as a queen in fifteenth-century India, as Marie Antoinette and as a Martian. She claimed to be familiar with the landscapes, inhabitants and language of the planet.

Siding with neither her admirers nor the sceptics, Flournoy treated her stories as products of her subliminal imagination, based on forgotten memories and unacknowledged desires. For the material she used in the narratives, her unconscious subpersonalities mined different layers of her past. In her examples of Martian speech, the syntactical pattern was based on French, her native language. After Flournoy's book appeared, a linguist demonstrated that much of her Martian vocabulary consisted of distorted Hungarian words, but this supported Flournoy's conclusions: Hungarian was her father's native language. In her Marie Antoinette stories she was going back to the age of sixteen; in the Hindu stories to the age of twelve.

Jung had discussed spiritualism with Bleuler, who was interested in psychical research, and, realising that Flournoy had made the subject academically respectable, he encouraged Jung to focus his thesis on seances. In 1935, saying that what differentiated his work most radically from Freud's was 'the idea of the independence of the unconscious', he claimed to have discovered this 'as far back as 1902, when I was engaged in studying the psychic history of a young girl somnambulist'. Helly had not been a sleepwalker, but Jung was working in the tradition of Charcot, who used hypnosis to study hysteria, and throughout most of the nineteenth century, 'artificial somnambulism', induced by hypnotism, had been regarded as the best way of gaining access to the unconscious mind. Even earlier, as Ellenberger points out, mentioning the scene in which the sleepwalking

Lady Macbeth gives away her secrets, interest in somnambulism had spread beyond medicine into literature and philosophy.

Giving the date 1902, Jung was referring not to the seances, which ended in 1899, but to the final stages of his work on his thesis, which was written – or so he claimed – from notes taken after each seance. The word *studying* has less relevance to the seances of 1895–9 than to the reading and thinking he did in 1901–2, after Flournoy's book was published. It served, as Sonu Shamdasani has shown, as the model for Jung's thesis.

Helly's absence and the gap of time made it easier for him to do what was expedient – to preserve an appearance of scientific objectivity and clinical detachment, though the words 'case' and 'patient' were incongruous with what had happened. Following Flournoy's example, he presented the 'spirits' as fragments that had split off from the medium's personality, and it is Flournoy's influence that makes him look at one of these, Ivenes, as a personification of the way in which Helly would like to mature. Or, as Shamdasani puts it, 'her subpersonality Ivenes represented a teleological automatism, the emergence of a personality in advance of her normal consciousness.'

Jung did not admit he had taken an active part in the seances, or even that he had gone on participating in them for four and a half years. 'The whole process arrived at its climax within four to eight weeks,' he writes, 'and the description of Ivenes and the other subconscious personalities refer in general to this period.' After this, he says, 'one could observe with one's own eyes all the gradations from somnambulism to conscious lying.' In fact, eighteen months had elapsed between the first seance and the birthday on which he gave her Kerner's book, and over three years between that and the last seance.

He said it was out of regard for his 'patient', whom he called 'Fräulein S.W.', that he was altering a few unimportant data and omitting various details, but the story he tells is substantially at odds with what happened. Giving Helly's age as fifteen and a half, he suppresses all the differences between the child who passed on the first message from her grandfather and the young woman who was desperate enough to perform conjuring tricks. Nor does he admit that one of the grandfathers was both hers and his, that the seances took place in his home, that he induced trances by hypnotising her, or that she was infatuated with him. More than anyone else, he had been in charge of the seances, but he now had to write as if he had been a detached observer.

He may genuinely have been more sceptical about spiritualism in 1901–2 than in 1895, but had Helly's 'conscious lying' altered his outlook? In a 1905 newspaper article he wrote that after examining eight mediums – six female and two male – he had concluded little could be expected from them. Everything that happened could be explained scientifically, and most mediums were slightly abnormal. One of the eight had been a fake. But did this tally with his private convictions? When had he decided that the contrasting voices belonged to fragments of Helly's personality? Was he trying to put spiritualism behind him when he argued that she had been repressing the emotions that came into play when she went into trances? Or was he posing as a sceptical empiricist?

The thesis refers to Freud's investigations of dreams when it explains how distraction can be bypassed by unconscious concentration: 'If a train of thought is initially rejected (consciously, perhaps) by a judgment that it is wrong or useless for the immediate intellectual purposes in view, the result may be that this train of thought will proceed, unobserved by the processes of consciousness, till the onset of sleep.' Jung argues that Helly's reveries were like dreams emerging from emotionally charged ideas that had entered her wakeful consciousness only briefly. Aware of the discontinuity between her shyness and her self-assertiveness, she had been repressing the two extremes and trying to keep a grip on the best parts of herself to play the role of Ivenes. The repressed elements then erupted into her hallucinations as autonomous personalities.

He explains the tapping sounds and the movements of the table as due to involuntary movements in her arm 'analogous' to certain hypnotic experiments in the waking state. He borrows Flournoy's word *cryptomnesia* to describe the process by which memories fade from consciousness and return during semi-somnambulistic trances. Trying to analyse the relationship of subpersonalities, such as the two grandfathers, to Helly's ego-consciousness, he suggests they were dramatised split-offs from her dream ego. When they taught Ivenes the secrets of the Beyond, praised her for being extraordinary and gave her opportunities to excel, they were gratifying her like a wish-fulfilment dream.

Jung uses Freud's term 'hysterical identification' for the state of being transported by one's interest in the object. Reveries can develop into hysterical delirium in which dream fantasies become hallucinations. The pathological liar who succumbs to his fantasies is like a child who loses himself in his game or an actor who loses himself in his role. 'The difference between this and the somnambulistic dissociation of the personality is only a difference of degree.'

If Helly had really been a patient, and if Freud had been supervising the case, Jung might have been told to let her speak out everything that came to mind until she could confront memories and perceptions that had sunk into unconsciousness and re-emerged during trances as images and ideas. He would later come to believe that integration could be achieved through bringing the contents of the unconscious into consciousness, but he had encouraged Helly to believe in her powers as a medium, hypnotising her into trances and taking part in the drama by questioning the subpersonalities as if they had nothing to do with her experience or with emotions she was trying to repress.

Even if he now believed he might have harmed her by encouraging her tendency to dissociation, he could hardly confess this in a thesis designed to win him a doctorate. Instead of following his argument about repression to its logical conclusion, he claimed to have helped her by talking to the subpersonalities. 'The individualisation of the subconscious is always a great step forward and has enormous influence on further development of the automatisms.'

This idea became basic to his theory. Later he would interrogate figures in his fantasies. Later still he would teach patients to interrogate figures in theirs. He called this technique *active imagination*. But he abandoned the term *subconscious*, talking instead of the *unconscious*, sometimes referring to un-conscious mental activity in the individual and sometimes to an external aggregate of forces, assuming it could act like nature or destiny on human life. His inclination to believe in what he called the independence of the unconscious is in line with his boyhood refusal to accept responsibility for such images as the giant penis and the divine turd. If they had presented themselves to him, it must be because some external power had implanted them in his mind. According to Anthony Storr, 'The delusion that external powers of some kind are implanting ideas into one's mind is one of the key symptoms of schizophrenia, known as "thought insertion".'

Jung's eighty-six-page account of the seances served as his inaugural thesis for his medical degree. Introduced as the 'First Assistant Physician in the Burghölzli Clinic,' he presented it before the Faculty of Medicine at Zurich in 1902, and it was approved on Bleuler's recommendation.

The thesis was then published. Though designed primarily to safeguard Jung, the deviations from the truth were also intended to conceal the identity of Helly and the Preiswerks. They failed to do this, and it caused a scandal when citizens of Basel read about a recognisable family in which the grandfather had waking hallucinations, while his brother was a feeble-minded eccentric who also saw visions, and his sister had fainting fits, 'followed by a brief somnambulism during which she uttered prophecies'. The medium's mother had 'a congenital psychopathic inferiority often bordering on psychosis', and one of her sisters was 'a hysteric and a visionary'.

What Jung told Sabina Spielrein about Helly suggests that his thesis may have been an act of 'revenge'. The initials he used – S.W. – may have been taken maliciously from Krafft-Ebing's *Textbook of Insanity*, where S.W. is a seamstress whose delusions of grandeur were aggravated by eroticism and coquetry. Atfter the thesis was published, there was a lot of gossip in Basel about the Preiswerks, and rumours about insanity in the family reduced Helly's chances of finding a husband; her sisters suffered in the same way. Helly became a seamstress and, with her friend Emmy Zinnstag, left Switzerland to settle in Versailles.

Seven

Wearing a Cardboard Collar

Knowing Jung had few friends in Zurich, an acquaintance of his family invited him to a fete in Winterthur, eighteen miles to the northwest, and it was there that he had his second meeting with Emma Rauschenbach. He was about twenty-seven, and she was about twenty, tall and slim, with her dark-brown hair in braids.

Now in his early forties, her father had gone blind when she was twelve, leaving his wife, Berta, with more control over the household and their two daughters. As the elder daughter, Emma was trying to share the extra responsibility with her mother.

A few months later Berta invited Jung to a ball at their summer residence. They had a beautifully situated estate at Olberg, outside Schaffhausen, with several acres of land, three gardeners, several carriages and two horses. The footmen wore green livery. Their home and their lifestyle could hardly have contrasted more strongly with those of the Jung family. The rooms were spacious, the furniture imposing, and the maids wore white caps with streamers and starched aprons.

He danced with Emma in the turreted courtyard, but did not make a favourable impression. He was wearing a cardboard collar, and his manners, like his clothes, were inelegant. Fortunately for him, this did not alienate her mother, who invited him to visit them again.

Afterwards, in August 1901, he wrote to Emma, asking her to marry him, but she told him she was engaged to a man in the village. Her mother liked Jung enough to arrange a meeting in a Zurich restaurant, where she explained that Emma was not engaged. Inviting him back to the estate, the Rauschenbergs sent their horse-drawn carriage to collect him from the railway station. He again proposed marriage to Emma, and this time she said yes.

Psychiatrists were rarely consulted during judicial proceedings, but in June 1902 a woman prisoner was referred to the Burghölzli. She had been standing rigid by the door of her cell and had ordered the wardress to give back the money she had stolen. Saying the food was poisoned, the prisoner refused to eat. Bleuler assigned the case to Jung.

The woman seemed to have lost her memory, spoke falteringly and gave no sign of feeling pain when he pricked her with a pin. Behaving as if she were in a grand hotel, she treated the prison staff like guests. She did not know her name, shouted gibberish as she became excited and, when questioned, turned away saying: 'Don't hit me.'

The problem of hysterical behaviour in prison had been highlighted in 1898, when Sigbert Ganser wrote about it in a psychiatric review. What came to be known as the Ganser syndrome was the apparent onset of insanity in prisoners who gave wild answers to the simplest questions, consciously or unconsciously trying to sidestep punishment by behaving insanely.

At first Jung made little headway with her, but after a few days he induced a state of hypnotic somnambulism by making some passes and closing her eyes. Giving her an empty glass, he made her believe she was drinking wine, and afterwards vinegar. Told that a pen wiper was an apple, she bit into it and said it was sour. He cured one of her headaches by hypnotising her, but failed to cure her amnesia.

One of his patients was a woman of sixty-five who had been lame in her left leg for seventeen years. When he first saw her, she was both holding on to her maid and using a crutch. He invited her to sit down and tell him about her disability. When he ran out of time, he interrupted her, saying he was going to hypnotise her. She immediately closed her eyes, and before he had done anything, went into a deep trance. When, after about twenty minutes, he tried to wake her up, she did not respond, and it took him fifteen minutes to make her come to. When she stood up, she could walk without any help, and when he tried to hand her the crutch, she rejected it.

Uncertain whether she was going to be all right, he told her to come back in a week's time. Once again she fell into a deep trance without being hypnotised, and she seemed perfectly fit when she left. Nearly a year passed before she came back, supported by the maid. He had students with him, but asked them to leave him alone with her. She then said she had a son in his early twenties. He had shown signs of talent, but was now a patient in the Burghölzli – an incurable catatonic. It was a case of transference: Jung had become the talented young man who needed help, and she did in fact help him. She let him cure her for the second time, and his success improved his reputation in the hospital.

Believing that schizophrenia produced a loosening in the nexus of associations, Bleuler sent one of his assistants, the twenty-two-year-old Franz

Riklin, to study work being done on the word-association test at a psychological laboratory which had been set up by the psychiatrists Emil Kraepelin and Gustav Aschaffenburg. Riklin's wife was one of Jung's cousins. The test, which had been invented by Darwin's cousin Francis Galton, and developed by the German physiologist and experimental psychologist Wilhelm Wundt, was already being used in the Burghölzli. Seeing patients individually, the doctor read out words from a list, one at a time, and the patients responded with the first word that came to mind. Using a stop-watch, the doctor recorded the interval between stimulus and reaction. Silences, hesitations, slips of the tongue, involuntary movements, changes of tone and volume provided evidence about their state of mind.

In the spring of 1901, after Riklin returned from Munich, Bleuler compiled a list of 156 stimulus words, and, wanting to compare normal and schizophrenic reactions, briefed Riklin and Jung to test normal subjects. Jung was keen to find out how easily people could be distracted between stimulus and response by external interference, such as noise, or by pre-occupations and unresolved conflicts. Instead of merely compiling statistics, he and Riklin introduced 'the distractibility factor', using it to check whether conscious or unconscious emotions were at work.

They tested sixteen men (seven of them uneducated) and twenty-two women (eight of them uneducated), all between the ages of twenty and fifty. Instead of limiting themselves to Bleuler's 156 stimulus words, they used 400 words, including 234 nouns and 82 verbs. One way of measuring distract-ibility was to have the subject make marks on paper with a pencil, keeping time with a metronome, which was speeded up after the first fifty marks; another was to use alcohol as a means of reducing concentration. Altogether they collected 12,400 associations.

Using a stop-watch to time the interval between stimulus and response, they found it was sometimes prolonged by internal distractions, which could also surface in awkward phrasing or visible emotional disturbance. Subjects might fail to respond, might be distracted by nearby objects, might become embarrassed or emotional, might forget something that had been said, or return to a question that had already been raised, instead of reacting to a new stimulus. These were all symptomatic of a 'complex' – a cluster of images and ideas around an emotional centre.

This had been discovered by Theodor Ziehen, who wrote about it in 1898 and invented the term 'feeling-toned complex', but he disapproved of what Jung and Riklin were doing – using the word-association test as a means of approaching the unconscious. The complex might involve intimate feelings that could be expressed through a quotation or words from a song, or the title of a story or book. As Jung and Riklin pointed out, 'the majority of complexes emerging in the association experiments relate to direct or transposed sexuality'

John Kerr has pointed out that they were using Freud's ideas on repression when they developed a means of testing conscious and unconscious emotions. Jung later wrote: 'The Devil whispered to me that I had the right to publish the results of my experiments and my conclusions without mentioning Freud . . . But then I heard the voice of my second personality: "If you do something like that, as if you didn't know Freud, it's cheating. You can't base your life on a lie." '

Lecturing in the autumn of 1904, Riklin, who was more Freudian than Jung, said the feeling-toned complex was 'repressed in the Freud–Breuer sense', but the first acknowledgment of indebtedness in the 194-page essay comes five pages before the end.

In the early autumn of 1902 Jung went to Paris. Psychiatry was more advanced in France than anywhere else, and Bleuler may have wanted him to study at the laboratory Jean–Martin Charcot had established during 1893 at the Collège de France. After Charcot's death, Janet had taken over, and Jung attended some of his lectures. He later stressed the importance of Janet's theory 'on "the lowering of the mental level" which has proved itself and has furnished an extremely fecund point of view for the study of these troubles . . . The investigations of Pierre Janet were particularly useful for the comprehension of functional troubles in the domain of the neuroses and above all of hysteria.'

Published in 1889, Janet's first book, *Psychological Automatism*, applied the word *automatism* to fragments of the personality that apparently become autonomous when the 'mental level' is 'lowered' by sleep or hypnotism. Because this 'splitting' appeared to be characteristic of the psyche, psychologists at the end of the nineteenth century were specially interested in spiritualistic media and others with a propensity for 'dissociation'.

Travelling to Paris, Jung acted as chaperone for Helly's sister Valerie, who could not have travelled alone. She had decided to live with Helly and Emmy Zinnstag, who were on the point of moving from Versailles to Paris, where they were going to work near the Madeleine. Helly, who had developed entrepreneurial qualities, now had twenty-two people working for her.

Though Jung was engaged to Emma Rauschenbach and wrote to her twice a week – they were to be married on St Valentine's Day, 14 February 1903 – he felt attracted to Helly, who was almost twenty-one. He wrote several letters to her before he left Paris, and the strength of his feeling is confirmed in a letter to Andreas Vischer. Their earlier roles were reversed, he said.

At the Collège de France he never met Janet but felt encouraged by the lectures to proceed along the paths he was exploring. Janet seemed to be scrupulous in collecting a maximum of information about each patient, using hypnosis when necessary to reach the core of the personality, or to deal with split-off memories of a traumatic event. He understood how hysterics put on a display of grandeur or guilt for the benefit of doctors and visitors, and he encouraged the tendency his writings had already inspired in Jung to think of mental illness as a dissociation of the self into subsidiary personalities which could 'take over'.

But Jung spent only two hours each week at Janet's lectures. Though he grumbled about the moral laxity of Paris life, he was not unaffected by it. He got up late and wandered through the streets, went almost every day to the Louvre, where he had a Franz Hals painting copied. He also did some painting of his own. He spent a few hours each week studying English at the Berlitz School and alongside his new passion for Helly, he became infatuated with a Jewish girl. Female patients had often made advances to him, but he had previously had little opportunity to discover how attractive he was to women who were not unbalanced.

Later, when they were working at association tests, he let Riklin test him. The tests went on till August 1903, and they wrote up the results. The subject, they said, had during this period formed an attachment to a young Jewish woman, which troubled him because his upbringing had been strictly Christian. Responding to the word 'kiss', he said: 'Never', and to 'love' he replied: 'Is useless.' His association with 'wedding' was 'misfortune', and 'sofa' made him think of the chaise longue in the Jewish woman's drawing room. On 27 December 1902, he gave the answer 'Yesterday' three times, after the stimulus-words 'kiss', 'love' and 'already', but the text explains that 'kiss' and 'yesterday' are not to be regarded as recollections because 'their relationship was not of this nature'. On the other hand, we are told that during the Christmas holidays the subject had been elated to receive a present from the woman.

If he felt troubled, it may have been partly because he was betraying Emma, and partly because he had harmed Helly. His new passion for her may have been inflamed by guilt feelings. In Paris, though he was short of money – he stayed in a students' hostel and his evening meal sometimes consisted of chestnuts roasted by a street vendor – he took her to Versailles, drove with her in a two-horse carriage and, to celebrate her twenty-first birthday, took her and two of her sisters to the theatre. The letter he sent Helly at the beginning of January is oddly and almost apologetically insistent. Does she really not have a free evening during the week? Could they chat and go to the theatre together? From his detailed account of the plays at

Sarah Bernhardt's theatre, at the Odéon and at Madame Réjane's, it seems he had already seen all three, but he would happily escort her to whichever she chose, or to the opera. He was keen to see her again before he left for London on the 19th, and from there he would probably go to Ostende before returning to Zurich for his wedding.

In London he saw the sights and improved his English by taking a private lesson every day. The international standing of the Burghölzli was so high that many English-speaking doctors came to study there, including the Welshman Ernest Jones and the American Trigant Burrow. If Jung had not been determined to become fluent in English, he would not have paid for private lessons when he was so short of money.

Helly survived for only nine more years. She died at the age of thirty, probably of tuberculosis, though according to Stefanie Zumstein-Preiswerk, what killed her was heartbreak.

Emma was not quite twenty-one when they married in February 1903. Her mother had encouraged her to opt for a situation in which she would be deprived of luxuries she had always taken for granted. They honeymooned on a cruise that took them to the Canary Islands, but, on returning to Zurich, had to live in the asylum. They were given a flat above the Bleulers'.

Emma's ideas of how a home should be run were naturally based on her experience of living in the house with the rose garden and the estate at Olberg with footmen in green livery and maids in white caps with streamers and starched aprons. Her parents' attitude to money could hardly have been more different from that of Jung, whose habits had been formed during his impoverished boyhood, and who now had control over her money and everything she owned. By Swiss law, a wife's assets belong to her husband.

Jung was ambivalent towards her wealth, which brought him professional independence. Without it, as he acknowledged, 'I should have been far more cautious in expressing my opinions, and many things would have gone another way.' But he never entirely outgrew the poverty he experienced during boyhood in the parsonages where he lived with his parents.

He and Emma could afford servants and their flat in the Burghölzli was large and self-contained, but they were living inside a hospital, and even at night, when the curtains were drawn, noises from patients would remind them where they were.

Jung's feelings about money were tangled. He was sometimes admirably generous, giving professional help without asking for fees, but he later made several transatlantic journeys to cultivate professional relationships with American multimillionaires. Anthony Storr has suggested this may have been partly because he was 'keen on making money for himself as a counterbalance to Emma's wealth'. The use of letters as scrap paper assorted oddly with his spending on the big house that was being built for him on the lakeside site he bought in Küsnacht.

Küsnacht was a small suburban village, much smaller and quieter then than it is today. Few industrial cities have such beautiful suburbs as Zurich, thanks to the lakes and mountains. On the eastern side of the lake, Küsnacht is five miles from the centre of the city – a fifteen-minute drive. But Jung was in no hurry to move, and four years later the house was still unfinished.

How did Emma feel about being a wife? There is some evidence in the answers she gave when she let Jung use her as a subject in the word-association test. In a paper he wrote during 1905, 'Subject No. 1' is described as a married woman who placed herself at his disposal in the most cooperative way. She was pregnant, and 'from time to time has feelings of nervous anticipation'. Commenting on her responses to stimulus words, he said she occasionally visited the asylum, had previously been in better financial circumstances, and sometimes 'feels this loss'.

The paper mentions the green lampshades in her present home. To the words 'swim' and 'cook' she reacted with 'learn'. She could not swim, had not yet learned much about cooking, and, being very musical, wished she could sing. Her reaction to 'despise' revealed anxiety that her pregnancy 'might by its various effects cause her husband to lose his regard for her'. She had read Zola's novel *Vérité*, in which a married couple become estranged after being idyllically happy. Tested with the words 'love' and 'duty', she responded to both with 'faithful'.

Jung's comment on her reactions is that while our ego-consciousness assumes itself to be in control of the association process, it is 'merely the marionette which dances on the stage, activated by a hidden mechanism'. He was echoing a metaphor Bleuler had used in a book review published the previous year: 'Our consciousness sees in its theatre only the puppets; in the Freudian world many of the strings that move the figures have been revealed.'

Instead of saying what she wanted to say, Subject No. 1 had revealed what she most wanted to hide. As Freud showed in his new book, *The Psychopathology of Everyday Life*, reactions that appeared to be haphazard were often symbolical acts. Associations reveal not only intimate secrets but important clusters of feeling that 'form the content of her pleasures and sufferings'. Her most powerful complex was the psychic equivalent of her pregnancy, 'which polarises her nervous anticipation and her love for her husband, together with slightly jealous fears'. But like Emma, Jung was revealing what he was eager to hide – secrets about his most intimate relationship.

She felt disconnected from the work he was doing, and thought she would never understand it. Talking to patients who were resistant to him or to analysis, he sometimes described her resistance, and how it was gradually overcome.

Another hurdle in his relationship with Emma was his belief in a disparity between male and female emotionality. 'Women must have emotions,' he said, 'or they can't see anything.' A man 'never has emotions for a purpose', whereas a woman's emotions 'are always for a certain purpose . . . Her real being is Eros.' When Jung said this in an English-language seminar during 1928, a voice from the audience called out: 'Don't make us feel inferior because we really feel superior!' He retorted: 'That's right, get emotional about it!'

He went on to say that there is 'nothing purposive' about a man's emotion.

It is only useful when through tremendous self-control, he can play his emotion when it is cold; then with that purposive element he can play and perform. But they are not really emotions at all. A woman works through her emotions, with every gift, as a man works with his mind – there is always purpose. While a woman's mind has the innocence and purpose-lessness of a natural product.

He believed the determining factors in the relationship between husband and wife were the man's earlier relationship with his mother and the woman's with her father. 'It is the strength of the bond with the parents that unconsciously influences the choice of partner, either positively or negatively.' Unwilling to admit how unsatisfactory her marriage is, a mother often binds her son to her as a replacement for her husband. The boy will later be driven either into homosexuality or into making a choice that is contrary to his true nature, selecting a wife who is either overbearing or so inferior to his mother that there can be no question of competition.

We cannot assume that Jung's generalisations about sexuality were based on his own experience, but we can make inferences about it from them. In 1922, invited to lecture about the lovelife of students, he pointed out 'a fact that applies to all early marriages': girls of twenty were usually older than men of twenty-five, though 'a girl can masturbate for years without knowing what she is doing'. There were many women, he said, 'whose real sexuality remains virginal for years, even after they are married. That is the reason why so many women have no understanding at all of male sexuality – they are completely unconscious of their own.'

The young man, who should be experimenting with his life, has probably had premarital experiences, and for these, 'the most inferior woman will do'. Respectable young men may become addicted to 'sexual fantasies of the lowest kind'. Even if these are repressed, they will later 'leap to the surface in their primitive form, much to the astonishment of the unsuspecting wife . . . Women are often frigid from the first day of marriage because their sensation function does not respond to this kind of sexuality.'

Like most men at this time, Jung had little interest in female sexuality. In a 1958 letter to a psychotherapist, an Englishwoman, who was 'worried by this peculiar fact that so many women are frigid', he wrote: 'I have noticed the same fact . . . I have tried during my voyages abroad in exotic countries to gather as much information as possible, and I reached the conclusion that mostly orgasm is connected with the expectation and even fear of conception.'

In the same letter he said there were two types – the 'married mothers' and the 'friends and concubines'.

> Marriage, statistically considered, increases the need of licentiousness, not only because matrimony gets stale, but also because of a certain psychic need which is associated with the hetaira-nature of the sex object. It is unfortunately true that when you are wife and mother you can hardly be the hetaira too, just as it is the secret suffering of the hetaira that she is not a mother. There are women who are not meant to bear physical children, but they are those who give rebirth to a man in a spiritual sense.

He took the term *hetairism* from Johann Jakob Bachofen, who used it for the earliest stage of prehistory, when humanity, he said, had lived in polygamous communities, and women did not know who had fathered their children. Jung wanted a wife and family, but also needed a sex object who could make him feel he was being reborn spiritually. He later used the term *femme inspiratrice* for this kind of woman.

He seems throughout his life to have recoiled from physical and emotional interdependence. In his 1932 seminar on Kundalini yoga he talked scathingly about the man who has been 'living in *participation mystique* with those he loves. He has spread himself over other people until he has become identical with them, which is a violation of the principle of individuality.' Jung first used the term *participation mystique* in *Psychological Types* (1919–21), taking it from the sociologist Lucien Lévy-Bruhl. Jung defined it as a 'psychological connection in which the subject, unable to differentiate himself clearly from the object, is bound to it directly by a relationship that amounts to partial identity'.

If you love other people, Jung wrote, 'you handle them as if they were yourself, and naturally there will be resistances'. The man who understands this 'knows when he loves that soon he will hate. Therefore he will laugh when he is going uphill and weep when he is going downhill, like Till Eulenspiegel.' A wily peasant in German folklore, Till liked walking uphill because he knew that going down would be easier.

In 1928, speaking in English, Jung said: 'Marriage in itself constitutes a resistance . . . Everything that lives together is influenced one by the other . . . the mana of one assimilates the mana of the other. This identity, this clinging together is a great hindrance to individual relationship . . . Since *participation mystique* is the usual condition in marriage, especially when people marry young, an individual relation is impossible.' The phrase 'individual relationship' is confusing, but Jung, always less interested in relationships than in the development of individuality, was ambivalent.

He never changed his mind about the damage done by marital inter-dependence. In 1959 he said: 'A marriage which is devoted entirely to mutual understanding is bad for the development of individual personality; it is a descent to the lowest common denominator, which is probably something like the collective stupidity of the masses.' Nor did he believe in equality between husband and wife. 'Ideally the man should contain the woman and remain outside of her . . . Basically speaking, however, man is polygamous . . . I think that the French have found the solution in the number Three.' He seldom talked about his marriage, but occasionally, in lectures, he made such generalisations as: 'If you study the ordinary psychology of marriage, you discover that most of the troubles consist in this cunning invention of irritating topics which have absolutely no foundation.' He does not appear to be thinking of conversational initiatives taken by the husband.

He also had an irrational aversion to childbearing. 'There are few things which have caused as much anxiety, unhappiness and evil,' he said in 1931, 'as the compulsion to give birth.' Twenty years later, confirming that 'I fully stand by my earlier remarks', he rationalised them as referring to the dangers of overpopulation.

Eight

Moon People

Nothing was more characteristic of Jung than his persistence. Where other doctors would assume a case was hopeless, he would go on talking, listening, demonstrating that his support was not going to be withdrawn.

A girl of nineteen had been in the asylum for two years with catatonia and hallucinations. When her brother, a doctor, brought her to Jung, she had cold, bluish hands, livid patches on her face and dilated pupils that barely moved. She said nothing. After weeks of sustaining a one-sided conversation with her every day for an hour, he heard her whisper a few words. Eventually, the pupils contracted, the livid patches disappeared, the hands grew warmer.

Gradually he coaxed her into talking about her life on the moon, where she was the saviour of the moon people. Four months later, thinking she could never go back to them after betraying their secret, she became manic. She was transferred to another asylum, but after two months she was calmer, and when Jung saw her, her apathy modulated into 'a rather lymphatic emotionality and soulfulness'. But she relapsed again, into an 'unusual epileptoid twilight state'. He went on seeing her, and, after a year, discharged her as cured.

Disregarding the orthodox assumption that psychosis was incurable, he started by gauging the extent to which a patient could 'stand his pathological material'. His natural inclination would be to protect himself from it by building a kind of wall, and Jung could either help to build it or try gently to demolish it, preparing to support him during the next onrush of psychosis. Some patients, he said later, 'came out of it as if out of a dream. They did not "coalesce" but retained their fluidity. If there are any congealed regions, you would find there: inaccessibility, lack of emotion, or inadequate emotions and complete immutability.' He liked to discharge them from the hospital as soon as possible 'as the hospital atmosphere is most contagious'.

None of his patients received more help from him than an eighteen-year-old Russian girl who arrived at the Burghölzli on 17 August 1904, after being treated at a private clinic in Interlaken. Sabina Spielrein was a rabbi's granddaughter who wore her hair in pigtails and dressed like a child. Sensitive, emotional, articulate and intermittently suicidal, she had uncontrollable bouts of laughing, weeping and screaming. 'She could no longer look anyone in the face, kept her head lowered, and when anybody touched her, stuck her tongue out with every sign of hatred.'

Her father was a merchant and her mother a dentist, both with a tendency to hysteria, while her brother had been 'severely hysterical' since his youth. After diagnosing 'psychotic hysteria', Jung was surprised when Bleuler told him to psychoanalyse her. What was he expected to do? Freud, who never treated psychotics, had introduced the term *psychoanalysis* in 1896, claiming he could bring to consciousness what had previously been unconscious. In *The Interpretation of Dreams* he argued that pathological ideas could be dispelled if traced back to their sources in the patient's mental life, and he promised to explain the procedure in a future work. Four years later the promise was still unfulfilled.

While Freud wanted wider recognition for himself and his ideas, he was proprietorial about analytical technique. Addressing the Society of Physicians on 12 December, he attacked the 'widespread and erroneous idea' that the technique of psychoanalysis was 'a simple one which can be practised casually'. It was absurd that a young assistant in a clinic should be instructed to analyse a hysteric. Even without the word 'young' (*jung*) it would have been clear he was denouncing the Swiss trespassers on his property.

Within four and a half months, Jung said he had analysed Sabina. He had apparently given her a session of one or two hours every other day. She was his first analysand, and we can glean something about what happened from what he wrote about the second:

> People with obsessions and compulsions are weak; they cannot keep their ideas under control. What they need is treatment that restores their energy, but the best treatment for their energy is to compel them, with a degree of ruthlessness, to uncover and expose to daylight the images their consciousness finds intolerable. This seriously challenges the patients' energy, and at the same time their consciousness begins to accept notions previously repressed.

Working as a neurologist, Freud had a couch in his consulting room, and, not wanting to go on using hypnosis, he made patients lie down. Pressing his hand on their forehead, he asked for the first idea or image that came to mind when the pressure was released. Using Janet's method of avoiding eye contact, Jung sat behind Sabina. He had already tried combining free association with the word-association test, and now he invited Sabina to talk about her troubles, expressing any odd thought or fancy that occurred. Listening carefully, he focused on hesitations and changes in subject matter, rhythm or volume.

When Sabina was about three, she had been beaten by her father on her bare bottom. She became excited, as she did when she saw her brother being smacked, but afterwards felt as if she had excreted on her father's hand, and for years, sitting on the floor, she tried to aim a turd at her feet, though she tried at the same time to hold it back, pressing her heel into her anus. This gave her 'blissfully shuddersome' feelings, which led to masturbation.

It enraged her to see punishment being inflicted, but the anger turned into sexual excitement. Once, when Jung casually said: 'Well, you have to obey,' he found he had aroused her sexually. Still more disconcerting was the realisation that he could no longer deny the existence of childhood sexuality.

After puberty had begun at the age of thirteen, Sabina could neither eat nor watch others eating without thinking of turds, and she could not look at her father's hands without becoming excited. When she had to eat with other people, she either laughed or cried out in disgust. She took refuge in unconcealed masturbation, and by the age of eighteen, she was alternating between fits of depression and bouts of manic rage. She kept her head bowed, and, when touched, stuck her tongue out. Her hunger for love exacerbated the pathological symptoms, and the psychic conflict culminated in what was then known as hysterical psychosis.

In childhood she had been scared of the plague, which she pictured as a tall dark man who would want to take her away. Behind this fantasy (she said later) lay a vague apprehension of sexual processes, but her childhood fears were still repressed after the 'analysis', though Jung explained what repression was. He also tried to improve her self-control, and lent her a copy of his thesis, which convinced her she had something in common with Helly.

Sabina was the first patient Jung invited to assist him with his work – a variation on Bleuler's technique of increasing the self-confidence of schizophrenics by giving them simple tasks to perform. Since she wanted to become a medical student, Jung enlisted her help on the essay he was writing, 'The Reaction-Time Ratio in the Association Experiment'. As his *Habilitationsschrift* (the paper that would qualify him to give unpaid lectures as a *Privatdozent* in the university), it was important to him, and she was surprisingly helpful. Still depressed and disoriented, she was astonished to hear him say: 'Minds like yours help to advance science. You must become a psychiatrist.'

He took her out for walks, and once, when she dropped her coat, he got the dust off for her by beating it with his stick. She threw herself at him furiously, tearing the coat from his hands. He had reminded her of being beaten by her father.

Jung talked about his marriage, and in one of Sabina's dreams, Emma said he was dictatorial and difficult. Hearing about this dream, he said it was hard to share a home with someone else, and when Sabina talked about the intellectual independence of women, he said she was exceptional. Emma was an ordinary woman, and was therefore interested only in what interested her husband.

Freud maintained that a doctor should never confide in a patient, but, against all the odds, Sabina made a rapid recovery. Perhaps for the first time, Jung was making full use of his ability to give a patient a more flattering image of herself than she could have formed without his help. In Switzerland, as throughout Europe at the turn of the century, even the most talented women rarely found opportunities to express themselves, but for the next fifty years, female patients would discover a new identity by looking at their reflection in his eyes. Arguably, these were women in need of spiritual rebirth, and in making it possible for them to achieve it, he was doing what their mother had failed to do for them, and his mother had failed to do for him.

In April 1905, eight months after being admitted to the hospital, Sabina enrolled at Zurich University. But because she gave the Burghölzli as her address, she was not allowed to begin her studies till she was discharged at the beginning of June.

Most patients stayed at the Burghölzli longer than Sabina, who was discharged within less than a year, and Jung had to wrestle with uncertainty about his feelings. She was now a medical student, but she was also a patient whose rapid recovery had been due partly to transference: she might relapse if he withdrew his support. This was both a reason for continuing to meet her regularly and a pretext for prolonging a friendship he seemed to need, much as he disliked her impulsiveness and eccentricity. 'Her character has a decidedly relentless and unreasonable aspect, and she lacks any sense of appropriateness and external manners, most of which must, of course, be attributed to Russian peculiarities.' At the same time, her Jewishness disturbed and excited him, while, for her, one of his attractions was his Teutonic appearance. He could hardly have looked less like the Jews and Russians she had known.

By now Jung was so eager to get in touch with Freud that he thought of sending Sabina for a consultation in Vienna. This would have been an auspicious beginning to a friendship or at least a professional connection.

Freud would have been presented with living evidence of Jung's success in his first attempt at psychoanalysis. But the two men did not make contact till over six months later.

Not yet thirty, Jung had in April 1905 been appointed the senior doctor, subordinate only to Bleuler, and in June he became director of the new outpatients department. When Riklin left to take over the mental hospital in Rheinau, Jung also became head of the psychology laboratory. Within five years of graduating, he had been promoted twice.

It was already apparent that Jung's thinking would not remain focused tightly on mental illness. In April, reviewing a book, he had predicted that any future history of hysteria would go 'far beyond the narrow limits of psychiatry and neurology. The further we penetrate into the problem of hysteria, the further its boundaries widen.'

His techniques could even be useful to the police. In September a distressed old gentleman consulted him about the eighteen-year-old boy who lived with him. Money was sometimes missing from the locked drawer where the old man hid it among his shirts, and he was not sure whether to blame his absent-mindedness. Jung offered to use the association test on the boy. First he prepared a list of stimulus words including 'drawer', 'burglary', 'sin', 'key', 'thief', 'shirt', together with words that had nothing to do with the situation.

The boy's response to 'give' was 'steal', and after answering 'burglary' with 'theft', he ignored the next stimulus word, and hesitated over the one that followed. The longest pause came after 'thief', to which he replied 'burglar', and he was slow in answering 'police' with 'thief'. The stimulus words 'arrest', 'jail' and 'false' produced long pauses before he answered with 'thief', 'prison' and 'rich' − responses that would have been incomprehensible unless he was stealing. He responded to 'month' with 'week' and to 'punish' with 'release', but then, disturbed by the combination of 'month' with the idea of punishment, hesitated before coming out with 'green' in answer to 'coloured'. When Jung called him a thief, he turned pale and protested his innocence before bursting into tears and confessing.

Jung told this story in an article, 'On the Psychological Diagnosis of Evidence'. The test could establish criminal guilt, but Max Wertheimer and Julius Klein, pupils of a criminal psychologist, Hans Gross, were claiming they had discovered it. Jung insisted he had been the first, and went on to attack those who had derided Freud without understanding his method, which 'ranks among the greatest achievements of modern psychology'.

Again and again in his use of the test, Jung was substantiating Freud's view of repression. Acknowledging indebtedness in a September paper, 'Experimental Observations on the Faculty of Memory', Jung argued that hysteria always involves repression, and dealing with his subjects' tendency to forget answers they had given when stimulus words touched on a complex, he compared the forgotten words with excuses. The evasiveness was due to the same sort of anxiety that produced what Freud called 'screen memories'. Memories of trivial childhood events lingered in the mind when traumatic experiences or unconscious fantasies were concealed behind them.

Appointed to the unpaid post of *Privatdozent* in psychiatry at Zurich University in the autumn of 1905, the thirty-year-old Jung delivered his inaugural lecture in October. He chose a safe topic: 'The Psychopathological Significance of the Association Experiment'. As in his fraternity lectures, he showed his interest in frontiers between intellectual disciplines. Is psychology a creed or a science? Experimental psychology was still in its infancy, growing up under the tutelage of philosophical psychology, which encouraged dependence on dogmas and axioms.

He argued that experimental psychology could produce laws – such as the law of association – no less solid than other scientific laws. If there was a demonstrable necessity about reactions provoked by stimulus words, the experiment would 'acquire the nature of something inexorable and causally inevitable', like a physiological experiment in which the nervous system is subjected to electrical stimuli. It could then be established that there were constants and variables in each application of the test. By now Jung had used over 25,000 stimulus words on 150 normal subjects, and one law he had discovered was that the quantity of associations depending on the sound of the stimulus word (as opposed to its meaning) was inversely proportional to the subject's attentiveness, which could be reduced by illness or exhaustion.

In Germany the term *experimental psychology* had a different meaning – it depended on experiments in self-observation by people who had been trained to observe themselves. Jung was attacked because untrained subjects could not be expected to remember what they had said. He had started interviewing subjects after the test, focusing on complexes that had been revealed, but he was challenged by a German psychologist. William Stern, who questioned the value of these interviews. In reply Jung conceded that the method was difficult and dangerous. For this reason, he said, he had used it on 'three people whose life and psychological constitution were known to me, and who were psychologically experienced, particularly in the observation of association'. Using the test on subjects without these qualifications, the experimenter would need knowledge of psychopathology. 'Only after assimilating Freud's method completely can one be secure in considering associations from a psychoanalytical viewpoint.' In its principles, at least, psychoanalysis was a teachable method, 'the practice of which is greatly helped by the association experiment'.

Since reactions were determined not by free will but by complexes, everyday occurrences were like stimulus words to which we reacted according to our nature. Our actions being determined by the psychological past that gave us our cerebral organisation, we would expose ourselves in the test as we do in our handwriting. He quoted a dictum by the criminal psychologist Wilhelm Weygandt: 'Tell me how you associate, and I will tell you who you are.'

Part Two

Crown Prince

Nine

Lusty Stallion

Before he met Freud in March 1907, Jung experimented in combining the word-association test with free association, hoping to shorten the time required for analysis. Though he had misgivings about Freud's emphasis on sexuality, it was clear that some of his patients were caught up in sexual repression. Freud was also right about what he called *transference* and Jung called *transposition*.

In five years at the asylum, Jung had worked hard, winning his patients' confidence and improving his position. His starting salary had been 1000 Swiss francs a year, but by 1905 he was earning 4000. He was achieving results that made his name almost as well known as Bleuler's, but their relationship was deteriorating. Perhaps Jung needed a different kind of father figure, now that he was a father himself. His first daughter, Agathe, had been born on 26 December 1904, and within four months Emma was pregnant again. Though his responsibilities as a husband and father were increasing, there was no apparent limit to what he could do. But he had not overcome his need for a father figure, and now that he could neither emulate Bleuler nor confide in him, he gravitated towards Freud.

During the spring of 1906, Jung dreamed that horses were being hoisted upwards on thick cables when one of the cables snapped and a powerful brown horse crashed to the street. As it bolted, another horse appeared beside it. Galloping, they were dragging a heavy log. The second horse disappeared before a rider came up on a horse that was small and dainty, like a rocking horse. By cantering in front of the brown horse, he slowed it down, but what saved them from being run over was the cab in front of the frightened horse. It was slowing him to a trot. There were children inside it.

Hoisting the horses upwards suggested that by hard work one can get to the top, and Jung identified with the brown horse. He had been planning a trip to the USA with Emma, who did not want him to go without her, but they had postponed it because of her pregnancy. She must be the second horse – they were matrimonially harnessed together, but he could still gallop. He associated the horses with a painting by Albert Welti of a married couple in bed under a cornice on which a lusty stallion is depicted, rearing up. Jung's ambitions were being thwarted both by Bleuler, who resembled the rider on the dainty horse, and by Emma's pregnancies.

The horse that symbolised sexuality was powerful but panic-stricken. Later on, corresponding with Freud, Jung equated the log with the penis, admitting his desire for a son, and suggesting that desire for the horse to be slowed down was 'just a screen pushed conveniently into the foreground in order to conceal an illegitimate sexual desire which must never be exposed in daylight'. He does not explain who was the object of this desire. Unable to ignore the dream, he wrote it down, together with an interpretation, and consulted Bleuler, who advised him against publication. He dictated a different interpretation to Emma.

In April 1906 he wrote to Freud, enclosing a copy of *Diagnostic Association Studies*, which had been published in 1905. In his letter of thanks, Freud said he had already bought a copy. He especially liked 'Psychoanalysis and Association Studies', 'because in it you confirm from your own experience the truth of everything I have said about the previously unexplored fields of our discipline. I am confident you will often be in a position to support me, but I will also be glad to accept correction.' For a first letter to a junior colleague, this could hardly have been more like an invitation to collaborate. But Jung let almost six months go by before replying.

On 27 May he attended a conference of neurologists and psychiatrists in Baden-Baden, where Gustav Aschaffenburg, who had helped Kraepelin develop the word-association test, attacked Freud's case history of Dora, saying it was immoral to explore a patient's sexual ideas. Jung argued that in many of Freud's cases, the sexual circumstances could not have been left out of account. 'We know only that we meet sexuality everywhere. Is there any other psychic factor, any other basic drive apart from hunger and its derivatives that is so important in human psychology?' Even if it could not be said that hysteria always had its origin in sexuality, this was true of 'an indefinitely large number of cases'. Jung claimed to be modifying Freud's dictum 'with the consent of the author'. But there is no evidence that this consent had been given.

In June Freud was to address a seminar of criminology students about the word-association test, and this was probably why he had bought *Diagnostic Association Studies*. Naturally, he preferred free association to the test. Three of its four main indicators, he said, were contained in his own technique, while nothing was added by the fourth – perseveration. Instead of forcing the patient forward with a new stimulus word, free association allowed him to stay on each topic as long as he needed to.

Freud's reservations did not deter Jung from paying tribute to him in the foreword to a new study of schizophrenia, longer than any of his previous writings and nearly twice as long as his thesis. After brief acknowledgments to Bleuler and Riklin, he praised 'the brilliant ideas of Freud', who 'has not yet received the recognition and praise he deserves'. Writing to him, Jung said: 'I approach *dementia praecox* and its psychology from your standpoint.' It was Freud, he wrote in *Diagnostic Association Studies*, who 'put dream analysis on the right track' by showing dreams to be symbolic representations of repressed complexes.

Unstinting praise for Freud was liable to offend Bleuler, whose *Affectivity, Suggestibility, Paranoia* had just appeared, and in a brief review Jung 'urgently' recommended the book to both psychiatrists and the general public. It proposed the term *affectivity* for emotion, feeling, sentiment – 'not only affects in the proper sense but the minor feelings or feeling-tones of pleasure and displeasure in every possible situation'. In *Diagnostic Association Studies*, Jung respectfully declared affectivity to be the essential basis of our person-ality. But the term has not survived, unlike *schizophrenia*, the word Bleuler introduced in a 1908 article to replace *dementia praecox*. The book he wrote in 1908, *The Theory of Schizophrenic Negativism*, was not published till 1911. Jung uses *dementia praecox*, and his title is *On the Psychology of Dementia Praecox: An Essay*. Kraepelin's textbook on psychiatry had distinguished between two forms of insanity – manic depression, in which periods of imbalance were followed by recovery, and *dementia praecox*, in which deterioration was inexorable.

But his admiration for Bleuler had evaporated. He had two sons, and Jung, who was nothing if not competitive, said: 'My chief is wholly conditioned by the fact that he has two boys.' Jung had wanted his second child to be a boy, but on 2 June Emma gave birth to another girl, who was christened Gret.

Discussing the horse dream – without saying whose dream it was – his book reveals his frustration. Hard work should be rewarded, but other horses were being hoisted up – colleagues whose promotion had nothing to do with merit. When the cable breaks, a new life begins for the horse who trots away, but his progress is blocked by the dainty horse, the log, which represents sexuality, and the cab, which contains the children Emma is producing. Jung could not see how he was going to overtake it.

One of the turning points in Jung's development was the discovery of 'distractibility'. A basic symptom of schizophrenia is a lowering of attention. Even catatonia is explained in these terms – no other conscious processes engage the patient's interest. Looking at results achieved by other doctors testing subjects whose attention was distracted, Jung was reminded of schizophrenics by the sequence of words and sentences. 'Superficial linkages noticeably predominated, reflecting the breakdown of logical connections,' and there were frequent repetitions. Language was misused when phrases were confused. Muddling 'as clear as daylight' with 'in broad daylight', one patient had said: 'It's as broad as daylight.'

Alert to nuances and modulations in language and tone, Jung picked up on what Freud had said about the inadequate feeling-tone in schizophrenia. Symptoms express thoughts that had been repressed because they would have been painful. Repressions determine both the delusions and the behaviour of the patient, who may no longer be able to take in new impressions. But imprisoned thoughts are chaotically liberated.

Replying to Jung's letter, Freud predicted: 'You will come much closer to me than you now think possible. Judging from your splendid analysis of a case of obsessional neurosis, you know better than anyone how cleverly the sexual factor can hide.' Though writing to a stranger, Freud mentions his age – fifty – and refers, invitingly, to 'those able to overcome their inner resistance and count themselves among my followers'.

Responding, Jung reiterated his misgivings about the emphasis on sexuality, and tried to 'abreact' a recent experience – this was his excuse for consulting Freud about Sabina Spielrein. Without divulging her name, he gave a brief summary of the case. Early in December he wrote to Freud again, implicitly accepting the implied invitation to become a follower. 'I leave our opponents a line of retreat,' he explained, 'with the conscious purpose of not making recantation too difficult for them.' Freud had used the word *we* impersonally – 'what we see . . .' 'Later on we shall find . . .' – but Jung was suggesting a strategy they should jointly adopt. They should not put too much emphasis on results: 'if we do, a rapid accumulation of material might show the therapeutic results in a thoroughly bad light, which would be damaging to the theory.'

In a friendly reply, dated only two days later, Freud almost promised to be flexible over points of disagreement. Left alone with his ideas, he said, he had become resistant to other people's. But he was aware of his fallibility. Jung politely riposted that he was the one who would need to be corrected. Nothing in his training had been more regrettable than lack of contact with Freud, and what was missing in Zurich was opposition. He would welcome criticism.

By now Jung was dangerously involved with Sabina, who said she could read his thoughts telepathically. He could read hers, but this was easy since she was always thinking about him. A year ago she had been fit only for life in an institution, but she trusted her guardian spirit, who said she would be able to do anything she liked.

Gently, without sapping her faith in her potential, Jung helped her towards a stable relationship with external reality, and the less unbalanced she became, the more he enjoyed her company. She said Wagner was the most psychological composer, capable of matching emotions with melodies that develop and blend in the same way. 'I'll show you,' Jung answered. 'I'm writing the very same thing.' And his eyes filled with tears. But he felt no love for her until long after she fell in love with him, and they loved each other long before they became lovers.

Her intention was to demand nothing. Obsessed with the idea of sacrifice, she felt more reverence for him than sexual desire. He admitted to desiring her, but said they must exercise self-control. Having a noble and pure friendship, they must not sully it with adultery, secretiveness and deception. Together, she believed, they could help other people, and she could help him towards even greater achievements. He identified her with his mother, while she identified him with her father and her brother. Showing her his diary, he said Emma was the only other person to have seen it.

Sabina's fantasies interpenetrated his, and they discussed her sense of being destined for greatness. She often felt flooded with energy, as if the whole of nature were speaking to her. Her fantasy was that Jung was descended from the gods, and that their child, Siegfried, would heroically blend Jewish and Aryan qualities. In spite of the name, which she intended symbolically, she was thinking of a daughter, but when Jung, who wanted to father a son, joined in the fantasy, he persuaded her the child would be a boy. At the same time, he reminded her their love must remain pure.

He was ambivalent about Jewish girls, however much they attracted him. He later said: 'I would never like to have children from a person who has Jewish blood.' But the difficulties of resisting Sabina were compounded by her certainty that she had powers as a clairvoyante, and by his willingness to believe her. What she wanted and predicted became inevitable.

His faith in her spiritual powers harked back to his childish faith in those of his mother. Sabina had a lot in common with her, and with Helly, who had chosen to make Ivenes Jewish. Like the Preiswerks and the Jungs, Sabina's ancestors had been spiritual leaders with pretensions to priestly insight into the secret workings of God's will. More articulate than either Emilie Jung or Helly, Sabina talked about 'the ancestor component' – a subject Jung had considered but never discussed. Were the dead alive in the living? Was Goethe present in Jung? Had the first Carl Gustav come to life through Helly? Was it coincidental that he had become involved with Freud and this Jewish girl who believed in fate? Her confidence in Jung's future greatness increased his impatience to meet Freud, who might help him to achieve greatness. In the meantime, he enjoyed discussing his destiny with Sabina.

A young assistant, Ludwig Binswanger joined the Burghölzli staff in June 1906. He was the nephew of Otto Binswanger, director of the clinic at Iena. Ludwig Binswanger took part in the word-association tests, and it was Jung who suggested them as the subject for his doctoral thesis.

Binswanger had been using not only a stop-watch but also an electric galvanometer. A subject he described as a female student may have been Sabina. Her reply to 'state' was 'Russia'. Given the cue 'jung' (young) she hesitated for twenty-four seconds before replying 'old'. The galvanometer reacted strongly both then and before she said 'answer' in response to 'ask'. Binswanger commented: 'Two strong complexes were aroused, which were important to her and still are.'

When Jung volunteered to be tested again at the beginning of 1907, Binswanger put electrodes under his hands in the first session and under the naked soles of his feet in the second. Noting that he responded to the cue 'will' with 'strive', to 'proud' with 'eminent', and to 'people' with 'ruler', Binswanger comments on his 'will to power'. In Basel, reproached by members of his family for being too proud, Jung had felt they were holding him back. Now he had the same feeling about Bleuler and the Burghölzli. He was being prevented from travelling. After dropping the idea of visiting England in April, he thought of going to see Freud in Vienna. 'Has a general feeling that "something is soon going to happen" '. The galvanometer 'points to the subject's great need of new "sensations" '.

Binswanger diagnosed eleven complexes. The one that centred on Goethe was 'an extremely powerful complex for the subject', who showed 'great embarrassment . . . at revealing this to the experimenter'. There was a *philosophical complex* as well as the *travel complex*, which had appeared in the horse dream, as had desire for a son, and frustration. Binswanger also diagnosed a *ruefulness complex*. Responding to 'ruefulness' with 'faithfulness', Jung may have meant that fidelity to Emma was frustrating his desire for Sabina, and answering 'cap' with 'put on', he may have been referring to contraception. Once he answered 'child' with 'have', and once with 'care – take it'.

When 'determination' came in response to 'sex', Binswanger took it to mean Jung was determined to have a son. His answer to 'divorce' was 'avoid', and to 'lie' he said 'belly', which was 'apprehended sexually and in the sense of "crawling on one's belly" to someone – something which is anathema to the subject, especially on scientific matters'. Binswanger concluded: 'We are dealing here with the complex of ambition, thirst for knowledge and "will to power".'

Binswanger travelled with Jung and Emma to visit Freud in Vienna during March 1907. Jung was already suffering the frustration he later described. 'In a university clinic, one must adjust to many factors which in private life one would prefer to ignore. But you can be sure of one thing: I shall never abandon any part of your theory that is essential to me, as I am far too committed to it.' He may have stopped in mid-sentence from offering too much: no one wants to abandon what is essential to him.

Freud, who normally saw patients from eight in the morning till eight in the evening, would have preferred them to come during the Easter holiday, but he promised to keep the whole of Sunday free, to give them dinner every day, spend the rest of the evening with them and take Jung to the meeting of the Wednesday Psychological Society. (Its name was changed in 1908 to the Vienna Psychoanalytical Society.)

The account of the visit in *Memories, Dreams, Reflections* neither mentions Binswanger nor tallies with what Jung said later that year to Ernest Jones, a young Welsh physician specialising in psychiatry and studying at the Burghölzli. The problem of what happened is further complicated by the testimony of John Billinsky about a meeting with Jung in 1957. A professor of psychology and a friend of Jung's closest associate, Carl Meier, Billinsky reports what he was told – presumably by either Meier or Jung. After Jung and Emma arrived at their hotel, Freud appeared with flowers, apologising for not inviting them to stay in his flat, where he had nothing but an elderly wife. Martha Freud was forty-five, and what he said about her embarrassed Emma.

The Jungs arrived at the flat in time for lunch on Saturday 2 March. It was Jung who did most of the talking, overjoyed at having Freud as his audience. According to Freud's eldest son, Martin, Jung 'never made the slightest attempt to make polite conversation with Mother or us children but pursued the debate which had been interrupted by the call to dinner . . . and Father with unconcealed delight did all the listening.' Martin Freud describes Jung as having 'a commanding presence. He was very tall and broad-shouldered, holding himself more like a soldier than a man of science and medicine. His head was purely Teutonic, with a small chin, a small moustache, blue eyes and thin close-cropped hair.'

Eventually the two men adjourned to Freud's study. Again Jung did most of the talking, perhaps because he found it hard to relax in Freud's company, but so did most of his friends. (Even after going on holiday with him in 1914, the Hungaren neurologist Sándor Ferenczi said: 'Your presence arouses inhibitions of various kinds that influence, and at times almost paralyse, my reactions and even my thinking.') After Jung had talked for about three hours, according to Jones, 'the patient, absorbed listener interrupted him with the suggestion that they conduct their discussion more systematically. To Jung's astonishment, Freud proceeded to group the contents of the harangue under several precise headings that enabled them to spend the further hours in a more profitable give and take.'

They went on talking till about two in the morning. 'In my experience up to then,' said Jung, 'no one else could compare with him. I found him extremely intelligent, shrewd, altogether remarkable.' He also thought Freud 'handsome', and said so for the rest of his life. He described Freud's face as being enormously likable, especially around the ears. Freud told Jones that Jung had a more sophisticated set of neuroses than anyone else he knew.

On Monday, Jung went back to Berggasse with Binswanger, who admired Freud's 'distaste for formality and ceremony, his personal charm, simplicity, natural openness and kindness, and, not least, his humour . . . To me it was a pleasure, albeit somewhat skeptical, to see the enthusiasm and confidence with which Freud responded to Jung, in whom he immediately saw his scientific "son and heir".'

Freud asked both men what they had dreamed overnight. Binswanger, who had a reputation as a womaniser, was told his dream meant he wanted to marry Freud's daughter, while Jung's was taken to reveal a wish to dethrone Freud and take his place. At fifty, Freud was rather young to be looking for a successor, but this interpretation suggests that the idea was in his mind, while Jung, believing something was 'soon going to happen', was on the lookout for opportunities.

Invited to Freud's club on Wednesday 6 March, Jung and Binswanger were the first non-Jews to attend, though the meetings had been held regularly in the flat since the autumn of 1902 for the discussion of psychoanalytic problems. The four founding members were Alfred Adler, Wilhelm Stekel, Max Kahane and Rudolf Reitler. The circle, which gradually grew larger, became the hub of the psychoanalytic movement.

Everyone who came had to speak, and names were picked out of an urn to decide on the order. Freud read part of a paper he was writing on obsessive actions and religious rituals. The compulsive habits of obsessional neurotics had an element of ceremonial in them, he said, and there was neurosis in the need to feel guilt as a sinner and to fend off retribution with reverence and ritual. The discussion centred on the anal eroticism of a male Russian student, and Freud elaborated on what he had said in his letter to Jung: stinginess and generosity might be connected with fixation on the anal zone, and this produced tendencies towards tidiness, cleanliness, conscient- iousness, obstinacy and concern over money matters.

Jung and Binswanger contributed little to the discussion. This was Jung's first confrontation with Freud's Viennese followers, and, like Binswanger, he was unimpressed – as Freud had anticipated. Taking Binswanger aside, he said: 'Now you've seen the gang.' According to Fritz Wittels, a doctor who

became Freud's first biographer, Freud had surrounded himself with me-
diocrities. 'He had little desire that these associates should be persons of
strong individuality, that they should be critical and ambitious collaborators
. . . He welcomed anyone who accepted his views. What he wanted was to
look into a kaleidoscope lined with mirrors that would multiply the images
he introduced into it.'

Freud was surprisingly friendly, but there was something odd about the
position of his sister-in-law, Minna, in the household. Four years younger
than Martha, Minna lived with the family and accompanied Freud on
summer holidays, while Martha stayed with the children. In the flat, Minna
had a sitting room of her own, but only a small bedroom next to the Freuds',
and going to the bathroom at night, she passed through their room. Jung and
Emma had noticed that Freud did not discuss his work with Martha. Minna
was better equipped to understand it. While Jung was in the flat, Billinsky
says, Minna took him aside. 'She was very much bothered by her relationship with Freud and felt guilty about it. From her I learned that Freud was in
love with her and that their relationship was indeed very intimate.' But
according to another account of the story, all Jung said was that Freud had
made advances to her.

Martha ran the household with tight-lipped efficiency, hated waste, and
seldom laughed. She was rigid about routines and meals, strict with
children and servants. Meticulous about domestic tidiness, she tried to
discourage the family doctor, Max Schur, from sitting down on the bed
when examining Freud, but her concern about appearances did not extend
to her coiffure, her clothes or even her figure, which had deteriorated over
the nine years in which she had borne six children. Freud admitted to
friends that Minna was his 'closest confidante', and the reason he gave for
not testing out his theories on his children was that the 'womenfolk' did
not like him to. In the spring of 1894, consulting another doctor about
chest pains and irregular heartbeats, he explained that Martha was 'not a
confidante of my death deliria'.

Jung and Emma spent six days in Vienna. Before leaving, he asked Martha to
send him a photograph of her husband. The Jungs went on to Budapest,
Fiume and Opatija, a seaside resort on the Istrian peninsula, where he once
again felt attracted to a Jewish woman – 'a compulsive infatuation' he later
called it. Writing to Freud at the end of March, he explained the delay with a
cryptic reference to the intensity of the feelings Freud had stimulated: 'until
recently the complexes aroused in Vienna were still in an uproar'.

Jung claims to have assimilated Freud's 'broadened conception of sexuality . . . up to a point', and to have tried it out in several cases. 'In general I

see that you are right.' He comes close to taking an oath of allegiance – from now on his 'foremost concern' will be to

> seek out methods for developing psychoanalysis with a maximum of precision, hoping in this way to lay the foundations for a scientific popularisation of your teachings . . . I am no longer plagued by doubts about the rightness of your theory. The last shreds were dispelled by my stay in Vienna, an event of the greatest importance for me . . . I hope my work for your cause will show you the depths of my gratitude and veneration.

He invited Freud to Zurich. 'A visit from you would be seventh heaven for me personally; the few hours I was permitted to spend with you were all too fleeting.' But Jung would later say: 'Freud consists of bitterness, every word being loaded with it. His attitude was the bitterness of the person who is entirely misunderstood . . . I noticed this in him the first time I met him, and always saw it in him.'

Their relationship had a strong erotic undertone. Early in 1907, before they met, Freud welcomed Jung's book on schizophrenia as 'the richest and most significant contribution to my labours that has ever come to my notice'. He then declared: 'The future belongs to us.' Jung's first letter after the meeting gave Freud what he had been waiting for – a pledge of support. His response was: 'You have inspired me with confidence for the future, that I now realise I am as replaceable as everyone else and could hope for no one better than yourself, as I have come to know you, to continue and complete my work.'

How would Freud have analysed behaviour like his own had he encountered it in a patient? Both men were overexcited about their new friendship, which would grow more intimate through correspondence than it could have done if they were meeting regularly. A lonely and insecure man who did not confide in his wife, Freud thought he had found a replacement for the man who had been his closest friend, Wilhelm Fliess. 'In my emotional life an intimate friend and a hated enemy have always been necessities.'

The friendship with Fliess had begun in 1887, after he married Martha. It was thanks to him that Freud acquired self-respect. 'When I talked to you, and saw that you thought something of me, I actually started thinking something of myself.' An ear, nose and throat specialist who worked in Berlin, Fliess was bizarrely cranky. Men, he believed, had a thirty-two-day biorhythmic cycle, like women's twenty-eight-day menstrual cycle, and menstruation was influenced by 'genital places' in the nose. But Freud hailed

Fliess as 'an even greater visionary than I am', and invited him to collaborate on *The Interpretation of Dreams*. 'I will change anything you want me to, and gratefully accept contributions. I am so tremendously grateful for what you are giving me by being the Other, a critic and a reader – and one of your quality at that. I cannot write without any audience at all, but do not in the least mind writing just for you.'

To provide facts Fliess could check against his scatty theories, Freud supplied the dates of Martha's menstruation, and, in the summer of 1893, said they were no longer making love. Later Freud admitted to a 'homosexual cathexis' in the friendship, which continued until 1904, two years before he started corresponding with Jung.

Given the luxury of a younger man's veneration, he felt free to be self-critical, as he now was in letters to Jung. At fifty-one, he still lacked the authority and the fame he acquired over the next ten years. He had no faith in himself as a leader. 'I'm certainly unfit to be at the helm. The splendid isolation of my formative years has left its mark on my character.' 'I wish I were with you,' he told Jung, 'taking pleasure in no longer being on my own and, if you need encouragement, telling you about my many years of honourable but painful isolation.' He would have enjoyed talking 'about my slowly growing conviction, which attached itself to the interpretation of dreams as to a rock in a stormy sea, and about the serene certainty that finally took hold of me, telling me to wait till a voice from the unknown multitude answered mine. That voice was yours.' The Fliess pattern was repeating itself.

Happy to find he was indispensable, Jung said he was 'living on the crumbs that fall from the rich man's table'. Freud lapped up the flattery, and reciprocated it.

> What you call the hysterical element in your personality, your need to impress and influence people, the very quality that so eminently equips you to be a teacher and guide, will come into its own even if you make no concessions to the current fashions in opinion. And when you have injected your own personal leaven into the fermenting mass of my ideas in still more generous measure, there will be no further difference between your achievement and mine.

The image is grotesque, implying parental equality between them, with Jung in the role of progenitor. Freud thought Jung was fit to be at the helm, and, intoxicated with each other, they fantasised self-indulgently about the power they would share once psychoanalysis was established internationally.

Though Jung later claimed he had never wavered in his resistance to

Freud's view of the libido, he underwent what he called a 'reformation of my psychological thinking'. After reading Freud's essay on *Gradiva*, a novella by the German writer Wilhelm Jensen, Jung wrote:

> One would have to be struck with sevenfold blindness not to see things now as they really are . . . Often I have to transport myself back to the time before the reformation of my psychological thinking to re-experience the charges that were laid against you . . . My thinking in those days seems to me not only intellectually wrong and defective but, what is worse, morally inferior, since it now looks like an immense dishonesty towards myself.

Fortified by confidence in their friendship, Jung began to think of abandoning his clinical work. Writing to Freud, he claimed (untruthfully) to have Bleuler's 'vigorous support' for a scheme to open a psychological laboratory, affiliated to the asylum but with a degree of independence. He would then be 'freed from the shackles of the asylum and able at last to work as I want . . . As I have seen from recent dreams, this change has its − for you − transparent metapsychological-sexual background, holding out the promise of pleasurable feelings galore. Anyone who knows your science has veritably eaten of the tree of paradise and become clairvoyant.'

Overcome by paradisal fantasies, Jung again mentioned the tree of knowledge when he wrote to Freud about two cases that supported his view of the libido. 'I'd like to make an amusing picture book in this style, to be enjoyed only by those who have eaten of the tree of knowledge.'

Freud, who wanted to start a psychoanalytical review, took his cue from Jung's jokey proposal of a picture book. 'Do you yet feel prepared to fight seriously for the recognition of our new ideas? If so the first thing would be to start a journal . . . A publisher can certainly be found; the editor can only be you, and I hope Bleuler will not refuse to join me as a director.' Within three months of meeting Jung, Freud was offering him a key position in the movement.

In the summer, wanting to avoid both Bleuler and Sabina, Jung took Emma to Geneva and Paris, where he saw Pierre Janet. Previously impressed and influenced, Jung now dismissed him as 'merely an intellect but not a personality, a hollow *causeur* and a typical mediocre bourgeois . . . These people are fifty years behind the times. It got on my nerves so much that I gave up the idea of going to London, where far, far less is to be expected.'

Twelve months had gone by since Jung completed his treatise on schizophrenia, but he had not prepared it for publication, and on 14 July he left Zurich again for three weeks of military service in Lausanne. Though he had a commission in the medical corps, he had to get up at five and work till eight in the evening 'as a medical jack-of-all trades, anointing feet, cutting out corns, treating diarrhoea'. He also took parades at which he had to inspect the genitals of five hundred men.

Returning to Zurich exhausted, he had to prepare a paper on hysteria for a September conference in Amsterdam. Writing the paper in August, he summarised Freud's ideas on the subject, and praised psychoanalysis for changing 'all the patient's thinking and feeling in such a way that his personality liberates itself gradually from the compulsion of the complexes'. He used Sabina's case history to show how Freud's ideas could be used clinically. His findings were 'true of an indefinitely large number of cases of hysteria which till now could not be delimited as clinical groups'.

Working under pressure, he let six weeks go by without writing to Freud, but the reprimand was flattering: 'My personality was diminished by the interruption in our correspondence . . . Your letters will carry me back to what for both of us has become the centre of interest.'

Jung responded by insisting on the depth of his commitment: 'It is my passion for the truth that makes me want to present your teachings in such a way as to produce a breakthrough. Otherwise my unconditional devotion to the defence and propagation of your ideas might appear in an extremely peculiar light, as would my equally unconditional veneration of your personality.' To demonstrate that his conversion was complete, he conceded that he had never encountered any complexes which were not sexual.

Freud was suffering from guilt feelings and self-hatred. Here he was, holidaying in a lakeside hotel, bathing and picking mushrooms in the woods, instead of attending the conference. But his absence would benefit both Jung and the cause. 'I have always felt there is something about my personality, my ideas and manner of speaking that people find strange and repellent, whereas all hearts open to you.'

In Amsterdam, hearts did not open. Jung's paper was too long, and he ignored the chairman's signals for him to stop. 'Ultimately he was compelled to,' reported Ernest Jones, 'whereupon with a flushed angry face he strode out of the room. I remember the unfortunate impression his behaviour made on the impatient and already prejudiced audience.' The next day, he preserved a sulky silence when several delegates attacked Freud. Writing to him again, Jung sneered at them as 'a ghastly crowd, reeking of vanity . . . I constantly feel the urgent need of a bath.' He repeated his request for a photograph of Freud – 'not as you used to look but as you did when I got to know you.'

Delayed by a bout of gastroenteritis, Jung's next letter reported that he and his Zurich colleagues had founded a Freudian Society of physicians. Its first meeting would be attended by about twelve members. Though he called Max Eitingon 'a totally impotent gasbag', Jung had got into the Freudian habit of analysing his own aggression: 'it occurs to me that I envy his uninhibited abreaction of the polygamous instinct.' Subduing his own polygamous instinct, Jung was still being faithful to Emma, and he sneered at Otto Gross, a maverick Freudian who contended that analysts should counteract transference by encouraging patients to be promiscuous. 'The truly healthy state for the neurotic is sexual immorality.'

Finally sending a photograph of himself, Freud asked for one of Jung in return. Not unaware of the erotic undertone in their relationship, Jung referred to it obliquely by consulting him about female patients. Referring anonymously to Sabina as one who had been cured of obsessional neurosis, he said she was making him an object of sexual fantasies, which tormented her. Because his role in them was morbid, she said, she wanted to cut loose from him and repress the fantasies. Should he go on with treatment that was giving her a sort of voluptuous pleasure, or should he discharge her? What did Freud do with cases like this? The idea of referring the case to Freud may already have been in his mind. In 1909 he drafted a letter with that intention, but did not send it.

He may have hesitated in October 1907 before posting the letter that contained the enigmatic sentence: 'When I was a boy, I submitted to a man I once venerated.' Admitting there was an element of sexual attraction in his feelings for Freud, Jung used the boyhood incident to explain the revulsion he felt not only against sexuality but against expressions of emotion. The 'erotic undertone' to his feelings for Freud was 'disgusting and ridiculous'. This 'abominable feeling' had its origins, he said, in the homosexual episode, which had made him uncomfortable about 'relations with colleagues who have a strong transference to me'. He therefore found it hard to speak about 'intimate affairs'. 'To my feeling at least, every intimacy (*Verkehr*) turns out after a time to be sentimental and banal or exhibitionistic.' This is not altogether dissimilar to the statement he made about the early sense of being abandoned by his mother when she was in the mental hospital: 'From that time onwards, I was always distrustful immediately the word *love* was mentioned.'

Talking much later about Freud, Jung said his friendliness had revived the old feeling of 'No, no, no, I don't want to belong to anybody. I don't want to be embraced.' Until he was in his thirties, at least, Jung was obviously apprehensive about emotional involvement, which affected many of his relationships with both men and women, even when emotion played only a small part in them.

He scarcely ever mentioned the homosexual episode except in his letter to Freud, and their relationship might have improved had Freud been capable of responding – like an analyst – as Jung obviously wished. Unfortunately for both of them, the subject was problematic to Freud, who had made a volte-face over the question of how often children were seduced by their parents. After explaining all hysteria in terms of childhood seduction – saying this was a common occurrence and that his own father was a pervert – he decided in 1897 that he had been misled by fantasies about seduction. Patients had been telling him what they thought he wanted to hear.

His reply to Jung's confessional letter has not been published, but he seems to have advised against taking the incident too seriously. In his letter of 8 November, Jung agrees that humour is now the only sensible reaction, and it is hard to decipher the subtext in Jung's letter of 20 February 1910 about homosexuality. From discussing resistance against the transference in analysis, the letter moves – quickly, confusingly and with an awkward jocularity – to prejudice against homosexuality:

> The homosexual resistances in men are simply astounding and open up mind-boggling possibilities. Removal of the moral stigma from homosexuality as a method of contraception is a cause to be promoted with the utmost energy . . . Homosexuality would be a tremendous advantage since many infererior men, who quite reasonably would like to remain on the homosexual level, are now forced into marriage . . . Thanks to our myopia, we fail to acknowledge the biological services rendered by homosexual seducers. Actually they should be credited with something of the sanctity of monks.

Ten

Ardent Freudian

Jung became Freud's closest friend, though they spent relatively little time together. They both found it easier to be intimate when writing letters than when face to face. The friendship was to last about seven years – longer than it could have done if the mutual need had been merely personal. Both benefited professionally: the alliance helped to propagate Freud's ideas, while the ideas helped both of them to international fame.

Though he would not have equated his Number One personality with the Freudian superego, Jung knew he was prone to an imbalance that needed correction, and experience at the giving end had shown how helpful psychoanalysis could be. Why waste his opportunity to consult an expert? He had confided in Freud about the German-American woman in Paris and now Jung wrote to him about Sabina's Siegfried fantasy. Though they were both familiar with the dangers of transference, they took exorbitant risks.

Not receiving an immediate reply to his letter of 28 October, Jung wrote again, admitting he was 'suffering all the agonies of a patient being analysed and envisaging all the possible consequences of the confession I made'. He invited Freud to spend Christmas with him and Emma. This would give them time for some analytical conversations, even if Jung did not lie down on a couch.

Freud's reply to Jung's first letter is missing, but addressing him as 'Dear Friend and Colleague' (instead of 'Dear Colleague') Jung acknowledged it on 8 November, saying it had 'worked wonders' for him, and agreeing that humour was the best means of dealing with the inevitable. Almost apologising for confessing so much, Jung explained: 'My religiosity, which used to be very lively, had secretly found some compensation in you, and I had to seal it with this.' Little could be gained by sidestepping the issue, but much could have been lost if they had confronted it.

In a mid-November letter, saying transference on a religious basis could end only in apostasy, Freud insisted he was unfit to be an object of worship.

He knew jokes could disguise the taste of unpalatable truths, but while willing to make his analytical expertise available to Jung, he did not draw on it for himself.

In November 1907, a new psychiatrist arrived at the Burghölzli – Abraham Brill, who had been trained in the USA. 'Under the wise guidance of Bleuler,' he wrote, 'and the aggressive inspiration of Jung, his chief assistant, everybody worked assiduously to test Freud's theories.' He was impressed by Jung's 'enthusiasm and brilliance', and by his commitment.

> Jung was at that time the most ardent Freudian . . . Jung brooked no disagreement with Freud's views; impulsive and bright, he refused to see the other side. Anyone who dared doubt what was certainly then new and revolutionary aroused his anger . . . Our conversation at meals was frequently punctuated with the word 'complex' . . . No one could make a slip of any kind without immediately being called on to evoke free associations to explain it.

The 'Psychoanalytic Circle' met every month. It contained some dissenters, 'but despite Jung's occasional impulsive intolerance, the meetings were very fruitful and successful in disseminating Freud's theories.'

After Brill had produced an English version of Jung's book on schizophrenia, Jung passed him on to Freud. Early in 1908 Brill went to Vienna, where he was commissioned to translate Freud's work into English. The task was beyond him, and psychoanalysis is still lumbered with some of his mistakes. Thinking of word tests in the hospital, he translated *freier Einfall* as 'free association', though *Einfall* means 'occurrence', and the point is that random thoughts should be admitted freely, while 'actual neuroses' is based on a misunderstanding of *aktuell*, which, like the French *actuel*, means 'current'.

At the end of November, one of the first English Freudians, Ernest Jones, spent a week at the hospital. He admired Jung's 'breezy personality' and his 'restlessly active and quick brain', though 'he could change his mood like a chameleon. One moment the big vibrant charming chairman of the group and the next a vociferous intervener, who, when confronted with opposition, put his case with a vigour which some thought – well – pretty rough. I liked him at the time. He did not mince his words.'

At one meeting, a Hungarian analyst suggested an international conference should be held in the spring at Salzburg or Innsbruck, both cities being about halfway between Vienna and Zurich. When Jung obligingly made preliminary plans for an international journal, Freud responded: 'That is a matter of life or death for our ideas.'

Jung was prepared to invest energy and time. 'We are on to a really good thing and can be glad of it.' In January he issued a circular saying an international congress would be held at the end of April in Salzburg, just after a three-day Congress for Experimental Psychology in Frankfurt. Delegates could travel from there to Salzburg on the 27th.

Jung considered himself strong enough to overwork with impunity, but in late January he succumbed to flu, and had not recovered by mid-February. Though he visited Baden several times for thermal baths, he could not throw off the malaise, which was inflamed by resentment at not having enough time for his own work. As well as organising the congress, he was giving time to pupils. 'They get ahead at my expense, while I am at a standstill.' Launching and editing the journal would mean investing even more time in 'our cause'.

Writing to Freud, Jung set a high value on 'the undeserved gift of your friendship'. Not wanting to repeat the Fliess pattern, Jung proposed: 'Let me enjoy your friendship not as one between equals but as that of father and son. This distance appears to me fitting and natural. Moreover it alone, so it seems to me, strikes a note that would prevent misunderstandings and enable two hard-headed people to coexist in an easy and unstrained relationship.'

Still meeting Sabina regularly, Jung was uncertain what he wanted. Kissing, cuddling, debating whether to make love, they still held back.

> We could sit for hours in silent ecstasy . . . My love for him transcended our affinity until he could bear it no longer and wanted 'poetry'. For many reasons I could not resist and did not want to. But when he asked how I envisaged what would happen next (because of the 'consequences') I said that first love has no desires, that I had nothing in mind and did not want to go beyond a kiss, which I could also give up if necessary.

Poetry was her euphemism for lovemaking. The titillation was intensified by the notion that their love was incestuous. In her dreams Jung was inter-changeable with her father and the brother who had been spanked, while his dreams identified her with his mother. Fantasies of incest constellated around the figure of Siegfried, who blurred in her mind with Jung and the child they would have.

The tension became intolerable, and when Jung decided to break off the sessions, she funnelled her anger into her diary. Her unconscious, she wrote, could want nothing that his rejected, but inflaming her desire by resisting her advances, he was making her play the male role while he played the female. He had revealed his desire for her child by showing her Binswanger's analysis of the word-test results, but she might lose the father by giving birth to the son.

Of the forty-two delegates at the Salzburg congress, more than half came from Vienna, six from Switzerland, including Bleuler and Riklin, five from Germany, including Karl Abraham and Otto Gross. Jung knew Abraham, who had been at the Burghölzli till he resigned in 1907. After visiting Freud in Vienna, he had settled in Berlin, where he became Germany's first full-time analyst. The two Britons were Ernest Jones and a surgeon, Wilfrid Trotter. 'My eastern contingent,' Freud had written, 'will probably be inferior in personal merit to your western contingent,' and Jung was suitably unimpressed with the 'degenerate and Bohemian crowd which did Freud little credit'. According to Jones, 'They were all practising physicians . . . and if their cloaks were more flowing and their hats broader than what one saw in Zurich, London or Berlin . . . that was a general Viennese characteristic.' But 'they were decidedly middle-class, and lacked the social manners and distinction I had been accustomed to in London.'

With Freud at the head of a long table, the meeting began at eight in the morning. Each speaker was limited to thirty minutes, except Freud, who would talk last. Jung spoke on 'Dementia Praecox', Gross on the cultural perspectives of psychoanalysis. He thought neurosis could be eliminated through social and cultural change. In the present situation, he said, sickness was unavoidable, and in refusing to disguise his own sickness, he was setting an example for other analysts. This was too risqué for Freud, who insisted: 'We are doctors, and doctors we must remain.'

Two years younger than Jung, Otto Gross was the son of Hanns Gross, who had been a judge for thirty years before he made criminology into an academic subject at the University of Graz. After studying medicine, Otto assisted his father's criminological research until he could no longer stomach the ex-judge's authoritarianism and his precept that punishment should be directed at the criminal, not the crime. He used the term 'criminal type' for 'degenerates' who had not yet committed a crime, but obviously would as soon as circumstances were propitious. Franz Kafka, who attended some of his lectures, may have picked up the seminal idea for *The Trial*, in which a man is arrested without having any specific charge laid against him.

In his schizophrenia book, Jung had referred to Otto Gross's articles, but Gross considered himself to be less of a writer than a talker and analyst. He encouraged patients to resist whatever they found oppressive, and, as Martin Green suggested in the 1970s, 'one sees how much he was for that moment what R. D. Laing or Timothy Leary is for us today.' Ernest Jones said Gross was 'the nearest approach to a romantic genius I have ever met . . . Such penetrative powers of divining the inner thoughts of others I was never to see again.'

Tall and slim with blond hair, blue eyes and an aquiline nose, Gross had charisma. Though shy with women, he sometimes became sexually involved with patients. A teetotaller and vegetarian, he was addicted to cocaine and morphine. He took a cure before he married at the age of twenty-six, but his father, who wanted him interned, wrote to ask whether Jung could take Otto to the asylum after the congress.

Though it was as a rebel against authoritarianism that Otto had joined the Freudians, he had begun to find Freud oppressively patriarchal. He felt most at home in Schwabing, a northern suburb of Munich where artists, anarchists and revolutionaries ate, drank, smoked, chatted and flirted in cafés that stayed open all night. It was a hotbed of decadence and promiscuity, but Gross approved of both, counting on them to produce a more liberal future. Acquiring followers and encouraging them to use narcotics, he eroded their moral scruples. He had supplied a suicidal woman with poison, and he had several illegitimate children. In 1906 he had met Frieda and Else von Richthofen. Frieda was married to a lecturer in English literature, Ernest Weekley, whom she later left for D. H. Lawrence, and Else was married to a teacher of political economy, Edgar Jaffe. Gross seduced both sisters, and Else bore him a son. He later told Frieda his Salzburg speech was the first fruit of their relationship.

Jung disapproved of him. 'Dr Gross says he cuts the transference process short by turning patients into sexual immoralists. He says transference to the analyst and its persistent fixation are just symbols of monogamy and therefore symptomatic of repression . . . But it seems to me that sexual repression is important and indispensable to civilisation, even if it is pathogenic for many people who are feeble.'

Indifferent to the feelings of his 'gang', Freud was going all out to prove psychoanalysis was neither a Viennese nor a Jewish phenomenon. Otto Rank was the only Viennese Jew invited to join the caucus Freud formed with the delegates from Zurich, the German Jew Karl Abraham, Brill, Jones and the Hungarian delegate, Sándor Ferenczi, who had started to practise psychoanalysis after reading *The Interpretation of Dreams* and had met Freud at the beginning of 1908. They agreed to set up an international organisation and publish a yearbook under the direction of Freud and Bleuler, with Jung as editor. This undemocratic decision was announced to the others, who were right to feel resentful. Was this how years of loyalty were rewarded?

Freud had let Jung persuade him to present a case history, and, speaking without notes, he talked about the patient who was to become known as the Rat Man. Freud started his talk at eight, 'and at eleven,' reports Jones, 'he offered to bring it to a close. We had all been so enthralled, however, at the fascinating exposition, that we begged him to go on, and he did so for another hour. I had never before been so oblivious to the passage of time.'

Instead of trying to placate his bristling Viennese followers, Freud peppered his speech with phrases calculated to please the Swiss. When his patient was told about a torture in which a basket of rats was strapped to the victim's buttocks, it was as if Fate 'had been giving him an association test: she had called out a complex-stimulus word and he had responded with his obsessional idea'.

Jung and Freud spent little time together, partly because Emmanuel Freud, a seventy-four-year-old half-brother, had arrived, uninvited. 'On balance,' wrote Jung, 'the results were very good.' Freud's talk had struck him 'as perfection itself. All the others were simply padding, sterile nonsense in the obscurity of inanity.' The letter ends: 'I beg you to have patience with me and confidence in what I have done so far. I always need to do a bit more than be just a faithful follower.'

Freud did not take this at its face value. 'I am quite sure that having moved a few steps away from me, you will find your way back, and then go a long way with me . . . I am satisfied to feel at one with you and no longer fear we may be torn apart. You will simply have to be patient with some of my idiosyncracies . . . We must not quarrel while besieging Troy.'

As requested, Freud committed Gross to internment in the Burghölzli, where Jung was to be his doctor. 'Do not let him out till October, when I will be able to take charge of him.' Jung's antipathy to him was soon eroded, and, giving him priority over other patients, Jung spent hours with him every day. Trying to cooperate, Gross reduced his drug intake, and once they went on talking for twelve hours, analysing each other. Gross passed on ideas he had picked up in Schwabing and Ascona, a resort on Lago Maggiore where radicals and bohemians congregated. His hostility to monogamy followed on from his rejection of patriarchal authority: wives and daughters should be liberated from commitment to a single dominant male.

Previously, Jung had been attracted by neither paganism nor bohemianism, but he told Freud his psychic health had benefited from conversations with Gross, 'an exceptionally decent chap with whom one can immediately get on very well as soon as one can get away from one's complexes . . . I completed the analysis yesterday. So far as I can see, all that remains is the residue from a rather long series of minor obsessions.'

Freud was sceptical, and Jung soon saw he had been too optimistic. Though Gross had moments of insight into his complexes, 'there is no development, no psychological yesterday for him; the experiences of early childhood remain indelible and overwhelming.' Jung had just arrived at a diagnosis of schizophrenia when, on 17 June, desperate for drugs, Gross escaped over the garden wall.

Jung called the experience 'one of the worst in my life, for in Gross I found only too many aspects of my own nature, so that he often seemed like my twin brother'. Freud understood only vaguely what this meant, but Jung had undergone something like a conversion. Even his relationship with Sabina was about to change.

He occupied himself by writing an essay on 'The Significance of the Father in the Destiny of the Individual'. Deprived of his new twin, he felt bereaved, which reminded him of his father, though he may have been thinking of Samuel Preiswerk when he said the father is 'usually the principal and dangerous focus of the child's fantasy, and if it ever happened to be the mother, I could see behind her a grandfather to whom she belonged in her heart'.

Discussing paternal influence on character structure, emotionality, values and lifestyle, he makes a preliminary foray into a question that will be crucial after the break with Freud: the relationship between psychology and religion. But in 1908 he followed Freud in taking ideas of divinity to derive from childhood feelings about the father, and regarded the child–parent relationship as basically sexual. 'We always try to deny the child's sexuality. But this is only because of wilful ignorance . . . In essence our biographical destiny is identical with the destiny of our sexuality.'

Gross's apologia for polygamy intensified Jung's hatred of authoritarianism. Would loving a Jewess be an act of rebellion? Sabina, who thought she had lost him, was astonished when, beaming with pleasure, he explained that he had gained insight into polygamy. He was going to stop suppressing his feelings, and apart from Emma, she was his dearest friend. 'You have no idea how much it means to me to be able to love someone I do not have to condemn to suffocating in the banality of habit, and who does not condemn herself to that fate.'

They made love and collaborated on a prose poem about Siegfried. 'For you I battled with the raging waves; now, as victor, I come brandishing my oars, and you shall be the prize.' Jung loved her for the magnificence of her passion, he said, and she had taken his unconscious into her hands.

As with Gross, Jung felt as if he had discovered a long-lost twin. Sabina was Sieglinde to his Siegmund. Together they were Siegfried's parents, while he also represented Siegfried, and Sigmund Freud was involved because she knew about their father–son intimacy. 'Here too the Christian is the "son" of the Jew. The latter is older and more independent. But here too my friend is my little son so that *volens-nolens* we are both married to Professor Freud.' Only thirty-nine years had passed since *Das Rheingold* was premiered in the year Cosima von Bülow, who had left her husband, gave birth to Wagner's illegitimate son, Siegfried.

Jung had misgivings, of course. He said they must find 'a clear way out of the turmoil we are in', and tried to conceal his anxiety at demands Sabina might make. What he needed, he said, was someone strong and unsentimental. She should be free and independent. He claimed to love Jewish women and to want a dark Jewish girl in his life, but she was jealous of the Christian wife who shared his home. For a while he almost persuaded himself Emma might accept Sabina as a friend, but instead she had to go on snatching at brief spells of togetherness, meeting him where nobody would see them, and reminding herself that Emma had failed to give him a son.

Sabina left in early August. She was going to spend the summer with her parents in Russia. Not hearing from her, Jung became 'somewhat hysterical', wondering whether 'the devil had got his hand in', and his mood went on 'shifting volcanically between grey and gold'. Her first letter cheered him up. 'I notice how much more attached to you I am than I should have thought possible,' and he asked: 'What does the old Bombuchina say to you? Is she glad you have become so pretty?' In early September he was urging her to hurry back to Zurich, though Freud was due there later in the month.

Freud's main objective in accepting the invitation, he said, was 'to persuade you to continue and complete my work by extending to psychosis what I have begun with neurosis. With your strong and independent character, with your Germanic blood, which enables you to command the public's sympathy more readily than I can, you seem more suitable than anyone I know for this mission.'

Freud arrived on 17 September to stay in the Jungs' flat for five nights, but Emma, who was in the eighth month of her third pregnancy, had not yet returned from holidaying with the two young children. Visiting the Burghölzli and meeting Babette, the old woman who boasted of being 'double polytechnic irreplaceable', Freud expressed surprise at Jung's willingness to spend so much time with someone so ugly. The two men talked about mythology. In mid-August Freud had written: 'One thing and another have turned my thoughts to mythology, and I am beginning to suspect that myth and neurosis have a common core.'

After Freud left on 22 September, Sabina was told that Jung's admiration for him had grown into genuine fondness, while Freud believed Jung 'has overcome his vacillation, adheres to the cause with no reservations and will go on working energetically on dementia praecox, following our approach'. To Jung he wrote: 'The days we spent so auspiciously together in Zurich have left me in high spirits.'

After another spell of military service in the barracks at Yverdon, Jung started a letter 'Lieber Professor Freud' instead of 'Sehr geehrter Herr Professor' ('Very Honoured Herr Professor'). Still anything but a committed Freudian, Bleuler could not stop Jung from involving himself in work that had nothing to do with his job. Freud was winning the tug-of-war for the thirty-three-year-old son: Bleuler agreed to become joint editor-in-chief of the yearbook, but as managing editor, Jung would effectively be working for Freud.

In October Sabina returned for the autumn term, but Jung left for another spell of military service. When they met in November, Emma was in the final stages of her third pregnancy, and on 1 December the baby was born – a boy. This put paid to Sabina's Siegfried fantasy – Jung had fathered a son without her.

Proud but exhausted, Emma was impatient to move into the new house, which was still not ready. If Jung felt guilty both about being unfaithful and about failing to put more pressure on the builders, his main anxiety was that a scandal might break. He now had a lot to lose. With his name on the cover, the first issue of the yearbook would be an international proclamation that he was Freud's adjutant.

The presence of a baby brother disturbed the four-year-old Agathli, who kept asking where babies came from, and refusing to believe in the stork. She started suffering from nocturnal terrors that reminded Jung of his childhood, and she became so angry with her parents that she threatened to move in with her grandmother.

The two girls ate with their parents, who had been talking about the recent earthquake at Messina. In spite of atlases and geological pictures Jung fetched from his study, Agathli felt sure that the mountains around Zurich were volcanic, that the earthquake would spread, that the house would fall down. It has been suggested by S. Rosenzweig that her mistrust of both parents may have derived from Emma's suspicions about Sabina. Without understanding what was going on, the child may have picked up her mother's insecurity. Jung tried to reassure Agathli by explaining that a mother is like soil and a father like a gardener who plants a seed, which goes on growing till the baby is born.

At two and a half, Gret was too young to be scared of earthquakes. More interested than her sister in orifices, and more resistant to pot-training, she laughed uproariously when she misbehaved at mealtimes, though Emma insisted that it was not funny. Gret took her revenge when a new dish appeared on the table. Refusing to taste it, she said it was not funny.

Unwilling to sacrifice his relationship with Sabina, Jung indulged in self-hatred:

Will you forgive me for being as I am? That in this way I insult you and forget my duties as your doctor? Will you grasp the fact that I am one of the weakest and most unstable of men? And will you hold back from revenging yourself with words or thoughts or feelings? I am looking for someone who knows how to love without punishing or imprisoning the man or sucking at him.

Could he see her at her lodgings on Tuesday between 9.15 and midday?

At this juncture he decided to give up his job. If a scandal broke, he would have to resign; if he resigned first, the scandal would be less damaging. Bleuler was not entirely unprepared for the news, and Jung agreed to go on working till March. He told Freud the birth of a son had coincided with success in rationalising the father complex and extricating himself from everyday dependence on a boss.

Freud was delighted. 'You will see what a blessing it is to have no master over you.' He might have pondered his own words more carefully if he had taken less pleasure in the feeling that he was now the master. 'We are certainly making headway. If I am Moses, you are Joshua, and you will take possession of the promised psychiatric land that I will glimpse only from afar.'

Sabina was not delighted about his resignation, and meeting her two days after his son was born, he said he wanted to withdraw from the relationship. She was shocked and incredulous. The next day he wrote a confused letter, insisting he could not go on deceiving Emma. 'When one is already married, it is better to commit the lie just once and pay the price than to repeat the experience again and again, again to lie and again to let someone down.' Arguing that she will be better off without him, he mixes fact and fiction in an unflattering self-portrait:

Unfortunately for me, my life means nothing to me without the pleasure of love, of tempestuous, constantly changing love . . . When love for a woman awakens within me, the first thing I feel is regret, pity for the poor woman who dreams of eternal faithfulness and other impossibilities and is due for a rude awakening . . . Give me back in the moment of my need some of the love and guilt and altruism I was able to give you when you were ill. Now I'm the one who is ill.

She was too dependent on him to give up the relationship, and, unable to break it off peacefully, he went on seeing her. Receiving less love and attention than she needed, Emma decided she had been too tolerant for too long. In mid-January 1909 Sabina's mother received an anonymous warning that she must step in to save her daughter from Dr Jung. When she wrote to him, he replied:

> I could more easily abandon my role as doctor since I felt myself to be under no professional obligation, as I had never charged a fee . . . A man and a girl cannot possibly continue indefinitely to have friendly dealings with one another without the likelihood that something more may enter the relationship . . . A *doctor* and his *patient*, on the other hand can talk of the most intimate matters for as long as they like, and the patient may expect her doctor to give her all the love and concern she requires. But the doctor knows his limits and will never cross them, for he is paid for his troubles.

His fee was ten francs per consultation, he explained, and he hoped Frau Spielrein would choose 'the prosaic solution'. But he soon regretted his hot-headed demand for money. With this letter in her possession, Frau Spielrein could be dangerous.

Jung told Sabina that from now on their relationship must be strictly that of doctor and patient. Writing to her mother again, he said:

> I have always told your daughter that a sexual relationship was out of the question and that my actions were meant to express my feelings of friendship. When this happened, I chanced to be in a very gentle and compassionate mood, and I wanted to give your daughter convincing evidence of my confidence in her and friendship in order to liberate her inwardly.

After staying away from him for three weeks, Sabina arrived in his consulting room, confused, with a knife in her hand, and when he grabbed at it, she resisted. 'Suddenly he went very pale, clapped his hand to his left temple: "You struck me." ' She found herself outside the room, weeping and sitting on a trolley, surrounded by people who wanted to know whether she was hurt. She had blood on her hand and her arm, but it was his. Apparently she had slapped his face before they struggled over the knife.

She ran away, leaving him acutely worried about letters he had written. Having accepted an invitation to see Freud in Vienna towards the end of March, he was afraid a scandal might have broken by then. Instead of confiding in Freud, he wrote no more letters till he received a telegram. He then blamed his silence on pressure of work and trouble with builders in Küsnacht.

Admitting an involvement with a female patient, he did not explain this was the woman he had discussed with Freud and described in his Amsterdam lecture. Claiming to have treated her 'with unstinting devotion' and cured her of 'a very awkward neurosis', he said she had

> kicked up a vile scandal just because I denied myself the pleasure of giving her a child. Towards her I have always played the gentleman, but in confrontation with my oversensitive conscience I do not feel entirely innocent, and that is what is most painful, for my intentions were always honourable. But you know how it is – the devil can use even the best of things for the manufacture of filth. Meanwhile I have acquired an indescribable amount of marital wisdom, for previously, despite all self-analysis, I had a totally inadequate idea of my polygamous components. Now I know where and how to lay the devil by the heels. These painful yet very salutary insights have given me hellish internal disturbance, but for that reason, I hope, have secured me moral qualities which will be greatly advantageous in later life.

Like a son telling his father he has done nothing wrong – and even if he has, contrition has already hurt him more than punishment could – Jung refers three times within four sentences to hell and the devil.

Freud noticed his 'lapse into the theological style'. In Nietzsche's view, 'The imagination of many Christian saints was dirty to an extraordinary degree; thanks to the theory that those desires raging inside them were actually demons, they did not feel too much to blame for them.' Jung felt the same compulsion as in childhood to blame an external power for his inclinations: 'Often we call it the hand of God or of the devil, expressing unconsciously but accurately a highly important psychological fact: that the power which shapes the life of the psyche has the character of an auton-omous personality.' Freud, who had been told about neither the penis dream nor the fantasy of the shitting God, made no comment on this important psychological fact.

In Vienna he met a neurologist from Basel, Arthur Muthmann, who said a woman had introduced herself to him as Dr Jung's mistress. Assuming this was the same woman, Freud assured Jung that neither he nor Muthmann believed her. 'To be slandered and scorched by the love with which we operate – such are the perils of our trade, which we are certainly not going to abandon on their account.'

Jung said he had no idea who the woman was. 'The story hawked around by Muthmann is Chinese to me. I have never really had a mistress and am the most innocent of spouses.' The letter jerks from marital infidelity to the idea of betraying Freud. 'Except for moments of infatuation, my affection is lasting and reliable. It is just that for the past fortnight the devil has been tormenting me in the shape of neurotic ingratitude. But I shall not be unfaithful to psychoanalysis on that account.'

Before Jung and Emma arrived in Vienna on 25 March, Freud had been invited to give six lectures on psychoanalysis at Clark University in Worcester, Massachusetts. Concealing his anxieties, Jung talked optimistically about the future of Freudianism in the USA.

This was the moment at which Freud decided to take up Jung's proposal that they should have a father–son relationship. Jocular but also serious, Freud offered to adopt him as his eldest son, formally 'anointing' him in an improvised ceremony as successor and crown prince. The biblical word *anoint* recurs in the first of Freud's subsequent letters to Jung, together with the phrase *in partibus infidelium* – 'in the land of the unbelievers'. Unlike Judaism, the psychoanalytic religion set no obstacle in the path of a patriarch who displaced his eldest son in order to adopt a Gentile as son and heir. Martin Freud had neither the right personality nor the ambition to take over leadership of the movement.

Overcoming his misgivings more quickly than he might have done if he had not been anxious about a scandal, Jung submitted to the improvised ritual. But, unable to relax, he steered the conversation into topics that could not fail to provoke disagreement – precognition and parapsychology. While Freud, who had little interest and no belief in either, explained his scepticism, Jung felt physically uncomfortable.

> And at that moment there was such a loud bang in the bookcase which stood directly beside us that we were both frightfully alarmed. We thought the bookcase was going to fall over on top of us . . . I told Freud: 'That's what's called a catalytic exteriorisation phenomenon.'
>
> 'Oh,' he said, 'that's pure nonsense.'
>
> 'No,' I retorted, 'you're wrong, Herr Professor. And to prove I'm right, I'm telling you now that we're about to hear another bang.'
>
> And indeed, the words were scarcely out of my mouth when the same noise came from the bookcase. To this day I do not know where my certainty came from. But I was sure the sound would be repeated. Freud just stared at me aghast.

He had lost all his elation. 'It is strange that you should have divested me of my paternal dignity, which divesting seems to have given you as much pleasure as I, on the contrary, derived from the investiture of your person.'

Left on his own, Freud realised the noise had been nothing more than a loud creak, caused by the weight of two Egyptian steles on the oak bookshelves in the neighbouring room, where they produced persistent creaking noises. He had never previously heard these in the other room, but subsequently he did. 'My credulity, or at least my willingness to believe, vanished with the magic of your personal presence . . . Accordingly I put my fatherly horn-rimmed spectacles on again and warn my dear son to keep a cool head, for it is better not to understand something than make such great sacrifices to understanding.'

The evening that disappointed Freud left Jung elated. 'That last evening with you has, most happily, freed me inwardly from the oppressive feeling of your paternal authority.' He could now think independently, and, remembering his intuition about the second noise, he had an idea that was going to be seminal. Perhaps there was 'some kind of special complex . . . that is universal and connected with man's forward-looking tendencies. If Psychoanalysis exists, there must also be a "Psychosynthesis" which creates future events according to the same laws.'

Freud could not have understood this use of the term *Psychosynthesis* unless he read Jung's letter in the perspective of Kant. In his copy of the *Critique of Pure Reason* Jung had made a marginal mark against the argument that *analytic* judgements (in which the subject contains the idea of the predicate) provide no new information, unlike *synthetic* judgements (in which the subject does not). Jung's cryptic sentence contains his first formulation of an idea basic to his later deviation from Freudian psychoanalysis, which, according to him, revealed nothing except past events that had been repressed.

It is more useful to understand what will happen in the future. 'In the same way that memory traces which sank under the threshold of consciousness long ago are demonstrably accessible to the unconscious, so also there are certain very fine subliminal combinations that point significantly towards future events, in so far as these are conditioned by our psychology.' He mentions Kant when he makes this point in *Symbols of Transformation*, and, as Paul Bishop explains, it is this distinction between analytic and synthetic judgements that provides 'the conceptual basis of what he saw as two entirely different psychologies'. Focusing on the origins of a neurosis, Freudian psychoanalysis could provide no new information, but Jung would 'deal with the trajectory of the neurosis and its implications for the future development of the patient'.

A revealing footnote in *Symbols of Transformation* suggests that the unconscious psyche may contain knowledge of the future. Forecasting that he will 'hardly be spared the reproach of mysticism', and pointing to history's ignorance of 'that which is hidden in the past and that which is hidden in the future', Jung uses the word *synthesis* for what can be predicted on the basis of dreams.

Eleven

Lakeside House

Jung moved into the new lakeside house in Küsnacht on 25 May 1909, but only four rooms were ready, though six years had passed since he bought the site. Emma and the children did not move in till 12 June.

The inscription above the front door was '*Vocatus atque non vocatus deus aderit*' – 'Called or not called, the god will be present'. It was taken from the *Collectanea adagiorum* of Erasmus, a collection of analects from classical writers. Jung had acquired a copy of the 1563 edition when he was nineteen.

In 1903, when he selected the site, he had already decided his future home should be close neither to the Burghölzli nor to the centre of Zurich. The architect was his cousin, Professor Fiechter, who lectured on architecture at the Federal Polytechnic, but in planning the building with him, Jung took many decisions for himself, which had helped to cause delays.

At last he had space where he could read, write, and smoke his pipe without being disturbed by unexpected visitors. He did not undervalue the help he had given to psychotic patients, but he had no qualms about abandoning this work. To a New York psychiatrist who questioned this decision, he said such cases 'can be treated, and even with the most obvious success, but such a success costs almost your own life. You have to make the most stupendous efforts to reintegrate the dissociated psychic entities . . . It is not too easy to cure a neurosis, but to cure a case on the borderline of D.p. is worse.'

He went on treating neurotics – if they came to Küsnacht.

Dr Jung's patients must take a little steamboat at a landing haunted by gulls and wild ducks, and then walk a good ten minutes to a yellow country house standing well within walls and gardens on the edge of the lake of Zurich. They must pull a shining brass bell, of old-fashioned mold, and while its fateful ring resounds through the house . . . meet the inspection of a group of skirmishing dogs.

An American patient reports:

> Guarding the house and making it even less hospitable was Jung's
> schnauzer, a rather disagreeable dog that always escorted one stiffly to
> the equally stiff front door. The house is a formal, typically bourgeois Swiss
> structure . . . It had that same closed-up, off-limits look of the well-to-do
> Swiss homes everywhere . . . Jung had warned me that people who are
> close to the unconscious must look out for his dog. The dog had a habit of
> biting such people. I was deep in the unconscious, as everyone else around
> Jung was . . . On entering his study, Jung amiably called it 'the chamber of
> horrors'. The little room was a clutter of stacked unread letters, notes in his
> handwriting, all kinds of papers, and books opened to special places . . . In
> the middle of the clutter was a rather worn, overstuffed, slightly flounder-
> ing leather chair. It was for the patient. The room had a look of hard,
> casual use and comfort. It was a private, warm, but small nest for a large
> man whose cultural and intellectual curiosity and quests knew no limits.
> The dog was part of it. He climbed in under Jung's desk, eyeing me . . .

Jung's mother had settled in Küsnacht, and in about 1909 Trudi moved in
with her. Jung had no secretary, and she had been doing some bookkeeping
and typing. She went to the house every Saturday to have lunch with him,
Emma and the children, but she did not talk much, and she led an
unadventurous life, never going outside Switzerland. She went on for
about sixteen years doing secretarial work for her brother, and, like her
mother, she was important to his children.

When Frau Spielrein demanded a meeting, Jung refused to see her, except
at the hospital. In May, noticing he suddenly went pale during one of his
lectures, a friend of Sabina's turned round to see her standing by the coat
rack, her face white. Nervous of losing her self-control, as she had when she
slapped him, she walked out, but came to another lecture, sitting opposite
him to watch him carefully.

Later in the month she wrote to ask Freud whether he would see her.
Instead of replying, he posted the letter to Jung: 'Weird! What is she? A
busybody, a chatterbox or a paranoiac? . . . If I do not hear from you I will
assume you know nothing.'

Jung now admitted she was the woman he had lectured about in
Amsterdam.

> Knowing from experience she would relapse rapidly if I withdrew my
> support, I continued the relationship over the years and found in the end I
> was morally obliged as it were to befriend her quite a lot until I saw that

contrary to my intentions a certain wheel was turning, and then I finally
broke with her . . . Like Gross she is a case of fighting against the father . . .
and I was trying to cure her *gratissime* with unquantifiable patience . . . My
first visit to Vienna had a very long sequel, first the compulsive infatuation
in Abbazia, then the Jewess popped up in another form, in the shape of my
patient . . . Throughout the whole business, Gross's ideas were floating
about too freely in my head.

Sabina was typical of the Russians: 'Little patience and depth, all quibblings
and vapourings – a good-for-nothing lot.'

Jung would not have been surprised if Freud had disinherited him.
Instead, he welcomed the chance to show clemency. No lasting harm
had been done, and if he had been ten years younger when he started out, he
might have had similar experiences. Women 'help us to develop the thick
skin we need and to control "counter-transference", which is after all a
constant problem for us.' This was the first time the term *counter-transference*
had been used. 'The way these women manage to charm us,' Freud went on
'with every conceivable psychic perfection till they have achieved their
purpose is one of nature's greatest spectacles.'

His leniency provoked a new outburst of contrition. 'It is too stupid that I
of all people, your "son and heir", should squander your heritage so
recklessly, as if I understood nothing about all these things.' But again
he implied that he had learned from his mistakes.

After the move to Küsnacht, Jung's practice expanded faster than he had
expected. In June, just as he finished a lecture, Sabina came up to him. He
tried to hurry away, but she seemed calm. Half believing what he was telling
Freud – that his feeling for her belonged to his 'Jewess complex' – he said
that in Vienna, he had been enchanted by Freud's youngest daughter,
Sophie, who was nearly fourteen, and that these feelings had been transferred to Sabina. Writing to Freud, though, he admitted he was largely
responsible

for the ambitious hopes of my former patient. Following my principle of
taking everyone extremely seriously, I discussed the problem of the baby
with her, talking theoretically, but Eros was of course lurking in the
background, making me impute all the other hopes and desires entirely to
my patient without noticing them in myself. When the situation became
so tense that the perseveration of the relationship could be rounded out
only by sexual acts, I defended myself in a way that is morally unjustifiable.
I wrote to her mother that I was not the gratifier of her daughter's sexual
desires but merely her doctor . . . Since I had until recently given the

patient my friendship and my full confidence, my action was a piece of knavery which I very reluctantly confess to you, as my father . . . I ask your pardon many times, for it was my stupidity that drew me into this imbroglio.

He asked Freud to assure Sabina he had now been told the whole truth.

Freud sent her a conciliatory letter. 'The fact that I was wrong and that the lapse has to be blamed, as my young friend admits, on the man and not the woman, satisfies my need to hold women in high esteem.' Still playing – perhaps overplaying – the role of indulgent father, he told Jung he would have been willing to forgive 'greater misdeeds on your part. Do not blame yourself for involving me; it was not your doing, but hers, and the matter has ended in a way satisfactory to all.' Jung had merely been oscillating 'between the extremes of Bleuler and Gross'.

In fact Gross's influence had pushed him closer not only to Sabina but also to Freud, who wrote: 'When I consider that I owe your ultimate conversion and profound conviction to the same experience with Gross, I cannot possibly be angry.' For a man who understood so much about wishful thinking, Freud was pathetically prone to it.

When Jung too was invited to lecture at Clark University, Freud was delighted. They could take the same boat, go for walks round the deck and have long conversations. 'This changes my whole feeling about the trip, and makes it important.' The university's president Stanley Hall also invited Sándor Ferenczi.

Before sailing from Bremen, Jung, Freud and Ferenczi met there on 20 August. After the nine years of abstinence Bleuler had inspired, Jung drank wine at lunch, and failed to allow for the effect it would have. In a conversation about prehistoric corpses that were being found in north Germany, he muddled them with peat-bog mummies that had been dug up in Belgium. Freud tried to change the subject, and when the inebriated Jung went on talking obstinately about corpses, Freud took the monologue to have the same meaning as Jung's first dream in Vienna – both expressed a desire for his death. When Jung rejected this interpretation, Freud fainted. He afterwards blamed this on exhaustion and alcohol, but the real cause, Jung suspected, was belief in a death wish against him.

During their eight days at sea, the three psychiatrists interpreted each other's dreams. One of Freud's was about Martha and Minna, but when asked what he associated with the dream, he refused to answer, saying he could not jeopardise his authority. The long sea journey was less relaxing than he had expected, and the strain affected both his bladder and his intestines, but he did not welcome Jung's suggestion that he would benefit from full-scale psychoanalysis.

In New York all three suffered from diarrhoea and stomach-ache but, undeterred, visited a palaeontology museum where, as Jung put it, 'all the old monsters, the Lord God's anxiety dreams of Creation, can be seen'. Meeting Ernest Jones, they went with him on a steamer excursion round the point of Manhattan. When Abraham Brill took them to Chinatown, Jung, who was unfamiliar with Chinese food, ate 'an unbelievable dish with chopped meat apparently smothered in earthworms'. On Sunday morning they took the train to Boston. 'The countryside was utterly charming,' Jung wrote, 'low hills, a lot of forest, swamp, small lakes, countless vast erratic rocks, tiny villages with houses painted red, green or grey with white-framed windows (Holland!) tucked away under big, beautiful trees.'

Arriving at Worcester in the evening, they called on Stanley Hall. 'A refined, distinguished old gentleman, almost seventy, he received us with the kindest hospitality. He has a plump, cheerful, good-natured and extremely ugly wife, who, however, serves wonderful food.' Her body temperature appeared to be much higher than her husband's, for in the mild September weather, she stood by the open window, fanning herself, while he stood warming himself at the fireplace, 'a state of affairs which inspired Freud to apt, fortunately private, commentary'. In the morning they moved out of the hotel into the Halls' house. 'Two pitch-black Negroes in dinner jackets, the extreme of grotesque solemnity, act as servants.' But no privacy was to be had anywhere. 'All the doors open, even the bathroom door and the front door; people going in and out all the time . . .'

Jung liked the 'real though plain elegance' of the university buildings, but the first session of the congress was so boring that Freud and Jung went out for a walk on the outskirts of the town.

In the third of his five lectures, Freud repeated his claim that as an investigative technique, psychoanalysis was superior to the word-association test. Of Jung's three lectures the first was on the test, the second about the recurrence of the same complex within the family, and the third on 'Psychic Conflicts in a Child'. He and Freud, who was lecturing the same morning about 'Little Hans', a sex-obsessed five-year-old he had treated, had arranged that Jung would produce a parallel case history by talking about the four-year-old Agathli, without using her name or mentioning that she was his daughter. Jung delighted the audience with his story of a girl – he called her Anna – who wanted to know where babies came from and balked when her parents said they were brought by a stork.

James Putnam, a Harvard professor who had come to hear Freud and Jung, said this lecture was 'full of personality, fire and life'. It was published in both English and German during 1910, but Jung made changes for the version that appeared in 1915. Finding less corroboration for the Little Hans story – Jung had cut down on the evidence of sexual precocity in the girl – Freud objected that 'the scientist did not entirely overcome the father'.

Liking Putnam, Jung praised his open-mindedness and his 'unflagging desire for objectivity', but the American who impressed him most was Henry James's older brother, William, who was in his sixties. A follower of Swedenborg, their father, Henry James Sr, had written on theology. After being privately educated, mainly by his father, William James studied medicine at Harvard, where he went on to become professor of psychology and philosophy. He spent twelve years writing *Principles of Psychology*, which, when published in 1890, established him as the leading psychologist in the country. His book *The Varieties of Religious Experience* was published in 1902.

He arrived one evening at the Halls' house after dinner. Interested in spiritualism, he had been experimenting with a medium, Mrs Piper, and had promised to bring some notes on what he had discovered. Putting his hand to his breast pocket and saying he had brought some papers which might be of interest, he pulled out a wad of dollar bills. Accidentally or deliberately he was showing his disapproval of the way Hall seized every opportunity to appeal for donations to the college. Apologising profusely, James produced the right papers from the other pocket. Writing to Flournoy about the evening, James said he 'met also Yung [sic] of Zurich, who professed a great esteem for you and made a very pleasant impression'. But Freud 'made on me personally the impression of a man obsessed with fixed ideas'.

At an evening ceremony on Monday the 13th, in front of about three hundred people, many of them wearing square, gold-tasselled caps and black or red gowns, Freud and Jung were awarded doctorates, Freud in psychology, Jung in education and social hygiene. 'We are gaining ground here,' Jung reported, 'and our following is growing slowly but surely.'

Drinking champagne at their final meal, Jung decided to resign from the teetotal societies he had joined. 'I confess myself an honest sinner and only hope I can bear to see a glass of wine without excessive emotion – an undrunk glass, of course.'

While in New York he had several meetings with a young alcoholic who had twice consulted him in Zurich, Medill McCormick. Jung had mentioned him in a letter to Freud, saying: 'Fate, which evidently loves crazy games, has just at this time deposited on my doorstep a well-known American (friend of Roosevelt and Taft, proprietor of several big newspapers etc.).' The McCormick family owned the *Chicago Tribune*, and Medill's cousin Harold Fowler McCormick was married to the daughter of the oil magnate and philanthropist John D. Rockefeller.

Jung discussed Medill with his wife Ruth, telling her the 'demon', who came from her husband's 'infantile relations with his mother', drove him to a 'wild and immoral life'. But in marriage, 'love could suppress the former immoral tendencies'. Writing to her, Jung had ignored Otto Gross's doctrines, but talking to Medill in New York, he relayed them. 'Jung warned me against being too good, and asked particuarly if I *felt* free. He rather recommended a little flirting and told me to bear in mind *that it might be advisable* for me to have mistresses – that I was a very dangerous and savage man, that I must not forget my heredity and my infantile influences and lose my soul – if women would save it.'

Jung confided in him about his own way of dealing with polygamous impulses, saying 'he quite permitted flirtations and had had one himself in this country'. Jung had also talked about his relationship with Emma, who at one time had 'thought she could not understand his science', Medill wrote, 'and paid no attention to it. Now she is his partner in his work.' This is an overstatement.

Before sailing back to Europe, Freud and Jung accepted an invitation to the Putnam camp at the top of Keene Valley in the Adirondacks. They responded differently to the primitive conditions and the lack of comfort: 'Freud assumed a philosophical smile as he forged through this richly varied world,' Jung wrote. 'I trotted along and enjoyed it.' In the evening he joined in the singing and enjoyed the games.

There may have been a connection between the size of Jung's new house in Küsnacht and the change in his image of consciousness, which he had previously pictured as a room, with the unconscious as a cellar, 'and then the earth wellspring, that is the body, sending up the instincts'. On the boat he dreamed he was in a big medieval house. Coming in from the street, he went down into a vaulted Gothic room, and from there into a cellar. Having thought he was at the lowest level, he found a square hole. With a lantern in his hand, he peered down to see a staircase. As in his dream about the enthroned penis, subterranean stairs led him down to the revelation of a secret. He found himself in an ancient cellar, possibly Roman, and looking through a hole in the floor, saw a tomb filled with prehistoric pottery, bones and skulls. Since the dust was undisturbed, he thought he had made a great discovery. The account he gave of the dream in a 1925 seminar differs from the account given in *Memories, Dreams, Reflections*, which says he saw only two skulls.

Discussing the dream with Freud, who asked whose skulls they were, Jung said they belonged to his wife and sister-in-law. He kept silent about his own interpretation of the dream, which was that the house represented

the psyche, with unconscious additions. The upper floor stood for consciousness, and the ground floor for the first level of the unconscious. The
cave represented the primitive world. The darkness of the lower levels
meant they could rarely be illuminated by consciousness. The dream, he
thought, 'pointed to the foundations of cultural history – a history of
successive layers of consciousness. My dream constituted a kind of structural
diagram of the human psyche; it postulated something of an altogether
impersonal nature underlying the psyche.' He says that this was his 'first
inkling of a collective *a priori* under the personal psyche'.

Twelve

Our Psychoanalytical Flag

Jung's dream about the four-storeyed house had encouraged his interest in mythology, and by mid–October 1909 he was 'obsessed with the idea of one day writing a comprehensive account of this whole area, after years of preparation and research, naturally . . . Archaeology or rather mythology has got me in its grip, it is a mine of wonderful material.'

He did not explain why he was conflating archaeology with mythology. Trusting his dream, and wanting to excavate material from his unconscious, he even visited archaeological sites where excavation might yield residue from the prehistoric past: 'All my delight in archaeology (buried for years) has sprung back into life.' But if a dream had sent him back to archaeology and mythology, the main traffic was to be in the other direction – images and motifs from his mythological reading presented themselves in dreams and waking fantasies.

He divided his energy between his reading and his private practice, which was growing, but he had spent a lot of money on the house. 'How would you feel,' he asked Freud, 'if I arranged things in such a way as to exploit the situation financially a little?' Freud suggested: 'Could you not announce a course of lectures – call it "An Introduction to the Technique of Psycho-analysis" – and let your "guests" enrol at a reasonable fee?'

Within two weeks Jung was asking a hundred francs for a three-week course, which means that with ten students he could have earned in three weeks as much as he was paid in his first year at the Burghölzli, but he immersed himself so deeply in mythology that he let twenty-seven days go by without writing to Freud. He read Herodotus, a book on Babylonian excavations, Richard Payne Knight's *Two Essays on the Worship of Priapus* and four volumes by the classical philologist Friedrich Creuzer, *Symbolism and Mythology of the Ancient Peoples Especially the Greeks*. 'Rich lodes open up for the phylogenetic basis of the theory of neurosis. Later I want to use some of it for the yearbook.'

Creuzer believed that through the Eleusinian mysteries priests or initiates had transmitted doctrines derived from ancient wisdom and superior to popular religion. Based on Pausanias and Plutarch, his accounts of the mysteries filtered into *Faust*. Goethe owned both editions of Creuzer's four-volume work, and Wagner owned the original edition. After visiting archaeological sites and reading mythology, Jung was convinced that

> a thorough understanding of the psyche (if possible at all) will come only through history or with its help. Just as an understanding of anatomy or ontogenesis is possible only on the basis of phylogenesis and comparative anatomy. For this reason antiquity now appears to me in a new and significant light. What we now find in the individual psyche – in compressed, stunted, or one-sidedly differentiated form – may be seen spread out in all its fullness in times past. Happy the man who can read these signs!

On New Year's Eve he wrote to Freud about 'the problem of antiquity'. 'Without doubt there is a lot of infantile sexuality in it, but that is not all. It seems to me rather that antiquity was ravaged by the struggle with *incest*, with which sexual *repression* begins (or is it the other way round?)'

Jung had never discarded what Professor Zschokke had taught him – that the growth of the human body reiterates the whole evolution of the race. If antiquity corresponded to the childhood of the individual, and if mythology could be read like a map of antiquity, Jung might arrive at exciting new insights into the psyche, the spirit, the soul. And if spiritualists were as close to the truth as he used to believe, why should he turn his back on the occult?

Though Jung had no respect for Helena Blavatsky, he owned some of her books and eighteen by G. R. S. Mead, all published by her Theosophical Society. A medium who had been trained in Tibet, she claimed that, together with Jesus, the Buddha and Mohammed, she had access to mysterious truths which had been known to the ancients but been preserved only partially by the great religions. She claimed to be in touch with Isis, and (like Jung) maintained there was no possible source in her knowledge or memory for the images that appeared to her 'inner eye'. In 1885, six years before her death, the London Society for Psychical Research declared her to be a fraud.

Founded in 1875 and based in New York, the Theosophical Society had branches all over the world, and its publications popularised a variety of subjects including Gnosticism, astrology, Eastern religions, Western philosophy, vegetarianism, clairvoyance and telepathy. One of the more scholarly Theosophical writers, G. R. S. Mead, edited the series *Echoes from the Gnosis*, which was intended 'to make more easily accessible for the ever-widening circle of those who love such things, some echoes of the mystic experiences and initiatory lore of their spiritual ancestry'.

Some of the heretical sects among the early Christians claimed to possess a special knowledge or *gnosis*. Different sects developed different forms of Gnosticism, but one of the basic tenets was that an incessant battle was being waged between the forces of good and evil. The universe came into existence when the original spiritual unity was split into a duality by an inferior demiurge and a female emanation of God. Imprisoned in the resultant cosmos, we are separated from God by space and time, but in each of us is a fallen spark of the divine substance, and our one chance of reuniting ourselves with Him is through *gnosis* derived not from cognition but revelatory experience.

In the case history of the Rat Man, Freud uses the phrase 'nuclear complex' for the child's earliest impulses towards parents and siblings. He was hoping Jung would arrive at the conclusion that mythology centred on the same impulses as the neuroses, but Jung was going in a different direction, thanks partly to Mead, and partly because his attitude to fantasy was changing.

He had habitually recoiled from it, though he could see it was integral to the creation of literature and art. 'As a form of thinking I held it to be altogether impure, a sort of incestuous intercourse, thoroughly immoral from an intellectual viewpoint.' He overcame his resistance 'through the process of projecting my material onto Miss Miller's'. Frank Miller was a young American writer with the same name as her father, and Jung read an essay of hers which Flournoy presented with an encomiastic introduction in the *Archives de Psychologie* during 1905. It was titled 'Some Instances of Subconscious Creative Imagination'.

She had travelled widely and, between 1899 and 1900, worked on literature and philosophy at the universities of Berlin, Lausanne and Geneva, where Flournoy was one of her teachers. The essay argued that in poems and fantasies which had presented themselves to her while she was semiconscious, the main 'inspiration' was the play of memory.

She had toured Europe and North America, presenting what she called 'a suite of three illustrated costume lectures on Russia, Greece and Scandinavia'. Appearing in costumes including those of a north Russian peasant girl, a medieval Boyar lady, a Greek peasant and a lady in classical Greece, she lectured about manners, customs and her personal experiences in the various countries, reading her own translations and reciting her own poems.

Quoting from her poems and fantasies, she traced them back to familiar literature or personal experiences. One of the fantasies was about an Aztec warrior, Chiwantopel, who had never found a soulmate. Suddenly a little snake kills both him and his horse. When Jung read her work, he saw in her 'a person who, like myself, had had mythological fantasies, fantasies and dreams of a thoroughly impersonal character'. Interpreting them as if she were a patient, Jung treats the snake as a symbol that has always had the same meaning. These symbols appear in dreams and fantasies, he says, because the subject is regressing to an archaic and nonverbal form of expression. The basic conflict is in the sexual drive that turns against itself. The snake represents the backward-looking incestuous urge, and the horse (as in his own dream about horses) forward-looking creativity. 'Sexuality destroys itself,' he said, meaning that the incestuous element must be sacrificed in order to liberate the creative and procreative impulse. This is where Sabina's influence merges with Frank Miller's. Jung, who subscribed to *Archives de Psychologie*, may have read her essay when it was published in 1905 and he dealt with it in his lecture at Herisau. As William McGuire has pointed out, the lecture was in effect the first draft of his book, *Transformations and Symbols*.

In one of her poems, the mixture of eroticism and religious feeling suggests that her image of God derives from her father, but the incest barrier had stopped her from wishing he could still cuddle her. In another poem, according to Jung, the desire of the moth for the sun represents her introverted sexuality. Her use of mythological themes indicates schizophrenic tendencies: unless she becomes less introverted, she will break down, he predicts in an intricate argument that shuttles between her essay and a variety of mythological motifs. Later, after returning to the USA, she did break down. She was diagnosed at Danvers State Hospital as a 'psychopathic personality with hypomanic traits', but the breakdown was quite different from the one Jung had predicted.

In the winter of 1909–10, taking myths to represent the common ground between the individual imagination and the consciousness of the race, Jung delegated to Sabina and two of his assistants – the twenty-four-year-old Johann Jakob Honegger and Jan Nelken – the task of studying mythology and collecting material that seemed thematically relevant from patients' delusions, hallucinations, fantasies and dreams. The son of a psychiatrist, Honegger was 'very intelligent and subtle-minded'. He had originally consulted Jung 'because of loss of reality-sense lasting a few days (Psychasthenia = libido inversion = Dem. praec.) Incidentally I am nudging him towards analysis so that he can analyse himself *consciously*; in that way he may perhaps forestall the automatic self-disintegration of Dem. pr.' As the medical historian Hans Walser points out, Jung was referring to 'the content of the psychosis' – ideas and images – not to a schizophrenic psychosis. The talented young man became a closer friend than anyone since Otto Gross. 'Hardly a day goes by without an exchange of ideas,' and they even discussed their dreams.

In 1959, when John Freeman was interviewing Jung on television, one of the questions was: 'Is there any one case that you can now look back on and feel that perhaps it was the turning point of your thought?'

'Oh yes,' he answered. The turning point was the discovery 'that there is an impersonal stratum in our psyche, and I can tell you an example'. The 'impersonal stratum' was what he usually called the *collective unconscious*, and his example was a story he often told about a schizophrenic patient who one day grabbed at the lapel of his coat and pointed at the sun, saying it had a penis. If Dr Jung moved his head from side to side, he would see. It was this penis that caused the wind.

Four years later, said Jung, he was reading about Mithraism, an ancient Persian religion based on sun worship. It explains the wind as coming from a tube that hangs from the sun and can be seen by those who look from east to the west. Since the patient could not have been familiar with Mithraism, his delusion must have come from the collective unconscious.

According to Jung, the conversation with the schizophrenic took place in 1906, and he went on telling the story for about fifty years, but in 1911, writing it up for the first time, he did not claim to have been involved in the conversation. It was reported to him by Honegger. But the 1930 essay 'The Structure of the Psyche' tells us it was Jung who had the conversation with a patient, and in the 1952 revision of *Symbols of Transformation*, he wrote: 'I once came across the following hallucination in a schizophrenic patient . . .'

John Freeman queried whether the schizophrenic might have been remembering something he had heard or read. 'Oh no,' said Jung. 'Quite out of the question, because that thing was not known . . . It was only published four years later, after I had observed it with my patient.'

Ein Mithrasliturgie by Albrecht Dieterich was published in 1903. It was the second edition of Dieterich's book that came out in 1910. Jung owned a copy of this edition, but, according to a footnote added to his *Collected Works* by the editors, 'he subsequently learned the 1910 edition was actually the second'.

His most dramatic account of the conversation is to be found in a 1936 lecture on 'The Concept of the Collective Unconscious'. While the personal unconscious, Jung says, 'consists for the most part of *complexes*, the content of the collective unconscious consists of *archetypes*'. He defines archetypal images as those with an archaic or primordial character, corresponding to familiar mythological motifs. Offering to show 'how the existence of the archetypes can be proved', he says that since they are 'supposed to produce certain psychic forms, we must discuss how and where one can get hold of the material demonstrating these forms'. One source, he says, is dreams, which may contain archetypal material; another is fantasies produced by deliberate concentration; a third is the delusions of paranoiacs.

The name of this patient was Schwyzer, and Jung claims to have found him standing at a window,

> wagging his head and blinking into the sun. He told me to do the same, for then I would see something very interesting . . . In his megalomania, he thought he was God and Christ in one person . . . His delusions were mainly religious, and when he invited me to blink into the sun like he did and waggle my head, he obviously wanted me to share his vision. He played the role of the mystic sage and I was the neophyte. He felt he was the sun–god himself, creating the wind by wagging his head to and fro.

Jung's former assistant, Carl Meier, who knew the man, describes him in a 1986 book, *Soul and Body*. He 'had a most vivid hallucinatory fantasy and used to hallucinate night and day'. They called him 'Dr Schwyzer'. In Meier's account, it was Honegger who had the conversation with him and reported it to Jung. Another member of the staff at the Burghölzli, Herman Nunberg, probably an unreliable witness, reported in his memoirs that the delusional idea came from Honegger himself, not Schwyzer.

Sabina, Honegger and Nelken found a lot of material. Honegger reported on a paranoid clerk who projected his complexes on his immediate surroundings and the entire world. He talked about the rebirth of the world, 'the complete identification of the universe with God (i.e. with the patient)', self-incubation, the transformation of the dead into stars, and a flat world surrounded by sea. Honegger concluded that the revival of ancient myths and cosmological theories represented 'a regression that goes back not only to the individual's childhood but to that of the whole human race . . . Cause of the regression is introversion of the libido.' Naturally, it was impossible to check whether patients were drawing on what they had learned from other people or from reading either publications of the Theosophical Society or other books, pamphlets, newspapers and magazines.

Encouraging him to analyse himself, Jung acted only as supervisor, and became fond of him. When Honegger left to take up a job in a psychiatric clinic near Geneva, Jung found his libido was 'whirling around looking for a suitable object'.

There were now two sources of disagreement between them. Feeling that Honegger was not working hard enough, Jung urged him to read more, and finish his thesis. And though he disapproved of Honegger's engagement to a girl called Helene Widmer, Jung took her on as his secretary.

At the beginning of February 1911, Honegger accepted a job at the psychiatric hospital in Rheinau, where he worked on his doctoral thesis. He wanted to be Jung's assistant, and Freud advised Jung to 'take him on and train him on the basis of his own nature', but Jung was reluctant to give him a job before he had his doctorate. Relenting, Jung took him on at the end of June.

Less than two months later on 28 March 1911, Honegger killed himself with a morphine injection. He was due to report for military service the next day. Jung wrote: 'The only motive was to avoid a psychosis, for under no circumstances did he want to give up living in accordance with the pleasure principle.'

After his death, Jung said he was 'trying to get hold of any manuscripts he may have left behind . . . so as to save for science anything that can be saved'. Five years later Jung wrote: 'His researches are in my possession and their publication in preparation.' But apart from a brief abstract in the yearbook, nothing by Honegger appeared in print.

Without complaining about the amount of time Jung spent on mythology, Freud revealed his irritation by making a Freudian error. In one of his letters he said he was so angry with his Viennese colleagues 'that I wish they had a single behind, so that I could wallop you with the same stick'. He had written *Ihnen* (you) instead of *ihnen* (them). And at a November meeting in Vienna, insisting that all hysteria came from memories accumulated between the ages of one and four, he attacked Jung's view that it might be hereditary or somatic in origin.

They were in agreement, though, about the basic subject matter of myths, which 'speak quite "naturally" of the nuclear complex of neurosis', Jung wrote. And as psychoanalysis grew more popular, they shared their elation. At a meeting of the Swiss psychiatric association, Jung reported, Bleuler and two other speakers had given papers on psychoanalysis. 'The psychiatrists' society is ours.'

Corresponding about mythology, they tried not to provoke each other, though Freud sometimes flexed muscles to remind Jung who was commander-in-chief. 'I do not think it would be good to plunge directly into the general problem of ancient mythology. It seems preferable to approach it in a series of detailed studies.' Another dangerous issue was the overlap between mythology and religion. Here Freud attempted a preemptive strike: 'It occurs to me that the ultimate basis of the human need for religion is *infantile helplessness*, which is so much greater in man than in animals. After infancy he cannot imagine a world without parents, and invents for himself a just God and a kindly nature, the two worst anthropomorphic falsifications he could have perpetrated.'

Jung did not shake off the hand on his shoulder, but did not let it guide him. In January 1910, lecturing to a student society on 'Symbolism', he distinguished between logical thinking, which involved words – the discourse being directed outwards – and 'analogical' thinking, which involved fantasy and emotion. This was wordless, pictorial and directed inwards. Telling Freud about the lecture, he said he had been trying 'to put the "symbolic" on a psychogenetic foundation, i.e. to show that in the individual fantasy the *primum movens*, the individual conflict, material or form, (whichever you prefer) is mythic, or mythologically typical.'

For Freud, there was no such thing as nonverbal thinking. Symbolism, in his view, was always secondary, derived from a system in which history, language and personality all played parts. But Jung, when analysing myths and symbols, paid less attention to context – historical, literary and linguistic. As John Forrester puts it, 'he made no distinction between the original and the derived versions of myths. Hence all myths resolved themselves into a uniform field of symbolic presentation.' In Jung's view, psychosis brings us into direct confrontation with the symbols that fill the unconscious, and these have more connection with mythology than with the individual.

To keep their alliance alive, Freud and Jung each turned a blind eye to the other's emotional make-up. Since Jung was nothing if not religious by temperament, it was as pointless to tell him the need for religion was based on infantile helplessness as to tell Freud that fantasy had origins outside individual consciousness. They went on trying to ignore areas of disagreement and to sustain their dialogue on quasi-military campaigning. 'I think we should raise our psychoanalytical flag,' Freud proposed, 'over the territory of normal love life, which is after all very close to us. Perhaps I will contribute a few pages to the yearbook.'

It was Jung who had to do most of the work on it, and, new to editing, he found the work tedious. Unlike Freud, who had enough literary talent to win the Goethe Prize, most contributors expressed themselves awkwardly and loquaciously. Aiming to have everything ready for the printer by the end of January, Jung had to do a lot of pruning and rewriting. Nothing, though, could hold him back from 'the overflowing delights of mythology, which I always reserve for the evening as dessert'. He pursued his 'mythological dreams with almost autoerotic pleasure'.

Not that this was his only erotic pleasure. According to Freud and Jolande Jacobi, he had started an affair with a Burghölzli nurse, a strong-minded Dutchwoman, a year older than he was. Rebelling against her father, owner of the Bols distillery, Maria Moltzer had escaped to work in a teetotal hospital, but if she was looking for a father substitute, she found it not in Bleuler but in Jung.

The affair precipitated a crisis with Emma. After years of sharing too little of Jung's day, she must have been pleased when, wanting to stabilise the marriage, he offered to analyse her. At first she responded well and believed their relationship would improve. But some kind of crisis developed, possibly because he had started a new affair, and it is possible that he could restore equilibrium only by agreeing to have another child.

Emma was pregnant again by the time he confided in Freud. Again, as when telling him about Sabina, Jung twisted the facts:

> This time I was not the one to be deceived by the devil, but my wife, who listened to the evil spirit and, without having any grounds, staged a number of jealous scenes . . . Unless there is a guarantee of mutual freedom, analysis of one's spouse is difficult. It seems to me that the prerequisite for a good marriage is licence to be unfaithful.

It was characteristic of him to deny the infidelity and tack on a justification for it, but Freud may have believed him. As Ernest Jones observed, 'Freud, despite his extraordinary genius in penetrating the deepest layers of the mind, was not a connoisseur of men.'

Emma had no reason, yet, to be jealous of another new patient, the twenty-two-year-old Toni Wolff. She was dangerously depressed after the death of her father, who had been forty when he married a woman of twenty. Like Sabina when she arrived at the asylum, Toni seemed to be bordering on madness. Another doctor might have failed to coax them back from the brink, but Jung, recognising the exceptional quality of their sensitivity and intelligence, helped them both to think creatively. He could not have done this if his own creativity had not been involved, and he was either failing or not trying to overcome his lingering doubts about the merits of monogamy. 'The ethical problem of sexual freedom is really tremendous, and worth the sweat of all noble souls.'

Since the Salzburg congress, the movement had been gaining impetus. The yearbook provided both a forum and a means by which Freud and Jung could exert their authority, but they had control over neither the hetero-geneous activities conducted under the psychoanalytical banner nor the heterodox views analysts were publishing. Jung's first proposal was to incorporate a review section in the yearbook, and Freud saw how useful this might be. 'You will reprimand the Viennese, and I will deal with the Zurich people when they wander off on their own. These reviews must express our personal convictions; this is an essay in literary dictatorship, but our people are unreliable and need to be disciplined.'

This could have led straight to the idea of setting up an international organisation. Provocatively, Forel had formed what was potentially a rival society – an association of European psychotherapists. But for the moment, mainly interested in censorship, Freud wanted to shelve the organisational problem by affiliating his supporters to another group. He asked Alfred Adler to prepare a memorandum about enrolling analysts in the Social Democratic Party.

Freud's junior by fourteen years, Adler had been an active member of the Wednesday psychology club since 1902, and Freud had a high opinion of the book he had published in 1907, *Studies of Organ Inferiority*. At the April 1908 conference in Salzburg, he read a paper on 'Sadism in Life and Neurosis'. But Sándor Ferenczi was developing a closer friendship with Freud, and on New Year's Day 1910 they discussed the problem of discipline. Writing to Jung the next day, Freud suggested they devote the next congress, which would be held at the end of March in Nuremberg, to such tasks as organisation. Jung gave the matter little thought until a month later, after hearing that Freud wanted Ferenczi to address the congress on 'organisation and discipline'.

Though Freud had dropped the idea of political affiliation, he was still in favour of merging with a larger group – perhaps the International Fraternity for Ethics and Culture, which was organised by a Bern chemist, Alfred Knapp. Jung was against this. 'I am now balanced so precariously between Dionysus and Apollo that I am wondering whether it would not be worth reintroducing some of the older cultural stupidities such as the monasteries.'

If they wanted to merge with another group, it should be 'nourished by the deep instincts of the race'. Religion could be replaced only by religion. Influenced by both Otto Gross and Nietzsche (who had influenced Gross), Jung questioned traditional ideas of good and evil. 'Do not we have to love evil if we are to escape from the obsession with virtue that sickens us and prohibits the enjoyment of life?' If psychoanalysis had a moral function, it was

to revive among intellectuals a feeling for the symbolical and mythical, to transform Christ cautiously back into the soothsaying god of the vine, which he was, and so absorb all the ecstatic impulses of Christianity with the single object of making the cult and the sacred myth what they used to be – a drunken feast of joy at which man can have the ethos and holiness of an animal.

Did this letter provoke doubts about the wisdom of putting Jung at the head of the movement? How would he use his powers if he wanted psycho-analysis to absorb 'all the ecstatic impulses of Christianity' and transform it gradually into the worship of Dionysus?

It might have seemed that Freud would find it easier to change his mind than to persuade his Viennese supporters to accept Jung as their president. But he never found it easy to change his mind, and if the letter caused him anxiety, he gave no sign of it in his reply. Without mentioning evil, Christianity or Dionysus, he abandoned the idea of merging with another group.

As Ernest Jones put it, Freud was too mistrustful of the average mind to favour democratic methods. 'He wished there to be a prominent "leader" who should guide the doings of branch societies and their members: moreover he wanted the leader to be in a permanent position, like a monarch.' Planning the *coup d'état*, Freud confided in only Jung and Ferenczi. The headquarters of the international organisation would be established in Zurich. Ferenczi formulated proposals that would give the president dictatorial powers. Members would be unable to publish scientific papers without his imprimatur. Already editor of the yearbook, Jung would control everything published under the banner of psychoanalysis.

Though Freud had put him in charge of administrative arrangements for the congress, Jung abruptly left for the USA after receiving a telegram from the wife of Medill McCormick, who had suffered a relapse. Leaving Honegger to take care of his other patients and (with help from Emma) to make all the final arrangements for the congress, he wrote to Freud: 'Now do not get cross with me for my pranks.' Without explaining who had sent for him or why he was obeying the summons, he said the trip would be good for his mental health.

It was Emma who wrote to Freud with an explanation. According to the reports, she said, the patient was suffering from either paralysis or mania, but Jung thought it 'possible that the trouble is psychogenic, and therefore followed the call. He urgently requests you not to worry about Nuremberg, as he will *quite certainly* be there.' When Jung arrived in New York, he found Medill had gone to Chattanooga in Tennessee, where he was riding about on a horse, trying to retrace Civil War battles with a relief map.

Jung returned in time for the congress, but too late for a preliminary meeting with Freud and Ferenczi. Had they been able to hold one, Jung might have advised them to be more diplomatic in handling the other delegates. In the early morning of 30 March, Karl Abraham was told what was about to happen, and a list of proposed rules for the new organisation was printed in a bookshop just in time for distribution during Ferenczi's talk. Finding it so easy to bully his gang into submission, Freud was not afraid of provoking resentment.

In his opening speech he argued that psychoanalysis could both alleviate suffering and contribute to communal enlightenment by curing neurotic disorders that led to social disorder.

Jung reported that Americans could benefit from psychoanalysis. They suffered from 'psychological peculiarities' which 'point to intense sexual repression'. This was the result of 'living together with barbarous races'. Black people had 'a suggestive effect on the laboriously subjugated instincts of the white race', which was being dragged down. Freud seems to have been ironic when he later congratulated Jung on 'the rich yield of your trip to America'. William McGuire thinks he was referring to 'the rewards of treating a rich patient'.

But nothing could have made Freud alter his plans for the succession. Following the lines Freud had laid down for his speech, Ferenczi divided the history of psychoanalysis into two periods – the heroic age in which Sigmund Freud had stood alone against his detractors, and the new age that had begun with the emergence of Carl Jung and the other Swiss Freudians. Freud later wrote that they had been 'the nucleus of the small band fighting for analysis to be recognised. The only opportunity of learning the new art and working at it practically lay there. Most of my present followers and co-workers came to me by way of Zurich – even those who were geographically much closer to Vienna than to Switzerland.'

Ferenczi's speech climaxed in the announcement of Freud's unilateral decision. Now that an International Psychoanalytical Association was to be formed, Dr Jung was to be president for the rest of his life, with the power to excommunicate anyone who ignored the rules.

Led by two founder members of the Wednesday Psychological Society, Adler and Wilhelm Stekel, the protests were so vehement that Freud postponed the vote until the following session. Before this was held, Stekel summoned his Viennese colleagues to his hotel bedroom for a discussion. Freud was not invited, but he made a melodramatic appearance in the doorway.

Most of you are Jews, which means you cannot win friends for the new teaching. Jews have to be satisfied with the modest role of preparing the ground. It's absolutely essential that I form ties in the scientific world. I'm getting on in years, and I'm tired of being incessantly under attack. We're all in danger . . . They won't even leave me a coat to my back. The Swiss will save me. They'll save you as well.

Freud was fanatical in his championship of Jung. 'When the empire I've founded is orphaned,' he told Binswanger, 'no one but Jung must inherit it – all of it. My politics, as you see, pursues this object consistently.' As Alphonse Maeder put it, 'He did notice that Jung was a genius-type, you see he had strength and was healthy. I mean, if you looked at those Viennese, they all looked like decrepit, strange people. No one had anything fresh.'

Eventually a compromise was evolved. Jung was to be president, but for only two years. When the principle of censorship was jettisoned, Adler and Stekel said they would launch their own journal, the *Zentralblatt für Psychoanalyse*, and after returning to Vienna, Freud made further concessions. Adler was appointed president of the Vienna Psychoanalytical Society, with Stekel as vice president, but Freud, who was to take the chair at all scientific sessions, persuaded them to accept him as 'director' of the *Zentralblatt*. 'They are badly shaken,' he wrote, 'and for the moment I am satisfied with the outcome of my statesmanship.' Later Adler and Stekel agreed to discuss every issue with him in advance, and to give him the power of veto.

Thirteen

Sleepless Nights

Not wanting to waste time on administrative chores, Jung passed most of them on to Franz Riklin, who had been appointed secretary, but worked grudgingly and inefficiently, while Freud was too far away to intervene. Bitterly resentful, he said it had been too early to form an international association.

> I was swayed by impatience to see you in the right place and by irritation at my own responsibilities . . . As it is, my dear son and successor, the first months of your reign have not turned out very well. I sometimes feel you have not taken your functions seriously enough and have not yet started to behave in accordance with your new dignity . . . Those who wish to rule must assiduously cultivate the art of winning people.

Replying, for once, by return of post, and promising to try harder, Jung said he was not worried by this 'period of depression'. Setbacks were 'a guarantee of unspoiled enjoyment, like a beautiful valley high in the mountains not yet discovered by Thos. Cook & Co.' But instead of devoting himself to psychoanalytical politics, he went on reading voraciously for his book on mythology.

Though Freud had warned him against plunging in at the deep end, he tried to find unifying themes in myth, folklore, religion, philosophy, literature, cultural history, psychoanalysis and his personal experience. Influenced by Nietzsche's *Birth of Tragedy*, he was hoping to discover something new about the Greeks: 'Through buried strata of the individual soul, we can come to grips with the living mind of the ancient culture, and thus achieve a stable viewpoint outside our own, from which we can understand the mechanisms of theirs.'

Polarised by the idea of Dionysus, and already contemplating the possibility of a break with Freud, Jung was turning towards Nietzsche;

he had been reading *On the Genealogy of Morals* and making pencil markings against key passages in Part Two. The section titled 'Guilt, Bad Conscience and the Like' explains bad conscience as 'the grave illness humanity had to contract when it underwent the most fundamental of all its transformations – when it finally found itself constricted by society and peace.'

Studying Jung's copy of the book, Paul Bishop found markings against the passages in which Nietzsche argues: 'All instincts which cannot be released outwards will turn inwards.' He equates this with the development of 'soul'. 'Originally as thin as if stretched between two membranes, the whole inner world expanded outwards and upwards, acquiring depth, breadth and height.' Bad conscience developed when aggressive and predatory impulses turned inwards. Imprisoned in what Goethe called 'the labyrinth of the breast', the instinct for freedom (which is identical with the will to power) turns against man's 'ancient animal self', and bad conscience becomes the womb of all imaginative activity. An illness in the same sense that pregnancy is an illness, it is bound up with a feeling of guilty indebtedness to ancestors and tribal forebears. This increases in proportion to the power of the tribe, and 'in the end the ancestor must necessarily be transformed into a god. Perhaps this in in fact the origin of gods, an origin therefore out of *fear*'.

Taking Freud's term libido, Jung widens it to mean what Nietzsche meant by *soul*. In *Symbols of Transformation* Jung gives a new meaning to the mythical theme of the hero's journey into the depths and his triumphant battles with monsters – consciousness must examine its own roots in symbols and stories that our ancestors originated.

Jung's gradually increasing hostility to Freud and his Jewish disciples intensified his sense of affinity with Nietzsche. Both men were sons of Protestant pastors who died young, and of women descended from generations of clergymen. While Freud appeared to have some of his roots in Jewish culture, Jung felt that in absorbing Nietzsche's ideas he was returning to his own roots. Writing to an American clergyman about growing up in Basel, where Nietzsche had been a professor at the university, Jung wrote: 'I grew up in an atmosphere still vibrating from the impact of his teachings.'

Like Jung and unlike Freud, Nietzsche had a deeply religious temperament which made him incapable of discarding Christianity completely, despite his objections to the church and its theology. What mattered even more to Jung was Nietzsche's interest in myth, and especially in Dionysus. Unlike Judaism and Christianity, Greek mythology 'deified *all* forms into a significant humanity'. There was no asceticism in it: the Olympian gods sanctified both good and evil. In the plays of Aeschylus and Sophocles, the hero had always, according to Nietzsche, been Dionysus confronting Apollo. In one note Nietzsche quotes the primitive German idea that all gods must die. He cherished 'the hope for rebirth of a Dionysus. Then everything will be Dionysus.'

Another influence on Jung is that of the Sanskrit scholar Friedrich Max Müller, who contended that among the *Aryans* – a term he popularised – all mythological systems were based on the orbiting of the Earth around the sun, and on the sun worship that developed from primitive man's perception of his dependence on it. Discussing solar mythology, Jung suggests that the longing for the sun has been turned towards God, but not the external God. 'To honour God, the sun or the fire is to honour one's own vital force, the libido. As Seneca says, "God is near you, with you, in you." God is our own yearning, which we honour.' And Jung approvingly quotes Seneca's belief that 'No good man is without a god . . . We do not, in fact, presume to specify which God, but it is certain that a God dwells within the breast of every good man.'

Encouraging indifference to the beauties of nature, Christianity was inferior to Mithraism. 'To me it seems we might still make some use of its ideas and especially of its great wisdom, which for over two thousand years has proved especially efficacious.' It identifies the god-hero Mithra with the sun. He kills the divine bull, whose death symbolically promises a blaze of fertility. According to Judaism and Christianity, there can be no union with God on this side of the grave, but Jung was gravitating towards the equation of God, father, son and fire.

Adducing evidence that Christians worshipped the sun during the fifth century, he argues that the idea of saintly haloes is a remnant from sun worship. The stories about the death and resurrection of a god or hero are all patterned on the sun's movement in setting and rising, while the Book of Job shows that forces of nature have two sides, creative and destructive. God is both creator and destroyer: He 'has simply turned his other side outwards for once, the side which man calls the Devil'.

Lecturing at a meeting of Swiss psychiatrists in the village of Herisau, near St Gallen, on 16 May 1910, Jung used this material – 'mythological stuff that won great applause'. He sent a text to Freud, who objected that what he had presented as a polarity between reality and symbolism was a polarity between reality and fantasy. 'The ancients, who lived in mythology, used to dream, and their dreams were the main source of their myths.' Mithraic images of self-sacrifice, which 'quite evidently derive from the killing of the animal ego by the human ego', should be seen as expressions of the way in which 'the sublimated part of the human being (the conscious ego) sacrifices (with regret) its vigorous drives'.

But for Jung it was significant that the symbol of fertility, the bull, was being killed by another sexual symbol. 'The self-sacrifice is at the same time voluntary and enforced (the same conflict as in the death of Christ).' The only possible reason for the conflict was the incest prohibition, which struck at the root of primitive sexuality by blocking the most convenient outlet for the libido. What was needed was a hero 'who can accomplish voluntarily what is demanded by the repression – i.e. temporary or permanent renunciation of fertility (the social background is unclear: overpopulation?) in order to realise the ethical ideal of subjugating the instinct.'

Freud warned Jung against trying to arrive at an interpretation of 'the whole façade'. It was important to take context into account, 'tracking down the origin of each element so as not to be led astray by later overlayings, duplications, condensations etc. In other words you should proceed as we do with dreams.' But Jung, who no longer dealt with dreams as Freud did, had never been less interested in listening to advice.

In September 1910, Sabina reappeared. She was writing a doctoral thesis, 'On the Psychological Content of a Case of Schizophrenia', and, influenced by Jung's work, had been studying a paranoiac woman who seemed to be talking gibberish. With perseverance and empathy, Sabina decoded what she was saying – the task being made easier by the woman's attitude to Jung. His good humour and his happy-go-lucky attitude, Sabina said, made everyone pursue him with their love, and the patient's fantasies centred on him. 'Dr J., who has prostituted me, is a friend of the Mormons – he wants to get married once a year.'

Impressed with Sabina's work, Bleuler said she should offer it to Jung for publication in the yearbook.

> The main result of our meeting was that we again loved each other fervently. My friend said we would always need to be careful not to fall in love again: we would always be dangerous to each other. He confessed that he had met no woman who could replace me. It was like having a necklace in which his other admirers were all pearls and I was the medallion. At first he was annoyed I had not sent him my essay ages ago, saying I did not trust him, etc. Then he became more and more intense. Finally he pressed my hand to his heart several times, and said this should mark the beginning of a new era.

She then had 'two bad nights. My love for him overwhelmed me with an insane glow. Sometimes I resisted violently, and at other times let him kiss every one of my little fingers and I glued myself to his lips, fainting with love.' But she could not face another bout of intense suffering. 'Better an absolutely pure friendship even *à distance*. That he loves me is certain,' though they could never be happy together because 'the thought of his wife and children would leave neither of us any peace'. But the fantasy of bearing him a child was still irresistible. 'Afterwards he could go back to his wife.'

Her thesis had thrown him into raptures, he said. It proved that psychotic thought mechanisms corresponded to patterns in myth. But his next letter was formal and cold: he was disappointed to find his name mentioned so rarely, and his work quoted so little. 'Good God!' she exclaimed in her diary. 'If only he had an inkling of how much I have suffered on his account, and how much I am still suffering! Is it surprising I was afraid to read his work, fearful of being enslaved by emotion all over again?' But he promised to work with her on the thesis till it was publishable, and offered to enrol her in the psychoanalytical association.

She wanted nothing more than to unite her life with his, 'so that I shall not just have the brief brilliance of a meteor'. But she refused to be

> just one of the many who languish for him, receiving in return his benevolent look and a few friendly words. Gazing up at him and rushing to carry out his every whim so as not to bring down his anger upon oneself! For if one ever leaves his vanity out of account, one must do bitter penance. He assumes a frigid, official tone, and who suffers from that? Not he, of course: he can dispose of his slight annoyance by working and can replace the love of one woman with the love of another. And it is certain that this woman will finally be humiliated. She will be the one who has to put up with tortured days and sleepless nights . . .

Taking the steamer to Küsnacht, she went to his house every morning, and they worked together on the essay, but she felt confused and ashamed. 'In the waiting room his children came running to meet me, two sweet little girls and a little boy . . . In front of the children I was small, powerless and "desire" seemed disgusting. What did I want, after all?'

He was also supervising the thesis of a beautiful Russian girl, Esther Aptekmann, whose eyes gleamed when she talked about him. Believing he loved her, she confided in Sabina, who had been told Esther was not 'one of those he could love'. But Sabina kept this to herself. Maria Moltzer was still on the scene, and another patient, Martha Böddinghaus from Munich, was infatuated with him. 'Naturally,' he told Freud, 'there is a loving jealousy over me between the two ladies.'

When Sabina arrived on the morning of 27 September, the door was opened by the maid, who said he could not see her. She was furious, but in the evening, hearing that Emma had given birth in the morning to another daughter, Sabina looked in the mirror. 'I was taken aback – that could not be me, that stony grey face staring out at me with black eyes that were burning and uncannily grim. It was a strong, baleful wolf lurking there coldly in the depths.'

Two days later they had a long talk. She said that in each person the father represents the 'ancestor component', which is often clairvoyant and more significant than conscious attitudes for the individual's fate. She had also been thinking about connections between the death wish and sexual desire for dissolution. Freud had not yet written about the death wish, but (as John Kerr points out) Sabina had read the work of Élie Metchnikoff, head of the Pasteur Institute in Paris and winner of the Nobel Prize in 1907. In *The Nature of Man* (1903) she suggested that a natural wish to die might assert itself at the end of a long life. Sabina had already started writing about the death wish.

There was no other woman and only two men (Freud and Gross) whose conversation had got Jung so excited. He showed her copies of his Herisau lecture on symbolism, of his most recent letter to Freud, and of Freud's answer.

> He said he was deeply moved by the parallels between our ideas and feelings. He said that awareness of this disturbs him, because this is how I make him fall in love with me . . . Certainly no other girl can understand him as I do, or can take him by surprise like this with an independently developed system of thought that is closely analogous to his own. He resisted, he did not want to love me. Now he has to, because our souls are profoundly akin, because even when we are separated, our joint work unites us.

The affinity depended partly on what they had both inherited from religious families. They believed the unconscious had prophetic powers, and they had both been reclaimed – she with his help – from schizoid experiences. They had both moved forwards to psychoanalytical theories, and the ones that preoccupied her now derived mainly from her work on the paranoiac woman, who reminded her of herself.

Obsession with disease, dirt, dissolution and death seemed intrinsic to the woman's sexuality. Her highly sexed Catholic husband had 'Catholicised' her – forced unwelcome ideas and experiences on her. In her psychotic delusions, as in her sexuality, 'antagonistic components' were at work, some destructive, some creative or transforming. Freud had noticed how people could both acknowledge what had been repressed and disown it. An emotion or a desire could be described in terms of its opposite, which would explain the association of sexual activity with death symbolism. It was this patient who led Sabina to the ideas she would later formulate in an essay on the death instinct.

Nietzsche had written: 'Whoever wants to be creative in good and evil must first be an annihilator and destroy values,' but Jung excitedly thought he and Sabina had discovered that what looks like destruction may be creation: something must die for something else to be born. She titled her essay 'Destruction as a Cause of Coming into Being'. Mentally, thanks to strength, intelligence and determination, they had both achieved a kind of rebirth from a kind of death, and they both believed that in schizophrenia, consciousness gives way to archaic patterns of thought when the rational ego is overpowered. But Sabina, as Lisa Appignanesi and John Forrester have pointed out, was combining *fin-de-siècle* biology with Freud's belief in the primacy of the sexual drive. In 'Destruction as a Cause of Coming into Being' she said the two basic drives were for self-preservation and for the preservation of the species through sexuality. Being a drive towards fusion, this has no regard for individuality, which means that both destruction and self-destruction are integral to sexuality, while repression is partly a matter of self-defence. But while Jung's collective unconscious was inimical to individual sexuality, Sabina's unconscious was collective because it was sexual.

Jung encouraged her to go ahead with her work on the death wish. But her preoccupation with it was not merely theoretical. At night, listening to violin music in the distance and brooding on her failure to find a man who would give her a baby, she felt worthy of nothing but a suicidal death. Perhaps she would swallow cyanide in front of Jung.

Their work had to stop when he went on holiday. In 1906 he had cancelled a holiday in America because Emma did not want him to go without her, but now he had no compunction about leaving her alone with her newborn daughter, Marianne, and the three other children, while he went to northern Italy on a cycling trip with a Munich doctor, Wolf Stockmayer.

In Verona they saw a statue of the god Priapus pointing smilingly at a snake which is biting his penis – an attack on one libido symbol by another. But on the way back, Jung dreamed he was surrounded by illustrious spirits from earlier centuries. It was reminiscent of his fantasy about having lived a distinguished life in the eighteenth century. Feelings of inadequacy survived from the dream to mingle with guilt feelings about the book he had not finished. Making excuses to Stockmayer, he caught the next train to Zurich.

The dream was beckoning him back to the period in which spiritualists had seemed better equipped than scientists to explain the psyche. After arriving in Zurich on 16 October, he wrote to tell Freud he was reworking the mythological material he had sent. Freud was corresponding with Bleuler, who had not joined the international association but said he wanted a meeting, though he could not get away from Zurich before Easter. Freud was so keen to have him as a member that he offered to visit Zurich over the Christmas holidays.

At the same time, Jung was thinking of travelling to Vienna, partly for a meeting with Adler and Stekel, the joint editors of the *Zentralblatt*. By the end of 1910, Adler's views were diverging quite blatantly from Freud's. As Henri Ellenberger points out, Adler, who was thirty-two when he met Freud, already had ideas of his own, and whereas Freud's main concern was to explain the turbulent psychic forces that could be seen at work in drama by the great tragedians, Adler, who had more of a social conscience, was more concerned with the everyday workings of human nature, and his first publication (in 1898) had been a pamphlet called *Health Book for the Tailoring Trade*. Jung, who admired neither Adler nor Stekel, wanted to claim presidential jurisdiction over their *Zentralblatt*.

In Jung's absence, Sabina had been praying for emotional independence, but she was still under his spell. In John Kerr's view, there is a section of *Memories, Dreams, Reflections* which refers to her without mentioning her name. Jung believed dreams could provide practical guidance on how to treat a patient, and he once dreamed he was puzzled by what a patient said till he realised she had an unusual father complex. Finding no evidence of a father complex in Sabina, he asked about her rabbi grandfather – a kind of Hassidic saint, reputed to possess second sight. Afterwards Jung told her that since her father had rejected Judaism, the fear of God had got into her, giving her a neurosis.

In another dream, a girl leaving a party in his house asked for an umbrella, and he knelt down as he handed it to her. Taking this dream to mean that Sabina had the makings of a saint, he told her about it. 'Because she had no mythological ideas, her most essential feature could not express itself. Her conscious activity was all directed towards flirtation, clothes and sex, because she knew nothing else. But she was really a child of God, and her destiny was to fulfil his secret will.' By reawakening mythological and religious ideas in her, he claims, he cured her neurosis. 'For she belonged to that type of person from whom spiritual activity is demanded.' Thanks to him, her life took on a new meaning.

Seeing Sabina in this perspective, he valued her more highly. Her faith in Siegfried had not been a mere projection of sexual desire; nor had her belief in her future greatness and in being fated to play a sacrificial role. Trying to awaken religious and mythological ideas in her, he was making his first experiment in countering neurosis by alerting patients to the presence of the numinous. But with Sabina, he inflamed both her desire for him and his for her.

By early November they were lovers again, and she was writing in her diary about their passionate 'poetry'. He loved her, he said, because of her magnificent pride, and because her thoughts ran parallel to his. But he would never marry her. Tempted though he was by the notion of changing his destiny and possessing such a splendid woman, he was fundamentally a philistine, he told her, who needed narrow limits and a typically Swiss lifestyle.

He confided in her about his feelings of isolation. He would never be given a professorial chair, never achieve worldly recognition. His relationship with Bleuler had been deteriorating, and when Bleuler wanted Jung to interpret one of his dreams in front of an audience, it turned out to be one in which he, instead of his wife, was suckling their child. Jung took it that the child represented him, and that Bleuler was refusing to acknowledge homosexual love for him.

Excited though Sabina was by his passion, she was nervous he might steal her idea of the death wish. He wanted to mention it in an article: what if he presented it as his own idea?

Her father had nothing against an illegitimate relationship: he respected her ability to tolerate disapproval and isolation. Though she hated the idea of being just a 'diversion' for Jung, their affair continued. Her whole being was 'suffused with love', and she prayed to Fate: 'Let me love him nobly.'

In bed he sometimes talked calmly and honestly, but sometimes 'reverted to the Don Juan pose I find so repellent. Though he considers me honest in love, he said I should belong to the category of women created not for motherhood but for free love.' In spite of what he had said about her spiritual destiny, he was not seeing her for what she was. But working with her on her thesis, he encouraged her to analyse echoes of myths in the paranoiac woman's delusions.

Sometimes, wanting to provoke Sabina or jolt her out of her solemnity, he seemed callous. While making love he was often tender and affectionate, but on 15 January 1911, the day before her exam, he said she would do well because she was in league with the devil. Unlike her, he sometimes said, he was dishonest in love, and often his reactions fell so far short of what she expected and needed that she went on brooding about the hypothetical man who, returning her love with all the strength of youth, would make her his wife and the mother of his children.

After taking her finals in mid-January, she left Zurich, and filed her thesis on 11 February. In psychiatry her result was so good it seemed to confirm her long-cherished belief that she was destined to achieve something exceptional. 'If there is a God-Father, let Him hear me now – no pain is intolerable, no sacrifice too great if only I can fulfil my sacred vocation . . . I'll try to leave myself entirely in the hands of divine might, to see whether I do not receive some message.'

Fourteen

Enough Women

Jung suggested that instead of travelling to see Bleuler in Zurich, Freud should meet him in Munich, and Jung would come there to spend a day with him. Delighted, Freud wrote to Bleuler, suggesting a Sunday meeting in a hotel. 'I find the intrigue delightful,' he told Jung. 'If he insists on coming Monday instead of Sunday, it will cost me a day's work. I will sacrifice it to him reluctantly, but to you willingly.'

Though he had so far found no limits to Freud's tolerance, Jung was not expecting it would extend to his work on the second half of his book, and he procrastinated, saying the material was still too disorganised to be readable. But Freud should 'be prepared for strange things unlike anything you have heard from me'.

When Bleuler agreed to a meeting in Munich on Christmas Day, Freud decided it would be more 'dignified' not to keep him in ignorance of his plan to see Jung afterwards. The meeting with Bleuler went so well that Freud predicted he would soon join the association, and Jung promised to maintain 'the correct attitude' towards him.

At the Munich hotel on 26 December, they discussed Jung's view of the sun-hero motif as an image of the ego's passage across the incest barrier in quest of succour from the libido. According to Jung, Freud asked him to promise he would never abandon the sexual theory, and became emotional, saying: 'You see, we must make a dogma of it, an unshakeable bulwark.' To the question: 'Against what?' he answered: 'Against the black tide of mud – of occultism.' As Jung saw it, 'unconscious religious factors' were erupting in Freud.

Jung later said it was in Vienna during 1910 that they had this conversation, but he did not go to Vienna in 1910, and it may have taken place at this meeting in Munich.

If the complaint about Freud – it was one Jung often reiterated – was not founded on fact, it is easy to see how the fungus of fiction grew. Barry

Silverstein has pointed to the possibility that Jung's memories of his father as a man who wanted him to believe – not to think – were sometimes projected onto Freud.

Their friendship, though, was still warm. Jung wrote: 'I still owe you a mountain of thanks for Munich,' and Freud told Ferenczi that Jung 'was magnificent and did me a power of good . . . I am more than ever convinced that he is the man of the future.' But he and Jung were both finding it harder to mask negative feelings, and some of Freud's jokes were dangerously barbed. In mid-January 1911, seeing a new production of *Faust*, Jung felt sure he was Goethe's great-grandson, and that the great man would have admired his work as 'continuing and even enlarging the ancestral line of thought'. This is what he told Freud, who then referred to Goethe as 'your little great-grandfather'.

Jung thought of his situation as analogous to Faust's: he could redeem himself in spite of his pact with the irreligious Freud. His duty was to complete the book in which he would penetrate the darkness of the psyche and track down libido symbols that reveal what we have in common with our forefathers.

Freud was puzzled by his secretiveness: 'I do not know why you are so afraid of my criticism on questions of mythology. I will be very glad when you plant the flag of libido and repression in that territory and return as a victorious conqueror to our medical motherland.' Trying to resume their war game, Freud was reasserting himself as commander-in-chief, situating mythology outside their homeland and showing impatience for Jung to have done with it.

In late February he said he was working on the incest problem: 'Something should come of it.' But in March he was astounded to find Freud had not only appropriated his ideas about direct and indirect thinking but, without permission, reported in print on his recurring dream about his dead father. In 'Formulations on the Two Principles of Mental Functioning' Freud contends that the primary and secondary mental processes are regulated, respectively, by the pleasure principle and the reality principle. Ignoring reality, neurotics are obeying the pleasure principle that dominates unconscious processes, but when the reality principle takes over, the ego turns from daydreams and fantasy towards external reality, while the sexual instincts move away from autoeroticism towards object love and procreation. Freud told the story of a man whose dead father kept reappearing in his dreams, unaware that he was dead. This pointed, said Freud, to the dreamer's feelings of guilt about death wishes he had been harbouring against his father.

Outraged, Jung protested only mildly. 'I have taken your pleasure and reality principle to heart, and have had to adopt your terminology for the time being . . . My only regret was that I did not have access earlier to this point of view.' Telling Freud about a schizophrenic he had been treating, he said the case had 'yielded some very strange fruits. I am struggling to understand them through a parallel investigation of incestuous fantasy and "creative" fantasy. Once my thoughts have matured, I must ask your advice.'

But he felt disinclined to ask advice, and went on making independent efforts to redefine *libido*, looking in myths and symbols for the emergence of what had been repressed. But whatever Freud's motives had been for writing 'Formulations', he had not wanted to alienate Jung or to pacify his Viennese supporters, who were no better than 'rabble'. He would 'feel neither alarm nor regret if one day everything here collapses'.

Reading Theosophical publications and working on the book that was to be called *Transformations and Symbols of the Libido*, Jung tried to forget his promises of loyalty to Freud, making only perfunctory efforts to report on progress:

At present I am looking into astrology, which seems indispensable for a proper study of mythology . . . Please do not worry about my wanderings in these infinitudes. I shall return loaded with rich plunder for our knowledge of the human psyche. For some while I shall have to inebriate myself on magic scents in order to plumb the secrets hidden in the depths of the unconscious.

Eighteen months earlier, he had said the faith of the obsessional neurotic in his own infallibility was only a step away from superstition, 'which in turn is only a special case of self-hypercathexis or rather weakness in adaptation (the two always go together). All superstition springs from this soil; it has always been the weak man's weapon of attack and defence. The enfeebled often go in for witchcraft – especially old women who have long since lost their natural witchery.'

On the other hand, thanks to Ferenczi, Freud was less sceptical about the occult than he had been at the time of the explosion in the bookcase. Ferenczi, who knew a medium in Budapest, had persuaded him to share a consultation, if only out of interest in 'thought transference'. In October 1909, Freud conceded: 'I am afraid you have begun to discover something big.' At the end of 1910 he invited Ferenczi to write on the topic in the yearbook. He never did, but gave a talk on telepathy to the Vienna society in November 1913. Freud now told Ferenczi that Jung wanted to 'lead a crusade' into 'the field of occultism'. 'I can see that you two are not to be held back. At least go forward in collaboration with each other; it is a dangerous expedition, and I cannot accompany you.'

He encouraged Jung. 'It is always right to go where your impulses lead. You will be accused of mysticism, but the reputation you achieved with *Dementia* will hold up against that for quite a time. Just do not stay for too long in the tropical colonies. You have to reign in the homeland.' Five weeks later, Freud said he had 'grown humble in matters of occultism since the great lesson I had from Ferenczi's experiences. I promise to believe anything that can be made to look reasonable. I shall not do so gladly . . . But my *hubris* has been shattered.'

Glad not to be reprimanded, Jung slipped back into the roles of son/ analysand. There had been 'another false alarm about being blessed with too many children. One tries every imaginable trick to stem the tide of these little blessings, but without much security. One scrapes along, so to speak, from one menstruation to the next.'

Brooding about Honegger, he compared him with a female schizo- phrenic patient. In both cases, he said, introversion of libido had produced a system of unconscious fantasies. These could be unearthed in analysis. It gave him the feeling of 'practising vivisection on human beings with strong inner resistance. Introversion seems to lead not only, as in hysteria, to a recrudesc- ence of infantile memories, but also to a loosening of the historical layers in the unconscious, thus giving rise to perilous formations which come to light only in exceptional cases.' Had he realised, he said, what was going on inside Honegger, it might have been possible to save his life. Reassuringly, Freud argued that unconscious fantasies were like carefully cultivated daydreams, and Honegger's system, 'if he had one', would have influenced the formation of his symptoms less than 'the aetiology and the motives and the rewards held out by real life'.

Jung was devoting most of his evenings to astrology. He made

horoscopic calculations to find clues about the core of psychological truth . . . Calculating the positions of the stars at the nativity of one lady produced a clear-cut character picture with several biographical details that related not to her but to her mother . . . It is possible we shall one day discover in astrology a great deal of knowledge that has been intuitively projected into the heavens. For example, it seems that the signs of the zodiac are character pictures – in other words libido symbols which depict the typical qualities of the libido at a given moment.

This prefigures his later work on typology, and shows he was still optimistic about mapping the psyche. Maybe mythology could provide a basis, or maybe astrology could. But the only danger Freud spotted was that Jung might get lost in 'the business of money making'. He parried the attack by

saying he had felt competitive: 'The sense of inferiority that often overwhelms me when I measure myself against you always has to be compensated by increased emulation.'

After seven years in Zurich, Sabina had finished her exams and settled in
Munich, where she worked on her death-wish essay. In her absence, Jung
often thought about her. Like Otto Gross's, her ideas, memories and
emotions interpenetrated his. Jung wanted *Transformations and Symbols of
the Libido* to absorb the energy that had gone into conversations with her,
but some of it reads as if he were arguing with her in her absence.

At the beginning of August, Sabina left Munich for Vienna. Submitting
'Destruction as a Cause of Coming into Being' for the yearbook, she wrote:
'Receive now the product of our love, the project which is your little son,
Siegfried.' Not wanting to think about her, Jung gave it only a cursory
reading. What she had written, he said, was courageous, far-reaching and
philosophical. Instead of appearing in the yearbook, it should be published
on its own. But he could not fend off her influence on his thinking.
Ambivalently trying to write the book that might precipitate a breach with
Freud, he argued that since modern fantasies correspond to mythological
motifs, they can be interpreted out of context. It is hard to disentangle Jung's
ideas from hers. Some were conceived and developed in their excited
conversations, and they would not have known afterwards who had
contributed what. Equating procreation with self-destruction on the
grounds that our descendants will take over from us, he was echoing her
point that destructiveness is integral to sexuality while expressing his own
feeling that his life was superfluous after the birth of his son.

He left on 11 August for a five-day educational conference at an institute
in Brussels. Given only twenty minutes to speak on the psychoanalysis of
children, he was intending neither to observe the time limit nor to court
unpopularity by defying the chairman. When he was interrupted, he said he
would like the decision to be taken by the audience. About two hundred
people were present, and the ovation was sufficient for him to go on. When
the chairman – director of an Antwerp institute for paedology – made a
second attempt to stop him, the audience again sided with Jung, who spoke
for nearly an hour.

After five days in Brussels, he took Emma into the Bernese Oberland for a
mountain tour. They returned on 28 August to Küsnacht, where a letter
from Freud was waiting. He had been 'working in a field where you will be
surprised to meet me'. Jung would be 'too shrewd not to guess what I am up
to when I say I am dying to read your "Transformations and Symb. of the
Lib".' Coming from the man who had written 'Formulations', this was

disconcerting. 'Together with my wife,' Jung wrote, 'I have been trying to solve the riddle of what you say.'

In 1910 Freud had started exploring primitive religion in *Totem and Taboo*, which was inspired partly by Sir James Frazer's *Totemism and Exogamy* and partly by an uprising of the Young Turks against Sultan Abdul Hamid II, who kept a harem guarded by eunuchs – the tyrannous father and the rebellious horde of sexually deprived sons. Wherever totems were found, Freud contended, there was a ban – as among Australian Aborigines – against sexual intercourse within the clan. Incestuous wishes that have been repressed eventually become unconscious, and primitive peoples punished them severely.

Jung would have only three weeks in Küsnacht before leaving for the International Psychoanalytical Congress to be held in Weimar on 21–22 September. Before it, Freud was coming to stay for three nights. James Putnam had also been invited to stay with the Jungs, and Freud gave him six hours of analytical sessions.

Though suffering from toothache, Freud seemed to want no sympathy, and, as Emma could see, the awkwardness between him and Jung had nothing to do with physical discomfort. Freud had read the first part of *Transformations and Symbols of the Libido*, but he had avoided the subject in his letters. Now he was in the house, confrontation must be imminent. But still he said nothing, and the tension increased.

Freud seemed less inhibited with Emma than with Jung, but what he wanted to talk about was his marriage. For a long time, he said, it had been 'amortised': nothing remained for him to do except die. He was fifty-five, and twelve years earlier he had already been saying: 'Sexual excitement is no longer of use for someone like me.' His only real pleasure, he told Emma, came from the children, who became more troublesome as they grew older. She wondered whether he was thinking of Jung as one of his children, but instead of asking, she suggested the children might benefit from analysis. He was too busy to analyse their dreams, he said, because of having to earn enough money for them to go on dreaming. She was sceptical about this, having found with Jung 'that the imperative "earn money" is only an evasion of something he is resisting'.

They left for Weimar on 19 September. To Alphonse Maeder, who travelled in the same railway compartment, their relationship seemed 'broken inwardly'. Jung was bringing Emma and four other women to the congress: Toni Wolff, Maria Moltzer, Martha Böddinghaus and Dr Beatrice Hinkle, who had opened a psychiatric clinic at Cornell Medical School after being City Physician in San Francisco.

Toni had been a patient for less than a year when Jung invited her to the conference, and she apparently remained a patient until about 1913. Jung referred to her, according to Carl Meier, who had left the Burghölzli to work as his assistant, as the one case of schizophrenia he had been able to cure.

Both Maria and Martha had been promoted to the rank of assistants, but in their loving rivalry, Maria had apparently emerged as the winner. According to Freud, Jung's affair with her lasted at least until the end of 1912, and she may also have been trying to analyse him. He had decided to be analysed by one of his assistants, and Freud suspected she was the one. A sexual relationship would have been no more of a deterrent than it had been in his analysis of Emma.

'We Viennese,' said Freud, 'have nothing to compare with the charming ladies you are bringing from Zurich.' Jung had also wanted Sabina to come, and when he arrived at his hotel – appropriately, he was staying at the Hotel Erbprinz (Crown Prince) – he had not yet given up hope. 'Only when you strive for other people's happiness will you enjoy happiness,' he told her. 'I can write to you in this candid and admonitory way because I have emptied my heart of all the bitterness that had accumulated against you . . . You should not under any circumstances fail to attend the congress.'

She may neither have wanted to confront Emma, Moltzer and Bödding-haus at close quarters nor understood why he wanted her to. Was he trying to flaunt his promiscuity? Otto Gross had certainly influenced him, and his mother is said to have appeared at the Burghölzli when he was working on word-association tests and said: 'There are not enough women in your life.'

How promiscuous was he actually being? We have Lewis Mumford's word for it that a friend of his was once in conversation with Jung, who said: 'When I die, probably no one will realise that the old man in the coffin was once a great lover.' Sabina believed he was taking full advantage of his popularity with women. 'Dr Jung is no hermit – he sees many other women besides me.' Jealousy seeped into her moral disapproval of the suffering he caused. 'I have just learned of a tragedy that occurred with a woman patient whom he first led on, then rebuffed, then people talked about other such "feats".'

We do not know what Freud felt about Jung's retinue. Martha Freud never attended congresses, and together with Lou Andreas-Salomé, who was there with a Swedish hypnotherapist, Poul Bjerre, the five women Jung had brought formed a small female enclave in a male assembly. A woman of fifty, highly intelligent and still good-looking, Lou Andreas-Salomé was the daughter of a Russian general, and Rilke had been one of her lovers. Freud's speech revealed the depth of Jung's influence on him. He said the unconscious contained 'not only infantile material but also relics from primitive man'. He paid explicit tribute to Jung, who 'has excellent grounds for his assertion that the mythopoeic forces of mankind are not extinct'.

Titling his speech 'Contributions to Symbolism', Jung argued that to understand schizophrenic delusions, historical parallels must be adduced, because the patient is 'suffering from the reminiscences of mankind'. Unlike the hysteric, the schizophrenic thinks in terms of ancient images that have universal validity. Rejected by a man, a thirty-four-year-old female patient had pictured him suspended from his genitals. The fantasy signified a sacrifice of sexuality, which should be seen in the perspective of ancient religious cults involving the sacrifice of the spring god by hanging or whipping, or the offering of the phallus as a sacrifice to the Great Mother. But it could equally well be seen as a nonreligious fantasy of revenge against the male organ.

Jung joined in the general discussion, and when someone objected that his jokes were too coarse, Freud riposted that it was a healthy coarseness. But according to Ernest Jones, Jung boasted that his reputation would eclipse Freud's. 'I was very astonished and naturally asked him why he did not analyse his father-complex instead of trying to live it out in such an inappropriate way. His mystical answer "It is my fate" showed me which way things were moving.'

Freud was retreating. By mid-October he was ready to concede it would 'soon be undeniable' that 'there is such a thing as phylogenetic memory in the individual'. Jung now maintained that when people claimed to remember the moment of being born or periods of sucking at their mother's breast, they were drawing on collective memories. He was happy to have Freud's agreement on such a fundamental point. Having offered Agathli at Clark University as a female counterpart to Little Hans, he now said her recent dreams seemed to be 'closely connected with certain Negro myths, in which this involvement in slimy stuff also occurs'.

Throughout most of October, while Jung was away on military service, Emma was hesitating about whether to approach Freud. He had confided in her about not sleeping with his wife: why not write to him? At the end of the month she mustered enough courage to tell him it was time for a candid confrontation with Jung.

Freud's reply to Emma was reassuring, and she wrote again, questioning whether he might be giving Jung too much. 'Does not a man often give a lot because he wants to keep a lot?' Freud was feeling old and morose, and resentful about feeling old and morose. 'Old age is not illusory. A morose *senex* [old man] deserves to be shot without remorse.' But why, at the age of fifty-five, did he feel so old? 'Why are you thinking of giving up already,' Emma asked, 'instead of enjoying your well-deserved fame and success? . . .

And do not think of Jung with a father's feeling – "He will grow, but I must decline" – but rather as one man thinks of another who, like you, has his own potential to fulfil.'

At her prompting, he wrote to Jung.

> One of the nicest works I have (re-)read is that of a well-known author on *Transformations and Symbols of the Libido*. In it many things are so well expressed that they appear to have taken on definitive form and in this form impress themselves on the memory. Sometimes I feel his horizon has been narrowed too much by Christianity, and sometimes he seems to be above his material, rather than in it. But it is the best thing this promising author has so far written, though he will do still better.

After this, Freud admitted how nervous he was about their rival claims to the same territory. To express ideas that might equally well have occurred to Jung would be to deprive him of them, and sometimes Freud started – and left unfinished – a letter to Jung in which he offered ideas and observations Jung might be able to develop. 'Why in God's name did I let myself follow you into this field?'

Jung had reason to feel anxious. As he told Freud in the middle of the month, 'The outlook for me is very gloomy if you too deal with the psychology of religion. You are a dangerous rival – if we must talk about rivalry. Yet I think it has to be like this, for a natural development cannot be stopped.' But he went on, provocatively, to say that the second part of his book contained 'a fundamental discussion of the libido theory . . . In my view the concept of libido as set forth in the *Three Essays* needs to be supplemented by the genetic factor to make it applicable to Dem. Praec.'

On the same day, 14 November, Emma was writing to Freud. Her letter shows how dependent she and Jung had become on Freudian terminology. It had not occurred to her, she said, that her last letter to Freud had really been addressed to the father image: 'I thought that, knowing the transference side of my father-attitude towards you, it would all be quite clear and do me no harm.' But she was not saying Jung should ignore him. 'Naturally one should recognise an authority, and if one cannot, it is only a sign of overcompensated insecurity.' She had at first thought the book had been delayed by Jung's fear of Freud's reactions, but that had been his excuse 'for not carrying on with the self-analysis that this work really involves'.

She even analysed her feeling of being overshadowed. How could she hold her own?

> I find I have no friends. Really, all the people we see are interested only in him, except for a few boring ones I find totally uninteresting. Naturally the

women are all in love with him, and with the women I am immediately categorised as the wife of the father or friend. But I urgently need people, and even Jung says I should stop concentrating on him and the children. But what on earth can I do? With my strong inclination to autoeroticism, I find it very hard, but it is also hard objectively because I can never compete with Jung. To emphasise this I usually have to talk extra stupidly when we are with people.

Jung was astonished to see an envelope addressed to Emma in Freud's handwriting, but she neither showed him the letters nor confided in him about their contents.

Sabina had settled in Vienna, where she surprised Freud by turning up at one of his Wednesday meetings. She said she had expected him to look malicious, and he did not. Instead of taking offence, he enrolled her as a member of the society. Without wanting to reject Jung, she was turning to Freud.

Giving a paper on the death wish at a meeting of the Psychoanalytical Society in Vienna, Sabina caused quite a stir. Her title was 'On Transform-ation'. Freud objected to her easy-going treatment of mythology, which might have been inspired, he said, by Jung. 'The presentation provides more opportunity for a critique of Jung because in his recent mythological studies he also uses mythological material at random.' His point was that 'surface versions of myths cannot be used uncritically for comparison with our psychoanalytical findings. We must work backwards to their latent original forms . . .'

He told Jung he had 'hit upon a few objections to your method of dealing with mythology, and I mentioned them in discussion with the little girl. I must say she is rather nice, and I am beginning to understand.' The little girl was twenty-five. 'What troubles me most is that Fräulein Spielrein wants to subordinate psychological material to *bio*logical considerations. This dependency is no more acceptable than one on philosophy, physiology or brain anatomy.'

He confronted Jung's challenge to the libido theory. 'I am afraid there is a misunderstanding between us – the same sort of thing as when you once said in an article that to my way of thinking libido is identical with any kind of desire, whereas actually I hold very simply that there are two basic drives and that only the power behind the sexual drive can be termed libido.' The article was Jung's September 1907 paper on Sabina's case history, which he had read in Amsterdam.

One of Freud's reasons for wanting to avoid a quarrel with Jung was that his relationship with Adler was rapidly deteriorating. Whereas Freud believed that relationships between siblings mattered less emotionally than relationships with parents, Adler took the opposite view, and the disagreement was exacerbated by the coincidence that he had always felt jealous of his popular elder brother, who had the same first name as Freud – Sigmund. By 1908, Adler had been criticising Freud's view of the libido's dominance in psychic life, and at the 1911 conference he suggested that Freud was overestimating the importance of sexuality. The term *inferiority complex* derives from Adler's psychology. The individual struggles to compensate for a feeling of inferiority which – in Adler's opinion but not in Freud's – may be organic in origin. Hunger for self-esteem leads to a striving for power.

After promising to publish Sabina's paper in the next yearbook, Jung asked Freud for more detail about his 'objections to my new method of dealing with mythology . . . so that I can turn your criticism to account in my second part,' which was to contain a chapter summarising all Jung's thoughts on libido theory. 'The essential point is that I try to replace the descriptive concept of libido by a *genetic* one. Such a concept covers not only the recent sexual libido but all those forms of it which have long since split off into unorganised activities. A little bit of biology was inevitable here.'

Though he told Sabina that Freud had spoken about her 'very positively', Jung's letter to her was unemotional. Writing again, no less coldly, on 23 December, he advised her to let Freud read her paper before she submitted it for the yearbook.

Jung felt that his whole libido was going into his book, and the final stages of writing were hectic. 'I am overwhelmed with work and grappling with the endless proliferation of mythological fantasies.' Having found numerous examples in myth of the hero's sacrificial renunciation of virility in favour of his first love object – his mother – and his subsequent rebirth through her womb, Jung argues that when Jesus told Nicodemus he must be born again, incestuous imagery was being used to redirect the libido. 'Let us remember that Christ's teaching ruthlessly separates man from his family, and in the conversation with Nicodemus we saw Christ's particular effort to activate the incest libido.' His intention was to 'liberate the Jew from his extraordinary fixation on the family, which implies not higher development but greater weakness . . . and produces as compensation the compulsory ritual and the cult of the incomprehensible Jehovah'. Here Jung was tilting at Freud, implying that his theory of the Oedipus complex was relevant primarily to Jewish families.

Having once praised Mithraism at the expense of Christianity, Jung now compares the treatment of sacrifice in the two religions. Christianity advocates 'that not only are the lower desires to be sacrificed but the whole personality. The Christian symbol demands total devotion, enforcing a genuine sacrifice of the self to a higher purpose.'

Muddled and indigestible, the writing suggests he may have had conscious or unconscious motives for not wanting his readers to understand fully. Possibly he was uneasy about his substantial indebtedness to the whiskery writer he had often seen in the streets of Basel – Johann Jakob Bachofen, who was not academically respectable. Whereas Freud maintained that memories of incestuous desires were repressed during infancy, Bachofen believed mankind had repressed memories of primeval matriarchy, and he takes the same view of myths that Freud takes of screen memories – vivid but apparently insubstantial, they lead back to indelible childhood experiences and fantasies. In Bachofen's view, myths preserved those elusive memories for the human race.

Another possible motive for Jung's obscurity was uncertainty about how much he had taken from Sabina. Writing disingenuously to her in March 1912, he said he had only just noticed the 'incredible parallels' between her work and his. Previously, he pretended, he had always thought her title was 'Distinction as a Cause of Coming into Being' (rather than 'Destruction as . . .'). The phrase would then be nonsensical. After receiving a furious reply, he conceded: 'The priority is yours . . . The death wish was apparent to you much earlier than it was to me. For obvious reasons!' What had happened was that they had unconsciously 'swallowed' part of each other's soul. But there was no need for her to worry. His book made such a different impression from hers that no one would accuse her of plagiarism. And he cautioned her that the reading public must never find out about this 'secret penetration of thoughts'.

Yet another reason for not wanting readers to understand him fully was uncertainty about his mental equilibrium The mother scene in the second part of *Faust*, he said, involved '*the deliberate introversion of a creative mind*, which, inwardly collecting its forces as it retreats before its own problem, immerses itself temporarily in the source of life to wrest more strength from the mother to complete its work'. He described this as 'playing with oneself like mother and child. It contains much feeble self-admiration and self-adulation.' Perhaps he found it hard to achieve what he called 'separation from the mother-imago, birth out of one's self, which reconciles all conflict through suffering'.

If Freud was worried about Jung's equilibrium, he hid his misgivings till early in 1912, when he confided in Ferenczi, who said Jung was being unbalanced by 'an infinite and unrestrained ambition which he expresses to you, his superior by far, in petty hatred and envy. His unfulfilled ambition may be making him *dangerous*.' Though he called himself a 'sentimental donkey', Freud did not want to quarrel with his crown prince and hoped at least their professional relationship would remain intact.

But the tension was increasing. Arriving in Zurich, a tiresome patient of Freud's – he called her his 'chief tormentor' – made an appointment with Jung. When she said Freud was remote and unconcerned, he sympathised, if only perfunctorily. Back in Vienna, she gave Freud her version of the conversation, and, upset, he told Jung he should remain 'reserved and merely receptive' instead of becoming involved with patients and 'giving a good deal' of himself.

Jung answered that the analyst should possess a freedom 'which the patient must acquire in turn . . . I think it is more a matter of our different lifestyles than of disagreement in principle.' Evading confrontation once again, Freud continued the argument in an article for the *Zentralblatt*, 'Recommendations to Physicians Practising Psychoanalysis'. Analysts should never volunteer personal information, never encourage new forms of sublimation and never lend books or articles to patients. Jung did all these things.

Freud went on trying to accept some of his new ideas, conceding that cryptomnesia could not explain the presence of mythological material in psychotic fantasies. Freud also told his Wednesday club that fears of castration might have phylogenetic roots.

Not knowing how to deal with his anxiety, Freud made a cryptic reference to it in a published statement – a summary in the *Zentralblatt* of a book by a French art historian. Freud told the story of a community that became disloyal to its founder, St Paul. It 'fell under the influence of a man named John, who had come with Mary, and promoted the cult of the Mother of God'. After losing money as result of Paul's preaching, the goldsmiths made money out of pilgrims who flocked to hear John. Few of his readers would have realised he was alluding to Jung's interest in Bachofen and mother goddesses.

Still immersed in mythology and astrology, Jung did little work for the international association. He did nothing to put the six national groups in touch with each other, or to prepare for the next congress. Sending him a prospectus for *Imago*, the review he was launching, Freud showed his annoyance: 'I would have been glad to see your name figure prominently in this journal and the *Zentralblatt*, but instead you hide behind your religious–libidinal cloud.'

Nor is Freud likely to have been pleased to learn that twenty former patients of Jung and Riklin had been organised into a 'Society for Psycho-analytic Endeavours'. On 13 February, Riklin chaired the first meeting, and the group agreed to meet once a fortnight. Jung told Freud the club had been started 'at the request of former patients . . . To me the experiment seems interesting from the viewpoint of the social bearing of psychoanalysis on education.'

In increasingly irregular letters, Jung sustained a friendly tone, but Freud was becoming bitter, as he showed when he belatedly heard Jung had been bitten by a dog, and asked whether he should worry about the dog's health. Jung apologised for his remissness as a correspondent, only to be told he should be psychoanalysed. 'Unquestionably I was demanding as a correspondent,' Freud conceded. 'Nor can I pretend I did not await your letters impatiently and reply promptly. I disregarded your previous indications of reluctance. But this time it struck me as more serious. I took myself in hand and quickly turned off my excess libido.'

Jung defended himself by quoting from *Zarathustra*: a good teacher is poorly rewarded by pupils who remain pupils. Freud was grudgingly conciliatory: 'If you think you want more independence, what more can I do than abandon my sense of urgency about our relationship, occupy my unemployed libido elsewhere and wait till you find you can tolerate greater intimacy?'

The friction was increased through Sabina. Jung had almost weaned himself away from emotional dependence, but there was a residue of malice. Telling Freud her paper for the yearbook was 'heavily overweighted with her own complexes', he quoted from Horace: 'The upper half is a lovely woman and the lower half a fish.'

Still fixated on Jung, she went in mid-April to consult Freud, who surprised her by offering to start analysing her in the autumn. Perhaps he could help her to 'drive out the tyrant'.

Fifteen

Giving His Throne Away

Ludwig Binswanger, who had witnessed the first meeting between Freud and Jung, was to play a role in their last quarrel. An appendix operation revealed he had a cancerous tumour; this was removed but, not expecting to survive for long, he wanted to devote his last weeks to writing an essay on Freud's significance for clinical psychiatry. Freud promised to help, and to keep his illness a secret. Binswanger lived on the edge of Lake Constance, in Kreuzlingen, forty miles to the northeast of Zurich, and planning to visit him there, Freud could have arranged a meeting with Jung.

As his views became less Freudian, Jung presented them to Freud more forcefully. In late April, he said incest was primarily a fantasy problem, and the veto had not been intended literally. 'The tremendous role of the mother in mythology is vastly more significant than the biological incest problem.' Following Bachofen, he explained that during the promiscuous matriarchal period, fathers counted for nothing, and the only point in making incest taboo would have been 'to consolidate the family (or piety or the social structure)'.

Freud was unimpressed. Without naming Bachofen, he indicated that he recognised Jung's source, and his next letter accused Jung of moving backwards: 'We have maintained that the origin of anxiety was the prohibition of incest; now you are saying the opposite: that the prohibition of incest originated in anxiety, which is very similar to what was being said before the advent of psychoanalysis.' Before writing this letter, he had decided not to meet Jung. 'During the Whitsun weekend I will be geographically closer to you. I am leaving on the evening of the 24th for Constance to see Binswanger. I am planning to return next Tuesday. The time is so short I will be unable to do more.'

Offended but not surprised, Jung did not back down. 'That you felt no need to see me during your visit to Kreuzlingen must be ascribed, I presume, to your chagrin at my development of the libido theory. I hope we will be able to arrive later on at an understanding on our points of difference. For some time to come, it seems, I will have to go my own way. You know how stubborn we Swiss are.'

Freud's reply was disingenuous. 'If you had come and spent half a day in Constance, it would have been a great pleasure for us all. I did not ask you to come because it is an imposition to ask someone to spend a holiday in this way if he has something better to do or wishes to relax. But I would have been pleased if you had thought of it yourself.'

After a silence that lasted over a month, Jung said he could 'understand the Kreuzlingen gesture. Whether your policy is justified will become clear from the success or failure of my future work. I have always kept my distance, and this will obviate any emulation of Adler's disloyalty.'

Freud regarded this note as 'a formal renunciation of our previously friendly relations', and, sending Ferenczi a copy, said he had given up hope of uniting Jews and Gentiles in the service of psychoanalysis. 'They separate like oil and water.' He told Sabina he had never liked her fantasy about 'the birth of the Saviour to a mixed union . . . The Lord in that anti-Semitic period had him born from the superior Jewish race.' She was trying to make peace between him and Jung, but, as Freud told her, 'there is no shortage of others who are trying to widen these chinks into a breach'. She would soon have to make a choice between Freud and Jung.

Their partnership could not have lasted so long without compromises that put a strain on both men, and Jung was no longer prepared to go on compromising. When he accepted an invitation to lecture at Fordham, a small Catholic university in New York, he asked Bleuler to take charge of the yearbook while he was away and warned Freud he was going to talk about the incest problem. The next congress could decide whether he should continue as president.

After writing the nine lectures in German, he had them translated for delivery in English. What he presented to about ninety American psychiatrists and neurologists was not an exposition of Freudian theory but a critique. He also held a two-hour seminar every day for a fortnight, gave clinical lectures at the Bellevue Hospital and the New York Psychiatric Institute on Ward's Island, addressed the New York Academy of Medicine, and gave an interview to the *New York Times*, reiterating some of what he had said in Nuremberg about the contamination of white Americans by blacks. Though his only visit to the American South had been the brief one to Chattanooga, he said:

I notice that your Southerners speak with the Negro accent; your women are coming to walk more and more like the Negro. In the South, I find what they call sentiment and chivalry and romance to be the covering of cruelty. The Southerners . . . treat the Negro as they would treat their own unconscious mind if they knew what was in it.

At Fordham, he presented his new view of the libido and his dissident division of individual development into three periods: a presexual phase which ends at about the age of three; a stage at which boys normally develop the Oedipus complex (a term he disliked) and girls develop the Elektra complex (a term he invented). In the third phase, the adolescent should direct his libido away from the family. If it leaks incestuously backwards, regression and neurosis ensue. Unlike Freud, who blamed all neurosis on damaging infantile experience, Jung thought its causes were always in the recent past. The earlier a bad experience seemed to have occurred, the more likely it was that memory was playing tricks.

Arguing that the intense emotions of childhood are not produced by the sexual libido, and that schizophrenic apathy is not due merely to withdrawal of sexual appetite, Jung redefined *libido* in terms of energy conservation. When too much libido is invested in one activity, too little goes to another, and the task of psychoanalysis is to adjust the balance.

Excessive fantasising could be equated with partial introversion and defective projection of libido outwards. Fantasies can be used as stepping stones towards spiritualisation, just as regression can be used in explaining the need for realistic adaptation to circumstances. While their intrinsic value is negligible, fantasies are like sunken treasure, because of the libido attached to them. The analyst must retrieve this for the patient's use in discharging his duties to life.

It is essential, then, that the analyst should himself discharge these duties. Unacknowledged infantile demands must not be confused with those of the patient, and to guard against this, analysts should be analysed. Those who deny this necessity are guilty of 'a Münchhausen psychology, and they will certainly get stuck. We need the objective judgement of someone else.' The implication was that Freud, analysing himself, had got stuck, and that Jung had not. But he did not say who had analysed him.

In the fifth lecture he argued that myths, like dreams, crystallise unconscious impulses, while solar myths contain fantasies about procreation, such as the notion that a mother must consume a child before she can give birth to one. In 'Red Riding Hood', the wolf eats a grandmother who reappears, alive, when his belly is ripped open. This parallels the story of Jonah and myths in which the sun is swallowed by a sea monster, only to reappear at daybreak. Mythological elements predominate in the childish psyche, Jung said, since the unconscious strata that once produced myths are still active.

In the growth of the analytic movement, the polarisation between Zurich and Vienna had been partly a matter of polarisation between Christians and Jews. If Freud and the Viennese were sometimes overhasty in alleging anti-Semitism, Jung was not always neutral, and these lectures, like *Transformations and Symbols of the Libido*, which had climaxed in a chapter on 'Sacrifice', contrast the two religions. Introducing his three stages of development, he suggests that the inner logic of renunciation in the second stage can best be characterised by the Christian symbol of sacrifice, though the Viennese used the ambiguous term 'castration complex' for the same phase. He also compared psychoanalysis with the therapy available in the confessional.

On this trip to the USA, Jung did not have to share the limelight with Freud, and being lionised helped to consolidate his self-confidence. In the interview for the *New York Times*, he felt entitled to moralise, almost like a preacher. America did not understand it was 'facing its most tragic moment: a moment in which it must make a choice to master its machines or be devoured by them'. Intent on succeeding in business, he said, Americans cultivated so much self-control that they broke down under the effort to maintain it. What he meant by psychoanalysis was 'the search back into the soul for the hidden psychological factors which, in combination with physical nerves, have brought about such a false adjustment to life'.

Lecturing to the Academy of Medicine, he said: 'A purely sexual etiology of neurosis strikes me as much too narrow'. James Putnam, who was in the audience, hoping to meet him afterwards for a conversation, was surprised to hear him say infantile fixations were virtually negligible as a cause of neurosis.

Putnam wanted to discuss a relation Jung was treating in Zurich. Thirty-eight, diffident, unattractive, unmarried and highly strung, Fanny Bowditch had become depressed in the winter of 1911 after the death of her father, Henry Pickering Bowditch, a close friend of William James. Asked for advice, Putnam had recommended Jung, who had impressed him at Clark University.

Arriving in Zurich early in 1912, she was treated simultaneously by Jung and Maria Moltzer, whose English was fluent. At first Fanny made headway, but, finding Jung had changed, Putnam wrote to her: 'I suspect that Dr Jung's very masterful ways may affect some of his patients more strongly than he realises himself, and you must not get dependent on him or hesitate to form critical judgments of him in your mind.'

In early December he wrote again, telling her not to be 'too much of a fly on sticking paper'. After all, Jung and Moltzer were only

humans with limitations and failings, like you and me . . . It is a fault in Dr Jung (*entre nous*) that he is too self-assertive and I suspect that he is lacking in some needful kinds of imagination, that he is, indeed, a strong but vain person, who might and does do much good but might also tend to crush a patient. He is to be learned from but not followed too implicitly.

Though strengthened by success in America, Jung was in a difficult position. He was president of the association, but how much longer would his schismatic views be tolerated inside it? New York would be a key city in the movement's future, and without planning his visit as part of an anti-Freud campaign, he was consolidating his reputation there.

The man who had invited him to Fordham, Smith Ely Jelliffe, had, together with William Alanson White, founded the *Psychoanalytic Review*, which they were co-editing, and, serialised under the title *The Theory of Psychoanalysis*, Jung's lectures might make more immediate impact on American readers than anything Freud had written.

During his eight-week absence from Zurich, Jung did not write to Freud. He stayed in the USA from mid-September till 26 October. He visited Chicago, Baltimore, where he saw the psychologist Trigant Burrow who had been at the Burghölzli, and Washington, D.C. Invited to St Elizabeth's Hospital by William Alanson White, who was its 'Superintendant', Jung seems to have spent at most three days in the hospital, the visit being made 'more in the capacity of observer than of physician'. When he told Freud that he 'analysed fifteen Negroes, with demonstrations', he was using the word *analysed* in a different sense from its usual meaning today.

He was later to make a lot of confusing statements about his visit to the hospital. In 1959 he talked to John Freeman as if it had been crucial to his discovery of the collective unconscious, and he often made out that he had gone to America in order 'to investigate the unconscious of Negroes', wanting to check whether collective patterns were racially inherited or were 'a priori categories of imagination'. He said the delusion about the sun's penis had 'prompted me to undertake various researches on mentally deranged Negroes'.

During a 1935 lecture he said their dream images had 'nothing to do with so-called blood or racial inheritance, nor are they personally acquired by the individual. They belong to mankind in general, and therefore they are of a *collective* nature.' One black patient – an unintelligent, uneducated man – had dreamed about a figure crucified on a wheel. 'It is the ancient sun wheel,' Jung explained, 'and the crucifixion is the sacrifice to the sun god in order to propitiate him, just as human and animal sacrifices formerly were offered for the fertility of the earth.' He later claimed he had 'been able to demonstrate a whole series of motifs from Greek mythology in the dreams and fantasies of pure-bred Negroes suffering from mental disorders'.

Like *analyse*, the word *objective* did not have the same meaning for him as it has for us. He called the collective unconscious the *objective psyche*, and did not discriminate in the way we do between objectivity and subjectivity. For him, a mental event might be no less real than an event that could be witnessed by other people. In the mind of the black patient, the crucified figure on the wheel may have had more to do with Jesus than with sacrifices to ancient sun gods, but even if Jung had no solid evidence to substantiate his theory of the collective unconscious, it does not follow that he did not believe in it. Like Moses and Rudolf Steiner, he had more faith in the voice inside his head than in the voices of other people.

Though Jung spent little time in the Washington hospital, the visit was the first step in a semi-anthropological investigation that would continue in journeys to Africa and Mexico. His interest in the dreams of black men seems to have been sparked by a sentence he read in a book about Australian Aborigines: 'What a savage experiences during a dream is just as real to him as what he sees when he is awake.' Jung quoted this in *Psychological Types*, and his reference to 'Australian Negroes' in a 1925 seminar suggests that he saw the American blacks in this perspective.

He often generalised about 'the primitive mentality' as if the same form of thinking were common to black American schizophrenics and Australian Aborigines, and as if they all belonged to the same category as prehistoric people. What appealed to him most in 'the primitive mentality' was that 'the inner and the outer tend to form one experience'. It seemed to him that 'primitives show a much more balanced psychology than we do for the reason that they have no objection to letting the irrational come through, while we resent it.'

He admired them for being bound to objects 'in a direct relationship which amounts to partial identity'. When he is ill, the Aborigine goes to the 'soul stone' that is full of healthy energy. When he rubs it, his sickness goes into it, and he then returns it to its hiding place among the rocks, where it can digest the sickness and be refuelled with healthy magic. He also performs ritual dances, and regards dancing as work. 'We would say one got strength from God through prayer, but the primitive gets strength from God by work.'

In America, Jung told Freud in November, he had done 'a very great deal for the spread of the movement . . . Naturally I also accommodated views of mine which deviate in some ways from conceptions that have existed hitherto, especially with regard to the libido theory. I found that my version of psychoanalysis won over many people who had previously been put off by the problem of sexuality in neurosis.' He had returned to the view he had taken before the 'reformation' in his psychological thinking.

He promised to send Freud an offprint of his lectures 'in the hope that you will gradually come to accept certain innovations already hinted at in my libido paper. I feel no need to let you down provided you can take an objective view of our common efforts.' Prefacing the published version of the lectures, he insisted he was not causing a split in the movement. 'Such schisms can occur only where faith is involved . . . I know my experience does not approach Freud's quite extraordinary experience and insight, but nevertheless I think some of my formulations do express the observed facts more aptly than Freud's version of them.'

Freud's reply began: 'Dear Herr Doktor, I greet you on your return from America, no longer as affectionately as last time in Nuremberg – you have succeeded in curing me of that habit – but still with considerable sympathy, interest and gladness at your personal success.' Jung could count on his objectivity, he said, 'and hence on the continuation of our relations; I still maintain that personal variations are quite justifiable and still feel the same need to carry on with our collaboration.'

In Jung's absence, Stekel had been causing trouble and refusing to resign as editor of the *Zentralblatt*. Annoyed that Jung had neither said how long he would be away nor appointed an acting president for the interim, Freud was planning to abandon the bulletin and replace it with a new journal. To settle the problem, Jung summoned the presidents of the six local societies to a meeting in Munich on 24 November.

There, going for a long walk together before lunch, he and Freud were holding their first conversation for nearly two years. Freud said he could not sustain a friendship in which Jung 'had conjured up the intimacy' only to brush it off. He was not what he had seemed – 'a born ruler, who, through his authority, could spare others many mistakes'. Even if this conversation had made an impact on him, Freud wrote afterwards, 'there is a core of disingenuousness in his being which will allow him to shake off these impressions.'

Over lunch they discussed an essay by Karl Abraham on the pharaoh Amenhotep IV, who was said to have introduced monotheism but had his father's name erased from monuments. Freud assumed he had felt parricidal, but Jung explained that his father and grandfather were thought to be divine. Removing the name of the old god encouraged support for the new religion. 'The story may be crude and even brutal,' Jung said, 'but it is true to nature. For the father already has a name, while the son has to go out and make one.'

'Possibly that is true of ancient times,' Freud answered, 'but not necessarily of this occasion.'

As Jung went on talking about Amenhotep, Freud fainted. This was the second time it had happened in Jung's presence. As Jung carried him to a sofa in the next room, 'he half recovered consciousness, and I will never forget the way he looked at me. In his weakness, he looked at me as if I were his father.' According to Jones, he also said: 'How sweet it must be to die.'

Freud blamed his weakness on an almost sleepless night and an upset stomach. Before leaving, Jung promised: 'You'll find me completely on the side of the cause.' But Freud compared him with Adler: they were both promoting their career in America by playing down the importance of sexuality. To one friend Freud said he had fainted because of an 'unruly homosexual component', and to another he blamed 'repressed feelings, this time directed against Jung as previously against a predecessor of his'.

Freud told Putnam the time spent with Jung had 'swept away a number of unnecessary personal irritations. I hope for further successful co-operation.' To Ferenczi he reported: 'The personal bonds, like the intellectual ones, will hold fast for years. No talk of separation or defection.' At the next meeting of the Vienna society, Freud claimed he was again on good terms with Jung, but Lou Andreas-Salomé was unconvinced: 'Freud has returned almost too refreshed and content from the trip to Munich. Is the rapprochement with Jung really as secure as it sounded on Wednesday?'

In his next letter, Jung claimed he at last understood the difference between them. From now on, he would know how to behave. 'Please forgive my mistakes, which I will not try to excuse or to extenuate . . . I am most distressed that I did not achieve this insight much sooner. It could have spared you so many disappointments.'

Freud found this letter condescending. Answering it, he admitted to 'a bit of neurosis I really ought to investigate', warning Jung that Ferenczi's critique of his libido paper would soon be published. 'I now think you have brought us a great revelation, though not the one you intended. You seem to have solved the riddle of all mysticism, showing it is based on the symbolic exploitation of complexes that have outlived their function.' He signed himself 'Your untransformed Freud'.

Infuriated, Jung accused Freud of underestimating him and misunderstanding his work. 'The majority of psychoanalysts misuse psychoanalysis to devalue other people and their progress by insinuations about complexes.' Across the top of the paper he scribbled: 'This letter is an unashamed attempt to accustom you to my style. So watch out!'

Writing to Jones in his quaint English, Freud complained: 'He behaves like a perfect fool, he seems to be Christ himself. The letters I get from him are remarkably changing from tenderness to overbearing insolence. He wants treatment, unfortunately by my last attack I have lost position of my authority.'

They no longer cared whether they upset each other, and Freud pointed out a Freudian error Jung made. Once again it was over the capital letter that differentiates *Ihrigen* (yours) from *ihrigen* (theirs). Wanting to say that even Adler's followers did not regard him as one of theirs, Jung had written 'one of yours'. Could he now be objective enough, Freud asked, to look at the mistake without getting angry?

This infuriated Jung.

> You go around sniffing out all the symptomatic actions in your vicinity, reducing everyone to the level of sons and daughters who blushingly admit to their deficiencies . . . You know of course how far a patient gets with self-analysis: not out of his neurosis – just like you. If you should ever get rid of all your complexes and stop playing the father to your sons and take a good look at your own weak spots instead of aiming continually at theirs, then I will mend my ways and eliminate the fault of being in two minds about you.

Two great analysts were accusing each other of neurosis. Jung promised to go on saying what he really thought in his letters, but to stand by Freud in public. The implication was that he would benefit from criticism, if only he was man enough to take it.

Freud told Ferenczi Jung was 'behaving like a florid fool and a brutal fellow, which he certainly is'. By now reconciliation was impossible. 'He seems all out of his wits,' Freud reported to Jones, 'he is behaving quite crazy. After some tender letters he wrote me one of the utter insolence.' And by the end of 1912, Jones was reporting on Jung's delusions of grandeur. Freud decided their friendship 'is not worth the ink'.

Without mentioning Jung by name, but making the allusion to him unmistakable, Jones reiterated the allegations in print under the title 'The God Complex: The Belief that One is God and the Resulting Character Traits'. 'The more unusual the method, the more it attracts him, giving him the feeling of possessing a key that is available only to the elect. For this reason he is apt to display great interest in the various forms of thought-reading, chiromancy, divination and even astrology, as well as in occultism and mysticism in all their branches.' Jones explained the delusion as due to 'a colossal narcissism'.

Taking the term *narcissism* from an English writer on the psychology of sex, Havelock Ellis, Freud had introduced it in 1910, explaining that homosexuals, choosing themselves as their love object, look for a young man they can love as their mother loved them. He seems to have accepted Jones's diagnosis of Jung, whom he apparently had in mind when he wrote *On Narcissism*, which was published in 1914. One of his intentions was to suggest that the concept of narcissism provided an alternative to Jung's nonsexual libido. The ego could be regarded as a reservoir which sends out libido to objects and absorbs it when it flows back. The narcissist withdraws emotional energy from external reality, turning it back on himself to become his only love object.

After six years of corresponding with Jung, Freud wrote his last letter on 3 January 1913: 'It is a convention among us analysts that none of us needs to feel ashamed of his residue of neurosis. But if one goes on behaving abnormally while shouting that he is normal, he may be suspected of lacking insight into his illness. I therefore suggest we abandon our personal relationship entirely.'

Jung's reply was: 'I never thrust my friendship on anyone. You yourself are the best judge of what this moment means to you. "The rest is silence." ' It might have been better to quote from *King Lear*. Intent on giving his throne away, the legitimate king would neither let his adoptive son rule nor behave like a mere subject. And though Jung had not only asked to be treated like a son, but had said that for a time 'I felt myself to be his son', it was a role he no longer wanted.

Local psychiatrists were meeting regularly twice a week – on Wednesday evening in Küsnacht and on Thursday evening at a room in the Restaurant Seidenhof in Zurich. We do not know when the group constituted itself as an association (*Verein*), but it had done so by 13 January 1913, when, for the first time, minutes were taken – by Toni Wolff, who was not then a member. Just over a year later, at the meeting on 30 January 1914, it was decided to co-opt two associate members who were not medically qualified: Toni Wolff and Maria Moltzer.

On 31 January 1913 the theme was Jung's theory of the libido, and his final contribution to the discussion was: 'Dreams provide answers through symbols, which must be understood. But we should not only see wish fulfilment in them – or else the analyst simply collaborates in the patient's fantasies. We must discover the objective of the unconscious, which never deceives people.'

In July 1913 Jung stepped up hostilities by writing to Freud in the first-person plural, implying a consensus among the Zurich analysts. Freud, he complained, had misunderstood their view on dreams. 'We fully admit the correctness of the wish-fulfilment theory, but we maintain that this way of interpreting dreams touches only the surface, that it stops at the symbol and that further interpretation is possible.'

As president of the international association, Jung was in a strong position. While trying to integrate revisionist ideas into psychoanalysis, he had not been thinking about his power within the movement. It had not even occurred to him that it might be possible to expel Freud and his supporters. But it occurred to them. What if Jung attempted a coup?

Ernest Jones had been the first to propose defensive action. What was needed, he suggested in August 1912, was a core group of loyalists, 'a united small body designed, like the Paladins of Charlemagne, to guard the kingdom and policy of their master'. Freud approved. 'What immediately appealed to my imagination was your idea of a secret council composed of our best and most reliable men.' The group was to consist of Ferenczi, Jones, Rank, Hanns Sachs (another veteran member of the Wednesday Club) and Karl Abraham. Freud gave each of them a Greek intaglio set in a gold ring.

But Jung was too disoriented to take any aggressive action, except possibly against himself. 'I felt fully suspended in mid-air, because I had not yet found what my position was.' And he later told a friend: 'I felt as though I had been banished from my father's house.'

It was hard to give patients the reassurance they needed. 'I decided for the time being not to make any presuppositions, but to wait for whatever they want to tell me . . . It soon became apparent that they reported sponta-neously on their dreams and fantasies, and I merely put a few questions "What occurs to you in connection with that?" or, "How do you mean that?" "Where does that come from?" ' He could not always conceal his own confusion. When a woman objected: 'But that's the opposite of what you said last week,' he answered: 'That may be so, but this is true, and the other was also true. Life is a paradox.'

He was sometimes 'so wrought up' that he had to 'eliminate the emotions through yoga practices'. He does not specify which yoga practices he used, but Sonu Shamdasani has noticed the resemblance between the 'savasana asana' of Hatha yoga and a technique he recommended to a patient for dealing with intense stress. He says Jung advised him to 'lie down flat on a couch or a bed and just lie quietly there and breathe quietly with the sense that the wind of disturbance blew over one'.

It can be argued that he should have stopped seeing patients until he regained his balance, but the analytical relationship involves a two-way traffic, and several of the most inspired therapists, including Freud, Jung, Wilhelm Reich and R. D. Laing, would have been less helpful to patients had they been more stable. Some of humanity's best healers have been healing themselves at the same time as their patients. Jung's dreams became so oppressive that he suspected a 'psychic disturbance'.

Had Jung consulted a doctor, he might have been advised not to travel, but in March 1913 he set out again for the USA, not to see Medill or Harold

McCormick, but Harold's wife Edith – John D. Rockefeller's daughter and a multimillionairess in her own right. Harold McCormick was president of a big company, Harvester International. She was slim, proud, wilful, with large, piercing eyes. Now forty-one, she had given birth to five children, but had been depressed since the death of her fourth, Editha, in 1903.

It was not until 1912 that she thought of consulting Jung, who was invited to Chicago for preliminary consultations after his Fordham lectures. He met her father, but when she offered to buy him a house in the USA so that he could bring his family and become her personal consultant, he refused. If she wanted to be his patient, she would have to settle in Zurich.

Neurosis played a bigger part than pride in stopping her – she was seized with panic whenever she tried to travel by bus or train. At the end of 1912, Maria Moltzer arrived in Chicago to give her preliminary sessions in her home, but Jung had to go back too. He gave her three weeks of daily analysis, but, according to her secretary, it was only when he hypnotised her that she made up her mind to settle in Zurich.

In New York he lectured at the Liberal Club in Gramercy Park, and revisited the asylum on Ward's Island. News of this visit reached Ernest Jones, who reported to Freud: 'His recent conduct in America makes me think more than ever that he does not react like a normal man, and that he is mentally deranged to a serious extent; he produced quite a paranoiac impression on some of the psychoanalytic psychiatrists on Ward's Island.'

Edith sailed to Europe with him, bringing her secretary, her fourteen-year-old son, Fowler, and her ten-year-old daughter, Muriel, together with his tutor and her governess. They took a suite in the grandest hotel on the lake, the Baur au Lac, which had been magnificently renovated at the turn of the century. The Swiss regarded it as the unapproachable stronghold of monarchs and royal families. Kaiser Wilhelm stayed there, as did the Empress of Russia and the King of Sweden. Liveried servants stood on duty, waiting to open doors for guests, but Jung insisted that Edith should learn humility by going down on her hands and knees to scrub the floors of her suite.

Early in 1912, Sabina had married Paul Scheftel, a doctor, but in the fourth month of her first pregnancy, she was still obsessed with Jung. Freud was unsympathetic: 'The reason you still love Dr J. so deeply, I imagine, is that you have not brought the hatred he deserves to the surface.'

Insisting that dreams could be prophetic, Jung sometimes found himself in conflict with patients over their interpretation. By June 1913, Fanny Bowditch felt in need of a holiday at home. Jung advised her to stay in Zurich, though, as usual, he was not going to see patients during the summer. She suspected him of cheating in his interpretation of her dreams and using them to support his argument, but it was not till the late autumn that she defied him and went to Boston.

Keeping abreast of the situation, James Putnam agreed that Jung was twisting the meaning of her dreams, and, disguising Fanny's identity, he told Jones that Jung had 'utilised her dreams as a means of deciding whether she ought to return to America for a visit. This seems queer, and the more so that during his absence just a little later, she analysed her own dreams, and came to the conclusion that a different meaning was to be asserted in this respect!' Writing to him again seven weeks later, Putnam called Jung 'a strong but egotistic man . . . under the necessity of accentuating any peculiarity of his own person for his own satisfaction'.

By the beginning of August 1913, plans were being made for the fourth International Psychoanalytical Congress, which was to be held in Munich during September, five years after the first congress in Salzburg. Freud was feeling more conciliatory. After studying the text of Jung's Fordham lectures, he pronounced them 'beyond all expectation good and harmless . . . From a distance I was on the whole seriously overrating the danger.' But he told Sabina he could hardly bear to listen 'when you go on enthusing about your old love and past dreams'. He had been cured of 'the last shred of my predilection for the Aryan cause, and would like to assume that if your child is a boy, he will grow into a staunch Zionist. We are and remain Jews. The others will only exploit us and will never understand us or appreciate us.'

Early in August Jung attended an international medical conference in London, where he repeated the lecture he had given in New York at the Academy of Medicine, distancing himself from Freud's view of neurosis, and urging that 'psychoanalytic theory be freed from the purely sexual stand-point. In place of it I should like to introduce an *energic viewpoint*.' None of his revisions, he said, entailed any change in psychoanalytic technique, but for the first time he used the term 'analytical psychology' for what he called 'the new psychological science'.

Back in Switzerland, he spent four days sailing on Lake Zurich with Albert Oeri and three other friends. Oeri entertained them by reading from Homer's *Odyssey* – the Circe and *Nekyia* episodes. The latter describes Ulysses's visit to the realm of the dead, and Jung would subsequently use the term *Nekyia* for the efforts he made while bordering on psychosis to recover unconscious material through dreams and fantasies. He was thirty-eight, and, according to him, the transition into maturity takes place between the ages of thirty-five and thirty-eight. He had lost his two surrogate fathers, Bleuler and Freud, but two other fatherly men helped him towards achieving professional independence and staking out the territory he would claim as his own – William James and Théodore Flournoy.

Until recently, the consensus of opinion was that their influence on him had been negligible in comparison with that of Freud, but this view has been cogently challenged by Sonu Shamdasani, Eugene Taylor and John Haule. Unlike Freud, who was temperamentally hostile to religion, James and Flournoy both helped to inspire Jung in the process of evolving techniques of psychotherapy that centred on the cultivation of a religious attitude.

Jung thought James, who had visited him in 1910, one of the most outstanding men he had ever met – aristocratic but unaffected. In *The Varieties of Religious Experience* he considered the lives of men who believed in an 'unseen order, and that our supreme good lies in harmoniously adjusting ourselves thereto'. He may have influenced Jung by his willingness to recognise subjective impressions as valid: the individual is entitled to believe in his psychic experiences, while the distinction Jung was to make between the *ego* and the *Self* may derive from James's differentiation between the *I* and the *Me*. The *Me* is the centre of selfish preoccupations, while the *I* is in ultimate control of the thinking. James even glances forwards to Jung's collective unconscious by suggesting that the current *I* recollects previous *I*s and *Me*s.

The influence Jung absorbed from James fitted well with the influence of Flournoy: they both thought of religious experience not as a relationship between man and God, but as something that filters through the subconscious or *subliminal* – a word they both used. 'If there be higher powers able to impress us,' said James, 'they may get access to us only through the subliminal door.' The psychology of religion, as Flournoy saw it, was not concerned with metaphysics but with human experience, psychological and biological.

Jung visited Flournoy several times in Geneva, where they talked critically about Freud as well as discussing somnambulism, parapsychology and the psychology of religion. 'I took over his concept of *creative imagination*, which specially interested me. I have learned a great deal from him.' While Freud was dynamic and penetrating, expecting 'to get something out of each case he treated, Flournoy wanted nothing. He was detached and objective.' Jung describes him as acting like a counterweight to Freud. He took Flournoy as his guest to the Munich congress, which was held on 7–8 September 1913.

Eighty-seven delegates attended. Surrounded by his supporters, Jung sat at a table opposite Freud's. Jones called the atmosphere 'disagreeable'; Freud called it 'fatiguing and unedifying'. Lou Andreas-Salomé, who came with Rainer Maria Rilke, reported:

> It is not so much that Jung diverges from Freud as that he does so as if he could rescue Freud and his cause *through* these divergences . . . A single

glance at these two shows which of them is more dogmatic and power-hungry. Two years ago there was robust gaiety and exuberant vitality in Jung's booming laughter, but his seriousness now is made up of pure aggression, ambition and intellectual brutality.

Yet, absurd though it was to think Freud might accept him as a mentor, Jung genuinely believed he could help the older man to overcome his neurosis if only he were willing to swap roles.

Jung took the chair, but did not join in the discussion of papers by Otto Rank and Alphonse Maeder on dream interpretation, though it was from Maeder that Jung had taken over the idea that dreams could be prophetic, expressing attempts by the unconscious to predict and solve problems that lie ahead. Finding himself face to face with Freud outside the lecture hall, Maeder held out his hand, only to have it ignored. But, catching his jacket pocket on a doorknob as he tried to hurry past, the accident-prone Freud could not free himself without help from the man he had just snubbed.

The crucial issue was whether Jung would remain president. There was no rival candidate, and though twenty-two blank ballots were handed in, fifty-two were cast in Jung's favour. Speaking 'On the Question of Psychological Types', he compared hysteria with schizophrenia. The hysteric attaches libido to other people by means of transference, while the schizophrenic turns libido inwards, sucking external reality into the delusion. In one case libido is being turned outwards or *extraverted*, in the other turned inwards, *introverted*.

Analysing dissimilarities between himself and Freud, he had concluded that he was introverted while Freud was an extravert. His new thesis had its roots in this idea, but it would have been undiplomatic to offer himself as an example of introversion, and he used Adler as a stalking horse, characterising him as less concerned with his patients' past history or the influence of their environment than with their dominating principles and 'guiding fictions'. At the opposite extreme, Freud, the extravert, had produced a theory 'which is essentially reductive, pluralistic, causal and sensualistic'. It is 'strictly limited to empirical facts, and traces back complexes to their antecedents and to simpler elements. It treats psychological life as consisting largely of reactions, and allocates the greatest role to sensation.'

What was now needed, he said, was a psychology that would be equally fair to both types, and he contended that both could be accommodated in the movement. But at the end of the conference, according to Freud, he and Jung parted 'with no wish to see each other again'.

Jung later told Sabina he had known since this congress that he had lost Freud: 'He wants to give me love; I want understanding. I want to be a friend on an equal footing; he wants to have me as a son. This is why he condemns everything I do and attributes to a complex everything that does not fit the framework of his doctrine.'

Part Three

Alarums

Sixteen

Creative Illness

Throughout the autumn of 1913, Jung was under strain. 'The pressure I had felt inside me seemed to be shifting outwards, as if there were something in the atmosphere: it actually seemed darker than before.' He had a vision of a flood in October, while reading a book in a train to Schaffhausen, which is close to the German border. The trance began as the train entered a tunnel. Looking down at a relief map of Europe, he watched the sea rise over the land. 'I saw the powerful yellow waves, floating fragments from works of art, and the death of countless thousands. The sea changed into blood. This vision lasted about two hours, overwhelming me, making me feel ill and ashamed of my weakness.' The duration of the vision is changed to one hour in the published text of *Memories, Dreams, Reflections* and in a 1952 interview, in which Jung says he was awakened by the conductor when the train arrived at Schaffhausen. Two weeks later, the vision returned, even more vivid than it had been the first time.

Proposing the term *creative illness*, Henri Ellenberger compares the solitude and depression in Jung's life during 1913–19 with Freud's period of what he called neurasthenia and hysteria. Two weeks after his trance, Jung's vision returned. 'Again the sea changed into blood, and an inner voice spoke: "Look at it, it's quite real, and that is how it will be. There is no doubt about that." . . . The vision did not release me from its grip.'

By now Edith McCormick was in Jung's thrall. Reminiscing about him, her son Fowler said: 'He was for me in my youth a father figure . . . of an intensely strong nature. In a sense the word *father figure* is too mild a term because one would call it more of a *God figure*.' In October 1913 his father, Harold McCormick, arrived in Zurich, hoping that six months of analysis would be enough for his wife, and that she would return with him to America, but she was not to be budged.

When Jung resigned in October as editor of the yearbook, it may have been because he felt disoriented, or it may have been the first calculated step in a campaign against his former ally. Bleuler's resignation followed. Renaming the book *Jahrbuch der Psychoanalyse*, Freud took over, with Abraham and the uncritically loyal Eduard Hitschmann doing most of the editorial work.

Knowing he would need a platform for himself and his supporters, Jung wrote to Alphonse Maeder on the same day he sent his letter of resignation to Freud: 'I shall not fail to create for the Zurich people a new organ in the style of the yearbook, perhaps called *Psychological Investigations*. Works of the Zurich School of Psychoanalysis. As it happens, Deuticke is willing to accept it. If our works are dropped from the yearbook, maybe the yearbook will cease to exist.'

The publisher Franz Deuticke was based in Leipzig and Vienna; the 'Zurich School' could now disseminate in Europe the revisionist ideas Jung had formulated in New York and London. *Psychological Papers* was the title he later chose. He had not intended to abandon the word *psychoanalysis*, but by May 1914, writing his foreword to the first volume, he was thinking in terms of a new movement. 'The present state of psychology seems to make it desirable that schools or movements have their own organs of publication.'

Though Bleuler resigned from the International Psychoanalytical Association, Jung could not count on his support as he could on that of Franz Riklin and Maeder. But nothing of his or theirs was ready for publication, and he devoted the first volume to papers by former students and loyal colleagues – Hans Schmid, a psychiatrist who lived in Basel, Josef Lang, J. Vodoz, and C. Schneiter. The others to rally around him were the four women he had taken to the congress, Toni Wolff, Maria Moltzer, Martha Böddinghaus and Beatrice Hinkle, together with Jan Nelken and Adolf Keller.

In his subsequent writing, the best description of his *Nekyia* is an account of what he calls 'godlikeness'. In any analysis that is 'pushed far enough', he says, the subject experiences this condition, which announces itself through such symptoms as

> dreams in which the dreamer is flying like a comet through space or feeling that he is the earth, the sun or a star, or that he is gigantically huge or dwarfishly small, or that he is dead, in an unfamiliar place, is a stranger to himself, or confused or insane. He may also undergo such bodily sensations as being too big for his skin or too fat, or hypnagogic sensations of continually falling or rising, of the body expanding, or giddiness. This state is characterised psychologically by a strange disorientation in relation to his personality; he no longer knows who he is, or feels completely sure that he is what he seems to have become. Common symptoms include intoler-

ance, dogmatism, euphoria, self-depreciation [sic] and contempt for people who have not been analysed, and for their views and activities.

If this were used as a criterion, it would have to be said not many analyses are 'pushed far enough'. But the passage is valuable as an account of Jung's experience. By using the phrase 'encounter with the unconscious', he made it sound purposeful, and he claims never to have forgotten he was conducting a scientific experiment. But according to Carl Meier, the breakdown could be classified 'phenomenologically . . . as a schizophrenic episode'.

Jung says he underwent a conversion in which he rejected scientific activity as he had previously understood it. He had not stopped believing in himself as a receiver of revelations, and the latest was that it had been wrong to make his soul into an object for scientific observation – to let himself be 'blinded by the presumptuous spirit of the times'. To regain his soul, he must stop trying to 'fend off' the other, more powerful spirit, 'the spirit from the depths of time immemorial and for all time to come'. He should never have doubted its superiority to a spirit that 'changes with generations and withers with the flowers of summer'. For the Spirit of the Times, the soul is 'something dependent on the person . . . a thing whose range we can grasp'. But the Spirit of the Depths knows that the soul is an independent, living being.

It was not a matter of deciding that from now on he would obey the Spirit of the Depths. No choice was involved – the spirit took hold of his mental activity and placed it 'in the service of the inexplicable and paradoxical, or rather what must appear so to the people of these times. He robbed me of the power to speak or write of anything that was not in his service – in the service of uniting sense and nonsense.'

The Spirit of the Depths was still in charge when Jung celebrated his fortieth birthday. If he assumed, from now on, that his patients' objectives should change when the first half of their life was behind them, it was partly because his own had changed. By his fortieth year, he said, he had fulfilled all his boyhood ambitions. He had achieved 'fame, power, wealth, knowledge and the best human fortune'. He no longer wanted more of 'these good things'. He had enough. 'I felt the spirit of the depths, but I did not understand him.'

This is how he puts it in the unpublished 'Red Book' – six hundred folio pages of typescript bound in red leather and illustrated with painstaking reproductions of paintings and drawings from the period of breakdown. Writing, drawing and painting were activities that helped him to regain a degree of control over turbulent fantasies, and he claims to have acquired the knack of catching unconscious material '*in flagrante*' by training himself to dream in a new way. 'What I did . . . was to make at night an exact reversal of the mental machinery I had used in the day . . . By assuming a passive attitude at night while at the same time pouring the same stream of libido into the unconscious that one has put into daytime work, the dreams can be caught and the performance of the unconscious observed.'

In a pre-Christmas dream he was with a small, brown-skinned man before dawn on a rocky mountain, and they were both armed with rifles. When they heard Siegfried's horn, they knew they must kill him. The first ray of the rising sun revealed him in a chariot made of bones as he drove down the slope, and they shot him. They were not going to be caught, because rain would wipe out all the evidence, but the feeling of shame lingered. When Jung woke up, he decided that if he could not understand the dream, he would shoot himself with the loaded revolver he kept in the drawer of his bedside table.

What stopped him from writing honestly about this dream was the need to keep silent about Sabina. He had been deeply involved in her Siegfried fantasy, but he says Siegfried represented his heroic idealism. 'It was my ideal of force and efficiency I had killed. I had killed my intellect, helped on to the deed by a personification of the collective unconscious, the little brown man with me. In other words I had deposed my superior function.'

He then elaborates on the repercussions involved in the idea of killing a hero:

> Dissolving an image means that you become that image. Doing away with the concept of God means that you become that God. This is so because if you dissolve an image it is always consciously, and then the libido invested in the image goes into the unconscious. The stronger the image, the more you are caught by it in the unconscious . . . The killing of the hero, then, means that one is made into a hero, and something hero-like must happen.

What happened was another fantasy, in which he became God. Those whose inferior function is 'hooked up with the collective unconscious' are only one step away from 'Godalmightiness . . . The person becomes more and more identical with the collective unconscious.' Like dreams, fantasy had to be interpreted: 'We look within and see if there is anything to be observed, and if there is nothing we may either give up the introspective process or find a way of "boring through" to the material that escapes us on the first survey.' If he could induce the trance state in a woman through hypnosis, he should be able to open himself out to visionary experiences. Once they started, he was no longer in control, but could he control the process of losing control? He told himself he was digging a hole. 'When I began on that hole I worked and worked so hard that I knew something had to come of it – that fantasy had to produce, and lure out, other fantasies.'

This led to an imaginary encounter with a bearded patriarch who introduced himself as Elijah and his beautiful blind companion as Salome. They had a black snake with them. Jung distrusted the girl, whom he took to be evil, and 'When Elijah told me he was always with Salome, I thought it was almost blasphemous for him to say this. I had the feeling of diving into an atmosphere that was cruel and full of blood.'

Digging further downwards, Jung visualised a Druidic altar and took himself to be in the underworld. Elijah smiled. 'Why, it is just the same, above or below.' Salome started to worship Jung, telling him he was Christ. The snake coiled around him, and holding out his arms as if being crucified, he restored her sight. But his face had become the face of a lion or a tiger.

> Awe surrounds the mysteries, particularly the mystery of deification . . . it gave the immortal value to the individual – it gave certainty of immortality. One gets a peculiar feeling from being put through such an initiation. The important part that led up to the deification was the snake's encoiling of me. Salome's performance was deification. The animal face which I felt mine transformed into was the famous [Deus] Leontocephalus of the Mithraic mysteries.

This was what he later had in mind when he spoke of 'self-deification'.

One factor in his disorientation was the loss of the two people who mattered to him most – Freud and Sabina. Both Jewish, they could both be associated with the Old Testament. Though he was to speculate at length about the meaning of Elijah and Salome – pointing out that in myth an old man is often accompanied by a young girl who represents the erotic while he represents wisdom – he never made the obvious equations. What made the double loss still harder to bear was that Freud was now analysing Sabina. Like dissidents who have been eliminated in a Soviet purge and vanish from new prints of old photographs, they are mentioned in none of Jung's accounts of his dreams and visions. It was as if he had forbidden himself to think about them

Laurens van der Post has suggested that for him 'to say that Salome was blind because the anima is incapable of seeing is really the unconscious way of confessing that he himself could not see the meaning of Salome'. Perhaps he saw it but did not dare to admit he was conflating Sabina with Lou Andreas-Salomé, who had dark hair and, being strikingly attractive and female, had been prominent among the audience at the Munich congress, where her sympathies were clearly with Freud.

Another fantasy figure was to develop out of Elijah, an old man with horns and wings. He was carrying a bunch of four keys. Jung called him Philemon and set a high value on their imaginary conversations.

> He expressed things I had not consciously thought. I recognised clearly that it was he, and not I, who was speaking. He explained to me that I dealt with ideas as if I had produced them myself, while in his view they possessed a life of their own, like animals in the woods or people in a room or birds in the air . . . So he gradually taught me psychic objectivity, the *reality of the soul.*

If a schizophrenic had used this argument, Jung might have explained that delusions did not have the same kind of reality as people, and if the psychotic had recurrent visions of a wise mentor, it would have been obvious that he felt in need of guidance. Dealing with his own delusions, Jung rarely drew on what he had learned in the Burghölzli.

But he did draw on what he read. When he said the atmosphere surrounding Philemon was 'Egypto-Hellenistic with a Gnostic coloration', it meant that Jung heard words which came from what he had learned about Gnosticism and mythology.

Ever since the episode of the shitting God, Jung had placed more faith in his dreams and visions than in Christian dogma. He always tended to mythologise his experience, and now that he was verging on psychosis, Gnosticism gave him a kind of licence. He later said that when he began to read the Gnostics, he felt 'as if I had suddenly found a circle of friends who had shared my experiences and could sympathise with me and understand the whole realm where I had been so lonely and isolated.' It was the same feeling that made myths and (later) alchemy attractive to him: images and patterns that surfaced in the writings tallied with images and patterns in his fantasies.

Even if he believes God has given him a Messianic mission, the schizoid may be capable of scientific discoveries. Isaac Newton had religious delusions and was, for a time, certifiably insane, but this does not invalidate his law of gravity. The history of cosmic theories may, as Arthur Koestler suggests, 'be called a history of collective obsessions and controlled schizophrenias'. It is easy to undervalue ideas evolved during schizoid periods. Some of the best insights into the workings of the human mind have come from men who were – like Coleridge, Baudelaire, Nietzsche and Rimbaud – sometimes deranged by drugs or delusions of grandeur.

The schizophrenic often personifies the contents of consciousness. Words become voices, and, holding silent conversations, he gives them names as if they were people. This is how Jung treated Philemon. 'At times he seemed almost physically real. I walked up and down the garden with him, and he was to me what the Indians call a guru . . . I could have wished for nothing better than a real, three-dimensional guru, a man with great intellect and ability who could have decoded for me the involuntary creations of my fantasy.' Philemon, he says, 'really gave me illuminating insights'.

He made his first appearance in a dream, sailing across the sky. Painting images that presented themselves, Jung worked in the Art Nouveau style, which does not necessarily mean he had originally visualised them in this style. It was conducive to concentration on detail, and he gained power over his dreams and visions by taking control of the detail.

While painting Philemon, he found a dead kingfisher in his garden. The German word for kingfisher, *Eisvogel*, also means halcyon – the seabird that was classically believed to breed in floating nests during the winter solstice, calming the wind and the waves. In his account of the dream, he says the old man had the wings of a kingfisher, but we do not know whether the word *Eisvogel* featured in the dream, or whether, still asleep, he made a connection between the man's wings and the bird. The idea may not have occurred till he painted the wings, or till he found the bird. Kingfishers are rare in Zurich, and he felt sure it was no coincidence, but, living in a solipsistic world, the schizophrenic tends to believe in ghostly links between unconnected events, making the paranoid assumption that everything refers to him. Later, reproducing these paintings in the 'Red Book', Jung gave Philemon no horns.

At the end of 1913 Jung was still having frighteningly apocalyptic dreams and visions. Whoever had analysed him had not inspired enough confidence to make him go back for help in warding off psychosis. The fear of madness was even greater than the fear that other people would think he was mad, but, as in childhood, he kept his anxieties to himself. His secretiveness was reinforced by his faith that he had almost superhuman powers of endurance. 'One thunderstorm followed another. That I survived was a question of brute strength. Others have been destroyed by them. Nietzsche and Hölderlin too, and many others. But there was a demonic strength in me.'

He was under constant tension. 'It often seemed as if gigantic boulders were showering down on me.' Resisting the bombardment, he felt he was obeying a higher will, and that if only he could hold out, he might make sense of seemingly senseless images. Confronting the tumult of images and imaginary voices, he tried to concentrate as intently as he had on patients at the Burghölzli. Making notes on his fantasies, he knew his language was high-flown and bombastic. His unconscious seemed to be in control of his prose style.

Several dreams involved subterranean staircases and caverns, which suggested that his fantasies were located somewhere underground. Perhaps he could grapple with them if he let himself drop downwards. He was nervous of psychosis, but on 12 December he was sitting at his writing table, he says, when he decided to take the risk. 'I let myself fall. It was as if the floor literally gave way underneath me, and I plummeted into dark depths.'

His account of what happened has been questioned by his son Franz.

> My father writes that he *chose*. I do not believe that he chose. I believe he had no choice. Can you imagine what it must be to think that you might be going mad? That you might fall forever into the void? . . . For years after he and Freud parted, my father could do no work. He placed a gun in his nightstand, and said that when he could bear it no longer he would shoot himself . . . For seven years he did nothing really except his painting . . . Think of my mother . . . Can you imagine living with a man who slept with a gun by his bed and painted pictures of circles all day?

Sometimes Franz was allowed to sit at the old library table, painting with his father. But only if the boy promised not to speak.

In the summer of 1914, the family went to stay with Emma's mother. 'All summer long,' Franz remembered,

> we played Indians against the English with my cousins. Father was the leader. He wore a Canadian mountie's hat and a pair of cowboy boots from his visit to America with Freud. He looked like a sheriff. We built teepees and huts big enough to sleep in, and each side had a horse. We would light fires and burn down each other's teepees and steal the horses. This was Father's idea. He played with us all the time, although his brother-in-law did not approve.

Sometimes Jung and the children dug wide tunnels in the earth and crawled into them.

Jung explains his resumption of childhood games by saying he was counting on his unconscious to cure him, and therefore needed contact with his childhood. But the narrative of *Memories, Dreams, Reflections* often presents afterthoughts as if they were integral to decision-making, and he probably had no clear objective when he found himself collecting stones and building a miniature village, with cottages and a castle.

Given dry weather, he played with stones every day after lunch until it was time to see patients, and often resumed the game afterwards in full view of passengers on passing steamers, who must have thought he was mad.

CREATIVE ILLNESS181

Sometimes Franz was allowed to help. 'Father would be down there fitting rocks together. He was a genius at that. He would build towers and houses and churches until he had whole villages. I would cut reeds for the roofbeams and fill the little houses with sand so that they wouldn't fall down. In the spring, when the lake rose, the little villages all disappeared.'

The breakdown induced a series of fantasies, but he tried to keep himself under control by making extensive notes. Uncritical followers accept the suggestion that he was heroically making a scientific expedition into what Mircea Eliade calls 'the womb of primordial life'.

Seventeen

The Woman Inside Me

It is not true that for seven years Jung did nothing but his painting. He never stopped seeing patients, though he handled them erratically. He maintained that an analyst should never bully, manipulate or even influence patients, but in mid-October 1913, he had reduced Fanny Bowditch to tearful submission when she returned from her holiday in Boston.

'Dr Jung emphasised again lately that I am untrue, fake and dishonest and he has even used the word *liar*.' He accused her of cowardice and of being 'faithless' to him. To find her life, he said, she must be willing to lose it.

> During these last days I've been down to the depths as never before and surely soon the uplift must come; the wonderful feeling of *Wiedergeburt* [rebirth] which keen suffering and a struggle for a higher life bring. I am, and always shall be, full of gratitude to Dr Jung for handling me with such absolute sincerity and seriousness – in my afterlife I may understand even more than I do now what it has done for me.

Instead of posting the letter to Putnam, she showed it Jung, who allowed her to send it, but not until five days later, when she added a postscript saying it belonged to a period of resistance which was over. She had been feeling 'hatred for Dr Jung with fantasies of shooting and stabbing him, and there were moments when I thought seriously of stopping analysis with him and going to Dr Riklin.' But Jung convinced her she must surrender her pride. She then 'felt a deep and overpowering love for him'.

Replying, Putnam asked her not to show his letter to Jung. 'The self-abasement reaction is "too easy" and becomes in its turn a sort of self-indulgence, like asceticism . . . There will be no harm in realising that he is also no god but a blind man trying to lead the blind, and that you are as much at liberty to criticise him as he is to criticise you.' Writing to Jones again, Putnam called Jung 'a strong but egotistic man . . . under the necessity of accentuating any peculiarity of his own person for his own satisfaction'.

Just as Philemon had developed out of Elijah, another figure developed out of Philemon. Jung called it Ka, which is a truncated form of his name, Carl. In ancient Egypt the *ka* was the embodied soul, and in this fantasy it was a demon that came from deep in the earth. Jung painted it with a glowing nebula of stars above its head, and a kingfisher's wing above the stars.

Worried that his painting might have nothing to do with science, he asked himself what it was.

> Then a voice inside me said: 'It's art.' I was astounded because it had never occurred to me that my fantasies had anything to do with art, but I thought: 'Perhaps my unconscious has formed a personality that is not me and which wants to express its own opinion.' I knew the voice came from a woman and recognised it as the voice of a patient, a talented psychopath who had a strong transference to me. She had become a living figure in my interior life . . . Emphatically and full of resistance, I explained to the voice that my fantasies had nothing to do with art. Then she was silent, and I went on writing. Then came another attack – the same assertion: 'That is art.' Again I protested: 'It is not. On the contrary, it is nature.' I was expecting to be contradicted and involved in an argument, but nothing happened, and it occurred to me that the 'woman inside me' possessed no capacity for speaking, so I suggested that she should use mine. She accepted the proposal and explained her viewpoint in a long statement. I was very interested that a woman should intervene from inside my thoughts. Probably, I thought, it is something to do with the *soul* in the primitive sense, and I wondered why the soul should be termed *anima*. Why should it be represented as feminine? Later on I came to see that this internal feminine figure plays a typical or archetypal role in the consciousness of a man, and I called it the *anima*.

Again he was emulating a medium. If Ivenes and the control voices had been 'split-off parts' of Helly, the anima that told him: 'This is art' was a split-off part of him, as were Elijah, Philemon, Salome and Ka. Artists are licensed to deviate from the facts, and wanting to think of himself as a scientist, Jung had been annoyed when Maria Moltzer said his work had artistic value.

It has sometimes been assumed that the voice was Sabina's, but there are strong indications in the material he dictated for *Memories, Dreams, Reflections* and in the published book that Shamdasani is right to contend that it belonged to Maria. 'In reality the patient whose voice spoke in me exerted a disastrous influence on men. She had succeeded in persuading a colleague of mine he was a misunderstood artist. He believed it and went to pieces. What destroyed him? His life was guided not by his own judgment but that of others.' The reference is to Riklin, who had talent as a painter, and in the words of Heinrich Steiger, a member of his group, 'Because he didn't seriously work as a medical doctor and more in painting etc., so he lost the big office.'

Jung went on doing his best to deal with his fantasies scientifically. 'I took great pains to understand each single image and its content – so far as this is possible – to classify it logically and above all realise it in life.' At the same time, he wanted to revive ancient wisdom. Goethe had written: 'Dare to throw open the gates where other men slink past.' In alchemical terms, he was a link in the golden chain formed by the series of wise men who join Earth with heaven. The first was Hermes Trismegistus, and Jung might become part of the chain if he could pass on wisdom learned from a prophet such as Elijah or a sage such as Philemon. In the margin of the 'Red Book' next to the picture of Philemon is a quotation from the *Bhagavad-Gita* translated into English and transcribed with a lettering pen: 'Whenever there is a decline of the law and an increase of inequality/ then I put forth myself for the rescue of the pious and for the destruction of the evildoers/ for the establishment of the law i [sic] am born in every age.'

In myth, the gods Zeus and Hermes arrived on Earth to test human piety. Asking for hospitality in Phrygia, they were turned away by everyone except an old couple, Philemon and Baucis. As a reward they were taken to the top of a mountain. From there they saw their homeland covered by a flood, and eventually they were turned into trees. Jung's vision of Switzerland's immunity to the flood water corresponds to this story, and he believed his Elijah-Philemon had independent existence as a guru whose wisdom could be passed on to others.

The relationship with Maria seems to have outlasted the one with Sabina, intertwining fantasies, ideas, preoccupations. Either Emma had been unable to share Jung's fantasies or had not been allowed to. During his breakdown, she could make little contact with him, and it was around this time that she finally did what she could not do at the time of her correspondence with Freud. To build an independent intellectual life for herself, she began to study Latin, Greek, physics and maths.

The woman who replaced Sabina was another soulful patient with big dark eyes, dark hair and a keenly intuitive intelligence. In material dictated for *Memories Dreams, Reflections* but not finally used, Jung described how he still felt involved with Toni Wolff after terminating her analysis. What he called a confrontation with the unconscious was a confrontation with madness, and Laurens van der Post, reiterating the euphemism, writes: 'This world of the unconscious which he was entering as a man, she had already endured as a woman. Thanks to Jung's guidance she had re-emerged, an enlarged and reintegrated personality.' In treating her, Jung had used what he had learned from working in the Burghölzli, studying the case of Frank Miller and working on *Transformations and Symbols of the Libido*. If the same patterns and images occur in madness as in myth, he could confront them by combining the roles of hero and narrator, screwing all his courage into the effort of holding his balance and keeping a logbook on the storm-tossed boat.

Toni had incredible, wild and cosmic fantasies, but he was too preoccupied with his own to cope with hers. Though he felt involved with her, he broke off her analysis, and did not then know what to do. One of the reasons he found her and Sabina irresistible is that, unlike Emma, they both matched his memories of the dark-complexioned maid who had looked after him in his mother's absence. After describing her, he wrote that this 'type of girl' became 'an aspect of my anima'.

He believed that every man inherits a collective image of women – his *anima*. He then projects this image onto the female companion he has chosen because intuition told him she would be capable of receiving his projection. Jung may have had Toni in mind when he wrote about the way in which a man can cut himself off from God and society, plunging himself into solitude and guilt, but can eventually expiate this guilt by giving 'his supreme good, his love, not to the soul but to a human being who stands for his soul, and from this human being it goes to God and through this human being it comes back to the lover, but only so long as this human being stands for his soul'.

It may have been Toni who took the initiative. According to Michael Fordham, she refused to go on with the analysis, saying he was too unstable and that what she wanted was a relationship. 'She more or less took him by the ear.' Another patient confirms that she acted on him like a brake, saving him from going over the edge. 'Without her he wouldn't have made it. She brought him back to reality.'

Though they became interdependent, his need for her, unlike hers for him, was temporary. As her sister Susanne Trüb put it, she was 'never totally in life', and never came fully alive except through him. Until 1940 she lived with her mother, and they ate all their meals together.

Isolation had never been more dangerous to Jung, but though he urgently needed an interlocutor, he did not immediately give in to temptation. He claims that he allowed a year to pass between ending her analysis and deciding to contact her again. The decision was prompted by a dream in which they were alone together in an Alpine valley, and she was vanishing into a mountain where elves were singing. His dreams were vivid and turbulent. One was about a woman who was stone from the waist downwards, but the upper half of her body was alive, and he was responsible for her condition, which resulted from an injection he gave into her spinal fluid.

His life seemed to be in danger, and, believing Toni could save him, he wrote to her. They did not immediately make love – as with Sabina, he had to undergo what was almost a conversion before he gave in to sexual temptation. An attack of cramp while he was swimming in the lake made him vow that if he survived, he would be her lover. Barely forty, he was already inclined to believe himself to be living inside a myth and to make vows like those of a warrior hero taking an oath to sacrifice the first stranger he met if only the gods would send a propitious wind.

Once they were lovers, he said, he infected her with his experience, which was awful, and, once inside it, she was helpless. Needing him as her centre, she depended on his insights, but her need was so desperate that he felt as if he were being torn in pieces. Sometimes he had to keep his balance by gripping the table.

His love for Toni, like his love for Sabina, was born out of transference, counter-transference and a discovery that their fantasies coincided, over-lapped, interlocked. Much later, after he had made her into an analyst, one of her patients said: 'She had a special gift: in her presence, inner pressure became images.' Functioning like a medium, 'she helped Jung see his images and talk with them'. Another patient of hers felt 'as if I were even nearer Jung's inner wisdom when I was with her than when I was with him in the flesh. She was in some way the inner side of his work . . . She mediated Jung's mind and intuitive ideas directly, for she had been part of their creation from the unconscious.'

A young patient described her as having 'very changeable looks, as so many intuitives do'. She 'could sometimes look beautiful and sometimes quite plain. Her extraordinarily brilliant eyes – mystic's eyes – were always expressive.' Some people found her unapproachable, and one man called her 'a ghost-like figure, gaunt, haughty and forbidding'.

Toni became virtually a member of the Jung family – the children addressed her as 'Aunt'. Fowler McCormick, who was shocked to see her and Emma cooking dinner together, had no doubt 'that this relationship was a torture . . . for Mrs Jung to bear'. What made it bearable, according to her son, was that she was 'sure of her femininity', while Toni 'never knew what it was to be a wife or mother'. Franz Jung described her as 'all spirit. It was almost as if she had no body.' But the household was surrounded by piously puritanic friends and demanding patients, and it was not easy for Toni to maintain her position. 'My God, she was courageous,' said one of her former patients. 'She just *made* them accept it.'

Her commonsensical pragmatism is clear from advice she gave a patient whose husband was being unfaithful. Why not invite the other woman to lunch?

You would then get to know her a bit, you might even *like* her . . .
Sometimes if a man's wife is big enough to leap over the hurdle of self-
pity, she may find that her supposed rival has even helped her marriage!
This 'other woman' can sometimes help a man live out certain aspects of
himself that his wife either can't fulfil or else doesn't especially want to. As
a result, some of the wife's energies are now freed for her own creative
interests and development, often with the result that the marriage not only
survives but emerges even stronger than before!

Toni may have been paraphrasing what Jung had said to her.

Van der Post admired her: 'I doubt whether any man is capable of a full
comprehension of what she was called on to endure, let alone measure her
achievements.' Her emotions fluctuated, as did Emma's. In one phase,
wanting Jung for herself, Toni tried to interfere in his family life; in another
phase, under the supervision of his assistant Carl Meier, the two women
took turns at analysing each other. According to him, Jung gave serious
consideration to the possibility of divorcing Emma, and there were three
times, according to Susanne Trub, when she was close to divorcing him. But
she relented – once when a storm blew up while he was on the lake and
almost capsized his boat. On both the other occasions too, he narrowly
escaped disaster. In the end Emma was generous enough to testify: 'I shall
always be grateful to Toni for doing for my husband what neither I nor
anyone else could have done for him at a most critical time.'

Buttressed by self-esteem, and unable or unwilling to differentiate between
the impulse to indulge himself and the prompting of his unconscious, which
he took to be infallible, Jung was ruthless with both women, putting them
under great strain, together with the children. One night, awakened by the
sobbing of his youngest daughter, he dressed and went out with Toni, saying
she could protect the family against emanations from his anima. And when he
had visions of Elijah and Salome, he said Salome personified the part of the
anima he had found in Toni. Having failed to find it in Emma, he said, he
needed it for the sake of his patients. To qualify himself for proper relationships with them, he must come to terms with his anima.

If Jung had been reminded by Helly of the olive-skinned maid, and by
Sabina of Helly, the dark, gentle, soulful Toni reminded him of all three, but
he was now the one who went into trancelike states, making contact with
dissociated parts of himself and treating them like real people. 'More than
anything else, it is a matter of differentiating between consciousness and the
contents of the unconscious. These must be isolated, as it were, and the
easiest method is to personify them and then put consciousness in touch with
them.' In his imaginary confrontation with his anima, he had felt, he said, as

if he were 'a patient in analysis with a female ghost'. Accepting the ghost as a lodger, he interrogated her

> whenever I felt my emotionality was disturbed and that I was plunged into restlessness. Then something was constellated in the unconscious. At such times I asked the anima: 'What's the matter with you now? What do you see? I'd like to know!' After some resistance, she invariably produced an image, and as soon as it was there, the disturbance or depression disappeared. The whole energy of my emotions was transformed into interest and curiosity about their contents.

Jung developed his theory of the anima with Toni in mind. 'Certain types of women seem to be made by nature to attract anima projections . . . The so-called sphinx-like character is an indispensable part of their equipment, also an equivocalness, an intriguing elusiveness . . . an indefiniteness that seems full of promise.' Such women are 'endowed with a naive cunning that is extremely disarming to men'.

In her own venture into female typology, Toni suggested that alongside the hetaira and the wife/mother there were two other types of woman: the amazonian and the mediumistic. The mediumistic type possesses less ego-consciousness than others. 'It carries and personifies the unconscious of other people or of its epoch . . . We know that the spiritual side of women is formed by the spiritual attitude of the father. The mediumistic type therefore not infrequently represents the unconscious, impersonal side of the masculine anima as so often happens between father and daughter.'

Less is known about Jung's relationship with Maria Moltzer, which may not have encroached on the triangle. Physically more like Emma, Maria had an intensity, an intelligence and a spirituality that rivalled those of Sabina and Toni. She seems, unlike Toni, to have been of little help during the breakdown, which may have enabled Toni to displace her.

Jung went on claiming scientific status for his activities, presenting samples of his dreams, fantasies and delusions as if they could be analysed microscopically. He thought humanity would benefit from what he was doing.

> There were things in the images that concerned not only me but many other people. That is how it became my duty no longer to belong to myself. From then on my life belonged to the public. The knowledge which concerned me and which I was seeking could not be found in the science of that period. I had to undergo the original experience myself, and

also try to establish the experiences on the soil of reality . . . It was then
that I dedicated myself to the service of the soul.

Those who say their life belongs to the public are usually suffering from
solitude or delusions of grandeur or both. In spite of his relationship with
Toni, in spite of sharing a home with Emma and the children, in spite of
being surrounded by patients, disciples and well-wishers, Jung was essentially
a solitary. For years, Toni could share his solitude, but as he recovered his
equilibrium, he outgrew his need for her, and their intimacy began to
dwindle. And though he had a genius for making close contact – as he had
with Otto Gross – there were few men who called him 'Carl', as Riklin did,
or spoke to him in the second-person singular.

During the breakdown he recognised 'the same psychic material that
forms the basis of psychosis and that is found in a lunatic asylum'. But he
took it to be the 'matrix of the myth-making imagination which has
vanished from our rational age'. His mission, he thought, was to restore
it. Though Frank Miller had tried to convert dreams, fantasies and visions
into art, and though other artists have drawn on this source more successfully
than she did, Jung, unlike Nietzsche, put art on a much lower plane than
religion, and once he had silenced the voice that told him he was doing
artistic work, he could tell himself he was working scientifically on his own
nightmares, fantasies and hallucinations. In this way he succeeded in staving
off madness, and his patients never lost faith in him. At the end of 1913,
sixteen days after Jung let himself 'plummet into the dark depths', Harold
McCormick wrote to reassure his father-in-law, John D. Rockefeller, that
Edith was 'in absolutely safe and trustworthy hands, for no finer man ever
breathed than Dr Jung'.

This did not tally with Jung's image of himself. He would have felt better
if he had not forfeited Sabina's respect. 'The tone of your letter touched me
to the quick,' he wrote in the spring, 'for I see that you too despise me.
Respect for the human personality and its motives should not be undermined by psychoanalysis. Because I fight for it, I must suffer much.'

Both in his dreams and when awake, he alternated between self-
glorification and self-abasement. In April, May and July he had the same
nightmare three times. In Sumatra with a friend, he was told Europe was in
the grip of a cold wave. It was midsummer when they went home, but the
land had been frozen to ice, as had the canals. Nothing green was visible
throughout Lorraine; human life had disappeared. But the third time he had
this dream, the ending was happy. On one tree the leaves had frozen into
sweet grapes, full of healing juices. Jung picked these and distributed them to
a large crowd. He was identifying with Dionysus.

Eighteen

Preaching to the Dead

After Emma gave birth on 14 March 1914 to their fifth child, a daughter they called Helene, the thirty-nine-year-old father was too disoriented to concentrate on either of them. His instinct was to withdraw: in April he resigned from his presidency of the International Psychoanalytical Association and from the university. Relieved he would not have to fight for leadership of the movement, Freud wrote to Abraham: 'You must have been just as surprised as I was at how meticulous Jung was in carrying out our intentions.'

At the university, after eight years of lecturing without a salary as a *Privatdozent*, he had expected to be offered a position on the staff, and hearing that his status was to remain the same, he withdrew. He would have found it difficult, in any event, to teach. 'For three years I could read no scientific books. This made me feel I could no longer keep up with the intellectual world.' But he neither gave up his private practice nor resigned from the association.

Feeling in need of a holiday, Jung went on a cycling tour of northern Italy with Hans Schmid, his junior by six years. The contrast between Schmid's personality and his helped Jung to develop his ideas about psychological types. If Schmid was a feeling extravert, he was a thinking introvert, and at first he equated feeling with extraversion, thinking with introversion. After the holiday, corresponding about typology with Schmid, who lived in Basel, Jung acknowledged: 'I owe a great deal of clarification to this interchange of ideas.'

The Jungs were now as close to the Schmids as to any other couple, except the Riklins. Jung was godfather to the Schmids' younger daughter, and the Schmids were Helene's godparents. But nine years later, sending a photograph of himself, Jung inscribed it 'To Herr Doktor Schmid'. According to their elder daughter, Marie-Jeanne, 'Frau Jung used to say she was rather sorry that Jung had no real friends.'

In the spring of 1914, Freud asked Sabina whether she would like her name to appear on the masthead of the new yearbook. This would indicate 'the clearest sort of partisanship' – something she might prefer not to proclaim 'at a time when you are still in love with Jung, when you cannot be really angry with him, when you see him still as the hero hounded by the mob'. She ought to 'throw aside as so much rubbish your infantile fantasies of the Germanic champion and hero'. These were fomenting her resistance to her background and her origins. Frustrated in childhood when she wanted her father to give her a baby, she had transferred the expectation to 'this phantom'.

Only eighteen months had gone by since Freud had told Ferenczi the personal and intellectual bonds with Jung would hold fast for years, but in his history of the movement, which was published in the yearbook during July, he wrote that with his 'modification' of psychoanalysis, Jung had 'given us a counterpart to the famous Lichtenberg knife. He has changed the hilt and put a new blade into it; yet because the same name is engraved on it, we are expected to regard the new instrument as the old one.'

After reading Freud's essay, Jung resigned from the association and started work on building himself an independent career. He already had a good foothold in the English-speaking world. The January 1914 issue of the *British Medical Journal* welcomed his revisionism as a return to 'a saner view of life', and he accepted an invitation to lecture in July at the annual meeting of the British Medical Association in Aberdeen. Talking 'On the Importance of the Unconscious in Psychopathology', he avoided the word *psychoanalysis*, substituting 'prospective psychology'. He referred to Freud briefly and laconically: 'To Freud we owe thanks . . . for having called attention to the importance of dreams.' The psychologist W. McDougall immediately wanted Jung to analyse him.

His approach to analysis had altered. By the spring of 1914, he was orienting sessions towards what he thought he had learned from the Spirit of the Depths, Philemon and Ka. Having always hungered for spiritual rebirth, he now thought he could guide patients towards it through the realm of primordial images. (He was not yet calling them *archetypes*.)

Dealing with patients, he put his new ideas into immediate circulation. His visions and fantasy figures reached the Rockefeller family. 'We must all fulfil our greater Destiny,' Edith told her father in June 1914. 'The great Divine Guardian Spirit cannot do things wrong.' Jung later described her as a 'latent schizophrenic'.

In the summer of 1914 he started applying spiritualistic ideas to clinical practice. His patients were taught how to make contact with their internal god through *active imagination*, a technique he had developed out of his conversations with figures in his fantasies, and indirectly out of his experiences with Helly. Though he was no longer using hypnotism, the trance state was involved, and, as Shamdasani has argued, quoting from William James and the Belgian psychologist Josef Delboeuf, suggestions from a doctor often exert more power than is apparent over the patient's behaviour. In *Principles of Psychology*, James shows that in hypnosis

> any sort of personal peculiarity, any trick accidentally fallen into in the first instance by some one subject, may, by attracting attention, become stereotyped, serve as a pattern for imitation, and figure as the type of a school. The first subject trains the operator trains the succeeding subjects, all of them in perfect good faith conspiring together to evolve a perfectly arbitrary result.

It might seem impossible that a girl who was not yet fourteen when the seances started could have trained Jung and effectively launched his school, but if Helly loved him, this would have increased her sensitivity to his suggestions, while the hypnotism may have reinforced the love. One of the early mesmerists, the Marquis de Puységur, found that his patient Victor Race not only carried out all his orders but seemed to anticipate what he was going to say next. As James goes on to say,

> With the extraordinary perspicacity and subtlety of perception which subjects often display for all that concerns the operator with whom they are *en rapport*, it is hard to keep them ignorant of everything he expects. Thus it happens that one easily verifies on new subjects what one has already seen on old ones, or any desired symptom of which one may have heard or read.

Teaching patients to isolate subpersonalities and enter into dialogue with them, Jung was letting them benefit from what Helly had done during seances and what he had done during his breakdown, but at the same time he was developing what he had learned in 1914 after reading a book by Herbert Silberer, a Viennese Freudian who committed suicide nine years later. Their indebtedness was mutual. Silberer used the term *imago*, which Jung had introduced, and developed Jung's theory of psychological types. Jung never acknowledged what he owed to an article Silberer had published in 1909 about efforts to think actively while in a drowsy state. What he called 'the autosymbolic phenomenon' could occur in the twilight between sleeping and waking. Without any exertion of willpower, thoughts were transformed into images that allegorised the ideas. As Dan Merkur has pointed out, Jung was following this lead when he developed 'active imagination'. But 'where Silberer had explored the unconscious symbolisation of conscious ideas, Jung sought the manifestation of symbols and ideas that had never before been conscious.'

He encouraged patients to make drawings or paintings of figures who appeared in fantasies, and then to interrogate them. In a note about her drawings, Fanny Bowditch wrote: 'I must learn to understand them and how each of them can be lived. Certain archaic tendencies and certain spiritual aspirations too low or too high to be lived . . . The possibility of developing from the very low to the very high. Of the value and importance of recognising one's archaic tendencies as part of oneself – loving them as being a part of one's soul.'

Tina Keller was in her late twenties, and married to one of the two Swiss pastors who had joined the circle of psychiatrists studying Freud under Bleuler. After the Munich conference, the other pastor, Oskar Pfitzer, sided with Freud, while Adolphe and Tina Keller attended the open evenings Jung was holding in his Küsnacht house. Suffering from anxiety attacks, she went to Jung for analysis in 1915, before and during her third pregnancy. He explained that instead of putting questions to him, she could put them to herself at home, 'for there are answers inside you if you really want those answers and are not afraid of them'. It was a matter of 'letting the unconscious come up'.

When she wrote out questions and waited in vain for answers, he told her: 'You know what prayer is.' She then began to write kneeling. The first results were 'a jumble of words without connection or meaning. Then gradually there came several different answers as if from different persons. I think I then started to write conversations between the different voices. It was painful to find these different voices inside me.' She oscillated between self-confidence and uncontrollable anxiety. 'Imagination had always con-jured up possibilities of danger; during analysis these apprehensions seemed to become more acute and at times the images I saw with my mind's eye took on an uncanny reality.'

Jung was teaching her to function like a medium, and eventually a tall, dark, straight-backed figure presented himself, saying he was her doctor. She was scared, but after each visitation, she made notes on what he said and did. He put his top hat on the floor, brim upwards, and, like a conjuror, pulled out a dead frog and some eggshells. He was disagreeably sarcastic, but sometimes his presence brought her close to orgasm. When she showed Jung what she had written, he laughed, which put an end to the fantasies, but they resumed when Toni Wolff took over as her analyst.

As Jung's idea of archetypes became clearer, it began to have more effect on the way he handled transference. Ernest Jones reported: 'The patient overcomes it by learning that she is not really in love with the analyst but that she is for the first time struggling to comprehend a Universal Idea in Plato's sense.' Tina Keller writes:

> Dr Jung never spoke of *transference* but obliged me to face the fact that I was *in love* with some quality or archetype which he represented, and had touched in my psyche. If and in the measure that I would be able to realise this unknown element in myself, then I would be free of him as a person . . . He said that what I brought was such an openness that he owed me some spiritual value that would fertilise my psyche and my *individuation* would be a *spiritual child*.

After a long period of keeping his religious inclinations to himself, Jung was making more use of them in clinical practice, trying to give nonbelievers a substitute for the religion they had lost. In 1958, describing his relationship with his guru, Christopher Isherwood wrote: 'I have arrived at this formulation: religion – as I understand it – means a relationship. Either directly with God, or with someone who has a relationship with God: belief in another's belief.' Jung was offering his patients an opportunity to believe in his belief. But Tina Keller and her husband formed the impression that the Spirit of the Depths had not entirely cured Jung of his narcissism. It had invaded his relationship with Sabina when he encouraged her to believe in the spiritual child they would have together, and it influenced the way he dealt with Tina Keller's transference.

On 10 July 1914 the Zurich association of psychoanalysts formally seceded from the International Psychoanalytical Association. Maeder was in the chair when fifteen of the sixteen members present voted in favour of the resolution. The reason given in the minutes is that in the yearbook Freud had unequivocally claimed psychoanalysis depended on the doctrines of a single individual. This was incompatible with 'the principles of free research'. Four months later, the Zurich group gave itself a new name – the Association for Analytical Psychology – and Jung accepted the presidency.

He was still in Aberdeen at the beginning of August, when Germany declared war on France. While the German army swept through Belgium, troop trains were given priority on the tracks, and panic-stricken tourists fought for space in overcrowded carriages. After several uncomfortable nights on trains that had been shunted into sidings, Jung succeeded in reaching Switzerland.

He felt more reassured than worried by the outbreak of war, which enabled him to regard his dreams and visions as prophetic. Speaking in English, later, he said: 'I had the feeling that I was an over-compensated psychosis, and from this feeling I was not released until August 1st 1914.' That was the day Germany declared war on Russia. His first obligation now, he said, was to probe the depths of his psyche to find out how far his experience 'coincided with that of mankind in general'.

If Jung had consulted Bleuler – who had, after all, written a book on schizophrenia – he might have been told his dreams and visions were symptomatic, even if Bleuler had not heard the rumours that the family described in Jung's thesis was the Preiswerks. On the other hand, if his experience 'coincided with that of mankind in general', he could think of himself as a leader. Leaders, as he said, are often schizophrenic or paranoiac:

It is precisely because these people often have fantasies and dreams that are collectively valid that they get followers. First they make a break with the world through their morbidity, then comes the revelation of a special mission, and then they begin to preach. People think of them as thrilling personalities, and women think it a tremendous honour to have children by them. By primitives they are imagined to be full of gods and ghosts.

Nor did he ever become more than superficially concerned about the slaughter and devastation. Writing in English during 1915 to Smith Ely Jeliffe, he said:

In these days the incurable wounded of the French and German armies pass through Switzerland. I have seen them yesterday. It is terrible. You have no idea how mad people in Germany, France and England have become since the war. In Switzerland we are rather normal. It is a most psychological war. It will leave certain traces in the European mind which will be of interest . . . The sky of Europe becomes more and more dark. We are in a pretty uncomfortable situation in our island . . . It is interesting to see how difficult it is even with us, to maintain the order against the madness of the people. The general madness is most infectious – you can hardly imagine this abyss of primeval foolishness which usurped the European mind. One sees no end.

Switzerland was an island in so far as neutrality isolated it, but in 1916, denouncing the war as 'an epidemic of madness', Jung did not claim immunity either for himself or for Switzerland. In the perspective of the European chaos, his own imbalance must seem negligible, and his patients took comfort from his presence as he talked about his ideas and preoccupations, showing them drawings he had done to illustrate dreams and visions. 'He often spoke of himself and his own experience,' wrote Tina Keller.

'One felt accepted into the very special atmosphere of the discovery of the inner world and of its mystery.'

The outbreak of collective madness made it impossible for them to go on trusting the criteria, values and institutions that had made life seem secure. 'I was one of a group gathered round an explorer trying to penetrate life's mysteries.' If the world outside Switzerland was destroying itself, 'a small group around Dr Jung participated in his vision of an inner world unfolding.' They felt privileged.

It was an unlikely habitat for multimillionaires, but instead of taking Edith home, Harold McCormick settled in Zurich, wanting to be analysed himself, and at the end of November 1914 he wrote: 'Dr Jung grows on me all the time.' But they did not share the hardships that war was inflicting on the Swiss. Since petrol was in short supply, doctors were the only private citizens allowed to drive cars, but after Edith's chauffeur had negotiated a deal with the General Staff, she was allowed to import petrol, tyres and spare parts, on condition that she sold some cheaply to the army.

When her mother died in the spring of 1915, Edith refused to go home for the funeral. She told her father. 'We cannot mourn for the beautiful spirit which has gone beyond us, for we know that it is living on and developing.' When Fowler was seventeen, she arranged for him to start analysis with Riklin, and when some of Jung's writings were about to appear in an English translation, she went through the proofs for him, making corrections.

Harold was becoming more than a mere patient. In the last week of August 1915 he joined Jung, Emma and Toni Wolff on a walking holiday in the mountains. 'There were only two or three times when things went for a little while wrong – "resistances" or "repressions" on my part but these were easily cleared by talking out.' Praising Harold for becoming more 'balanced', Jung said it was hard to know from his behaviour whether he was an extravert or an introvert. Jung, he decided, was 'as nearly perfect . . . as a man can be', and Harold was delighted with the changes he could see in himself. He had the impression of knowing himself and liking his own company more than ever. He was told he had been in the habit of feeling too much and thinking too little, while Edith's tendencies were in the opposite direction. Following Jung's advice, he tried to think more, and she tried to feel more.

But Jung was spending less time with the McCormicks than with Riklin, Toni, her younger sister Susanne, and two of Susanne's lovers: the psychiatrist Hans Trüb, who later married her, and a Russian, Emilii Medtner, younger brother of the composer Nikolai Medtner. Emilii had married in 1903, but his wife, Anna, was now pregnant by Nikolai. Emilii had extraordinarily piercing eyes: Jung said he had seen nothing like them except on canvases by Botticelli and Filippo Lippi. He also said Emilii resembled Hindenburg. After consulting Bleuler in 1913, he had been referred to Jung, who diagnosed 'intellectual hypertrophy' and started seeing him five times a week. He said Medtner was the most modern man he had ever met, combining the psychology of an eighteenth-century German with the 'modern yet archaic' psychology of a Russian.

Medtner thought Jung had saved him from going mad, but he did not regard Jung as entirely sane. Goethe, he said, had foreseen psychoanalysis as 'a psychic cure in which insanity is sent in to cure insanity'. Jung, wrote Medtner, 'says I am fair with everybody, too fair, but entirely unfair to myself, especially to Konrad. It is terribly amusing and pleasant to hear him say how he quarrels with Konrad (his own Konrad, that is) – how he consults him, defers to him, pampers him.' In Carl Spitteler's 1906 novel *Imago*, Konrad is the body.

When Jung was not in Zurich, Medtner was analysed by Maria Moltzer, whom he described as 'penetrating, businesslike and sly'. She and Jung both tried to make him less intellectual in order to develop his spirituality. His talent for intimacy bordered on genius, and he made more impact on Jung than any male patient since Otto Gross. Jung enjoyed his company and they talked to each other in the second-person singular. Nikolai said: 'It is very healing for me that Jung is so cheerful, even though he is so terribly self-absorbed and complex.' If we are to believe a letter Emilii later sent to Anna, he succeeded in seducing Toni. He also impressed Edith McCormick, who wanted him to be her secretary and settle in Chicago. He refused, but she let him persuade her that 'sick Russia' could be healed by Jung, and she agreed to pay for a Russian translation of his books.

Edith and Harold were used to being courted by people who needed money, but they had never been more eager to give than they were to Jung. The Association for Analytical Psychology was still meeting in the Restaurant Seidenhof, but the possibility now emerged of making it into something more like an English or American club – at this time there were no clubs of this sort in Switzerland.

In the centre of the city Harold found a building big enough to serve as a clubhouse for analysts and patients, with space for accommodation and a restaurant, as well as for lectures and seminars. It was in Löwenstrasse, and Edith rented it for two and a half years, which cost $120,000. Borrowing more than half from a bank, she had expected to repay the debt quickly, but went on subsidising running costs that were surprisingly high, and by March 1920, she was over $800,000 in debt. 'This work is unique in the history of mankind,' she told her father. 'For a cause such as this I would willingly make a bigger loan.'

Remaining the 'proprietor' of the club, she took decisions about policy, decoration, furniture and arrangements of the rooms, orienting everything to her own taste and her memories of exclusive American clubs. Installing a billiard table, she employed a hostess, a cook, three servants and a main-tenance man, and Emilii Medtner persuaded her to give him a salary as club librarian. The policy was to exclude nonmembers and have only twenty members.

Even when more members were admitted, the restaurant and accomm-odation were too expensive for most of them, and another problem was that the club had two functions, one social and the other partly educational, partly therapeutic. Previously, patients had seldom seen each other, except in Jung's waiting room, and, as Barbara Hannah tells us, he 'increasingly felt that they needed a social group as a *reality* basis for what they were learning in psychology . . . and he began to feel the need for opportunities to get to know his patients and their reactions in a setting nearer to outer life than the consulting room and the analytical hour.'

Though he disapproved of group analysis, he did think 'he could learn much more about certain aspects of his patients by seeing them in a group than by what they told him during their hours'. Or as he said, 'We know enough about how someone who has been analysed reacts to someone who has not, and vice versa, but what is not known is how analysed people interact . . . We know nothing about the collective function of individuals and its conditions.'

More concerned with the social activities, Edith tended to forget that patients differed in class, taste and outlook from her circle of acquaintances in Chicago. Her son Fowler remembered 'very clearly Father feeling how little most of the members at that time . . . knew about social life and how to have a sociable time. Father used to laugh about some of the efforts to have joyous evenings and how they fell flat. It was all considered to be trivial and too light.'

According to the minutes for the inaugural general meeting of the Psychological Club on 26 February 1916, most of the preparatory work had been done by the McCormicks, the Jungs, Hermann Sigg, E. P. Teucher and Toni Wolff. Although Jung was the pivotal figure, he wanted neither to be president nor to be involved in running the club. He may have been remembering how Freud had refused to be president of the interna-tional association. Jung offered the club presidency to Alphonse Maeder, who had taken over from him as president of the association, but he objected: 'In the background, all the strings are in your hand. Only what you want will be done. Only what you say will be accepted.' The presidency was finally given to Emma. Sigg was appointed treasurer, and Irma Oczeret secretary.

Maeder remained a member of the Association for Analytical Psychology – the group of analysts that now replaced the Zurich Psychoanalytical Association. In a circular letter dated 20 April 1916, Jung invited him, together with Riklin, Toni, Maria Moltzer, Herbert Oczeret and Dr C. Schneiter to attend regular fortnightly meetings in the clubhouse on Saturday mornings, starting on 13 May. 'At each meeting a formulation will be made on the basis of the collective discussion, and minutes will be kept.' The Psychological Club kept its premises in Löwenstrasse until 1919, when it moved to the house that is still its base, in Gemeindestrasse, near the Kunsthaus and the Schauspielhaus – the art gallery and the theatre.

The devil, who often featured – not just metaphorically – in Jung's thinking, played a prominent part in his mental confusion. In November 1915, without equating him with Freud, Jung evoked the devil to describe the desire to understand reality on a scientific and materialistic level. A fourteenth-century saint, Birgitta of Sweden, had given him insight into devils, he said; she had learned from a vision that their bellies were swollen because their greed was boundless. The desire to *comprehend* was the desire to devour.

> The devil's will lurks in the desire to understand, ethical and human though it sounds . . . Understanding is a frightfully binding power, at times a true murder of the soul . . . The core of the individual is a mystery, which is wiped out as soon as it is 'grasped' . . . The symbol wants to protect itself against Freudian interpretations, which are really such pseudo-truths that they never fail to be effective . . . 'Analytical' under-standing of our patients can have a wholesomely destructive effect, like a corrosive or cauterisation, but on sound tissue it is damagingly destructive. It is a technique we have learned from the devil . . . The threatening and dangerous thing about analysis is that the individual is apparently under-stood: the devil eats away the soul which, naked and exposed, robbed of its protective shell, was born like a child into the light.

He may have been remembering Dostoevsky's Ivan Karamazov, who says: 'I made up my mind long ago not to understand. If I try to understand anything, I shall be false to the facts, and I am determined to stick to the facts.'

In 1916 Jung had a fantasy that his soul had flown away from him, had withdrawn into the unconscious, or into the collectivity of the dead. There it was the soul that gave forms to residue from ancestors – the collective contents of the unconscious. 'Like a medium, it gives the "dead" an opportunity to materialise.'

Not long afterwards, Agathe saw a white figure passing through her room. Gret had the blanket snatched off her bed twice, and Franz had a nightmare about the devil. At five the next afternoon, the doorbell started ringing. Jung could see the bell moving, but nobody was at the door. The house was full of ghosts, and he challenged them: 'For God's sake, what's all this about?' They answered in chorus: 'We have come back from Jerusalem, where we could not find what we were seeking.'

The haunting came to a climax the next afternoon. 'The air was thick, I can tell you! Then I knew it was going to happen. The whole house was packed, as if there were a crowd in it – crammed with ghosts. They were standing there, all the way to the door, and one could hardly breathe.' But they dispersed as soon as he started writing.

We are not intended to read this as a mixture of fantasy and delusion, but as objective facts about the soul and about a series of events that could have been witnessed by anyone who happened to be present. When he wrote down his fantasy that his soul had flown away from him, he meant it had withdrawn into the unconscious, which corresponded to the collectivity of the dead, where the soul, he thought, gave form to residue from ancestors – the collective contents of the unconscious. 'Like a medium, it gives the "dead" an opportunity to appear.'

It is questionable whether his children would have corroborated what he said about the ghosts. Franz's age is given as nine, though the book says this happened during the summer of 1916, when he was only seven. But the experience – whatever it was – made Jung write something different from the records of dreams and fantasies which were all he had produced for three years. He completed *Septem Sermones ad Mortuos (Seven Sermons to the Dead)* within three days by a process akin to automatic writing. The sermons, he said, fell unexpectedly into his lap like a ripe fruit. He attributed them to 'one of those great minds of the early Christian era which Christianity obliterated'. He was referring to the Gnostic Basilides, who lived in Alexandria during the second century AD, but there are contradictory accounts of what he taught – one in Hippolytus and the other in Irenaeus – and here his name is not much more than a pseudonym. Outlawed by the Christian Roman emperors, Gnosticism survived in Syria and Persia, where it was absorbed into Manicheism, founded by the third-century Persian Mani, who taught a dualism grounded in independent cosmic powers of good and evil: evil is a substance; spirit represents light and matter darkness.

Jung's starting point was the sentence that presented itself to him in the vision about crusaders who said they had come back from Jerusalem, where they had failed to find what they were seeking. Like patients or parishioners, they wanted Jung to explain the meaning of life. Sermons had, in reality, sometimes been preached to the dead: this is said to have happened in Basel when Paul Achilles Jung was a priest there.

According to the first of Jung's *Seven Sermons*, the essence of created being is dissimilarity – the principle of individuation. He contrasts the emptiness of material things with the *pleroma*, which contains the sum total of God's powers and emanations. Confined within time and space, we are distanced from the pleroma, but we have certain polarities in common with it – between good and evil, light and dark, life and death.

The second sermon affirms the existence of a god superior to both God, who represents fullness, and the devil, who represents emptiness. The superior god, Abraxas, is equated not only with the concept of efficacy but also with the unknown and unconscious. Abraxas produces both truth and falsehood. But for the real Basilides, Abraxas had been identical with the inferior demiurge – neither the supreme god nor a unification of good and evil. There is no Gnostic precedent for Jung's version of him, or for the assertion that divinity exists inside the individual soul.

The last sermon affirms that salvation or rebirth can be achieved by looking inwards. At the zenith of the inner world is a star which is our guiding god. This star or sun or god should be the goal of our pilgrimages. Our relationship with God takes place within the individual soul.

At the end of the seventh sermon, the ghosts go gratefully away in search of their inner gods. In Jerusalem they had heard only doctrines like those preached by Paul Achilles Jung, but now, thanks to his son, they are enlightened. Believing his unconscious had been shaped by familial experience, Jung thought it was for him to fulfil tasks neglected by his ancestors. 'I could well imagine I might have lived in earlier centuries where I encountered questions I could not yet answer; that I had to be born again because I had not fulfilled the task given to me . . . Perhaps it is a question that preoccupied my ancestors, who could not answer it.'

Though it was a relief that Jung had resumed writing, he could not always control his behaviour when he was with other people. In the clubhouse, according to Tina Keller, he 'could be vulgar' and 'made fun of people in an unfeeling way'. Shocked, she 'avoided going to any of the social gatherings'. When he was in the audience at a lecture, he would make loud interpolations. 'That doesn't exist at all.' Or, sitting next to Toni Wolff, he would whisper and giggle with her. When other people were performing, he liked to draw attention back to himself.

According to Alphonse Maeder, he had the same fault that he criticised in

Freud: 'he couldn't bear his collaborators to be independent.' In the autumn of 1916, when the club held its first banquet in the new building, Maeder's after-dinner speech infuriated him, and Fanny Bowditch joined in the argument, telling Jung: 'You really have lied here.' Livid, he stalked out of the room, and when she followed him, he told her: 'Here blood will flow.' Maeder then suggested they should spend the evening together the next day. Jung agreed, but they did not talk about the quarrel.

In an unpublished report on 'The Welfare of the Psychology Club', Harold McCormick declared misgivings about 'the spectacle of orthodox religious circles fighting among themselves' over questions that strike onlookers as unimportant. The existence of the club intensified Jung's problem's with male patients and followers. It seemed to them that he was favouring the women, choosing them as his 'assistants' and delegating important work to them. Maria Moltzer was allocated patients of her own, and they made their payments directly to her. She 'worked quite independently and quite efficiently', Jung said. There is evidence that like Toni and Sabina, she became a good analyst, but as he went on alienating more of his male colleagues, he replaced them by promoting female patients whose only qualification was the experience of being analysed and attending the lectures and seminars.

The most disastrous of these promotions was that of Edith McCormick, who was still a relatively new patient. She rarely ventured outside the hotel, and her chauffeur's only job was driving her to Küsnacht and back. Her patients came to see her in the hotel, and by November 1916, she was spending six hours a day with them. In March 1919 she reported to her father: 'New patients are coming to me all the time and I have had some fifty cases now. I hear in a year twelve thousand dreams . . . It is so beautiful to see life and joy come into the eyes of those who have come to me so hopeless and seemingly lost!'

The main reason for her popularity was that she gave money to patients who convinced her they needed it. A young musician was presented with a villa in the centre of the city, and an attractive young Austrian with enough money to buy Swiss citizenship. She stopped going to see Jung, and cancelled appointments with other patients in order to spend more time with the Austrian. Soon she was overheard telling Harold he must never come into her rooms without being announced by her secretary. When Jung warned her about the danger of scandal, she retorted: 'This is my problem, and I can do what I please.'

She encouraged her chauffeur, a married man, to start an affair with her pretty secretary and to stay with her overnight. 'If your unconscious causes you to love several women,' Edith told him, 'you need not feel any guilt.'

Nineteen

The Importance of Going Astray

In 1916, writing on what he called the *transcendent function*, Jung said it fused inner and outer experience, or conscious and unconscious thinking. He rejects psychoanalysis and free association in favour of singling out strands of unconscious thinking by lending them voices and by listening to inner voices as if they were people. 'It took me a long time,' he said, 'to adapt to something in myself that was not myself – that is, to the fact that there were in my individual mind parts that did not pertain to me.' But this is what he had been doing ever since the dream about the giant penis and the fantasy about the shitting God.

What he did during his creative illness was refine his technique for dealing with the something that was not himself. 'If you can isolate these uncon-scious phenomena by personifying them, that is a technique that works for stripping them of power.' He had not been trying to gain power over Elijah and Philemon any more than Helly had over the grandfathers and Ivenes, but his technique of buttonholing his anima or cross-questioning his visions was in line with his experience of seances. 'For the understanding of the unconscious, we must see our thoughts as events, as phenomena. We must have perfect objectivity.' This is not what most people mean by objectivity, but he meant that the dreams and fantasies belonged to a reality that had existed before the individual who was cross-questioning them.

According to Ellenberger, 'The termination of a creative illness usually occurs rapidly and is followed by a short phase of euphoria, a feeling of exhilaration and a need for activity . . . When the outcome of such an experiment is successful, it is manifested in a permanent change of person-ality.' Jung emerged from his years of withdrawal with increased self-assurance, though he also had 'an increased propensity to intuitions, psychical experiences and meaningful dreams. It is another characteristic of those who have lived through such a spiritual adventure to attribute a universal value to their own personal experience.'

The main value of Jung's experience lay in the power it gave him to rescue other victims of disorientation. Like the child terrified by the disembodied head outside his mother's room, by the fear that Jesus might eat him, by a father who chanted at funerals, by black-clad uncles in clerical collars and Jesuits in female disguise, the adult Jung did not always want to distinguish between hallucination and reality, even retrospectively. Had the house been full of ghosts? Had Philemon been walking with him in the garden and giving him new information? These questions are irrelevant if mental events are no less real than events other people can witness.

At the Burghölzli he had helped schizophrenics by talking to characters in their delusions. He now helped himself by talking to characters in his own, and when he felt most at risk, he would lie down and do yoga exercises, but he went on giving advice to patients, and lost few of them.

In the book *Jung's Treatment of Christianity*, Murray Stein has analysed the pattern recurrent throughout his life. There were three stages. The

> persecutory inner object would be defended against by the use of paranoid thoughts and fantasies, which would function to place it 'out there'; the crisis would then be followed by an experience of relief and restoration; and the final step would be an attempt to integrate the good and bad sides of the self, often in a symbolic formulation (paintings of mandalas, concepts of God as *unio oppositorum*, psychological theories).

In childhood Jung's precarious sense of identity had made impulses to blasphemy and obscenity seem so dangerous that he externalised them with the paranoid image of a God who was himself guilty of aggression, blasphemy and obscenity. What seems odd is that none of Jung's subsequent experience of mental illness made him question his early assumptions about God's method of communicating with him.

The idea of an autonomous unconscious, which derives from these notions, survived throughout Jung's intellectual development. We needed neither Freud nor him to tell us that our willpower has no control over our dreams. But in formulating his theories of archetypes and the collective unconscious, Jung argues that the psyche exists outside place and time.

If everyone shares the same psyche, we have no criterion for establishing the validity of what people present as psychic events. Are the delusions of a schizoid psychiatrist less pathological than those of a schizophrenic patient? Stein contends that Jung's 'particular personal psychic structures' were 'keyed in' to 'deeper dynamics and energy structures in the collective unconscious'. It is our responsibility, he says, to 'recognise the archetypal dimension upon which these personal dynamics rest, and which they reflect'.

Proposing a 'constructive' method of dream interpretation, Jung criticised Freud's 'reductive' analysis. Citing a dream about a Celtic dagger that once belonged to a patient's dominating father, he said a Freudian analyst might focus on her fantasies about the phallic weapon and her involvements with men weaker than her father. Jung saw the dagger as part of her heritage. Passive and self-pitying, she had led a frustrating life, but she was entitled to fulfil herself no less than her father had. The transcendent function is 'an individual-collective phenomenon which in principle agrees with the direction of life anyone would follow, if he were to live in a completely unconscious, instinctive way'.

Like her, many people repress their instinctive life, but, bypassing the critical faculty, constructive analysis can release unconscious fantasies. Instinct can subvert conformism, and, in Jung's opinion, Nietzsche had liberated himself by writing *Zarathustra*. From then on 'the secret counteraction of the unconscious' became more apparent in his work.

To unchain fantasies and achieve dissociation of consciousness, people who are 'visual types' should 'concentrate on the expectation that an inner image will be produced'. Observing it carefully, they can make notes or sketches. 'Audio-verbal types usually hear inner words, perhaps mere fragments of apparently meaningless sentences.' While the insane hear the inner voice clearly, it is less distinct to the sane, but they can gain control over their fantasies by writing. To follow his advice is to do what artists and writers of fiction do, but 'the danger of the aesthetic tendency is overvaluation of the formal or "artistic" value of the fantasy-products; diverted from the real object of the transcendent function, the libido is sidetracked into purely aesthetic problems of artistic expression.' The symbolic meaning of the writing or drawing is lost when it is analysed intellectually.

He was not concerned about the extent to which dreams, fantasies and semiconscious images change as soon as conscious effort is exerted. To him this was only a matter of clarifying something that had been vague.

> Often the hands can solve a riddle that is baffling the intellect. By shaping it, one goes on dreaming the dream in greater detail in the waking state, and the initially incomprehensible, isolated event is integrated into the sphere of the total personality . . . The less the initial material is shaped and developed, the greater is the danger that understanding will be governed not by the empirical facts but by theoretical and moral considerations.

Jung would ask new patients to write down some of their dreams, illustrating the narrative if they could. At the first session he read through these written reports as if they corresponded exactly with the experiences of the sleeping mind. But writing a dream down involves the intellect.

He regarded dream analysis as 'the central problem of the analytical treatment, because it is the most important technical means of opening up an avenue to the unconscious'. Dreams, he insisted, are 'objective facts' and they are independent of our willpower but they are 'as difficult to read as the facts of physiology have always been difficult to read . . . The more interesting dreams are very thrilling, but they are easier to understand than the minor ones.' The only significance of these is private, and perhaps there had been no 'big' dreams of public importance since a Roman senator's daughter dreamed the goddess Minerva appeared in her dream to complain that her temple was being neglected. When this was reported to the senators, they decided to have the temple rebuilt.

Generally Jung tended to treat dreams as if they were statements in a foreign language, sometimes difficult to translate but never untranslatable. The losses involved in treating them like this could hardly have been explained more clearly than he explained them himself at the end of his life when he said that an inner experience which consists of 'spontaneous natural emotion or *ekstasis*' is 'the complete opposite of a methodically construed imitation'. It 'has a tendency to succumb again and again to the sensualism and rationalism of consciousness, i.e. to literal-mindedness. The result is that one tries to repeat a spontaneous, irrational event by a deliberate, imitative arrangement of the analogous circumstances which had apparently led to the original event.' Dreams resist any attempts to solidify them through writing or painting.

'The Transcendent Function' remained unpublished till 1957. The *Septem Sermones* had not appeared in print; and Jung was not lecturing at the university – which means he had made no public statement since his crisis. His first lecture to the faculty (which had been reconstituted as the Zurich School for Analytical Psychology) was on 'The Structure of the Unconscious'. He also gave a script to Flournoy, who, later in 1916, published a translation of it in the *Archives de Psychologie*. This was Jung's first appearance in print since 1914.

He does not explicitly contradict anything he had said about the transcendent function, and he claims that 'access to the collective psyche means a renewal of life for the individual', but his approach is cautious, and he focuses on obstacles in the way of understanding the collective psyche. Again using Adler as a stalking horse, Jung picked up the term he had applied to a pathological state involving delusions of superiority – *godlikeness*. Jung applies it to his concept of a collective unconscious. There are two levels in the unconscious, he contends: personal and impersonal. Everyone is born with a brain that 'makes him capable of a wide range of mental functioning which is neither developed ontogenetically nor acquired'. The mind is neither self-contained nor wholly individual. There are a collective mind, a collective soul and a collective psyche, by which he meant nonindividual thinking, nonindividual feeling and the nonindividual psychological functions as a whole. Since there were 'differentiations corresponding to race, tribe and even family, there is also a collective psyche limited to race, tribe and family over and above the "universal" collective psyche'.

Jung explains the dangers of trying to fuse the collective and the personal psyche in analysing a patient's unconscious. It can be

> injurious both to the patient's life-feeling and to his fellow men, if he has any power over his environment. Through his identification with the collective psyche he will infallibly try to force the demands of his unconscious upon others, for identity with the collective psyche always brings with it a feeling of universal validity – 'godlikeness' – which completely ignores all the differences in the psychology of his fellows.

Jung may have been telling himself not to abuse his power over people who believed he could put them in touch with the god inside them, but he was also trying to contradict rumours that he was unstable.

According to him, the neurotic participates more fully than the normal person in the life of the unconscious. By reinstating what has been repressed, analysis enlarges consciousness to include 'certain fundamental, general and impersonal characteristics of humanity'.

> Repression of the collective psyche is essential to the development of the personality, since collective psychology and personal psychology exclude one another up to a point. Individual personality is based on a *persona* – the mask worn by the collective psyche to mislead other people and oneself into believing that one is not simply acting a role through which the collective psyche speaks.

In schizophrenia, the unconscious usurps the reality function, substituting its own reality. For the sane patient, there are two possible escapes from the condition of godlikeness. One is to restore the persona through a reductive analysis; the other is to 'explain the unconscious in terms of the archaic psychology of primitives'.

Some of these ideas are developed in a paper dated October 1916 and titled 'Adaptation, Individuation, Collectivity'. It discusses the problem of

how much the individual should cut himself off 'from personal conformity
and hence from collectivity'. Organised religion is an obstacle to individuation: no one can become wholly himself without cutting himself off from
God. This involves both guilt and expiation. 'But inner adaptation leads to
the conquest of inner realities, from which values are won for the reparation
of the collective.'

His differentiation between personal and collective unconscious is clearer
in 'The Role of the Unconscious', an article he wrote in 1918 for the
monthly review *Schweizerland*. While the personal unconscious contains
material that has been repressed or forgotten, the contents of the collective
unconscious come from the inherited brain structure. Though no ideas are
inherited, the unconscious is 'above all the world of the past, which is
activated by the one-sidedness of the conscious attitude'. When the conscious mind becomes unbalanced, the unconscious tries to reassert the needs
that are being ignored.

Defending belief in spirits and witchcraft as 'actually more sensible than
the academic views of modern science', Jung explained that spiritual
elements took sensuous form when projecting themselves to the primitive
psyche, 'whose reflexes are purely animal – a thought *appears to him*, he does
not think it.'

In spite of Maeder's decision, Jung went on confiding in him over the next
few years about the club and his arrangements with Edith. 'I agreed with
the idea of the club,' he said, 'because it struck us as being of the utmost
importance to find out . . . whether we had made mistakes in our analysis
of the collective function. I have already learned an enormous amount in
the club.' Without specifying how his freedom was restricted by the deal
he had done with Edith McCormick, he said restrictions would last only
two years.

Some of the members resented the ways in which she used her financial
power. In November 1916, answering a questionnaire Emma circulated,
Maria Moltzer wrote: 'It seems to me the present club is incurably ill . . . A
club cannot survive unless it is financed by its members . . . The present
members should find it disgraceful to be parasitic.' She made proposals for
changes to the club's statutes, but these were not implemented, and she
eventually resigned her membership.

Toni Wolff, who became head of the lecture committee, acquired
considerable influence. Later, in his introduction to her *Studies in Jungian
Thought*, Jung wrote: 'She also helped me to carry out, over a period of forty
years, a "silent experiment" in group psychology, an experiment which
constitutes the life of the Psychological Club in Zurich.'

It was at the club that Jung met the thirty-eight-year-old Hermann Hesse, who had been doing library and editorial work in Bern for German prisoners of war until March 1916, when the death of his father precipitated a breakdown. Hesse was sent to Sonnmatt, a private clinic near Lucerne, where, in May, he had the first of twelve analytic sessions with the thirty-three-year-old Josef Lang, a former student of Jung's and a contributor to his 1914 compilation *Psychological Transactions*. Bringing Hesse to the club, Lang introduced him to Jung.

Hesse had been interested in psychoanalysis since about 1914, when he read work by Freud and Adler. Praising Freud's originality in a book review, he had defended him against his 'embittered opponents', without mentioning Jung by name. While Lang was analysing him in Lucerne, Hesse read *Transformations and Symbols of the Libido*. At the same time, the war was giving a new meaning to the term *collective unconscious*: his generation was caught up in the wholesale slaughter. Hesse had another fifty sessions with Lang, some of them lasting three hours.

A shy, heavily built man with a big head, Lang uninhibitedly applied what he had learned about 'active imagination', and this was to influence Hesse, who was writing again by July, reassessing both his work and his relatives – some had been missionaries – from the perspective of Jung's book. Surviving fragments from Lang's diary tell us how he spoke to patients. On 23 October 1917 Hesse was told he would 'hear the voice that calls out from the primordial depths of the earth the Laws of the Magma in whose springs I reign. You will learn from me the Laws of the Dead, which will become the Laws of the New Age.'

Two days later Lang said he was a labourer inside Hesse's psyche, hammering at the ice encrusting his soul. 'I seek to approach you in order to touch.' The next day he developed the metaphor. 'I am hammering within the mine shaft that contains me, giving me no light I do not radiate myself. You hear my hammering in the roaring in your ear. Your heartbeat is the hammering of my arms longing to be freed.' The reference is to the psyche, but the connotations are sexual, and he reminded Hesse of his mission as a writer, which was to 'chisel from the rocks of your soul the primordial signature of men which you must teach them: the tablets of the Law of what is to come'.

Like Svengali with Trilby – or Jung with Helly – Lang offered Hesse a chance to break out of his solitude, sharing ideas, emotions and experiences. He was encouraged to think he could work like a medium: 'Go quietly to sleep,' Lang urged, 'for I am always close to you. Day and night I am often sending the rays of your thoughts into the dark well of your soul where I seek to approach you in order to touch.' Hesse would be able to read the runes. This is an invitation to a shared experience of the collective unconscious where dead ancestors merge with the future.

Lang's rhetorical pleading may have been crude and unprofessional, but he was the direct cause – and Jung the indirect cause – of what Stefan Zweig called 'the astonishing and important metamorphosis and deepening in Hesse's poetic nature'. No one could have been more deeply predisposed to benefit from analysis, and the sixty-two sessions with Lang had an intro-verting effect. As Hesse said in a 1918 essay, the artist could be provided with three 'confirmations', establishing the objective value of his questionable games and fancies, leading him to a richer relationship with his own unconscious, and teaching him to confront his repressions more honestly and impartially.

Hesse's *Demian* was the first Jungian novel. (Later examples are Morris West's *The World Is Made of Glass*, which features Jung, Toni and Emma among its characters, and, on a higher level of achievement, Robertson Davies's *The Manticore*.) In the traditional German *Bildungsroman* the young hero progresses towards maturity, learning from his mistakes and from wise preceptors. Though *Demian* belongs to this tradition, the preceptors are not entirely separate from the hero, Emil Sinclair, whose name suggests a combination of sin and enlightenment. His friends Demian and Pistorius appear to be partly imagoes – images generated subjectively and perceived according to Sinclair's needs – while Demian's mother, Frau Eva, corre-sponds to Sinclair's anima. Without exception – and without acknowl-edgement – all the insights these characters offer Sinclair are based on Jung's ideas.

The main theme is stated in the prologue: 'Each man's life is a way towards himself . . . Till the end everyone goes on carrying residue from his birth – slime and eggshell from a primeval world.' But, as Sinclair discovers, 'Nothing in the world is more disturbing to a man than following the path that leads him to himself.' Jung's ideas of individuation and the collective unconscious are being crystallised into fiction. In November 1917, while having the last of his sessions with Lang, Hesse was working at the novel, which he completed by the end of the year.

His speed in absorbing Jungian ideas was due partly to influence that had already permeated him from thinkers who had influenced Jung, including Bachofen, St Augustine, Nietzsche and William Blake. Persecuted by the school bully, Sinclair is coaxed away from the Pietistic morality of his parents by Demian, who says it would not be wrong to kill the bully. The mark on Cain's forehead may signify that he is different from other men, not that he is evil.

In a dream Demian orders Sinclair to eat the coat of arms on the keystone of the arch above the main entrance to his house. It features a heraldic bird which, in the dream, begins to devour him from inside. Later he sends Demian his painting of a sparrowhawk struggling to free itself from a dark terrestrial globe as if from a giant egg. 'The egg is the world,' Demian replies. 'Whoever wants to be born must destroy a world. The bird flies to God. The god is called Abraxas.' Sinclair reads the note in a classroom, where he hears the name Abraxas during a lesson on Herodotus. 'Roughly speaking,' says the young teacher, 'we can think of the name as that of a godhead which has the symbolic task of uniting the divine and the diabolical.' *Septem Sermones ad Mortuos* had not been published, but Jung probably gave a copy to Lang, who may have introduced Hesse to Abraxas.

The counterpart to Lang in the novel is Pistorius, an organist, who redefines the relationship between the internal and the external. 'When we hate someone, we're hating in his image something that's inside ourselves . . . The things we see are the same things that are in us.' Uninhibitedly eclectic, Hesse even incorporates the metaphor of hammering. Conversations with his friend 'struck at the same point inside me with a gentle, constant hammer-blow'. Pistorius talks about Mithraic ritual and about fire worship. Together he and Sinclair lie on the floor, staring into the dying embers; and when a slender flame shoots up, it looks like the head of the sparrowhawk. Without using the terms 'phylogenetic' or 'collective unconscious', Pistorius explains: 'What constitutes each one of us is the whole contents of the world, and just as our bodies carry in them all the stages of existence, back to the fish and still further, we have in our souls everything that ever lived in the human soul. All the gods and devils there have ever been, whether for the Chinese or the Greeks or the Zulus, they are all inside us as possibilities, as desires, as outlets.' Pistorius then produces a book on zoology to show Sinclair 'a function from early periods of evolution' still active inside him.

Dreams, says Demian, can be prophetic. Some concern the whole human race, and his recent dreams suggest the old world is about to collapse. 'I can smell death. Nothing new happens without death.' This is how the novel introduces the war, in which Demian is mortally wounded and Sinclair, hit by shrapnel, has a vision of a godlike figure with Frau Eva's features and shining stars in her hair. Finally realising his own face is identical with that of his dead friend, Sinclair has come to terms with the god inside him.

The novel is written in the first person, and publishing it in 1919 under the pseudonym Emil Sinclair, Hesse did not reveal his authorship until June 1920. Lang sent a copy to Jung, who wrote to Hesse in December 1919. Instead of being troubled, as most people would have been, by the shameless plagiarism, Jung was delighted to find so many of his formulations fitting snugly into a system devised by another mind. He called the book 'masterly as well as veracious', praising the ending

> where everything that has gone before runs truly to its end, and everything with which the book began begins over again – with the birth and awakening of the new man. The Great Mother is impregnated by the loneliness of him that seeks her. In the shellburst she bears the 'old' man into death and implants in the new the everlasting monad, the mystery of individuality.

During the war Jung did several stints of military service, sometimes six weeks or so at a stretch. The Geneva Convention of 1864 had been revised in 1906, and it ruled that prisoners of war who escaped into Switzerland must be interned in camps. From 1917 till the end of the war, Jung was commandant of the British internees at a camp in Château d'Oex, not far from Lausanne. There were some brown-skinned, turbaned Gurkhas among the prisoners.

Expenses were paid by the British government, and discipline was lax, officers being allowed to live with their wives in hotels and report to the camp twice a week. Because invalids could be repatriated, and because there were sometimes outbreaks of dysentery and tuberculosis, Jung's medical savoir-faire was useful, and he was glad of the chance to practise his English. His duties left him with plenty of free time, and he invited his Russian patient Emilii Medtner to stay at the camp.

Making sketches in a small notebook, Jung found himself drawing circular patterns and believing they represented the restoration of inner peace to the self. He called them by the Sanskrit word *mandala* (circle). The circular form had always appealed to him, and he found it soothing to go on drawing these figures. 'The archetype that is constellated represents a pattern of order which is superimposed on the psychic chaos like a psychological viewfinder marked with a cross or a circle divided into four. Each element then falls into place, and the seething confusion is protectively encircled.' This idea was important to him: 'I knew that in finding the mandala as the symbol of the self I had achieved the most that was possible for me.' Involving concentric circles, many of the mandalas Jung painted imply a unity that embraces the whole of created life. In thinking of them as symbols of the self, Jung was assuming that individuality should be complete in itself and independent of relationships with other people.

Talking to prisoners in Château d'Oex helped to reorient him, but it was still hard for him to distinguish between psychic and physical events, especially when someone claimed powers of clairvoyance. The wife of an interned British officer told him snakes in her dreams always meant illness, and she had dreamed about a huge sea serpent. When an epidemic of Spanish flu broke out, he thought he had proof that dreams could be prophetic.

Sabina was still trying to make peace between him and Freud. She told Jung that he was

> still capable of growth. You could understand him perfectly if you want to, i.e. if your personal emotion does not get in the way . . . You should have the courage to recognise him in all his greatness, even if you cannot agree with him on every point, even at the cost of giving him credit for some of your own achievements. Only then would you be completely free, and only then would you emerge as the greater man. You will be amazed to see how much your whole personality and your new theory will gain in objectivity through this process.

Startlingly perspicacious, this is an early pre-echo of what Michael Fordham wrote after Jung's death: 'If his main life's work was in the end to be founded on a personal and scientific incompatibility with Freud, there are those who believe, like myself, that this was a disaster, and in part an illusion, from which we suffer and will continue to do so until we have repaired the damage.'

But by 1918 damage was unavoidable. They had both entrenched themselves in anger, and while Freud was surrounded by supporters, Jung was isolated. He took little comfort from the continuing correspondence with Sabina, who now believed that for most patients Freud's methods were more effective, and from May 1916 until October 1917. Jung had been starting letters 'Frau Doktor' and signing himself 'Dr Jung'. In a letter of January 1918 she told him: 'Strange to say, I no longer dream of Siegfried, and I think this has been the case because I showed Professor Freud my analysis of the Siegfried dream.'

It upset Jung that she had let Freud into the secret of the fantasy they had shared about Siegfried. 'Freud's opinion is a sinful rape of the holy,' he wrote in April 1919. 'It spreads darkness, not light . . . Only out of the deepest night is new light born. Siegfried is that spark.' This was six years after his dream about killing Siegfried.

His last letter to Sabina was written in the third person:

> The love of S for J alerted the latter to something he had previously suspected only vaguely – a power of the unconscious that shapes one's

destiny, a power which later led him to things of the greatest importance. The relationship had to be 'sublimated', because otherwise it would have led him to delusion and madness (the concretisation of the unconscious). Occasionally one must go astray, simply in order to survive.

Generosity and vindictiveness are both on display here. At the same time as he acknowledges her importance to him, he says the relationship would have driven him mad. Calling his own behaviour unworthy, he does not apologise. He implies her love had been unreciprocated, and that he was the one who did all the sublimating.

Unable to agree, she went on thinking about him, and had a dream about him as a syphilitic Don Juan. But her published account of it is suitably camouflaged. This was her bitter last word on the most passionate relationship in her life.

Part Four

Excursions

Twenty

Cooking in the Rain

When the war ended in November 1918, Switzerland was much better off than neighbouring countries, and Jung, liberated from his duties as camp commandant, was free to consolidate his success.

The activities of the Psychological Club helped him to build up his practice. His energy was prodigious, and seeing most of his patients three times a week, he started work at 7.30 in the morning. Most of his patients, like Freud's, were women, but while Freud's were mostly under forty and neurotic, Jung said: 'About a third of my cases are not suffering from any clinically definable neurosis, but from the senselessness and aimlessness of their lives. I should not object if this were called the general neurosis of our age. Fully two-thirds of my patients are in the second half of life.'

Distancing himself from Freud's view of consciousness, he had evolved his own ideas of what analysis should achieve. He concentrated on what he called 'individuation' – the process of fulfilling potential by integrating opposites into a harmonious whole. His idea of mental health derived partly from memories of the splitting in his mother's personality and his own, partly from memories of subpersonalities in spiritualism and schizophrenia. If madness divides the self, sanity is unity.

According to Freud, neurosis starts during the first five years of life, and analysis helps by freeing infantile material from repression and bringing it under conscious control. Jung concerned himself neither professionally nor privately with the problems of childhood. When his son Franz asked for advice on how to bring up children, he was told: 'Let them grow, like trees.' Since Jung never discussed his psychology at home, this answer was neither helpful nor comprehensible, but it was not flippant or meaningless. In his view, integration did not necessarily involve consciousness, and he some-times thought of it as exemplified by a tree, which, if nothing goes wrong, grows into its preordained shape.

By the beginning of the 1920s, the proliferation of psychoanalytic ideas was making people anxious about whether their selves were divided. In a letter to John Middleton Murry about the fiction she was reviewing for the monthly he edited, the *Athenaeum*, Katherine Mansfield complained about the ' "mushroom growth" of cheap psychoanalysis everywhere. 'Five novels one after the other are based on it; it's in everything . . . these people who are nuts on analysis seem to me to have no subconscious at all.' They made it harder for her to feel confident about the stability of her own identity. We all seem to have hundreds of selves. 'What with complexes and suppressions, and reactions and vibrations and reflections – there are moments when I feel I am nothing but the small clerk of some hotel without a proprietor who has all his work cut out to enter the names and hand the keys to the wilful guests.'

If Jung could teach people how to reunite the scattered fragments, he would be answering an urgent need, but, unlike the maturity that Freud proffered to his patients, the individuation Jung cultivated did not depend on the elimination of neurosis, which could be useful, in his view, to people who had been evading responsibility, had been arrogant or had acquired false values. 'Thank God he became neurotic!' was what he would some-times say of a patient. Habitual attitudes, he maintained, were nearly always carried too far, and if one side of the personality overwhelms another, the neglected side reasserts itself through dreams and symptoms. Differentiating between the ego and the self, he said the ego is only the centre of consciousness. The self should shift to take both conscious and unconscious demands into account.

Jung later argued that neurosis is 'by no means just a negative thing – it is also something positive . . . In the neurosis is hidden one's worst enemy and best friend.' We should 'accept the neurosis as our truest and most precious possession'. Instead of trying to get rid of it, we should 'find out what it means, what it has to teach, what its function is . . . We do not cure it – it cures us.' Anyone who took the opposite view was guilty of 'a soulless rationalism reinforced by a narrow materialistic outlook'.

Jung was reading voraciously as he worked on *Psychological Types*, which was to be published in 1921. The enormous range of reference shows how carefully he had studied Gnosticism, Tertullian, Origen, Lao Tse, Meister Eckhart, *The Shepherd* by Hermias, which dates from AD 140, a Latin translation by Ficino of *De Insomniis* (*Concerning Dreams*) by Synesius, the Christian bishop of Ptolemais and pupil of Hypatia, Rousseau, Schiller's *On the Aesthetic Education of Man*, Carl Spitteler's *Prometheus and Epimethus*, Worringer's *Abstraction and Empathy* and Otto Gross's books.

But alongside the reading, Toni's influence was pivotal. According to Carl

Meier, 'she was responsible for the most important parts in his books . . . I know from the two of them that many parts of the *Types* are due to her insistence on clarifying this or that . . . She could be a hard taskmaster.'

Jung called himself a Kantian. 'Epistemologically,' he wrote, 'I take my stand on Kant,' and in lectures, seminars and letters he referred to Kant more than to any other philosopher. In a letter of 1957 to a Swiss doctor, he said Kant had made it impossible 'to think that it lies within the power of man to assert a metaphysical truth', and in a second letter Jung explained: 'All that I have written you is Kantian epistemology expressed in everyday psychological language.' But in the first chapter of *Psychological Types*, 'The Type Problem in Classical and Medieval Thought', he tries to outmanoeuvre Kant by claiming that psychology can 'unite the idea and the thing without doing violence to either'.

In 1787, introducing the second edition of his 1781 *Critique of Pure Reason*, Kant said: 'I had to nullify *knowledge* in order to make space for *faith*.' We can know only what we experience, but we can conceive of transcendental ideas, which he called 'things-in-themselves' or 'concepts of pure reason' or *noumena*, as opposed to *phenomena*, which exist tangibly and visibly in time and space. Without denying the existence of God or the soul, Kant denied their existence as *phenomena* – belief in them can have no empirical foundation. Distinguishing between *pure* and *practical* reason, Kant was differentiating between the thinking based on experience and the kind that consists of making logical connections between concepts.

Jung set himself the task of achieving 'a psychoanalytic cure for faith and disbelief' by offering psychological insight into the old religious myths and symbols. By filling them with new contents he thought he could liberate them from 'the depressing results of doctrinal oppressiveness'.

Working with psychotics in a mental hospital, he had succeeded better than most of his colleagues in winning patients' confidence by taking their delusions seriously. If a woman said she had been on the moon, he not only listened but chatted as if she had been visiting a country that interested him. In his theorising, as in his clinical practice, he accorded factual status to mental events. He argued that reality consists of 'a reality in ourselves, an *esse in anima*'.

He then tried to bridge between the noumenon and the phenomenon by using this *esse in anima* as if Kant had licensed him to regard mental events as phenomena. Since the notion of God is a 'psychological fact', says Jung, the only important question is 'whether it occurs just once, often or universally in human psychology. The datum which is called "God" and is formulated as the "highest good" signifies, as the term itself shows, the highest psychic value.'

Kant would not have wanted his name to be used in support of the phrase 'psychological fact' and the habit of treating fantasies, visions, dreams and hallucinations as if they were empirically real. Jung sometimes said there are 'two kinds of truth', but they do not correspond to Kant's pure and practical reason.

For Jung, an image of God is a 'psychic fact', and in this way he disguises a noumenon as a phenomenon, though the image is not grounded in time or space. As Stephanie de Voogd has shown, his Kantianism is 'both self-contradictory and self-defeating', while 'Jung's distinction between the noumenal God and the image of God becomes pointless as well as misleading'. As she says, Jung seems to be at cross-purposes with himself when he insists that on the one hand psychic manifestations are real and on the other, 'only psychic'. Marilyn Nagy concludes that his thinking was in line with the 'radically subjectivistic neo-Kantianism' favoured at the end of the nineteenth century by 'religionists who hoped thus to defend religious truths from the reductionist conclusions of scientists'.

If Jung had genuinely taken his stand on Kant, he would have acknowledged that archetypes and the collective unconscious are both noumena, and that nothing can be asserted about either. Instead he spoke about 'the phenomena I have termed archetypes', and claiming a parallel between psychology and microphysics, concluded that the unconscious psyche 'exists in a space-time continuum where time is no longer time and space no longer space'.

Aniela Jaffé said: 'Fundamentally his entire work is to be understood as a psycho-religious statement, a progressive interpretation of the numinous by which man is consciously or unconsciously filled, surrounded and led.' It is hard to reconcile this with the claim she made in her Introduction to Memories, Dreams, Reflections – that his private life was founded in belief in God, while 'as a scientist Jung was an empiricist' who 'limited himself to facts and what could be demonstrated'.

On Sundays and during holidays Jung sometimes took the children hiking, boating and camping, though this had not yet become popular. At Château d'Oex he had acquired some tents made for British army officers. Emma, who did not enjoy camping, rarely accompanied them on these expeditions. Hating flies, she once put up flypaper in a tent, only to get her hair caught on it. But when she stayed at home, she worried endlessly about how Jung was looking after the children.

Sometimes he camped with them on an island at the mouth of the Linth Canal, at the northern end of Lake Zurich. He now owned four boats: two sailing boats, a rowing boat and a canoe. He had designed one of the boats himself – a fast-moving two-masted yawl with red sails. The bigger sailboat – the *Pelican* – had a cabin large enough for three of the children to sleep in it. He enjoyed spending the night on the boat or in a tent, organising them into collecting firewood from the forest, drawing water from the lake, buying supplies in Schmerikon – twenty minutes away by rowing boat – and burying food in the ground to keep it cool.

They spent a summer holiday (1919 or 1920) in the Engadine, where he took them down every day to play games of the sort he used to play himself. Together they constructed a network of canals in the sand and stones. At home, loving to work with his hands, carving or doing carpentry, he taught them to build model boats and miniature cities.

Agathe and Gret were never to forget what he called their 'North Pole journeys'. Ignoring bad weather, he took them boating and camping in winter. On the lake, when it was foggy, Franz had to blow on the horn every two minutes. If the boat was becalmed in the middle of the lake, Jung told the children to annoy the wind by making a lot of noise with their oars.

Sometimes they would sleep in a tent for four successive weeks, braving the rain, the wind and the freezing cold. He liked cooking out of doors, and when it was raining, the children would have to hold an umbrella over him. Once, wearing an old hat and an oilskin coat, he spent seven hours cooking a pike in the rain, worrying more about keeping the fire alight than about the wet and shivering children inside the tent. Rain was seeping into it.

When his five children were growing up, Jung spent more time with his son than with his daughters, who were mostly kept at a distance. Snapshots show Emma with the girls, all wearing long white dresses and watching while Jung and Franz build little villages with stones.

Franz, who became an architect, remembered a boat trip after the end of the First World War when he was about ten and his eldest sister fourteen. Jung loved sailing on Lake Zurich, but he rarely took the girls. One day when he did, they landed at a village on the way home, and he bought them all cakes. After mooring the boat in the little harbour at the end of their garden in Küsnacht, Marianne, who was eight, ran across the lawn to her mother. 'Just look! Franz's father bought me a little cake.' Emma had to explain that Franz's father was also her father.

The other children, though not confused about his identity, were uncertain of where he stood in relation to Christianity. His second daughter, Gret, who was born in 1906, has said:

When I was about twelve or so, I didn't pray any more because I thought it wouldn't please him, because he always made fun of theologians, and he was very pleased because my elder sister and I – we should have gone to church on Sunday, and we didn't . . . I thought he wasn't religious at all, and it was only through reading his books that I discovered he'd been a religious man.

What was hidden from his children and other visitors was revealed to strangers if they were patently believers. A woman who had worked on the New Testament was told: 'Go on talking about the religious aspects of my work. They are the most important parts.' And once, discussing the value of prayer, he asked: 'Why do I have to talk about God? Because he is everywhere. I am only the spoon in his kitchen.'

Jung sometimes exchanged letters with his daughters when he was travelling. In July 1919 he was in London to speak at three meetings, and replying to a letter from Marianne, he mythologised the city for her, saying the river flowed alternately upwards for six hours and downwards for six. Every day about fifty thousand cars passed the big house where he was staying, and the King's golden throne and sceptre were in a castle with a high tower. 'By day the crown is in the tower on top and you can see it, in the evening it sinks down with the sceptre into a deep cellar which is shut with iron plates.'
    It was six years since he had stayed in London, and he enjoyed being in a city with a population twice the size of Switzerland's. After learning so much English during the war, he no longer needed a translator for his lectures, and from now on, English would become increasingly important in his professional life. He had learned it at school and had often spoken it at the Burghölzli, where English and American doctors came to train.
    In July he addressed the Society for Psychical Research on 'Psychological Foundations of Belief in Spirits', and the Royal Society of Medicine 'On the Problem of Psychogenesis in Mental Disease'. He also spoke on 'Instinct and the Unconscious' to a joint meeting of the Aristotelian Society, the Mind Association and the British Psychological Society.
    Like his Zofingia lectures and the 1925 seminar in which he spoke about 'Australian negroes', all three papers reveal an abhorrence of materialism and a nostalgia for 'the ancient metaphysical account of nature'. Denying that intellect could comprehend reality, he regretted the loss of spirituality that ensued on the loss of primitive naivety. It was not as if psychic phenomena occurred less frequently in the modern world. 'The only difference is that where the primitive speaks of ghosts, the European speaks of dreams and fantasies and neurotic symptoms, and attributes less importance to them than the primitive does.'
    This word *primitive* will go on recurring frequently in Jung's pronouncements. In 1923 he will reaffirm his conviction that 'we cannot possibly get

beyond our present level of culture unless we receive a powerful stimulus from our primitive roots. But we shall receive it only if we go back behind our cultural level, thus giving the suppressed primitive man in ourselves a chance to develop.' Indefatigably and simplistically contrasting primitivity with modernity, he kept reminding audiences and readers that in losing touch with our spirituality, we had paid too high a price for any progress we might have made. He never stopped feeling nostalgic for the kind of thinking that had been extirpated from 'the West' by rationalism, materialism and scientific progress. He loved the pre-Newtonian idea of a unitary world with a coherent divine intention behind it. If everything in existence is planned by a single intelligence, everything must be relevant to everything else, even if the relevance is not discernible to us. The presuppositions and predilections revealed in his Zofingia lectures reappear in his 1931 essay 'Archaic Man'.

The main influence on his thinking about 'the primitive mentality' was the work of the French sociologist Lucien Lévy-Bruhl, whose books *How Natives Think, Primitive Mentality* and *The 'Soul' of the Primitive* were published in France between 1910 and 1927. Whereas Sir James Frazer's *The Golden Bough* (published in twelve volumes between 1895 and 1915) rests on the assumption that the mental functions of primitive people are the same as ours, but not so well used, Lévy-Bruhl believed that they think in a different way because their mental processes are conditioned differently by the group.

Two of his key terms – Jung frequently used them in French – are *représentations collectives* and *participation mystique*. Imposed on the individual by the group, collective representations are not merely mental notions. In illiterate societies, there is less abstraction, less conceptualisation, and more mystical belief in invisible forces. The perception an individual forms of an animal is inseparable from the collective representation which endows it with magical powers and mythical connotations. Because the natural and the supernatural worlds are believed to interpenetrate, the natural is not observed separately.

What Lévy-Bruhl called the *law of participation* is the principle that a thing can be itself and something else at the same time. Things and creatures participate in one another, sharing the spirit called *mana*, while all matter is believed to be fundamentally the same. Because nothing is fortuitous, accidents can always be explained, though not without reference to the supernatural, and since we must defend ourselves against hostile forces, techniques need to be supported by rituals. Since supernatural powers reveal themselves in dreams, illness (or death) and luck, a remedy may be ineffective or a skilfully made canoe may sink unless the right incantations have been uttered.

'Archaic Man' shows how strongly Jung was attracted to the spirituality of this primitive world as Lévy-Bruhl describes it. Disliking the modern habit of exorcising mysteries by explaining everything scientifically, Jung thought it healthier to blame death on witchcraft, sorcery or magic than on old age, disease or accident. Lévy-Bruhl writes about the interpenetration between the visible and invisible worlds:

> This explains the place held in the life of primitive man by dreams, omens, divination in a thousand different forms, sacrifices, incantations, ritual ceremonies and magic. This accounts for their habit of ignoring what we call secondary causes and concentrating on the mystical cause as the only really effective one. A man contracts an organic illness, is bitten by a snake, crushed by a falling tree, eaten by tiger or crocodile, but for the primitive mentality . . . it is without doubt because a sorcerer had 'doomed' and 'delivered' him . . . The fatal tree or animal has been only an instrument.

This is one of the passages Jung paraphrases in 'Archaic Man'. If a nocturnal creature such as an anteater ventured into the daylight, he says, efforts would be made to placate the demonic forces that had produced the deviation from normality. 'Thanks to our one-sided emphasis on so-called natural causes,' Jung writes, 'we have learned to differentiate what is subjective and psychic from what is objective and "natural". For primitive man, on the contrary, the psychic and the objective coalesce in the external world.' The oldest maternal uncle of the man who had seen the anteater should sacrifice a bull.

In the archaic world, said Jung, 'everything has soul, the soul of man, or let us say of mankind, the collective unconscious, for the individual has as yet no soul of his own.' Introducing the sacrament of baptism, Christianity had separated the individual from the world by giving him a soul as if it were his personal property. But for archaic man, 'each relatively independent part of the psyche has the character of personality' and 'it is personified as soon as it gets an opportunity for independent expression . . . As soon as an autonomous component of the psyche is projected, an invisible person comes into existence.' Life, in other words, was like a nonstop seance.

This nostalgia for the time when everything had soul is comparable to T. S. Eliot's mournful conviction that something 'happened to the mind of England' between the time of John Donne and the time of Tennyson. 'A thought to Donne was an experience; it modified his sensibility.' Tennyson and Browning did not 'feel their thought as immediately as the odour of a rose'. What had developed during the seventeenth century, Eliot believed, was a 'dissociation of sensibility . . . from which we have never recovered

. . . While the language became more refined, the feeling became more crude.' Our two greatest masters of diction, Dryden and Milton, 'triumph with a dazzling disregard of the soul'. But Donne, when he looked into his own heart, had penetrated more deeply: 'One must look into the cerebral cortex, the nervous system and the digestive tracts.'

The 'dissociation of sensibility' had separated thought from feeling, and when Jung, after his 1938 visit to India, said that Indians do not think, he meant that like 'primitive' man, they *perceived* the thought. 'The primitive's reasoning is mainly an unconscious function, and he perceives its results.' What troubled Jung was not so much a dissociation of sensibility as a dissociation of spirituality. Finding that people were looking *only* at the cerebral cortex, the nervous system and the digestive tracts, he wanted to heal the sickness in the modern soul by persuading us not to forget that the savage side of our nature is still there. If he had succeeded in confronting his own madness without breaking under the strain, he could probably reconcile other people with the most disruptive parts of their nature.

There was one area where Lévy-Bruhl's influence merged with that of Sabina Spielrein, who believed in 'ancestor components'. For the primitive, said Lévy-Bruhl, death is not the end of life. The dead man has a double existence as a corpse and as a new arrival in the world of the dead, and he can live again in this world if a newborn child is given his name. There was also an affinity between the stories told by mediums about travel through space while in the state of trance and the primitive belief in a double which can travel during dreams while the body lies asleep.

Lévy-Bruhl stayed with Jung in Küsnacht, and they were both contributing editors of the quarterly *Charakter*, which was published in Berlin from 1932, but Jung was influenced only by the first three of Lévy-Bruhl's six books on primitives. In the three he published between 1931 and his death in 1939, *Primitives and the Supernatural, Primitive Mythology* and *Primitive Mystical Experience and Symbols,* and in his posthumously published notebooks, he took account of the criticisms provoked by his first three. He was accused by Marcel Mauss, who introduced the term *social anthropology* into France, of using the word *primitive* too loosely for heterogeneous societies. In his last three books he generalised less, and in the notebooks he explicitly abandoned the idea that there is any such thing as 'a primitive mentality distinguishable from the other by *two* characteristics which are peculiar to it (mystical and prelogical). There is a mystical mentality which is more marked and more easily observable among 'primitive peoples" than in our society, but it is present in every human mind.' But Jung rejected the later developments in Lévy-Bruhl's thinking, saying he had been unnecessarily intimidated by critics. Dismissing their criticism as unwarranted, Jung went on bundling Hottentots, Hittites and *Homo erectus* together.

Siding with Marcel Mauss and Lévy-Bruhl's other critics, Claude Lévi-Strauss's book *The Savage Mind*, which came out in 1962, made it virtually impossible to go on believing in 'the primitive mentality' or in *participation mystique*. 'The savage mind,' says Lévi-Strauss, 'is logical in the same sense and the same fashion as ours, though as our own is only when it is applied to knowledge of a universe in which it recognises physical and semantic properties simultaneously . . . Its thought proceeds through understanding, not affectivity, with the aid of distinctions and oppositions, not by confusion and participation.' Like Jung, Lévi-Strauss was fascinated by myth, magic, ritual and clan organisation, but he was rigorously objective in looking at the ways in which 'primitive' peoples have organised their ideas about nature and their place in it.

Jung introduced the term *archetype* in his paper on 'Instinct and the Unconscious'. Assuming that 'every psychic content must possess a certain energy value in order to become conscious at all', he took the unconscious to be 'the receptacle of all lost memories and of all contents that are still too weak to become conscious'. This was the 'personal unconscious', which he characterised as a relatively thin layer immediately beneath consciousness. Further down we find the

> inborn forms of 'intuition,' namely the *archetypes* of perception and apprehension, which are the necessary *a priori* determinants of all psychic processes. Just as man's instincts compel him to a specifically human mode of existence, so the archetypes force his ways of perception and apprehension into specifically human patterns. The instincts and archetypes together form the 'collective unconscious'.

Like the instincts, which had nothing to do with individuality, archetypes were 'collective phenomena'. If nothing determined our mode of apprehension, he said, it would be impossible to explain the uniformity of our perceptions. The determining factor, which he called the archetype or *primordial image*, could be described as the instinct's perception of itself 'in exactly the same way as consciousness is an inward perception of the objective life-process'.

Around 1912 he had been using the term *primordial* for images that occurred in both mythology and fantasies of psychotic patients. Mythology now played a part in his idea of archetypes. Gods, heroes, spirits and magic might come to the fore. 'In the great religions of the world we see the perfection of those images and at the same time their progressive encrustation with rational forms . . . Just as everybody possesses instincts, so he also possesses a stock of archetypal images.'

His idea of a collective unconscious had been prefigured by Nietzsche's suggestion in *Human, All Too Human* that 'asleep and dreaming we traverse the thought of earlier generations . . . We still reason in our dreams in the way primeval men reasoned when they were awake.' For Jung the idea was connected with Haeckel's theory that the lifelong development of the human body goes through the same stages as the evolution of the race. He never discarded the ideas he had absorbed in medical school or the formulation he made in 1912, when he said the newly born human mind was already seeded with the potential of fantasies identical with myths. 'Just as our bodies retain the residue of obsolete functions and conditions in many of their organs, so our minds, which have apparently outgrown those archaic impulses, still carry the marks of evolutionary stages we have traversed and re-echo the dim bygone in dreams and fantasies.'

Lecturing in London, he made no mention of heredity, but he later said the archetype was 'a potentiality handed down to us from primordial times in the specific form of mnemonic images or inherited in the anatomical structure of the brain'. While no ideas are inborn into the collective unconscious, the archetype 'is a figure – a demon, a human being or a process – that recurs constantly throughout history and appears wherever creative fantasy is expressed freely'. Each archetypal image contains 'a little piece of human psychology and human fate – residue of the pleasures and sorrows that have been recurrent throughout our ancestral history'. Their course is 'like a riverbed in the psyche, where the waters of life swell suddenly into a torrent'.

Whenever we meet modes of action that are uniform and recur regularly, he tells us, we are dealing with instinct; whenever we meet modes of apprehension that are uniform and recur regularly, we are dealing with archetypes. He says he borrowed the notion from St Augustine, that for Plato things were only copies of archetypes or model ideas, and that Kant reduced archetypes to a limited number of categories of understanding.

This is confused and confusing. The Forms in *Phaedo* and other dialogues by Plato are available to the intellect but not the senses. They are both paradigms and universals, whereas Kant presents his categories not as being independent of experience but as presupposed by it. The muddle extends into Jung's use of the term 'primordial image', which he took from Kant. The glossary of 'Definitions' in *Psychological Types* says an image is primordial when it has an archaic character and accords with familiar mythological motifs. The primordial image, Jung says, is the precursor and matrix of the idea, but under *idea* he quotes Plato, who defined it as the prototype of all

things, and Kant, who saw it as 'the archetype of all practical use of reason
. . . a rational concept with no counterpart in experience'.

By 1917 Jung was writing about *nodal points* or *nonpersonal dominants* in the
unconscious, and in 1926 he wrote: 'Not only are the archetypes, apparently, impressions of ever-repeated typical experiences, but, at the same
time, they behave empirically like agents that tend towards the repetition of
these same experiences.'

Many of his statements confuse form with content – a difficulty he tried to
resolve by introducing the term *archetypal images*, intending to reserve the
word *archetypes* for the form, which he said was noumenal, while he would
treat archetypal images as phenomenal. But though he believed, with Kant,
that nothing can be said about noumena, he had a lot to say about
archetypes, and sometimes he forgetfully called them phenomena.

He also speaks of archetypes as ' "pathways" gradually traced out through
the cumulative experience of our ancestors'. This is a vivid image, which
would be useful if he had not kept confusing the path with the journey, or
the riverbed with the water. He regarded the collective unconscious as a
repository of memories that induced tendencies to behave in a certain way –
but also did a great deal more than that. In 1927, writing on 'The Structure
of the Psyche', he said:

> The collective unconscious contains the whole spiritual heritage of
> mankind's evolution, born anew in the brain structure of every individual.
> His conscious mind is an ephemeral phenomenon that accomplishes all
> provisional adaptations and orientations . . . The unconscious . . . is the
> source of the instinctual forces of the psyche and of the forms or categories
> that regulate them, namely the archetypes. All the most powerful ideas in
> history go back to the archetypes. This is particularly true of religious ideas,
> but the central conceptions of science, philosophy and ethics are no
> exceptions to this rule. In their present form they are variants of archetypal
> ideas.

This confuses inborn patterns with patterns formed by habit, suggesting that
behaviour standardised by generations of ancestors forms a template which is
imprinted on every newborn mind. In 1929 he wrote:

> The existence of the collective unconscious means that individual con-
> sciousness is anything but a *tabula rasa* . . . it is in the highest degree
> influenced by inherited presuppositions. . . . The collective unconscious
> comprises in itself the psychic life of our ancestors right back to the earliest
> beginnings. It is the matrix of all conscious psychic occurrences. And

hence it exerts an influence that compromises the freedom of consciousness in the highest degree, since it is continually striving to lead all
conscious processes back into the old paths.

Although he often returned to the problem, it was mostly to repeat what he
had already said. He never succeeded in sorting out the muddle.

In England, Jung spent his weekends in an Aylesbury valley, staying in an
isolated two-storey farmhouse surrounded by twisted orchard trees. For
years the estate agent had been unable to let it, but it had eventually been
rented by a young Scottish doctor, Maurice Nicoll, who had twice stayed in
Zurich to study with Jung. Nicoll was rarely in the cottage when Jung stayed
there.

   At night he found there was an unpleasant smell in his stuffy bedroom,
and he sometimes heard a creaking noise or dripping water, but if he lit a
candle, the inexplicable smell vanished, and the sounds stopped. Two village
girls told him the house was haunted, and he had his worst experience on a
windless night when he was disturbed by persistent rustling, banging and
creaking. The moonlight was bright enough for him to see that on the
pillow beside him was 'an old woman's head. Wide open, the right eye
glared at me. Below the left eye, half her face was missing.' He jumped out
of bed, lit a candle and spent the rest of the night in an armchair. He dates the
episode as occurring in the summer of 1920, but it was in 1919 that he gave
the lectures in London, and this dating is confirmed by the letters of Maurice
Nicoll.

   A believer in black magic, Nicoll was 'at the time trying to serve Hecate,
but I felt the presence round me of evil'. Jung talked to him 'a lot about the
possibilities of psycho-material-transformation – i.e. if a man puts his psychic
genius into a bit of wood, the wood stands up to him, and in fact it is an
example of psycho-transformism.' Talking to the Society for Psychical
Research, he had said: 'I see no proof whatsoever of the existence of real
spirits, and until this proof is forthcoming I must regard this whole territory
as an appendix of psychology.' Spirits were 'either pathological fantasies or
new but as yet unknown ideas'. But did he believe this? And did he think he
had put his psychic genius into the manikin he had carved out of the ruler?

In *Psychological Types* he developed the typology he had introduced at the
congress in 1912, equating the introvert with the thinking type and the
extravert with the feeling type. Schiller had written: 'Man unquestionably
carries within himself the potentiality for divinity.' For every introvert, Jung
explains, nothing matters more than the abstraction and conservation of the

ego, while for the extravert, 'the god is the experience of the object, complete immersion in reality'. According to Jung, Schiller and he were both introverts, while Goethe, like Freud, was an extravert.

Alongside Schiller, a key influence was William James, who was, as Jung acknowledged, a pioneer in human typology. In his 1890 book *Principles of Psychology* he had contrasted the 'analytic' kind of thinking with the 'constructive' kind, and in his 1907 book *Pragmatism* he had postulated a polarity between 'tender-minded' and 'tough-minded' characters. Jung devoted twenty-one pages of his *Psychological Types* to an analysis of what James had written.

It seems to have been Jung's relationship with Maria Moltzer that brought him round to thinking there were more than two types. The dual classification survives into his 1917 *Psychology of the Unconscious Processes* and into its second edition, which came out in 1918. The first mention of an 'intuitive type' occurs in the 1921 book *Psychological Types*, where he acknowledges in a footnote that 'The credit for having discovered the existence of this type belongs to Miss M. Moltzer.'

Now, dividing everything into four categories, Jung subdivided extraversion into thinking and feeling; introversion into sensation and intuition. To most people the words *sensation* and *feeling* are almost synonymous, as they were for Schiller, though Jung's differentiation between them was based on an essay by Schiller, 'The Aesthetic Education of Man', which describes an instinct that 'confines the upwardly aspiring spirit to the world of sense'. Our personality is extinguished while we are dominated by sensation, and we are no more than 'a filled moment of time'.

In Jung's analytical psychology, God is 'an unconscious content, a personification in so far as he is thought of as personal and an image or expression of something in so far as he is thought of as dynamic. God and the soul are essentially the same when regarded as personifications of an unconscious content.' Jung advances his argument for soul as a personification of the unconscious by quoting Meister Eckhart, who interprets Christ's words 'The kingdom of heaven is like a treasure hid in a field' by saying 'The field is the soul, wherein lies hidden the treasure of the divine kingdom. In the soul, therefore, are God and all creatures blessed.' God is the power working within the soul, which never loses its intermediary power, conveying forces from inaccessible parts of the unconscious mind to the conscious mind.

This is how God becomes integral to the collective unconscious. In a series of 'Definitions' at the end of the book Jung equates *psyche* with the totality of conscious and unconscious psychic processes, while *soul* is defined as 'a clearly demarcated functional process that can best be described as "personality" '. Although the concrete contents of the psyche are lacking at birth, the potential contents are given

> by the inherited and preformed functional disposition. This is simply the product of the brain's functioning throughout the whole ancestral line, a deposit of phylogenetic experiences and attempts at adaptation. Hence the newborn brain is an immensely old instrument, fitted out for quite specific purposes, which does not only apperceive passively but actively arranges the experiences of its own accord, and enforces certain conclusions and judgements.

Because the introvert, Jung contends, withdraws libido from the external object, he is more strongly affected than the extravert by the archetypes, which are precursors of ideas. While the extravert is slow to recognise similarities between things, the introvert, more at home with abstract thinking, focuses less on individual objects than on general characteristics. Reason can develop ideas into concepts which are not based on experience but are the underlying principles of all experience. There is a danger of confusion here, but for Jung, if the meaning of a primordial image is formulated in an idea, its essence is not derived or developed but exists a priori as a psychological determinant. 'In this sense Plato sees the idea as a prototype of things, while Kant defines it as the "archetype (*Urbild*) of all practical employment of reason", a transcendental concept which as such exceeds the bounds of the experiencable.' These primordial images can be awakened from their slumber 'like invisible stage managers' who draw the stuff of experience into their empty forms.

Jung had written nearly three quarters of the book before he settled down to his main task of describing differences between the four types of extraversion and introversion.

There are, according to Jung, four functions – thinking, feeling, sensation and intuition – and we are unbalanced when we let one of these dominate our dealings with the world, leaving the others to atrophy. The 'extravert thinking type' rejects both activities that depend on feeling and irrational phenomena such as religious experiences. Jung regarded Freud as an example of this type, which is more common among men.

The 'extravert feeling type' is to be found mainly among women, whose feelings are based more on external circumstances than on subjectivity. Any thoughts that would disturb these are rejected and they are ready to believe they love a man if his age, income and social position make him appear suitable. Compulsive pleasure-seeking is characteristic of this type, together with the suppression of anything painful or unpleasant.

The 'extravert sensation type' is similar in its repression of subjectivity and its lack of intellectuality, but it is more likely to cultivate a crude hedonism or an effete aestheticism. Intuitions, which are mostly repressed, may reassert themselves in the form of projections.

In the 'extravert intuition type' sensation is generally repressed as intuitions are formed about relationships between things, and these become more important than things themselves. Facts are valued only as a means of going beyond them, and things are discarded as soon as they have led to a new combination. Many entrepreneurs and politicians belong to this type, but it is more common among women, who exploit social situations. But the object may finally take its revenge, causing phobias, hypochondria and absurd bodily sensations.

In the introvert, subjective determinants are the most important, and the archetype functions when conscious ideas are absent or inhibited. In the 'introverted thinking type', he says, thinking always leads back into the subject. There is less concern with new facts than with new views, and the idea will often have a mythological streak or an air of whimsicality. People of this type follow their own thinking inwards, ignoring criticism. They are impractical, with a horror of publicity, and, not knowing how to curry favour, they often have bad experiences with rivals. They are so scrupulous that they clutter their prose with qualifications, and readily allow themselves to be brutalised and plagiarised. Jung assigned both Kant and Nietzsche to this category, though they could hardly have had less in common.

Jung saw the 'introverted feeling type' as being more common among women than men, but it was this type, in his view, that had a decisive influence on modern art. The subjective factor revealed itself in exaggerated, tasteless forms of expression bordering on caricature.

'Introverted sensation types' are guided less by the object than by the intensity of subjective sensation it excites. He gave no examples of this type.

'Introverted intuition types', such as mystical dreamers, artists and cranks, focus on the background processes of consciousness. Jung assigned both William Blake and himself to this category. Not everyone would agree that he was an introvert, but he argued that the world saw him as one.

Twenty-One

There Is Greatness in You

By the beginning of the 1920s, Jung had stabilised his triangular relationship, but it altered both Emma and Toni. Carl Meier says Emma 'underwent the most spectacular transformation during their married life. More so than any of the women I saw.' Meier later played the neutral role at sessions of what he called 'group analysis', in which he and the two women discussed their dreams.

Dignified and good at concealing pain, Emma was scrupulously polite when Toni came to Küsnacht. Unquestionably, the children suffered, but Emma and Toni behaved with dignity, camouflaging their frustration, while their tolerance of each other was sustained by realisation that neither of them could have made Jung monogamous. As she told Freud in 1911, Emma had given up hope of keeping him to herself, and the Sabina episode had illustrated the therapeutic value of sexual involvement.

It could also be said that the Swiss dialect cemented the triangle. This was what Jung spoke with Emma, Toni and the children. His three other languages – German, English and French – were associated mainly with work, for which he would seldom use Swiss German, except when talking with Toni or Swiss patients.

At first he discouraged Toni from becoming an analyst, saying the poetry she wrote was as good as Goethe's, and that she would realise more of her potential as a writer. But she became one of the best analysts working with him. One patient praised her 'genius for accepting with a unique calm the most extraordinary ideas and fantasies from the unconscious'.

Though she became Jung's foremost collaborator, his image – like his domestic life – depended more on Emma, who was always available when he needed to be seen in public as a married man. One of her many functions at dinner parties was to kick him under the table when he became too pompous or self-indulgent. Michael Fordham was having dinner with them and some friends when the conversation settled on children's dreams. Jung launched into a monologue, but Emma, who sometimes said he knew nothing about children, intervened: 'You know very well that you are not interested in people, but your theory of the collective unconscious.' That, says Fordham, 'was the end of Jung for quite a time, and he sat reflectively eating his meal while the conversation continued between the rest of us.' Fordham tells the story to show 'she was no downtrodden wife, but could be very outspoken and hold her own against him'. Carl Meier said: 'She could react very very violently and strongly. She was a tremendously forceful person . . . She could put her foot down and attack you face to face, and ask you to be honest.'

Three servants ran the household and looked after the children, who spent a lot of time in each other's company but little in that of their parents. The younger ones went to bed immediately after supper, while the older ones had to sit at table after the meal. Emma often went into the garden or the library with Jung, but they were not allowed to follow. In the morning, Agathe would do her younger sisters' hair and help to look after them.

On evenings when their parents were entertaining, the children were sent to the small house where their grandmother and their aunt Trudi had been living since 1909. Though Emilie Jung regularly got up at five in the morning, she never went out, except into the garden. She did a lot of needlework, and, weather permitting, spent much of the day out of doors. For the five children, who saw so little of their father, it was a consolation that their grandmother and aunt were always available. But the old lady enjoyed telling them ghost stories, which scared them, and afterwards their aunt often had to walk home with them.

When one of the girls started going out with a boy, his elder brother put an end to their friendship by saying he should have nothing to do with a girl whose father was in touch with insanity. And if she tried to tell Jung about a dream, he looked at her over his spectacles in such a way that she stopped. He was never prepared to discuss dreams or psychology with the family.

Like Emma, Toni subordinated her needs to Jung's. She may have been temperamentally predisposed towards self-denial. She regarded herself as a 'mediumistic' woman, the type that 'carries and personifies the unconscious of other people or of its epoch'. While the other type – it was not until later that she increased the number of types to four – 'encounters certain difficulties in its attempt to realise and express itself', the mediumistic type 'possesses less ego-consciousness than the other, and it is the one that most easily loses'.

Within ten years of moving into the new house, Jung felt the need for an alternative space. Encroaching on his domestic peace were a growing retinue of patients, a wife, a mistress, three servants and five children between the ages of sixteen and five. So he began searching for a site where he could either have something built or build it for himself. An island would have been ideal, and he made efforts to buy the nearby island of Schmerikon, where he had enjoyed several camping holidays, but negotiations came to nothing.

Feeling restless in the spring of 1920, he was glad when a friendly Zurich businessman Hermann Sigg, who was planning a trip to Tunis, invited him to go along. Now forty-five, Jung had never visited a country where he could not speak the language, and though he had been in the USA he felt as if he had never had a chance 'to see the European from outside'. In African coffee houses and public places, he watched gestures and listened to tones of voice without understanding what was going on. He soon came to disbelieve in 'what the European takes to be Oriental calm and apathy'. Behind it he perceived 'a restlessness or even an agitation I could not understand'.

Leaving Sigg in Tunis, he went southwards with a guide, to Sfax, and then to the oasis city of Tozeur. Watching white-clad men embracing each other or holding hands as they strolled underneath date palms, he was reminded of homosexuality in ancient Greece. Few women ventured into the streets, and the ones without veils were prostitutes.

On his first morning in Tozeur, Jung was woken at sunrise by camels, sheep, donkeys, dogs and drums. Between the hotel and the mud-brick houses, about a hundred camels were sitting, surrounded by black-bearded men in white burnouses. A caravan had arrived. With arms outstretched, men were dancing to music from drums and a woodwind instrument that sounded like bagpipes. They had come from the Sahara to do a day's voluntary work for the tribal elder, a holy man, who rode up on a mule, wearing a green robe and a white burnous. Having no hat, Jung improvised a turban with a towel. The Marabout welcomed him with a handshake. Leading the war against starvation, the Marabout controlled the communal land. In return for supplying voluntary labourers, villages benefited in turn. Drumming, singing and dancing fortified the workers' resistance to the heat, and by midday a dam had been constructed.

To Jung, whose predilection for the primitive was being boosted, his pocket watch symbolised Western decadence. For the Arabs, life was timeless. Had any real progress been made since the Middle Ages? 'With lighter baggage we continue our journey with increasing speed towards doubtful goals, making up for the loss of gravity and the corresponding *sentiment d'incomplétude* with the illusion of our successes, such as railways, steamships, aeroplanes and rockets.' The Arabs were 'closer to life' than we are. 'Much that is human is alien to the European, who is largely rational, and he takes pleasure in this without realising that he is living with less intensity and that in consequence his primitive personality is condemned to an underground existence.'

In 1920 Jung began lecturing in English to a small group of sympathetic students. The English seemed to be more receptive to his ideas than Germans, who were more Freudian in orientation. He also held discussions in his Küsnacht home with about six of these students, including Esther Harding, Helton Godwin Baynes and Eleanor Bertine. Esther Harding, who came from Shropshire, had been an intern at the Royal Infirmary in London, the first English hospital to accept woman interns. Known to his friends as Peter, Baynes was thirty-eight, even taller than Jung, attractive and friendly. He had been a rowing blue at university. He settled in Zurich during 1929. Eleanor Bertine was an American doctor in her middle thirties.

These meetings led to an invitation for Jung to conduct his first seminar outside Switzerland, at Sennen Cove in Cornwall. Organised by Constance Long – his hostess on his first visit to London in 1914 – it was attended by about a dozen people, including Baynes and Esther Harding. Using a book called *Authentic Dreams of Peter Blobbs*, Jung discussed his approach to dreams. Depending less on free association and more on what he called *amplification*, he was filling out his interpretation by introducing religious symbolism and material from myth.

Members of the audience were all staying in the same boarding house, where in the evening they played games. Jung had not only begun to dream in English, but he sometimes succeeded in winning word games.

At the end of the two weeks, he stayed on in London, where he held regular meetings with members of the group. Working on *Psychological Types*, he read from his first draft, looking perplexed as he paced up and down. Sometimes he muttered: 'This is difficult.' He seems to have stayed on for a few months. Writing in December 1920 to Albert Oeri, whose mother had died, he says he has been neglecting correspondence because of work that accumulated during his long absence in England.

As Jung's fame grew, women flocked to him from all over the world, bringing money and a desire for dependence. Men came too, but not so many. Nietzsche wrote that people become believers when they find they need to be commanded. Without being religious, many of Jung's followers almost worshipped him, and felt better when he was instructing them in how to live. They were convinced he could help them to be themselves.

'All kinds of people big and small,' wrote one, 'found through him their uniqueness.' His greatest quality as an analyst, according to another patient, was the sense he gave of accepting everything that came up in the session 'not only rationally, intellectually, but with his whole being. He never reduced material from the unconscious to something infantile; he always asked himself: "Now where does it lead to?" He gave us a feeling "There is a greatness in you, and we must serve this." ' Another remembered 'his marvellous laugh, which shook the room and made everyone want to laugh with him. He had a courtesy which a grand seigneur of the eighteenth century would have.' All three patients went on to become Jungian analysts.

He had begun to accumulate a retinue who would remain loyal, but some were borderline cases who could not have lived without him, except in an asylum. In these people, according to Jolande Jacobi, the collective unconscious was too close to consciousness. In Jung they 'found a partner for this part of their life'. Without him, life would have become 'meaningless and then disturbing'.

Outsiders noticed the high proportion of women among his patients and followers. One of his answers was: 'What's to be done? Psychology after all is the science of the soul, and it is not my fault if the soul is a woman.' But in his view, it was only the male soul that was female; the female soul was 'not of an affective nature . . . Consciousness in women corresponds to emotionality in men, not to their intellect. Mind constitutes the soul or *animus* of a woman, and just as a man's *anima* consists of inferior relatedness, full of emotion, a woman's animus consists of inferior judgements or opinions.' (By *inferior* he meant relatively undeveloped.) In a 1928 seminar he said that a woman can be analysed only through her emotions. 'One can only talk to her so-called mind as if to a library, perfectly dry.' But he also held that 'Women are far more "psychological" than men. A man is usually satisfied with "logic" alone. Everything "psychic", "unconscious" etc. is repugnant to him; he considers it vague, nebulous, and morbid.'

Women at this time were generally excluded from the professions and, as one member of the circle put it, it was assumed that they had no soul. Himself no feminist, Jung maintained that women who took up a masculine profession were injuring their femininity. The qualities that endeared him to women were not so different from those that had alienated young men from him at university and had made him apologise to his fraternity brothers for being considered rude, uncivil, insolent, cheeky and unmannerly. But there was a strain of masochism in these women, and Jung did not always succeed in concealing his impatience.

With so many of them clamouring for his attention, he was too busy to give them fifty-minute sessions three times a week, though he now took his first patient at seven in the morning. Even if there had been less pressure on his time, a session with him would have been quite different from one with

Freud, who let patients free-associate, which meant letting them talk about whatever was on their mind – dreams, fantasies, guilt feelings, marital relations, indigestion, clothes, children, memories of childhood, business problems, anxieties and trivialities. He concentrated mainly on their relationships with their past and with other people, but Jung concentrated on their relationships with themselves, God and the universe.

While Freud's patients had nothing but individual sessions, lying on a couch, seeing his face only briefly after they arrived and before they left, Jung's had a series of face-to-face conversations. Most of Freud's were Viennese or were living in Vienna, while most of Jung's came to Zurich because of him and either stayed at the Hotel Sonne in Küsnacht or found lodgings in the vicinity.

One of them wrote to her husband: 'Today I had my first lesson with Dr Jung; it really is a lesson.' Nor did the teacher–pupil relationship change. Five months later she wrote: 'Had my last lesson with Dr Jung Monday at 5 to 6 p.m. and was dismissed with "go home and live it now".'

Since private lessons were uneconomical, he started giving seminars, which virtually made patients into students, but, as in analytical sessions, he not only explained his ideas and theories but reminisced about experiences, dreams and visions.

> His method was to use each theme, sequence or symbol as a springboard from which to launch into an exposition of his theories, speculations and vast erudition. He ranged not only throughout the global field of psychiatry but also over present-day social and political subjects, as well as historical and mythological material. He covered philosophy, psychology, medicine, economics, and folklore. He reported his experiences at home and abroad, his prejudices and opinions on many diverse subjects. He had opinions about practically everything, and dwelled especially on the personality structure of Americans, Orientals, Teutons, Jews, Blacks – Goethe, Nietzsche and especially Heraclitus . . . One purpose of this method is to offer the patient a way to stand back a little from his problems and see them as a little less personal, as though projected on a screen, more universal and more human.

Lectures were followed by questions and discussion. The club became rather like a college, with his personality at its centre. Patients paid ten dollars an hour, and their lives revolved around their relationship with him.

Like Sabina, Toni, and later Emma, several female patients graduated to combining the roles of student, assistant and collaborator, eventually winning the right to analyse patients of their own. In curing them and giving them a vocation, Jung was making them both more self-reliant and more reliant on him. Struggling to emancipate himself from Freud, he had twice quoted Nietzsche's maxim that a teacher is poorly rewarded by the pupil who remains dependent. But he did not always discourage those who developed a long-term need for him.

Feeling they had come to life more fully than ever before, many of them felt scared of a future without him. Does this mean he was a guru? In a 1996 study of gurus, *Feet of Clay*, Anthony Storr focuses chiefly on Gurdjieff, Baghwan Shree Rajneesh, Ignatius Loyola, Rudolf Steiner, Jung, Jim Jones, David Koresh and Freud. In spite of their heterogeneity, many common denominators come into view.

They were all charismatic, narcissistic and authoritarian. Doubt is akin to anxiety, and their followers gladly sacrificed their freedom for the luxury of being told what to do. Part of a guru's appeal lies in his certainty of being right, and part in making other people feel instantaneously and intimately understood. Most of these eight men claimed to have spiritual insight based on personal revelation, and to have gained esoteric knowledge from travelling to remote or inaccessible places. They all had a lonely boyhood, followed, early in adult life, by what Ellenberger called 'creative illness'. Though capable of dominating other men, they could not sustain a friendship; capable of seducing women, they could not continue a sexual relationship as a partnership between equals. Rejecting conventional religion, they all (except Freud) offered what Rajneesh called 'a religionless religiousness' – spiritual insight based on a religious attitude. What Storr says of Jones could equally well be said about most of the others: they illustrate 'the difficulty in defining the borderlines between conviction, delusion, confidence trickery and psychosis'.

Their allure lay partly in their mysteriousness. The secretiveness that looked like a screen for esoteric knowledge helped them to hide past experiences they could not afford to disclose. Their followers must never be allowed to see the mesh of conviction, delusion, confidence trickery and psychosis. In 1934 Jung was asked whether there was any 'secret knowledge' behind his writings. His answer was:

I have had experiences which are, so to speak, 'ineffable', 'secret' because they can never be told properly and because nobody can understand them . . . 'dangerous' because 99 per cent of humanity would declare I was mad if they heard such things from me, 'catastrophic' because the prejudices aroused by their telling might block other people's way to a living and wondrous mystery.

But like the other gurus, he could liberate his followers from the burden of freedom. According to the Grand Inquisitor in Dostoevsky's *The Brothers Karamazov*, Jesus made a mistake in the wilderness when he refused to deprive people of their freedom. 'Men are tormented by no greater anxiety than to find someone speedily who will take over that gift of freedom with which the unfortunate creatures were born. But no one can take over their freedom without appeasing their conscience.'

Jung sometimes said women gave themselves fully to analysis, while men tried to use it for other purposes. An American woman formed the impression that Swiss women had been brought up to believe men knew the answers. Some of the Swiss women tended to let Jung define their female nature for them instead of finding for themselves. Thinking women could not function without male support, they tended to think his thoughts instead of their own, while he gave the impression they should model themselves not on other women but on his *anima*.

Jung could alternate mercurially between showing enormous respect for other people and making despotic demands that would alter their way of life. In one of his last letters, he accused himself of failing in the main task he had set himself – 'to open people's eyes to the fact that man has a soul, that there is buried treasure in the field and that our religion and philosophy are in a lamentable state'. In fact he succeeded in bringing a new soulfulness to many people and in giving them faith in the work they must do on themselves to unearth the buried treasure.

At the beginning of the twenties, his attitude to transference was changing. In the 1921 essay on 'The Therapeutic Value of Abreaction' he says nothing is more helpful than 'the doctor's efforts to enter into the psyche of his patient, thus establishing a psychologically adapted relationship. For the patient is suffering precisely from the absence of such a relationship . . . In the same measure as the doctor assimilates the intimate psychic contents of the patient into himself, he is in turn assimilated as a figure into the patient's psyche.' The patient is seeing him 'not as he really is, but as one of those persons who figured so significantly in his previous history'. The projections must be 'consciously recognised' and 'submitted to a reductive analysis before all else'.

There are two dangers. One is that neurotics are encouraged to brood on the past. Instead of being wasted on blaming their parents and castigating themselves for past mistakes, their energy should be focused on the present and the future. 'The real issue is the moral achievement of the whole personality.' The other danger is that sexuality may invade the relationship between doctor and patient, and be accepted as a compensation for their failure to understand each other. The doctor should not give an exclusively sexual interpretation of dreams and fantasies.

Jung's practice went on growing. Among the Americans to arrive in Zurich were Joseph and Jane Wheelwright, who made the journey from San Francisco with Jane's schizophrenic aunt and her husband, having been told Jung was the one doctor who might be able to help her. Jung was busy, but 'because of the distress of the patient's husband and the long, arduous trip, he spent hours, between lectures, at intermissions, after hours, to help in any way he could. Incidentally, although the husband was a rich man, there was no charge for this extra time.'

It struck Joe that 'an awful lot of tottering old things were coming in and out of the consulting room', and in the end Jung explained that he already had too many 'floating cases' – patients hopelessly attached to him who would lapse back into psychosis if he stopped seeing them. He was liable to become angry when asked why he devoted so much time to these old women. From this Joe concluded that he was covering up what might have been a problem for him, and that he had a 'special feeling for unattractive women'. 'This has nothing to do with me,' Jung said, and he told one woman he liked: 'I am not a bit interested in you. But I care a great deal about your soul.'

Joe had been a jazz musician, a reporter and a teacher. Now he decided he wanted to be an analyst, but Jung's response was: 'Oh God! It happens over and over again . . . The patients say "I want to do what you do". Jung decided not to take Jane's aunt on, and the family went back to San Francisco. But Joe and Jane would return in 1931.

Freud's patients rarely saw each other, and they could not hope that they might one day be collaborators or colleagues, but Jung was surrounded by people who saw more of each other than they did of him, though he was the centre of the circle and their main subject of conversation. His charisma was so great that many patients – men as well as women – wanted to change their lives in order to be more like him.

But he did not have the same effect on men as on women. 'Women fought each other to get close to him,' one said, 'and men railed against him because of imagined neglect.' One of the women who became dependent, a student of philosophy, used to dream she was a child sitting on his knee or that he was a giant, holding her in his arms. It felt like being in the arms of a god who swayed with the wind, putting her to sleep.

At the beginning of 1921 Hermann Hesse arrived in Zurich. In spite of – or perhaps because of – borrowing so much for *Demian*, he had afterwards turned his back on Jung. Reviewing two of Freud's books in June 1920, and glorifying him as the founder of a new science, Hesse attacked Jung for rejecting him while exploiting his theories and making a philosophy out of

his science. Hesse had been exploiting Jung's theories and making philosophical fiction out of his psychology.

In 1921 Hesse made another volte-face. He was living in Montagnola,
where he had acquired a palazzo, and though his future wife, Ruth Wenger,
was in Zurich, taking singing lessons, he intended, when he arrived, to stay
only briefly. It was not her presence but Jung's that made him change his
mind.

He settled near the forest on the Zürichberg, where he tried to work on a
novella about a painter called Klingsor. After accepting an invitation to read
some of his poetry at the Psychological Club, he was so impressed with
Jung's response that he started going to him for analysis. Giving it priority
over the novella, Hesse took time for two long walks every day between the
forest and Küsnacht. In a letter to the Dadaist Hugo Ball and his wife, he
said: 'My psychoanalysis is causing me a lot of trouble, and Klingsor often
feels old and incorrigible. The summer no longer belongs to him. I shall stay
on here. I have bitten into fruit that must be finished. Dr Jung impresses me
very much.'

'Analysis,' he told the Balls, 'has become for me a fire I must pass through
but which hurts very much . . . Already duties and dangers have emerged
which I can scarcely yet confront.' And in another letter he compared the
methods and techniques of the early monks with those of analysis, which
'can fundamentally have hardly any other objective than to create an internal
space in which God's voice can be heard'. In his novels *Siddhartha* (1922) and
Steppenwolf (1927) he developed this idea of internal space where conflict
gives way to transcendental vision.

In the summer of 1921, Hesse could not yet transpose his experience into
fiction. Concentrating, with Jung's help, on his own psyche, he wrote diaries
and verse. He sent Jung some of the verse, and in Zurich during January
1922 read from the diaries to a literary club, the *Lesezirkel Hottingen*. This
attracted an unsympathetic review in the *Neue Zürcher Zeitung*, and Jung
wrote: 'You have given the Hottingen literary fraternity a touch of the
horrors with your wide-ranging autobiography . . . For someone like me,
who never reads poetry, your poems are simply beautiful.'

Soon after this, Hesse abruptly severed contact with the man he had found
so impressive. He broke off the analysis, perhaps because he lost faith in Jung
or perhaps because he was scared of being overwhelmed by the influence.
Hesse spent most of his life in Switzerland, often going to Zurich and
remaining friendly with Josef Lang, but not with Jung.

When *Psychological Types* came out in 1921, Hesse gave it an enthusiastic
review, but within a year he had stopped reading Jung's books – 'since
analysis later no longer interested me very much,' he said. 'I have always

respected Jung, nevertheless have never been as impressed by his writings as by Freud's.' At the club, he said, Jung had made a good impression on him, 'but at that time I began to realise that any real relationship to art was beyond analysts; they lack the necessary wherewithal for this.'

Early in the summer of 1922, Esther Harding arrived in Küsnacht to be analysed by Jung. She had already attended his seminars, and now she kept daily notes on the sessions. Calling consciousness 'the superior function' and unconsciousness the inferior one, Jung told her that only her superior function was under her control. United to the collective, the inferior function was her master, and she must adapt herself to it.

She was an extravert, he told her; therefore her language was thin and scanty. In talking to her, he said, he had two problems. One was to 'cut down' his thought, and the other was to 'take up a feminine attitude'. To sit still and tune in patiently to a female viewpoint, he went on, a man must adapt his attitude. A lover, who would automatically call 'on the eternal image of the feminine in himself', would find himself becoming tender and using baby-talk. But a husband would not do this for his wife – 'for she is only his wife' – while an analyst 'has got to learn the feminineness of a man, which is not his anima'. But he 'mustn't let his masculinity be overwhelmed, or this will call out the animus in the woman'. Most of the time she would have to fight her animus. In so far as she identified with it, she would tend to project it into him. 'And then if you battle with him who is demonic, *I* call my demon, my anima, to my aid, and it is two married couples fighting. Then you have a hell of a row.' Esther Harding was a feminist and a lesbian. It might have been dangerous to tell a heterosexual woman that he was making more effort to adjust to her femininity than he did to his wife's.

Though constantly surrounded by admiring women, Jung never again got himself into so much trouble as he had with Sabina. He found it easy to inspire mood changes. He could move from provocative intimacy to reverential solemnity such as his father might have assumed in the pulpit. It was not only in the *Septem Sermones* that Jung adopted this tone, and if Esther Harding's notes are accurate, some of his thinking and some of his cadences derived from Luther's translation of the Bible via Nietzsche's *Zarathustra*. 'Be afraid of the world, for it is big and strong, and fear the demons within, for they are many and brutal; but do not fear your Self, for this is yourself.' He was echoing Zarathustra when he told her: 'If you feel afraid, be brave enough to run away.'

Advising her on how to fend off demons, he said words could be creative and powerful in the spiritual realm. 'God spake and created from the chaos and here we are all gods for ourselves. But use few words here, words that you are sure of. Do not make a long theory, or you will entangle yourself in a net, in a trap.' The main gist of his advice was that she should find enough courage to break through the barriers erected by habit and convention. She might sometimes feel unstable, but if she could stop living mainly for other people, she would discover a new, self-regulating self. 'Thus, vice too, if entered into sincerely, as a means of finding and expressing the self, is not vice, for the fearless honesty cuts that out.'

She began the next session by saying that 'something wonderful had happened'. Jung's talk on the animus relationship had 'cleared things up, so that much had clicked into place'. She now felt different. He warned her against responding to the voice of the animus as if it were the voice of God. 'When we are not aware of the negative aspect of the animus,' she wrote afterwards, 'we are still animal, still connected to nature, therefore unconscious and less than human . . . If we are conscious, morality no longer exists. If we are not conscious, we are still slaves . . . He said that if we belong to the secret church, then we belong, and we need not worry about it, but can go our own way.' This idea of a secret church is one that Hesse had borrowed: in *Demian* the sign of membership is the mark of Cain.

In September 1922 there was a serious row in the Psychological Club. Hans Trüb, though he had not become a psychiatrist until 1920, had been elected president in 1921, the year Edith and Harold McCormick went back to the USA. (A farewell banquet had been held for them on 10 September.) In their absence, Jung had become more autocratic and self-indulgent, breaking rules and giving himself so much freedom to reiterate his opinions that Trüb was provoked into tabling a motion of censure, which, to Jung's intense annoyance, was seconded by Maeder. This time, Jung not only stalked out of the room but resigned from the club, together with Emma and Toni.

The quarrel precipitated a breakdown in Trüb. Without Jung he lost all sense of his identity. Overwhelmed with guilt feelings, he felt disoriented by the idea that the self had an archetypal dimension and that God was contained in it. Its main relationship must therefore be with itself. His senior by only fourteen years, Jung had been a father figure, but what Trüb now lacked cannot be summed up so simply.

The books that would eventually help him to recover his equilibrium led him further away from Jung. In 1923 he discovered Martin Buber's philosophy. The central idea is that the self can be developed only through relationships – not only with people, but with objects, plants, scenery. There are two kinds of relationship: I–It, and I–Thou. While an *It* is merely a passive object of observation, there is interaction with a *Thou*, and it is through interaction that the self comes fully to life. The everlasting Thou is God, who can be glimpsed through encounters with other Thous. Accepting an invitation from Trüb to lecture at the club, Buber spoke there at the beginning of December 1923.

Hermann Graf Keyserling was a Russian aristocrat who had escaped from his native Livonia after the Revolution, married Bismarck's granddaughter and contributed to the *Kreuzzeitung*, the newspaper of the Prussian conservatives' radical right wing. Travelling in India, he concluded that Indian wisdom was 'the profoundest in existence', and yoga struck him as superior to any Western 'path to self-perfection' through 'the enlargement and deepening of consciousness'. He understood that to the Indian mind, psychic phenomena are more real than physical events. This was a point that would later be made by Jung. One of the first Europeans to work systematically towards a synthesis between Eastern and Western thinking, Keyserling founded a college in Darmstadt, the 'School of Wisdom', and Thomas Mann had written an open letter in support.

A friend of Keyserling's, Oskar Schmitz, attended some of Jung's seminars, and came to the conclusion: 'With the Jungian system the possibility enters for the first time that psychoanalysis can contribute to the higher development of man.' In 1922, after Schmitz had got Keyserling interested in Jungian psychology, Jung was invited to lecture at the college.

On the podium he gave the impression of being less modishly intellectual than the other speakers, who included the philosopher Max Scheler and Leo Frobenius, an expert on ancient religion. One member of the audience, Olga Freun von König-Fachsenfeld, found herself moved by what Jung said, and when she saw him striding away from the lecture room 'like a sturdy peasant, his hat pushed back to the scruff of his neck,' it seemed to her that his 'earth-rootedness' was 'the guarantee for the credibility of his psychology'.

When Schmitz's book *Psychoanalysis and Yoga* presented them both as techniques of self-improvement, Jung objected that Eastern ideas should not be shipped into Western culture. The Chinese had 'gone through an uninterrupted development from the primitive state of natural polydemonism to polytheism at its most splendid and, beyond that, to a religion of ideas within which the originally magical practices could evolve into a method of self-improvement'. When the Romans brought Christianity to the Germanic tribes, they had still been 'in the initial state of a polydemonism with polytheistic buds . . . Like Wotan's oaks, the gods were felled and a wholly incongruous Christianity, born of monotheism on a much higher level, was grafted onto the stumps. Germanic man is still suffering from the mutilation.'

We progress to a higher cultural level only by taking a step backwards, allowing 'the suppressed primitive man in ourselves to develop'. We must 'let God himself speak despite our only too understandable fear of primordial experience'. Jung was trying 'to educate patients and pupils to the point at which they can accept the direct demand made on them from inside'. In the early twenties, as today, Oriental styles and religious practices were attractive to the younger generation, but Keyserling failed to understand the dangers 'of building a new house on the shaky foundations of an old one, or pouring new wine into old bottles'.

In Darmstadt Jung met a former missionary who had spent much of his life in China. Richard Wilhelm knew more than Schmitz about Chinese yoga, but he was more realistic about the problems of importing it. Wilhelm, who had studied with a Chinese master of the Confucian school, Lao Nai-hsuan, struck Jung as seeming 'totally Chinese, in his gestures as well as in his handwriting and speech . . . He had adopted the Oriental viewpoint' and 'prided himself on never having baptised a single Chinese'. Or, as Keyserling put it, 'What happened to him in China was like what happens to a woman who, when she marries, changes not only her name but her nationality, and finds fulfilment in that . . . His fatal illness was nothing but the external expression of the impossibility for him of continuing with the life he had to live in Germany.'

Although Jung had studied neither the language nor the history of China, he revered 'a civilisation thousands of years old which has grown organically out of primitive instincts without that brutal morality that is so suitable for us as Teutonic barbarians who have only recently been civilised.' Unlike Westerners, the Chinese never denied 'the paradoxicality and polarity' of life. 'The opposites always balance each other – a sign of high cultural achievement.'

Jung was impressed by Wilhelm's story about a drought which lasted so long that the suffering villagers sent for a rainmaker. After demanding a cottage on the outskirts of the village, the old man stayed indoors for three days. On the fourth day a heavy downpour of rain was followed by snow, which was unusual at that time of the year. Asked what he had done, he said nothing. Coming from a place where everything happened as it should, he could see the villagers were 'out of providence and out of themselves'. He therefore wanted to stay as far as possible from the centre of the village, and once he was in Tao again, the rain came. The word *Tao* means approximately *way* or *path*. Wilhelm usually translated it as *Sinn* (meaning). Tao can be seen as 'the ongoing, self-renewing and purposive energy of life, continually creating as it moves'.

Jung called his encounter with Wilhelm 'one of the most significant events of my life . . . Indeed, I feel myself so very much enriched by him that it seems to me as if I have received more from him than from any other man.' He also said: 'I see Wilhelm as one of those great Gnostic intermediaries who brought the Hellenic spirit into contact with the cultural heritage of the East and thereby caused a new world to rise out of the ruins of the Roman Empire.'

Wilhelm was equally impressed by Jung:

> Chinese wisdom and Dr Jung have both descended independently of each other into the depths of man's collective psyche and have there come upon realities which look so alike because they are equally anchored in the truth . . . The congruity between the Swiss scientist and the old Chinese sages only goes to show that both are right because both have found the truth.

Wilhelm had devoted ten years to studying and translating the *I Ching*, a series of oracular statements which may have originated in the second millennium BC. They are believed 'to represent a configuration of time: a dynamic cluster of images which shapes experience and perception. Together the texts and the hexagrams give a rhetoric of the possible modes of change.' According to Chinese tradition, the spirits form the 'living soul' of the book, and the symbols 'comprehend the light of the gods'. Stimulated by consultation, the book can 'reach the depths . . . grasp the seeds . . . penetrate the wills' of everybody.

Wilhelm published his German version in 1924. Already interested in the book before the end of the twenties, Jung had been working with an English translation that had come out in 1882, but he deepened his familiarity with the text when Wilhelm came to stay with him.

As a translator, Wilhelm was meticulous – his first complete German draft was translated back into Chinese for Lao Nai-hsuan to check it – and his knowledge was vast, but he has been accused of 'philological credulity'. He believed that Confucius had made additions to the *I Ching* in the sixth century BC, but this idea has since been discredited. The book had been derided by Western scholars as a collection of obsolete magic spells, and Jung knew it had frequently been 'put to superstitious use', but he saw it as embodying 'the living spirit of Chinese civilisation, for the best minds of China have collaborated on it and contributed to it for thousands of years'.

The oracular pronouncements are arranged through a set of sixty-four six-line figures called hexagrams, some of them broken, some unbroken. Each one can be changed into its opposite according to the yin-yang polarity principle. After formulating a question, you divide a bunch of forty-nine yarrow stalks into two piles. The number of stalks in each pile guides you to a hexagram, which guides you to a text.

Jung sometimes consulted it. Instead of using yarrow stalks he cut himself a bunch of reeds, and after devoting hours to them and the book, felt sure the fall of the reeds was not determined purely by chance. Too engrossed at first to take notes, he surmised that something in his psyche was affecting the action of his hand as it divided the stalks. He sometimes used the *I Ching* with patients, as he did when consulted by a young man with a mother complex. Though strongly attracted to a girl, he was afraid she might turn out to be no less overbearing than his mother. Jung made him divide the reeds, and his hexagram – number 44, 'Coming to Meet' – pointed to the text: 'The maiden is powerful. One should not marry such a maiden.'

Throughout his nonstop war against materialism and scientism, Jung regarded the *I Ching* as 'an Archimedian point from which our Western attitude of mind could be lifted off its foundations'. The Chinese mind was concerned with 'what we call coincidence', while 'what we worship as causality passes almost unnoticed . . . The matter of interest seems to be the configuration formed by chance events at the moment of observation.' The sixty-four hexagrams were 'the instrument by which the meaning of sixty-four different yet typical situations can be determined'. If the alternative principle to causality was what Jung later called synchronicity, the only criterion of its validity in the *I Ching* was 'the observer's opinion that the text of the hexagram amounts to a true rendering of his psychic condition. It is assumed that the fall of the coins or the division of the bundle of yarrow stalks is what it necessarily must be in a given situation.'

Twenty-Two

Tangible Silence

In February 1923, after only two days of illness, Jung's mother died at the age of seventy-five. He was in Castagnola on Lake Lugano when the news reached him. He took the night train from Lugano, but did not feel sad on the journey home. 'I heard nonstop dance music, laughter and joyful noises, as if celebrations were going on for a wedding . . . With the gay dance music and happy laughter it was impossible for me to give myself over to grief.'

The bereavement came while he had no contact with the club. His impulse was to cut himself off still further, and he resumed the search he had begun the previous year for an isolated piece of land. Remembering that as a student he had made summer pilgrimages to an isolated crypt behind the vineyards in Reichenau, he felt hungry for the same tomblike stillness, the same solitude. 'By temperament,' he wrote, 'I despise the "personal," any kind of "togetherness".' Wanting to build a kind of retreat with his own hands, he eventually found a lakeside site almost as inaccessible as the crypt. It was on the same side of the lake as Küsnacht, but at the other end, much further away from the city, between the villages of Bollingen and Schmerikon. He did not drive a car till the end of the twenties, and, given favourable winds, it would take about four and a half hours to sail there from Küsnacht. Or he could take a train and walk the last part of the journey.

Words and paper were too flimsy for the statement he felt driven to make about bereavement and rebirth – it would have to be in stone. He wanted to build an alternative mother, a space for spiritual growth. He said the experience of building was like being reborn in stone. What he had in mind at first was 'an African hut where the fire, ringed by a few stones, burns in the middle, and the whole life of the family is played out around this centre. Basically primitive huts realise an idea of wholeness.' But once he had started putting the walls up, he did not want the building to 'huddle too close to the earth', and it was then that he decided to add a second storey, but he started painting the walls before they were finished.

After spending six weeks in a quarry, where he was taught how to cut the heavy rocks and to move them, he did much of the building himself, with help from members of the family and two workmen. People on passing boats saw a big man at work in a bright-blue linen overall or drill trousers stuffed into laced boots, or wearing a leather jacket and an old blue apron. After seeing him wash his jeans 'with his powerful arms in a tub of water', a journalist described how 'every cell and fibre of his physical being' seemed to participate in every task he undertook, intellectual or physical.

The building work was completed in the spring of 1924. His indifference to physical comfort was extraordinary. Isolation, for him, was a luxury, but the only other one was the magnificent view across the lake. He put no floorboards and no carpet on the uneven stone floor. In a severe winter the heavy oak door would be covered with ice, but he wanted no electricity; his source of heat was the fire. He had one bright lamp for reading, and no telephone. Water had to be fetched from the lake and boiled – later filtered. It was not till eight years later that, after employing a water diviner to find a spring, he installed a hand pump. As he said, 'If a man of the sixteenth century moved into the house, only the kerosene lamp and the matches would be new to him; with everything else he would know what to do.'

Jung was serious – or at least half serious – about providing a home for the souls of his ancestors:

> I can tell you the doyen of that corps chuckled when he again found himself in the accustomed frugal rooms, smelling of smoke and grits, and occasionally of wine and smoked bacon. As you know, in olden times the ancestral souls lived in pots in the kitchen. *Lares* and *penates* are important psychological personalities who should not be frightened away with too much modernity.

Here he had a more direct relationship with pots, pans and cooking utensils that at Küsnacht. According to Ruth Bailey, his housekeeper during the last years of his life, he not only said good morning to each of his saucepans, pots and frying pans, but made her greet them. 'They understand and appreciate it,' he told her. Regarding them as friends, he thought it natural to chat with them. Modern materialism might have chased all the spirits and goblins away from the countryside, but here he tried to reinstate them. He patted the tall green-tiled stove in his Küsnacht study, telling visitors: 'It's human.'

Consciously or semiconsciously, he was modelling his life on that of primitive man, as characterised in the early work of Lévy-Bruhl. He was not merely being playful when he made gestures in the direction of appeasing invisible forces, and his resistance to gadgets and innovations is sometimes reminiscent of the fear shown in 'simple societies' to everything that comes from outside. Lévy-Bruhl quoted from a missionary, H. Newton, who described the fanatical conservatism of the natives in his book *In Far New Guinea*, published in 1914. After missionaries had persuaded them to slaughter pigs in a more humane way for an annual feast, some of the older people sent a deputation to say that at least one pig must be killed in the old way because the mango trees might bear no fruit if they did not hear the squeals.

At Bollingen Jung scrubbed himself every day with a hard brush, sunbathed in the open air, went for long walks in the hills. Pots, pans, plates and cutlery had to be washed in the lake, and though he saw little of his neighbours, it was clear from what he did see that they regarded him as a crazy intruder.

He went to bed at ten and got up at seven but spent a long time preparing breakfast, which usually consisted of coffee, salami, fruits, bread and butter. Sometimes he would bake corn, sometimes cook bacon and eggs. He would usually start eating at nine, drink tea at two or three in the afternoon, and have a substantial meal in the evening. For the washing-up, water was heated indoors on the fire and brought outside in a basin to where the dirty crockery and cutlery would be washed. A great deal of time was spent before and after meals on preparations and tidying. In Küsnacht Jung insisted on having pots, pans and cooking implements put in their proper place, but here it was still more important because it was always so dark inside the building, even with the shutters open during the day, and with the oil lamps lit at light. He could find everything in the dark – provided that it had been put where it belonged.

He made the surrounding land into a garden. He enjoyed cutting wood and growing vegetables; he felt fully alive when doing manual work in the open air. He spread manure and planted potatoes. He carved alchemical figures and quotations on the walls and on blocks of stone 'to make these troublesome things steady and durable'. To help stagnant water reach the lake, he used a shepherd's spade to widen the banks of rivulets.

The isolation was conducive to almost trancelike reflection, which Jung achieved more readily here than in Küsnacht. Stories were told about how long he stayed motionless. According to one, a bird helped itself to some of his hair for a nest; according to another, a bird sat on his head for ten minutes. He was motivated by faith in the collective unconscious. Given silence that was almost tangible, it seemed possible to make contact with thoughts that were centuries old, to experience trees and birds as an extension of himself. It was easy to feel humble when chopping wood or carrying water from the lake to the fire, and in his old age he went on sculpting as if possessed by a demon. Images from his dreams were becoming solidly three-dimensional.

When messages or images came up from his unconscious he would write, paint, sculpt or carve. According to Meier, the mantelpiece here was one of his first carvings, and sometimes, sitting outside the building and staring at the rough surface of the stone wall, he saw shapes that seemed to be staring back at him, almost challenging him to bring them into existence as bas-relief. A face he sculpted like this he called 'the Trickster'. 'By carving him out I discovered his identity. I have thought I have laid him, but I was obviously wrong again.' The grin on the features is amiably diabolical, and when Jung made mistakes in some astrological calculations intended to illustrate his theory of synchronicity, he complained that 'the whole experiment has indeed been bedevilled'.

Another figure was a kneeling woman. While he was carving her out, the hindquarters of a mare appeared in the stone behind her, and her hands then seemed to be reaching out for its milk.

> The woman is obviously my anima in the guise of a millennia-old ancestress. This afflux of anima energy immediately released in me the idea of a she-bear approaching the back of the anima from the left. The bear stands for the savage energy and power of Artemis. In front of the bear's forward-striding paws I saw, adumbrated in the stone, a ball, for a ball is often given to bears to play with in the bear-pit. Obviously this ball is being brought to the worshipper as a symbol of individuation . . . The whole thing, it seems to me, expresses coming events that are still hidden in the archetypal realm. The anima, clearly, has her mind on spiritual contents. But the bear, the emblem of Russia, sets the ball rolling.

Throughout the rest of his life, he devoted a lot of time to sculpting, carving and painting, but insisted he was not producing works of art. 'I only try to get things into stone of which I think it is important that they appear in hard matter and stay on for a reasonably long time. Or I try to give form to something that seems to be in the stone and makes me restless. It is nothing for show . . . There is not much of form in it.'

He felt no affinity with contemporary artists and writers. He said: 'Picasso's psychic problems, so far as they find expression in his work, are strictly analogous to those of my patients.' The paintings struck Jung as schizophrenic: 'The main characteristic is one of fragmentation, which expresses itself in the so-called "lines of fracture" – that is a series of psychic "faults" (in the geological sense) which run right through the picture. The picture leaves one cold, or disturbs one by its paradoxical, unfeeling and grotesque unconcern for the beholder.'

He was equally hostile to modernism in poetry and the novel. 'Contemporary literature,' he wrote, 'particularly German, is to me the epitome of boredom coupled with psychic torture.' Though there is undisguised acrimony in his attacks on contemporary artists, his bitterness usually appeared to be unconnected with any feeling that he was himself an artist *manqué*. But writing about Hermann Broch's 1945 novel *The Death of Virgil*, he admitted he was

> *jealous* of Broch because he succeeded in doing what I had to forbid myself on pain of death. Whirling in the same underworld vortex and buoyed ecstatically up by the vision of elusive images, I heard a whisper telling me I could make it 'aesthetic', while knowing all the time that the writer in me was just embryonic and incapable of genuine artistry . . . Despite this constant awareness, all kinds of resentments have grown up inside the artistic homunculus in me, who has obviously been deeply upset by my refusal to press the poet's wreath on his brow.

Lecturing in 1922 'On the Relation of Analytical Psychology to Poetry' he maintained that there were 'two entirely different modes of creation': introverted and extraverted. Schiller's plays are examples of the introverted literature that expresses the writer's intentions, while in *Zarathustra*, Nietzsche let his material take him over. (Eight years later Jung substituted the terms *psychological* and *visionary* for the two modes of creation.)

Though the extravert or visionary writer may think he is swimming, he is being swept along by an unseen current. We should see the creative process as an autonomous complex implanted in the human psyche. Saying 'the writer's consciousness was in abeyance during the period of creation', Jung is implicitly comparing him to a medium whose voice is taken over by a spirit, or a dreamer whose mind is relaying images and stories that have nothing to do with conscious memories or intentions. A writer, according to Jung, may switch from one mode to the other: Nietzsche's carefully crafted aphorisms are generically different from his tempestuous *Zarathustra*. In the greatest art, the creative process consists in the unconscious activation of an archetypal image. 'By shaping it, the artist translates it into contemporary language, making it possible for us to find our way back to life's deepest springs.'

Jung explained his dislike of modernity by arguing that

> we have plunged into a cataract of progress, which pushes us forwards into the future with increasing violence the further it drags us away from our

roots . . . But it is precisely the loss of this perspective, our rootlessness that
has given rise to the 'discontents of civilisation' and to so much haste that
we live more in the future and its chimerical promises of a golden age than
in the present. Our whole background of evolutionary history has not yet
caught up with it . . . We refuse to recognise that everything better is
bought with something worse.

He did not always know whether he was awake or asleep. In the winter of
1923, thinking he could hear footsteps all round the tower, he slipped into a
dream about a crowd of peasant boys laughing and prancing about in dark
clothes. The dream went on recurring till the spring.

Emma and the children were rarely invited here, while Toni, who was
allowed to visit him, had to put up with the lack of comfort. Over the
entrance he chiselled the words: *Philemonis Sacrum – Fausti Poenitentia*
('Shrine of Philemon – Repentance of Faust'). Faust had caused the death
of Philemon and Baucis, the only people who still honoured the gods, and as
Jung wrote in 1942, 'suddenly and terrifyingly I realised I had taken over
Faust as my heritage, and moreover as the champion and avenger of
Philemon and Baucis'. He took this idea as seriously as if *Faust* had been
a chronicle of historical events. Returning to a simple lifestyle not unlike
that of the old couple, Jung was trying to reinstate a way of life in which we
understand ourselves through the gods.

Now that he had the tower, he would no longer want to go camping.
Bollingen would provide the same holiday from the comforts and gadgets of
contemporary civilisation. He had four bunk beds in the tower – later five.
During weeks when the children were allowed to help with the building
work, some of them would sleep in tents outside, and they had all their
meals in the open air.

During the summer of 1923 Peter Baynes organised a Jungian conference in
a Cornish village, Polzeath. He and Esther Harding collected an audience of
about thirty Jung enthusiasts, including Swiss and Americans. This time Jung
brought Emma and Toni with him. They all stayed in Polzeath's only hotel,
while Jung lectured and held seminars in the village hall. His subject was
'The Technique of Analysis'.

Finding that free association led back to sexuality or the lust for power, he
advocated what he now called *controlled association* to enrich the symbolism
and compensate for the one-sidedness of the conscious attitude. Discussing
tranference, 'which brings up all the dirty, perverted and repressed material'
of the unconscious, he formulated some ideas that would become central to
his thinking. When collective elements enter the transference, he said, it

means the patient has been living under outworn collective ideas, which should be replaced by a new ruling principle.

He discussed a young man's dream about the imminent death of a king. The anima was released in her black, instinctual aspect, and only a black magician was wise enough to follow her. Though he found the key to paradise, he could not unlock the gates. For this a white magician was needed. Jung took the dream to be prophetic, indicating worldwide ideological changes. Regarding the dream as 'full of wisdom', he felt sure the young man, had he been a patient, would have begun to respect the unconscious.

Twenty-Three

Dark-faced Men

Superficially, the world has become small and known . . . There's no
mystery left . . . Yet the more we know, superficially, the less we
penetrate, vertically. It's all very well skimming across the surface of
the ocean and saying you know all about the sea. There still remain the
terrifying under-deeps, of which we have utterly no experience.

This was not written by Jung but by D. H. Lawrence in an essay on New
Mexico, where he spent a lot of time between 1922 and 1925, when he was
in his late thirties. He called it picturesque, with 'old Spanish Red Indian
desert mesas, pueblos, cowboys, penitentes, all that film stuff'. But this is
how he goes on:

I think New Mexico was the greatest experience from the outside world
that I have ever had . . . It was New Mexico that liberated me from the
present era of civilisation, the great era of material and mechanical
development . . . I had no permanent feeling of religion till I came to
New Mexico and penetrated into the old human race-experience there
. . . A vast old religion which once swayed the earth lingers in unbroken
practice there in New Mexico, older, perhaps, than anything in the world
save Australian aboriginal taboo and totem, and that's not yet religion.

Jung had not read this essay when, in the winter of 1924, he was invited to
the USA by George Porter, a rich businessman, art collector and philanthropist, married to a Frenchwoman who had been involved in the
Theosophy movement. Jung wanted to visit the Pueblo Indians in Taos,
and Porter financed the trip, made the arrangements and offered to
accompany him – a proposal Jung accepted.

Before leaving Zurich on 10 December, Jung contacted Harold and Edith

McCormick, who had divorced, and Fowler, who was now twenty-five. Though he had still been a boy when they last saw each other, Jung invited Fowler to join him and Porter on their journey to New Mexico. In Bremen on 13 December Jung boarded a steamer for New York with Fowler.

In Chicago by Christmas, Jung divided his time between Harold and Edith. From there, he went on with Porter and Fowler to the Grand Canyon. 'I *saw* the Canyon,' he wrote in a letter, 'but I say nothing about it.' What he said later was that it gave him the same 'feeling of awe' he got when walking into a cathedral.

The three men were joined by Jaime de Angulo, an expert on American–Indian languages, who had met Jung in Zurich during 1923. He had taught at Berkeley and done fieldwork among Californian Indians. His former wife Cary had gone to Zurich in 1922 to study with Jung. During 1924 de Angulo had been in Taos with Lawrence, who was now in Mexico.

Jung knew the Indians had been driven into a ghetto existence. Forced to live on reservations where churches had been built, they were under pressure to convert. But for them, Taos was still the heart of the world. Arriving on 5 January 1925 in the pueblo, Jung found two groups of square, reddish adobe brick houses separated by a stream flowing down from the sacred mountain. The spokesman for the Indians was a member of the pueblo council whose English was fluent. He chatted with Jung after they had climbed up rough wooden ladders to the fifth storey of the main building. 'I could talk to him,' Jung claims, 'as I had seldom spoken to a European.' But he was not what Jung says he was, 'a chief of the Taos Pueblos'. His name was Ochwiay Biano – Blue Mountain Lake.

White people always want something, he said. They are uneasy and restless. In fact they are mad, always thinking with their heads, while Indians think with their hearts. 'This Indian,' says Jung, 'had struck our vulnerable spot and noticed something to which we are blind.'

While other Indians appeared on the roofs, wrapped in their woollen blankets and gazing at the sun, which was rising higher in the sky, Jung questioned him about religious mysteries. Not allowed to discuss them, he had to answer evasively or remain silent, but he became excited when talking about the sun. How could there be any other god? Obviously, the sun is our father. Alone in the mountains, could a man build a fire without help from the sun? If their religion was stamped out by the Americans, the world would fizzle out, because every day their prayers were helping their father to travel across the sky.

Europeans, wrote Jung, would sneer at this man's naivety. 'Knowledge does not enrich us, but distances us further and further from the mythic world in which we once felt at home.' Apparently unaware that Mexican Indians had used human sacrifice to fuel their father's journey, he was so impressed that forty-five years later he was still quoting what Biano had said. Jung made an equally strong impression on him. Afterwards they sporadically corresponded, and Biano kept a picture of him on the wall above his fireplace.

Jung went on to visit Indians who lived more primitively in caves and small houses in the Canyon de los Frijoles, between Taos and Santa Fe. When Fowler told him American blacks were being employed to cut down trees in the forest outside New Orleans, he wanted to meet them, and the three Europeans arrived there on 9 January 1925. Fowler never forgot a moment in a New Orleans restaurant when Jung impulsively tossed his hat up on the blades of the revolving fan on the ceiling.

He went on to Washington and New York, where he spoke to a small audience at the 59th Street flat of Dr Kristine Mann, founder of New York's Analytical Psychology Club. He talked about racial psychology and morphological changes in American and Australian skulls. Generalising, as he had on his 1912 visit, about the national character of the Americans, he accused them of ruthlessness, lack of reverence, indifference to ancestors and a 'single-mindedness' that would be impossible for Europeans.

Jung may afterwards have wished he had tried while in the USA to contact Fowler's second cousin, Medill McCormick, who killed himself on 24 February.

George Porter would shoot himself exactly two years later. In his final letter to Ruth McCormick, Porter confessed he had always been in love with her husband. He left stock with a face value of left $20,000 to Jung, but it turned out to be worth almost nothing.

That summer, Jung took part in three seances held at the Burghölzli or in the house of Professor Rudolf Bernoulli, a friend of Bleuler, who also attended, as did the parapsychologist Baron Albert Schrenck-Notzing. The medium was an Austrian boy, Rudi Schneider, whose journal for the seance on 25 June 1925 contains the signature 'C. G. Jung, Psychoanalyst'. According to Schrenck-Notzing's research secretary Gerta Walther, nothing significant happened at the first or third seance, but at the second, human limbs materialised and telekinetic phenomena were observed. Jung later claimed to have

> seen objects moving that were not directly touched and moreover under
> absolutely satisfactory scientific conditions . . . all the objects that appar-
> ently moved by themselves moved as though lifted, shaken or thrown by a

hand. In this series of experiments, I, together with other observers, saw a hand and felt its pressure – apparently the hand that caused all the other phenomena of this kind. These phenomena have nothing to do with the 'will', since they occurred only when the medium was in a trance and precisely not in control of his will. They seem to fall into the category of poltergeist manifestations.

In another letter he confirmed his belief that 'certain archetypal figures of the unconscious literally appear as ghostly controls with materialisation mediums'.

In a thoughtful book about Rudi Schneider, Anita Gregory gives us her conclusions after analysing journals in which he provided accounts of 269 seances. Most of them seemed to have been monotonous, but he gave the impression of being fundamentally honest, and though she found little reliable-seeming evidence for the materialisation of complete human figures, she found plenty for 'partial materialisations, notably a hand and fingers, and greyish-whitish quasi-gaseous masses'.

Jung was less interested at this time in ordinary personal relationships than in telepathic contact or contact with spirits. Esther Harding, who came to Küsnacht in the spring after hearing him lecture in New York, had an analytical session in which, talking dismissively about sexuality and friendship, he said the only lasting relationship was one in which two people were linked as if by an invisible telegraph wire. 'I call it to myself the golden thread.' But the veil of maya, or illusion, may stop us from recognising it. The only way to penetrate beyond maya is through individuation, which is impossible without relatedness, just as relatedness is impossible without individuation. The individuated state, he said is made up of three realities – God, the self and relatedness. In Christian terms the three realities are God, the spirit and heaven.

Jung may have spent too much time in the tower. Visting him in 1924, Smith Ely Jelliffe had formed an unfavourable impression. 'I was amazed to learn how narrow his vision was for the general situation and how one-sided (sic) he had developed his interests. I felt he had really ceased to be a physician.'

This is a charge that has to be taken seriously. Addressing a conference on the question of whether Analytical Psychology is a religion, Anthony Storr made the point that in reading through Jung's collected works, any psychiatrist 'must be amazed by the lack of reference to the symptoms of neurosis with which every psychiatrist is familiar. If you consult the index to the 16th volume, *The Practice of Psychotherapy*, you will find no entry for *anxiety*, no entry for *compulsion*, only two entries for *hysteria*, only two entries

for *depression*, one of which is a footnote, and only one entry for *phobia*.'
Throughout the first nine years of his career as a doctor, he had more contact
with schizophrenics than neurotics, but after 1909, none of his patients had
been incarcerated, and though he maintained that many neurotics were
schizophrenics in disguise, this does not resolve the problem of whether he
had 'really ceased to be a physician'. Storr points out, Jung was mainly
interested in altering his patients' outlook.' Analytical psychology, Storr
concludes, 'is certainly closer to being a religion than it is to being a medical
treatment for neurosis.' Jung might not have liked this formulation, but he
said that as a doctor, he encouraged belief in immortality, especially in older
patients, and took all religions to be 'therapies for the sorrows and disorders
of the soul'.

Jung was going to celebrate his fiftieth birthday on 26 July 1925. By the age
of forty-five he had, as Peter Homans argues in *Jung in Context*, evolved all
his original ideas, and, as Homans concludes, 'they underwent little significant change thereafter'. To read through his collected works, his
correspondence and his interviews is to read through innumerable reiter-
ations of the same points, illustrated with the same stories. Though Jung
went on reading alchemical and theological books – and rereading the Bible
– most of his work was done on the periphery of psychology. His thought
processes were mainly oriented towards alchemy, the archetypal, the supra-
human and the primitive.

The birthday was celebrated in Swanage, Dorset. He recalled the evening
in a letter written three years later: 'There was a beautiful sunset, the
waterfowl called to one another, a chill night wind came down from the
mountains, and I drank an extra bottle of wine and smoked a birthday cigar.'
There are no mountains in the area, but he had got into the habit of
mythologising his past.

He was in Swanage for a seminar on 'Dreams and Symbolism'. A large
tent had been pitched in the middle of a hayfield for the meetings, and Jung
lectured for a couple of hours each day to an audience of about fifty people.
But the weather was unfriendly, and most of what he said was accompanied
by the loud patter of rain on the canvas.

Until Freud rediscovered it, he said, the art of dream interpretation had
been lost since the antique period. Pythagoras had pointed forward to the
notion of a collective unconscious by teaching that dreams came from the
all-pervading mind of God. Jung contrasted two series of dreams, one from a
young man and the other from a middle-aged woman. Hers were personal
in character, and he was more interested in the young man's, which were full
of *représentations collectives*. 'To have a great dream,' he said, 'is a revelation of

the new aspect of the world, but it is dangerous. To have a trivial dream is more normal, more ordinary; but where triviality is the disease (as it was with the woman patient) it would be an advantage to have deep dreams.'

After the final meeting with the group, Jung stayed in London to give three lectures for the New Education Fellowship. He always felt at home in England, and sometimes said: 'If I have lived before, I am sure I was an Englishman.'

After one of his lectures, he was invited to dinner with the novelist H. G. Wells in his Regent's Park house. When Wells asked what went on in the mind of a schizophrenic who became delusional, Jung explained at length how the psychotic projected his own ideas onto other people and events. As he talked, Wells, who had been expansive, appeared to become smaller. He was concentrating so hard that he seemed to 'shrink back in his chair as though sucking in my words in a most incredible way'. At the end of the evening Jung felt exhausted, and had no desire to meet Wells again.

But what he had said led to Wells's novel *Christina Alberta's Father*, which Jung could then use when talking about the collective unconscious. 'Mr Preemby, a complete nonentity, recognises himself as the point of inter-section of all ages, past and future. This knowledge is not too dearly bought at the cost of a little madness, provided that Preemby is not in the end devoured by that monster of a primordial image – which is in fact what nearly happens to him.' Wells also described the evening with Jung in his 1926 novel *The World of William Clissold*.

In March an attractive young American doctor had arrived in Küsnacht from England, where he was doing biochemical research at Cambridge. Two years earlier, reading *Psychological Types*, Harry Murray had been fascinated by the suggestion that type creates a predisposition towards certain intel-lectual attitudes, and he had written to Jung, asking for an interview. But when they discussed the book, Jung gave the impression of having lost interest in typology, which made Harry start talking about his emotional confusion as if he were a prospective patient.

His wife, Josephine, a rich, pretty, extravert Bostonian, had brought their daughter to Cambridge for the year, and another American family was there – Will and Christiana Morgan, with their son. Harry felt strongly attracted to Christiana, who was beautiful and soulful, and had already been unfaithful to Will with Harry's younger brother.

After a few minutes, Jung interrupted abruptly to start talking excitedly about the anima. Using vivid, earthy, concrete language, he confided in the young American about Toni as his anima figure, and described individuation as the process that brings unconscious material under conscious control.

Seeing Harry as a thinking intuitive type, Jung felt an affinity with him. Harry's boyhood, like Jung's, had been dominated by a powerful mother, and Josephine sounded like Emma – good-looking, practical, stable, capable of running a household efficiently. Jung's intuitions were quick to tell him that Harry would soon have to choose between two routes into the future. He could continue to base his life in the conventional way on marriage and family, or he could choose a more uncomfortable route parallel to the one Jung had chosen. Perhaps Christiana would turn out to have the same talent as Toni for putting a man in touch with his unconscious.

Harry was astonished that Jung was so friendly. Every day for three weeks they spent at least an hour together, and at weekends they sailed on Lake Zurich, stopping to eat at lakeside restaurants. Harry was too conservative not to be shocked when he was invited to tea in the tower with Emma and Toni, but it was impressive that they gave no indication of rivalry. They struck Harry as similar, both dark and diffident.

Though already half in love with Christiana, he was scared of damaging both her marriage and his, as well as his daughter, her son and his career. Jung surprised him by comparing adultery with the German invasion of Belgium in 1914. Violating a treaty, the Germans overran a defenceless country 'because they had to'. Going to bed with Toni, Jung said, he was morally in the wrong, but the infidelity had been inevitable, and it was better, afterwards, neither to make excuses nor to pretend he had behaved well. This was how he had once talked to Sabina.

Should Harry 'trust himself to Jung'? He insisted that patients should not hold him responsible for what happened to them. When you come to Zurich, he said, 'you take your life into your hands'. But it was impossible to ignore either Jung or what he said. Harry, as he wrote later, '*experienced* the unconscious, something not to be drawn out of books'.

Feeling sorry for Toni, he did not intend to exploit Christiana in the same way, but he wanted Jung to meet her, and they arranged that she should come to Küsnacht later in the year. Josephine and their daughter (who was also called Josephine) were in San Remo, where Harry joined them in April. 'He was absolutely hypnotised by Jung,' wrote Josephine in her diary, 'and impenetrable.' But he soon blurted out his new insights, and she vowed: 'never again would I let him go off alone.'

When he talked to Christiana, she was outraged by the idea of a triangle. But over the next weeks, she and Harry became more intimate. 'We spoke to each other through Melville,' she wrote in her diary. Reading *Moby-Dick* on the boat while crossing the Atlantic in the summer of 1924, Harry had taken Captain Ahab's struggle with the white whale to represent rebellion against paternal authority, while the dangerous and mysterious ocean seemed to stand for the unconscious. Melville, writing in 1851, had penetrated it, Harry thought, 'with more genuine comprehension than any other writer'.

Afterwards, reading his 1852 novel *Pierre* in a Jungian perspective, Harry had been confronted with a reflection of his own situation. If the white whale had seemed archetypal, Pierre appeared to be driven by his anima into sacrificing his marriage to his fixation on his darkly introverted half-sister, Isabel, who reminded Harry of Christiana. Talking to her through Melville was dangerous.

The twenty-seven-year-old Christiana Morgan arrived in Küsnacht during September. If Harry had reminded Jung of himself, Christiana, who was better-looking than Sabina or Toni, had comparable depth, intensity and spirituality. He liked her, but she found, as Harry had, that Jung had little talent for listening. As a young doctor at the Burghölzli, eager to learn all he could about the nature of the psyche, he had concentrated for hours at a stretch on whatever schizophrenics said. Now, having formed clear-cut ideas about the unconscious, he wanted patients to learn from him. Confronted with a case, a piece of evidence, a system or a theory, he could no longer look at it objectively and open-mindedly. Reluctant to abandon or modify theories he had adopted, he usually declared he had found new confirmation for them.

He let patients talk about anything that seemed to come from the collective unconscious, but Christiana found him unresponsive to what she said about herself, her parents, Harry and other individuals. 'From the beginning,' writes the biographer Forrest Robinson,

> Harry and Christiana had been put off by Jung's failure to deal at all closely with their personal histories . . . They were disturbed that his attention seemed fixed almost exclusively on the ways in which their lives confirmed his 'universal' theories. In Christiana's case particularly, he asked very few questions before launching into an analysis of her personality type.

Letting her answer his questions only briefly, he said men should be primarily thinkers, but feeling should be the dominant function in women. She had unbalanced her life by subduing her feelings and relying on her intelligence.

Other patients encountered the same resistance when they wanted to give him facts about family background and emotional relationships. When Aniela Jaffé started talking about her mother, his response was: 'Don't waste your time.' An American with a mother-fixation was told:

You've got a lulu of a neurosis, but you seem rather intelligent and you seem to have a lot of good will and everything . . . There's going to be an awful lot of stuff about your mother. You've got the look of a mother-drowned guy, somehow. Well, all that stuff just bores me to the extreme . . . Why don't you just work with Toni Wolff? She likes that stuff, and we'll just talk about the collective stuff.

He started going to Toni three times a week, and to Jung once or twice. Jung's view was that 'we should never let our self-confidence or self-esteem depend on the behaviour of another person, however much we may be humanly affected by him. Everything that happens to us, properly understood, leads us back to ourselves . . . dependence on the behaviour of others is a last vestige of childhood.' His system of thought, as Peter Homans writes, placed his followers

> at the centre of a cosmological epic and encouraged them to view their past traditions and surrounding culture exclusively in terms of the struct-ures and processes of their own consciousness. In doing so he gave them occasion to think endlessly about themselves, and he blunted their capacities for achieving social distance interpersonally.

Not that he could altogether avoid having to deal with relationships between men and women, but his interventions usually pivoted on assumptions about inequality between the anima and the animus. It was inconceivable to him that sexual interdependence can lead to a partnership based on reciprocity. Before meeting Christiana, he had made up his mind what her function should be in Harry's life. Whatever she had to say about herself, her past, her anxieties, her dreams, nothing would have altered his view that her destiny was to be a *femme inspiratrice*. 'He has a chance to become an adult through you, but it will be difficult for him. Rebirth for him will be like destruction. You are a pioneer woman – your function is to create a man.'

Impressed, she told Jung 'how calm Harry's face was after he'd seen you'.

'Yes,' said Jung. 'I gave him a hell of a good time. I let him look through my telescope. I showed him heaven. I knew he'd fall back into all sorts of infantile things, but at least he has seen . . . You're an animus woman, and so you're an anima woman for man . . . The problem with you is your negative thinking, which will be hard for him because his thinking is creative.'

Whatever misgivings she had about the difficulty of making Jung listen to her, she admired his charismatic self-confidence and his indifference to

conventional morality. She decided he 'has indeed the true fire. I never
dreamed that anyone could talk so directly or so instantly to the spirit or the
core. There is a fine comprehension and a large sweep about it all, rather a
splendid fearlessness. I had the curious feeling of having ages of New
England ancestry quietly and noiselessly taking flight after two hours of
conversation with him.' He seemed to be 'attempting a new way. There is
no question that he is the prophet. And the new way means the reconciliation of the thought of the present day with the spirit.'

But he had not worked out the full philosophy. 'Let's do it, Harry! To go
on with what Jung has begun would be the biggest thing that could be done
at the present time.'

Visiting the Colonial Exhibition at Wembley Jung had seen a display about
tribes under British rule. This made him want to penetrate further into
Africa. His appetite for primitive culture and religion had been stimulated by
the visit to the pueblo, and though he did not see himself as a pioneering
anthropologist, he would not have laid the plans he did if anthropology had
established itself as a subject of study. The universities of Columbia and
Cambridge had opened anthropological departments in 1896 and 1904, but
it was not till the 1920s that Bronislaw Malinowski, a pupil of Wundt,
started publishing his books about his researches in the Trobriand Islands off
the eastern tip of New Guinea, and there was no general interest in primitive
culture. Jung also wanted to explore mythological material in the dreams of
tribal people.

He invited Peter Baynes to join him on the African expedition, and
discussing where they should go, they decided on the foothills of an extinct
volcano called Mount Elgon or Masaba in the land of the Kavirondo, near
the border between Kenya and Uganda.

Later, still, undecided about the expedition, Jung consulted the *I Ching*
and landed on the fifty-third hexagram, which deals with development and
gradual progress. He concluded that the unconscious approved of his
intentions, but in the commentary on the third line of the hexagram he
read: 'The wild goose gradually approaches the plateau. The man goes forth
and does not return.' Was he being warned that if he went on the
expedition, he would not return alive? Perturbed, but not deterred, he
spent six weeks learning Swahili, assuming that almost everyone in East
Africa spoke the language.

Peter Baynes arranged for the British Foreign Office to sanction their
safari as the 'Bugishu Psychological Expedition'. The letters BPE were
stamped on their provision crates. The third member of the party was
another American, an ex-patient in his mid-twenties, George Beckwith.

Though he had a flat in Paris and a manservant, he was not enjoying life, and Jung had not enhanced his faith in the future by telling him he had been allocated a leaky vessel for the journey between birth and death. Unlike most of Jung's admirers, Beckwith was not too respectful, and Jung enjoyed being told: 'You're an old humbug with hair like feathers. Anyway it needs brushing before you go out.'

After going to England, Jung sailed for Mombasa on 15 October 1925. The second port of call was Malaga, where Baynes and Beckwith were to join him. Baynes's second wife was so passionately against his going on the expedition that she threatened to commit suicide if he went. Baynes discussed her with Jung, who advised him to ignore her threats. He did so, and she killed herself while he was packing. Which did not stop him from accompanying Jung on the trip. What Baynes could not control was his depression, which was stressful for the other two men. Jung was better than Beckwith at concealing his irritation.

They sailed from Port Said to Mombasa through the Red Sea together with a lot of young Englishmen about to take up Foreign Office posts in East Africa. The young people, who danced and played games on board, called the two doctors and Beckwith the three Obadiahs – the title of a popular music-hall song. Some of the young men exchanged addresses with Jung and Baynes, who were disconcerted to learn how few of their new friends survived the tropical diseases. The man who had sat opposite Jung at the table died within two months from malaria, pneumonia and amoebic dysentery.

The three Obadiahs arrived in Mombasa on 12 November. 'The whole town consists of huts thatched with grass. Negroes and Indians everywhere. Tall coconut palms.' They took a narrow-gauge train into the interior.

> The earth there is quite red, and red dust swirled about the train so that our white clothes turned red all over. We saw wild Masai with long spears and shields, they were quite naked and had only an ox skin on. They had bored through the lobes of their ears and hung such heavy brass rings in them that the lobes were 10 cm long. The women wear iron rings round their ankles, sometimes up to the knee. We travelled through jungles where monkeys sat in the trees, then we came to unending plains with whole herds of antelope and zebra – two ostriches raced the train.

In Nairobi, the capital of Kenya, they stayed at the New Stanley Hotel. After buying two guns and four hundred cartridges, they hired four black servants and a cook. On 11 November Armistice Day was celebrated at the hotel with a dance, and a pleasant-looking thirty-year-old Yorkshirewoman

Carl at the age of 6

Paul Jung with his wife Emilie.

Carl in his late teens with his parents and his sister, Gertrud, aged about nine.

The church and the parsonage at Laufen, where Carl lived until he was four.

The attic in the parsonage at Klein-Hüningen. This is where Carl hid his manikin.

Throughout his life, Jung loved boats, rivers and lakes. Here at the age of 17 he is seen with two friends on the Old Rhine near Basel.

Jung's cousin, Helly Preiswerk, had dark, penetrating eyes, and a clever, alert face. He encouraged her to believe in herself as a medium.

The Burghölzli was both an asylum and the psychiatric clinic of Zurich University. In 1899 there were four doctors to look after 340 inmates. Jung, who started his career there, is pictured outside the building in 1901 (*below*).

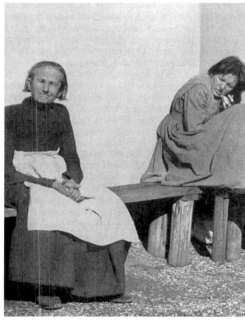

Two catatonic patients at the Burghölzli during the 1920s.

Jung was 27 when he married the 20-year-old Emma Rauschenbach in 1903. They are seen here in the year they married.

Freud had to be asked more than once before he would send Jung this photograph in 1907. It had been taken the previous year.

Jung with Emma and four of their five children – (*from left to right*) Franz, Agathe, Marianne and Gret – at Château d'Oex in 1917.

Left: Jung with Hermann Göring's cousin Dr Matthias Göring in 1934. In 1936 Jung invited Göring to co-edit the *Zentralblatt*, the organ of the General Medical Society for Psychotherapy.
Right: Jung with Leo Baeck at the 1947 Eranos Conference.

Jung with Mircea Eliade, an expert on mythology, at the 1950 conference.

Above: Jung on his travels, pictured here holding a 'palaver' with Elgonyi tribesmen in the border region between Kenya and Uganda in late 1925.
Below: In Egypt during 1926.

Jung started building his 'tower' at Bollingen in February 1923, completing the work in the spring of 1924, but he went on adding to it over the next 32 years, stopping only in 1956, five years before he died.

Staring at the rough surface of the Bollingen wall, Jung imagined half-formed figures which he completed by chiselling them into reliefs. He called this smiling face 'the Trickster'.

Jung was never happier than when at Bollingen, sitting by the lake.

Jung with Toni Wolff. According to his assistant, Carl Meier, 'she was responsible for the most important parts of his books.'

Father Victor White. None of Jung's male colleagues, assistants or collaborators ever had such a close relationship with him.

Jung with Emma at Eranos. After her death in 1955, the inscription he wrote for her tombstone read: 'Oh vase, sign of devotion and obedience'.

Jung in 1944.

Jung on the terrace at the Casa Gabriela.

Jung with Jolande Jacobi, who once made him so angry that he threw her down a flight of stairs.

Olga Fröbe-Kapteyn at the Casa Gabriela overlooking the Lago Maggiore.

Jung at the moment of leaving the Casa Gabriela.

Jung sitting with Aniela Jaffé at his favourite spot on the terrace wall.

Jung giving one of his Eranos lectures.

Jung's house at Küsnacht, and his study.

approached Jung. 'Do you mind if I sit here? I won't say a word.' They had seen each other on the boat from Hamburg, but had not spoken. Keeping her promise, she said nothing till he started a conversation.

Her name was Ruth Bailey, and she had been engaged twice, but both men had been killed in the war. Her youngest sister was about to marry an English engineer working for a railway company that refused to give him any leave, and their mother had agreed to the marriage on condition that Ruth should chaperone her sister till the wedding. Knowing that her future brother-in-law was intending to dance with them alternately, Ruth escaped by saying she was going to sit with Dr Jung – making it sound as if she knew him.

In the morning, while the sisters and the fiancé were having breakfast, Jung went across to their table. 'Young man, you can't have two wives, even in Africa. We want Miss Bailey to have breakfast with us.' He led her away and afterwards invited her to go in a rickshaw on a shopping expedition. Like Beckwith, she endeared herself to him by not being overawed, but Beckwith was annoyed at having to spend so much time with Baines while Jung chatted with Ruth.

His account of how she came to join the expedition is different from hers. According to *Memories, Dreams, Reflections,* the three men had left for Mount Elgon, and after climbing a narrow path, they found themselves in Masai territory, where a letter was waiting for them from the governor of Uganda, asking them to take care of an English lady whose itinerary was the same as theirs – she was going through the Sudan and Egypt back to England. In fact, she was due to sail back to England from Mombasa, and according to an interview she gave in February 1969, she was staying with her sister and her new brother-in-law in Turbo when a runner arrived with an invitation for her to join Jung in the camp. She would have to make a 250-mile journey, and her brother-in-law was against it.

The three men had travelled as far as they could by rail. At the end of the line, Jung was sitting on a provision crate when he was joined by a pipe-smoking Englishman who had spent forty years in Africa. 'You know, mister, this here country is not man's, it's God's country. So if anything should happen, just sit down and don't worry.'

Driving towards Mount Elgon and stopping when the road turned into a dirt track, they found they were at the government station for the Nandi district, outside the bungalow of the assistant district commissioner, Francis Hislop. He describes Jung as burly with a reddish-brown country face and grey hair that made him look older than he was. Hislop gave them tea and, hearing their plans, warned them against entering the territory of the Karamojong and the Sabei without a permit from the provincial commissioner at Mbale. Both tribes had their own language, he said, and Jung would need an interpreter. His knowledge of Swahili would be less useful than he was expecting – the more primitive the tribe, the more materialistic its language. For expressing abstract ideas or emotions, the Karamojong and Sabei languages would be even worse than Swahili. And when Jung asked about the Elgon caves, Hislop explained that tribesmen used them as cattle shelters. Covered in dung, the floors had become a home for millions of fleas.

The semi-official status of the 'Bugishu Psychological Expedition' made it easy to recruit bearers, and the safari was given a military escort of a corporal and two privates. The region, which had first been explored in the 1880s, still had few visitors. After passing through stretches of jungle and tramping along native trails, they reached the Masai, and pitched camp not far from a kraal consisting of a few huts and a *shamba*, or yard. Here the white visitors respected the custom that stopped them from speaking to the women. A conversation would have been regarded as an act of intimacy. The tribesmen hunted and took care of the cattle, while the women looked after the children, the goats and chickens, who lived in the same round huts. The women had a clear-cut role in the tribal economy. 'The concept of "equal rights for women" was born into an age in which such a partnership has lost its meaning.'

Though they stayed several weeks, Jung spoke to none of the women except the one who was introduced to him – the sister of a young man called Gibroat. She had four children, and her husband, who wandered about with his herds, had another wife with six children. The three adults each had a hut within forty yards of the other two. Liking the woman, Jung thought her security and self-assurance 'depended to a large extent on her identity with her visible wholeness'. She was a paragon of stability.

> I asked myself whether the masculinisation of the white woman is not connected with the loss of her natural wholeness (*shamba*, children, livestock, own house and home) as a compensation for her impoverishment, and whether the feminisation of the white man is not a further consequence. The more rational a society is, the less difference there is between the sexes.

He wholeheartedly approved of the inequality.

Central Africa was making a deep impression on him, and he thought of his weeks with the Elgonyi as 'one of the loveliest times of my life . . . Thousands of miles separating me from Europe, the mother of all devils, who could not reach me here – no telegrams, no telephone calls, no letters

. . . My liberated spiritual forces flowed happily back into primeval expanses.'

Curious about the doings of the white men, the natives squatted outside
the camp all day, watching. Jung's headman arranged a 'palaver' every
morning and found a mahogany stool for him to sit on while the others sat
on the ground. 'The chief has men with whips who whip everybody down
if they don't sit down at once.' Jung had to begin by saying a mantra. The
man who replied to him had to speak from his position on the ground in a
low, unemotional voice. 'If a man speaks too loudly, somebody comes with
a whip . . . As soon as there is emotion, there is danger of fighting and
killing.'

Hislop had been wrong to say none of the tribesmen understood Swahili.
Frequently pausing to consult a dictionary. Jung could communicate with
them. But though he offered cigarettes, matches and safety pins, none of
them would discuss his dreams. They never had any, they said. And when he
questioned the old *laibon* (medicine man), whose cloak was made from the
skins of blue monkeys, he said there had been a time when dreams told the
laibon about war and sickness, and when rain would come, and where the
herds should be driven. But dreams were no longer needed, because the
English knew everything.

Going outside their huts at dawn, the men either spat or blew vigorously
into their hands before raising them towards the sun. Unable to explain
why they did this, they said everyone worshipped the sun as it rose. Only
then was it God, as was the moon when it appeared as a slim crescent.
Saliva contained the personal mana, the power of healing, magic and life,
while breath was wind and spirit. The act of raising the hands was a
wordless prayer, and so long as sunlight prevailed, ghosts and evil spirits did
no harm.

The travellers survived several dangerous episodes on the trip, but the
worst came on the return journey. In a Sudan village a local chief made what
seemed like a friendly offer – he would give a dance for Jung and his
companions. Armed with lances, clubs and swords, sixty tribesmen appeared
in the evening, followed at some distance by women and children. Singing,
dancing and drumming in the mixture of firelight and moonlight, the men
advanced threateningly towards the fire, brandishing weapons.

Uncertainly, Jung and Baynes joined in the dance. Jung swung his whip
and smiled back at the smiles on the African faces. The rhythm of the
drumming and dancing quickened as the sweating natives stamped, sang and
shouted, growing more excited. When Jung signalled it was time to stop, the
chief ignored him, even when he made signs to indicate sleep. He then
swung his whip threateningly, giving a friendly laugh at the same time, and –

knowing he would not be understood – swore at the top of his voice in Swiss German.

The natives laughed, stopped dancing, gradually dispersed. For some time drumming was audible in the distance. The whip-cracking and the swearing in Swiss German had probably saved their lives. According to the district commissioner, two white men had recently been killed by the tribe.

Twenty-Four

Negotiating with Heaven

Never before had Jung absented himself for so long from his patients. After being away for three months in the winter of 1924–5, he took a summer holiday, as usual, and stayed on in London after the seminar in Swanage. He left Zurich again in mid-October for his African trip, and after his fiftieth birthday had sharpened his alertness to the quantity of time and energy consumed by his practice, he was still unsettled fourteen months later. 'Patients eat me,' he told an American analytical psychologist, Frances Wickes, writing in English from Sils Maria. 'But my resistances against them are gathering like thunderclouds. I should write much. I have not said yet all I ought to.'

She tried to sympathise, only to be rebuffed: 'Don't worry about myself. I am on my road and I carry my burden just as well as I can do.' Wanting to think of himself as primarily a scientific researcher, he was permanently ambivalent towards patients. Did he owe them more time than he gave them? He always took long holidays – three weeks in the spring, a summer holiday from mid-July till mid-October, and a Christmas holiday. Though he was not greedy for money, he accepted more patients as his fame increased, and as his stamina dwindled, he offloaded more work on collaborators, seeing patients less frequently and resisting demands for more time. One woman, for instance, was allowed to see him only once a fortnight, and this was reduced to once a month.

It was partly to evade them that he went to New Mexico and Africa, and they resented the two long absences. If they had settled in Zurich for his sake, how could he behave so irresponsibly? They waited impatiently, but when he arrived, some no longer wanted him as their analyst. Tina Keller, for instance, had found that working with Toni Wolff, she had been able to resume the series of fantasies he had interrupted by laughing at her.

Like Jung during his breakdown, Tina benefited from Toni's talent for converting pressure into fantasy. Tina was encouraged to think that 'latent possibilities which had had no chance to express themselves could be discovered and channelled'. Toni's presence was 'conducive to the acting-out of the drama'. 'I also have a remembrance as if there were movements, as of shadowy figures in the room.' Toni told Tina to show the spirits she was not going to let them confuse her. 'If this spirit has something he wants to tell you, he must put it into such words as a modern woman can understand. It is his business to translate.'

Toni was less irascible than Jung, and more accessible. He got angry if an overanxious patient tried to make contact while he was on holiday, but Toni gave Tina her summer telephone number. In her first session with Jung after his return from New Mexico, Tina said she had been given more help than he would have given her. Apparently pleased, he said it was a woman's privilege to accompany patients into dark places – a man tended to remain aloof. Nor was Tina alone in her admiration of Toni as an analyst. Joe Wheelwright says: 'Toni was the best analyst I ever had; better than Jung in my estimation.'

Recommending her to one patient as likelier than Emma to be helpful, Jung said: 'You need someone who is clever like a serpent. Not someone who is without fault, like a pigeon.' But despite her talent for coaching patients in the technique of active imagination, Toni did not practise it. According to Barbara Hannah, 'not only had she no ability to do active imagination, she had not the slightest wish to experience the unconscious at first hand. She had no doubt whatsoever of its objective existence, but no inclination to go into it herself.' According to Marie-Louise von Franz, 'Very split people and people threatened by a latent psychosis cannot do active imagination at all.'

In the late twenties and thirties, Jung did not absent himself so much. Nothing if not a star performer, he contented himself with patient–pupils who doubled as audience and supporting actors. Closeted with them, one by one, in his untidy study, he knew that what mattered was the personal confrontation. 'Faced with the patient, you see at once, if you are not totally blinded, that all theorising is absurd. Everything depends on how you strike the patient as a human being. In the end, the personality is the most powerful therapeutic agent.' Sometimes he enjoyed the interaction, and many felt that while they were with him, they were no longer self-contained. 'Once in his presence,' wrote Jane Wheelwright,

one felt as though all the surrounding matter had turned into whizzing molecules . . . Everything stirred. Reality blurred, conversation happened unplanned. I felt someone, not me, spoke through me, and someone, not Jung, was speaking through him. There was also the feeling of being swept into the depths to a perilous, dangerous underworld, but since Jung had descended into this strange world and emerged, so could I . . . Two people were caught in a vice that was forcing them to undergo an important rearrangement of themselves that had a significance – some meaning far beyond them.'

Believing her sanity to be precarious, she had always kept her fears to herself, but perhaps because he had been over the edge, he knew how to make her feel safe. 'He made a grab in the air towards me with both hands as if catching a football, and then hugging it to himself said, "Now I have it and you will not fear any longer." As I remember it, the fear disappeared at that moment.'

'He speaks of the Unconscious as "the other side"', another patient wrote, 'which gives me the same feeling I used to have when, as a little girl, I heard grown-ups speak of heaven. You feel at once that he has great respect for it, and is perfectly capable of entering into negotiations with the forces of its fury and feeling.'

He was usually flexible in presenting his ideas. Analysing a patient is like directing an actor in that nothing can be gained by winning an argument. What matters is not intellectual conviction but emotional adjustment and the developing transference. In lecturing as in analysis, it was good to overcome resistance, but better not to arouse it, and Jung would not talk to an audience of strangers as he would to followers. Writing to a pastor, he said: 'I always have to tread the path of science and experience, quite irrespective of any tradition, in order to get my patients to acknowledge spiritual truths.' His patients were his parishioners. *Septem Sermones ad Mortuos* had prefigured the whole of his subsequent career. If Paul Achilles Jung had failed to give his parishioners what they needed, Carl Gustav Jung would expiate his father's sins of omission.

Naturally, he felt ambivalent towards people who year after year counted on him for emotional support. To one unsuccessful applicant for an appointment, he wrote: 'Anyone who solved the conflict for you would have got the better of you, for he would rob you of a reward on which all self-respect and manliness are ultimately grounded.' Was Jung getting the better of his patients? Robbing them of self-respect and manliness or womanliness?

In his first session with the American Jane Wheelwright, he asked her about her attitude to him. 'Painfully aware of the people around him who had become hopelessly enmeshed in his aura and who had apparently lost their identity in the sticky gluey substance of the transference,' she was determined not to lose hers, and she said he could be a catalyst. He agreed to play this role, but found it gave them insufficient contact. 'Not long afterwards I heard him say in a gently pleading way from deep down in his humanity, "Can't you see me as a human being?" '

Accepting the roles that patients projected often involved histrionic performance. 'A girl comes to me – I'm the mother. An hour later, another arrives – I'm the lover. Then a man comes, and I'm his great-grandmother . . . And I can tell you, if a deputation arrived tomorrow and offers me the crown of Switzerland, I'd seriously consider whether I have the right to refuse the role of King of Switzerland.'

He gave genuine help to those questing for a meaningful life. 'He enriched and amplified and verified our roots and course of historical development by searching out worldwide human common denominators lying in the deepest unconscious religious strata of the human psyche.'

A successful American designer who became a patient early in 1926 was uncertain at the age of thirty-nine whether to continue with his career. Robert Edmond Jones had worked with the Barrymores and designed sets for ten of Eugene O'Neill's plays. He was being analysed by the eclectic Smith Ely Jelliffe, whose technique derived from Freud and Adler, and he may have referred the case to Jung.

In Küsnacht Jones settled into the Hotel Sonne, about fifteen minutes' walk from Jung's house. Given regular sessions, he found Jung 'got down right the first days deeper than Jelliffe ever got . . . It is as quiet as the grave in this little hotel, nothing to do but to have dreams and to interpret them. God only knows which is worse. When you go in for this for all it is worth, it is fearful – simply *fearful*. Right down in the swamp with the demons.'

Seldom reluctant to talk about his own dreams and visions, Jung showed his paintings to Jones, who was impressed by their theatricality. Because he found it easy to draw or paint figures that appeared in his dreams, Jones was at an advantage over other patients, and by practising 'active imagination', he made rapid headway. When he had arrived, he wrote, 'I was *in articulo mortis* and now, well, people who see me simply can't believe their eyes.'

This is typical of the praise travelling round the world by word of mouth and by letter. It increased the pressure on Jung's time, and his dependence on his 'assistants'. In the absence of any equivalent to what was later called 'training analysis', he made intuitive judgements about which patients could be trusted to analyse others. Recognising that Jones had talent for both recording visions and sending himself into trances, Jung made him coach other patients in the technique. Becoming familiar with each other's fantasies, they shared 'the pictures and stories that emerged from the trance state, greeting each other in the streets of Zurich with "How's your Indian?"

"Are you still in the cavern?" or "What's your magician up to today?" '

Patients promoted to the rank of analyst naturally used Jung as their model, and Toni seems to have spent a lot of analytical time on teaching her patients Jungian theory, though she was more flexible than he was when they wanted to discuss anxieties and relationships. So many patient-students were English-speakers – mostly American – that the seminar in English became a regular Wednesday event, starting at ten with a break at eleven for a 'second breakfast' with tea, canapés and general conversation till Jung resumed lecturing. What happened when he finished has been described by Jane Wheelwright:

> He took off down the street with a bevy of females in tow. One of the women, a very pretty society lady Jung tried in vain to help find herself, usually hooked her arm into his. She called him 'Uncle C.G.' The plainer ladies (obviously hating the pretty one) and a few men . . . were shyer, following at a more respectful distance. All of them were on their way to a coffee place where he would continue psychological discussions.

They were encouraged to cultivate their visions. Instead of listening passively to an internal voice, they should enter into dialogue. A friend who had felt unsettled since a trip to South America was advised:

> The first question to be addressed to the Invisible would be: 'Who or what has come alive in S.A.? Who or what has entered my psychic life and caused disturbances and wants to be heard?' To this you should add: 'Let it speak!' Then switch off your noisy consciousness and listen quietly inwards and look at the images that appear before your inner eye, or listen to the words the muscles of your speech apparatus are trying to form. Write down what comes next without criticism. Images should be drawn or painted assiduously, no matter whether you can do it or not. Once you have got down at least fragments of these contents, you can reflect on them *afterwards*.

Teaching patients the technique of 'active imagination', Jung had no intention of making them into artists, but he was empowering them to function in a similar way, drawing on their imagination and their creativity as few of them had since childhood. They found it both pleasurable and frightening to make contact with subpersonalities, as Helly had in the seances.

Complexes, he said, had 'a certain willpower, a sort of ego', and that 'in a schizophrenic condition they emancipate themselves from conscious control to such an extent that they become visible and audible. They appear as visions, they speak in voices which are like the voices of definite people.' He often compared these visions and voices with those found in literature: 'Any novelist or writer will deny that these characters have a psychological meaning, but you can read a writer's mind when you study characters he creates.'

Most writers do not deny this, and some have a ritual or routine for entering the trancelike state that comes spontaneously to others. Virginia Woolf wrote in her diary: 'The only existing life is the imaginary one. Once I get the wheels spinning in my head, I don't want money much, or a dress, or even a cupboard, a bed at Rodmell or a sofa.' Writing *Three Guineas*, she worked at her desk only in the mornings, but her mind went on with the job. 'I must very nearly verge on insanity I think, I get so deep in this book I don't know what I'm doing. Find myself walking along the Strand talking aloud.' In 1931, finishing *The Waves*, she 'reeled across the last ten pages with some moments of such intensity and intoxication that I seemed only to stumble after my own voice, or almost, after some sort of speaker (as when I was mad) I was almost afraid, remembering the voices that used to fly ahead.'

In June 1926, when Christiana Morgan returned to Küsnacht with her husband William, they settled into the Hotel Sonne, where they spent some of their time with Robert Edmund Jones, who was already an acquaintance.

Christiana had an exceptional talent for active imagination. At school she had produced elaborately detailed drawings and paintings. Between 1921 and 1924 she attended classes at the Art Students' League in New York, not only drawing and painting, but also modelling in clay, carving in wood and sculpting in stone. Talking to her, as he had to Sabina and Toni, about his own fantasies and visions, Jung warned her she would need a strong 'ego stance'.

Teaching her how to achieve a trancelike inwardness, he told her to objectify with her retina.

> Then instead of keeping on trying to force the image out, you just want to look in. Now when you see these images you want to hold them and see where they take you – how they change. And you want to try to get into the picture yourself – to become one of the actors. When I first began to do this I saw landscapes. Then I learned how to pull myself into the landscapes, and the figures would talk to me and I would answer them.

She must involve herself more in the images and then paint them as beautifully as she could. She would liberate herself by gaining power over them. The paintings should be kept in a finely bound book, which would represent 'the silent places of your spirit where you will find renewal. If anyone tells you that this is morbid or neurotic and you listen to them – then you will lose your soul – for in that book is your soul.'

In one of her dreams, a nursemaid told her she had two Jewish fathers. One was Christ, Jung explained, and the other was her former lover, the Zionist leader Chaim Weizmann. The Jews, said Jung, 'enter our consciousness through a hole – the hole being the lack of any religion for our animal nature – our nature-forming selves. The Jews have domesticated their instincts – they are not savage as ours are – so your inferior animal self says – you are Jewish – you have given up nature.'

Jung came to regard Christiana as a prophet with an important message for the world. Her visions, he said, were a sacrament, containing 'material for the next two or three hundred years. It is a great *document humaine*. It is the rushing forth of all that has hitherto been unconscious.' In one she saw herself being physically united 'in the blood' with a dark god who transformed her into a snake, entered a church and climbed up on the cross.

But Jung went on reprimanding her for thinking more than a woman should, instead of feeling. She was not an intellectual, he insisted. Her wisdom was not her own – nature's wisdom was speaking through her. Her thoughts were not real thoughts but feelings in disguise.

Sometimes he criticised her fantasies as thin: she should participate more actively. Wanting her to compare hers with his, he told her about one in which he was writing when a man looked over his shoulder. A gold dot jumped out from his book, hitting the man in the eye. When the man asked him to remove it, he made it a condition that the man should tell him exactly what he wanted. Assuming that fantasy figures always *wanted* something, he taught her to squeeze information out of them.

By the end of October, she was dreaming – unhappily – that she was seeing Jung for the last time. In a November dream he admitted he had always loved her and started to embrace her. Though thrilled, she felt anxious about Toni Wolff. In December she again dreamed she was seeing him for the last time. She asked for advice on what to do, but his answer was deliberately confusing. She wept, clung to him, kissed him goodbye. Holding her away from him, he kissed her on the neck. Her impression was that he wanted her to pick up the ball and run with it as if playing football.

Unlike dreams, visions occur during the waking state, and visions, according to Jung, have nothing in them that would be encountered during everyday life – no aunts, cars, emotions or personal involvement. Finding he was more interested in visions than dreams, Christiana did her best to please him. If his visions had been influenced by those of Frank Miller, and by his interpretation of them, Christiana's may have been influenced by what he told her about both.

Something he left out of account was the influence he unintentionally exerted on the dreams and the active imagination of his patients. Mikkel Borch-Jacobsen has suggested that much of the evidence Freud accumulated in support of his seduction theory was provided by patients who were trying – without knowing what they were doing – to oblige him. 'The "influenc-ing machine" that he had put into motion was working *all too* well, so well that he could no longer believe in the stories he had extorted from his patients.' Writing about hysterical nuns in his 1952 book *The Devils of Loudun*, Aldous Huxley explained their behaviour in terms of sexual starvation, fantasy and a patient–doctor relationship with the exorcist, for whom they obligingly provided symptoms that seemed to confirm his diagnosis. A similar process may have been at work in Jung's patients. Aware (or half aware) how avid he was in collecting material that supported his theories, they could count on having his undivided attention if they supplied suitable dreams and visions.

Between July 1926 and May 1927 Christiana's visions teemed with imagery that seemed archetypal – divine, human and animal figures, real and mythical, stallions, bulls, pigs, sphinxes, goats, snakes, birds, scarabs, dragons, giants, wise old men. Jung said her inferior function – feeling – was speaking to her like an oracle. She was feeding her soul with libido, using her inner eye to see the life behind life. When she asked what he had done to produce her visions, he said: 'I just simply muddled you, so that your directed will could flame up and become conscious.' Heartened, she went on painting prolifically. Later, for the printed version of the seminars Jung gave in 1930–4 about her visions, Harry Murray was asked to comment, but the editors cut some of his remarks about Jung's pleasure that love for him had produced the visions, though they kept the statement that unless love had been involved, it would be impossible to explain why 'a woman . . . contrary to her entire previous existence, suddenly manifests such a notable degree of industry and persistence, such willingness . . . to be exploited in the service of her doctor's search for truth'.

In 1926–7, judging from what Jung said later, he was less interested in analysing her than in collecting evidence to illustrate his theory about the unconscious. To an unbiased observer it might have seemed that some of her images reflected desire that had been frustrated – a powerful black stallion, a beautiful dancing youth, a bull drinking from a goblet she held out, a virile black god singing under a tree with fruit in his hands, a man playing a long flute, a Swiss boy who offers her music lessons. But Jung focused on the gods, such as Abraxas, and the wise old men. He explained the stallion as an 'animus horse' or 'libido in a certain opinionated form'. He used the word *opinionated* to condemn female defections from Eros to Logos. Men were entitled to think and hold opinions, but, according to Jung, women could only opinionate.

> The animus is a figure personifying the opinionating of a woman . . . Unrealised, ready-made opinions, spoken with authority. I know women who have an opinion about everything . . . Everything that falls into the unconscious is possessed by the animus. He is there with open mouth, and catches everything that falls down from the table of consciousness, and the more she is unaware of the other side, the more powerful he is.

If she dreamed about a Satanic Christ or a green-eyed giant, these were only projections of the animus that interfered with the womanly feelings she should be having. The anima was useful, necessary, beautiful, but the animus was like a hunchback who followed a little girl everywhere, spoiling all her pleasures by saying something evil. In one of Christiana's visions, a Jew was performing beautiful music, and an ecstatic Indian appeared in another. Jung interpreted both figures as personifications of female opinionating. He seemed less concerned to find out the meaning of the dreams and visions than to hammer home the point that she was an 'animus woman'.

His interest in her dwindled when she left Zurich and her visions no longer conformed (as he put it) 'to the rules'. Harry suspected that their 'unlawfulness could conceivably be due to the absence of the law-giver'. During the summer of 1927, while Jung was on holiday, she joined Harry in Munich, and showed him the paintings she had done. His admiration for them carried them towards a passionate consummation of their desire for each other. Jung had helped them both, though not in the way he had wanted to. He had liberated them from the moral scruples that had stopped them from becoming lovers.

Jung was critical of Harry, and when she described her vision of a burning naked goddess with snakes instead of hair, Jung told her about the snake in his vision of Salome. Reminded of Sabina, he was soon talking about Siegfried: 'You are like Brünnhilde. You have never been broken in. There ought to come to you a Siegfried who would break through your ring of fire – who would make you into a woman.' He told her to make Harry realise that 'no religion has so violated eros as Christianity', and that 'sexuality is the *sine qua non* of spirituality'. She spent the days recording her visions and the nights with Harry. Her last painting before they left Munich was of their entwined bodies encircled by a black snake wearing a crown.

After returning with Harry to Zurich in October, she told Jung she had never felt so alive. The analysis had been crucial, but he still showed little interest in what she wanted to say. What had emerged was a love based on sexual and intellectual rapport – what Harry described as 'a relationship that was mutual, that was double, as it were, that went back and forth'. But for Jung, the completion of the self had nothing to do with love or reciprocity. To Harry he wrote: 'Your life is yourself. Nothing matters but the completion of the self.' The main problem was one of rebirth. A man needs two mothers, and the second must be a *femme inspiratrice*. Christiana's function, he repeated, was to create Harry.

Jung could never forgive her for refusing this role, and in 1931, when the relationship appeared to be cooling, he advised Harry to discard her: 'I can't be sorry for you, because you learn and experience, and you got rid of a bother – a thing that became a nuisance.' Useful though they could be, women were expendable.

But Christiana became his star patient. On evenings out, drinking beer with his students, he often said she was his Olympus. His series of seminars on her visions went on for four years, and the characterisation of the *femme inspiratrice* by Ina May Greer, a Jungian who knew Christiana well, throws light not only on her but on Toni and Sabina – and on Jung. Indifferent to external reality, the *femme inspiratrice*, who immerses herself in the unconscious, may exert the magnetism that self-absorption sometimes produces. Other people may be profoundly inspired, or may be alienated by her preoccupation with her inner experiences. But she becomes dependent on others, condemned to being an 'introverted Anima woman . . . Alone she has no fruits. She perishes without a creative lover who will bring ideas and people to her and enfold her.'

Christiana would acknowledge her indebtedness to Jung: 'I bless him with every breath I draw, for had he not been through *his* experience, *we* could never have had ours.' But her words are chosen carefully: she and Harry had benefited less from his theories than from the practical example he set.

The analysis ended abruptly in early November, partly because of the way he dealt with the transference and partly because he scared her by saying she had a major role to play in the history of human spirituality. The spirit lived in Christianity, he told her, until it was formalised by the church. Then the life went out of the spirit because it had become general. It came back to life in the crusaders, who had the mystery of the Grail. Then it lived it Protestantism under Luther. The music of Bach expressed belief in the new freedom. Then came the Rosicruceans, who soon died out. Then the alchemists. But where is spirit now? 'The spirit forced itself through me and it forced itself through Freud. Freud refused it but it came to him. He's a great prophet. Of course his followers just use his *theories* to shut the door even tighter than before on the spirit. But in this age it is absolutely impossible for this to happen.'

She left Zurich before Christmas. They corresponded for a year, but only one of his letters to her has been published. At the end of 1927, acknowledging the drawings she had sent, he said:

> In early December your face haunted me for a while. Thank you for everything. *'Don't blame me!'* You are always a living reality to me whereas other former patients fade away into oblivion . . . But my dear, dear [he crossed out the second 'dear' and added two exclamation marks] Christiana Morgan, you are just a bit of a marvel to me. Now don't laugh, there is nothing to laugh about. You were quite right in scolding me. Yours affectionately, C.G.

We do not know what had happened, and all Harry Murray was prepared to say was that Jung's feeling verged at times on 'libidinous affection'.

Twenty-Five

His Magic Wand

'We Europeans are not the only people on the Earth,' Jung told audiences. 'We are just a peninsula of Asia, and on that continent there are old civilisations where people have trained their minds in introspective psychology for thousands of years . . . These people have an insight that is simply fabulous.'

In the 1920s, most Europeans assumed that civilisation in China and India was backward not only scientifically but psychologically – that the unconscious had not been discovered until Freud wrote about dreams. On the contrary, said Jung, psychoanalysis was 'only a beginner's attempt compared with what is an immemorial art in the East'. All Freud's ideas about sexuality had been 'matched or surpassed by Hindu writings on the subject . . . while the idea of indeterminacy, newly broached in the West, is the very basis of Chinese science.'

Not that Jung was the first builder of bridges between the two cultures. As he said, 'The intrusion of the East is rather a psychological fact with a long history behind it. The first signs may be found in Meister Eckhart, Leibniz, Kant, Hegel, Schopenhauer and E. von Hartmann.' A heretical Dominican who lived in the late twelfth and early thirteenth centuries, Johannes Eckhart believed in a mystic union between God and the innermost recesses of the soul, where there was a spark, he said, capable of participating in God's timeless existence. 'God must be born in the soul again and again.' Jung regarded him as a believer in letting things happen, in letting go of the self and acting through nonaction. The most serious problems in life, says Jung, are all insoluble: the way to deal with them is to outgrow them.

Leibniz's critique of Western decadence had depended partly on Confucian ideas imported by Jesuit missionaries, and some of the Romantics, disillusioned with European values, had found inspiration in India and Buddhism. Jung was interested not only in the dogmas and stories in Oriental religions, but in techniques and disciplines such as yoga and meditation. For us, said Jung, 'the essence of that which works is the world of appearance', while for the Indian, the world 'is a mere show or façade, and his reality comes close to being what we would call a dream'. This is, of course, simplistic.

To both Christians and nonbelievers Jung recommended the discourses of the Buddha: 'They offer Western man ways and means of disciplining his psychic life, thus remedying an often regrettable defect in the various brands of Christianity.'

His visits to Africa and New Mexico had reinforced his conviction that 'certain contents of the collective unconscious are very closely connected with primitive psychology . . . Deep down in our psyche there is a thick layer of primitive processes . . . closely related to processes that can still be found on the surface of the primitive's daily life.' He was glad to see that 'our psychic situation is now being influenced by an irruption of the Oriental spirit'.

His enthusiasm for Indian legends had begun in childhood, and before completing *Transformation and Symbols of the Libido*, he read widely in Buddhist, Taoist and Vedic literature. *Psychological Types* showed that he felt most at home with the Gnostics and the early Church Fathers, but as he had shown when he talked to Christiana, he wanted to believe in an unbroken tradition of spirituality connecting the Middle Ages to modern times, and if this golden chain had been severed in the West, perhaps it was still intact in the East.

Richard Wilhelm fortified his belief that it was. Having read Jung's work with admiration, and having completed a German translation of a Chinese alchemical treatise that was over a thousand years old, *The Secret of the Golden Flower*, Wilhelm invited him to write a commentary for publication with the text.

For many people, the word *alchemy* has connotations of charlatanism. We think of elaborate medieval glass retorts and gullible aristocrats financing fraudsters who promise to enrich them by transforming base metals into gold. But alchemy appealed to Jung as being 'rather like an undercurrent to the Christianity that ruled on the surface. What it is to this surface is like what the dream is to consciousness, and, just as the dream compensates conscious conflicts, alchemy strives to bridge the gaps left by Christianity's oppositions.' Most damaging of these, in Jung's view, was the opposition between good and evil. 'Good is equivalent to the unconditional imitation of Christ, and evil is its hindrance.' In Christian symbolism 'there is a rift running through the world: light wars against night, and the upper against the lower.' And Christianity's insistence on the unity of the Trinity was numerically significant. 'Since olden times, not only in the West but also in China, uneven numbers have been regarded as masculine and even numbers as feminine. The Trinity is therefore a decidedly masculine deity.'

The Secret of the Golden Flower reminded Jung of Herbert Silberer, who had written about the emergence of images in the twilight state between sleeping and waking. He had found symbolical representations of patricide and infantile sexuality in alchemical texts and offered a psychological interpretation of them, but Jung did not warm to the subject of alchemy until fourteen years later, when he read Wilhelm's translation.

What surprised him most was that Taoist alchemists appeared to have practised something like 'active imagination'. As in Wilhelm's story about the rainmaker, results had been achieved by doing nothing – by waiting passively for things to happen. 'Consciousness is forever interfering, helping, correcting, and negating, never leaving the psychic processes to grow in peace . . . To begin with the task consists solely in observing objectively how a fragment of fantasy develops . . . The conscious mind raises innumerable objections, in fact it often seems bent on blotting out the spontaneous fantasy activity in spite of real insight.'

But alchemical language is 'not so much semiotic as symbolic: it does not disguise a known content but suggests an unknown one, or rather this unknown content suggests itself. This content can only be psychological.' Read like this, *The Secret of the Golden Flower* 'formed a living parallel to what occurs in the psychic growth of my patients, none of whom is Chinese'. Taking over Silberer's idea that the language of the alchemists had been coded, Jung surmised that their real concern was with self-discovery and transformation of the personality. Projecting desires and fears into experiments, they had psychic experiences that were inseparable from their work.

It was not long after this that the Romanian scholar Mircea Eliade arrived independently at a similar position. He came to believe that 'the traditional science of alchemy works not only upon the matter under transmutation but on the soul'. Gold was 'the symbol of perfection, of freedom, of immortality'. The alchemist was like the yogi, 'who does exercises in order to master both his body and his spirit'. Eliade points out that the alchemists claimed their objective was similar to that of the major esoteric and mystical traditions. In China, alchemy was intimately related to Taoism, in India to yoga and Tantrism, in Hellenistic Egypt to *gnosis*, and in the West to Hermeticism and mysticism.

If he had not felt excited, Jung would not have written such a long introduction to *The Secret of the Golden Flower*, but he was prevented by his ignorance of Chinese from immersing himself in the text as he had in the medieval texts he so lovingly expounded and analysed in *Psychological Types*. Sonu Shamdasani quotes the scholar Gopi Krishna, who objected that 'despite the unambiguous nature of the statements in the work', Jung found nothing in it except 'material for the corroboration of his own ideas'. He simply reiterates them without even summarising the Chinese text or explaining how it corresponds with his views. Less acerbic, the great Chinese scholar Joseph Needham says Jung and Wilhelm 'are not exactly wrong but not exactly right either'.

What appealed to Jung most was the emphasis on the circulation of the light. 'The circulation is not merely movement in a circle but means, on the one hand, the marking-off of the sacred precinct and, on the other, fixation and concentration . . . Action is reversed into nonaction; everything peripheral is subordinated to the command of the centre.' The circular movement has 'the moral significance of activating the light and dark forces of human nature, and together with them all psychological opposites of whatever kind they may be'.

In his view, mental and physical activities never escape from dependence on archetypes, but the unconscious can be disruptive. What we need is a means of reuniting what has been divided. 'The beginning, where everything is still one, and which therefore appears as the highest goal, lies at the bottom of the sea in the darkness of the unconscious.' Here, in 'the germinal vesicle' consciousness and life are still united. In the Chinese text, as in other alchemical texts, he interpreted references to the process of ennobling and refining in terms of consciousness as it develops by taking in elements from the unconscious. Precious gold grows from the lead of the water region, leading to a union between consciousness and life.

When images of gods and demons emerge from the unconscious, the psychiatrist, he says, need not question whether there is any reality in them. 'They are fragmentary psychic systems that either appear spontaneously in states of ecstasy, making powerful impressions, or otherwise, in mental disturbances, become fixed in the form of delusions and hallucinations, undermining the integrity of the personality.'

The Tibetan Book of the Dead warns us against these murky figures. The dead should not confuse them with the pure white light emerging from the divine body of truth. But while Jung maintained that gods were born because the human psyche needed them, he detested the Western habit of ignoring them. Our religion is really monotheistic belief in consciousness, but if we pretend to have no knowledge of 'fragmentary autonomous systems', they 'behave like any other repressed contents . . . The effect they go on exerting can no longer be understood . . . They become an inexplicable source of disturbance, and we finally assume it must exist somewhere outside ourselves.'

The treatise inspired him to reconsider Lévy-Bruhl's idea of *participation mystique* as the hallmark of the primitive mentality. 'When there is no consciousness of the difference between subject and object, an unconscious identity prevails.' (Jung may have been thinking of his own childhood identification with the stone he sat on.) Westerners might think themselves superior to the Africans for whom the night bristles with ghosts and gods, but many of us suffer from a lifelong identification with our parents, or accuse other people of the faults we cannot see in ourselves.

What Jung believed he had done for himself and wanted to do for his patients was to shift the centre of gravity from the ego, which is merely the centre of consciousness, to the self, which is between consciousness and the unconscious. 'If the transposition is successful, it does away with the *participation mystique* and results in a personality that suffers only in the lower storeys, as it were, but in the upper storeys is singularly detached from painful as well as from joyful happenings.'

It was *The Secret of the Golden Flower* that kindled Jung's passion for alchemy, and from the following year onwards he devoted an enormous amount of time to collecting and studying ancient texts, saying: 'Our profession is such that one has to deal with many subjects. But this gives one a feeling of being an amateur in all things. That's why I wanted to study at least one area thoroughly, down to its roots – and that was alchemy.'

He often claimed that alchemy had supplied his need for a link between Gnosticism and analytical psychology, 'which now has a historical foundation. It was given substance by the possibility of a comparison with alchemy, and by intellectual continuity with Gnosticism.' He argued that the 'practical, chemical work' of the alchemists 'was at the same time a psychic activity that can best be compared with what we call active imagination' and that some of the Gnostic symbolism 'may well have been based, originally, on some visionary experience, such as happens today not uncommonly in psychological treatment'. But in what he holds out for us as a chain of tradition, several links are missing.

Though it was not until after the First World War that Jung studied the Gnostic writers in depth, his interest in them was evident, as Dan Merkur shows, in his doctoral thesis (1901–2). While his technique of active imagination has some of its origins in Helly's seances, it may also derive partly from other experiences involving the occult. In the late nineteenth century, as Merkur tells us, the Hermetic Order of the Golden Dawn had been teaching two techniques of visualisation known as *pathworking*. They could both be performed either consciously or in a state of trance. In the active variety of pathworking, occultists planned the imagery they were going to visualise, but in the passive variety only the starting points were planned, and visions could develop spontaneously.

Madam Blavatsky canvassed the idea that Gnosticism was an antecedent of occultism, and though much of the Gnostic literature Jung read was published by her Theosophical Society, he cultivated his image as a scientist who would have no truck with mysticism, and this may help to explain his reticence about active imagination. Written in 1916, his essay 'The Transcendent Function' was not published until 1957. Though he was making regular use of active imagination, he mentioned it only briefly or cryptically in published writings. Marie-Louise von Franz regarded it as '*the* most powerful tool in Jungian psychology', and attributed his refusal to publish 'The Transcendent Function' or whatever else he wrote about active imagination to awareness of 'how far removed these documents were from the collective, conscious view of his time'.

After working on *The Secret of the Golden Flower*, Jung discovered a great deal of alchemical imagery in patients' dreams. When looking for connections between dream material and the dreamer's conscious memories of events preceding the dream and associations with it, the analyst has to focus on what the patient knows, but when looking for connections with residue in the collective unconscious, the analyst is free to introduce Mithraic sun wheels or anything else that *he* knows about.

If Jung's new absorption in alchemy coincided with a rich harvest of alchemical images in patients' dreams, his explanation was that after being repressed by Christianity, alchemical ideas were naturally rising to the surface in a period when the church was declining and losing its grip on the imagination.

What would have been harder to explain was why he encountered so little material from prehistory. Human life is probably about four million years old, though the first written records date from about 3500 BC. In 1816 a Danish archaeologist, Christian Thomsen, classified early human cultures according to the materials used for tools and weapons. The Stone Age, which he divided into Palaeolithic, Mesolithic and Neolithic periods, was followed by the Bronze Age and the Iron Age. It was in Neolithic times that agriculture and the domestication of cattle began. If Jung was right about collective memories, all these primitive cultures would have left residue that could surface in dreams. Though alchemy was practised from ancient times till the Middle Ages, this is a relatively short period, and if there was no 'influencing machine' in operation, it would be hard to explain why he found so much alchemical symbolism in dreams and so little material from prehistory.

In spite of his enthusiasm for 'the primitive mentality', Jung was not interested — as Lévy-Bruhl was in his later work — in studying differences between different periods of primitive culture, and though he claimed that Arnold Toynbee, who wrote a ten-volume *History of the World*, accepted the existence of archetypes, Jung showed less interest in what Toynbee had to say about early civilisations than in his lack of religious faith. 'I would like to ask Mr Toynbee: Where is your civilisation and what is your religion? What he says to the masses will remain – I am afraid – sterile, unless it has become true and real in himself. Mere words have lost their spell to an extraordinary extent.'

According to Ruth Bailey, Toni Wolff thought Jung was wasting his time on alchemy, but Toni gave a sympathetic account of his work in a 1946 talk to the Psychological Club, arguing that for the alchemists, 'the transformation of substances coincided with or even caused an equal transformation in the operator, and it was by means of imagination and meditation that the operations were performed.' She seems to agree with Jung that the initial phase of *nigredo* – 'making black' – corresponds with confronting the shadow, and that there is a correlation between integration of the self and the struggle to conjoin the evil parts with the indestructible substance or the philosopher's stone. The alchemists wanted to rescue the spirit trapped in imperfect nature. The intuition that led them away from orthodox Christianity led them towards the part of man which is nature and towards the reality of the psyche.

Jung acknowledged that most of the alchemists had been misguided. Their experiments had been 'an obvious result of the literal-mindedness of the adept, who tried to cook, melt and distil "symbolic" substances'. But 'the obviously absurd chemistry of alchemy was a half-conscious blind for a very real spiritual longing.'

In 1926, lecturing in Augsburg on 'Spirit and Life', he described spirit as a psychic experience beyond the scope of ego-consciousness. It could neither be explained rationally nor proved to exist in the external world. Encouraged by the Chinese text, Jung was becoming less tentative: 'Without soul, spirit is as dead as matter, for both are artificial abstractions; but originally we regarded spirit as a volatile body and matter as not being without soul.'

Later, lecturing in London during 1935, he said that the process of individuation could not be completed without the objectification of 'impersonal images'. The objective was

to detach consciousness from the object so that the individual no longer places the guarantee of his happiness, or of his life even, in factors outside himself, whether they be persons, ideas or circumstances, but comes to realise that everything depends on whether he holds the treasure or not. If the possession of that gold is realised, then the centre of gravity is *in* the individual and no longer in an object on which he depends. To reach such a condition of detachment is the aim of Eastern practices, and it is also the aim of all the teachings of the Church.

This is to claim support from both Oriental religion and the Christian church for what he had said to Harry Murray: 'Your life is yourself. Nothing matters but the completion of the self.'

After Jung's long estrangement from the Psychological Club, his seminars in English resumed during the autumn of 1928. As before, he held them regularly on Wednesday mornings during term time. Lectures and seminars bulked so large in the club's activities that it had become almost collegiate in character, and it seemed natural for the year to be divided between terms and holidays. He had about thirty people in the audience, mostly American and Swiss, with a few British. Talking in English, he sounded almost American, and he was obviously enjoying himself.

Wearing a suit and looking like a bank manager or a stockbroker, he would come in clutching a brown portfolio, and, as an American woman reported, there was always a suspenseful silence as he stood, grave and silent, studying his notes 'as a sailor might look at his compass, relating it to the psychological winds and waves whose impact he has felt on his passage from the door . . . By some magic yet to be explained, Dr Jung manages within the first five minutes to get vitally on the wire of everyone present.'

He looked like an expert in the art of living. Striding up and down as he spoke, sometimes stopping by the blackboard to chalk up Greek roots or diagrams of the heavens or symbolic inscriptions from ancient monuments, he was friendly, entertaining, stimulating. He combined benevolence with provocativeness as he confronted students with a series of challenges, encouraging them to talk, telling stories, changing the subject abruptly between dreams and practicalities, appearing to take as much interest in other people's experience as he aroused in his own.

Between the autumn of 1928 and the spring of 1930 he devoted thirty sessions to the dreams of a male patient, a middle-aged businessman. Jung had become even more anti-Freudian than he had been in 1925, when he talked about dreams in Swanage. 'Dreams are objective facts,' he insisted – not invented by the dreamer. 'I handle the dream as if it were a text I do not understand properly, say a Latin or a Greek or a Sanskrit text, where certain words are unknown to me or the text is fragmentary, and I merely apply the ordinary method any philologist would apply in reading such a text. My idea is that the dream does not conceal; we simply do not understand its language.'

But dreams do not consist merely of language. Penile erections and facial twitching during sleep indicate emotional excitement that is quickly for-gotten, while any written account of a dream is likely to introduce more continuity than the experience possessed and is unlikely to deal adequately with its visual, tactile and emotional components.

Jung habitually told patients to write out their dreams. The businessman had also been asked to record his associations, and to illustrate his dreams with drawings, which were mimeographed and distributed to the group. Generally Jung seems to have taken little account of the tricks memory played with dream material. Having no recollection of dreaming about Africa while he was there, he confidently asserted that Africa had never featured in his dreams.

But his lectures were invariably entertaining and stimulating. He used dream analysis to make connections between mythology and history, astrology and Einsteinian relativity, Gnosticism and spiritualism. His dream analysis 'includes journeys with age-old seers into the fearful reaches of the collective unconscious and concrete very human questions such as how to make a success of marriage'. But he often spoke in terms of opposites. The polite businessman will achieve wholeness only if he can recognise within himself and his dreams the primitive apeman hungry for rape and violence.

On Wednesdays there were two sessions of two hours with an interval for tea and sandwiches. Wanting to make members of the class feel more relaxed and more familiar with each other, Jung introduced what he called 'the Alleluia Game', a variant on pig-in-the-middle. One member sat in the centre of a circle while the others went on throwing a knotted napkin past him till he caught it. Jung said later that 'clubs were a kind of family of which he was "father". It was not healthy if the family had no quarrels, so if he thought that there was calm, he would take steps to upset it. A family quarrel would then ensue and everything would then come to life.

In 1928 Toni Wolff began her long reign as president of the club. Previously the presidency had often changed hands, but for nineteen years it was continuously in the hands of a woman sensitive to Jung's wishes, and almost ferocious in enforcing them. 'The club tiger' was one of her nicknames. Jung wanted the club to remain small and to have the highest possible calibre of members. He always attended the lectures given on alternate Saturday evenings, and he often lectured himself, trying out his theories on a sympathetic audience.

In private analytical sessions he was equally friendly, entertaining and stimulating as he impressed patients with the extent of his arcane knowledge. He enjoyed making unexpected leaps from history to astrology, from mythology to alchemy, from Gnosticism to quantum physics. He would sometimes pull a book down from his shelves to show a patient photographs of ancient monuments, or engravings, etchings, diagrams illustrating an archetypal pattern.

While some patients were frustrated by his lack of interest in their childhood and their personal relationships, others were greatly helped by the transference he encouraged and by the impression that he had magical powers. Some were reminded of a medieval sorcerer, and one showed him a painting she had done of herself with the lower half of her body trapped by rocks on a beach. In a fantasy, she had shouted to him for help, and he had released her by touching the rock with his magic wand.

Many benefited from sensing an affinity between themselves, him and the medieval alchemists, theologians and mystics he seemed to resemble. Encouraging patients to paint and draw, he studied their work sympathetically, usually interpreting it in terms of their quest for personal wholeness. After looking at a woman's paintings, he 'showed me Jakob Boehme's representation of his experience in the old manuscript, a wonderful battered old book. The representation showed two half circles back to back, one dark, one light, and a heart between.' (This is reproduced in the *Collected Works* on page 297 of volume 9, part 1.) Striving to unite his opposites, Boehme had succeeded only in getting them back to back, but Jung had done better. He

> said that in one of his mandalas he had united his and had sought for others' experience throughout history. He then spoke to me of the isolation of such experience. As I handled Boehme's book I felt, for just a fleeting moment, the isolation relieved by a companionship of suffering and individual experience of consciousness . . . For just a moment I sat with those two great men of such different epochs.

This feeling was not only comforting but also therapeutic. Jung went on to talk

> of man's experience of the opposites, of woman as the Yin principle, of evil, of Eve, of spirit and flesh, and I saw it as a man describes it, as I had often seen it before from woman's side. I felt in easy and true rapport with Dr Jung, a great man who had wrestled with his own soul and stood before the opposites till they met in him. At the same moment I experienced that same opposition from the side of woman, not as man sees her and experiences her, but as she is in her being. I felt the 'essence' from the side of flesh and Yin going over to comprehend the Yang . . . I felt as woman-earth, receptive to the masculine principle. But I also felt something more, something new . . . Yin trying to rise up into Yang and find its meaning there.

She always looked back on this session as a turning point in her life.

In 'The Structure of the Psyche', Jung's 1928 revision of an essay published the previous year in a symposium edited by Keyserling, he claimed he could prove conclusively that 'supra-individual psychic activity actually exists'. Giving 1910 as the publication date of the Dieterich book that came out in 1903, he again retold the story of Schwyzer, the paranoid schizophrenic who pointed to the sun's penis. Stories tended to become more elaborate as he reiterated them, and the point Jung added now was that the man believed himself to be Christ.

In this essay Jung also claims that the whole psychic organism 'corresponds exactly' to the human body. 'In its development and structure, it still preserves elements that connect it with the invertebrates and ultimately with the protozoa. Theoretically it should be possible to "peel" the collective unconscious, layer by layer, until we come to the psychology of the worm and even of the amoeba.' Though he lived till the 1960s, Jung never outgrew the ideas he had imbibed in the 1890s from lectures in 'comparative anatomy'. Shortly before he died, he wrote that 'just as the human body represents a whole museum of organs, with a long evolutionary history behind them, so we should expect the mind to be organised in a similar way rather than to be a product without history'.

Though 'The Structure of the Psyche' had been printed during 1927 in Keyserling's symposium, Jung read it out when he went to Vienna in February 1928 to lecture to the Kulturbund, a prestigious cultural society. The invitation had come from its vice president, Jolande Jacobi, a Hungarian of thirty-eight married to a prominent lawyer. They had escaped from Budapest in 1919 after a communist takeover. When she gave a lunch party for Jung, he talked about the *I Ching* and impressed her by writing out all sixty-four hexagrams from memory.

He had not been in Vienna since he and Emma visited Freud in 1909. He told the press that a 'debt of gratitude' obliged him to 'honour Freud and Janet', ignoring Bleuler, and implying Freud had been no more important to him than Janet. He praised Catholicism, saying no creed was more closely akin to psychoanalysis, and that Catholics were less neurotic than Protestants and Jews.

Discussing differences between Freud's ideas and his own, he talked of a 'flight back to the primitive', generalising as he so often did about the contrast between contemporary neurosis and the naturalness of 'the primitives'. Tutankhamen's tomb had been discovered in 1922, and he said the excitement this aroused, like 'the craze for Negro dances, the Charleston and jazz', reflected nostalgia for 'the joys of the Golden Age, which let us be natural and graceful and conscious of our strength, delivered from the bane of our time, the neuroses'. The primitives were better than we are at releasing the powers that lie dormant in every human being. A hidden artist 'slumbers in every man. Give him a chance to bring to light the pictures he carries unpainted within himself, to free the unwritten poems he has shut up inside him, and yet another source of psychic disturbances is removed.'

H. G. Wells was in Switzerland during 1928, and he visited Küsnacht to resume his acquaintance with Jung. Wells believed that with the decline of Christianity, the metaphysical basis for morality was collapsing. According to Jung, 'he rubbed his nose with his finger, which meant: Then we ought to know or smell what we can do now.' Talking about the conversation later, Wells said:

> I didn't get the hang of too much of it . . . But he seemed to speak of that Old Man of his as if he were a kind of collective human being we were all in touch with in one way or another. Sounded suspiciously like God to me. Never understood why he sidestepped the word so often. And look at that stuff about the Anima. I've always known I had a beautiful young girl trying to break out from inside me!

When Emma Jung gave a talk to the Psychological Club about the effect of character type on relationships with other people, some of her statements seem to have been based on her relationship with Jung.

She compared the introverted sensation-thinking type to a photographic plate – 'everything to which it is exposed leaves its mark on it'. One of the biggest drawbacks was lack of spontaneity. 'He appears to be opaque, aloof or indifferent, to be not spontaneous and responsive . . . Because he usually has too little time, or it is too much effort to form a genuine reaction, he gets used to examining only the foreground of the picture or he says nothing at all, and he then appears to be superficial and impersonal.' She never said she or I – always he or him.

Being 'oriented to the facts', the sensation-thinking type 'tends to see everything as static and unchangeable, and he becomes confused, disappointed or irritated when something which he has considered to be genuine and seriously meant turns out to be simply a thing of the moment'. Another means of taking shelter from 'too massive or overwhelming impressions' is by 'pretending not to notice, so his partner thinks he hasn't seen anything'. Another strategy was

> mimicry, in which one adapts oneself as much as possible to a situation or a person. This can be active empathy, but it can also happen entirely automatically, sometimes out of laziness because he does not want to take the trouble of realising what his own situation is, and sometimes out

of fear of offending another or creating an awkward situation. If this
happens with very powerful impressions, there can be such total adaptation
that the individual can be totally blotted out, so to speak . . . In this sense
of mystical identification, one is of course simply not there in the sense of
being a partner in the relationship. There is also a tendency, especially for
introverts, to linger in this condition because it can be a very blissful state.
All in all, the sensation type is therefore a difficult, awkward and tedious
partner.

There can be no question of total adaptation to the intuitive, who may be
'helpful . . . in showing new possibilities', but he 'can also have a negative
and paralysing effect when he is always telling you what you could or should
do. It is also irritating to have him poking his nose into everything and
feeling you out, or when he, under the assumption that we are unaware,
points out his marvellous intuition to us and draws our attention to things
which are all too familiar.'

'Woman in Europe' was the title of a 1928 magazine article by Jung, but
Emma was not one of the women he had in mind. The article started with a
quotation from Nietzsche's *Zarathustra*: 'You call yourself free? . . . There
are some who threw away their last value when they threw away their
servitude.' Jung argued that it was difficult for Western women to live by
their principles because of the pressure on them to rely on their masculine
side. 'Masculinity means knowing what one wants and going all out to
achieve it. This lesson, once learned, can never be forgotten without
enormous psychic loss.'

The Dean of Chichester's unmarried daughter Barbara Hannah was in her
late thirties and living in Paris, half-heartedly trying to paint. Drawn to
Zurich by the article, she arrived during January 1929 and found the fifty-
three-year-old Jung impressive.

Except for his grey, almost white, hair, he still looked a young and
exceptionally vigorous man . . . He was a tall man, about six feet, two
inches, and broad, but with little spare flesh. His eyes were dark brown and
he always wore gold-rimmed spectacles. He had a habit, however, of
looking at people over the rims of the glasses and then one saw that his eyes
were not really very large; they were rather on the small side but
extraordinarily expressive. He could convey more with an almost im-
perceptible wink than anyone else I ever saw . . . His forehead was high,
though not unpleasantly so, as it sloped slightly backward, and his nose and
chin were very decided.

Disconcerted by 'that indefinable look of the complete, natural human being', she bent down to pat his large grey schnauzer, Joggi, which provoked the question: 'Did you come from Paris to see the dog or me?'

Having been given to understand he was willing to take her on as his patient, she was dismayed to be told: 'Oh my God, you bore me,' but she submitted meekly when he passed her on to Emma, who passed her on to Toni. Finally sent back to Jung, she told him a dream about being in a ditch. 'AH!' he roared. 'You've ditched both of them and now, you hell-cat, you want to get me in the ditch. I knew you were a hell-cat. That's why I passed you on. But I tell you what I will do. I will take you on again on the understanding that if you do get me in the ditch too, it's up to you to get me out.'

She liked being bullied, and counted herself lucky he did not yet have a car. He was depending on trains and his bicycle for journeys between Küsnacht, Bollingen and Zurich, but sometimes she was allowed to chauffeur him. He did not learn to drive until the Easter holidays of 1929. He then bought two cars – a red two-seater Chrysler and a big Dodge for travelling with the family. Emma and Toni soon followed suit, but Toni, who bought herself a large Chrysler at the end of the year, had great difficulties in passing the test, though she had driving lessons every morning before breakfast. The gardener, Müller, was given lessons too, and one of his jobs, from now on, was to look after the cars.

Barbara Hannah had got to know Jung much better by the time she was invited to stay at the tower for two days in December 1929, but this was thanks to Toni, who had spent a month during the summer with the Hannahs in Sussex at the cathedral close and at their country house. Since Toni lived with her mother, who was too conventionally Swiss to return the hospitality by inviting a stranger to stay in her house, Toni persuaded Jung to invite Barbara Hannah to Bollingen.

Arriving on a cold evening, she found him cooking in the kitchen, wearing a long Oriental robe and looking like 'an old alchemist at work among his retorts . . . I seemed to be back in the Middle Ages, with the lamp and firelight making a small illuminated circle in what struck me that evening as a huge circular circumference of darkness.' In fact the kitchen was quite small. Fanatical about cooking, Jung would sometimes use sixteen ingredients in a sauce. He liked adding wine to meat, which he cooked not only with the bone, but also with the fat and gristle. Lean veal or chicken upset him. 'This is not meat.'

He said nothing when she arrived, and she was too timid to break the silence. It seemed to her that two or three hours passed before she said: 'I am scared stiff,' and he replied only with a faint smile. Eventually he gave her a drink, which he called a 'sundowner'. When the three of them finally sat down to eat and drink at the round table, the silence continued, apart from 'a few appreciative gruntlike murmurs'. Jung, who had never discarded his mother's belief that conversation was disrespectful to good food, said: 'Oh, well, you already know how to enjoy your food, that is *one* thing I shall not have to teach you!'

When they had fetched water from the lake and washed the dishes, they sat down to play a card game, and in the morning they went for a long walk in the woods on the hill.

Over the years he went on inviting patients to meals, and their reactions were often similar to Barbara Hannah's. A woman described her dinner there in May 1934 after he had added to the building:

> I remember the damp, stony medieval look and smell of the inside of the house, and Dr Jung sitting by the fireplace with a stocking cap on his head, stirring a stew in a big iron pot. We ate the stew later at a refectory table in another stone-floored room. Dr Jung gave us a lot of wine and made us all quite drunk in a pleasant way, and all I can remember is everyone telling jokes . . . Only when we had finished our second helping of stew and might have been ready for another, he asked us to a guess what a certain kind of meat in it could be. We guessed heart, lungs, and all kinds of unusual things and finally had to give up. He then revealed it was dried cow's udder; and after that no one seemed to want any more. Great joke! He threw the rest to the dogs under the table – another medieval gesture.

Over the next ten years Jung would make a serious attempt to place himself at the head of the psychotherapeutic profession by incorporating elements from Freud's and Adler's psychology into his own. In an essay titled 'Problems of Modern Psychotherapy' he defined analytical psychology as 'embracing both psychoanalysis and [Adler's] individual psychology as well as other endeavours in the field of "complex psychology" '.

In his form of analysis, he says, there are four stages: confession, elucidation, education and transformation. Secrets or repressed emotions are like sins that need to be confessed, so that the patient can regain his wholeness and become independent of the doctor. For this to happen, the transference – which is a form of fixation – must be explained. In the third, educative, stage the patient is drawn out of himself to attain normal adaptation. The fourth stage involves change in the doctor, resulting from 'the counter-application to him of whatever system is believed in, and with the same persistence, consistency and uncompromisingness as he applies it to the patient'.

Jung claims that 'the momentous discovery of the unconscious shadow side in man' forced the Freudian school 'to deal even with questions of religion', and that 'this latest advance' makes the doctor's ethical attitude into an 'unavoidable problem'. He must examine himself in a way that involves 'a view of the psyche radically different from the merely biological one which has prevailed hitherto'. Analytical psychology, Jung declared, has finally gone 'beyond itself to fill the hiatus that has previously put Western civilisation at a disadvantage in comparison with the civilisations of the East'.

Twenty-Six

The Purity of Divine Dirt

For the carnival of February 1930, Jung wanted a masked ball to be held for the Psychological Club in Zurich's Hotel Sonnenberg. The club's resident housekeeper, Anni Ammann, dressed as an angel, and her costume was only one of many religious images that appeared during the evening. This pleased Jung, who thought his psychology must be pushing club members in the right direction.

His own masks and costumes – he changed three or four times – did not stop people from recognising him and encircling him. Barbara Hannah's Jungian explanation of this is that 'the opposites were so much united in him, and he was by this time so whole, that more one-sided people were inevitably drawn to him to get at least a glimpse back into their own lost wholeness'.

She was one of the members later chosen to give a lecture at the club, and, with her long-standing admiration of Emily Brontë, she took *Wuthering Heights* as her subject, saying it illustrated the process of individuation. Instead of rewarding her with the praise she expected, Jung seemed angry. 'There is no such thing as a process of individuation without a conscious individual to live it in himself; it *is* the individual himself.'

'What about the alchemists?' she parried.

'They describe something totally unconscious to themselves which they really believe they are seeing in their retorts, and your girl knew even less than they did. As to your mentioning the Zen masters in connection with her, it is inconceivable that you can be so stupid.'

Jung clarified his attitude to literature in a 1930 lecture, 'Psychology and Literature', which repeated much of what he had said in 1922 when lecturing 'On the Relation of Analytical Psychology to Poetry', but protested more strongly against 'the reduction of art to personal factors'. Great literature, he said, draws its strength not from individual experience but from the life of mankind, while great poets, such as Dante, Goethe and Nietzsche, speak 'with the voice of thousands and tens of thousands, prophesying changes in the consciousness of their period'. It is when consciousness becomes lopsided in a society, or when wrong-headed attitudes become dominant, that archetypal ideas rise to the surface in dreams and artistic vision. 'A great work of art is like a dream,' and it meets the psychic needs of the public.

He had invincible faith in a nonhuman power that intervenes benevolently in human affairs to correct the balance. Like a medium, the great artist must simply allow himself to be taken over, and Jung characterises him as a man with some inadequacy in his personality, or an inability to adapt. His creativity monopolises his energy, draining him of his humanity. If he behaves like a neglected child, becoming ruthless, selfish and vain, it is because his ego has no other way of maintaining its vitality.

Jung lectured on 'Psychology and Literature' in several cities, including Munich, where the publisher Daniel Brody was in the audience. In 1927 his company, Rhein-Verlag, had published a German translation of James Joyce's *Ulysses*, and though Joyce had not been mentioned, Brody thought Jung might have had him in mind. In 1930, Stuart Gilbert's book on *Ulysses* was being translated into German, and Brody invited Jung to write a preface. He accepted, but wrote that when reading Joyce's book, he had fallen asleep twice before he reached page 135. Asking 'who is Ulysses?' he answered:

> Doubtless he is the symbol of that which makes up the totality, the oneness, of all the single appearances of *Ulysses* as a whole, Mr Bloom, Stephen, Mrs Bloom, and the rest, including Mr Joyce. Think of it; a being that is not merely a colourless crowd-soul composed of an indeterminable number of ill-assorted and antagonistic individual souls, but is also made up of houses, street processions, churches, the Liffey, several brothels and a crumpled note on its way to the sea – and yet possesses a perceiving and reproductive consciousness!

When Brody showed him what Jung had written, Joyce, thinking it would make Jung look silly, told Brody to go ahead and print it, but the piece remained unpublished until 1932, when Jung rewrote it, and, in a letter to Joyce, praised Molly Bloom's final monologue as 'a string of veritable psychological peaches. I suppose the devil's grandmother knows so much about the real psychology of a woman, I didn't.' And in his book *Mysterium Coniunctionis*, written between 1941 and 1954, Jung approvingly quoted the verdict of Ernst Robert Curtius, who called *Ulysses* a work of the Antichrist. Jung compared Joyce with Sir George Ripley, an obscure sixteenth-century alchemist, 'for neither author had any inkling of the dubious nature of what he was doing'.

Jung preferred the fiction of Hugh Walpole, the popular author of *Mr Perrin and Mr Traill*, which had established a fashion for novels about schoolmasters. In July 1930, when Walpole lectured in Zurich, Jung attended, and they had supper together afterwards. In his diary Walpole wrote: 'He's like a large genial English cricketer . . . he delighted me with his hatred of hysterics.' Afterwards Jung wrote to him, praising his 1912 novel *The Prelude to Adventure* as a 'psychological masterpiece'. People like Walpole's hero should more often be given 'the chance to commit a decent murder . . . Minor crimes done by the right people have ordinarily a wonderfully humanising effect, a decided moral improvement.'

In October 1930 Jung gave a seminar in German on Christiana Morgan's visions, and at the end of the month he started a series of seminars on them in English. By taking her dreams and visions out of chronological order, he jettisoned any possibility of charting her development during analysis. By any reckoning, she had become more fully herself, but he was not setting out to show how he had helped her.

He described her as a typical intellectual, 'exceedingly rational' with a 'one-sided development of the thinking function and therefore an inferior feeling function'. His primary concern in the seminars, he said, was with individuation, and his main theme would be 'the development of the transcendent function out of dreams'. He wanted, as always, to produce evidence in support of his theories, and he was involved, naturally, with the needs of his audience, which consisted largely of patients, together with assistants and analysts who were still in analysis. So it was natural for him to talk almost as if he were analysing his audience collectively. According to one member of it, Elizabeth Sergeant, he was addressing the needs and the complexes of each individual in the room.

Because Christiana had been cut off from the unconscious, he said, it had been painful for her to move downwards into it. He looked back on her analysis as a process of initiation. She needed 'to know more about the inside of the mountain'. Without trying to empathise with the frustrations of women in a paternalistic society, he commented that they 'often pick up tremendously when they are allowed to think all the disagreeable things they denied themselves before'.

As Christiana dug her way down from New England puritanism to primary instinctuality, her regression had struck him as archaeological: 'The feeling is archaic and has all the advantages and disadvantages of an archaic function. The inferior function is generally characterised by traits of primitive psychology.' He portrayed what had gone on as a journey backwards and downwards through ancient matriarchal mystery religions to the deepest level of vegetation, where she represented herself as a tree rooted in the earth with arms branching into the heavens. She resumed the journey forwards and upwards through classical, Mithraic and Christian mysteries.

Though he wanted to concentrate on the individuation process, his focus was mainly on the symbolical and archetypal. He said her 'dreams started with personal stuff, all sorts of resistances and wrong attitudes, but when all that was settled, they began to come to the fundamental things and to prepare very carefully that attitude most favourable for the production of the symbols which brought about the solution of the problem.' But it was simplistic to call her attitudes 'wrong', and he never solved the problems caused by her relationship with her father.

Searching, as always, for interiority and for ways in which a collective unconscious might be at work, Jung required his audience to share his assumption that reality and external circumstances were mutually exclusive. 'I omit personal details intentionally because they matter so little to me. We are all spellbound by those external circumstances and they distract our attention from the real thing.'

One of the reasons for his interest in Indian philosopy and in Tantric yoga was that he saw them as aiming at a 'connection between the specific nature of the non-ego and the conscious ego. Tantra yoga then gives a representation of the condition and the developmental phases of this impersonality, as it itself in its own way produces the light of a higher suprapersonal consciousness.' Feeling in tune with the Tantric view of the human body as microcosm of the universe, he wanted, as Sonu Shamdasani puts it, 'to develop a cross–cultural comparative psychology of inner experience'. He believed that 'in the course of the years, the West will develop its own yoga, and it will be on the basis laid down by Christianity'. But Jung's interest in yoga was more psychological than philosophical or religious. Yoga, he said, 'was originally a natural process of introversion', and it could 'lead to characteristic inner processes of personality changes'.

Before discussing Kundalini yoga in a lecture he gave during October 1930, Jung had studied *The Serpent Power*, a 1919 translation from the Sanskrit of Tantric texts with commentary by Sir John Woodroffe, writing under the pseudonym Arthur Avalon. The copy of the first edition in Jung's library contains extensive annotations. *Kundala* is a Sanskrit word meaning 'coiled up', and Kundalini is divine female serpent power. The devotee imagines the power to be inside him, coiled supine, like a sleeping serpent, at the base of his spine in the deep place known as the *muladhara* (root base). This is the lowest of seven chakras, or centres of psycho-physical energy. Aroused by a mantra, the divine power travels upwards through the spiritual channel inside the spine, touching the chakras. Each one is pictured as a lotus. The seat of earth, *muladhara*, is imagined to be crimson with four petals. The next, *svadhisthana*, which is level with the genitals, is the centre of sexual energy. Level with the navel, *manipura* relates to anger, conflict and mundane needs. Most people's lives are governed from these three centres, while the higher ones represent higher modes of experience. In *anahata*, the heart chakra, thinking and feeling can mingle. *Visshuddha* is the throat chakra, a centre of creative energy, and located between the eyes is *ajna*, the focus of bliss. Here the devotee can see the Lord. The highest chakra is *sahasrara*, and after bringing each lotus to full bloom, the divine energy arrives here, at the centre beyond duality, where all opposites are joined.

Eight months after Jung's Kundalini lectures, Wilhelm Hauer came to lecture on yoga at the Psychological Club. Hauer had spent five years in India as a missionary. As a professor of Indian studies and comparative religion at the university of Tübingen, he published many of his lectures, and Jung read one on 'Yoga in the Light of Psychotherapy'. The Indologist Heinrich Zimmer called him 'most unreliable as a scholar and as a character as well, but endowed with a demoniac, erratic vitality made up of primitive resistances and ambitions'. But Carl Meier thought him 'a very nice chap'.

In the first week of October 1932, at Jung's invitation, he gave a series of seminars on Kundalini. According to Barbara Hannah, 'we all got terribly out of ourselves and confused', but according to Meier, he was lucid enough and there was no general confusion. Hauer was convinced, he told Jung, that 'for psychotherapy as a whole, the way lies in the direction at which you are pointing'; and Jung, who said he was 'aware of the profound congeniality between my view and yoga', accepted the dedication of his new book, *Yoga as a Way of Healing*. Hannah gives the impression that Jung improvised the four seminars he gave between 12 October and 2 November to rescue his audience from the confusion Hauer had caused, but in fact Jung's lectures had been carefully planned. Copying from the illustrations in *The Serpent Power*, Hauer's wife had done seven large paintings of the chakras, and after being used during the seminars, they were eventually given to the Jung Institute, where they were kept on permanent display.

As Sonu Shamdasani suggests, Jung may have been influenced by Hauer, who said: 'I understand an inner reality only in so far as I have it within myself.' It had to become 'absolutely living in my own consciousness'. Jung took pride in having liberated himself 'from the Indian way of looking at things. I find I do not reach the inner meaning if I do not look at them in my own way, from my own point of view.' Jung reminded Heinrich Zimmer of Zen Buddhist masters who taught wordlessly with gestures and attitudes.

The master 'watches you and leaves you to your own way, and he guides you, as far as possible, by silently and involuntarily exhibiting his own way'.

In a 1926 book on Hindu art, Zimmer had focused on mandalas and similar forms in his interpretation of idols, but he did not meet Jung until 1932. They were both at the club in Zurich for one of the lectures, and at the buffet afterwards Zimmer asked for his opinion on the Hindu idea of the transcendental self that underlies both the conscious personality and the unconscious. Jung's reply was to pour gin from a bottle into Zimmer's glass of lemon squash until he said, 'Stop, stop, thank you.' He had made Zimmer tell himself to stop talking and come down to earth – at least, that was how he interpreted the way Jung had poured the gin. Staying with him in Küsnacht over the weekend, Zimmer decided he had at last met 'the master magician alive . . . the most accomplished embodiment of the big medicine man, of the perfect wizard, the master of Zen initiations'.

While some forms of yoga are designed to eliminate the passions, Kundalini aims to reach through them towards the spiritual objective, shifting attention from the normal targets of the passions to the energy in them. Heinrich Zimmer put it well: 'This tide of passion itself may be the baptising water by which the taint of ego-consciousness is washed away . . . the hero (vira) floats beyond himself on the roused but canalised current.'

Jung's attitude to Kundalini was ambivalent. Acquaintance with it was invaluable – 'otherwise you cannot realise the self, and the purpose of this world had been missed.' He quoted St Paul: 'It is not I that live, it is Christ that liveth in me.' But he took the view that Kundalini was one of those Eastern systems of thought which 'inhibit the natural growth and development of our own psychology, therefore one has to make really heroic attempts to stand up against these symbols, in order to deprive them of their influence'. The danger, from his point of view, was that patients would try to immerse themselves in the unconscious. 'You must keep outside, detached, and observe objectively what happens.' His duty – so he believed – was was protect them from the kind of 'inflation' that would result if the ego mistook itself for the self. He explained: 'Nobody understands what the self is because the self is just what you are not – it is not the ego . . . The ego discovers itself as a mere appendix of the self . . . The ego is always far down in the *muladhara* and suddenly becomes aware of something up in the fourth storey, above, in *anahata*, and that is the self.'

Though Nietzsche had set a high value on the body – Body is a mighty sage, says Zarathustra – Jung shied away from the physical in his Kundalini seminars, as he had in those on Nietzsche. He ignored both Kundalini's celebration of the body and what Mircea Eliade called 'a sort of religious rediscovery of the mystery of woman'. Heinrich Zimmer confirms that

Tantrism 'insists on the holiness and purity of all things', including the 'five forbidden things' which are incorporated into certain rituals: wine, meat, fish, dried grain and sexual intercourse. Some ceremonies incorporate them symbolically, and some literally, just as the erotic terms in Tantric texts can be interpreted in either way.

If Jung had given members of his audience more freedom to forge their own relationship with a form of yoga most of them were encountering for the first time, some would have been able to make more use of it than others, but he magisterially maintained: 'The concept of Kundalini has for us only one use, that is, to describe our own experiences with the unconscious, the experiences that have to do with the initiation of the suprapersonal processes.' He treats what Tantric yoga terms the awakening of Kundalini as if it were identical with what he called psychic objectivity. To be realistic about our experience, he said, we need to detach ourselves from it, and the symbols of the chakras 'afford us a standpoint that extends beyond the conscious . . . It is as if a superconsciousness, an all-embracing divine consciousness, surveyed the psyche from above.'

With his habits of thinking diagrammatically and mapping the individual body in relation to the macrocosm, he liked the notion of the chakras, but he was more interested in adapting Kundalini yoga to fit analytical psychology than in expanding analytical psychology to accommodate new insights that might have been gained. He interfered surgically with the symbols, making Kundalini energy into the anima and rearranging the chakras. 'We begin in our conscious world, so our *muladhara* might be not down below in the belly but up in the head.' He equates it with ego-consciousness, while moving *svadhisthana* downwards to make it into the unconscious. 'In the East the unconscious is above, while with us it is below, so we can reverse the whole thing, as if we were coming down from the *muladhara*, as if that were the highest centre.'

On the other hand, Jung's treatment of Kundalini made an enormous impact on many of those who heard him speak, and some of his patients produced new symptoms that may have been suggested by their experience. The seminars on Christiana's visions had been suspended, and the Kundalini seminars were not irrelevant to the visions, which had similarly suggested a spiritual journey in bodily terms, representing movement both downwards and upwards − exploration of the depths and ascent to spiritual heights. There was a patient in the audience who was either having or soon started having dreams and symptoms that would suggest a connection with both Christiana and Kundalini.

Another man, who had not yet met Jung but later became a Jungian analyst, had his first encounter with Kundalini through reading about it, and the awakening of Kundalini struck him as corresponding to experiences of his own

> with similar noises & sensations which were truly terrifying, & mixed up also with highly mystical ones, also of course Psychosexual, that I'm wondering whether something of the same kind may have been happening to me – the devilish outcome of an almost divine experience. We in the West are so lacking in the true religiosity that we have lost the threads, & get good things so muddled up with bad that we have lost the purity of divine dirt.

The brief immersion in Tantrism seems to have intensified Jung's impatience with atheistic materialism. Like Hinduism, Christianity offered an alternative perspective. 'To it, too, the world is only a preparation for a higher condition, and the here and now, the state of being involved in this world is error and sin.' The function of prayer and ritual was to liberate humanity 'from the merely personal state of mind', and the ascension of Jesus represented 'the desired end, that is, being lifted above the personal and into the suprapersonal'. In the West, non-Christians were at a disadvantage in seeing the here-and-now as the only reality.

Kundalini offered an alternative to the 'peculiar duality and even duplicity' of human psychology, where 'the two aspects form a bewildering crisscross'. From one viewpoint 'all the personal things are the only meaningful things', and from the other 'the personal things are utterly uninteresting and valueless, futile, illusory . . . We could not possibly judge this world if we had not also a standpoint outside, and that is given by the symbolism of religious experiences.'

Historical events could not be explained adequately, he maintained, in political and economic terms. The war of 1914–18 was 'a psychical phenomenon. If you are looking for the causal root of it, it could not possibly be explained as arising out of the reason of man or out of economic necessity . . . It was simply the time when that thing had to happen from unknown psychical reasons. Any great movement of man has always started from psychical reasons.' Politicians should take decisions in accordance with this principle. During the 1914 war, according to Richard Wilhelm, the Japanese leaders regularly consulted the I Ching on 'important affairs of state'.

But in an article or book or public lecture, Jung would not have been so dogmatic. He was addressing a small audience which had accepted his premises. When he returned to the subject of Christiana's visions on 2 November, he said: 'You know I must refrain entirely from speaking of the personal life of our patient because it leads nowhere; if you begin to think of her as a personal being it will lead you astray. These visions are not to be understood in a personal way, for then it would be nothing but the subjective foolishness of one person.'

But Jung was once again forced to think of her as a personal being when Harry Murray arrived in Zurich, as did a Harvard colleague who had come under Christiana's spell – Ralph Eaton. When Eaton had visited her home, which was near Harvard, she showed him some of the paintings she had done for Jung, but she rebuffed his advances. Wanting to consult Jung about the abortive relationship, he came to Zurich, and when he attended some of the seminars, he recognised the material Jung was using. Eaton went back to Harvard, tried to see her, suffered a psychotic breakdown, escaped from hospital and killed himself.

Like Christiana's analysis, the seminars ended badly. 'The case is getting more and more complicated,' said Jung. 'Things are getting reversed in a very peculiar way.' With only a perfunctory discussion of transference and counter-transference, he put the blame on her. She was too young, too unsettled, incapable of making the right contact with him. But the seminars repeated the pattern of the analysis: like Christiana, the audience was at first involved and then alienated as Jung became increasingly irritable and increasingly critical of the visions and dreams he was using. 'I cannot tell you how bored I was, how terribly uninteresting I found them. For a long time they got on my nerves, I couldn't touch them.'

It was not from Eaton but from Harry – during a reunion which followed a period of separation – that Christiana finally found out in 1933 that Jung had failed to conceal her identity. She had not only given permission for the seminars to be held but had provided pictures. But she was outraged to find he had failed to preserve her anonymity, and the seminars, which had started in October 1930, had to stop. Held on 21 March, the last one was the eighty-seventh in the series. He had discussed forty-four of her dreams and visions.

When the seminars were published as a book, Harry – invited by the editor to contribute a 'postscript' on Christiana – was critical of the way Jung had handled the material. His talks had been 'devoted to the study not of a particular case but of a set of *universal* self-transforming processes'. Christiana's interpretation of her visions 'was nowhere near the focus of her doctor's commentary'. Harry had no doubt 'that love was the key to it all', but Jung was so preoccupied with the theme of individuation that he forgot why Christiana had been willing to undergo so much suffering. 'It wasn't in his being,' said Harry, to take this into account.

The Kundalini patient, who was in her mid-twenties and was having an affair, had been born in Java and had spoken Malay as a child, though her parents were European. Jung was her third analyst. The second, a woman, had broken off the treatment after a week. She had three dreams about crossing a frontier, and said in the third that she had nothing to declare. The customs official then searched her handbag to find two beds or two mattresses – Jung gives different accounts of the dream. When he interpreted this to mean she had been hiding her bourgeois desire for a conventional marriage, she 'produced the most violent resistances', and behind them was 'a most singular fantasy of a quite unimaginable erotic adventure that surpassed anything I had ever come across'.

He lost patience with her, and the analysis made no progress till he had a dream about catching sight of her at the top of a castle on a hill. Having to look up at her in the dream made him feel bad about looking down on her – disapproving of her – and their discussion about this made her start dreaming again. In the first dream a white elephant was emerging from her genitals. She soon developed symptoms of uterine ulcers, and then a hypersensitivity in the bladder. The next symptom was higher in the body – intestinal spasms. The symptoms went on moving upwards, to the colon, the ileum, upper sections of the small intestine, and she finally felt as if the top of her skull was softening. She thought the fontanelle was opening and a bird with a long beak was going to pierce through it to her diaphragm.

Jung says he found 'an explanation of all those things I had not understood in the patient's dreams and symptoms' in the *The Serpent Power*, and claims it was 'quite impossible that the patient knew the book beforehand'.

Twenty-Seven

Hitler Is a Medicine Man

As Isaiah Berlin reminds us, opposition to the values of the French Enlight-enment is as old as the movement itself. Voltaire believed that progress in the arts and sciences was counteracting 'ignorance, superstition, fanaticism, oppression and barbarism', while Rousseau blamed civilisation and its institutions for destroying the simplicity and spontaneity that were natural to man, corrupting the life of natural justice.

Rousseau neither believed savages were noble nor wanted men to slide back into their primitive state, while Jung was not alone in sympathising with the Mexican Indians and Africans whose indigenous culture had been crassly destroyed by missionary Christianity, but what the two men had in common was that they both saw cultural achievement as antithetical to natural human need. While condemning the chains a corrupt civilisation had put on humanity, Rousseau believed that natural impulses would lead only to good behaviour, that conscience was a 'divine instinct that would speak only with the voice of Reason'.

Thinking more simplistically in terms of a polarity between the civilised and the primitive, and lamenting the disappearance of a *Weltanschauung* in which all strata of experience were interconnected, Jung believed that by demanding rational explanations for everything that happened, we had erected an artificial barrier between the psychic and the objective.

In the archaic world, said Jung, when an important psychic component is projected onto an individual, 'he becomes *mana*, exceptionally effective – a sorcerer, witch, werewolf or something similar'. According to the mana theory, 'all these extraordinary effects are produced by something like a power that is widely distributed through the world . . . Being is a field of force. The primitive idea of mana has in it, as you can see, the beginnings of a crude theory of energy.' The underlying question, as formulated by Jung, is: 'Does the psychic in general – the soul or spirit or unconscious – originate in *us*, or is the psyche actually outside us in the early stages of conscious evolution in the form of arbitrary powers which have intentions of their own?' Jung found this 'not altogether inconceivable . . . Since the human body is made up by heredity from innumerable Mendelian units, it does not seem impossible that the psyche is built up in a similar way.' He did not feel uncomfortable with the notion that 'instead of being something in its own right, human individuality is the accidental product of forces in the natural environment'.

In spite of all the pressures on his time and the complexity of the arrangements that had to be made, Jung had been managing without a secretary. He had written letters in longhand and kept no copies, while accounting had been erratic. Barbara Hannah says that in her first year or two (1929–30) 'I do not think . . . I ever got a correct bill, and the mistakes were always in my favour!' At first it had sometimes been Emma who helped Jung with secretarial work, and sometimes his sister Trudi. In April 1931, his twenty-one-year-old daughter Marianne took over. New cupboards were installed in the old nursery to transform it into an office.

In the spring of 1932 he arrived at a better solution to the problem. Hans Schmid had died at the age of forty-four, and his elder daughter, Marie-Jeanne, needed to earn a salary. Fluent in French and English, with some knowledge of psychology, she was a good organiser, and, unlike Marianne, she had learned shorthand. In theory, her working hours as Jung's secretary were from eight in the morning till six in the evening, with a break at twelve for lunch with him and Emma. In practice, Marie-Jeanne often had to work through her lunch hour and stay late in the evening. Since Jung had known her as a child, she was one of the few adults he addressed in the second-person singular, while she called him 'Herr Professor'.

He dictated some letters and made her write others, including letters of thanks for present, many of which had never been opened. He usually signed all these letters without reading them. Once every two weeks she went to Bollingen, taking the typewriter and the correspondence that had accumulated in Küsnacht. Reluctant to deal with it, he barely said hello, which was less disconcerting once he had explained why her appearance invariably put him into a bad mood. It was because most of his correspondence bored him. At the end of her first twelve months in the job, he said: 'You are playing the perfect secretary, and it is just sickening.'

One of her tasks was to clean his pipes. He had a large collection of Kobler pipes, whose hollow stem contained a metal spiral which could be dipped in water. This cooled the smoke, and much of the nicotine remained in the metal, which became dirty and smelly. She used petrol to clean the stems once every six weeks. He mixed his tobacco himself, using English, Dutch and Swiss. The tobacco tin was called Habakkuk; he liked giving names to inanimate objects.

Though Jung never again abandoned his patients for so long as he had in 1924–6, he was always liable to assert his freedom by disappearing abruptly. In March 1933 Markus Fierz, a professor of chemistry at the Swiss Federal Polytechnic (*Eidgenossische Technische Hochschule*) was about to go on a Mediterranean cruise. 'Why don't you come with me? I'm starting tomorrow from Zurich station at eleven a.m. I'm travelling first class, which means there's always a second bed in the compartment.'

At first Jung demurred. How could he abandon his patients? They needed him from hour to hour. But the next day he was at the station in time to catch the train. 'I've realised that somebody who's tired and needs a rest, and goes on working all the same is a fool.'

Travelling by train and boat, they visited Alexandria, Athens and the Greek islands. The shared experiences strengthened their friendship, and Jung took two decisions. One was to to resume lecturing at the Polytechnic and give a course on 'General Psychology'. The other was to sell Fierz some of the land at Bollingen, so that he could build a house there. 'It's friendship,' Jung said, 'but not just that. I've realised that by itself one family isn't strong enough to defend this beautiful lakeside area against the growing pressure of village and state to free the lake for the public, and to make a pathway just in front of my tower.'

From the islands they sailed to Palestine. Jewish refugees were arriving from Germany, where Adolf Hitler had come to power at the end of January. This was Jung's first glimpse of what the new regime was doing to the Jews. In October 1929, the stock market had crashed on Wall Street, and violent repercussions were felt all over Europe, except in Switzerland. In Germany, where the Nazis soon profited at the polling booths, and in Austria, groups of youngsters were to be seen wandering from place to place, but if they tried to enter Switzerland, they were stopped at the borders. 'It seemed that nothing troubled Switzerland,' wrote one of Jung's American patients. 'Like Shangri-La or the Magic Mountain, it was high up and mysterious and somehow magical or mystical, otherworldly, untroubled.'

Jung had been taking an interest in Hitler's personality. In 1932, when his photograph was often appearing in the newspapers, Emilii Medtner sent Jung a clipping, which prompted a preliminary character analysis:

A too intensive unconscious sphere as counterpart to a somewhat blocked conscious sphere – therefore too much distance between the conscious and unconscious. Higher up too purely intellectual, below too much like a

primeval forest. A kind of pre-war Russian soul. He is thinnest at the
centre of the face . . . so there is a split into oppositional pairs . . . no
balance but a tendency towards obsession. The eyes express: discharge of
the unconscious in fantasies he then tries to interpret.

On 12 May 1933, Freud's books were among those burned by the Nazis in
Berlin. Within weeks of Hitler's appointment as chancellor, intellectuals
were under pressure to pledge their loyalty, while foreigners were banned
from sitting on the central executive of any medical society. The head of the
Berlin Psychoanalytical Society was Max Eitingon, a Russian Jew who had
taken Polish nationality. He was succeeded by a non-Jew, Felix Boehm, but
the man who took charge of the society was an Adlerian neuropsychiatrist
from Wuppertal who had been practising as a psychotherapist, Professor
Matthias Göring. He was Hermann Göring's cousin. Most German psychoanalysts were Jewish, and when some were expelled, the others resigned.

Jung seldom commented on public events, but long before swastikas and
other symptoms of neopaganism had erupted on the skin of the body politic,
he had mentioned the 'chthonic quality' of Germans, who had been only
half civilised by Christianity. Still unredeemed, their darker half 'remains
connected with the residue of the prehistoric age, with the collective
unconscious, which is subject to a strange and constantly increasing activation'. Since the French Revolution, Europe's respect for Christianity had
dwindled, he wrote in 1916, and 'the "blond beast" is likely to become
more threateningly audible as it paces about in its subterranean prison'. Not
long after the end of the First World War, he said that in the group, as in the
individual, the first effect of regression was the reawakening of infantile
attitudes. Panic-stricken people cluster together, looking for father images
that appear in a mythological setting. Group formations deteriorate into
tribes, held together by mystical doctrines and by a chief or medicine man.
Hitler was a kind of medicine man.

The Nazis were going to stigmatise psychoanalysis as a Jewish science.
This would be Jung's second chance to benefit from not being Jewish. Freud
had thought he needed a Christian president for his international association,
and now, after setting up a rival orthodoxy, Jung suddenly had powerful and
unscrupulous allies. In Germany it seemed likely that analytical psychology
could displace psychoanalysis. Putting all Jewish doctors and lawyers out of
work at the same time as banning work by Jewish writers, composers and
artists, the Nazis needed to rally as much support as they could from
intellectuals and educated people, not only inside Germany but in other
German-speaking countries.

So far, there were no indications of the territorial aggression that would change the map of Europe, but the psychological map was already changing. The General Society for Psychotherapy had been founded in 1926 for doctors using different psychiatric techniques. In 1928, when Jung joined, over 80 per cent of the 399 members were German. Among the ex-Freudians were Alfred Adler and Wilhelm Reich. The others included Georg Groddeck, Karen Horney and Matthias Göring.

The society's journal, the *Zentralblatt für Psychotherapie*, was founded in 1930, the year that the German psychiatrist Ernst Kretschmer was elected president and Jung vice-president. One of the president's jobs was to edit the *Zentralblatt*, and when Kretschmer came under pressure to align it and the society with Nazi ideology, he resigned. On 21 June 1933, Jung took over as president, and in the autumn it was arranged that he would control the international edition of the *Zentralblatt*, while Matthias Göring would be in charge of the aligned German edition.

Jung had accepted an invitation to give five seminars on dreams in Berlin. On 26 June, the day of the first, he was interviewed on Radio Berlin by a former pupil, Adolf Weizsäcker, who introduced him as 'the most progressive psychologist of modern times' and sneered at the 'destructive' psychology of Freud and Adler. Coming from 'a Protestant parsonage in Basel', Dr Jung naturally had a more positive approach.

Knowing what was required, Jung provided it. He condemned Freud and Adler as 'hostile to life'. In their psychology, 'a single individual standpoint – such as sexuality or the striving for power – is set in critical opposition to the whole phenomenal world. In this way a part of the phenomenon is isolated and corroded [*zersetzt*].' Here Jung chose a word that often featured in propaganda against the Jews, and he used it again in one of his Berlin seminars, saying a dream is a message that should not be 'corroded'. For both the radio audience and the seminar, the word would have signalled agreement with the Nazis.

When Weizsäcker asked Jung for his opinion on 'personal leadership' as an alternative to democratic government, he said it was natural for a mass movement to 'culminate organically in the leader [*im Führer*], who embodies in his whole being the meaning and purpose of the popular movement. He incarnates the nation's psyche, and he is its mouthpiece.' *Im Führer* means both 'in the leader' and 'in the Führer'.

He went on to say the 'aimless chit-chat of parliamentary deliberation' might 'drone on' in 'times of aimless quiescence', but it was 'perfectly natural that a leader should stand at the head of an elite'. In earlier centuries the elite had been formed by a nobility, which 'believes by the law of nature in blood and exclusiveness of the race'.

His answers to Weizsäcker's questions were opportunistic, as was the editorial he wrote in the *Zentralblatt*, arguing that it was no longer right to 'gloss over the differences which really do exist between Germanic and Jewish psychology, and which have long been familiar to all intelligent people'. Here too there is ambiguity – he could be referring to either mental make-up or psychological theory. Or both.

Though not admirable, Jung's behaviour is understandable. He disliked what he saw of the Nazis – especially Goebbels – but he did not know how long they were going to be in power. Now that Freud was handicapped by age (he was seventy-seven) and by Jewishness, analytical psychology could overtake psychoanalysis, at least in the German-speaking world, and Jung, who was not yet fifty-eight, could become the leading depth-psychologist if he managed not to antagonise Germany's new rulers.

He found the prospect alluring, and later felt the need to defend his behaviour. He said he had wanted to keep an open mind about the Nazis. 'Every archetype contains the lowest and the highest, evil and good, and is therefore capable of producing diametrically opposite results . . . With my medical attitude towards such things, I was in favour of waiting, for it is an attitude that allows no hasty judgements. does not always know from the outset what is better, and is willing to give things "a fair trial".'

This implies that he was never a sympathiser: but writing in the *Zentralblatt*, he combined praise for the movement with derision for Freud's view of the unconscious:

> Where was the unheard of energy and tension when there was as yet no National Socialism? It lay hidden in the German soul, in that depth which is anything but the garbage bin of unresolved childish wishes and unresolved family resentments. A movement that seizes a whole people has ripened in each individual. Medical psychology must take into account not just the diseased aberrations of the individual but the creatively active forces of the soul, not just an obscure section but in the significant whole.

Speaking to the Kulturbund in Vienna during November 1932, Jung argued that 'the great liberating deeds of world history have originated from leading personalities and never from the inert mass that is always subordinate, needing a demagogue if it is to move at all. The plaudits of the Italian nation are addressed to the personality of the Duce, while other nations lament their great lack of a leader.' Publishing this in 1934, after Hitler had come to power, Jung added, 'since this sentence was written, Germany too had found its leader.'

In the mid-thirties Jung even approved of Hitler's S.S. 'The S.S. men are

being transformed into a caste of knights ruling sixty million natives . . .
There is no more ideal form of government than a decent form of oligarchy
– call it aristocracy if you prefer.'

There is evidence of anti-Jewish prejudice in his conversation. In 1933 he
had his first meeting with Michael Fordham, a twenty-nine-year-old
psychiatrist who had heard about him from Peter Baynes. He was at first
sceptical about Jung's theories, and, working on a paranoid schizophrenic,
told himself that if Jung was right, it would be possible to find his patient's
delusions in Sir James Frazer's book *The Golden Bough*. 'I did find them, and
my sceptical resistance broke down.'

Deciding that he wanted Jung to analyse him, Fordham sent a letter
explaining that since he had no money, he would have to pay for the analysis
by finding work in Zurich. At Jung's suggestion, he travelled out to meet
him, and in the train found himself in the same carriage as a young Jew, who
talked about the persecution in Germany. Mentioning this conversation
when he met Jung the next afternoon, Fordham found the word *Jew* 'was
like the stimulus word in an association test that hid a complex, and for about
three quarters of an hour, Jung delivered a long discourse on the Jews, their
history and their difference from Christians and Europeans'. He talked about
'parasitic elements in Jewish psychology'. What, asked Jung, had the Jews
fed on during their forty years in the wilderness? And since they were not the
same as other people, they should wear different clothes.

Eventually Fordham interrupted to remind Jung why he had come. It was
out of the question, Jung said. Foreigners could not work in Switzerland.
Fordham's annoyance at having made the journey for nothing was defused
when Jung invited him to a seminar in the morning, and then, during the
coffee break, picked him out for a friendly chat.

The habit of generalising about the Jews was to continue throughout
Jung's life. In a 1951 letter he said that if pride was 'the specific Greek vice',
cupidity 'falls to the lot of the Jews'.

When he was in his last year at school, Toni Wolff's nephew Pablo Naeff
was invited to bring some of his classmates to Bollingen. Most of the
youngsters were boys, but among them was Marie-Louise von Franz, the
eighteen-year-old daughter of an Austrian nobleman.

> Suddenly out of the bushes, what seemed an enormous man came with a
> dirty shirt and dirty trousers and gold-rimmed spectacles and I thought
> 'what an incredible face he has!' He was very friendly. I felt terribly shy and
> he just shook our hands and said 'I haven't finished cooking. You boys go
> down and look at the lake and my sailing boat down there.' And then he

called me and said 'Could you cut these cucumbers up?' In great excitement I did and cut my thumb and the blood ran into the cucumber. And Jung just roared with laughter and gave me a bandage and so everything began.

After giving them all lunch, he talked about his ideas. Telling them about a patient who said she had been on the moon, he insisted that she really had. 'For minutes I thought "Now am I crazy or is this man crazy? I can't see what he's driving at." Until I realised that for him the soul was real, and I became tremendously enthusiastic. We stayed until midnight and he poured a lot of wonderful burgundy down us and so I came home completely happy.'

The Greek word *eranos* means a banquet to which each guest contributes something – possibly a speech, a poem or a song. The creator of the Eranos Conferences was Olga Fröbe-Kapteyn, a neurotic widow who had once been a circus rider in Holland. Her father had left her a big house, the Casa Gabriele, with extensive grounds at Moscia, a village outside Ascona, on the shores of Lago Maggiore. She led a secluded life there, studying Indian religion, but in 1928 she impulsively had a conference hall built, big enough to seat two hundred people. It was linked to her villa by a terraced garden. She did not know how she was going to use it.

It was probably in 1928 that she went to Connecticut and offered to collaborate with Alice Bailey, leader of the Arcane School. According to Alice Bailey's unfinished autobiography, Olga Fröbe-Kapteyn offered to start a spiritual centre, 'and that it should be undenominational, nonsectarian and open to esoteric thinkers and occult students of all groups in Europe and elsewhere'.

Early in 1930, Olga Fröbe-Kapteyn sent out invitations to 'a Summer School for the study of Theosophy, Mysticism, the Esoteric Sciences and Philosophies and all forms of spiritual research'. In her opening speech on 3 August 1930, she declared the centre open, expressing the hope that 'gradually a nucleus may grow up around it, a Tree with many branches, rooted in the Supreme One, Who enfolds all beings'. The centre's motto was taken from the *Bhagavad-Gita*: 'However men approach ME, even so do I welcome them, for the path men take from every side is MINE.'

During the first summer school, Alice Bailey lectured on 'Man and Superman', 'The Occult Significance of Speech', 'The Stages in Meditation' and 'The Religion of the New Age'. Other speakers included Roberto Assagioli, the neurologist who had withdrawn from psychoanalysis to originate psychosynthesis, and Alexander, Grand Duke of Russia, who spoke on 'Spiritual Education'. A young Hindu officiated at the house-blessing ceremony, and the villa was named Casa Shanti.

Though she responded to the beauty of Lago Maggiore, Alice Bailey had misgivings based on her belief that the area had once been 'the centre of the Black Mass in Central Europe'. She withdrew from the summer school before Jung became involved. Olga Fröbe-Kapteyn met him in 1930, when they were both at the School of Wisdom in Darmstadt. She talked to him about the summer school, and he was interested in her project, but the turning point for her was encouragement from a historian of religion, Rudolf Otto, whom she met in 1932.

Planning events for the summer of 1933, she decided that the theme should be yoga and meditation, Eastern and Western. When she invited Jung to be one of the speakers, he refused, but changed his mind when she told him who the other speakers were. 'You devil! You've invited all my friends and colleagues. Of course I'll come.'

He talked without notes on 'The Empirical Basis of the Individuation Process'. Because Olga Fröbe-Kapteyn disliked argument, she had decreed there would be no discussion at any of the sessions. The whole morning was devoted to one lecture and the afternoon to another, with an interval in the middle of each. She gradually became more dependent on Jung, convincing herself that he could heal her with his presence or by laying his hands on her. Mary Bancroft has described her when she was in conversation with him:

> She was dressed as always – big hat, loose garment too long to be fashionable, and around her neck chains or beads of 'things' of esoteric significance. I got the impression that she was in possession of some mysterious talisman – and Jung in his way was *it* – the talisman. She struck me as one of those people who float through life an inch or two off the ground.

Twenty-Eight

This Jewish Gospel

No Swiss group had been formally constituted for the International General Medical Society. Needing a president for it, Jung approached Alphonse Maeder in January 1934 but he did not want to be involved, and in March, writing to the Dutch president, J. H. van der Hoop, Jung said Maeder 'intends to do nothing in this matter, as he is now devoting himself entirely to the Christian work of conversion in the Oxford Movement'. A Swiss group was finally formed in January 1935 with a committee that included Jung and Meier.

Göring sent Jung a conciliatory letter, suggesting foreigners should take 'a psychotherapeutic view of the situation in Germany', and Jung decided to stay on friendly terms with him, even when he saw his own name under a manifesto in the December 1933 issue of the *Zentralblatt*, recommending *Mein Kampf* as a basic text for all psychotherapists, and saying all members must be loyal to National Socialism. The manifesto had been written by Göring, and was intended for the German edition. The review was published in Leipzig, and, claiming he was only nominally the editor, Jung said the manifesto had appeared in the main body of the review without his knowledge or permission.

He was attacked in the *Neue Zürcher Zeitung* by the psychiatrist Gustav Bally for advocating 'the super-psychology of the racial psychologists'. Jung defended himself by arguing that psychotherapy was 'above politics' and professing 'complete inability to understand why it should be a crime to speak of "Jewish" psychology'. 'Are we seriously to believe that a tribe which has wandered through history for several thousand years as "God's chosen people" was not put up to such an idea by some quite special psychological peculiarity? If no differences exist, how do we recognise Jews at all?'

Did he think assimilated modern Jews were recognisably different from everybody else? Were they no different from the tribal Jews who thought

God had chosen them? In March 1934, Jung wrote a cautiously worded letter saying he did not want to denigrate Jews but to 'single out and formulate the mental idiosyncracies that distinguish Jews from other people'.

According to Thomas Mann, Jung was 'striking the wrong pose'. Mann had settled in Küsnacht during the autumn of 1933 after exiling himself from Hitler's Germany. Apparently he wanted to meet Jung, and they did meet, but only once. Jung said Mann reminded him of South American vampires who flew around at night and sucked blood from the toes of sleeping people. Mann thought Jung's 'self-justifying article' in the *Neue Zürcher Zeitung* was 'most unpleasant and disingenuous, even badly written and witless . . . He ought to declare his "affiliation" openly.'

In the *Zentralblatt*, Jung elaborated his argument that neither Freud nor Adler was 'a universally valid representative of European man'.

> The Jews share this peculiarity with women: because they are physically weaker, they have to aim at chinks in their enemy's armour, and thanks to this method, which has been forced on them throughout the ages, Jews are strongest where others are weakest. And because their civilisation is more than twice as old as ours, they are much more conscious of human weaknesses – of the shadow side of things – and therefore much less vulnerable in this respect than we are. Thanks to their experience of an ancient culture, they can live on friendly and even tolerant terms with their weaknesses, while we are still too young not to be 'deluded' about ourselves . . . The Jewish race as a whole – in my experience at least – possesses an unconscious which can be compared with the Aryan only to a limited extent.

Categorising European non-Jews as Aryan – a word popularised in the nineteenth century by the philologist Friedrich Max Müller – the statement rests on uncritical acceptance of the doctrine that they belong to a different race from Jews, and on a mindless assumption, not uncommon at this time, about the relative strength of Aryans and Jews.

Freud had assumed that Jung was an anti-Semite who had overcome his anti-Semitism in order to be a Freudian. But in May 1933, writing about his first encounter with Freud's work, Jung claimed: 'I suspected at once that this partly diabolical sexual theory would turn people's heads, and I have sacrificed my scientific career in doing all I can to combat this absolute devaluation of the psyche.'

Jung's *Zentralblatt* article suggests that Jews, regardless of nationality, background and education, are all somehow conditioned by having three thousand years of civilisation behind them. In these generalisations, he does not differentiate between the personal unconscious and the collective. In

1911 he had believed some of Agathli's dreams to be 'closely connected with certain Negro myths, in which this involvement in slimy stuff also occurs', but he was now saying Jews and Aryans did not share the same unconscious.

He was obviously writing with one eye on the Nazis when he praised the 'still youthful Germanic peoples' who may go on to create 'new cultural forms which still lie dormant in the darkness of every individual's unconscious – seeds bursting with energy and capable of powerful expansion'. But the Jew had always been too nomadic to create 'a cultural form of his own and so far as we can see he never will, for his instincts and talents can develop only with a more or less civilised nation as his host'.

Thomas Mann agreed that neurosis was 'a precious part of the soul', but accused Jung of 'revolting behaviour'. His earliest attacks on Freud's 'rationalism' had no political overtones, but to fire a broadside against 'soulless rationalism' in 1934 was to imply

a total rejection of rationalism, long after the moment has come for us to fight on the side of rationality with every ounce of our strength. Jung's thought and his statements tend to glorify Nazism and its 'neurosis'. He exemplifies the irresistible tendency of people's thinking to bend itself to the times – he is a high class example. He swims with the tide. He is intelligent, but not admirable. Anyone in these times who wallows in 'soul' is old-fashioned, both intellectually and morally.

Eight years later, looking back on Jung's behaviour, Mann said he 'was always a half-Nazi'.

Jung was developing the attack on 'Jewish psychology' he had made during 1927 in a footnote he added to the 1916 essay on 'The Relations between the Ego and the Unconscious', and in the autumn of 1934 he was preparing a new edition:

To accept the conclusions of a Jewish psychology as generally valid is a quite unforgivable mistake. None of us would think of applying Chinese or Indian psychology to ourselves. The cheap allegation of anti-Semitism that has been levelled at me on the basis of this criticism is about as intelligent as attacking me for being prejudiced against the Chinese.

Trying harder than Mann realised to 'swim with the times', Jung wrote in February 1934 to a founder of the Berlin Institution, Wolfgang Kränefeldt:

The Aryan people can make the point that with Freud and Adler specifically Jewish viewpoints are preached publicly, and, as can be proved

similarly, viewpoints that are essentially corrosive [*zersetzend*] in character.
If the propagation of this Jewish gospel is acceptable to the government,
then so be it. The alternative possibility is that this would not be acceptable
to the government.

His continuing use of the word *corrosive* suggested willingness to preach the
Aryan gospel. Not that his attitude was consistently anti-Semitic, but he
often returned to the argument that Jews were different in their unconscious
from non-Jews, and that in so far as Freud's ideas were valid, they were
relevant only to Jews.

In May 1934 at the annual congress of the General Medical Society in Bad
Nauheim, Jung was in the chair when Matthias Göring was reading a paper
that said *Mein Kampf* 'has to be called a scientific book', and he expected all
members to study it. They would recognise that the Führer 'has something
most of us lack: Jung calls it intuition. It is more important than all science.'

Writing at the end of 1935 to Erich Neumann, a supporter who later
settled in Israel, Jung said: 'The "cultivated" Jew is always on the way to
becoming a "non-Jew" '. He usually reminded Jewish patients 'that it stands
to reason they are Jews'. Perhaps they would need no reminder if they lived
in Palestine, but 'Jews in general have lived *much longer* in other countries . . .
I can scarcely feel my way into a psyche that has not grown up in any soil.'

A year later, writing in English to Abraham Roback, author of *Jewish
Influence in Modern Thought,* Jung asked for information on the 'experiments'
Roback said he had made 'about the mental differences between Jews and
non-Jews . . . There is indeed a marked difference which has to do with the
age of the race.' Jung had 'found something very similar in Hindus, namely
an extension or extensibility of the consciousness into the subconscious
mind'. In Jews 'the tendency of consciousness to autonomy' entailed the risk
that it would be cut off 'almost entirely from its instinctive sources'. In this
respect, Freud was typical, which explained why he was so pleased with 'the
re-establishment of the communication with the instincts', while non-Jews
are not pleased because they 'experience it as a restriction of moral freedom.
That explains the peculiar leaning of Protestant parsons to Freudian analysis.
In their hands it is a beautiful means to show a brand-new category of sins to
people.' In a letter to Hauer, Jung claimed that having treated so many Jews,
he could 'recognise the relation of their racial psychology to their religion'.

The *Zentralblatt* went on publishing anti-Semitic articles until 1939,
supporting Hitler and the Nazi party while deriding the mentality characteristic of Jews and 'Jewish psychology'. In 1936 Jung appointed Göring as
co-editor, on the understanding that the *Zentralblatt* would not be censored
or prevented from reviewing books by Jews. In 1939, when the Germans

introduced Italian, Hungarian and Japanese groups into the society and refused to guarantee its exemption from 'Aryan regulations', Jung stayed on as president. He did not resign until 1940. He should have been succeeded by the vice president – an Englishman – but Göring, overriding this rule, moved the headquarters to Berlin, where the *Zentralblatt* was brought into line with Nazi ideology.

When charged, as he frequently was, with anti-Semitism, Jung sometimes grew so indignant that he advanced even more provocative generalisations. 'I cannot see why the Jew, unlike any so-called Christian, is incapable of assuming that he is being criticised personally when one has an opinion about him . . . No one who is a Jew can become a human being without *knowing* that he is a Jew, since this is the basis from which he can reach out to a higher humanity.' The premise for this statement is that some Jews are not yet human, while others are, but they start on a relatively low level.

Returning to the subject of Freud, Jung wrote:

> It is typically Jewish that the Jews can utterly forget that they are Jews despite the fact that they know they are Jews . . . So when I criticise Freud's Jewishness I am not criticising the *Jews* but rather that damnable capacity of the Jew, as exemplified by Freud, to forget his own nature. Actually you should be glad that I think so rigorously, for then I speak in the interest of all Jews who want to find their way back to their own nature.

Jean-Paul Sartre took a similar position in his 1944 essay 'Reflections on the Jewish Question'. Jews cannot be authentic unless they live out fully their condition as Jews. But he later repudiated the statement as anti-Semitic. The Jewish recipient of Jung's letter, Dr Gerhard Adler, went on to become an editor of his collected works – a fact which is sometimes taken to prove that Jung had nothing against Jews.

In the spring of 1934, when Christiana Morgan put a stop to the seminars about her, they had been running for two and a half years. The Wednesday-morning seminars, which had started in 1925, had been so popular that there was no question of abandoning them. According to Mary Bancroft, the audience consisted mainly of 'doctors, analysts, college professors or students of esoteric subjects'. Jung now let them choose a new topic; some of the ideas were proposed by members of the audience. It seems to have been Martha Sigg who suggested Nietzsche's *Zarathustra*, and the new series started in May.

Jung sat at one end of the room with Toni Wolff on his right and Emma opposite him in the front row. Each chair was labelled with the name of the person who was going to sit on it, and remained empty if that person was absent. If anyone in the mainly female audience did not know what to expect, she was soon given a clue:

> If you think that *Zarathustra* is easier than those visions, you are badly mistaken, it is a hell of a confusion and extraordinarily difficult . . . These chapters of *Zarathustra* are sort of sermons in verse, but they have some analogy with the visions in as much as they are also evolutionary incidents. They form a string of experiences and events, manifestations of the unconscious, often a directly visionary character: and therefore it is probably recommendable to follow the same technique in the analysis as we have applied to the visions.

To Jung's audience this approach was perfectly acceptable, but, like his dismissal of Emily Brontë as 'your girl', it shows how indifferent he was to literature. In the creation of both *Wuthering Heights* and *Zarathustra*, inspiration and hard work had been as intimately interdependent as breathing in and breathing out. While breathing in or being inspired, the writer feels no more in control of the text than if someone were dictating it. Some passages may never be rewritten, but others will be cut or shortened or elaborated or rebalanced and restructured — a different part of the mind comes into play when the writer is finalising the relationship between the parts and the whole.

Trusting the unreliable biography of Nietzsche by his sister Elisabeth, and remembering a passage he had quoted in his essay on cryptomnesia from a book Nietzsche wrote when he was going mad — *Ecce Homo* — Jung stressed the feverish speed at which he wrote. It took him only ten days to rewrite his preliminary sketches for the first part of *Zarathustra*. But he also revised, and he went on working at the four parts between January 1884 and December 1885.

Frank Miller's fantasies — like Christiana Morgan's — could validly be discussed as if they had been thrown up more or less directly by the unconscious, but these were not great works of art. Like all the best users of the German language, including Wittgenstein, Nietzsche was a stylist, and the 'visionary' content of *Zarathustra* is inseparable from the style and rhythms in the prose. Forgetting this, Jung assumed that Nietzsche would have arrived at a better understanding of his own work if only a good analytical psychologist had been on hand to help him.

In both his 1922 lecture 'On the Relation of Analytical Psychology to Poetry' and his 1930 lecture on 'Psychology and Literature', Jung had used

Zarathustra as his prime example of work in which 'the writer's consciousness was in abeyance during the period of creation'. To impute the authorship of such work to an autonomous complex or an archetype is to ignore not only the writer's skill, but also the connection between the text and his personal experience. On finishing *Zarathustra*, Nietzsche said it 'contains the most sharply focused image of me as I am *after* I have unburdened myself'.

He had just been humiliated by Lou Salomé, and the pain was still intense. Loving her and believing she would be his spiritual daughter, he had fantasised about establishing a *ménage à trois* with her and her friend Paul Rée. Nietzsche's agony would have lasted longer if he had not been able to create an imaginary son – Zarathustra. 'Unless I can learn the alchemist's trick of turning this filth into gold,' he wrote, 'I am lost.' His alchemical retort was his imagination, and the urge for vengeance was irrepressible, but the main drive was towards mockery. 'It is not anger but laughter that is lethal,' says Zarathustra.

There may be less comedy in the book than Nietzsche intended, but Jung's approach is so solemn that he misses what comedy there is, and ignores the parody of biblical syntax and cadences. Nietzsche's reversal of Judaeo-Christian values is couched in a style that pokes fun at the parables and paradoxes of the New Testament. Comic irreverence and irony are integral to the conception of Zarathustra as an anti-Jesus – a saviour who preaches self-transcendence and prophesies a future in which humanity will redeem itself without any help from heaven.

Nietzsche maintained that Buddhism and Christianity had 'taught fanaticism in a period when willpower was exhausted. Once a man becomes convinced that he needs to be commanded, he becomes a believer.' This sentence points to a side of Nietzsche Jung could not have ignored if he had been committed in good faith to exploring Nietzsche's intentions. Though many passages of *Zarathustra* are obscure, and though he kept asking the group what Nietzsche meant, he was uncritical in accepting suggestions from disciples who were even more Jungian than he was, and no less eager to find corroboration for what he had taught them.

In his 1922 lecture, he had said: 'The only aspect of art that can be a subject of psychological investigation is the process of artistic creation – not what constitutes the essential nature of the work of art.' He stuck to the notion that consciousness can be suspended while a writer's creativity is requisitioned by the collective unconscious. This entailed overlooking both Nietzsche's appetite for revenge and the ways in which this book picks up motifs and techniques he had already begun to develop. He had never come so close to writing fiction, and never sustained a persona for so long, but had already used characters to make statements he did not want to make in his own voice. One of these comes in his 1882 book *The Joyful Wisdom*, in which a madman proclaims that God is dead. It is as misleading to talk as if this statement had come directly from Nietzsche as it is to equate him with Zarathustra. He had good reasons for introducing characters.

Jung's main failure was to engage seriously with Nietzsche's efforts to go beyond Christian ideas of good and evil. 'Truly,' says Zarathustra, 'I tell you good and evil exist only temporarily . . . He who will create in good and evil must be a destroyer first, and smash values. So the greatest evil belongs to the greatest goodness, but that is what is creative.' Instead of blessing the meek, the merciful and the peace lovers, Zarathustra favours the great despisers, those who 'do not want to have too many virtues'. He mocks the Christian ideals of brotherly love and turning the other cheek.

Ignoring Nietzsche's organic disease of the brain, Jung writes as if he went mad as a consequence of his arrogance in thinking he could manage without Christianity. 'Being identical with Zarathustra, who is also Wotan, he is half divine and above humanity.' Jung never engaged with Nietzsche's most trenchant criticism of Christianity, which is to be found not in *Zarathustra* but in the two later books *Beyond Good and Evil* (1885–6) and *On the Genealogy of Morals* (1887), which attack Christian virtues as belonging to a herd morality based on timidity. 'Life itself *essentially* consists of dispossessing, injuring, overpowering the foreign and the more feeble, suppression, severity, imposing one's own forms, annexing and – at least and at mildest – exploiting.' Religions like Christianity and Buddhism teach the humble to delude themselves that their piety and their docile acceptance of suffering qualify them for membership of a higher order. The Judaeo-Christian morality is a slave morality, the outcome of an ethical revolution, fuelled by the malice 'of those who are incapable of taking action and make up for it by means of an imaginary revenge'. The weak look pityingly at the strong, thinking 'They know not what they do.'

Genealogy shows how ideas of good and evil had evolved as the dominant groups in society used their name-giving prerogative to glorify themselves and their qualities while denigrating those of other groups. 'Good' had been cognate with 'noble', 'bad' with plebeian. The association of nobility with high-mindedness and baseness with social inferiority still exists in most languages.

Nazism was making itself felt all over Europe, and even the Eranos Conference was not immune to it. One of the speakers in 1934 was Wilhelm Hauer, who had spoken on Kundalini at the club in 1932. He published a periodical, *Kommende Gemeinde*, in which he had welcomed National Socialism as a 'new faith'. In the same year, he founded the

German Faith Movement, presenting it as more compatible with National Socialism than Christianity, which was tainted by the Semitic origins of its founder, Jesus of Nazareth. In 1934 one of the other speakers at Eranos was the Jewish philosopher Martin Buber, who lectured on 'Symbolic and Sacramental Existence in Judaism'. Hauer was lecturing on the self in Indo-Aryan mysticism. Ignoring the rule that there should be no political discussion at Eranos, he spoke up for Nazism during an exchange with the audience, and Buber tactfully steered the discussion towards Meister Eckhart. Hauer was never again invited to Eranos.

At the end of September 1934, following the advice of a friend, James Joyce consulted Jung about his schizophrenic daughter, Lucrezia. Jung had her moved into a private clinic in Küsnacht, where she seemed at first to be making headway. Most of her previous doctors – she had already had nineteen – had failed to engage her in conversation, but Jung succeeded. She soon seemed happier, and started to put on weight.

He blamed her condition on her father, saying they were 'like two people going to the bottom of a river, one falling and the other diving'. Her happiness was short-lived, and her faith in Jung soon fizzled out. 'To think that such a big fat materialistic Swiss man should try to get hold of my soul.'

According to Jung, Joyce and Lucrezia were 'a classic example' of his anima theory.

> She was definitely his *femme inspiratrice*, which explains his obstinate reluctance to have her certified. His own anima, i.e. unconscious psyche, was so solidly identified with her that to have her certified would have been as much as an admission that he himself had a latent psychosis . . . His 'psychological style' is definitely schizophrenic, with the difference, however, that the ordinary patient cannot help himself talking and thinking in such a way, while Joyce willed it and moreover developed it with all his creative forces, which incidentally explains why he himself did not go over the border. But his daughter did, because she was no genius like her father, but merely a victim of her disease.

This can be read as an indirect comment on Jung's use of his creative forces to conquer the psychosis that had threatened him in childhood and after the breach with Freud.

To Jung it seemed that Nietzsche, Joyce and Freud had something in common. In an essay on 'Sigmund Freud in His Historical Setting', Jung wrote: 'Like Nietzsche, like the Great War and like James Joyce, his literary counterpart, Freud is an answer to the sickness of the nineteenth century.'

Jung accused him of borrowing the concept of sublimation from the alchemists, and using it to deal with the accumulation of repressed incest wishes and other anomalies in the psyche. Sublimation was the alchemists' trick of turning what is base into what is noble, but physicists had not yet solved the problem of how to 'convert energy without consuming a still greater quantity of energy'.

This essay was one of the nine by Jung he included in the fourth volume of his *Psychologische Abhandlungen*, together with two by Kränefeldt. The volume was titled *The Reality of the Soul*, and subtitled *Applications and Advances of the New Psychology*. Published in 1934, it was reviewed by Hermann Hesse, who found that Jung had 'become professorial', and sent him a copy of the review.

Hesse defended Freud's use of the term *sublimation*, but, in reply, Jung said that not only patients but also doctors were liable to mistake repression for sublimation. Replying at length, Hesse agreed that 'sublimation is in the last resort also "repression" ' but maintained there were cases of 'successful repression' in which instincts were 'channelled into a lofty field of culture though not properly belonging to it, for instance art. Within our category of art, we artists perform a true *sublimatio*, not by will or from ambition, but by grace.'

Jung objected that there was no sublimation in artistic activity because 'it is not a question of transforming a primary instinct but rather of a primary instinct (the artistic instinct) gripping the whole personality to such an extent that all other instincts are in abeyance.'

The physicist Wolfgang Pauli, who was to win the Nobel Prize in 1945, had been in Zurich since 1928, when, at the age of twenty-eight, he was appointed professor for theoretical physics at the Federal Polytechnic. The previous year, his mother had poisoned herself after finding out that her husband was being unfaithful. Before he had recovered his equilibrium, Pauli married a cabaret singer, but the marriage lasted only about twelve months, and in the winter of 1931–2 he was in a desperate state.

When Jung started lecturing at the Polytechnic in 1933, Pauli's father, worried by the wild risks his son was taking, advised him to consult his new colleague. Talking about him anonymously in a 1935 lecture, Jung described him as an intellectual so one-sided that his unconscious became 'troubled and activated; so it projected itself into other men who appeared to be his enemies . . . once he got thrown out of a restaurant and beaten up'.

Jung claims to have noticed immediately that Pauli was 'chock-full of archaic material', and in order to make sure he could 'get that material absolutely pure, without any influence from myself', he referred the case to a young doctor, Erna Rosenbaum, 'who was then just a beginner and did not know much about archetypal material'. Jung did not mention that he was analysing her while she was analysing Pauli, which means she was learning about archetypal material.

But by 1935, Pauli was keenly on the lookout for something Jung might be able to give him. One of Pauli's dreams around this time was about a man who looked like Einstein and demonstrated that quantum mechanics dealt with a one-dimensional intersection of a two-dimensional reality. What was missing, as Pauli understood when he woke up, was the archetypal contents of the unconscious.

It is questionable whether the dreams he described to Erna Rosenbaum were influenced by his interest in Jungian ideas or by an unconscious desire to give Jung something in return for what he wanted. Using these dreams ten years later in the 1944 book *Psychology and Alchemy*, Jung described him as 'a young man of excellent scientific education', and stressed that 'this education was not historical, philological, archaeological or ethnological. Any references to material derived from these fields came unconsciously to the dreamer.' The anthropologist John Layard, who was analysed by Jung, was impressed by his account of the dreams in the book and believed for a time that they came from the collective unconscious. But Layard later concluded: 'This is part of Jung's falsification of data in support of the collective unconscious being independent of personal relationships.'

For ten months, it seems, Erna Rosenbaum went on taking notes while Pauli talked about his dreams. It is hard to make out what happened after that. According to Jung, he took over, and, reporting on the case in 1939, he said Pauli 'got into order again because he gradually accepted the symbolic data, and now he leads the religious life, the life of the careful observer. Religion is careful observation of the data. He now observes all the things that are brought to him by his dreams; that is his only guidance.' But according to Marie-Louise von Franz, Jung never analysed Pauli, who again started drinking heavily at the end of the analysis with Erna Rosenbaum.

Pauli was interested in Jung's theory of the archetypes, and had long discussions with him about subatomic physics. It was at the beginning of 1934 that Louis de Broglie introduced the term *antiparticle* for a particle with the same mass as another but opposite values for its other properties. The positron is the antiparticle of the electron, and interaction between them involves their annihilation, together with the emission of energy in the form of radiation. Later on in 1934, Pauli, collaborating with Victor Weisskopf, demonstrated that certain subatomic particles must have antiparticles.

In 1927 de Broglie had introduced particle-wave duality for matter: an electron or any other subatomic particle can behave as either a particle or a wave. This excited Jung because it meant that what looked liked two phenomena might in fact be one phenomenon seen under different conditions.

In pre-Einsteinian physics (as in chemistry), the truth seemed to consist of facts that could be demonstrated in laboratories: to hold that spiritual truths were more important involved Jung in rejecting material facts, as he did in his Zofingia lectures. But subatomic physics seemed to involve the scientist in acts of faith. Atoms might be invisible and intangible, but atomic explosions were more powerful than any other kind. The crucial field of activity had become as invisible as God. Excitingly, it looked as if spiritual speculations could claim citizenship of the same realm as scientific thinking.

In their different ways, Jung and Pauli were both interested in causality and acausality. For Einstein, everything had to have a cause. 'God does not play dice,' he insisted. Jung had always disliked the principle of causality. In a 1928 seminar he had called it 'the modern prejudice of the West'. The East, he said, 'considers coincidences as the reliable basis of the world rather than causality. Synchronism is the prejudice of the East.' The following year, in the same series of seminars, he said that what looks like a coincidence may actually be the occurrence at the same time of two events which 'express the same time content'.

It was not until May 1930 that he invented the word *synchronicity*. He was talking about the *I Ching*.

> I found that there are psychic parallelisms which simply cannot be related to each other causally, but must be connected by another kind of principle altogether . . . It seems as though time, far from being an abstraction, is a concrete continuum which possesses qualities or basic conditions capable of manifesting themselves simultaneously in different places by means of an acausal parallelism, such as we find, for instance in the simultaneous occurrence of identical thoughts, symbols or psychic states.

This idea interested Pauli. And in a series of informal conversations, he talked about his dreams to Jung, who said they showed 'the patient always tried to evade his emotional needs. As a matter of fact, he was afraid they might get him into trouble, for instance into marriage, and into other responsibilities, such as love, devotion, loyalty, trust, emotional dependence and general submission to the soul's needs.'

In an April 1934 essay on 'The Soul and Death', Jung said that under certain conditions the psyche was capable of breaking through the barriers of space and time because one of its essential qualities was 'its relatively trans-spatial and trans-temporal character'. He would have enjoyed discussing this with Pauli, but he had just married again, and his new wife, Franca, never forgave Jung for putting him into the hands of such an inexperienced analyst as Erna Rosenbaum.

He had been meeting Jung every Monday, but in July he wrote to say that in spite of problems which had not been resolved, he wanted to break off the weekly conversations, to stop analysing his dreams, and to work on developing his feeling function from his daily experience in life.

In October, he sent Jung an essay by the German physicist Pascual Jordan, who was trying to explain telepathy in terms reminiscent of *An Experiment with Time*, the book by J. W. Dunne which 'postulates an infinite number of time dimensions roughly corresponding to Jordan's "intermediate stages" '. Jordan contended that senders and receivers in the same conscious space are observing the same object, and it struck Jung that 'if individual consciousnesses are blotted out in the unconscious, then all perception in the unconscious takes place as though in a single person'.

For two years Jung had little contact with Pauli, who wrote to him again in February 1936, saying he was feeling more stable, though he had at first found life difficult after breaking off the weekly sessions. At the beginning of 1939 he wanted to resume them – without paying for them – but in September, he and his wife left Switzerland for the USA.

Jung was often asked what he believed about death, and in 1934, with his sixtieth birthday approaching, he took the view that if the individual's nature is gradually unfolded over the first twenty years of his life, the last twenty should be spent on preparing for death. In his essay 'The Soul and Death', Jung may have been referring to himself – he modulates from 'one' to 'I' – in the passage about the time

> when one is alone at night and it is so dark and silent that one neither hears nor sees anything but thoughts that add and subtract the years, and the long line of disagreeable facts that ineluctably indicate how far the hand of the clock has progressed, and the gradual, irresistible approach of the dark wall that will eventually engulf everything I love, possess, wish for, hope for and strive for.

Religions are 'complicated systems of preparation for death', and in the two 'greatest living religions, Christianity and Buddhism, the meaning of existence is consummated in its end'. Far from being products of the human intellect, religions 'have developed, plant-like, as natural manifestations of the human psyche'. That is why 'religious symbols have a distinctly "revelatory" character; they are usually spontaneous products of unconscious psychic activity.'

Even if death extinguishes consciousness, it does not necessarily terminate the psychic process – 'the psyche's attachment to the brain can be affirmed with far less certitude today than it could fifty years ago'. Since telepathic phenomena were 'undeniable facts', the psyche must be capable of breaking through barriers of space and time.

Five years later, Jung referred to this essay after a pastor, Fritz Pfafflin, described a telepathic conversation he had with his brother when the brother, who was in Africa, was killed in an accident. 'Spatial distance is, in the psychic sense, relative,' Jung declared. 'This nullification of space proceeds with great speed, so that perceptions of this kind occur simult- aneously with the accident.'

It seemed to him 'that only what we call consciousness is contained in space and time, and that the rest of the psyche, the unconscious, exists in a state of relative spacelessness and timelessness'. Jung had no doubt that the dead can 'entangle themselves, so to speak, in the physiology (sympathetic nervous system) of the living. This would probably result in states of possession.'

Twenty-Nine

The Thieves Were Redeemers

Returning to Germany in May 1934 and March 1935, Jung took the chair at the seventh and eighth annual congresses of what had formerly been the General Medical Society for Psychotherapy. The largest national group was the German one, which was controlled by the Nazis, and to stop them from controlling the whole society, Jung reorganised it at the beginning of 1935 as the International General Medical Society for Psychotherapy. Groups of analysts in the Netherlands, Denmark and Switzerland had been affiliated under his presidency, but there was still no group in Freudian Austria.

Jung was careful to remain politically neutral in his speeches, and in his editorial for the 1935 issue of the *Zentralblatt* he mentioned neither psychoanalysis nor analytical psychology, speaking only of *medical psychology*, and saying it should be 'accounted a specialised subject on its own'. But at a symposium on 'Psychotherapy in Switzerland', he attacked 'the Freudian spirit of sectarianism' which had 'put the greatest obstacles in the way of an Austrian group'.

Writing to a clergyman, he compared the psychiatrist with the 'pastor of souls', whose parishioners 'expressly demand to be spiritually arranged from above downwards'. Without working from metaphysical premises, Jung had to help 'people in whom I cannot implant any values or convictions from above downwards. Usually they are people whom I can only urge to go through their experiences and to organise them in a way that makes a tolerable existence possible.'

In practice, the distinction between the two functions was less clear-cut. Many of Jung's patients made no secret of their wish to be rearranged spiritually from above downwards, and he never quite gave up the role he had assumed in his *Septem Sermones ad Mortuos*, of preaching to those who had lost faith in the sermons of clergymen like his father. Talking to patients, though he never explicitly equated the psyche or the unconscious with God, he tried to shepherd lapsed Catholics back to their religion. 'Psychology in this context therefore means only the removal of all those factors which hinder final submission to the authority of the Church.'

Sometimes he characterised religions as psychotherapeutic systems, and he noticed that few practising Catholics approached him for help. Having a director of conscience and a rigorous system of confession, they did not need him. But he was ambivalent about the Oxford Movement – the Catholic revival that continues as Anglo-Catholicism. He praised it for giving people 'all those collective alleviations they do not possess or cannot create for themselves, together with a shared religious confession'. But at other times he scathingly attributed its success to 'a *psychologie des foules* with a prognosis to match'.

In 1923 his building at Bollingen had consisted of a single tower, but he had made additions to it at four-year intervals. In 1927 he added a small hallway, a living room, a workroom and a guest room on the upper level; in 1931 he built a second tower, which he intended to 'represent' Toni Wolff. He completed his work in 1935 with what he described as 'a courtyard and a loggia, forming a fourth element separated from the unitary threeness of the house. So in the course of twelve years a quaternity had arisen.' He had an open fireplace in the loggia, and in summer did most of his cooking here. He spent a lot of time sitting outside, and though few boats passed, he had begun to feel the need for an enclosed space.

Visitors now had to knock at the door of the courtyard, and Jung never opened it himself, unless he was there alone, which rarely happened. Now sixty, he was finding it a strain to climb the steep stairs to the bunk beds, and he needed help with felling trees and cutting wood for the fire. His regular assistant was Hans Kuhn, who sometimes brought drinking water from his home, half a mile away. Otherwise, water from the lake had to be boiled for drinking. No effort was involved in being alone with Hans, who made no demands and never asked questions about psychology. Jung told him he did not need it. When they burned new wood, it made a variety of noises, and sometimes they played the game of trying to frighten each other, saying they could hear a poltergeist.

In August 1935 Jung gave his third Eranos lecture, on 'Dream Symbols in the Individuation Process'. Later he expanded his text into 'Individual Dream Symbolism in Relation to Alchemy', the second part of his 1944 book *Psychology and Alchemy*, interpreting a series of Wolfgang Pauli's dreams. Though he insists it is essential to 'give up all preconceived opinions when it comes to the analysis and interpretation of the objective psyche, in other words the "unconscious" ', his interpretations are nearly all based on his theory that archetypal images find their way from the collective unconscious into dreams. A hat is 'round like the sun-disc of a crown', while passengers on a train are taken to represent unconscious components of the dreamer's personality because, standing in front of a window, he blocks their view. When feminine figures appear, Jung assumes they 'point to the feminine nature of the unconscious', and he quickly identifies a veiled woman as the anima. 'Personification always indicates an autonomous activity of the unconscious.'

One of the alchemical texts Herbert Silberer had analysed was the 1625 *Guldenen Traktat vom philosophischen Stein* When a young, black-bearded man appeared among a group of white-bearded philosophers, Silberer had been uncertain whether he was the devil, but Jung seems to have encouraged Pauli to identify a man with a pointed beard as Mephistopheles, though the dream was set in America, where Pauli was looking for an employee with a pointed beard, and was told everyone had such an employee.

Invited to give five lectures in London at the Tavistock Clinic between 30 September and 4 October 1935, Jung arranged to stay with his friend E. A. Bennet. This was going to be unlike any of his previous experiences of lecturing in England. At Polzeath, Sennen Cove and Swanage, audiences had been small but had been on his side before he started speaking. For the 1935 lectures, which were organised by the Institute of Medical Psychology, the main initiative had been taken by its director of studies, Dr J. A. Hadfield. The audience would consist of about two hundred people, mainly doctors and psychiatrists who might be pro-Freudian.

Jung impressed them by being able to speak so fluently and colloquially in English with no script and no notes. His intention, according to the psychiatrist Charles Rycroft, was to give the impression of being

> a direct man, down-to-earth even when scaling the heights or plumbing the depths, a countryman more at home with peasants and aristocrats than with urban middle-class intellectuals, too virile and familiar with the facts of nature to have much time for those sex cases which so interested Freud, but none the less, as befits a pastor's son. heir to the Christian spiritual tradition.

Ever since 1909, when he had thought his dream about the house 'constituted a kind of structural diagram of the human psyche', Jung had often used diagrams in lectures and seminars, unintentionally illustrating his tendency to think about consciousness and unconsciousness in terms of space. In the London lectures he called one of his diagrams 'the cross of the functions'. The ego is at the centre, and for the 'thinking type' of person, feeling is the inferior function (below on the diagram) and thinking the superior function. 'That comes from the fact,' he said, 'that when you think, you must exclude feeling, just as when you feel, you must exclude thinking.' This is questionable. In his diagram he places Sensation (S) and Intuition (I) on either side of the ego (E). You can often tell from people's eyes, he said, whether they are intuitive. If they are, 'they only glance at things – they do not look, they radiate at things because they take in their fullness, and among the many things they perceive, they get one point on the periphery of their field of vision, and that is the *hunch*.'

People who are most secure in their feeling are most insecure in their thinking. 'The inferior function is always associated with an archaic person-ality in ourselves; in the inferior function we are all primitives . . . There we have an open wound, or at least an open door through which anything might enter.' He illustrated this with another diagram, using a vertical line to represent the threshold of consciousness. On one side is an area of con-sciousness that relates to the *ectopsychic world*, the external world ruled by the four functions, but on the other side is a *shadow world* where the ego is 'somewhat dark' and we are 'always discovering something new about ourselves'. On this *endopsychic* side of the threshold, the first function is memory, and the second is 'the subjective components of psychic functions'. The third – and here he no longer wanted to use the word *function* – is what happens when 'the inner side of a man takes hold of him'; and the fourth 'endopsychic factor' is *invasion*. 'Here the shadow side, the unconscious side, has full control so that it can break into the conscious condition.'

But, as he insisted, overwhelming emotions are not necessarily path-ological. 'There are other undesirable things in the world which are not pathological, for instance, tax-collectors.' Introducing Jung's second lecture, Dr Hadfield praised his sense of humour.

It was in this lecture that he introduced the subject of archetypes and the collective unconscious, quoting the cases of the black Southerner who had dreamed about a man crucified on a wheel, and the Swiss schizophrenic who thought there was a tube hanging from the sun. 'The deepest we can reach in our exploration of the unconscious mind,' Jung declared, 'is the layer where man is no longer a distinct individual, but where his mind widens out and merges into the mind of mankind . . . where we are all the same.'

His diagram of the psyche is like a target: a series of concentric circles with the collective unconscious in the centre, the personal unconscious next to it, and then eight circular bands representing endopsychic and ectopsychic spheres. The outermost band represents *sensation* because 'by it a man gets information about the world of external objects. In the second circle, *thinking*, he gets what his senses have told him.' He then gets a *feeling* about things, and finally an *intuition* about how they will develop. The inner bands surrounding the personal unconscious represent *memory, the subjective components of the functions, affects* and *invasions*. Of these four, the outermost is the easiest, and the innermost the hardest, to control by willpower.

After a few anecdotes to demonstrate differences between French and German national character – 'The German nation is characterised by the fact that its feeling function is inferior' – Jung went on rather abruptly to explain word-association tests, though he no longer used them unless he was investigating a suspected crime. He devoted the whole evening to them, saying almost nothing he had not been saying thirty years ago, and telling the same stories.

At the end of the lecture, some of the questions were more critical than any put the previous evening, and Jung did not try to conceal his annoyance. One doctor was told: 'I should like very much if you would pay more attention to what I say,' and another was told off for being indiscreet. After asking what would happen if *mystic* and *fourth dimension* were used as cues in the association test, he had gone on to suggest Jung believed there was no personal unconscious – 'only a relative unconsciousness which depends on a relative degree of consciousness'. Jung was 'moving in fluid medium of relationships and Freud in a static medium of unrelated entities. To get it clear, Freud is *three-dimensional* and Jung is, in all his psychology, *four-dimensional*.'

Jung's response was 'You are right, but you should not say such things . . . Freud is seeing the mental processes as static, while I speak in terms of dynamics and relationship. To me all is relative. There is nothing definitely unconscious; it is only not present to the conscious mind under a certain light.' He had used diagrams in both lectures, but this had been 'a static presentation of something that is functionally moving'.

This discussion troubled Jung, and he talked about it at the beginning of his next lecture, using it to illustrate his definition of *complex*:

> an agglomeration of associations – a sort of picture of a more or less psychological nature – sometimes of traumatic character, sometimes simply of a painful and highly toned character . . . If, for instance, something is very important to me, I begin to hesitate when I attempt to do it, and you have probably observed that when you ask me difficult questions . . . I have a long reaction time. I begin to stammer, and my memory does not supply the necessary material. Such disturbances are complex disturbances . . . somehow associated with physiological reactions, with the processes of the heart, the tonus of the blood vessels, the condition of the intestines, the breathing and the innervation of the skin.

A complex had 'the tendency to form a little personality of itself. It has a sort of body, a certain amount of its own physiology.' Since it can divert us from our intentions, 'we really are forced to speak of the tendencies of complexes to act as if they were characterised by a certain amount of willpower . . . Where then is the ego that belongs to the willpower of the complexes?' Leaving his question unanswered, he said: 'Our personal unconscious, as well as the collective unconscious, consists of an indefinite, because un- known, number of complexes or fragmentary personalities . . . Therefore you can understand a writer's mind from the characters he creates.'

The seances of 1895–9 had launched him on this track, and he was brave enough to mention spiritualism, saying: 'Unprejudiced people are inclined to believe that the spirits are the ghosts of a deceased aunt or grandfather or something of the kind, just on account of the more or less distinct personality which can be traced in these manifestations.'

Talking without a script, he was free to change direction at any moment, and when he was halfway through this lecture, he switched abruptly to dreams, reprising what he had told his seminar ten years earlier, and using the same analogy of translating a foreign text:

> I do not want to know the complexes of my patients. That is uninteresting to me . . . I want to know what a man's unconscious is doing *with* his complexes. I want to know what he is preparing himself for . . . Therefore I handle the dream as if it were a text which I do not understand properly, say a Latin or a Greek or a Sanskrit text, where certain words are unknown to me or the text is fragmentary . . . The assumption that a dream wants to conceal is a mere anthropomorphic idea.

In the discussion, he extended his relativism into ethics:

> We also do not feel quite right when we are behaving perfectly, we feel much better when we are doing a bit of wrong . . . There must be some people who behave in the wrong way; they act as scapegoats and objects of interest for the normal ones . . . This is the deeper meaning of the fact that Christ as the redeemer was crucified between two thieves. These thieves in their way were also redeemers of mankind . . .

It is our weakest function, he said, that gives us our closest connection with the unconscious. 'Only through our feebleness and incapacity are we linked up with the unconscious, with the lower world of the instincts and with our fellow beings. Our virtues only enable us to be independent.'

In the fourth lecture he discussed the connection between archetypes and disease. In ancient Greece, as in the East, therapy had sometimes depended on 'raising the mere personal ailment into a generally valid situation . . . The myth or legend arises from the archetypal material that is constellated by the disease, and the psychological effect consists in connecting the patient with the general human meaning of his particular situation.' If he felt isolated, his therapist could speed up his recovery by renewing his feeling of connectedness. 'When other people are in the same hole as I am,' said Jung, 'I feel much better.' A lost battalion might be in as much danger as one lost soldier, but morale would be higher.

Similarly, patients found it reassuring to be told that figures in their dreams were archetypal. If the dreamer is a neurotic, he can then assume that many other people are involved in a similar neurosis. Identifying the individual with the community, the symbol of the city with four gates represents indestructible wholeness. In New Mexico, Pueblo Indians treat sickness by making a sand-painting of a mandala with four gates, and the patient undergoes a sweat-cure in the centre of it.

When he took questions, Jung again had to compare his view of the unconscious with Freud's. He said he had been 'on excellent terms with him until I had the idea that certain things are symbolical'. He conceded that 'what Freud says agrees with many people, and I assume that these people have exactly the kind of psychology that he describes.' Jung's following 'consists presumably of people who have my psychology. I consider my contribution to psychology to be my subjective confession. It is my personal psychology, my prejudice that I see psychological facts as I do.' With some of his patients, he said,

> I have to make a Freudian analysis and go into all the details which Freud has correctly described . . . People who have the capacity to adapt and are successful are more inclined to have a Freudian psychology, because a man in that position is looking for the gratification of his desires, while the man who has not been successful has no time to think about desires.

Though Jung regarded himself as adaptable and successful, 'I cannot say I have a Freudian psychology because I never had such difficulties in relation to desires. As a boy I lived in the country and took things very naturally, and the natural and unnatural things of which Freud speaks were not interesting to me . . . But I know exactly how I could make myself neurotic: if I said or believed something that is not myself.' He then came back to their disagreement over the unconscious: he saw it as 'a vast historical storehouse'. But for Freud it was 'chiefly a receptacle for things repressed'.

He was too diplomatic to repeat his assertion that Freud's psychology was suitable for Jews and his for Aryans. Instead, he said Freud's was useful to those in quest of sex, and Adler's to those in quest of power. But he added: 'I never could bring myself to be so frightfully interested in these sex cases. They do exist, there are people with a neurotic sex life, and you have to talk sex stuff with them until they get sick of it and you get out of that boredom . . . It is neurotic stuff, and no reasonable normal person talks of it for any length of time. It is not natural to dwell on such matters.' We should emulate the reticence of primitive people. 'They allude to sexual intercourse by a word that is equivalent to "hush". Sexual things are taboo to them.'

Talking about transference, he showed how far he had moved since 1921, when he had said nothing was more helpful in therapy than the emergence of a psychologically adapted relationship after the doctor had made efforts to enter into the patient's psyche. He had since come to the conclusion that far from being useful, transference was usually a hindrance – 'a condition of personal contamination through mutual unconsciousness'.

He said little in the lectures about politics, but explained Hitlerism by quoting Bernard Shaw: 'This creature Man, who in his own selfish affairs is a coward to the backbone, will fight for an idea like a hero.' Of course, Jung glossed, 'we would not call Fascism or Hitlerism ideas. They are archetypes, and so we would say: Give an archetype to the people, and the whole crowd moves like one man, there is no resisting it.'

Michael Fordham, who was now chairman of London's Analytical Psychology Club, had invited Jung to lecture for it, and, accepting, he had asked for a small audience. Finding himself confronted with a large one, he showed his annoyance by delivering his lecture in what Fordham described as 'a dull and sometimes scarcely audible voice'.

Now in analysis with Baynes, Fordham found he was making so little headway that he wanted to discuss the situation with Jung, who received him in a hotel bedroom while dressing for dinner. 'He was changing his trousers. This did not seem at all inappropriate, but rather like being treated as one of a family.' Jung agreed he should find a new analyst.

Generally Jung travelled by boat, but in 1935 he flew back to Zurich. In his opinion, air travel was too fast, and passengers left bits of their psyche behind. Even in the fifties, when air travel had become cheaper and more popular, he advised patients not to fly, saying they would not be fully present in the experiences they had on arrival.

Thirty

The Incompetent Mind of the Masses

It would be impossible, Jung maintained, to exaggerate the importance of the anima when emotions are at work in a man. 'She intensifies, exaggerates, falsifies and mythologises all emotional relations with his work and with other people of both sexes.' In 1936 he introduced the term *syzygy*. Anyone, he asserted, 'who does not know the universal distribution and significance of the *syzygy* motif in the psychology of primitives, in mythology, in comparative religion and in the history of literature, can hardly claim to say anything about the concept of the anima.' Used in astronomy, biology and Gnostic theology, the word means conjunction of opposites, and Jung most often used it apropos the anima and the animus.

Throughout history, he believed, humanity had encountered *syzygys* in the pairing of male and female deities and of such concepts as yin and yang.

> We can safely assert that these *syzygys* are as universal as the existence of man and woman. From this fact we may reasonably conclude that man's imagination is bound by this motif, so that he was largely compelled to project it again and again, at all times and in all places . . . It is indeed easy to show that the divine pair is simply an idealisation of the parents or of some other human couple, which for some reason appeared in heaven.

Assuming that willpower has no control over the psyche, Jung believed the unconscious sent out determining influences which 'guarantee in every single individual a similarity and even a sameness of experience and also of the way it is represented imaginatively'. This entitled him, he concluded, to equate archetypes with mythological motifs. The archetypes were 'normal religious factors' which were 'present in every man'. 'Anyone who succeeds in putting off the mantle of faith can do so only because another lies to hand.'

A talent that should not be undervalued is Jung's ability to apply these ideas when helping people who had not yet come to terms with the incurable madness of someone they loved. In February 1936 a friend of Mary Foote, Eleanor Du Vivier, consulted him about her eldest son, a brilliant fresco painter who was incarcerated in a French sanatorium.

She liked Jung and described him as 'big, fat, old, bespectacled, the kind of man who gives you all his attention . . . Everything that I needed to be told I was told, and with such insight and spirituality that I, at last, understood – not only understood but accepted. The man is inspired, really.' She had brought photographs of her son at various ages, and studying them sympathetically, Jung explained that some children were born with a predisposition to schizophrenia. 'In this case it is unmistakable, nothing could have saved him . . . He couldn't meet the world, he was turned in . . . too busy with God and things eternal, with intuition . . . All his trouble was he was constantly being pulled back into a reality which had nothing to do with him.' She took comfort from the idea that her son was occupied with something real that was more important than business or the activities that fill most people's lives.

In March 1936, the *Neue Schweizer Rundschau* published an article by Jung on 'Wotan'. The character of the god, he suggested, explains more about Nazism than any analysis in terms of political, economic and psychological factors. Wotan was the god of storm and frenzy, the magician who released passion and belligerence, the master of occult knowledge. He was taking possession of a whole nation and reducing it to a state of fury: the Germans were in a state of *Ergriffenheit* – possession. Hitler was obviously possessed, and it might look as if he had the country in his grip, but an individual had no power over the social, political and psychic storm that was blasting like a hurricane on German civilisation. 'The rouser of this tempest is called Wotan.' He had remained passive while Christianity appeared to be in the ascendant, but Germany was a land of spiritual catastrophes, vulnerable to the god of rage and frenzy.

The essay contains an approving reference to Hauer's German Faith Movement, which was now in its fourth year. Those who had joined it, said Jung, were 'decent and well-meaning people'. He remained friendly with Hauer, who came to give a series of six lectures at the Psychological Club in 1938.

Summing up Jung's attitude to what was going on in Germany, Jolande Jacobi said: 'His idea was that chaos gives birth to good or to something valuable. So in the German movement he saw a chaotic (we could say) precondition for the birth of a new world.' He may have been remembering Nietzsche's dictum that chaos gives birth to a dancing star.

But he encouraged patients to cultivate their anti-Semitism. 'He was very strong about the Jews,' said Irene Champernowne.

> You know that there was . . . a great collective problem that we could all make the Jews our shadow because we were jealous of them and their position. And he also pointed out that they were such opportunists that you really had to be quite clear that you were being exploited if you felt you were, and stand firm else you would be caught in a pogrom. So he used to encourage negativity toward the Jews in us.

She was practising as an analyst in London, where immigrant Freudians were competing for the same patients, and she says Jung told her: 'If you have any feeling against Jewish people . . . be clear. Keep it up. Don't let it go down. Because if you do you'll be caught in a pogrom.' As if anti-Semitism were the best weapon of defence against refugees who might otherwise join forces to persecute Christians.

Having accepted an invitation to lecture at Harvard in September 1936, Jung had told Olga Fröbe-Kapteyn he would have to miss the Eranos conference in August. At first she seemed willing to accept the bad news, but later, visiting him in Küsnacht, she presented him with an ultimatum. If he did not come in 1936 and come regularly, she would abandon the conferences. Surprised, he gave in, and she was surprised to have won the argument.

So in August Jung made his fourth appearance at Eranos, where he had become pivotal. When lectures ended and the audience streamed out into the garden, he would usually sit on the garden wall, and the speaker would usually be surrounded by a smaller ring of admirers than he was. Some speakers were disconcerted to find he was giving a 'psychological' explanation of what they had just said.

Puritanic by nature, Olga Fröbe-Kapteyn had an intense relationship with him. She was possessive about him, and on the terrace she rarely allowed any other woman to sit at the round table where she ate with him and the other speakers. Certainly he had helped her with his advice, and until war broke out in 1939, she helped him by travelling around Europe in pursuit of photographs relevant to the archetypal and alchemical themes that interested him. They were collected in an archive at Eranos.

She was also helpful to some of his patients. Like several of the other women who interested him, she was gifted mediumistically, and when he sent patients to her, all she had to do, apparently, was remain passive. When they were left alone with her in a room, images appeared to them. 'It happened to me once in her house,' said Liliane Frey. 'I just suddenly began to have visions.'

Harvard University was holding its Tercentenary Conference on Arts and Sciences in September. A row broke out when it was announced that Jung was going to be one of the speakers, and to be awarded an honorary degree. One contributor to the university newspaper, the *Harvard Crimson*, complained that his scientific integrity had been 'partially stifled under the Nazis' thumb', but Harry Murray defended him. Many people were saying he had been supporting the Nazis against the Jews. Embarking on a study of Jung's work in 1937, the critic Walter Benjamin accused him of leaping 'to the rescue of the Aryan soul with a therapy reserved exclusively for it'. This 'auxiliary service to National Socialism' had 'been in the works for some time'.

Expecting journalists to bombard him with political questions as soon as the boat arrived in New York harbour, Jung prepared a statement:

As a psychologist I am deeply interested in mental disturbances, particularly when they affect whole nations. I want to emphasise that I despise politics wholeheartedly . . . I am convinced that 99 per cent of politics are mere symptoms and anything but a cure for social evils. About 50 per cent of politics is definitely obnoxious inasmuch as it poisons the utterly incompetent mind of the masses. We are on our guard against contagious diseases of the body, but we are exasperatingly careless when it comes to the even more dangerous collective diseases of the mind.

For the ceremonial award of an honorary degree, Jung was required to wear academic clothes, and, having brought nothing suitable, he went to a theatrical costumier and hired what a Southern senator would have worn: a frock coat, a string tie and a broad-brimmed black hat. But part of the ceremony was held in the Yard, and when it began to drizzle, black dye from the hat streaked down Jung's face and his shirt.

One of the other speakers at Harvard was Franklin Roosevelt, who had won the second term of his presidency by virtue of his New Deal, a programme of measures to counteract effects of the worldwide economic crisis. He impressed Jung as being 'a strong man, a man who is really great'. Jung thought him too strong to be a democrat. 'Make no mistake, he is a force – a man of superior and impenetrable mind, but perfectly ruthless, a highly versatile mind which you cannot foresee. He has the most amazing power complex, the Mussolini substance, the stuff of a dictator absolutely.'

There were two kinds of dictator – 'the chieftain type and the medicine-man type. Hitler is the latter. He is a medium. German policy is not made; it is revealed through Hitler. He is the mouthpiece of the gods as of old. He says the word which expresses everybody's resentment.' That was why the Germans were so sensitive to criticism from outside. 'It is blasphemy to them, for Hitler is the Sybil, the Delphic oracle.'

Afterwards, Jung and Emma spent a week at Bailey Island, off the Maine coast, where they stayed in the beachside house shared by three of his female followers, all doctors – Eleanor Bertine, Esther Harding and Kristine Mann. Having agreed to give a seminar on the island, he was expecting a small audience, but over a hundred people came to hear what he had to say about dreams. He based the talk on his 1935 Eranos lecture.

This was his first visit to the USA since 1925, and he spent the next week in New York, lecturing and seeing private patients. His visit climaxed in a public lecture at the Plaza Hotel. The subject was the collective unconscious, and the large audience included not only the most loyal of his local supporters but also his most hostile critics.

He wanted to illustrate what he had to say with lantern slides, and the man who had volunteered to operate the projector turned out to be nervous and accident-prone. The more mistakes he made, the more frantic he became. He dropped slides on the floor, showed some upside down and many in the wrong order. Forced to wait on the rostrum, pointer in hand, while the man struggled with the projector, Jung succeeded at first in remaining calm, but only at first. He afterwards said: 'I was analysed tonight if never before.'

He left New York on 3 October, and on the boat back to Europe, with his mind now focused on European politics, he wrote the lecture he was going to deliver in London, at the Tavistock Clinic in October. Using the title 'Psychology and National Problems', he argued that mankind was 'caught in one of the worst moral crises the world had ever known'. Generalising about misery and disorder in Russia, Germany, Austria and Italy, he diagnosed 'infantile and archaic psychology' in people's behaviour – 'infantile inasmuch as they always look for the father, and archaic inasmuch as the father-figure always appears in a mythological setting'. They therefore regressed to 'primitive tribal associations that are held together on the one hand by a chief or medicine man, and on the other by a sort of mystical doctrine, the tribal teaching'.

Man in the group, said Jung, 'is always unreasonable, irresponsible, emotional, erratic and unreliable. Crimes the individual could never stand are freely committed by the group being . . . The larger an organisation, the lower its morality.' Nations are 'inaccessible to reasonable argument, they are suggestible like hysterical patients, they are childish and moody, helpless victims of their emotions. They are caught in every swindle . . . they are stupid to an amazing degree, they are greedy, reckless and blindly violent, like a rhino suddenly roused from sleep.' Without apparently realising he was echoing Nietzsche's *Zarathustra*, he said: 'When a monster group first called itself a democracy, it did not think that its former ruler, now dethroned, would turn into a ghost. Yet he did. He became the State.' (A case of cryptomnesia.)

Germany, he went on, was 'the first country to experience the miracles worked by democracy's ghost, the State'. In Germany, as in Russia and Italy, men had come 'out of nowhere . . . and each of them said like Louis XIV, *"L'État c'est moi."* They are the new leaders . . . inconspicuous nobodies previously, but equipped with the great spirit voice that cowed the people into soundless obedience.' He then described Hitler. In private life he was 'a shy and friendly man with artistic taste and gifts. As a mere man he is inoffensive and modest, and has nice eyes.' But 'when the State-spirit speaks through him, he sends forth a voice of thunder and his word is so powerful that it sweeps together crowds of millions like fallen autumn leaves'.

Involving three million people, the neopagan movement in Germany 'can only be compared with the archetypal material exhibited by a case of paranoid schizophrenia . . . It does not go as far as collective hallucinations, though the waves of enthusiasm and even ecstasy are running high.' The swastika was a form of mandala, which could be interpreted as 'a projection of an unconscious collective attempt at the formation of a compensatory unified personality . . . The almost personal authority and apparent efficiency of the State are, in a sense, nothing else than the unconscious constellation of a superior instinctual personality which compensates the obvious inefficiency of the conscious-ego personality.'

Jung arrived at the Nietzschean conclusion: 'Order is always a cage. Freedom is the prerogative of a minority and it is always based on the disadvantage of others.' Describing the septuagenarian writer Miguel de Unamuno as 'one of those Spanish liberals who undermined the traditional order in the hope of creating greater freedom', Jung quoted his apologia for Franco: 'It is not any more a question of Liberalism and Democracy, Republic or Monarchy, Socialism or Capitalism. It is a question of civilisation and barbarity. Civilisation is now represented in Spain by General Franco's army.'

But Unamuno's support for Franco was short-lived, and on 12 October, the day after the *Observer* published an article by Jung, reiterating his argument, the Spanish writer turned against Franco. He was arrested and survived only till the end of the year. But Jung continued to support Franco after his army stormed into Barcelona in January 1939 and the Spanish government withdrew to Figueras.

While Jung was in London, Peter Baynes introduced him to a brilliant bisexual anthropologist with keen eyes and an aquiline nose, John Layard. He was forty-five and had lived in Berlin, where he met W. H. Auden. The man who introduced them, David Ayerst, thought of Layard as a man who could heal others while himself being in need of healing. At Cambridge, he had been befriended by the psychologist and anthropologist W. H. R. Rivers, who took him to do fieldwork in the South Pacific at the same time as Bronislaw Malinowski was in the Trobriand Islands.

Afterwards, before he could write up his discoveries, Layard suffered a nervous collapse which left him paralysed, but the paralysis was cured in London by the American psychologist Homer Lane, who believed in 'Original Virtue'. Human nature is innately good, and people who indulge their impulses fully are not only liberated from neurosis but are behaving ethically. Impressed by what Layard told him about Lane, Auden wrote: ' "Be good and you will be happy" is a dangerous inversion. "Be happy and you will be good" is the truth.'

Layard had a brief affair with Auden, his junior by sixteen years, and they remained friends. Auden was sleeping with several young male prostitutes. Going to bed with one he regarded as belonging to Auden, Layard found he was impotent, and afterwards shot himself in the head. The bullet failed to kill him, and he took a taxi to Auden's digs, where he asked his friend to finish him off. Though he had been encouraging Layard to kill himself if he wanted to, Auden refused to take the risk of being hanged.

Feeling abandoned by both his titled barrister father and by Homer Lane, who had died, Layard had gone to Berlin in search of psychiatric help, and went afterwards to London. There he was treated by Peter Baynes, who talked to him about Jung and to Jung about him. By the time they met, Layard was married, but the relationship was already deteriorating.

His first impression of Jung – so he said later – was that he could not 'hold a candle' to Homer Lane, but Layard liked him enough to ask whether he could come to work with him in Zurich. Did he mean, Jung asked, to work on anthropology or work on his problem? On his problem, he said, and they arranged that he should go the following year.

During the first week of 1937 Jung visited Nazi Germany as one of the two main speakers at a conference on 'Fundamental Questions of Spirituality and Spiritual Leadership' at Königsfeld in the Black Forest. The other main speaker was a theologian, F. Staehelin, who was to become a Lutheran bishop.

According to the official report, Jung immediately impressed his audience as being 'very independent, very open-minded . . . He unmasks the fervour and ill humour with which many pious people destroy themselves and others.'

In the discussion at the end of his lecture, he was asked who his patients really were. Taken by surprise, he answered:

> I am Herr Jung and nobody else, and here is Miss So-and-so. It would not be pleasant if one could not treat such sick persons. Besides, I have a certain enthusiasm for work . . . If some kind of idiot arrives at the door, it arouses the explorer in me, the curiosity, my spirit of adventure, my compassion. It touches my heart, which is too soft, as it usually is with people of my size. They try to hide it, but like fools, they fail, and I enjoy seeing what I can achieve with these crazy people.

The organiser, Rudi Daur, afterwards paid tribute to his 'refreshing honesty' and 'wonderfully earthy matter-of-factness'.

In October 1937 the International General Medical Society congress was held in Copenhagen, where, according to Carl Meier, Matthias Göring tried to arrange a meeting in Berlin between Jung and Hitler. Jung was invited to attend a big military parade before meeting the Führer.

Meier travelled with him to Berlin, where they shared a hotel bedroom, and on the night before the meeting, it was searched by the Gestapo. At the parade, Jung was within a few yards of Hitler, but the meeting was cancelled at the last minute. 'I think it was Jung who backed out,' said Meier, 'because I was asked in case Hitler refused to see Jung, would I go? I never found out exactly whether it was Jung or Hitler who backed out.'

It is hard to believe this. It would have been in character for Hitler to change his mind, but not to prefer a consultation with an assistant. Jung's comment, after being so close to Hitler, was that it would have been impossible anyway 'to talk to that man because there is nobody there'. But Jung did not want to declare himself an opponent of Nazism: 'You never know how these forces of the unconscious begin to arise, something good may come from it. Give them a chance.'

He must have gone on thinking about what would have happened had the meeting taken place. He said that when he had a patient acting under the command of 'a power within him, such as Hitler's Voice, I dare not tell him to disobey his Voice . . . All I can do is attempt, by *interpreting* the Voice, to induce the patient to behave in a way which will be less harmful to himself and to society.'

The same month Jung gave his three Terry Lectures at Yale University in New Haven. He had an audience of three hundred at the first, he said, and six hundred at the second. At the third, three thousand people were trying to get into the auditorium, and the police had to be called.

The title was 'Psychology and Religion' – he wanted to 'demonstrate the existence of an authentic religious function in the unconscious'. For him the word *religion* had less to do with creed or ideology than with the observation of 'certain dynamic factors that are conceived as "powers" – including spirits, demons, gods, laws, ideas and ideals'. The invisible presence of the 'numinous' could cause 'a peculiar alteration of consciousness'.

The Latin word *numen* means the divine power, and Jung used the word numinous in the same sense as the Protestant theologian Rudolf Otto, whose 1923 book *The Idea of the Holy* describes religious experience as a nonrational but objective sense of the numinous – a fascinating and awe-inspiring mystery that implicitly promises exaltation and bliss. Jung, who often used the word *numinous*, sometimes said that what mattered in therapy was that patients should be introduced to the numinous. 'The approach to the numinous is the real therapy, and inasmuch as you attain to numinous experiences, you are released from the curse of pathology.'

At Yale, discussing the psyche, he said that though its connection with the brain was 'undeniable', it was 'a fatal mistake to regard the human psyche as a purely personal affair'. When symbols such as quaternity crop up in their dreams, people ignorant of the symbol's history 'took it to symbolise *themselves* or rather *something in themselves*. They felt it belonged intimately to themselves as a sort of creative background, a life-producing sun in the depths of the unconscious.' The source of this proprietorial error was 'the prejudice that God is *outside* man'. It was clear to Jung that 'the quaternity is a more or less direct representation of the God who is manifest in his creation. We might therefore conclude that the symbol spontaneously produced in the dreams of modern people means something similar – *the God within*.' It also 'points directly . . . to the identity of God and man'.

Reluctantly conceding that dreams could be sent by either God or the devil, the medieval church had claimed the right to arbitrate in cases of uncertainty. Immediately after challenging the authority of Rome, Protestantism had begun to 'experience the disintegrating and schismatic effect of individual revelation'. But the modern Protestant has 'a unique spiritual opportunity for immediate religious experience'. It is not so easy for the Catholic to 'make himself conscious of sin', because confession and absolution are always available 'to ease excess of tension'.

Talking about archetypes, Jung equated them with motifs in mythology and folklore that 'repeat themselves in almost identical form'. They 'presumably derive from patterns of the human mind that are transmitted not only by tradition and migration but also by heredity'. The term *archetype* had been used 'since the first centuries of our era' by Cicero and Pliny, while Nietzsche had advanced the theory of the collective unconscious when he said: 'In sleep and in dreams we pass through the whole thought of earlier humanity . . . This atavistic element in human nature is still apparent in our dreams, for it is the basis on which the higher reason has developed and goes on developing in the individual.'

Jung's supporters held a farewell supper party for him, and he made an impromptu speech, discussing whether analytical psychology was a religion. 'Today archetypal contents, formerly taken care of satisfactorily by the explanations of the Church, have come loose from their projections and are troubling modern people . . . Life has gone out of the churches and it will never go back.'

Though he insisted he was not a religious leader – 'I have no message, no mission' – the speech ended like a sermon: 'Be human, seek understanding, seek insight, and make your hypothesis, your philosophy of life. Then we may recognise the Spirit alive in the unconscious of every individual. Then we become brothers of Christ [*sic*].'

By comparing this use of the phrase *archetypal contents* with his definition of archetypes in the lectures, we can see how hard it was for him to decide whether to restrict the term *archetype* to form. In 1926 he had thought archetypes 'behave empirically like agents' that encourage the re-enactment of 'ever-repeated typical experiences'. In 1927 he said 'the collective unconscious contains the whole spiritual heritage of mankind's evolution, born anew in the brain structure of every individual . . . All the most powerful ideas in history go back to the archetypes.' He also spoke of archetypes as ' "pathways" gradually traced out through the cumulative experience of our ancestors'. In 1929 he said 'inherited presuppositions' limited our freedom of consciousness by 'striving to lead all conscious processes back into the old paths'.

In 1935 he spoke of 'inborn images', but he kept changing his mind about whether images could be inborn. In 1940 he declared: 'Archetypes are not determined as regards their content, but only as regards their form, and then only to a very limited degree . . . The representations themselves are not inherited, only the forms, and in that respect they correspond in every way to instincts, which are also determined in form only.' But in a 1943 reworking of a 1917 essay he went back to the assumption that images were dormant in the collective unconscious. 'The greatest and best thoughts of man shape themselves on these primordial images as on a blueprint . . . The archetype is a kind of readiness to produce over and over again the same or similar mythical ideas.'

Jung had received an invitation from the British government to visit India. The University of Calcutta had been founded in January 1913, and an

Indian Science Congress was to be held in celebration of its twenty-fifth anniversary. In 1926 Jung had gone to Kenya and Uganda on his own initiative, but the decisions to visit North Africa in 1920, New Mexico in 1925 and India in 1938 were all prompted by invitations, and though ten years had elapsed since he had embarked on his study of alchemy, he was not entirely free to focus on new experiences. In North Africa he still had an appetite for them, but in India he was eighteen years older, more tired and less observant. Instead of being on the lookout for substantial new experiences, he wanted to find new substantiation for conclusions he had already formed. Engrossed in the *Theatrum Chemicum*, he took the first volume with him, and did not always want to go ashore when the boat stopped.

In New Mexico he had enjoyed Fowler McCormick's company, and once again he had chosen Fowler – now thirty-nine – as his travelling companion. They had known each other since 1913, when Fowler was fourteen, but it was only now that Jung suggested: 'Well, Fowler, why don't you call me C.G. instead of Dr Jung?' He left Zurich in December 1937, and they spent three months together in India.

The first city they explored was Bombay, which Jung described as 'a jumble of incidentally piled-up human habitations. These people carry on an apparently meaningless life, eagerly, busily, noisily. They die and are born in ceaseless waves, always much the same.' It seemed to Jung that 'the still youthful British Empire' would leave a mark on India, but fail to change its 'majestic face'. What seemed to confront him was 'immeasurable age with no history'. And if there was no recorded history, it scarcely mattered. All India's native greatness was 'anonymous and impersonal, like the greatness of Babylon and Egypt'. Everything and everyone had 'lived a hundred thousand times before . . . Even India's greatest individual, the unique Gautama Buddha, was preceded by more than a score of other Buddhas and is still not the last.'

Jung had come to India with a lot of preconceptions about the Indian mentality. Some of these derived from his belief in a polarity between East and West. He wanted to believe there was no split between thinking and feeling in the Eastern consciousness, that spirituality pervaded the world of the senses. 'The Indian can forget neither the body nor the mind,' he wrote, 'while the European is always forgetting either the one or the other.' The Indian 'not only knows his own nature, but knows how much he himself is nature'.

It is dangerous to generalise about 'the Indian' as if all Indians were the same, but Jung seems to have been looking at people in streets, temples, bazaars with his mind already made up about their priorities. The Indian 'wants to liberate himself from nature, and therefore tries to achieve through meditation the condition of blankness and emptiness'. Jung also assumed that for 'the Indian', the world 'is a mere show or façade, and his reality is more like what we would call a dream'. This appears to be based not on conversations with Indians he met but on the assumption that there had been no dissociation of sensibility or spirituality in India. 'The collective introverted attitude of the East did not permit the world of the senses to sever the link with the unconscious and psychic reality was never seriously disputed.' But Jung provides no evidence for his conclusion that the majority of ordinary Hindus look at the world as if it were a mere show, and that they practice yoga and meditation. From his reading, as we can see from citations in *Transformations and Symbols of the Libido*, Jung acquired considerable knowledge of Oriental mysticism, but his interest was in the esoteric, not in the everyday life of the average Indian.

He had repeatedly stressed the need to reintegrate 'primitivity' into consciousness. Looking at India from the perspective of his usual dichotomy, he saw it as 'one example of a civilisation which has brought every essential trace of primitivity with it, embracing the whole man from top to bottom'. Everything in India seemed 'dreamlike' because one gets pushed back into the unconscious, into that

> unredeemed, uncivilised, aboriginal world, of which we only dream, since our consciousness denies it . . . In the mental make-up of the most spiritual you discern the traits of the living primitive, and in the melancholy eyes of the half-naked illiterate villager you divine an unconscious knowledge of mysterious truths.

Heinrich Zimmer, who had never visited India, had been interested for years in Shri Ramana Maharshi, the most outstanding of the 'holy men', and the first question Zimmer put to Jung after his return was about this man he had not wanted to meet. 'He is of a type that has always existed and always will. Therefore it was not necessary to seek him out . . . He is merely the whitest spot on a white surface.' To understand the pleasant simplicity that pervades the spiritual life of India, 'it is enough to read an Upanishad or any discourse of the Buddha. What is said there is said everywhere: it speaks out of a million eyes, it expresses itself in countless gestures, and there is no village or country road where that broad branched tree cannot be found where the ego struggles for its own abolition.'

Trying to generalise about 'Eastern religious practice' and to define what it had in common with 'Western mysticism', Jung suggested that the goal of both was 'the shifting of the centre of gravity from ego to self, from man to God'. Comparing Ramakrishna and Shri Ramana Maharshi – mainly on the basis of a conversation with one of Shri Ramana's disciples, 'a man who had absorbed the wisdom of the Maharshi with utter devotion, and at the same time had surpassed his master' – Jung judged Ramakrishna to be more profoundly affected by Western attitudes than Shri Ramana, who had struggled harder to extinguish his ego in his self. For 'the modern Indian', Jung tells us, self, or *atman*, 'is essentially synonymous with "God" '. Ignatius Loyola's spiritual exercises – Jung lectured on them at the Polytechnic – had been aimed to subordinate the possession of an ego to possession by Christ; Shri Ramana wanted a dissolution of the ego in the atman. As Jung saw it, the only difference between Christian mysticism and Oriental philosophy was terminological. Shri Ramana spoke of the body as 'this clod'.

One of Jung's problems in India was ambivalence about whether he was entitled to absorb influence. 'I had to make do with my own truth . . . It would have seemed to me like thievery if I had wanted to learn from the holy men and to accept their truth for myself . . . In Europe too I must not borrow from the East but must live out of myself – out of what my inner being tells me, or what nature brings me.' Though he had read a lot about Indian philosophy, religion and mythology, the trip gave him – at the age of sixty-two – his first direct confrontation with an alien civilisation that had developed beyond the primitive stage.

Of the Indian religions, Buddhism attracted Jung most. 'For Buddha the self stands above all gods, a *unus mundus* which represents the essence of human existence and the world as a whole . . . Buddha saw and grasped the cosmogenic dignity of human consciousness; for that reason he saw clearly that if a man extinguished that light, the world would sink into nothingness.'

Jung watched a group of Japanese pilgrims marching towards the stupas of Sanchi, where Buddha delivered his fire sermon. Each pilgrim carried a gong, and chanting *Om mani padme hum*, they struck their gongs each time they reached the word *hum*. They bowed outside the stupas, and marching twice around the statues of Buddha, they sang a hymn and bowed before each one.

In Calcutta, where Jung was due to receive an honorary doctorate on 7 January 1938, he was invited to a series of dinners and receptions. At these he enjoyed seeing women dressed in saris. 'It is the most becoming, the most stylish and at the same time, the most meaningful dress ever devised by women . . . Women's fashions with us are mostly invented by men.' Instead of emphasising femininity, they were 'trying to create the adolescent hermaphrodite, an athletic semimasculine body, despite the fact that the body of the Northern woman already has a painful tendency to bony coarseness'. In contrast, Indian women seemed to live off their Eros principle.

Jung and Fowler visited several temples to Kali, where there was plentiful evidence that animals had been sacrificed. Fowler says 'the places were filthy dirty – dried blood on the floor and lots of remains of red betel nut all around, so that the colour red was associated with destructiveness.' The colour then began to feature in Jung's dreams. When he succumbed to amoebic dysentery, Fowler took him to the English hospital in Calcutta. The illness, according to Fowler, had two causes. One was the intensity of Jung's irritation at finding people were more familiar with Freud's work than with his; the other was the dirty floors in temples.

In general he applauded the Indian integration of sexuality into religion. The obscenities in the Black Pagoda of Konarak were explained by a pandit as a means to spiritualisation, and when Jung objected that the young peasants were having their heads filled with sexual fantasies, the answer was: 'These unconscious fellows must be reminded to fulfil their karma.'

Hinduism struck him as being less spiritual and less advanced than Islam. 'The cult is one wailing outcry for the All-Merciful. It is a desire, an ardent longing and even greed for God; I would not call it love. But there is love, the most poetic, most exquisite love of beauty in these old Moguls.' In a 1925 seminar Jung had described Eros as the god of relatedness and Logos as the god of form; in Agra, seeing the Taj Mahal, the finest temple of love ever built, he said Islam was founded on an experience of Eros, while in other religions Logos had been the determining principle.

After returning to Switzerland, Jung discussed Indian attitudes with Pastor Walter Uhsadel, professor of theology at Hamburg University. Pointing to a copy of a stained-glass window representing the Crucifixion, Jung said: 'You see, this is the crux for us.' In India, he said, it had struck him that 'the Oriental wants to get rid of suffering by casting it off. Western man tries to suppress suffering with drugs. But suffering has to be overcome, and the only way to overcome it is to endure it. We learn that only from him' – pointing to the figure of Christ. Jung expressed a similar opinion in a letter of September 1937 to Subramanya Iyer. 'I believe that misery is an intrinsic part of human life, without which we would never do anything.' What we should do is help people to endure misery.

According to Fowler, the experience of India, and especially of the Kali temples, gave him an 'emotional foundation . . . for the conviction that evil was not a negative thing but a positive thing . . . The influence of that experience in India, to my mind, was very great on Jung in his later years.'

Jung arranged for John Layard to stay in Küsnacht at the Hotel Sonne, and at their first analytical session Layard was surprised (as Harry Murray had been) to be treated like a close friend. Jung did most of the talking, confiding in him about Toni Wolff and how good she was in bed. Her father had run a business in Japan, and Layard formed the mistaken impression that she had been brought up there and learned Japanese sexual techniques.

Jung talked about his own life throughout most of Layard's first two sessions, but when they turned to his dreams, he found the interpretations enlightening. Though he felt in need of more time than Jung was giving him, and resented the division of the year into terms and holidays, Layard said at the end of his first term that he would like his wife, Doris, to come out for analysis. By now Jung was in such demand that even his assistants were overworked, and in 1936 Liliane Frey had started working, under supervision, as an analyst, though she had herself not started analysis with Jung until 1934. But he did not like to turn patients away, and without consulting Emma, he offered to have Doris analysed by her.

Layard would have to find somewhere he could live with Doris and their three-year-old son Richard. In one of Layard's dreams, the three of them were standing at equal distances from each other in a circular room. Richard was close to the gas fire, and when his nightclothes burst into flames, his mother made no effort to save him. Layard was slow to move, but he was beating flames out of the child's clothes as he woke up.

In *Faust* Part Two, said Jung, a child goes up in flames, which represent healing and redemption. He did not want to discuss the dream in terms of relationships and circumstances, though what mattered to Layard was his jealousy of his son, and guilt-feelings about his reluctance to save the boy's life.

He arranged for Doris and Richard to stay with him at the Sonne, but once they were settled in, it was suddenly impossible to make headway in the analysis. Jung struck him as being uncommitted to it, unwilling to give it enough time, or to take a transference. Believing Toni to be Jung's anima, Layard asked for simultaneous sessions with her, assuming these would give him additional access to Jung, who refused at first but eventually agreed.

Going to her for the first time, Layard talked on the assumption she would know Jung had discussed their intimate relationship with him, but the situation soon became embarrassing when, after describing one of his dreams, Layard talked about her visits to Bollingen. Baynes had said Jung built the tower for her, but she said: 'What has Bollingen got to do with me?'

Nonplussed, Layard asked: 'Don't you go there sometimes?'

Her reply was: 'What has that got to do with you?'

He soon came to think she hated him. Nor was Jung willing to discuss these difficulties. Layard concluded that their relationship as lovers was no longer as good as Jung had made it out to be.

Developing a strong transference to Jung, as so many people did, Layard had two homosexual dreams. In one they were lying down together with their clothes on in an empty theatre before the curtain had risen. Describing the dream, Layard knew he was asking Jung to pay more attention, but his only response was: 'We cannot discuss that.'

Layard drew another blank when he told Jung he had once wanted to have sex with Doris in a Sussex church.

'You can't do a thing like that. That's desecrating the church.'

Layard thought it could be regarded as a way of joining opposites together, but the analytical relationship went on deteriorating.

One day he made Doris go to keep his appointment with Jung, while he went to see Emma, but nothing could have saved the situation, and at the end of the second term they went back to England, defeated. Layard wondered whether Jung had been disappointed when he said he did not want to work on anthropology in Zurich, but on his emotional problems. Perhaps, as some of the other patients suggested, Jung wanted to learn more about anthropology.

Layard had noticed a parallel between Jung's fourfold division of the psyche and kinship systems in Malekula – patriarchal and matriarchal. He showed Jung a section of his unpublished book titled 'The Incest Taboo and the Virgin Archetype'. Tribe and settlement are divided into four, as in the basic pattern of a square or circle divided by a cross. The population is divided into patrilineal and matrilineal 'moieties'. Every man belongs to his father's moiety, and the woman he marries must not belong to his mother's, which means he can take a wife only from the opposite matrilineal *and* patrilineal moiety. Jung took all this over, with due acknowledgment, in 'The Psychology of the Transference'.

Layard's disillusionment did not stop him from running Jungian discussion groups in Oxford during the war and practising as an analytical psychologist, or from returning to Zurich after the war for as many sessions as the ageing Jung was willing to give him.

Part Five

The Grail and the Bomb

Thirty-One

The German Psychosis

When Jung was in his sixties, he paid no less attention to dreams than during his boyhood. Of all his experiences in India, none made more impact than a dream he had in his Calcutta hotel, while recuperating after being discharged from hospital. He was in a castle courtyard on a narrow island south of England. A celebration was going to be held for the Grail, which was still on another part of the island, in a small, uninhabited house. Friends accompanied him on the quest, but the island was divided by a channel, and, exhausted by the long walk, they fell asleep, leaving him to swim across.

He took the dream to mean he had a mission unconnected with India. 'Seek rather for your fellow men the healing vessel, the *servator mundi*, you urgently need. You are in danger of ruining everything the centuries have built.' This was the archaic language in which he spoke to himself. Another man might have felt more amused than challenged by a dream about saving humanity with a heroic deed, but Jung had never stopped seeing himself as a hero, and in reality – as later in *Memories, Dreams, Reflections* – he tended to push his life towards the dimension of myth.

Previously, he had tried through psychology to give people contact with the numinous. Never entirely jettisoning orthodox Christianity, he had not given it precedence over the other belief systems he had studied. But for the next twenty-four years, his formidable (but dwindling) energy would be focused mainly on the history, traditions, symbols and rituals of Christianity.

Lecturing at Yale, he had said: 'Life has gone out of the churches and it will never go back.' He now changed his mind: the trend was reversible, and he was the man who could reverse it. If Nazism was a symptom of spiritual sickness, his duty was to save civilisation from Wotan-oriented paganism. Since this could not be done by imposing Eastern religion on Western culture, the best chance was to cure Christianity of the disease that had driven his father to despair and premature death. People no longer responded to the images of wholeness in the rituals, dogmas and traditions preserved by the church. Unlike him, its spiritual leaders had no experience of direct contact with God. Surely this, combined with the knowledge and skill he had acquired, would empower him to reach the other half of the island.

Nietzsche's influence now began to recede, as Jung turned back towards Christianity. In his *Psychological Approach to the Trinity*, which he delivered as an Eranos lecture in 1940 and expanded in successive revisions, finally publishing it in 1948, he said Nietzsche provided a foretaste of the self-importance that inflates a man who tries to deify himself. Awareness of 'the religious problem' can save us from putting 'the divine germ within us to some ridiculous or demoniacal use'. We should remember we are 'no more than the manger in which the Lord is born. Even on the highest peak, we shall never be "beyond good and evil".' Zarathustra had proclaimed new commandments inscribed on new tablets, but Jung tells us not to ignore the old commandments. Ignoring the risks of self-importance and inflation, he braced himself for the task of reviving the convalescent church by translating dogma into psychological theory.

In the book he titled *Jung's Treatment of Christianity*, Murray Stein uses both meanings of the word *treatment* as he analyses the 'intensely personal aspect' of Jung's 'therapeutic attitude towards Christianity'. With Freud and psychoanalysis, says Stein, Jung 'repeated what he had done with his father and his father's religion'. His understanding of

> the complexity of projection and perception in the transference/ counter-transference process can accommodate the dual realisation that while his writings on Christian themes were indeed dealing with the cause of his father's spiritual illness (and therefore with Jung's strong feelings about his victimised parent), they were also an attempt to treat the profound problem in Western culture – the conflict between tradition and modernity – which both his father and he had inherited.

In March 1938, when the Germans marched into Austria, Jolande Jacobi was in danger. Jewish by birth, she had become a Catholic, but this would not protect her from the Nazis, and her prominence in the Kulturbund would make it hard for her to escape notice. At the age of forty-four, wanting to become an analyst, she had written to ask Jung whether he would train her.

More intelligent, more critical and more assertive than most of the women who surrounded him, she was likely to cause friction, and, to discourage her from coming, he told her to study for a doctorate. Undeterred, she enrolled as a student of psychology at the university in Vienna. She was within four months of graduating when Austria was annexed, and after her flat had been ransacked by the Gestapo, she escaped to Budapest, where she again wrote to Jung, asking for asylum.

Though few of his assistants had a university degree, let alone a doctorate, he refused to relent. Risking her life, she returned to Vienna, staying in a friend's house and putting on a veil, as if she were in mourning, whenever she went out. After graduating, she went to Zurich in October 1938, and Jung finally admitted her to his circle. She was forty-nine.

A Jew with better reasons for expecting support was Vladimir Rosenbaum, a young lawyer who had helped Jung when he was being accused of anti-Semitism, and again when he was turning the General Medical Society into an international organisation. Wanting to be sure its constitution allowed him to offer Jewish analysts individual membership, Jung went secretly to Rosenbaum's house for advice.

Later, after fighting in Spain against Franco, Rosenbaum was arrested for contravening Switzerland's neutrality, and was imprisoned for four months. He did not know afterwards whether he would be welcome at meetings of the Psychological Club. At first Jung encouraged him to go, and he attended lectures, including one by a Nazi who said Jews were people of the desert, and the law of the desert was hatred. Soon after this, Rosenbaum received a letter from Jung, telling him to stop coming. When he asked for a face-to-face conversation, Jung invited him to Bollingen, but made him stay outside the building. 'Being wounded,' said Jung, 'even a wild animal hides somewhere to die.'

Rosenbaum answered: 'Goodbye, Herr Professor,' and never spoke to him again.

One of Jung's ambitions was to unite the various schools of psychotherapy under a single institute. He had built the foundation for this enterprise in his 1929 essay 'Problems of Modern Psychotherapy', and, following the example of Woodrow Wilson, who had formulated 'Fourteen Points' for the League of Nations, Jung listed fourteen points for acceptance as 'Views Held in Common' by 'all psychotherapists, working along the lines of psychological analysis'.

In May 1938, a Teaching Institute for Psychotherapy was founded at Zurich University with Jung as president and a 'curatorium' of nine doctors in charge. One of the intentions was to encourage cooperation between rival analytical schools, and two Freudians who regularly attended meetings were Gustav Bally and Hans Banzinger. They were among the lecturers, as were Jung, Alphonse Maeder and H. W. Maier. Meetings were held every fortnight in Jung's house, and guests were invited.

As Andrew Samuels has shown, Jung was trying to establish himself as 'the dominant psychological theorist of the day', and at the end of July, when he presided over the congress of the International General Medical Society, which was held in Oxford, he spoke about his efforts to achieve cooperation between different analytical schools. But it was hard to be conciliatory when German delegates kept trying to interpolate Nazi propaganda. In 1939 Jung's fourteen points were listed in the *Zentralblatt*.

He was the first psychologist to be awarded an honorary doctorate of science by the university, but his speech of acceptance embarrassed Michael Fordham, who found it 'flowery and unusual to English tastes'. Afterwards, 'as he came down with the university dignitaries, Jung gave his close assistant C. A. Meier an enormous wink which convulsed Meier and several others besides . . . It seemed like a calculated insult to the university. I don't think so, however; it was just Jung unable to resist being a gamin and showing his humorous disrespect for ceremony.'

In June, Freud and his family had left Nazi Vienna to settle in London, and on 1 August, prompted by E. A. Bennet, Jung arranged for the conference to welcome him by telegram. Freud's diary mentions 'the obligatory greetings telegram to which I have responded with a cool answer'.

In October, receiving an American journalist, H. R. Knickerbocker, in Küsnacht, Jung talked at length about Hitler and Mussolini. Unlike Mussolini, Hitler scarcely existed as a man. While Mussolini's role disappeared behind him, Hitler disappeared behind his role. Watching a parade of goose-stepping German soldiers, Mussolini enjoyed it 'with the zest of a small boy at a circus . . . It really is a most impressive step.' But Hitler 'made upon me the impression of a sort of scaffolding of wood covered with cloth, an automaton with a mask, like a robot . . . During the whole performance he never laughed; it was as though he were in a bad humour, sulking.'

Studying photographs of him taken after his invasion of Czechoslovakia, Jung had thought: 'The outstanding characteristic of his physiognomy is its dreamy look . . . there was in his eyes the look of a seer.' He was 'the loudspeaker which magnifies the inaudible whispers of the German soul until they can be heard by the Germans' unconscious ear'. Seventy-eight million people had projected their unconscious into his. 'If he is not their true Messiah, he is like one of the Old Testament prophets: his mission is to unite his people and lead them to the Promised Land.'

Of course he would break his promises, just as England and France would ignore their pledges to Czechoslovakia. 'No nation keeps its word. A nation is a big, blind worm, following what? Fate perhaps. A nation has no honour, it has no word to keep . . . Hitler is himself the nation. That incidentally is why Hitler always has to talk so loud, even in private conversation – because he is speaking with 78 million voices.'

In Jung's view, 'the only way to save democracy in the West – and by the West I mean America too – is not to try to stop Hitler . . . I say let him go East . . . Let him go to Russia . . . Instinct should tell the Western statesmen not to touch Germany in her present mood.' Jung's advice to the American people was to stay out of the war. 'Keep your army and navy large, but save them. If war comes, wait.'

Jung's *Collected Works* omits many of his contributions to the *Zentralblatt*, including the greetings sent in April 1939 to Matthias Göring on his sixtieth birthday. Together with Carl Meier and O. Curtius, Jung signed an open letter congratulating Göring on the conferences he had organised in Germany.

Throughout most of the 1930s, Jung had been working with patients eight or nine hours each day, unless he had to give a lecture or a seminar. He was lecturing three times a week: once in English at the club and twice in German at the Polytechnic, where he talked about Indian thought. Discussing a Tantric text – the *Shri-Chakra-Sambhara Tantra* – he made comparisons with alchemical works, especially those in the collection called the *Theatrum Chemicum*. Still studying alchemy alongside theology, he set such a high value on his time that when Toni Wolff arranged an auction at the club to raise money, he suggested that an hour should go under the hammer, and bid for it himself till the price had gone above a hundred francs – ten times as much as patients normally paid an hour.

By the beginning of 1939, halfway through his sixty-fourth year, he felt so tired and overworked that he cut down on his activities, and in February, after five years of talking about Nietzsche, he suspended the seminars. He was intending to resume them in the autumn, but too many of his American and English students went home before war broke out.

Invited by the Royal Society of Medicine to lecture in early April, he took Emma to London, and also Barbara Hannah, who could act as their driver. Emma had been studying the legend of the Grail and wanted to visit the West Country. According to tradition, Joseph of Arimathea, who had collected Jesus's blood in the Grail at the Crucifixion, had brought it to England and founded the first church – at Glastonbury.

Jung's lecture was so well received that Barbara Hannah enquired in the car whether his anima had been dancing on his forehead. About seven years previously he had used this phrase to mean he had been showing off during a lecture in Germany: 'I positively felt my anima dancing on my forehead and fascinating the audience on her own.' Annoyed by her question, he got out of the car without thanking her for giving him a lift, but at lunchtime the next day he said: 'Of course it was like that last night.'

Emma wanted to visit not only Glastonbury but other places, such as Tintagel and Banbury Rings, associated with King Arthur, who in some of the stories had sent his knights in quest of the Grail. Barbara Hannah drove the Jungs to West Byfleet in Surrey, where Peter Baynes and his third wife, Anne, took over as drivers. But Jung did not want to spend much time in England, partly because war seemed imminent, and partly because he was impatient to be in Bollingen. About to write a commentary on Tibetan texts collected and translated by W. Y. Evans-Wentz under the title *The Tibetan Book of the Great Liberation*, he said it would be hard to finish it before term started. 'Nevertheless, I can't do it straight from here or I shall not be able to get into its atmosphere, so I must stare at the lake for some days.'

In July, when a meeting of the society was held in Zurich, he offered to resign from the presidency. With delegates representing groups in Switzerland, Germany, the Netherlands, Sweden, Denmark and Britain, the pro-Nazis were in a minority, but Göring announced that three new groups had been formed in pro-Nazi countries – Italy, Japan, and Hungary. Once they were accepted, he would be able to swing a majority vote in favour of any motion he wanted to pass.

Hoping to minimise tension between Nazis and anti-Nazis, the English vice president, Hugh Crichton-Miller, proposed that the Dutch doctor J. H. van der Hoop should take over the presidency, but Göring objected that this was a slight to Germany. Jung then agreed to stay on as president, but Hoop, who had been trying to stop Nazi sympathisers from joining the society, must have been bitterly disappointed when Jung appointed Göring co-editor of the *Zentralblatt*. This may have been intended to show he was not going to be intimidated by accusations of pro-Nazism.

At Eranos that summer, what he called 'a feeling of Last Judgment' was in the air. After his visit to Munich in September 1938, Neville Chamberlain had been congratulated on averting a war, but by the summer of 1939 Hitler's designs on Danzig showed how fragile the peace was. The theme for the conference was 'The Symbolism of Rebirth in the Religions of all Times and Places', but conversations veered uncontrollably towards politics, and conditions were abnormal. Olga Fröbe-Kapteyn's garden had been flooded when the lake overflowed its banks during the freak thunderstorms of the late summer, and much of the land was still under water.

One of the speakers was Heinrich Zimmer, who had already left Germany. His father-in-law, the writer Hugo von Hofmannsthal, was of Jewish descent, and, giving up his chair in Heidelberg, Zimmer had accepted a lectureship in Oxford. One morning, Barbara Hannah was driving the Jungs and a German friend of Emma's up the hill to the hotel. When they stopped to buy a newspaper, the German woman said England and France were 'determined to have a war'. Jung laughed when Hannah ordered her to get out and walk up the hill.

Jung talked with the American multimillionaire Paul Mellon and his attractive thirty-five-year-old wife Mary, who had both been writing to him, asking to be taken on as patients. Mary suffered from asthma, which, it was suspected, might be psychogenic in origin. They had attended one of his seminars and one of his Terry Lectures at Yale, where, impressed by his informality and matter-of-factness, they had invited him to dinner in a New Haven restaurant. Mary's first words to him were: 'Dr Jung, we have too much money. What can we do with it?' He impressed them both, especially when the waiter left a bottle of Chianti on their table and went away without opening it. Jung produced a hunting knife from his pocket, used the corkscrew to open the bottle and poured the wine.

During the conference, the Mellons offered to help Olga Fröbe-Kapteyn. Paul described her as 'a very powerful, mysterious sort of woman, brim full of all kinds of mystical learning', but she had been finding it so hard to fund the conferences that she was intending to sell the Casa Gabriela. Jung vehemently opposed this idea, and the Mellons volunteered to contribute funds. Eating lunch with her and Jung on the terrace at her round table, they finally succeeded in arranging appointments with him. Giving them a fifteen-minute interview each, he said Mary had a terrific animus problem – 'It was the horse in her that was on the rampage, and she should be given more freedom to kick out.' He agreed to analyse them both.

Talking about Hitler's ungovernable rages – when a Red Cross official had tried to argue with him, he ripped down curtains from the window – Jung said his madness had infected the whole German people: 'They are all possessed like Hitler and absolutely unapproachable.' After the pact between Germany and Soviet Russia was signed on 23 August, Jung dreamed that Hitler was the 'Devil's Christ', the Antichrist, but that, as such, he was 'God's instrument'. In a letter he wrote in English on 2 September, Jung said: 'Hitler is approaching his climax and with him the German Psychosis.'

When the conference ended, the Mellons drove to Zurich, where they stayed at the palatial Dolder Grand Hotel before renting a flat near the club for themselves and their young daughter Cathy. But Paul was more critical than Mary of the set-up.

One unfortunate feature of Jung's system in those days, and, indeed, probably throughout his career, was that there was no way of knowing which analysts were approved by him, or had been trained by him, or trained at all . . . I always found his attitude towards his pupils and analysands puzzling. It was sometimes hard to distinguish between his elderly lady patients and those other ladies who claimed to be analysts.

But Paul enjoyed his sessions with Jung. 'He was quite easy to talk to. There was a good deal of the peasant about him, and he was very direct. He also had a very good sense of humour.'

It was hard to make plans. 'I'm living provisionally,' Jung wrote. It was uncertain whether Switzerland would be allowed to remain neutral. 435,000 men had been mobilised, including Jung's son Franz and three of his four sons-in-law. The wives and children all settled in the big Küsnacht house with Jung and Emma.

On 3 September Britain and France declared war on Germany. And on the 23rd, Freud died in London at the age of eighty-three. Some of the resentment Jung had accumulated spilled into the long obituary he wrote for the Sunday supplement of the *Basler Nachrichten*.

It starts by saying that the cultural history of the last fifty years was inseparably bound up with Freud's name. But every subsequent sentence either denigrates Freud or damns him with faint praise. This may not have been Jung's intention, but, as he often explained, a complex can make us deviate from what we intend.

Though Freud's work had affected every other sphere of contemporary thinking, the 'exact sciences' had remained untouched. Freud was above all a 'nerve specialist', with no training in psychiatry, psychology or philosophy. Psychoanalysis owed its origins to Charcot and Janet, while it was Breuer who had discovered that pathogenic 'ideas' derived from the memory of early experiences that had been traumatic. Freud's psychology had never escaped 'the narrow confines of nineteenth-century scientific materialism', while his 'inadequate philosophical equipment' had prevented him from exploring its foundations. He had 'always remained a physician' who 'constantly had the clinical picture of neurosis before his mind's eye'. That was why he kept pointing to 'what this demonically obsessive picture forced him to see – the weak spot, the unacknowledged desire, the concealed resentment, the secret, illegitimate fulfilment of desire deformed by censorship'. He made the unconscious appear to be full of elements that had rightly been rejected by the conscious mind.

The 'rigid one-sidedness' in his theory had been 'backed by an often fanatical intolerance'. The revelation he had been granted 'took possession of his soul and never let go'. Being 'possessed by a demon', he had been capable of 'carrying the torch of knowledge only part of the way'.

This was not, of course Jung's last word on Freud. In October 1940 an American who had given up his business to become a patient of Jung's, queried his assertion that Freud was an extravert. Replying (after a ten-month delay) to the letter, Jung reconsidered his position and introduced the possibility of categorising a man's work differently from his personality. 'What I meant to say was that Freud's theoretical view is extraverted . . . Personally a creative man can be an introvert, but in his work he is an extravert and vice versa.' Freud's 'general way of living was a genuinely introverted style'. Describing him as 'neurotic all his life long', Jung wrote: 'I myself analysed him for a certain very disagreeable symptom which in consequence of the treatment was cured.' (Probably Jung, who used the word *analyse* more loosely than Freud did, was referring to their analysis of each other's dreams on the trip across the Atlantic, but I have found no justification for the word *treatment* and no evidence that any disagreeable symptom was cured.)

'Originally,' Jung went on, 'he was a feeling type and he began later on to develop his thinking, which was never quite good in his case. He compensated his original introversion by an identification with his creative personality, but he always felt insecure in that identification, so much so that he never dared to show himself at the congresses of medical men. He was too much afraid of being insulted.'

In December 1939, Jung made one of his rare attempts at political inter-vention, writing to two members of the National Council with the suggestion that every Swiss male between eighteen and sixty should be considered 'mobilised' whether liable for military service or not. They should all receive the same salary from the state, and whatever they earned in excess of it should be used for the public good. This would stop soldiers from feeling that they were being financially exploited at the same time as having to risk their lives.

At the beginning of the First World War, he had decided that his main duty was to explore the depths of his own psyche, and throughout the Second he went on believing the battles that mattered most were internal. 'One could say that the whole world with its turmoil and misery is in an individuation process.' If only people understood this, they would not be at war, 'because whosoever has the war inside himself has no time and pleasure to fight others'.

Thirty-Two

Trinity + Devil = Quaternity

In the spring of 1940, Switzerland's neutrality seemed precarious. German troops were gathering on the other side of the frontier. The Maginot line of French fortifications between Switzerland and Luxembourg was reputed to be impregnable, but the Germans could bypass it by marching through northwestern Switzerland. If they did, Zurich would not have been defended. Guisan's emergency plan was to withdraw behind the line formed by the Jura Mountains, the Walensee, Lake Zurich and the river Limmat. The Swiss army dug into the cliffs, building caves from which they could defend the mountains.

But the Jungs, who had nothing to lose by going south for an April holiday in Ascona, invited the Mellons to join them. Mary had to stay in Zurich for an appendicitis operation, but while she was convalescing, Paul accepted, and went for walks in the mountains above Locarno with Jung. Back in Zurich by the end of the month, the Mellons went to Bollingen on the 29th for tea, but they left for the USA at the beginning of May.

Switzerland was in danger while the Germans advanced rapidly through Belgium and Holland to attack France. As Jung said, Zurich was 'threatened with complete destruction', but he saw signs of discord between Hitler and Mussolini. 'It looks as if Italy prefers an undisturbed Switzerland. Even the dictators mistrust each other.'

Emma had expected that Jung would refuse to leave his practice, but after being told his name was on the Nazis' blacklist, he took her, his eleven grandchildren and his daughters-in-law to a boarding house at Saanen, three or four miles from Gstaad, in the Bernese Oberland. 'We have here the feeling as if one were sitting on a box of dynamite that might go off in the next moment,' he wrote in English to a woman who invited him to settle in California with Emma and their family till the war was over. 'Yet one is quiet because it is a great fatality.'

Some of his patients moved into a Gstaad hotel, where he gave them a weekly session or two, returning throughout most of the summer for midweek sessions with patients in Küsnacht. After France surrendered in June, the Germans were unlikely to invade Switzerland, and Jung went back to dividing his time between Küsnacht and Bollingen. 'These were strange, memorable drives,' wrote Barbara Hannah, who travelled with him twice to Küsnacht, 'through a fully armed countryside, on roads that were almost empty except for military traffic.' Jung felt constricted. 'Up to the present moment Bollingen has escaped – together with Switzerland – the general destruction, but we are in prison. You don't see the walls but you feel them.'

The government had recommended citizens to lay in stores of food, saying the country could support itself if consumption was reduced by 20 per cent. Bread and most other foods were rationed, but, having land of his own, Jung could grow corn, potatoes, beans and, later, wheat, as well as poppies, yielding seeds from which oil could be extracted.

When the annual meeting of the society was held in Vienna, Göring pressed for the acceptance of the Italian, Japanese and Hungarian groups, though formalities had not been completed. As co-editor of the *Zentralblatt*, he was in a strong position, which became stronger when Jung again offered his resignation. Gladly accepting it, Göring said he was too old to understand political developments, and that he had been using the *Zentralblatt* as a Jungian publication. Carl Meier was still secretary-general, and he should have been in charge of running the society's affairs, but he got no answer when he wrote to Göring, outlining the legal status quo, and there was no effective resistance when Göring moved the society's headquarters from Zurich to Berlin. Jung had twice been president of an international organisation, and twice he had lost control.

Because Switzerland's frontiers were closed to foreigners, the Eranos Conferences might fail to survive, and Jung wrote for financial help to the Pro Helvetia Foundation, a department of the Swiss Arts Council, arguing that their demise would be 'an irreplaceable loss for the spiritual life of Switzerland and for the international relations and forces that emanate from Switzerland'. In 1940 only a token conference could be planned, and only one lecture was announced – the mathematician Andreas Speiser on 'The Platonic Doctrine of the Unknown God and the Christian Trinity'.

In her opening speech, Olga Fröbe-Kapteyn said that if neither the speaker nor the audience had come, she would have celebrated Eranos on her own. But as it turned out, there were two speakers: Speiser's talk prompted Jung to give an impromptu reply. Reconstructed from memory and from notes taken by members of the audience, 'On the Psychology of the Dogma of the Trinity' appeared in the Eranos yearbook for 1940–1, and he went on developing it over the next seven years. In 1948 it reappeared, revised and expanded, under the title 'A Psychological Approach to the Dogma of the Trinity'.

Believing that Christian symbols and tenets derived less from logical thinking than from archetypes, Jung submitted them to the same treatment he had given the narrative in *Zarathustra* – analysing them as if they were dreams or visions. Reworked for publication in 1948, his Trinity essay prefigured *Answer to Job*, which he wrote in the spring of 1951.

The Trinity enigma had concerned him throughout most of his life. 'Of course,' he said in a 1930 seminar, 'we know that it is the Christian formula for the supreme value, the supreme idea, the supreme motive, but the fact that the supreme value should be symbolised by the Trinity, as being three in one, is in itself mysterious. It has always shocked me.' He went on to say that he used to argue with his father about the Trinity. If it was perfect, why was the devil still free to do evil? 'I said that when a person has a bad dog, the police interfere. But when God or the Trinity lets such a dangerous devil roam about amongst quite nice people, nobody is there to punish God for it, which is an outrageous thing; what is not allowed to man should not be allowed to God.' Already, twenty-one years before he wrote *Answer to Job*, he was holding God responsible for the evil deeds that cause the innocent to suffer.

In a letter written during April 1932 he said the Trinity concept had resulted from the eagerness of 'the old theologians to push God outside the sphere of psychic experience into the Absolute . . . Man was therefore separated from him most effectively, so that he could not manage without the intercession of *Ecclesia Mater*.' But it was 'incorrect to assert that the Christian Trinity has no mother goddess in it. The Mother is simply veiled by the Holy Ghost (Sophia) which is the connection between Father and Son.'

In his 1937 seminar on *Zarathustra* and again in his 1937 lectures at Yale, Jung had made the point that 'whereas the central Christian symbol is a Trinity, the formula presented by the unconscious is a quaternity. In reality the orthodox Christian formula is not quite complete.' He developed this argument in the 1940 Eranos lecture and his reworkings of it. The Trinity contained no representation either of the feminine or of evil. What was needed, of course, was a quaternity. 'Quaternity forms the logical basis of any judgement . . . There are always four elements, four prime qualities, four colours, four castes, four ways of spiritual development, etc.'

The life of Jesus, the god-man, had revealed much that had been unknowable so long as God was indefinable and indivisible. Becoming the Father and simultaneously becoming a man, he revealed the secret of his divinity. As the third term common to Father and Son, the Holy Ghost rounds out the Trinity, confirming the exclusion of the female element. (This deviates from the position he had taken seven years earlier about the veiling of the Mother.)

The New Testament contains no explicit reference to the Trinity, although, operating under the surface, an archetype is throwing up such triadic formulae as 'The grace of the Lord Jesus Christ, and the love of God and the Communion of the Holy Ghost be with you all.' The medieval mind assumed that the psyche had the same structure as the Trinity, but the modern mind 'reverses that procedure and derives the Trinity from the psyche'. The history of the Trinity is seen as the emergence of an archetype that 'moulds the anthropomorphic conceptions of father and son, of life and of various people into an archetypal and numinous figure, the Most Holy Three-in-One'.

If humanity is to achieve psychic wholeness, it must learn how to integrate images of God precipitated by the unconscious to 'compensate or complete the prevailing mood or attitude'. The man who is 'merely conscious', consisting only of ego, is nothing more than a fragment.

If evil was excluded from the idea of God and from the Trinity, its reality was being denied. Christianity had two ways of dealing with the problem. One was to insist that evil was only the absence of good, and this 'makes it a shadow that has only a relative existence, dependent on light'. The other was to personify it as the devil, but the Bible failed to explain how evil originated, or why God had given him so much power and done so little to protect mankind. According to one Gnostic view, Christ was God's second son, and the first was Satanael – the name means Satan-God. The central symbol, the cross, was unmistakably a quaternity, but the Church Fathers had angrily resisted the idea that a fourth figure should be added to the Trinity.

Anyone else would have understood there was no prospect of persuading the Vatican to replace it with a quaternity that included the devil. But Jung pointed optimistically to quaternity symbolism in medieval representations of the Virgin's coronation. The dogma about her Assumption was not going to be promulgated until November 1950, but there was already a new doctrine that her body had been taken into heaven together with her soul. Could the church take another step towards enlightenment?

As Christ's adversary, the devil gave us our first insight into the polarity between heaven and hell, and if he is Christ's brother, the same archetype is at work as in the story of Cain and Abel – the archetype of the hostile brothers. Cain's 'Luciferian nature' is evident in his 'rebellious progressiveness'. Lucifer was 'perhaps the one who best understood God's intention of creating a world and who carried out that intention most faithfully.

Rebelling against God, he became the active principle of a creation that confronted God with its own counter-will.' According to Jolande Jacobi, Jung had used a similar argument in the thirties when he told people not to be overhasty in condemning the evil of Nazism. Evil is the bringer of light, he said, and Lucifer means light-bringer.

In his Terry Lectures, Jung had quoted one of his favourite alchemists, Gerard Dorn, who noticed that after the second day of Creation, the day God separated the upper waters from the lower, he did not say 'it was good', as he did every other day. Was this because evil, together with 'confusion, division and strife', originated in the dualism he had just created? In the Trinity essay Jung suggests that the idea of an Antichrist was probably connected with 'the astrological synchronicity of the dawning aeon of Pisces' and with 'the increasing realisation of the duality postulated by the Son, which in turn is prefigured in the fish symbol . . . It is a question of preconscious, prefigurative connections between the archetypes themselves.'

The antagonism between Christ and the devil implies conflict that humanity must endure till 'good and evil begin to relativise themselves, to doubt themselves and the demand is made for a morality "beyond good and evil". Such an idea is out of the question 'in the age of Christianity and the realm of Trinitarian thinking.' Thesis and antithesis cannot be viewed together without 'cooler assessment of the relative value of good and the relative non-value of evil'.

Though he alludes to Nietzsche's *Beyond Good and Evil*, Jung was not interested in his approach to the problem of how concepts of good and evil had originated and evolved. In Nietzsche's 1887 book *On the Genealogy of Morals*, the perspective is historical and linguistic. (Michel Foucault's 'archaeology of knowledge' in the human sciences is a continuation of Nietzsche's genealogical examination of morality.) But Jung's appetite for theological discussion was still insatiable, and he argues as if it should be possible to establish historical facts about what happened on the second day of Creation.

Writing to Peter Baynes in the summer, Jung said 1940 was 'the fateful year for which I have waited more than 25 years'. Since 1918 he had known that 'a terrible fire would spread over Europe'. He was reminded 'of the enormous earthquake in 26 BC that shook down the great temple of Karnak'. What they were experiencing now was 'the premonitory earthquake of the new age'.

At sixty-five, he said it was 'difficult to be old in these days. One is helpless. On the other hand one feels happily estranged from this world. I like nature but not the world of man or the world to be . . . I loathe the new style, the new Art, the new Music, Literature, Politics, and above all the new Man.' The connection between his alienation and his loathing of contemporary art is explained in a later wartime letter. 'When the earth quakes, there are only abrupt and disjointed fragments . . . It is much better for modern art to paint the thousand-hued debris of the shattered crockery than to try to spread a deceptive quietness over the bottomless disquiet. The grotesque, the ugly, the distorted, the revolting perfectly fit our time.'

Though he often spoke of feeling old, he still had plenty of stamina, and still channelled a lot of energy into outdoor pursuits – chopping wood, gardening, sailing and hiking in the mountains. 'I can vouch for it that nothing is more invigorating and therapeutic than mountain air.'

He had to stop himself from overworking. 'I must watch out that the creative forces do not chase me round the universe at a gallop . . . Gently, attentively and assiduously, I have to persuade myself not to do too much . . . The secret of growing old properly, it seems to me, is to consume oneself prudently and avoid being consumed.'

Just before the Nazis occupied France, the head of the new American Office of Strategic Services (OSS), Allen Dulles, arrived in Switzerland to recruit agents. One of the women who interested him, both sexually and professionally, was a thirty-six-year-old American, Mary Bancroft, who had lived in Zurich since 1934, after divorcing an American businessman. Her second husband was an accountant. She had attended some of Jung's lectures at the Polytechnic before going into analysis, first with Toni Wolff and then with him. When she told him Dulles wanted to involve her in espionage, he advised her to say yes.

The war was making him even more religious, and more inclined to give the psyche priority over external events. To Peter Baynes he said: 'Don't think please, that I am callous in not mentioning the horrors of our time. I am confirmed in my fundamental disbelief in this world.'

He was immersing himself progressively in theological reading and in correspondence with clergymen. He prided himself on his friendships with 'high-ranking clerics who appreciate my labours', and he specially enjoyed conversations with a Catholic priest, Dr Gallus Jud, 'an intelligent and scholarly man, who gives me a chance to get thoroughly acquainted with the Catholic mind. It is wonderful to see medieval mentality still at its best.'

His thinking – like his handling of his patients – was conditioned by lack of interest in specific circumstances and personal emotions. He saw everything as dependent on archetypes and collective forces. Since evil was rampaging all over the world, the best way to fight it, he decided, was through the most powerful of all international institutions – the Christian church. But before it could exert substantial influence on world affairs, it would have to be changed, and Jung was never more unrealistic than in believing he could change it.

Resuming his lectures at the Polytechnic in November 1940, he discussed the psychology of alchemy, and in the spring of 1941 he gave two talks at the club 'about the main symbolism of the Mass (sacrifice and transubstantiation)'. In August he used the same material in his Eranos lecture on 'The Symbol of Transformation in the Mass'.

Christianity's ultimate purpose, he said, was to democratise enlightenment about the self and the individuation process. Once this had been the prerogative of shamans and medicine men, later of physicians, prophets, priests and initiates of mystery cults. The Mass is 'the culmination of a process that began thousands of years ago'. The symbolism of the ceremony represents the union of imperfect parts into a perfect whole. The wine and the bread represent the masculine and the feminine part of Christ. By becoming man and retaining his divinity, Christ involves man in the process; by celebrating the two miraculous transformations in a ritual, the priest renews their efficacy.

Looking for pagan counterparts to the symbolism, Jung picked on the Mithraic ritual of sacrificing a bull who represents the god, on the Aztec practice of making a dough god, who is symbolically killed, divided up and eaten, and on the visions of a third-century Gnostic, Zosimos. One of his visions was of a priest who had been scalped, dismembered and transformed into spirit. At the end of the vision, his eyes fill with blood. He changes into a manikin and eats his own flesh.

Though this vision, unlike the Mass, is a raw product of the unconscious, both derive from the archetype of sacrifice, which should not be explained in moral terms. Jung saw the crucifixion not as an expiation of humanity's sins but as a symbolical transformation of instinctual man into spirit. If he is to achieve enlightenment, he must be submitted to the painful process known in alchemy as *divisio*, *separatio* and *solutio*. 'Every step forward along the path of individuation is achieved only at the cost of suffering.'

When properly performed by the priest and fully understood by the congregation, the Mass fuses them with Christ so that 'the soul is assimilated to Christ and on the other hand the Christ figure is recollected in the soul. It transforms both God and man, since the Mass, at least by implication, repeats the whole drama of Incarnation'. What is sacrificed is the ego, and since 'the relation of the ego to the self is like that of the son to the father, we can say that when the self requires us to sacrifice ourselves, it is carrying out the sacrificial act on itself.' Everything depends on the self-transformation of the psyche through the conscious integration of unconscious drives.

Languishing in human darkness is an Enchained One, says Jung, and our understanding must go down to lead him back into the light.

Christ was once whole, but having either lost his wholeness or given it to mankind, he can regain it only through man's integration. The alchemists had paved the way for the realisation that the mystery of transubstantiation depended less on magical than on psychological processes, but 'the psychologist can do no more than describe a psychic process whose real nature transcends consciousness . . . The ethics of the researcher require him to admit where his knowledge ends.'

Open-minded about miracles, Jung considered the possibility that Switzerland had been saved from the Germans by the intervention of Niklaus von der Flüe. 'My son is an officer in a Catholic infantry regiment. He told me that his soldiers had the collective vision of the blessed brother Niklaus von der Flüe, extending his hands towards the Rhine to ward off the German troops approaching our frontier . . . It is nice to have such protective saints.'

While nonbelievers, unless they were actively involved, could do nothing to influence the course of the war, believers could pray, and Jung had no hesitation about recommending this. In September 1943 he told an anonymous correspondent that prayer is

> highly necessary because it makes an immediate reality out of the Beyond we imagine and reflect on, and it transposes us into the reality of the ego and the obscure Other. Hearing yourself speaking, you can no longer deny that you have addressed 'It'. The next question is: What will become of You and Me – the transcendental You and the immanent me? Frightening and inescapable, the way of the unexpected is opened – the way of what is not to be expected, but there is hope of a favourable twist or a defiant 'I will not be destroyed by God's will unless my will reinforces it.' Only then, I feel, is God's will made perfect . . . I belong with it, a tremendously heavy milligram without which God has made his world in vain.

His view of the collective unconscious shifted simultaneously. Before the war, he had not insisted it was nonhuman, as he did in May 1940. 'You trust your unconscious as if it were a loving father,' he grumbled. 'But it is *nature* and cannot be made use of as if it were a reliable human being. It is *inhuman* and needs the human mind to function usefully for man's purposes.'

Though Switzerland enjoyed a higher standard of living than its war-torn neighbours, Jung's life was not unaffected. Food was rationed, and fuel for central heating was in short supply – 'General state of health therefore much better.' He no longer ran a car: petrol was unavailable to ordinary citizens, and he did not apply for special treatment.

'At times I feel old and rotten,' he told Mary Mellon in the spring of 1941, but he may have been trying to discourage her from thinking about him so much. She had been dreaming about 'twin children, twin men, twin Jungs', and from the beginning of July, when Paul joined the army – though the USA seemed unlikely to become involved in the war – she was left on her own. Though Paul was more critical of Jung than she was, the Bollingen Press, the publishing company they had founded together at the end of 1940, was to centre on Jung's work, and her plan was to disseminate his ideas. The first two publications were to be a collection of papers read at Eranos conferences and an English translation of the *I Ching*.

In the middle of August she dreamed about being with Jung 'in a foreign place'. He looked different – thinner, harder, 'and his hair was Prussian looking. He still loved me, but apparently I was the source for some kind of information all of which was found in the past correspondence of Jung and myself. These were the things Jung was betraying me with.' When he took her in his arms, she said: 'This is not the Jung who wrote the green letters to me.' She had the feeling that everything would be all right if only Toni Wolff were present. 'He had always told me of the devil in every man and I was seeing his . . . After he finished loving me his face changed again and he went on with his work. I was so very sad and hopeless because I believed in him still.'

She enclosed her account of the dream in a letter written twelve days later. Eager to hear his reaction to it, she confessed to having 'a strong feeling that you would like to see me as much as I want to see you . . . Tell me if you ever do because it would help me to know it sometimes. Anyway the grass is green and the fire still burns.' She signed the letter: 'All my love to you, Mary.'

He replied that he often thought of her, and often wished he could see her. The dream meant she had a living image of him. Her letters emanated immediate warmth, and something like a living substance, which made him emotional, and he might do something foolish if they were on the same side of the Atlantic. They had a living connection 'through the non-space' – an unconscious identity – which was dangerous, because it could alienate her from herself. He signed the letter 'Affectionately'.

When she became pregnant again, she wrote: 'Somehow, somewhere, someway – you are in this child too. It is as if I had been twice impregnated, for had it not been for the brutal and spiritual anguish which you and I have forced me to go through, I do not believe I would ever have conceived again.' It was 'the result of the miraculous year I spent with you'. But she had not lost her identity, like 'those around me who have also been touched by you'. The people who 'live and breathe Jung' had taken up a pattern 'based on your ways, your likes and dislikes, your mode of living, speech – and to my great amazement – even your handwriting. I have had letters from one or two in the N.Y. Psychological Club – and I swear I had to look twice to see if it weren't yours.' She signed the letter 'With all my love to you, Dr Jung, Mary'.

Over two months elapsed before he replied with a letter signed 'I remain, yours cordially, C. G. Jung.' He had always thought of Paul, he said, as a man waiting to be picked up by something not yet in sight. He enjoyed hearing from the other side of the Atlantic. Life was moving forward like the ticking of a clock that could never be wound again.

A month after his Eranos lecture on the Mass, Jung had to lecture on Paracelsus, who was born on 7 September 1541 at Einsiedeln, to the south of Lake Zurich. To celebrate the four-hundredth anniversary, the Swiss Society for the History of Medicine arranged a festival there. Jung chose 'Paracelsus the Physician' as his title. Four weeks later, on 5 October, he lectured in Basel, where his title was 'Paracelsus as a Spiritual Phenomenon'.

He found it easy to empathise with Paracelsus, whose driving force was compassion. 'Compassion is the physician's schoolmaster,' he maintained. The son of a doctor, he lost his mother when she was young, but he was left, as Jung puts it, with two mothers – the church and nature. He held that knowledge about disease was pagan, coming as it did from 'the light of nature'. He believed there were two kinds of knowledge: eternal and temporal. One comes directly from the light of the Holy Spirit, the other, coming from nature, is both good and bad. It 'is not from flesh and blood, but from the stars in the flesh and blood'. God the Father created man 'from below upwards', but God the Son 'from above downwards'.

A healer, said Paracelsus, should gather knowledge from a variety of natural sources, and from the lore which taught that a sickness could be diagnosed from the sickness of metals. A doctor should also be a philosopher, an alchemist and an astrologer – the inner constellation corresponds to that of the stars.

Jung respected the mixture of conservatism and radicalism in Paracelsus, who was conservative about Christianity, alchemy and astrology, but sceptical and rebellious. 'What immediately strikes us on reading his work is his bilious and quarrelsome temperament. He raged against the academic physicians all along the line.' Believing in cosmic correlations, he thought the stars in the human body copy the stars in the sky. 'The physician should proceed from external things, not from man.' He should be both an astrologer and an alchemist. How could he know what caused ulceration if he did not know what made iron go rusty? But above all, Paracelsus believed in magic, intuition and empathy. 'Thus the physician must be endowed with no less compassion and love than God intends towards man.'

For the festival in Einsiedeln, Jolande Jacobi was invited to speak on 'Paracelsus and Women'. By the autumn of 1941, the danger of German invasion had receded, and the president of the festival was surprised to receive a warning from Jung that she had been an intimate friend of Kurt von Schuschnigg, the Austrian chancellor who had tried to stop Hitler from occupying his country. 'What would our great neighbour say if a friend of Schuschnigg spoke at a Swiss festival?'

Forced to withdraw, she afterwards said: 'I always regarded Jung as a Pétainist . . . He always wanted not to get into difficulties with people.' Head of state in the part of France that was not yet occupied, Marshal Pétain was collaborating actively with the Germans. According to Jacobi, Jung had once said: 'You know the great difference between you and me is that I am a coward and you are unusually brave for a woman.'

She was not deterred from continuing with *The Psychology of C. G. Jung*, a summary of his work. He was nervous it might erode sales of his books, but he checked through her text and discussed it with her before it was published in 1942. It contains a diagram rather like one he had used earlier to represent layers of consciousness, but he modified it to sort out a problem that had arisen over the collective unconscious. Was there only one for the whole of humanity, or did Jews have a different one from non-Jews? This time the lowest layer in the diagram represents 'the unfathomable, the central force out of which at one time the individual psyche has been differentiated'. The seven layers above this refer (in ascending order) to memories lodged in animal ancestors, in primitive human ancestors, in population groups, in the nation, in the tribe, in the family and in the individual. By bringing 'animal ancestors' into the picture, he was clarifying a point that had been ambiguous, but it would follow that the fragments of memory which surface in our dreams could contain residue from the experience of prehistoric apes.

Hitler had defeated France with astonishing speed – the armistice was signed in June 1940 – but his offensive against the USSR started in June 1941, and on 7 December, Japanese warplanes attacked American ships in Pearl Harbor. After the raid, there could be no doubt that the most powerful country in the world would be fighting on the side of the Allies.

Five weeks earlier, it had seemed unlikely that Moscow would hold out against the besieging German army, and for everyone who wanted Hitler to be defeated, nothing better could have happened than the Japanese air raid, but Jung was not pleased. On 20 December he wrote in a letter: 'I begin to feel my age and whenever I get a bit too tired I also feel my heart and that is decidedly disagreeable and makes me cross with the whole world, which is damnable anyhow. I went through a period of black depression during the first four days. Only yesterday I began to feel human again.' The four days were the first four after the air raid.

America's involvement in the war had a consequence he could not have predicted. The Bollingen Press had been reconstituted as the Bollingen Foundation, which would make it easier to collaborate with other publishing houses, and everything appeared to be progressing until it was decided that the foundation should suspend all operations outside the USA till the war was over. The government had passed a Trading with the Enemy Act, which imposed heavy penalties on anyone convicted of dealing directly or indirectly with enemy aliens.

In 1943 Jung and his old friend Albert Oeri were briefly involved in an unofficial effort to stop the war. Several high-ranking Nazis, including Heinrich Himmler, had been alarmed by Hitler's irrational behaviour, and, conspiratorially, they became involved in an initiative that gathered momentum when a doctor prepared a medical report on Hitler without any cooperation from him, and without examining him. It confirmed that his condition was pathological.

In possession of this report, Himmler encouraged the SS leader Walter Schellenberg to take soundings through connections in Spain, Sweden and America. What interest would there be in negotiating a peace settlement with or without Hitler's consent? Schellenberg used a German doctor, Wilhelm Bitter, as his emissary to Switzerland, where he approached Jung, Oeri and Carl Burckhardt, a historian and diplomat who lived in Geneva. Jung was preparing to send one of his English students to London, when the initiative collapsed, and, expecting to be shot if he went back to Germany, Bitter stayed in Switzerland.

In February 1943 Jung started corresponding with a student who reviewed his new book, *Problems of the Unconscious*, in *Der Zürcher Student*, and sent him a copy of the review. 'Much in Jung is still the romantic vision of a creative spirit,' Arnold Künzli had written, 'occasionally at the expense of scientific empiricism.' And, reviewing a psychological book by another writer, he mentioned 'the romantic character of the unconscious in C. G. Jung'.

Intensely annoyed, as he always was when accused of being unscientific,

Jung defended himself with more vigour than dignity. Was his young critic aware he had been awarded seven honorary doctorates? How had he deviated from the methods of empirical science?

Künzli was glad of the opportunity to exchange letters. He was writing a thesis on the problem of angst in Kierkegaard; and, answering a second letter in which Künzli posed psychological questions, Jung denounced 'that moaner Kierkegaard', together with Heidegger, James Joyce, Hegel and Nietzsche, who 'drips with outraged sexuality'. Philosophy still had to learn it was '*made by human beings* and depends to an alarming extent on their psychic constitution . . . There is no thinking *qua* thinking, at times it is a pisspot of unconscious devils . . . Neurosis addles the brain of every philosopher because he is at odds with himself.' But this lesson had already been learned. Nietzsche says every philosophy is an autobiographical statement.

In mid-March Jung wrote to Künzli again, explaining what he would have said had he been Kierkegaard's analyst. 'I would have told Kierkegaard straight off: "It doesn't matter what *you* say, but what *it* says to you. To *it* you must address your answers. God is immediately with you and is the voice inside you. You have to have it out with that voice." ' This would have silenced the philosopher and made him into a different man,

> but a *whole* one not a jangling to-and-fro of unpleasant fragmentary souls . . . Neurosis does not produce art. It is uncreative and inimical to life. It is failure and bungling. But the moderns mistake morbidity for creative birth – part of the general lunacy of our time . . . Neurosis is a protracted crisis degenerated into a habit, the daily catastrophe ready for use.

In November 1943 Jung received an emissary from a publisher interested in an English edition of his collected works. Herbert Read was a prolific writer of poetry, art criticism and literary criticism. His novel *The Green Child* may have been written under Jung's influence, and in a 1943 book, *Education through Art*, he argued that Jung had been more successful than Freud in interpreting 'those collective phenomena which take the form of myth and symbol'.

Since 1937, Read had been a literary adviser to the publisher George Routledge, and in 1938 he bought a partnership in the company. It did not merge with Jung's English publishers, Kegan Paul, until 1947, but the two firms were already operating jointly. For an English translation of Jung's collected works, the USA would form part of the market, and a lot of negotiation would have to be done before Anglo-American co-publication could be arranged, but in principle, Jung was agreeable.

Thirty-Three

What Happens After Death

Walking in the snow on 11 February 1944, the sixty-eight-year-old Jung slipped and broke his fibula. Taken to a private hospital, the Klinik Hirslanden, where his ankle was plastered, he was given a bed and told not to move; but after ten almost motionless days, he disobeyed orders, which brought on a severe heart attack – a triple thrombosis in the heart and lungs. He refused to eat and showed little interest in surviving. Emma decided she should move into the hospital, where she was given a bed next to his.

Retrospectively he would call the illness 'a most valuable experience'. It had given him 'a glimpse behind the veil. The only difficulty is to get rid of the body, to get quite naked and void of the world and the ego-will. When you can give up the crazy will to live and when you seemingly fall into a bottomless mist, then the truly *real* life begins with everything which you were meant to be and never reached.'

After the heart attack he had a series of visions. On the point of leaving the earth, he could see the whole of India from a great distance and, less clearly, Persia, an Arabian desert, the Mediterranean and the northeastern coast of Africa. In another dream or vision he was floating in space with a huge block of dark stone shaped like a magic lantern. There was a doorway in the stone, and, wearing a white gown, a black Hindu sat silently on a stone bench in the lotus position. As Jung approached the doorway, he felt as if everything belonging to his earthly existence was being stripped away, but he consisted of everything that had happened, and needed nothing he did not have.

A priest-physician arrived with a message: people were saying he must not be allowed to leave. He was disappointed at having to go back, instead of joining 'the people in whose company I belonged . . . Life and the whole world struck me as a prison.' In another dream he was floating in the stratosphere while at least thirty women were clamouring for his return.

He was not allowed to sit up in bed until eight weeks after the accident.

On the same day, 4 April, his doctor, Theodor Hammerlei-Schindler, was taken ill, and when he died of septicaemia, Jung thought the doctor's life must have been taken in exchange for his.

He spent five months in the hospital. Many people were dreaming about him, having fantasies or visions, believing in synchronistic connection between their experience and his. There was an epidemic of virulent flu, and one infected woman pictured him telling her he had decided to go on living, so she should get back inside her body. Another flu victim, finding that her watch and her clock had stopped at the same time, wondered whether he had died at that moment.

According to Swiss etiquette, illness concerned only the family, and it was bad form to keep other people informed about the patient's progress. Nothing if not conventional, Emma kept all the news to herself, and some anxious women in the inner circle believed their sufferings helped to call Jung back into the world of the living. After he recovered, he gave orders that in any future illness, regular bulletins should be issued about his condition.

Before the accident, he had been working with Marie-Louise von Franz on the book he had started in 1941, *Mysterium Coniunctionis: An Enquiry into the Separation and Synthesis of Psychic Opposites in Alchemy*. The title refers to the alchemical unification in a symbolical marriage of opposite qualities – hot and cold, moist and dry, active and passive. Jung was pursuing his argument that the alchemists, who believed self-knowledge and piety to be indispensable for the discovery of the philosopher's stone, had envisaged a process of transformation that was not only physical but psychic. The stone was 'called on the one hand cheap, immature, volatile, and on the other precious, perfect, solid . . . The *materia* is visible to all eyes, the whole world sees it, touches it, loves it, and yet no one knows it.'

In questing for a combination of opposites, the alchemist, like the analyst, had been trying to fuse inner and outer experiences, to integrate the unconscious into consciousness. Though this is what Jung had been contending for at least fifteen years, he now declared that he would never have understood it but for the dreams and visions brought to him by his illness.

Discharged from the hospital in July, he was reluctant to part with his blissful dreams and visions, but felt certain that he knew more than he had before about the afterlife, and that consciousness survived. 'What happens after death,' he wrote in a letter, 'is so indescribably glorious that our imagination and our feelings are inadequate to form even an approximate notion of it . . . Sooner or later all the dead become what we also are . . . The dissolution of our time-bound form in eternity brings no loss of meaning.' And according to *Memories, Dreams, Reflections*, the 'rule of opposites' will not be totally absent from the afterlife, which will be 'grand and terrible, like God and like the whole of nature that we know'. Nor will suffering be entirely absent from it.

While he was convalescing at home, Emma did not allow Toni Wolff inside the house, though she was still president of the Psychological Club. From now on, she was kept at a distance, not only by Emma, but also by Jung.

Preoccupied throughout most of 1944 with his inner life, Jung paid little attention to the bombs falling on Germany or the progress of the Allied troops who had landed in France and Italy. Without quite believing, as he had in 1914, that inner and outer events were blending in his consciousness, he still believed in his prophetic intimacy with the archetypal forces that governed the war, and his followers were happy to see a synchronistic connection between his recovery and the victory of the Allies.

One event that concerned him was the plot to kill Hitler on 20 July 1944. One of the conspirators was General Erwin Rommel, and another was Mary Bancroft's friend Hans Gisevius, but the crucial role was played by a colonel, Claus Count von Stauffenberg, Chief of Staff to the commander of the army reserve. Not wanting to become involved, Jung kept silent, and did not reveal his attitude until after Stauffenberg had been shot. He and Gisevius were in Jung's opinion no better than Hitler − what they wanted was absolute power. They were all 'lions fighting over a hunk of raw meat'.

In reality von Stauffenberg was an idealist − courageous, sensitive, cultured and enterprising. He loved the Germany that had been destroyed by the Nazis. Though he had lost his left eye, his right hand and two fingers of his left in the Tunisian campaign, he organised the plot that came closer than any other to ridding Germany of Hitler. But in Jung's view, 'it is probably just as well that the putsch failed'.

To believe that archetypal forces determine events is to devalue both individual initiatives and historical developments. In his 1936 essay on Wotan, Jung had maintained that the unfathomable depths of the god's character explained more about National Socialism than economic, political and psychological factors.

Jung's disposition had, if anything, become even more religious since the heart attack and the ensuing visions, but in September 1944 he dealt brusquely with a Catholic who tried to coax him into the church:

My dear Sir! *My pursuit is science*, not apologetics, not philosophy, and I have neither the capacity nor the desire to found a religion. *My interest is scientific, yours evangelical* . . . These two standpoints are mutually exclusive so that any discussion is impossible. We talk at cross purposes and charge

through open doors . . . As a Christian of course I take my stand on the
Christian truth, so it is superfluous to want to convert me to that . . .
Though I know little of Catholic doctrine, the little is enough to make it
an inalienable possession for me. And I know so much about Protestantism
that I could never give it up.

As a doctor, he said, he frequently had to help 'victims of the great schism of
our time', but it was irritating that a man who had read his books so
carelessly should think himself capable of leading him to 'the goal and
consummation' of his life's work. 'And where are you leading me? To the
very spot I started from – to the Christianity which is still medieval. It not
only failed four hundred years ago but is now more of a failure than ever and
in the most terrible way.'

Ambivalence becomes evident, though, when he admits to wishing he
could find 'a scholarly Catholic collaborator who with understanding and
goodwill would correct my theologically defective mode of expression, so
that I could avoid everything that looked even remotely like a criticism, let
alone a devaluation of Church doctrine'.

In December 1944 it was secretly decided to limit the number of Jewish
members in the club. The initiative seems to have come mainly from Toni
Wolff, who was still president, and Linda Fierz David, but it could not have
been implemented without Jung's support. Dated 7 December, the appendix to the bylaws stipulated that 'when possible', the quota of Jewish
members should be limited to 10 per cent, and of 'guests' to 25 per cent.
The document was signed by members of the executive committee, but not
circulated to members.

Various attempts have been made to justify the decision. One is that the
club could have been dominated by 'foreigners'; another is that if the Nazis
invaded Switzerland, Jung might have been sent to a concentration camp if
there were too many Jews in the club. But by now the war was virtually
over.

In February 1945, twelve months after the accident, Jung said he was still
'practically an invalid, recovering very very slowly from all the arrows that
have pierced me on all sides'. In April his doctors pronounced him fit to
resume his normal routine, but he cut his hours of analysing from six a day to
two or three.

With the war in its final stages, he made a series of statements about
Hitler's Germany, and, giving an interview to a Swiss journalist, he said the
psychologist should avoid making 'the popular sentimental distinction
between Nazis and opponents of the regime'. Collective guilt was a fact,

and the task of therapy was to make the Germans admit this. The 'general psychic inferiority of the Germans' had produced a 'national inferiority complex which they try to compensate by megalomania'. It was no accident that Goebbels had been 'branded with the ancient mark of the demonised man – a clubfoot. Ten per cent of the German population today are hopeless psychopaths.'

In a more considered statement, published in June, he elaborated on this accusation, saying that the sight of evil kindles evil in the soul, that everyone in the vicinity of a crime suffers with the victim as the air is poisoned. The Swiss were innocent, but Switzerland was a small country. If its population were multiplied by twenty, 'our public intelligence and morality would automatically be divided by twenty as result of the damaging psychic and moral effects of living in a mass society . . . Do we seriously imagine that we would have been immune?' Reliance on the state meant that a whole nation was 'on the way to becoming a herd of sheep . . . The shepherd's staff soon turns into an iron rod, and the shepherds become wolves.'

Spreading the blame widely, he attacked European civilisation, as he often had before. What was wrong with art? What about atonal music and 'the blatantly pathological element in modern painting'? What about the 'far-reaching influence' of Joyce's *Ulysses*? 'Here we already have the germ of what became a political reality in Germany.'

Nor could Jung resist another reference to his 'pueblo chieftain' and his travels, which had helped him to look at Europeans with critical detachment. The white man was nervous, restless, pressured, unstable. The gods had been dragged down, transformed into demons and dispersed, thanks to scientific enlightenment. But it had failed to destroy psychic factors corresponding to the old gods – suggestibility, fearfulness, prejudice, superstition – the qualities that had made it possible for the German to be *possessed*, as if by evil spirits.

War had continued in the Far East after the surrender of Germany in May, and three months later, on 6 and 9 August, the US Air Force dropped atomic bombs on Hiroshima and Nagasaki. Jung was ambivalent: 'Perhaps the invention of the bomb and the actual use of it in war proceeded from a worldwide unconscious impulse to limit the surge and growth of populations throughout the world.'

But the scale of the slaughter reinforced the effect of the Grail dream, which had made him believe he could save humanity. 'Now that mankind possesses the instrument that can bring the world to an end, it will assuredly use it unless a third world war comes soon and smashes the power of those nations that might *also* develop the atom bomb unless – *and this is the only hope* – the great reversal comes, a universal retreat from Marignano.' At the

Battle of Marignano, in 1515, the French King Francis I had crushed
Switzerland's hopes of remaining a major European power.

'As I see it, only a worldwide religious movement could fend off the
diabolical drive towards destruction. That is why the question of the Church
grips me so urgently, for the Church is the only worldly authority where
spirit in the religious sense moves the brute masses. The Church would have
its *raison d'être* if it could save humanity or at least civilisation.' This idea is
echoed in a 1948 letter: 'I am persuaded that the Christian Church is one of
the most powerful instruments for keeping the great masses more or less
right in the head.'

He often thought about the atom bomb, wondering whether it could
annihilate humanity, and in 1948, meeting a man who had worked on the
Manhattan Project, Jung asked whether the whole Earth could be destroyed.
The answer was that it could. 'Jung sat focused, having listened closely to
each word, absorbing. Suddenly he lifted his hands and smote his left palm
with his right fist, saying "Good!" with finality. Somehow the subject was
settled, and we never had any further explanation of what he may have
meant.'

His only chance of fulfilling his mission was to form an alliance with the
church. But it would have to be on his terms, and the changes he wanted
were so radical that he implicitly compared himself to Luther.

> A tremendous revolution in Christianity is long overdue. Four hundred
> years ago it was Germany who performed this service for the world. The
> unconscious is pure nature, which means that behind the bad foreground is
> a natural reality, beyond good and evil. It always depends on human
> understanding whether the archetypal content of the unconscious assumes
> a favourable or unfavourable form.

He would need a collaborator inside the church, and if he prayed for one, it
must have looked as though God was responding when, shortly after Jung's
seventieth birthday, a package arrived from an English Dominican who had
been put in touch by a Jungian analyst, Gerhard Adler. Father Victor White
enclosed a paper on 'The Frontiers of Theology and Psychology', together
with two articles and a review of a book by a psychoanalyst. One article was
titled 'St Thomas Aquinas and Jung's Psychology', while the other, 'Psychotherapy and Ethics', proposed a synthesis between Thomistic theology
and analytical psychology.

Thomism is a philosophical and theological movement based on the ideas
of the thirteenth-century preacher Thomas Aquinas, who wrote comment-
aries on both the Gospels and Aristotle. Until the 1960s, Thomism was the

Catholic church's official philosophy, and it was held that the truths of theology were compatible with the truths of philosophy.

White's letter contained the phrase: 'The task before us is gigantic indeed.' This astonishing use of the first-person plural is reminiscent of Jung's first letters to Freud. A stranger was writing to an older man, a famous doctor, with an implicit offer of collaboration.

White, who was forty-two, taught at the Dominican college of Blackfriars in Oxford. After entering the order at the age of nineteen, he had studied Thomist philosophy for four years, and then theology. But suddenly, in 1940, he decided theology was meaningless. 'I could not get my mind onto it, or anything to do with it, except with horror, boredom and loathing.' Given 'compulsory leave of absence' from Blackfriars, he was not allowed to go within six miles of Oxford.

In 1940–1 John Layard was running three Jungian discussion groups in Oxford. Still under the influence of Homer Lane, he held that the whole of the psyche was good – an idea that impressed White, who of course had misgivings. In a note dated 5 December 1940, he said Layard's account of the Fall was 'ultimately dualistic and Manichean . . . There is a considerable likelihood that Jungians by going beyond their empirical data and making metaphysical and meta-psychical affirmations which are demanded by their data, may lay the foundations for a religion or ersatz-religion which, so far from complementing Christianity, may contradict it radically.' But he called Layard 'the magician', and started analysis with him in 1941. Banished from Oxford, White was living exactly six miles away, and made the journey with a cap pulled down over his forehead and his chin muffled in a scarf.

No less influenced by his new patient than White was by him, Layard went on to found the Oxford University Society for Psychology and Religion. After being reinstated by his superiors, White gave one of the society's first lectures, 'The Frontiers of Theology and Psychology'. This was among the texts he sent to Jung in 1945.

In spite of some reservations, White had become involved with Jungian ideas. He had read Jung's 1928 article on 'Psychoanalysis and the Cure of Souls', which said Catholicism was rich in rituals that 'work like a vessel for receiving the contents of the unconscious'. These rituals could 'gather the lower, instinctual forces of the psyche into symbols, and in this way integrate them into a hierarchy of the spirit.' Churchmen provoke transference when they penetrate into the consciousness of parishioners, but unlike the priest, the Protestant clergyman 'has no form which he can substitute for his own person'.

In 1937, lecturing at Yale, Jung had argued that Protestants were given better opportunities than Catholics 'for immediate religious experience', but in the winter of 1945, writing to a Protestant clergyman, he expressed a preference for the Catholic church and the religious practice 'that proves the existence of a need for fixed and immovable ideas and forms'. Protestantism was 'dynamic but unbalanced'. It 'dissolves into countless subjectivisms'. It was neither a church nor a counter-church, though it was 'by its very nature anti-ecclesiastical. A Church must have a common foundation, and that foundation certainly is not the Bible nor is it the figure of Christ, which has provoked the most divergent views among theologians themselves.'

From the early thirties, White had aspired to be one of the Thomists who did for the modern period 'what St Thomas did for his'. It was necessary to integrate 'all modern discoveries and scientific achievements . . . into the Thomist synthesis for the good of man and the glory of God'.

White was approaching Jung at the right moment. Since the end of his relationship with Freud, thirty-two years earlier, Jung's only collaborative partnership with another man had been the brief one that was ended by Richard Wilhelm's premature death. But after reading the lecture and the articles by Victor White, he was excited by the prospect. Though he had corresponded with several Catholic churchmen, he wrote:

> You are the only theologian who has really understood something of what the problem of psychology in our present world means. I sympathise fully with you when you say: 'The task before us is gigantic indeed' . . . and I would surely be among the first to welcome an explicit attempt to integrate the findings of psychology into the ecclesiastical doctrine.

Insisting that it was unjust to accuse him of 'repudiating the divine transcendence altogether', he explained why he had been so circumspect when dealing with educated people. 'I cannot "tell" my patient. I have to seek him and I must learn his language and think his thoughts, until he knows that I understand him correctly. Then only is he ready to understand me and at the same time the strange language of the unconscious, that tells him of eternal truths, and incidentally he will discover that he has heard similar things before.'

The end of the war made it possible to revive the Bollingen Foundation, and Jung resumed contact with Paul and Mary Mellon. In September he wrote to tell her about his illness and to ask for some Granger pipe tobacco. Replying at great length in November, she said she wanted to publish a 'Library of Alchemy' and his complete works. She told him to stay as well as he could 'during this hard winter to come. I am sending you eleven pounds a week made up of butter, fats and sugar.'

His reply was mainly negative. He had promised the English-language rights to Herbert Read, he thought a 'Library of Alchemy' would be too uncommercial, and if she sent food parcels, he had to surrender ration points when collecting them from the post office. But he accepted her offer of a belated present for his seventieth birthday – a book by Paracelsus. 'From all I could find out about it,' she wrote, 'it is a very rare book, containing 10 parts to the British Museum's 4 . . . It comes to you with my great love.' She was happy to be in touch again, and to have a publishing connection. In a postscript she wrote: 'I can feel all through me how I will feel when I lay eyes on you again.'

The Mellons started negotiating with Kegan Paul to co-publish Jung's complete works in English on both sides of the Atlantic. Herbert Read said his company could not commit itself to the project without financial guarantees from the USA and it was agreed that Bollingen would pay all the expenses of translating and editing the books. Jung wanted Michael Fordham to be editor-in-chief, and Mary, who was planning to attend the 1946 Eranos Conference, suggested a meeting there with Jung, Read and her associate editor, John Barrett, an elegant young man who had invested in the Madison Avenue art gallery owned by John Becker, who had given her her first job.

But on 17 July she cabled Jung to say that after consulting the *I Ching*, she had decided against coming to Ascona. Severe asthma attacks had put a strain on her heart. In October 1946 she and Paul were returning from a hunt when another attack started. The atomiser she used for relief had been broken. She was taken home and put to bed, but a new attack overstrained her heart, and she died. She was forty-two.

Thirty-Four

Call Me C.G.

Forced to stay inside neutral Switzerland throughout the war, Jung had felt impatient to travel, but at the beginning of 1946, he was not well enough to risk a long journey. 'My cardiac infarct has left me with a lasting scar and a corresponding low cardiac performance.' Recovering slowly, he had to push his correspondence 'very much into the background so as not to overload myself'.

His daily routine revolved around two hours of work in the morning, 'and in the afternoon a rest plus a visitor'. But he was well enough to go sailing again, and to exercise. He swam in the lake at seven in the morning, and went out twice a day for a forty-five-minute walk. Another form of exercise was gardening. In Switzerland, as in Britain, food rationing did not end with the end of the war, and in the spring of 1946, the bread ration was reduced to 250 grams a day. Jung, who had been growing potatoes, beans and corn, went on digging his potato patch, as well as growing wheat and poppies.

He did not complete his work on *Mysterium Coniunctionis* until 1954, and it is not surprising that, written over fourteen years at a length of six hundred pages, it sometimes loses momentum. Drawing on his wide reading of mystical texts from different cultures and periods, he found the same motifs, patterns and polarities often recurred. He compared alchemical symbols with symbols from classical mythology, folklore, the Kabbalah and writings of the Church Fathers.

He agreed with Herbert Silberer that the *coniunctio* or union of opposites was the 'central idea' of the alchemists. Even when they spoke of 'uniting' iron and copper or sulphur and mercury, the formation of an amalgam was partly symbolical. 'Iron was Mars and copper was Venus, and their fusion was at the same time a love affair.' Substances seemed hermaphroditic, and they had a numinous quality.

Success in combining them had produced an active principle, sulphur, and a passive principle, salt, as well as a mediating principle – mercury or

Mercurius. The union can occur only through a medium: Mercurius is the soul that mediates between body and spirit. In this trinity, the supreme opposition is between male and female, and a totality can be produced only by their synthesis – not by the quaternity of the four elements, earth, air, fire and water. Far from being just the medium of conjunction, Mercurius also consists of what is being joined. He is the essence or 'seminal matter' of man and woman.

In the beginning, God had created one world – *unus mundus* – but he divided it into heaven and Earth. In *Physica Trismegisti*, the sixteenth-century alchemist Gerhard Dorn had described the bond of matrimony as 'the medium enduring until now in all things, partaking of both their extremes, without which it cannot be at all, nor they without this medium be what they are, one thing out of three.'

This made it clear – to Jung – that Mercurius was identical with the *unus mundus*, 'the original non-differentiated unity of the world or of Being . . . the primordial unconscious. The Mercurius of the alchemists is a person-ification and concretisation of what we today would call the collective unconscious.' The *coniunctio* was 'nothing less than a restoration of the original state of the cosmos and the divine unconsciousness of the world'. It was equivalent to the union of yin and yang in Tao.

Materialism and science had combined to produce a 'causalism' that made us want to gain knowledge by 'breaking everything down into individual processes'. This distracts us from the *unus mundus*, though J. B. Rhine's experiments in telepathy, clairvoyance and precognition had validated what Jung called the synchronistic principle. 'Events must possess an *a priori* aspect of unity.'

Jung, who felt a strong yearning for this paradisal unity, responded to Dorn's vision of a future in which the whole human being would merge with the *unus mundus*. He pictured a return to 'the potential world of the first day of creation when nothing was yet *in actu*, i.e. divided into two or many, but was still one . . . the eternal Ground of all empirical being, just as the self is the ground and origin of the individuality, past, present and future'.

This passion for the *unus mundus* helps to explain why Jung was so excited by the promulgation (in November 1950) of the dogma about the Virgin's bodily ascension. Calling it this 'the most important religious event since the Reformation', he saw it as a response to 'a deep longing in the masses for an intercessor and mediatrix who would at last take her place alongside the Holy Trinity'. Thanks to Pope Pius II, Mary was now 'functionally on a par with Christ, the king and mediator,' while Protestantism was left 'with the odium of being nothing but a *man's religion*, which allows no metaphysical representation of woman'.

The Assumption was 'really a wedding feast, the Christian version of the *heirosgamos*, whose originally incestuous nature played such a great role in alchemy. Traditional incest always indicated that the supreme union of opposites expressed a combination of things that are related but dissimilar.' For over a thousand years, by equating physicality with the feminine or passive principle, the alchemists had been preparing for the dogma of the Assumption of the Virgin, which was grounded neither in the Bible nor in the first five centuries of Christian tradition. The Pope had taken an 'irrevocable step beyond the confines of historical Christianity', and this was 'the strongest proof of the autonomy of archetypal images'.

Jung's thinking about consciousness had been altered by his closeness to death. There was no question now of denying that Jews had access to the same collective unconscious as everyone else. He was provoked into reformulating his ideas by a Protestant theologian who contended (in an essay) that the visions of Niklaus von der Flue must have come either from his unconscious or from a metaphysical God. No, said Jung, not his unconscious. The personal unconscious varies from man to man, but the collective unconscious 'is like the air, which is the same everywhere, is breathed by everybody and yet belongs to no one'. It was from this that 'everything psychic takes shape before it is personalised, modified, assimilated etc. by external influences'.

In the summer, Jung received a parcel of three books from a psychiatrist in Los Angeles, Fritz Künkel, a convert from Adlerian psychology to Jungian. The books were by Stewart Edward White, a prolific American who had progressed from adventure stories to *The Betty Book* (1937) and *Across the Unknown* (1939) which both recorded statements made by his wife, Betty, during trances. After her death, she communicated with him through a medium, as he explained during 1940 in *The Unobstructed Universe*. Jung read all three books 'conscientiously', and decided the last was 'really important', though 'written in a ghastly style'.

Two years later, in a foreword for the German translation, he contended that like dreams, the 'communications of "spirits" are *statements about the unconscious psyche* . . . *The Unobstructed Universe* may therefore be regarded as offering valuable information about the unconscious and its ways.' Betty, he declared, was the 'real begetter' of the book. While she was alive she had exerted 'educative' influence on everyone around her, and she was now striving, like other spirits, 'to develop man's consciousness and to unite it with the unconscious'. The beginnings of American spiritualism had 'coincided with the growth of scientific materialism', which showed that spiritualism 'in all its forms has a *compensatory* significance'.

The spirits 'favour an energic conception of the psyche', which tallies with the findings of analytical psychology, and 'the unobstructed universe' is the single cosmos formed by the combination of human consciousness with the Beyond. 'The dead are not in a different place from the living,' while 'the conscious and the unconscious psyche are one, but are separated by different amounts of energy. Science can agree with this statement.' Information from Betty confirmed 'the primitive view', in which 'the land of dreams is also the land of the dead and of the ancestors'.

Jung's letter to Künkel says Betty is 'more probably a spirit than an archetype', though 'archetypes can behave exactly like real spirits'. She was collaborating with Lady Anne, a sophisticated sixteenth-century Scotswoman who 'behaves towards Betty as the mother archetype (the Great Mother) behaves towards the ego in the psychology of women. She represents the feminine aspect of the self . . . If Betty were nothing but an anima, in the case of a man there would have to be a masculine figure corresponding to Anne, namely the Wise Old Man.'

It seems less likely that the Betty books modified Jung's ideas than that they made him less reluctant to discuss them. Writing later in the month about Kristine Mann, who had died in November 1945 at the end of an extremely painful illness, he says that if she had committed suicide,

> I would have thought that this was the right thing to do. As it was not the case, I think it was in her stars to undergo such a cruel agony . . . Our life is not made entirely by ourselves. The main bulk of it is brought into existence out of sources that are hidden to us. Even complexes can start a century or more before a man is born. There is something like karma.

In the hospital, three or four months before she died, she had seen a powerful light shining in her room. It left her with a lasting sense of peacefulness, and in Jung's opinion, her spirit left her body at the time of the vision. He was no longer reluctant to hypothesise about what happens after death. 'As far we know at all there seems to be no immediate decomposition of the soul. One could almost say on the contrary.'

In November 1946, Jung talked on the BBC's Third Programme about 'The Fight with the Shadow'. He had used the tern *shadow* in his 1937 lectures at Yale, arguing that people are morally worse than they imagine. 'Everyone carries a shadow, and the less it is embodied in the individual's conscious life, the blacker and denser it is . . . If it is repressed and isolated from consciousness, it never gets corrected, and is liable to burst forth suddenly in a moment of unawareness.'

In the broadcast he said Hitler 'represented the shadow, the inferior part of everybody's personality, in an overwhelming degree'. He was 'the most prodigious personification of all human inferiorities. He was an utterly incapable, unadapted, irresponsible, psychopathic personality, full of empty infantile fantasies, but cursed with the keen intuition of a rat or guttersnipe.'

Jung had brought out a book titled *Essays on Contemporary Events: Reflections on Nazi Germany*. It contained his 1936 essay 'Wotan' and a 1941 lecture on 'Psychotherapy Today', together with his more recent denunciations of Hitler, and a new introduction. His object was to show he had never been anti-Semitic or pro-Nazi. Writing to Mary Mellon, he had revealed more than he intended when he explained that 'Freudian Jews in America' had accused him of being a Nazi. 'This rumour has been spread over the whole world . . . It is however difficult to mention the anti-Christianism of the Jews after the horrible things that have happened in Germany. But Jews are not so damned innocent after all – the role played by the intellectual Jews in prewar Germany would be an interesting object of investigation.'

Jung had another serious heart attack in November, but instead of being taken into hospital, he convalesced at home. Of the many letters he received from well-wishers, none moved him more than one from Victor White, who was praying for him and sent gramophone records. Still in bed, Jung wrote in pencil: 'Dear Father White, Thank you for your dear letter . . . The *aspectus mortis* is a mighty lonely thing when you are stripped of everything in the presence of God. One's wholeness is tested mercilessly.'

Medication was disorienting him. 'An accumulation of drugs however necessary, has made a complete mess of myself. I had to climb out of that mess and I am now whole again . . . I am no more a black and endless sea of misery.' But he was feeble, and uncertain how long he could survive.

> Death does not seem imminent, though an embolism can occur anytime again. I confess I am afraid of a long drawn-out suffering. It seems to me as if I am ready to die, although as it looks to me some powerful thoughts are still flickering like lightnings in a summer night. Yet they are not mine, they belong to God . . . Please write again to me. You have a purity of purpose which is beneficial.

In White's next letter, Jung was invited to call him Victor, and he responded: 'I hope you will reciprocate by calling me C.G. which is the current designation of my unworthy "paucity". '

By the spring of 1947 he was inclined to blame the second heart attack on tension between practical work with patients and 'creative scientific work'. After all, he had only a limited amount of creative energy. To Eleanor Bertine, before she came to Switzerland, he wrote:

> I am no longer capable of delving into the mysteries of your private psychology, as the remnant of my creative power has to be reserved for my own use . . . And when you do analysis you have to do it by application of your creativeness . . . In my illness I found that there was a mountain of thoughts which I should get into shape and of which I hadn't known that they existed. I'm not trying to catch up with my unconscious fertility. I have a feeling as if I were the ancestral mother of the rabbits.

The heart attack, he calculated, had cost him 'a tidy half year'. By mid-April he was feeling 'almost as well as I did before my illness', but he did not want to see John Layard, who arrived in Zurich, eager to resume what had been interrupted by the war. Told he would have to wait six months between each session with Jung, Layard settled for sessions with Jolande Jacobi, Carl Meier and Liliane Frey.

Impatient to do analytical work of his own, he started what he described as 'a big illegal practice' with other people who were 'lying around all over Zurich'. After settling there because of Jung, they had been frustrated because he was too old, too ill and too busy to give them enough time, and because he was reluctant to discuss personal problems. His reputation had gone on growing as his stamina and patience dwindled, while his early homosexual trauma still made it harder for him to accept a strong transference from a man than from a woman. Layard was one of those who suffered from this resistance to transference.

Yielding to persuasion from Emma, Jung finally agreed to see the desperate Englishman every day for ten days on condition they had no psychological discussion. They sat in deck chairs, and so far as Layard could remember afterwards, Jung did nothing but praise himself and attack Freud. Before they had met ten times, Jung announced: 'This is the last time I shall see you.'

It was probably Jung who suggested that the scholar Gershon Scholem, an expert on Jewish mysticism, should be invited to the Eranos Conference in the summer of 1947. Having heard that Jung had sympathised with the Nazis, Scholem consulted his friend Rabbi Leo Baeck about whether to go.

Baeck, who had met Jung at Keyserling's School of Wisdom in Darmstadt, had heard rumours to the same effect, and on his first visit to Zurich after being released from the concentration camp at Theresienstadt, he refused an invitation to call on Jung. But when Jung came to his hotel, they talked for two hours. According to Scholem:

> Jung defended himself by an appeal to the special conditions in Germany but at the same time confessed to him: 'Well, I slipped up' – probably referring to the Nazis and his expectations that something great might after all emerge . . . Baeck said that in this talk they cleared up everything that had come between them and that they parted from one another reconciled again.

Scholem then accepted the invitation to Eranos, and Baeck, who went too, stayed with Jung in Küsnacht for two weeks in 1947.

John Mellon and John Barrett had come to the conference, and on 25 August, after a session of bargaining, Jung secured a royalty of 15 per cent on the first five thousand copies, and 20 per cent on the rest. He signed the contract for the co-publication of his collected works in English by Kegan Paul and the Bollingen Press. Wanting a native German-speaker to be editorially involved, he proposed Gerhard Adler, and it was agreed that Read, Fordham and he should be co-editors.

Mellon and Barrett went on to London for a meeting with Read, Fordham and Adler. The six of them agreed that the translator would be Richard Hull, a former medical student who had turned to journalism and poetry. During the thirties he had lived in Munich and translated Rilke. The decision was taken without consulting Jung, who might have proposed Barbara Hannah for the job. She had completed a translation of *Psychology and Alchemy*, which was the book Jung wanted to appear first in the English series. When he heard that Hull had been chosen, he wrote angrily to Fordham, saying he wanted to be consulted in future before any decisions were made.

Soon after finishing the first translation, Hull was taken into hospital with a severe attack of anterior poliomyelitis paralysing both arms and both legs. He was kept in hospital for eight months but, while lying on his back, started dictating the next translation, *The Psychology of Transference*, to his wife. When Jung read a chapter of his *Psychology and Alchemy* translation, he preferred it to Barbara Hannah's, which he found 'awkward', but she was retained as consultant.

Six days before Christmas, Jung wrote to Victor White about his reluctance to start work on the book that would eventually be called *Aion*. It was only after he had written the first twenty-five pages that 'it began to dawn on me that Christ – not the man but the divine being – was my secret goal. It came to me as a shock, as I felt utterly unequal to the task.'

But he was encouraged by a dream in which his small fishing boat was sunk, and a giant provided 'a new, beautiful seagoing craft about twice the size of the my former boat . . . My further writing led me to the archetype of the God-man and to the phenomenon of synchronicity which adheres to the archetype.'

He went on to describe another dream about three priests. One of them had a remarkable library. Doing some kind of military service, Jung had to sleep in a barracks where each bed had to accommodate two men, and he had to share one with 'a most venerable looking, very old man with white locks and a long flowing white beard. He offered me graciously one half of the bed and I woke up when I was just slipping into it.' This echoed a much earlier dream about declining to share a bed with an old man.

Replying at the end of December, White said he would 'not dare to comment'. Though he had clear ideas about the dream, he kept them to himself. But his next letter described a vision that brought him misgivings about his reticence. It was about sharing a meal with Jung on a Friday. Asked to pass him the fish, White replied: 'Hell! YOU don't have to eat fish today.' Jung did not answer, but looked disappointed, reproachful and ill.

Interpreting this to mean it was wrong to hold back from offering spiritual advice to his non-Catholic friend, the priest for once took the risk of being gently critical: 'There is one thing you have written which has rather worried me, and more so since I have come to know and love you personally. (Permit me to be quite frank about it.)'

Jung had written about the stoicism Protestants need to handle their sense of sin with no help from confession or ritual. Without mentioning that Jung was in the same position, White reminded him that consolation was not the only function of absolution and ritual. Was there not an element of arrogance in the Protestants' belief that they needed no help when coming to terms with their sins? Aristotle had written: 'The solitary man is either a beast or a god.'

Friendlier than White's other letters to Jung, this one was more out-spoken. They had reached a point at which their friendship could grow closer, but Jung withdrew into silence, as he often had during his corre-spondence with Freud. He let four months go by without writing to White, and then, instead of confronting the main issue, he explained that for him, faith was a matter of having great respect for all the major religions, including Christianity. 'I feel the same kind of respect for the basic teachings of Buddhism and the fundamental Taoist ideas.' Rebuffed by the long silence, White must have been saddened by this letter that put Buddhism and Taoism on the same level as Christianity.

As the world acclimatised itself to the return of peace, more Americans and Britons arrived in Zurich, eager to make contact with Jung, but, now in his seventies, he did not have the stamina to resume the seminars in English, and he could neither involve newcomers in the activities of the club nor pass them on to his collaborators.

In 1946 Jolande Jacobi suggested that what was needed was some kind of institute, but Jung resisted the idea. The alternative proposed at a general meeting of the club was that a bureau should be set up to organise lectures and social events. Toni Wolff and Carl Meier proposed that Jolande Jacobi should be in charge, but she was unpopular, and a petition was drawn up asking for a second meeting.

When this was held, Jung, who enjoyed springing surprises, surprised everyone by arguing that a bureau would not be enough. What was needed was an institute. He told Jacobi his only objection to a C. G. Jung Institute was that it gave too much prominence to his name. 'It is not easy to get accustomed to the thought that "C. G. Jung" designates not merely my private person but something objective as well.'

Asked why he was no longer opposed to the idea of an institute, he said: 'They would start one between my death and my funeral in any case, so I think it is better to do so while I can still have some influence on its form.' His capitulation was consistent with an old Chinese maxim he often quoted: 'Say what you think *once*, and if no one listens, retire to your estates.'

The functions of the institute, as outlined in a booklet that was printed, would be teaching, training and research. A full-time training would be provided for future analysts, who would be given lectures, seminars and a training analysis. Jung appointed the first board of directors, which included Jacobi, Liliane Frey, Carl Meier and the analyst Ludwig Binswanger. The lecturers would include Emma and Toni. Before classes started in the Gemeindestrasse building during April 1948, thirteen students were accepted, all British or American, and it was agreed that the teaching was to be in English.

In his opening address on 24 April, Jung named 1912 as the year he discovered the collective unconscious. That was the year he met black psychotics in Washington. He paid tribute to Richard Wilhelm, Heinrich Zimmer, the Hungarian expert on myth Karl Kerényi, Victor White and J. B. Rhine, as well as to Carl Meier, Toni Wolff, Jolande Jacobi, Marie-Louise von Franz and others.

At the celebration banquet, which was held in one of Zurich's old guildhalls, Jung said that whenever he wanted long hours of introversion, he made Limburger cheese dressing. Talking about the relationship of women and men to Eros and Logos, he said: 'Damn it, woman *is* Eros, *is* relationship, *is* the secret mystery! If she doesn't live that, she is nothing. And man must have the adventurous mind. Or what is he?' All we have to give the world and God is ourselves as we really are. 'Most of us want others to do it for us, to carry us along. Jesus crucified was a man fully carrying his own serpent side.'

The youngest of the students was a shy twenty-seven-year-old American, Robert Johnson, who was allocated Jolande Jacobi as his analyst. In her aggressive way, she responded to one of his dreams by saying it belonged to a much older man, and he had no right to dream it. Annoyed, he gave up the analysis, and asked for an hour with Emma.

After listening to his account of the dream, she said little, but the next day he was summoned to Küsnacht, where Jung took him into the garden and talked for nearly three hours. Johnson, whom he had never previously met, said almost nothing, but he was told what to do with the rest of his life. He should spend most of his time alone, never join any groups, have a room that he used exclusively for inner work. Nothing else mattered. The collective unconscious would protect him, and he need do nothing in life except contribute to its evolution. Of the four elements in the dream, one was less developed than the others, and Jung was emphatic about the importance of making the trinity into a quaternity.

Johnson felt at home with Jung, who seemed to be, like him, an introverted feeling type. 'Only later when I was with him in groups of people did I learn that he was quite different from me in type and that his gift to me was in leaving his own natural typology and engaging me in my own.'

Johnson went on to found a retreat centre near San Diego and to run it. With the righteous ruthlessness of a prophet, Jung had taken charge of his life without even letting him talk. Emma's account of the dream had sufficed to tell him which commandment he must pass on from the collective unconscious.

Many of the other students, naturally, wanted an audience with the great man, and Toni Wolff told them: 'One can ask for anything one wants if one can take No as an answer.' Some of them were waiting for him on the patio in Küsnacht, 'when around the corner of the house came a handsome, tall, robust man, dressed in old clothes, a straw hat on the back of his head, shirt sleeves rolled up and carrying a hoe. There he was . . . My first feeling was – This is what it means to be a human being.' This was the reaction of a young American, Luella Sibbald, who later spent an hour with him. She went into the room knowing what she wanted to talk about, and though he was the one who set the agenda, she later wrote: 'What his words set in motion that day has been central since then.'

Jung could do something almost indescribable, validating a part of the self that was hard to develop and impossible to discard. Laurens van der Post, a South African soldier, explorer and writer who spent a formative period with the San Bushmen of the Kalahari, had what he called a ' "dreaming" area of myself which I had carried about with me for forty years'. When he met Jung, he felt that he was coming into contact not just with a set of ideas and not just with another man who had visited Africa, but with 'what Jung was in himself . . . He had a genius for propinquity.' Van der Post felt reassured: he had been right to have faith in the dreaming area.

By the end of his seventy-first year, Jung had started thinking more about mortality. 'I realise now very often that I am doing a certain thing for the last time . . . It has happened for the first time that I could not plant my potatoes and my corn any more and weed has overgrown my piece of black earth as if its owner were no more.'

His fragility increased his pessimism about the postwar world. 'Switzerland has become an island of dreams amidst ruins and putrefaction. Europe is a rotting carcass. Towards the end of the Roman Empire they made attempts and had insights similar to mine.'

In June 1948, not long before his seventy-third birthday, Esther Harding, who had last seen him before the war, found he had aged – his face was 'a little thinner, with harder lines and planes, throwing the width and height of the head into greater prominence. Hair a little thinner, softly wispy around his head. He spoke of it, calling it his "feathers". "Yes, my head is growing feathers. But the barber won't cut it." '

He still liked wearing leather shorts, and a woman in a group invited to tea on the terrace during the summer of 1948 afterwards remembered almost nothing about Emma, who spoke quietly in the background with one of the older women. But Jung still had star quality. 'Smoking a pipe, he came out of the house with vigorous motion, and sat, centre stage, as though with a friendly purpose'. 'Fully at home in his energetic body full of intention,' he was 'dynamic and virile, focused and aware. I liked his defying the stereotypes of age; I liked his bare knees and his open readiness to attend to what we had to say . . . I think all of us there felt a little more alert and dramatic in his presence.'

At the beginning of September, Victor White came to stay at Bollingen, and while he was there, Jolande Jacobi called. She was with Jung when the priest came out, bringing tea. Seeing a small man wearing spectacles, a big hat, a jersey, striped shorts, sandals and no socks, Jacobi asked: 'Since when have you a valet?'

Later in the month, when White wrote to him, Jung did not reply, but in mid-December, he complained it was a long time since he had heard from the priest: 'I confess to have a feeling as if when you were in America a door had been shut, softly but tightly.' White wrote again, and Jung apologised for his oversight. 'That's how the inferior function behaves.'

It seemed to him at the beginning of 1949 that the main reason for the ups and downs in his health was that he did not 'know what one can or cannot do when one will soon be 74 . . . Twice a day I have to tell myself: not too much! Snail's pace and a rest in between and a change of snail-horses . . . I am like an old car with 250,000 km on its back but unable to shake off the memory of its 20 horsepower.'

Hesitating about whether to write a foreword for the English translation of Richard Wilhelm's version of the *I Ching*, he decided to consult the book. According to tradition, it was the mysterious intervention of spiritual agencies that made the yarrow sticks or coins fall in a meaningful way, and he questioned it 'as one questions someone before introducing him to friends: one asks whether or not this would be agreeable to him.' It directed him to the fiftieth hexagram, the Cauldron. The food contained in this ritual vessel is to be understood as spiritual nourishment, and he interpreted the text to mean the *I Ching* felt undervalued. Perhaps the English translation and his foreword could help to bring it the honour it deserved.

What he most relished was the escape it offered from the preoccupation with causality. The Chinese seemed more concerned with 'the configuration formed by chance events at the moment of observation'. He often consulted the book, and described himself as 'a jealous lover of the *I Ching*'. He believed in it as '*the* book that teaches you your own way and the all-importance of it. Not in vain has the book been the secret treasure of the sages.' 'It is always right,' he said. He considered the possibility of writing a commentary, and decided not to, but his foreword was crucial in popularising the *I Ching*. In Wilhelm's translation it sold better than any of the other books published by Princeton University Press. It was thanks to Jung that it became popular and influential in the West, regularly consulted by thousands of people.

He often reissued and revised earlier publications. The history of one essay is especially revealing – 'The Significance of the Father in the Destiny of the Individual'. In the 1908 version he explained that early ideas of divine figures derived from children's feelings about their father, and that this relationship was basically sexual. 'In essence,' he concluded, 'our biographical destiny is identical with the destiny of our sexuality.'

When the essay was reissued in 1927, fourteen years after his break with Freud, he left the text unchanged. 'Nothing in it is actually wrong,' he wrote in his foreword to the new edition, 'merely too simple, too naive.' But at the end of 1948, preparing the third edition, he made substantial changes. No longer interested in sexuality as a factor in children's relationship with their parents, he thought archetypes shaped the destiny of the individual. The father's personality was unimportant, but the father archetype merged the imago of God with the images of the father and other paternal figures.

Still using the same four case histories to demonstrate that paternal power could be overwhelming, he now insisted it had its source in the archetypal base. It is the destiny of the individual to worship and obey the figure on whom he projects the idea of divine power. First it will be the biological father, later other father figures and a God imago. This is to disregard differences in personality – those, for instance, between a feeble father who prefers his wife to take all the decisions and a drunken bully (like Hitler's father) who terrorises both wife and children. Ideas of salvation were 'not rationalisations of a father-complex but archetypally preformed mechanisms for the development of consciousness'.

If Jung had once adored his father and later had a 'religious crush' on Freud, the archetypal transference must have been at work in both surges of emotion. For himself, as for other people, Jung tended to depersonalise personal history, shifting the focus away from individual characteristics and specific circumstances. 'Previously, the personality appeared to be unique, as if rooted in nothing,' he wrote, but he now believed in 'a general human precondition, the inherited and inborn biological structure which is the instinctual basis of every human being'. In political, social and economic history, as in personal relationships, everything could be explained in these terms. 'Provided for, and, as it were, imprinted on this inherited structure, every normal human situation has already occurred countless times in our long ancestral history.'

When students of the institute staged a cabaret during a banquet in a Zurich hotel, they mimicked their lecturers and analysts, reducing the audience to howls of laughter. Meier was ridiculed, and not even Emma was spared from the satire, but Jung was. This did not please him. 'But where am I? What is the matter with you? You don't dare to tease me in that way? That's awful!'

He had taken to using a gold-headed cane, and he now stayed in his chair when he lectured, standing up only to point with his stick at one of the diagrams displayed on a board or pinned to a wall. But he still gave the impression of being robust and energetic, and he was still tremendously popular with the students, unlike Toni Wolff. According to an American who studied at the institute for three years, she was unapproachable, and resembled 'a ghost-like figure, gaunt, haughty and forbidding. No smile ever crossed her face in class, in fact she betrayed no emotions of any kind. Questions were answered in clipped tones which made the questioner feel small, even stupid for having asked the question.'

Though some of the students liked her, most seem to have found her reserved, dignified and rather distant. She seemed taller than she was, wrote a young American woman, 'sitting ramrod straight behind her desk in what I remember as a rather high-backed chair . . . But despite her aristocratic bearing and her impeccably tailored clothes, Miss Wolff was one of the most down-to-earth practical human beings I've ever known.' Convinced, as

Jung was, that the collective unconscious is partly responsible for what we do, she was good at making patients feel less guilty about failure and less vain about success.

Many patients regarded her as the best analyst they ever had, even when Jung was one of the others. Returning to Zurich after an absence of twelve years, Joe Wheelwright 'went to Toni like a homing pigeon. I sat down in her consulting room, took one look at her, sitting with her feet on the pillow that she used as a footstool, and her long fingers holding her long cigarette holder, and burst into uncontrollable sobbing.' She let about ten minutes go by before she asked: 'What is it?' and by the end of the analytical hour, he felt he was again in control of his life. But he also found her status had been affected by the existence of the institute: 'She was no longer the leading figure in the analytic community.'

In June 1948, the Bollingen Foundation had donated a thousand dollars to set up an annual poetry prize. The Library of Congress's Fellows in American Letters were appointed to act as judges, and it was announced in February 1949 that the first prizewinner was Ezra Pound, who was currently incarcerated in St Elizabeth's Hospital, Washington. Charged with disseminating propaganda on behalf of the enemy during the war, he had been found insane.

Though Jung had nothing to do with the judges' decision, he was attacked during June 1949 in the *Saturday Review of Literature*, which said he had been actively pro-Fascist and had been involved in a conspiracy to inaugurate 'a new authoritarianism'.

In the public controversy that ensued, the American journalist Dorothy Thompson sided with him. She wrote to him in September, condemning the 'mendacity and malice' of his critics. Replying, he expatiated on his rather muddled political forebodings. 'Russia is certainly on the warpath, and it is only fear of those who are in the know that is holding her back.' Any country that accumulated weapons would be tempted to use them, but 'we should not even try to overcome Russia, because we would destroy ourselves, since Russia is – as it were – identical with our unconscious, which contains our instincts and all the germs of our future development.' The underlying problem was 'the development of science and technology, which has destroyed man's metaphysical foundation'.

It was on grounds of strategy, not principle, that he was opposed to using the bomb. 'But what are you going to do with that mass mentality of the leaders, mostly downright criminals or lunatics (of the reasonable variety. Particularly dangerous!)? How could you deal with Hitler? Well it is the same with Russia. Nothing short of the atom bomb will register there.'

Thirty-Five

Jesus and Satan Are Brothers

In the Küsnacht house, at the end of October 1949, Emma, who was sixty-four, slipped on a carpet and fell, causing a serious fracture in her right shoulder. She had to stay in hospital for about two months, and life became increasingly difficult for Jung, who succumbed to gastric flu while his secretary Marie-Jeanne Schmid was ill. When he turned to Ruth Bailey for help, she gladly came to stay in the house and look after him. Since 1925, after their meeting in Africa, she had been coming to spend at least part of every summer in the house, except during the war.

By now, his relationship with Toni had cooled, and he did not try to hide this from Ruth. Toni came to have tea at the Küsnacht house regularly on Wednesdays, 'and to begin with they used to have it in the library, the two of them, and then when it was summer and I was there, and Emma was in hospital, they used to have it in the garden.' Soon, he no longer wanted to be left alone with Toni. One day he told Ruth to stay and have tea with them. 'And I thought "Oh my goodness," I didn't know what to do. He said, "You pour out for us." And then when we finished tea and we were talking, he got out his little paperback book and started to read it and didn't take any notice of her. I felt ever so sorry for her. I thought that was awful.' And after Toni had gone, Ruth told Jung off for his bad manners.

One evening, she was playing cards with him in the drawing room when Toni arrived. Just as 'the door slid back she heard me say, "You are an old cheat, CG. You cheat. You wouldn't play with us in England, we wouldn't have you cheating like that." And the door was hastily shut, and she disappeared. To say this to God was terrible, wasn't it? . . . I blundered in where angels feared to tread because out it came, and, of course, that was what he liked – he roared with laughter.' According to Aniela Jaffé, he also cheated when playing patience. 'It had to come out right.'

Jaffé and Ruth did not like each other, but Jung enjoyed Ruth's company. He loved sailing, and Emma, who did not, encouraged Ruth to go with him. At first she was scared of pulling the wrong rope, and he was apt to start shouting when he lost his temper, but, better than most people at standing up to him, she said: 'God, I won't be your cabin boy any more.'

He did most of the cooking, making Emma and Ruth prepare the vegetables. The docile Emma always obeyed instructions unquestioningly; but Ruth was more liable to argue. Toni Wolff was no good at assisting him when he was cooking. One evening he sent her into the garden for a few chives to be sprinkled on the soup. She came back with enough to fill a large bowl, and his rage reduced her to tears.

In the paper 'Some Bearings of Religion on Analytical Psychology', which he wrote in 1942, three years before meeting Jung, Victor White had already voiced misgivings about his attitude to the problem of evil. While agreeing with Jung that the devil should not be ignored, White denied that this tendency was 'something endemic to original and authentic Christianity itself', and took Jung to task for assuming that Christianity had fulfilled its historic function and outlived its usefulness. 'The mistake would seem to be largely due to a failure to grasp the real significance of the definition of evil, found in many Christian philosophers, as "the privation of good". So far from implying, as Jung seems to suppose a denial of the reality of evil, it precisely supposes it, and confirms his own conception of the opposites.' The Catholic doctrine of *privatio boni* is that evil, unlike goodness, has no substance or reality of its own. It consists merely of the absence of goodness. But Jung believed that evil had existed before man, who could therefore not be blamed for it.

Disagreement over the problem of evil is older than Christianity. If the whole universe was created by God, evil was either created by him or created subsequently by some other mighty force. And if God is omnipotent, omniscient and perfect, why did He either create it or tolerate its existence after making His creatures so vulnerable to it? The story about Eve and the apple sidesteps the question of why an all-knowing God failed to give his creatures enough willpower to resist the temptations He knew they would encounter. If He was the designer of human flesh, he designed the carnal pleasures that were going to be irresistibly attractive.

Plotinus, the third-century founder of Neoplatonism, was a contemplative who ignored Christianity and tried to achieve contact through personal goodness with a supreme principle, the One or Good, which is beyond being, the highest of three universal principles or *hypostases*. The next is Intellect, and the third is Soul. Just as the sun emanates light, he believed, everything that has power must exert it by emanating something less powerful, and the goodness that is emanated by the One becomes weaker as is moves downwards and outwards into being. The thing that has no residue of good in it is matter. Matter is evil, but that does not mean evil is a substance, as it was for Mani. For Plotinus evil is the consequence of manifestation and distance from the Good.

The idea of *privatio boni* was evolved in the fourth century by Augustine as he made his way from Manichean dualism into Christianity. Influenced by Plotinus, he contended that everything God makes is good – for a thing to be bad is for it 'to fall away from being and tend to a state in which it is not'. Evil is neither a substance nor a force, but it comes into existence when something goes wrong with what God created.

The orthodox Christian cannot deviate from the idea that God is wholly good. Gnosticism and Manicheism were heretical, and it could be argued that Jung and White should both have known they would always be at loggerheads over the problem of evil. But it is easy to see how much they both wanted to find a way of compromising, or at least agreeing to disagree. It was not merely that they liked and admired each other. They both believed passionately that the church could not function adequately in the modern world unless it caught up with modern psychology.

The fifth chapter of Jung's *Aion* (the word is the Greek for *aeon*; the book is about archetypes and symbols in the Christian aeon) is titled 'Christ, a Symbol of the Self', and the first sentence compares the eschatological events foretold in the New Testament with 'the dechristianisation of our world, the Luciferian development of science and technology and the frightful material and moral destruction caused by the Second World War'. In the Apocalypse predicted in the Book of Ezekiel and the Book of Revelations, the Antichrist will be in charge of the calamitous events that overtake us.

That Jung's thinking has been affected by conversations with White about *privatio boni* is evident from the way in which Christianity is arraigned for splitting the Christ symbol into a positive Christ and a negative Antichrist. Christ is still 'our culture hero' who 'embodies the myth of the divine Primordial Man, the mystic Adam', but the Christ image lacks wholeness when evil is funnelled off into the figure of the Antichrist. Failing to represent the psychological forces in the soul, Christian symbolism gives too little help to the believer striving to achieve wholeness by integrating the opposites.

Wolfgang Pauli later objected that the chapter which deals with *privatio boni* leaves out

everything that seems to me important and interesting about the idea of *privatio*. (Apparently it is to him uninteresting and unimportant.) The impression is given that *privatio boni* is an early Christian invention

(Bizarrely, Plotinus is not even mentioned in this context!) while the opposite is true, that the concept of *privatio* is very old and the doctrine of *privatio boni* grew organically into later Platonism.

Pauli arrived by a different route from Jung's at his rejection of the doctrine.

Reviewing the Eranos yearbooks of 1947 and 1948 in *Dominican Studies*, White accused Jung of confusion and 'quasi-Manichean dualism'. The 'great scientist' had been making an 'infelicitous excursion . . . outside his orbit'. His 'neo-gnosticism' was 'a regression to a bygone immaturity and one with which the genuine achievements and discoveries of scientific depth-psychology need and should have nothing to do, except perhaps as an escapist disease which calls for cure.'

On New Year's Eve, Jung wrote a long and affable letter to White, saying 'I guess I am a heretic,' and in a letter of 4 May 1950, White conceded that their argument about evil had 'reached deadlock'.

By the spring of 1950, Jung knew Emma was dying slowly of cancer, but she did not know. In March they took a fortnight's holiday together, staying at a small hotel in Ascona, the Casa Tamaro. Wanting to meet him, Buffie Johnson, who was working on a book called *Great Goddess and Her Sacred Animals*, was invited to the hotel. Told they were in the lounge, she peeped through the curtains on the glass door to see them reading together.

He was now seventy-five and she was sixty-five. In the mornings the three of them went for walks along the quay by the lake, and the Jungs 'seemed to be very much at peace with each other'. At teatime they regularly received visitors from Zurich. In the evenings the three of them sat in the lounge. It was Jung who did most of the talking, and his favourite subject was his experiences in Africa.

Paying his first visit to the Eranos Conference in the summer of 1950, the historian of religion Mircea Eliade found that Olga Fröbe-Kapteyn did not provide enough food for her guests. Most of them were resigned to feeling hungry most of the time they were there, but he heard that someone had sent the Jungs a cooked chicken, which they had secretly devoured.

She was more generous in providing drink, and one evening when they were in a merry state, Jung flirted with her, pronouncing a mysterious formula as he put one of his rings on her finger. It was inscribed ABRAXAS. In the morning she grumbled that he, as a psychiatrist, should have done nothing to increase her dependence on him. 'I did not do it,' he answered. 'It was my Self that did it.'

At the conferences, the beauty of the scenery, the convivial atmosphere and the flow of drink combined to induce a relaxation that sometimes made it hard for guests to control aggressive impulses. Jung and Herbert Read had often disagreed vehemently about Picasso and modern art, but the closest they came to quarrelling was in August 1952, when Read was lecturing at Eranos and Jung, who had never enjoyed listening passively, behaved as he sometimes did at the club when he was in the audience at a lecture. Read became aware of a sound like growling in the middle of the auditorium. It became more thunderous, and then Jung started yelling in German: 'That's mine . . . That's yours . . . That's mine.' Accusing Read of plagiarism, he eventually stood up and stamped out of the room. He went upstairs, and angry pacing could be heard for some time on the floor of the room above.

Their friendship survived, and Read went on editing Jung's collected works, but the argument about modern art continued. Jung was less interested in looking at individual works by contemporary artists than in diagnosing an unhealthy tendency towards fragmentation. Picasso, in his view, misunderstood

the primordial urge, which does not mean a field of ever so attractive looking and alluring shards, but a new world, after the whole has crumpled up . . . The great problem of our time is the fact that we don't understand what is happening to the world. We are confronted with the darkness of our soul, the Unconscious. It sends up dark and unrecognisable urges.

Jung had introduced his concept of synchronicity during 1930 in his obituary for Richard Wilhelm, and in February 1933, writing to a German pastor, had affirmed his conviction that 'a door exists to a quite different order of things from the one we encounter in our empirical world of consciousness . . .' Present in the deeper layers of the unconscious were 'things that cast doubt on the indispensable categories of our conscious world, namely time and space'. Eight weeks later, in another letter to the same pastor, he mentioned 'a (scientifically unknown) factor that evidently has the tendency to realise itself in human life'. But he remained silent about synchronicity until 1951, when he made it the subject of his Eranos lecture.

He might not have maintained this silence for so long if Wolfgang Pauli had stayed in Switzerland, but he was working in the USA at the Institute for Advanced Study in Princeton. On the other hand, the silence might have lasted even longer if Pauli had not returned to Zurich after winning the Nobel Prize in 1945: he not only encouraged Jung to write about synchronicity but collaborated. Titled 'Synchronicity: An Acausal Connecting Principle', Jung's main statement on the subject was published in a 1952 book, *The Interpretation of Nature and the Psyche*, which couples it with an essay by Pauli, 'The Influence of Archetypal Ideas on the Scientific

Theories of Kepler'. A German mathematician and astronomer whose life spanned the end of the sixteenth and the beginning of the seventeenth century, Kepler made important formulations about planetary movement, and Pauli believed that the symbol of the trinity had dominated his ideas and his belief in the three-dimensionality of space, while quaternity had been the principal motif in the thought of his English contemporary, the alchemist Robert Fludd. Quaternity suggested the possibility of a fourth dimension, and in Pauli's view, the relationship between space and time had been seriously misunderstood.

Before the book was published and for the next five years, Pauli read drafts of what Jung wrote on the subject, and made suggestions. Not altogether happy with the word *synchronicity*, Pauli preferred to speak of 'meaningful correspondences [*Sinnkorrespondenzen*] under the influence of an archetypal, acausal ordering'.

In their different ways, he and Jung were both interested in the analogy between synchronicity and radioactivity. Pauli wrote:

> A radioactive substance creates a gaseous substance throughout the laboratory. So too does a synchronicity spread out to many people . . . The radioactive phenomenon moves from an unstable initial condition of the atom to a stable end condition. By analogy, the synchronistic phenomenon as archetypally grounded goes from an unstable conscious condition to a stable one, with the unconscious in equilibrium as the synchronicity disappears.

Jung began to speak of archetypes as having a 'field of force' and to redefine them as transcendental ' "arrangers" of psychic forms inside and outside the psyche'. Pauli was exerting an influence both on his language and on his view of the archetype. In his foreword to Victor White's *God and the Unconscious*, he had written that the theologian and the empiricist 'appear to speak the same language', but it 'calls up in their minds two totally different fields of associations'. In a 1952 letter, he said: 'Our language is a faithful reflection of the psychic phenomenon with its dual aspect "perceptual" and "imaginary" . . . The language I speak must be ambiguous, must have two meanings in order to do justice to the dual aspect of our psychic nature. I strive quite consciously and deliberately for ambiguity of expression.' Only ambiguous language could do 'equal justice to the subjectivity of the archetypal idea and to the autonomy of the archetype'.

Thanks to Pauli, Jung's language was becoming less ambiguous and more scientific, though his thinking was shifting towards parapsychology. According to Max Planck's quantum theory, there is no smooth continuity in natural processes but a series of unpredictable jerks. The archetype, said Jung, was like a radioactive atom, except that it consisted of qualitative – not quantitative – relationships. What excited him most of all was the idea that the psyche and matter might be different aspects of the same reality, with archetypes as its governing principles.

Pauli's support would have been more valuable had he been more stable. There was little justification for the claim Jung had made in 1939 that, thanks to analysis, Pauli 'got into order again because he gradually accepted the symbolic data'. He still felt that his intellect and his emotions were pulling him in different directions. In a letter written during the summer of 1954, he said he was aware that having reached 'the limits of what might be knowable in the framework of contemporary knowledge', he had 'approached the realm of "magic" ' and risked 'a regression into most primitive superstition'.

Pauli was feeling insecure about his identity, and in his dreams, the same stranger kept challenging his right to go on working as he was. In 1949 he dreamed a conference on physics and mathematics was being held on the upper floors of a house where a course on cookery had been announced under his name. A fire broke out, and after escaping from the building, he found a taxi which was being driven by the stranger, who promised to take him where he belonged.

A year later, still dreaming about the stranger, he wrote to Emma Jung about him. Using Jungian terminology in a letter dated 16 November 1950, he explained the figure as both a bringer of higher knowledge and a spirit of nature. Unless what he said was accepted, he made himself 'known by every means such as synchronicities, depression or misunderstood affects . . . The stranger is the archetypal background constellated by the system of scientific concepts of our time . . . He is the preparer of the way of the quaternity, which he follows. Women and children follow him gladly, and he some-times teaches them.'

Using alcohol to ward off depression, Pauli sometimes lapsed into irrationality. One of Jung's favourite examples of synchronicity was a story in which a patient was describing a dream about a golden scarab when an insect rapped at the window and turned out to be a scarabaeid beetle – a common rose-chafer. Pauli contributed the suggestion that this incident might have occurred during an equinox. That, he said, was when most synchronicities occurred, and he improvised a 'thought experiment' in which the stranger appeared to Jung after the scarab incident and said: 'I congratulate you, doctor. You have finally succeeded in producing a radioactive substance. It will be exceptionally beneficial to the health of your patient.' The stranger then explained about radioactive decay and the 'rest activity' of radioactive substances.

In order to give himself more time for dreaming, Pauli was sleeping a lot, but though they sometimes seemed valuable, his dreams unsettled him, and he approached Marie-Louise von Franz, who had been helping him by doing translations from Latin. What he now wanted from her, he said, was a 'philosophical discussion' about his dreams. 'He made it clear that he did not want analysis; there was to be no payment. I saw that he was in despair, so I said we could try. The difficulties began when I asked him for the associations which referred to physics. He said, "Do you think I'm going to give you unpaid lessons in physics?" ' She thought it might be because he was 'too proud to admit he needed a real analysis' that he 'arrived at the conclusion that Jungian psychology should be transformed into a philosophy and not used as a framework for therapy'.

She had just turned thirty-six when Pauli wrote in January 1951 to say he had fallen in love with her. The stranger was in favour of their having a relationship, but nothing was going to be straightforward. In April he told her 'we should more entertain the *amor ccelestis* than the *amor vulgaris*'. These were the terms used by the fifteenth-century Italian philosopher Marsilio Ficino for spiritual and carnal love. Pauli was still too inhibited to risk either love or transference. In a postscript to the letter he wrote: 'I defend the thesis that the future of Jung's psychology does not lie in therapy and the hands of doctors, but in natural philosophy, that is to say it in any case leads to the Faculty of Philosophy.' He may have been trying to persuade himself that what felt like emotion thrown up by the unconscious was actually a problem that needed discussion in general terms.

To explain the kind of claim he wanted to make on her, he wrote down a piece of active imagination in which a Chinese woman, who represented the anima, took a ring from her finger, let it float in the air, and called it 'the ring i' – *i* signifying the imaginary element. 'The ring with the i,' he said, 'is the unity beyond particle and wave, and at the same time the operation that generates either of these.' He wanted it to symbolise love that united the couple in a process of individuation, but when she asked: 'What does the ring i mean to you?' he refused to give his associations.

Later, in a letter to Markus Fierz, Pauli said Jung appeared to agree that the future of his ideas lay not so much in therapy as in a 'unified holistic conception of nature and of the status of man within it', and that it was necessary to formulate a new definition of the archetype, which 'represents nothing other than the probability of psychic occurrences. It is to a certain extent the figurative given result of a psychic statistic.'

It seemed to Pauli that his needs and Jung's were complementary. 'More and more,' wrote Pauli, 'I see the key to the whole spiritual situation of our time in the psycho-physical problem.'

In work for publication Jung had usually avoided such terms as *fourth dimension* and *synchronicity*, but in the spring and summer of 1951, these ideas became central to his work. In May, while he was chiselling at an inscription, it occurred to him that 'consciousness is only an organ for perceiving the fourth dimension, i.e. the all-pervasive meaning, and itself produces no real ideas'. Jung had never felt more inclined to embrace this pre-Newtonian belief in a unitary world permeated by a coherent divine intention. It is consistent with the assumption that creative writing consists of taking dictation from the collective unconscious. Perhaps there was 'something like an "absolute knowledge" which is not accessible to consciousness, but probably is to the unconscious, though only under certain conditions'.

Jung's *Answer to Job* was written quickly, like the *Septem Sermones ad Mortuos*, but the ideas had been fermenting for a long time. 'This book has always been on my mind,' he told Mircea Eliade, 'but I waited forty years to write it. I was terribly shocked when, still a child, I read the Book of Job for the first time. I discovered that Yahweh is unjust, that he is even an evildoer.'

Using the word *counter-transference* for the 'highly charged emotional relationship to Christianity . . . which occurs within the context of his therapeutic designs' on it, Murray Stein sees Jung as both the analyst and 'the angry son who brutally confronts the Father with his own shortcomings. These are precisely the roles he played earlier with his own father and with Sigmund Freud and psychoanalysis.'

He often thought about the Book of Job, and in a letter to a clergyman at the end of 1945 he wrote: 'For every thinking man the question arises: What about God's omniscience? Above all, what about his morality? He dickers with the devil, allows himself to be hoodwinked and, out of sheer insecurity, torments the wretched Job . . . What does it mean when he calls on God to help him against God? And how does this conception of God square with the New Testament one?'

About a year before writing his *Answer to Job*, he dreamed that his father was a distinguished scholar. Opening a big Bible, the pastor started interpreting a passage so eruditely that neither Jung nor two other psychologists could follow. The pastor then led the way up a narrow staircase into a circular auditorium like Sultan Akbar's council hall. Offering to take his son into the highest presence, the pastor knelt to touch the floor with his forehead. Jung followed suit, but, less humble, left a space between his forehead and the floor.

In the spring of 1951, the critical gap widened while he was in bed with a liver disorder. He regarded his *Answer to Job* as 'a *tour de force* of the unconscious. It still goes on rumbling a bit, rather like an earthquake.'

'If there is anything like having the scruff of one's neck seized by the spirit, it was the way this book came into existence.' It condemns 'divine savagery and ruthlessness'. If God was omnipotent and omniscient, why did he make innocent people suffer? How can the modern Christian come to terms with 'the divine darkness that is unveiled' in the story of Job?

Jung took it that evil was something that had come into existence at a specific moment. Could man be held responsible for it, or had it been created it by God? The answer, could be found, he believed, in the Scriptures. ' "The Evil One" existed before man did as one of the "Sons of God" .' Jung took this to be a historical fact, and to be crucial. Ignoring all the references to Jesus as God's only son, he insists that he had an elder brother, Satan, who was a trickster. It may have been his idea to put a serpent into the Garden of Eden.

There are references in the Old Testament to the Messiah, but the name Jesus is of course never mentioned, and *Answer to Job* does not explain where Jung found this story about the brothers. But in 1955, three years after his book came out, he wrote a 'Prefatory Note' in a periodical, *Pastoral Psychology*, published in Great Neck, New York. Here he refers briefly to Clement of Rome, who 'taught that God rules the world with a right hand and a left hand, the right being Christ and the left Satan'. For a fuller explanation we must turn to the foreword Jung had written in March 1951 for R. J. Zwi Werblowsky's book *Lucifer and Prometheus* (London, 1952). In Clement, says Jung, 'we meet with the conception of Christ as the right hand and the devil as the left hand of God, not to speak of the Judaeo-Christian view which recognises two sons of God, Satan the older and Christ the younger.'

St Clement probably lived in the second half of the first century. According to tradition, he was a disciple of St Peter, and was the third or fourth bishop of Rome. The First Epistle of Clement is addressed to the church at Corinth, but Jung's reference to 'the Judaeo-Christian view' is misleading. The idea never found its way into the main tradition of Judaeo-Christian dogma.

In the Book of Job the 'Sons of God' are divine members of his heavenly assembly, but it is only in this book – not in the Old Testament as a whole – that Satan is given a coherent identity. The Hebrew word *satan* could refer to any human adversary or accuser, as it does in the books of Samuel and Kings. In Numbers it is used for the divine messenger sent to stop Balaam from cursing Israel.

Certainly the Book of Job presents God in an unfavourable light. It might have been useful to approach the text by trying to analyse the mentality and the motivation of the anonymous Israelite who wrote it. He bears a literary resemblance to the Marquis de Sade, whose novels are parables suggesting virtue is punished and vice rewarded, but Jung writes as if the events had actually occurred and as if they reveal the truth about Jahweh.

This is the Israelite name for God, and it frequently occurs in the Old Testament. Job, who seems to live in north Arabia, does not call God by this name, but Jung uses it for the Old Testament God, who described himself as jealous and took brutal revenge on the enemies of his chosen people. Out of respect for its holiness, the name Jahweh was not usually pronounced after about the third century BC. Readers of the Hebrew text usually substitute Adonai (Lord), and the artificially constructed name Jehovah makes its first appearance in Christian texts of the sixteenth century.

In the Book of Job, although Jahweh regards Job as 'perfect', he does not dismiss Satan's malicious allegations against him. Instead, Satan is allowed to test him with any suffering short of death. If Jahweh had chosen to 'consult his omniscience' – a phrase that often recurs in Jung's book – he would have known the accusations were groundless, but the innocent man is punished with a series of disasters. He loses his wife, his children, his servants, his wealth and his livestock. His skin erupts in ugly sores. Jahweh breaks at least three of his Ten Commandments, and often behaves as if he is not *compos mentis*. But instead of cursing him, and instead of believing the 'comforters' who say he would not have been punished if he had not sinned, Job confronts Jahweh's contradictory nature, and in this way gains the upper hand. As described in *Answer to Job*, his enlightenment resembles that of the young Jung, who understood that a God who shits on his own cathedral is not altogether benevolent.

But He is not immoral. All this is 'the behaviour of an unconscious being who cannot be judged morally'. It is naive, says Jung, to assume that the creator of the world knew what he was doing. He was not a conscious being. The 'nonsensical doctrine of the *privatio boni*' would never have been necessary if we had admitted that evil can emerge from 'divine unconsciousness and lack of reflection'. In *Memories, Dreams, Reflections* Jung will develop this idea that God was unconscious when he created the world.

Some of Jung's anger is directed against the Christ of the Apocalypse, who 'behaves rather like an ill-tempered, power-conscious "boss" '. Jung would afterwards make his usual disclaimer – that he had not been writing about God and Christ but about the way they are presented in the Scriptures. But it is hard to reconcile the passionate invective with his premise that 'no statement can be made about God'. His *Answer to Job* would not have been written unless he believed the Book of Job made an accurate statement about divine injustice. We can have an image of an unjust God, but an image cannot be unjust.

It has often been observed that the character of God changes between the Old Testament and the New: the vengeful God becomes the God of love. If Jung had genuinely been referring to the God image whenever he mentioned God, he would have looked at the change in terms of human perception. Instead, he argues that God's nature changed, and that the turning point was his realisation that he was inferior to Job. 'He raises himself above His earlier primitive level of consciousness by recognising that the man Job is morally superior to Him and that therefore He has to catch up and become human himself.' It was Job who prompted God's decision to incarnate himself as Christ.

The decision, according to Jung, also involves Sophia, the Apocryphal female figure representing divine wisdom. She is not mentioned in the Book of Job, but Jung sees her as a split-off aspect of the God image that had been repressed until Jahweh had to acknowledge his inferiority to Job. Since he cannot allow things to go on as they are, Jahweh 'remembers a feminine being who was no less agreeable to Him than to man, a friend and playmate from the beginning of the world, the firstborn of God's creatures, a stainless reflection of his glory and a master workman'. After helping him to create the world, she was excluded, like Adam's first wife, Lilith, from the biblical narrative, but her reappearance in heaven 'points to a coming act of creation . . . God desires to reincarnate Himself in the mystery of the heavenly nuptials – as the chief gods of Egypt had done from time immemorial – and to become man.'

Jung is proceeding as if what he calls an 'autonomous psychic content' could take a series of decisions continuing over a period of more than a thousand years – between the Ten Commandments, which were probably written before 1000 BC, and the Gospels, which date from roughly AD 50 to 125. The Book of Job has been dated as belonging to the fourth century BC, which would mean that if God had already decided to become human, he postponed his incarnation for over three hundred years.

What Jung calls 'the answer to Job' is the cry of despair from the cross – 'My God, my God, why hast Thou forsaken me?' It is then that 'his human nature reaches divinity; God then discovers what it means to be a mortal man and drinks to the dregs the sufferings He imposed on His loyal servant Job.' The life of Christ is precisely what it had to be 'if it is simultaneously the life of a god and a man'. It is symbolical, 'rather as if Job and Jahweh were combined in one personality'. And in the Lord's Prayer Jesus was reminding his Father not to revert to his earlier primitive level. Never again must He succumb to those 'devastating fits of rage'.

Jung regards Christ's work of redemption as 'the reparation of a wrong done by God to man'. God had behaved irresponsibly, but his behaviour was 'no worse than what has already been alleged against Him if we accept that the son had to be tortured to death on the cross just to appease the anger of the father. What sort of father would rather have His son slaughtered than forgive the fallible creatures who have been misled by His beloved Satan?' God cannot be a paragon of goodness. He still 'hesitates to use force against Satan. Presumably He is unaware of the extent to which his own dark side favours the evil angel.'

One of Jung's questions is why does God need man? He later wrote in a letter: 'Man is the mirror God holds up to himself, or the sense organ with which he apprehends his being.' And in another letter Jung suggested that 'God needs us as regulators of his incarnation and his coming to consciousness' because 'in his boundlessness he exceeds all the bounds for becoming conscious'. These statements would be difficult to construe if we substitute 'the God image' for 'God'.

The book was finished before the first hydrogen bomb was exploded on 6 November 1952, but it had been obvious since 1945 that humanity could be annihilated. Jung viewed the new weapons in the perspective of the Apocalypse – the prophecies in the Bible remind us that God wants us to be scared of him. 'He fills us with evil as well as with good . . . and since He wants to become man, the resolution of His antinomy must take place in man.' Man could no longer wriggle out of his responsibilities, 'for the dark God has slipped the atom bomb and chemical weapons into his hands, and given him the power to void on his fellow creatures the apocalyptic vials of wrath.'

About six months had passed since the Chinese occupied Tibet in October 1950 and began to destroy its theocracy, but God's tolerance of this played no part in provoking Jung. Later, asked why he had never protested, he answered: 'In such matters I usually wait for an order from within. I have heard nothing of the kind.' The only public event that impinged on his treatment of the Job story was the promulgation (in November) of the dogma about the Virgin's bodily ascension. For Jung this parallelled the return of Sophia to the heavenly regions.

His motives for writing his *Answer to Job* were mixed. In mid-April, when Anthony Storr met him, he said: 'What I'm writing now is pure poison. But I owe it to my people.' Storr was 'taken aback . . . for I knew that no ordinary psychiatrist would talk like that of "my people" '.

Though Jung often resented demands made on him by patients and followers, it was not just a one-way dependence. The performance he gave extended beyond his behaviour into his writing. He was influenced by their transference, their expectations and their use of him as a role model. He could never escape from the image they formed of him, and he did not discourage the intense interest they took in revelations that might be offered to him in dreams. While his patients were in the usual danger of having dreams likely to interest their psychiatrist, he may have been in more danger than most psychiatrists of having dreams that would interest them.

Lecturing on synchronicity at Eranos in August 1951, Jung said he did not want to begin with a definition, but immediately went on to define it as '*a meaningful coincidence* of two or more events, where something other than the probability of chance is involved'. His first example was having a telephone conversation in which a number mentioned was identical with the number on a tram ticket bought earlier in the day, and finding the same number on a theatre ticket in the evening.

His second example was a story about a day in his life – 1 April 1949. After making a note about a figure that was half man, half fish, he ate fish for lunch. There was a conversation about making someone into an 'April fish' (April fool). An ex-patient showed him pictures of fish, and, that night, another ex-patient dreamed about a big fish. A few months later, when he was writing about these coincidences, he found a dead fish on the wall by the lake.

The next anecdote was about a student who before holidaying in Spain dreamed about a carriage in a Spanish city with two cream-coloured horses. Arriving in Spain, he recognised the city, the carriage and the horses of his dream. He told the story about the arrival of the rose–chafer, and, after mentioning Swedenborg's telepathic view of the fire in Stockholm, Jung proposed three categories for all these phenomena – a noncausal connection between a psychic state and an external event; a psychic response to a simultaneous event too distant to be perceived; an accurate psychic forecast of a future event. In fact, only the rose–chafer episode was an example of coincidence. The other stories, as Colin Wilson points out, are about precognition, telepathy and extrasensory perception.

After introducing the three categories, which camouflaged this flaw in his argument, Jung proceeded to summarise a 'statistical experiment' he had made, analysing 180 marriages in terms of astrological conjunctions and oppositions. Previously sceptical about astrology, he now affirmed his belief in it, and redefined synchronicity as 'an acausal connecting principle' designating 'the parallelism of time and meaning between psychic and psychophysical events'.

Rhine had already 'demonstrated that space and time, and hence causality, are factors that can be eliminated, with the result that acausal phenomena, otherwise called miracles, appear possible'. Leibniz, the last of the medieval philosophers to offer a 'holistic' explanation of the universe, had held that four principles were at work – space, time, causality and correspondence. He believed God had pre-established a complete and eternal harmony between mental and physical events. Jung wanted the principle of synchronicity to replace 'the obsolete concept of correspondence, sympathy and harmony'. When an archetype prevails, he said, we can expect '*acausal correspondences*, which consist in a parallel arrangement of facts in time'.

Though intellectually more cautious than he had been in the twenties, when he said that for Paracelsus, as for primitive man, 'nature swarmed with witches, incubi, succubi, devils, sylphs, undines, etc.', Jung was no less attracted to this notion of correspondence. Man contained everything present in the universal macrocosm. 'Everything outside is inside, everything above is below. "Correspondence" reigns over everything in the larger and smaller circles – an idea that culminates in Swedenborg's *homo maximus* as a giant anthropomorphisation of the universe.'

This was the last of the fourteen lectures Jung delivered at Eranos. In the thirties he and Emma had stayed at a villa in the hills and had walked to Moscia every morning. Latterly Olga Fröbe-Kapteyn had given them a room on the first floor of the Villa Eranos, where the meetings were held.

Congratulating her in 1951 on her seventieth birthday, Jung thanked her for 'countless evenings overflowing with stimulation and information, providing just what I so much needed, that is personal contact with other fields of knowledge'. Eranos had been, above all, a forum for exchanges of ideas between protagonists of Eastern and Western spirituality.

As usual, Jung was surrounded by admirers. One member of the audience remembered him

> walking up the path, sort of stooped, his white coattails and baggy grey trousers, wispy white hair, pipe in hand, enjoying the moment and the place which is one of great beauty. He often came down to the water's edge, but not for long could he just enjoy the blue of the water and sky, for where he was there was also a little group; so after a bit he'd turn and trudge up the walk to his quarters above the seminar room.

Afterwards he expanded his lecture material into 'Synchronicity: An Acausal Connecting Principle', which was published in the same 1952 book as the essay on Kepler by Wolfgang Pauli. What Jung offers as 'empirical experience and experimentation' consists largely of anecdotes, some of them taken from *The Unknown*, a book published in 1920 by Camille Flammarion, whom he describes as an astronomer. Discussing telepathic precognition of death in terms of probability calculus, Flammarion found that the odds were

1:804,622,222 in favour of the authenticity of 'a particularly well-observed instance of "phantasms of the living" '. And when he was writing about wind-force, he says, a gust of wind blew all the papers off his table and through the window.

Like Jung's story about fish, this is so inconclusive as hardly to be worth telling, but Jung seems to be less interested in synchronicity as such than in the relationships of mind and matter, and of a nonpersonal psyche and human action. But he does not focus unequivocally on either of these subjects. Arguing that the eleventh-century Persian physician Avicenna and the thirteenth-century scholastic philosopher Albertus Magnus had both been familiar with synchronistic events, Jung refers to the belief they shared that anyone in a state of violent emotion can produce magical effects by wishing evil.

> The appropriate hour or astrological situation or another power coincides with such an inordinate emotion and we then believe that what this power does is being done by the soul . . . Everyone can influence everything magically if he falls into a great excess . . For the soul is then so full of desire that she seizes of her own accord or the better and more meaningful astrological hour that rules over the appropriate things.

Jung took this to be 'the quintessence of primitive magic and of the corresponding phenomena like Nazism, Communism, etc.'

The underlying question is whether a single force is controlling everything that happens in the universe, and making every event meaningful. Jung writes at length about the *I Ching*, which appears to operate on a principle at odds with sequentiality and causality. Those who consult it are frequently impressed with the results they get, but, wanting something that could be measured statistically, Jung turned back to the astrological experiment he had mentioned in the lecture, now going into great detail, providing tables and graphs, while admitting he had made some miscalculations.

The tables and graphs assort oddly with the stories, and Pauli found them unhelpful, but Jung comes back to what he seems to have at heart in a story about a woman who almost died after childbirth and saw herself looking down from above at the consternation of the doctor, nurse and relations at her bedside. Seeing beautiful, flowery parkland, she knew she was at the gateway of another world, but resisted the temptation of entering. After recovering consciousness, she found her observation of the people in the room had been accurate. Without mentioning his own near-death experience, Jung seemed to value both hers and his as providing reassurance about life after death.

One of the most unequivocal statements in his essay is: 'We must completely give up the idea of the psyche's being somehow connected with the brain, and remember instead the "meaningful" or "intelligent" behaviour of lower organisms that are without a brain.' He was interested in the seventeenth-century alchemist Sendivogius (Michal Sendiwoj) who maintained that though the soul functions in the body, most of it is located outside the body. At the beginning of the thirties Jung had written: 'There is no reason why one shouldn't suppose that consciousness could not exist detached from a brain.' Now he affirmed that it could.

Thirty-Six

She Was a Queen

Answer to Job was going to cause a furore, but the people closest to Jung responded positively. Erich Neumann found it 'the most beautiful and deepest of your books . . . it is a dispute with God, similar to Abraham's when he pleaded with God about the destruction of Sodom. In particular it is – for me personally – also a book against God who let 6 million of "his" people be killed, for Job is really Israel too.'

Saying Neumann had put his finger 'on the right spot', Jung asked him to imagine 'the arrogance I had to summon up to be capable of insulting God'. God, he went on, 'is a contradiction in terms, therefore he needs man in order to be made One . . . God is a disease man has to cure. For this purpose, God penetrates into man . . . God has to show himself in his true form, or man would be everlastingly praising his goodness and justice and so deny him admission.'

When Victor White read the book during a visit to Bollingen in August 1951, he formed the impression that Jung was not going to publish it. Two months later, hearing the German text was going to press, he wrote to tell Jung he was looking forward to reading it again. After doing so during the spring of 1952, he called it 'the most exciting and moving book I have read in years, and somehow it arouses tremendous bonds of sympathy between us, and lights up all sorts of dark places both in the Scriptures and in my own psyche'.

The same letter expressed eagerness to find an area of agreement about the *privatio boni*, 'which must affect one's value-*judgments* on almost everything (alchemy, gnosticism, Christ and anti-Christ, the Second Coming, the whole orientation of psychotherapy) without there being any dispute about the *facts*'. By *facts* he meant what Jung called 'psychological facts' – the existence of good and evil.

Maintaining what he mistakenly believed to be a Kantian distinction between two kinds of truth, and treating archetypes as if they were phenomena, Jung argued that they prompted religious and metaphysical statements. 'I have no arguments against these facts. I only deny that the *privatio boni* is a logical statement, but I admit the obvious truth that it is a "metaphysical" truth based upon an archetypal "motif".' Here he came closer than usual to formulating what might have been the basis for a treaty. Given acknowledgement of the *privatio boni* as a metaphysical truth with an archetypal foundation, White might have accepted that they had at last found amicable grounds for agreeing to disagree. But Jung could not – or did not – stop himself from adding that while it might be a ' "metaphysical" truth', it was 'illogical, irrational and even a nonsense'. He had missed a chance of making peace.

Upset, White replied tersely: 'There is surely nothing religious or archetypal in my motivation, nor anything illogical or transcendental, when I call an egg "bad" because it *lacks* what I think an egg ought to have.' He could not think of a 'single empirical example of real or alleged "evil" in which the *privatio* definition is not verified – any more than I can think of an empirical darkness which is not a *privatio* of light'. They had got stuck, he said, in 'the deadlock of assertion and counter-assertion . . . We move in different circles, and our minds have been formed in different philosophical climates.' Nothing is odd about this conclusion except that it had taken nearly seven years to reach it.

Jung's next letter quoted the metaphor of a Jesuit he had met: evil was a disintegration or decomposition of goodness. Decomposition would make a good egg into a bad one smelling of hydrogen sulphide. This is only a paraphrase of what St Augustine had said, but, trapped in the deadlock, Jung ended with a reassertion: 'because it belittles and derealises Evil', the doctrine of *privatio* 'weakens the Good, because it deprives it of a necessary opposite'.

None of Jung's male colleagues, assistants or collaborators had ever had such a close relationship with him, but although White came to stay at Bollingen for ten days during the second half of July, their liking and respect for each other had been frayed by the dispute. In the last stages of their friendship, Jung had to realign the balance between allegiance to Protestantism and inclination towards Catholicism. He hated the schism between the two religions. 'The fact that I as a Christian struggle to unite Catholicism and Protestantism within me is chalked up Pharisaically against me as blatant proof of characterlessness. It seems to be an extreme nuisance that psychology is needed for such an undertaking.'

In February 1952 an attack on Jung appeared in the German monthly *Merkur*. Writing on 'Religion and Modern Thinking', the septuagenarian Jewish philosopher Martin Buber called him 'the leading psychologist of our day', but blamed him for helping to precipitate 'the eclipse of God'. As he had explained in his 1923 book *I and Thou*, Buber believed in God as 'the eternal Thou', and held that we achieve authenticity only by confronting him directly. If *Gnosis* was knowledge, what mattered to Buber was *devotio*: bringing faith alive through mutual confrontation with God.

Jung had 'overstepped the boundaries of psychology' by defining religion as 'a living relationship with psychical events independent of and beyond consciousness in the darkness of the psychical hinterland'. This would mean that religion cannot be regarded as a relationship with a primordial being and presence that remains transcendent. If God is an 'autonomous psychic content', he has no reality outside the human psyche. Jung contends that 'metaphysical statements are *statements of the psyche* and are therefore psychological', but every statement is psychological when considered with regard to its origin, not its meaning. If the soul experiences only itself, not God, there is no I–Thou confrontation, and Jung is proclaiming a new religion of psychic immanence.

Buber had read the unpublished *Septem Sermones and Mortuos* and found they expressed a tendency characteristic of Jung. In the Gnostic god Abraxas 'good and evil are bound together and, so to speak, balance each other'. Jung was inclined to let conscience be overruled by belief in the unity of good and evil. The place of God is usurped by the individuated self. In effect, Buber argued, Jung was saying 'the important thing for the "man of modern consciousness" is to stand in no further relations of faith to God.' Instead of letting our conscience discriminate between right and wrong, good and evil, he wants the soul to be integrated in the self that unifies good and evil.

Jung wants the self to include others, but in Buber's terms, this can only be done by making them into an *it* instead of a *Thou*. 'A being becomes Thou for me only when, recognising its unincludable otherness, I give up any claim to incorporate it or integrate it into my soul. This holds good for God as for man.' Since the self, according to Jung, 'cannot be distinguished from an archetypal God image', self-realisation is equivalent to the incarnation of God. Jung is treating the Judaeo-Christian concept of God from a Gnostic viewpoint, making the Old Testament God into a semi-satanic demiurge.

In May *Merkur* printed a rejoinder by Jung, who repudiated the charge of Gnosticism but did not try to answer all the points Buber had made. Jung denied that he possessed 'the gift of faith' and reformulated the point he had made so often – that when he spoke about God, he was referring only to 'psychic models'. Buber might believe he was involved in 'a living relationship with a divine Thou', but it was only with 'an autonomous psychic content that is defined in one way by him and in another by the Pope'.

Jung also suggested that Buber's criticism could be dismissed as that of an orthodox Jew, but in the rejoinder he wrote for *Merkur*, Buber explained that his view of revelation, which had nothing to do with any orthodoxy, was based on the idea that 'human substance is melted by the spiritual fire which visits it, and there now breaks forth from it a word, a statement which is human in its meaning and form . . . and yet witnesses to Him who stimulated it and to His will.' Atheism, he argued, was less dangerous than Jung's modern version of Gnosticism, which tended to 'deify the instincts instead of hallowing them in faith'.

Jung usually spoke about 'the God image' in the singular, though he was aware that Moses, Augustine, Luther, Buber and the Archbishop of Canterbury had not formed the same picture of God. Challenged by a Swiss doctor, Bernhard Lang, to say whether God was merely a component of the human psyche or a transcendental power, Jung replied with an argument that could have been used to challenge his surviving faith that God had sent him his childhood visions. The God-concept is 'grounded on archetypal premises, corresponding essentially to the instincts'. An archetype was an inherited structure with a 'natural numinosity' that made it seem to have 'a life of its own, different from my life. We then say: God has appeared.'

In his next letter to Lang, Jung went further:

> I am sorry to say that everything people assert about God is nonsense, for no one can know God. Knowing means seeing something in such a way that everyone can know it, and for me it is totally meaningless to profess a knowledge that only I possess. People like this are found in the madhouse . . . Because this so-called knowledge is illegitimate, inner uncertainty makes it fanatical and generates missionary zeal . . . When you ask me whether I am a believer, I must answer 'no'.

But within four weeks he told Aniela Jaffé: 'What we are dealing with here is the living will of God. Since it is always stronger than mine, I find it always confronting me . . . God presents me with facts I have to get along with.' And in the 1959 television programme, when John Freeman asked whether he believed in God, he said: 'Now? Difficult to answer. I *know*. I don't need to believe. I know.' Four years earlier he had responded in the same way to the same question from another interviewer: 'All that I have learnt has led me step by step to an unshakeable conviction of the existence of God . . . Therefore I don't take his existence on belief – I know that he exists.'

In his private correspondence, Jung made many unequivocal affirmations of religious faith. 'I wanted the proof of a living spirit and I got it. Don't ask me at what a price . . . I know that my way has been prescribed to me by a hand far above my reach . . . I am only trying to be a decent tool.' In a 1955 letter he said: 'I find that all my thoughts circle round God like the planets round the sun, and are as irresistibly attracted by him. I would feel it the most heinous sin were I to offer any resistance to this compelling force.' Later in the year, he wrote: 'I consider myself a Protestant and very much so!'

Though the octogenarian Jung liked Franz's son Peter, and generally enjoyed having his grandchildren playing in the vicinity, he did not get to know all of them so well as Emma did. Given to understand he was always preoccupied with work, Franz's sons Andreas (who had been born in 1942) and Lorenz (born at the end of 1943) never tried to initiate conversations with him and scarcely got to know him till the sixties, when Andreas was told to make three appointments for conversations with his grandfather.

The boys often stayed at Bollingen, but Jung sometimes paid so little attention to the presence of other people that, emptying his chamber-pot out of the window one morning, he narrowly missed Andreas. Like Andreas, Gret's son Wolfgang, who was born in 1932, had memories of being told his grandfather was an important man who must not be disturbed.

When he took the boys sailing, Jung was the first to clamber on board, and, once seated, he gave orders like a captain. Total obedience did not stop him from shouting and swearing. Some of his commands were oriented to invisible powers. The spirits might switch the wind off if anyone seemed pleased with it, and when it dropped, the boys had to say: 'How lucky we are that it's windy!' Then the spirits would cooperate.

In September 1952, after working as his secretary for twenty years, Marie-Jeanne Schmid left to get married. She was replaced by a woman who had been analysed in the twenties, first by Baynes and then by Jung – Una Thomas. Marie-Jeanne spent an afternoon briefing her, and then Una Thomas was on her own.

Her first afternoon was difficult because Jung and Emma took a siesta after lunch until four, which was also the maid's rest time. So Una had nobody to ask when people came to the back door, begging. She had to work till six. The Jungs had tea at four, and then he dictated letters till five, when he saw people for an hour. In the morning he wrote, using a pen. He wrote his longer letters in full, giving her the manuscript to copy. Short letters he dictated.

In the last quarter of his eighth decade, his capacity for work was dwindling, and his sensitivity to noise increasing. 'I fear new ideas as they demand too much work from me.'

In the winter of 1952–3 he suffered from tachycardia. Throughout 1953 his heartbeat became increasingly irregular, and his sleep was disturbed if he worked too hard or grew anxious. The most he could safely manage was four three-hour stints of writing a week.

Toni Wolff was thirteen years younger than Jung, and it had never occurred to him she might die first, though she had suffered since the war from arthritis, contracted when she worked as an ambulance driver for the Red Cross. And, ignoring the advice of doctors, she smoked thirty or forty cigarettes a day. 'We must have a vice,' she said, 'and I have chosen smoking as mine.'

Though deeply unhappy to be playing a smaller role in his life, she had gone on working with undiminished devotion, first for the club and later for the institute. In the second week of March, she impressed her colleagues when she tested herself by preparing written answers to all the questions candidates had to answer in an examination. 'One never knows whether one is on top of the situation,' she said, 'and one owed this to the candidates.'

On 19 March 1953 she was telling Jung about her summer-holiday plans, and on that night she died. Emma broke the news to him. He grieved for three days before he resumed working.

Under a gingko tree that had been given to him by students of the new institute, he carved a small stone bas-relief in her memory. The tree had been imported from China, and he arranged four sets of Chinese characters vertically on the stone, meaning:

> Toni Wolff
> Lotus
> Nun
> Mysterious

He kept a photograph of her on the table of his study, but he said that personal guilt is always involved when someone dies prematurely. She had stubbornly refused to surrender her oneness. After his visit to India, he had 'become many', which meant he had become objective, but she had refused to divide herself, and could never accept any other man. This implies that the only guilt involved was hers, but he may have felt guilty too. Some of her friends thought she had died of a broken heart, and by saying she could never accept any other man, he acknowledged that the quality of her life had changed when he distanced himself from her. Like Simone de Beauvoir, who did not survive for long after Sartre's death, Toni had little appetite for life without a close connection to the one man who mattered.

Her death heightened his awareness of mortality and his advancing age.

'The temporariness of life is indescribable. Whether you are watching a cloud or cooking soup, you do everything on the brink of eternity.'

Victor White was due to address the Analytical Psychology Club in London on 23 November, and earlier in the month he wrote a challenging letter. Did Jung think Christ was no longer adequate or valid as a symbol of the self?

Jung answered at length. Without being symbolically invalid, Christ represented only half the self. The evil half had been cast off before the incarnation. 'The *problem of the shadow* . . . Christ versus Satan, is only the first step on the way to the . . . unity of the self in God.' We are 'still within the Christian aeon and just beginning to realise the age of darkness where we shall need Christian virtues to the utmost'. Being committed to the principle of *imitatio Christi*, the church should 'be maintained until it is clearly understood what the assimilation of the shadow means. Those that foresee must – as it were – stay behind their vision in order to help and to teach.' This is what Jung wanted White to do.

His own mission was different.

> Somebody is entrusted with the task of looking ahead and talking of the things to be. This is partially my job, but I have to be very careful not to destroy the things that are. Thus, making the statement that Christ is not a complete symbol of the self, I cannot make it complete by abolishing it. I must keep it therefore in order to build up the symbol of the perfect contradiction in God by adding the darkness to the *lumen de lumine* . . . We are actually living in the time of the splitting of the world and the invalidation of Christ.

If White had still had any residual faith in the possibility of mediating between Jung and the church, this letter would have undermined it. He sent only a brief reply, and, speaking to the club on 'Good and Evil', said it is possible to describe light without mentioning darkness, but not to describe darkness except as the absence of light. 'That there are privative opposites cannot well be denied, and it is difficult for me to see why it should be illogical to classify good/evil as such.' Though the doctrine of *privatio* had never been specially important to him, he had thought analytical psychology confirmed it by setting such a high value on the integration of the personality and the emergence of a transcendent function in which consciousness transcends everyday contradictions.

But White was still under the spell of Jung's personality. Though his initial enthusiasm for *Answer to Job* evaporated, he was slow to digest its implications. He could understand why Jung had written the book, but not why he had published it. Did he not really want a *rapprochement* with the church? Catholics would never accept 'this new myth, symbol, doctrine – or whatever it is – of the Dark or Evil God . . . for ourselves it is *psychologically* impossible . . . We cannot know it otherwise than as a projection – and precisely *not* what we call "God" or the pattern for our living and the standard and measure for all things.' In an earlier letter he had said: 'I just do not understand what is to be gained by the publication of such an outburst . . . I can only see harm coming of it, not least to my own efforts to make analytical psychology acceptable to, and respected by, the Catholics and other Christians who need it so badly.'

White had committed himself deeply to his alliance with Jung, jeopardising his standing in the church. In spite of the care he had taken and the reservations he had expressed, he had got himself into trouble. After his book *God and the Unconscious* was published in 1952, the Vatican ordered that sales should be suspended. In the autumn of 1954 he was sent to California, where he could do less harm. It was there that he wrote his review of *Answer to Job* for the Oxford periodical *Blackfriars*.

Jung's behaviour, he said, was that of 'a spoilt child', and White may have been referring not only to Job but also to Jung when he criticised 'the ingenuity and power, the plausibility and improbablity, the clear-sightedness and blindness of the typical paranoid system which rationalises and conceals an even more unbearable grief and resentment'. He professed uncertainty about whether Jung is 'pulling our leg or is duped by some Satanic trickster into purposely torturing his friends and devotees'. (He had seen Jung's bas-relief of the Trickster at Bollingen.) And he wondered 'how many, Job-like, will venture to observe that the Emperor has appeared in public without his clothes.'

Jung was deeply wounded but unrepentant. In early April he told White: 'You should be glad that somebody thinks about God at all.' White was making 'the mistake of Libra people: they are afraid of anything disturbing the balance. But they can maintain it only by "studying what troubles them".' He should understand that redemption is to be found 'only on the middle ground, the centre of your self, which is just as much with as against God . . . It is as a matter of fact a product of the opposites in God.'

The friendship ended with an episode reminiscent of 'the Kreuzlingen gesture' – the phrase Jung had used for Freud's lack of eagerness to see him when visiting Binswanger forty miles outside Zurich. White, who was coming to the institute during April, had always stayed at Bollingen when he visited Zurich. In April Jung said he would be at Bollingen when White arrived, 'but when we return at the beginning of May, I should like you to stay with us in Küsnacht'. There they would not be alone together.

White wrote to him about 'problems arising from publication of "Answer to Job" ', and without explicitly cancelling the invitation, Jung mentioned in his letter of 6 May that Emma was going to need 'careful nursing for several weeks to come', and added: 'Since I am the cause of much discomfort to you, I am not sure whether you care to see me or not. Please put conventionality aside and do not feel under any obligation.'

White did not come to stay, but wrote again on 25 May. 'For myself, it seems that our ways must, at least to some extent, part. I shall never forget, and please God I shall never lose, what I owe to your work and friendship.' Though he afterwards wrote to Jung occasionally, he received no reply for over four years.

Even in his late seventies, Jung was revising his work for republication, and in 1954, preparing a new edition of the 1946 essay 'On the Nature of the Psyche', he added an eight-page 'Supplement', returning to the question of contents in the archetypes. Though ideas cannot be inborn, he insisted, archetypes are 'typical forms of behaviour which, when they become conscious, naturally present themselves *as ideas and images*, like everything else that becomes a content of consciousness'.

Still wanting to make statements about archetypes as if they were phenomena, not noumena, Jung used the analogy of atomic physics to justify his procedure. His theory of the archetypes might be no more than a hypothesis about observed products of the unobservable unconscious, but in atomic physics too, inferences are made about unobservable events.

In psychology, as in physics, observations are coloured by the presence of the observer, or, as Jung formulated it with help from Pauli, the observer had uncontrollable effects on the system observed, with the result 'that reality forfeits something of its objective character and that a subjective element attaches to the physicist's picture of the world'. After reading Jung's draft for the supplement, Pauli made a comment that was incorporated as a footnote. He agreed that 'the epistemological situation with regard to the concepts "conscious" and "unconscious" seems to offer a pretty close analogy to the undermentioned "complementarity" situation in physics'. But whereas physics had to 'abandon in principle any objective understanding of physical phenomena', it should be possible to 'supplement the purely subjective psychology of consciousness by postulating the existence of an unconscious that possesses a large measure of objective reality'.

Encouraged by Pauli's contribution, Jung went on to speculate about archetypes, saying they are not merely psychic. Experiments in telepathy and the frequency of synchronistic phenomena suggest that 'psychic processes stand in some sort of energy relation to the physiological substrate . . . The use of the term *libido* in the newer medical psychology has surprising affinities with the primitive mana. This archetypal idea is therefore far from being only primitive, but differs from the physicist's conception of energy by the fact that it is essentially qualitative and not quantitative.'

The psyche must have an aspect under which it would appear as mass in motion. If there is no pre-established harmony between physical and psychic events, they must interact, which would force us to believe in 'a psyche that touches matter at some point, and, conversely, a matter with a latent psyche'. If the profession had followed Jung, psychology would have been moving towards a sychronistic account of the interrelationship between the mind and the brain.

In the autumn of 1955 Aniela Jaffé took over as his secretary. He had known her for twenty years. After starting an analysis with Liliane Frey, she transferred to Jung in 1937, and he let her pay for it by doing part-time work for him. Ten years later, she was appointed secretary of the Jung Institute in Zurich, where she learned a lot about Jungians and their needs. A month before she started working at his home, he 'initiated' her. She must never be irritated at his anger, he told her, or his occasional 'grumbling', roaring and cursing. Nor must she try to make herself indispensable – he was familiar with the tricks women used to gain power over men.

A new cook had been engaged, and on Jaffé's first morning, he dictated details of the lunches and dinners he wanted for the next seven days. One of her jobs was to organise the bulky archives he kept on a variety of subjects including flying saucers. He collected journals and clippings from newspapers that reported sightings of UFOs – unidentified flying objects – all over the world, as well as letters, dream accounts and notes on the phenomena. He also received reports from a woman who acted as secretary for a Swiss organisation that recorded observations of them. The material on UFOs filled several bookshelves and five or six large files which she put into two drawers. One evening, when she was at home, he searched in vain for one of these files. Anyone else would have telephoned her to ask where it was, but Jung disliked using the telephone, and she had to adapt to his attitudes. 'Jung never ruled out the possibility that life knew better than the correcting mind, and his attention was directed not so much to the things themselves as to that unknowable agent that organised the event beyond the will and knowledge of man.' If he could not find his tobacco jar, he would say it had been 'magicked away again'. He was jocularly echoing a phrase used by a patient at the Burghölzli, but he believed objects had a will of their own, and it was better not to look for them when they disappeared. They would turn up when they wanted to. His principle was: 'Don't interfere,' and if a smouldering match flared up in the ashtray, he would be annoyed if Jaffé tried to blow it out. He preferred to watch: it might set light to some of the other rubbish. Like Lévy-Bruhl's primitives, he believed that since nothing happened by accident, any unusual event had religious significance. He was therefore permanently on the lookout for the unexpected.

In 1954 the Swiss weekly *Die Weltwoche* had printed Jung's written answers to a journalist's questions about UFOs. Four years later, after another journalist happened to read the piece, the press took up the story, and articles appeared all over the world, calling Jung a believer in flying saucers. He issued a disclaimer, which was ignored, so he wrote a short book called *A Modern Myth: Of Things Seen in the Skies.*

He said he 'felt compelled, as once before when events of fateful consequence were brewing for Europe, to sound a note of warning'. He was referring to the warning he had issued during 1936 in the essay 'Wotan'. He now wanted 'to warn those few to whom I can make myself heard that events are in store for mankind which signal the end of an aeon'. The Christian era had begun with a shift toward the constellation of Pisces, but around the year 2000 the solar system would enter Aquarius, which symbolised the union of opposites. The Christ–Antichrist conflict would give way to the aeon of the reconciler, the Holy Ghost.

Without having seen a flying saucer, Jung had no doubt that other people were seeing them and dreaming about them. Unquestionably, flying saucers had 'become a *living myth*', which had a compensatory significance as a 'response from the unconscious to the present conscious state, or to anxiety over the apparently hopeless world political situation, which at any time may lead to a universal catastrophe'. Assuming the attitude of the majority could 'activate an archetype', he was crediting the unconscious with the power of a benevolent god to intervene in human affairs when consciousness became lopsided.

Since the first atom bomb had exploded in 1945, humanity had been so vulnerable that even irreligious people were asking fundamental questions, and perhaps those who did not were being 'visited by "visions", by a widespread myth'. In a less materialistic period, 'innumerable parsons would already have been preaching about the warning signs in heaven,' but 'we cannot get back to that limited world view that used to leave room for metaphysical intervention'. In the modern world it was for the analytical psychologist to interpret a new myth, which 'is essentially a product of the unconscious archetype and is therefore a symbol'.

The archetype that had been activated was the Self, which was taking 'the traditional form of an epiphany from heaven'. Consisting of both consciousness and unconsciousness, the Self was identical with Jesus. If he were to 'trespass into metaphysics', he said, he would have to call the Self Christ since he was living in the West. In the Far East he would have called it 'atman or Tao or the Buddha'. But belief in Jesus as the son of God was 'on the point of evaporating. Untold millions of so-called Christians have lost their belief in a real and living mediator.'

'The religious longing for wholeness' was indestructible. Though it played 'the least conspicuous part in contemporary consciousness', it was stronger than the instincts for sex and power. (At the age of eighty-three, Jung had not stopped arguing with Freud and Adler.) What the striving for wholeness wanted, said Jung, was 'to free the individual from the compulsion of the other two instincts', which 'have always stood in the way of man's higher development'.

Summing up his position, he said we know 'with tolerable certainty' that flying saucers 'possess a surface which can be seen by the eye and at the same time throws back a radar echo'. He felt certain of their existence: 'By all human standards it hardly seems possible to doubt this any longer.' We were living through a global legend clothed in visual form. Shaped like mandalas, flying saucers were 'spontaneously appearing circular images of unity, which represent a synthesis of opposites within the psyche'. The reason most people failed to see them was that they were incapable of believing in the possibility of a redeeming supernatural event.

Jung's eightieth birthday fell on 26 July 1955, a Wednesday, but celebrations started on Saturday the 22nd with a big family lunch, followed by a boat trip to Schmerikon with thirty-eight people on board, all members of the family except Ruth Bailey and E. A. Bennet. Jung's two great-grandchildren were too young to come. One of the grandsons made a speech from a typed script, and the entertainments included a quiz about the great man.

When the boat stopped opposite the tower at Bollingen, three of the boys dived unexpectedly into the lake from the roof over the deck. In Schmerikon a feast had been prepared at the Hotel Bad. A huge ham was presented to Jung, who pulled out his pocket knife to carve the first few slices. Fritz Baumann made a speech, and the children staged a series of sketches, including a parody of life at Bollingen and a pastiche of a radio programme about analytical psychology.

On Monday morning there was a celebration at the Dolder Grand Hotel, with speeches and the presentation of the *Codex Jung*, a valuable collection of Gnostic documents bought from a Belgian dealer who had acquired them in Egypt. In the evening a dinner was held for about seventy-five people. Bennet was given the place of honour at Jung's right hand, and Michael Fordham was seated to the right of Emma.

On Wednesday morning there was a meeting at the Institute about the formation of a new international association, and about two hundred people had reserved places on the steamer chartered for a trip on the lake in the afternoon. When the boat stopped at Meilen, Jung 'stepped on board, chuckling over the grand surprise he had given everyone. He sat on deck while members of the party clicked their cameras mercilessly in his face, and then got off at Rapperswil.'

In the evening the local band played in the garden of Jung's house, and he twice joined in the dancing, once with Emma and once with one of his daughters. After the band stopped, children and adults played the piano and sang. Afterwards, Jung brought in records of 'Negro spirituals' and sat next to the gramophone, nodding his head in time with the music.

He was sent a huge variety of presents. From London the Society of Analytical Psychology sent a cricket ball mounted on a wooden base. The ball had been used in a match under the title 'Freudians versus Jungians'. The Jungians had won by five runs.

Emma, who was suffering from uraemia, had undergone surgery in the spring. At times she looked very grey, but one day Una Thomas told her: 'It's nice to have you looking so much better and so well.' She did not answer.

At breakfast on Tuesday 23 November 1955, when she said she thought she was going to die, Jung told her not to think of such things, but later in the morning a medical report arrived, holding out no hope. After hesitating about whether to tell her, he decided he should. She seemed undisturbed and perhaps relieved. Ever since her operation, she had been preparing for death.

Bennet was due to arrive in Küsnacht before lunch on Wednesday the 26th, and Jung had invited him to stay at the house, but, meeting his train in Zurich, explained why he had arranged for him to stay with one of his daughters. Over lunch, Jung talked about schizophrenia as 'a protection from the shadow, and usually the collective shadow'. He also talked about his boyhood dream of the shitting God, and about recent dreams in which he saw dead friends – 'death is in the air.'

At ten o'clock on Thursday morning Emma told the two daughters who were with her: 'I'm going to go. I'm going to die now. I'm going to say goodbye to you right now.' Half an hour later, she was dead. They had been married fifty-two years.

When Jung led the family into the church at Küsnacht for the funeral service, he was erect and composed. The Fordhams had come out to be with him, and to attend the funeral. 'She was a queen,' he told them after the service, and started weeping. He seemed to have become smaller – shrivelled. 'He just looked like a little old man.' At the lunch, which was held in the house, he was calm and friendly, but made it clear he wanted to be left alone.

He was eighty, but still behaved like a boy. At Bollingen he dug up a potato to show the Fordhams how big it was, and he could not conceal his pride in having an outside lavatory in a hut.

He lost little time in telephoning Ruth Bailey to arrange for her to settle in the house as his companion and housekeeper. This would give him more freedom than depending on the family. He told Barbara Hannah to answer any questions Ruth might ask about psychology, 'but *never* to begin the subject yourself or in any way rub in *anything* about it'.

For some time he was too depressed to dictate letters, but Aniela Jaffé dealt with his correspondence, writing in the first person. 'I read my tentative answers to him – sometimes he corrected a word or a sentence, sometimes it was all right.'

The inscription he put on Emma's grave was 'Oh vase, sign of devotion and obedience.' He asked Marie-Louise von Franz to take over the book she had left unfinished, on the Grail legend, and it came out in 1960.

The Stuttgart periodical *Universitas* published Jung's article 'A Psychological View of Conscience' in 1958. Freud, who had said the superego consisted of a consciously acquired stock of customs, values and precepts, was, in Jung's view, thinking of archetypes when he conceded that it contained 'archaic vestiges'. But for Jung, conscience had nothing to do with consciousness. It existed autonomously before the moral code was evolved. It was a manifestation of mana, 'of the "extraordinarily powerful", which is characteristic of archetypal ideas'. It 'falls within the sphere of the collective unconscious, exemplifying an archetypal pattern of behaviour reaching down into the animal psyche'. Conscience can appear in the form of compulsions and obsessions, but not all of these are good. 'Beside the positive, "right" conscience is the negative "false" conscience called the devil, seducer, tempter, evil spirit, etc.'

In 1957, twenty-four years after the tower was built, Jung made his last additions to it, adding the upper part of the second tower, the containing wall, the loggia in the courtyard and the top storey.

Bennet, who came to spend the first half of July with him and Ruth, enjoyed the isolation and the quasi-medieval simplicity of their life. They sometimes carried out the heavy wooden table to eat dinner by the lake, afterwards sitting outside or in the loggia, reading by the light of a paraffin lamp. When it rained, they sat in the small room at the bottom of the second tower.

The fireplace occupied almost the whole of one wall, and adjoining the other walls was a tiled stone seat with cushions on it. They sat 'with our chairs absolutely jammed together reading by the light of an old lamp suspended from the ceiling . . . If only those who read his books could see C.G. here, in his shirt sleeves and an old pullover, and socks (with a hole in them!)' He did much of the cooking himself,

> crouching on one of the small chairs . . . He is very particular indeed about every detail of the cooking. We had pork chops, and he made the sauce for these with flour and water and a glassful of wine. Then he made the salad at the table, cutting up tiny bits of garlic and mixing these on the wooden spoon with some salt and pepper (I think). Then we had some crushed plums (a puree) which came from the garden at Küsnacht, and some kirsch.

At the age of eighty-three Jung was still vigorous. A summer visitor to Bollingen was shown into the garden, where she heard wood being chopped behind a wall. The sound stopped before she saw a 'strong-bodied, white-haired eighty-three-year-old man in his green workman's apron, seated before the chopping block'. He told her he had found the way to live there 'as part of nature' in his own time. 'When a man begins to know himself, to discover the roots of his past in himself, it is a new way of life.'

Everyone, he maintained, 'should have his own plot of land, so that the instincts can come back to life. To own land is psychologically important, and there is no substitute for it . . . Everything around me is part of me, which is why a rented flat is disastrous.' Big cities were 'responsible for our uprootedness'. It was because the Swiss lived in small cities that they were 'mentally more balanced and less neurotic' than most other Europeans. 'Human existence should be rooted in the earth.'

A man who met him in February 1959 described him as 'a little stoop-shouldered', with 'wispy white hair . . . His gestures and words were solemn and elegant, but underneath there was a burning enthusiasm which indicated his extraordinary vitality . . . His eyes were penetratingly observant.'

He did not want Ruth Bailey to know he was using a catheter. The family would not let him risk the operation that might have obviated the need for it. When he needed a new one, it was Müller and not Ruth who was sent to the chemist.

Thirty-Seven

Mythification and Auntification

In the early 1960s, when Jung stipulated that *Memories, Dreams, Reflections* should not be published till after his death, he may have been forgetting he would have no jurisdiction over the final revisions.

At first, he had intended neither to write an autobiography nor to let a biography be written. Throughout the latter part of his life, many potential biographers made overtures to him, only to be rebuffed. But in 1956, the publisher Kurt Wolff propositioned Jolande Jacobi about conducting a series of interviews and writing a biography. She refused, but suggested the job should be done by Aniela Jaffé. Discussing this idea with Jung, Jacobi eventually succeeded in persuading him.

He started spending an afternoon each week dictating material to Jaffé, who took shorthand notes and typed them up verbatim. Judging from the surviving typescripts – which can be seen at the Library of Congress in Washington – they worked in this way from January 1957 until May 1958.

Towards the end of 1957, he was invited by a former member of the Zofingia fraternity, Gustav Steiner, to write a short memoir for a Basel periodical, the *Basler Stadtbuch*. Sending a negative reply to the letter, Jung formulated a principle that would be crucial to the book. He said: 'All memory of outer events has faded, and perhaps the "outer" events were not the real ones, or were real only in so far as they coincided with inner phases of development . . . Conversely, my recollection of "inner" experiences has become livelier and more colourful.' Jaffé quoted from this letter in her introduction, and Jung reiterated the point in his Prologue. This also features the word *myth*. 'In the eighty-third year of my life I have undertaken to tell the myth of my life. I can however only make direct statements, only "tell stories". Whether they are true is not the problem. The only question is whether it is *my* fable, *my* truth.' Is he giving himself *carte blanche* to conflate fiction with fact? The problem of accuracy is not solved simply by asserting it is not a problem.

Though the emphasis of the title is on the subjective element, the majority of the reminiscences are about external events, and only a naive reader would trust the elaborate reconstructions of dreams. Many of these had already been used more than once in books, lectures and seminars. Variation between different versions reminds us how elusive dreams are, with their mixture of images, words, sounds and feelings. A verbal account, even if produced immediately after waking up, can only approximate to the experience, and the dreams recounted in *Memories, Dreams, Reflections* are unmistakeably reinforced with details evolved by the conscious mind either at the moment of writing (or dictating) or in earlier efforts at reconstituting the dream material.

Talking to patients, students and admirers, whether individually or in groups, Jung had found that they were more amused than shocked by an unexpected reference to sex or the bodily functions. Throughout the second half of his long life, he was surrounded by people who idolised him, clamoured for attention, used him as their role model. They naturally affected his image of himself, but he alternated between playing the great man and sabotaging his own performance with behaviour designed as an antidote to excessive reverence.

But the book was not being written just for patients, disciples and 'Jungians'. Partly because he was aspiring to the form of myth, his salty sense of humour rarely made itself felt in the material he dictated, and in the end product, there is still less evidence of it. He often tended to idealise his former self, reconstructing past events as if he had consistently behaved with high principles, phenomenal foresight, admirable self-control and exemplary generosity.

As secretary of the Jung Institute, Aniela Jaffé had earned only a small salary, and one of his motives in letting her write *Memories, Dreams, Reflections* was to provide a pension for her without putting money aside for it – she would receive royalties on the book. It was like a reversal of the bargain they had made when he accepted labour instead of cash for her analysis.

It would be her job to construct a coherent narrative from the accumulation of dictated material. It was not clear whether the book was to be written in the first person or the third, but she was to write it, and his name for the project was 'the Jaffé enterprise'. But when he discovered how much he enjoyed reminiscing about his childhood, he broke off, deciding to write about it himself. He was not intending to give her what he wrote, but she persuaded him that the best way to publish it would be to let her incorporate it in her book. He wrote about a third of it, as well as making additions to what she wrote. In April 1960 he said: 'I regard the pieces in it written by myself as a contribution to the work of Mrs Jaffé. The book should appear under her name and not mine, as it does not represent an autobiography written by me.' In May Herbert Read wrote to John Barrett, saying that when the book came out, Aniela Jaffé would have to be named as author, and they must use the formula: 'with contributions from C. G. Jung'.

At the end of November 1960, six months before he died, Jung attended a meeting with Jaffé, Read and Barrett. Confirming that he regarded her as the author, Jung signed a declaration that she was to be credited with authorship.

He was always ambivalent towards the book, which was both his and not his. The end-product is neither an autobiography nor a biography, though its status as autobiography was not seriously challenged until Alan Elms wrote about it in *Uncovering Lives* and Sonu Shamdasani in 'Memories, Dreams, Omissions'. If Jung's insistence on posthumous publication was intended to make him feel detached, the stratagem failed, and he became passionately concerned about the image that would be projected. Early in 1960, talking to Richard Hull, he coined the word *Tantifizierung – auntification* – to describe what was being done to the text. Throughout his life, he had prided himself on being earthy and outspoken, but Aniela Jaffé, who was prim and prudish, was imposing cuts and introducing euphemisms he no longer had the stamina to oppose. The narrative was in the voice of a maiden aunt.

Given a typescript, Hull found Jaffé had made a lot of deletions and alterations to stop Jung from appearing blunt or crude. Hull became more deeply involved in the project when asked to translate the chapters Jung wrote. (Jaffé's chapters were translated by Richard and Clara Winston, who are credited on the title page with translating the whole book.) Hull soon discovered Jaffé was not the only source of the auntifying interference. Before and after Jung's death, textual changes were made at the instigation of his family – mainly his son Franz, his third daughter, Marianne, and her husband Walter Niehus, who all felt strongly about family privacy. Franz has said it would be 'a form of prostitution' to let the world into his father's secrets, and Hull used the term 'family falsifications' to describe Niehus's 'wholesale cutting' of a section about Jung's adolescent religious preoccupations.

The typescript used for the Pantheon edition – Jung wanted the English translation to appear before the German original – can be seen at the Francis Countway Library in Boston. Editorial changes were made in four different colours. Aniela Jaffé worked in red, and the initials CGJ are to be seen in the margin against some of her revisions. This presumably means that Jung was consulted; the emendations without his initials may have been made after his death. Richard Hull worked in purple, and the black markings are by

Richard Winston. There are also markings in pencil by 'W.S.' (Wolfgang Sauerlander, an editor) who also transcribed corrections by Hull and Jaffé.

On one level, Aniela Jaffé did a good job. The book was an immediate bestseller in Switzerland, and it became more popular than any other book with Jung's name on its spine. (In German the word *von* can mean *by*, *from* or *of*, and the German edition was titled '*Träume, Erinnerungen, Gedanken von C. G. Jung* Aufgezeichnet und herausgegeben von Aniela Jaffé' – '*Memories, Dreams and Reflections of C. G. Jung* recorded and edited by Aniela Jaffé'. The English edition might have made a slightly different impact if the publisher had not put Jung's name above the title, which obviates the need to translate the first *von*.)

The book still exerts a lot of influence. The biographical information that has been disseminated about Jung mostly derives from it directly or indirectly. It has magnetised many readers into Jungian analysis, and some into becoming Jungian analysts.

One reason for its success is that it is more accessible than Jung's books, and since it is written in the first person, we can easily forget we are not listening to his voice. Unintentionally, he had trained Jaffé to impersonate him. She was familiar with the image he wanted to project, the style he liked to write in and the feelings he wanted to evoke. After her ten years at the Jung Institute, she was second to none in her knowledge of what his followers wanted from him. When she took over as his secretary, he had not recovered from the loss of Emma. Ailing and depressed, he had little energy to spare for his voluminous correspondence. When Marie-Jeanne Schmid was his secretary, he had not always read through the typed letters she produced from his dictation. He had merely signed them. And with Jaffé, he signed letters she had not only typed but composed. Of the letters he signed between 1957 and 1961 we do not know how many had been written by her. If she enjoyed literary ventriloquism, she must have enjoyed writing *Memories, Dreams, Reflections*. She was sculpting a monument.

During the thirties, she had been one of the female admirers who pursued him to Eranos conferences in Ascona, knowing that even if they got no chance to be alone with him, at least he would be surrounded by fewer admirers than in Zurich. When lectures were over, he would sit on the garden wall, 'and in a flash,' wrote Jaffé, 'we were clustering around him like bees around a honey pot'. She did not know what a privileged bee she was, or how high she would fly. The Jung that has become familiar to the world is made from her beeswax.

The balance of editorial power was already shifting before he died in 1961. In January 1957, he was totally in command. He was a demanding and irascible master, and even if he began to tire quickly and to contradict himself, it did not occur to her that she would later be able to ignore his wishes when adding and subtracting material.

His family was hostile to the project. During a dictating session in the spring of 1958, he mentioned that his children disliked the idea that biographical facts should be disclosed to the rest of the world. Conceding that their attitude was the conventional one, he said he wanted no truck with convention.

If the text was already being censored before he died, the auntifiers had more freedom afterwards. The situation deteriorated still further when Kurt Wolff died – now there was no one to restrain them. Not that Wolff and Jung had ever been in agreement about the book. With his eye on sales, Wolff had wanted Jung to write it himself, and, if he refused, it could still be made to look like an autobiography.

One of the mistakes made by Jaffé and the other auntifiers was to forget that readers draw conclusions not only from what is put in but from what is left out. It has often been observed that apart from Jung, only three characters come to life in *Memories, Dreams, Reflections* – his parents and Freud. About Emma, the book contains almost nothing except the comment: 'After my wife's death in 1955, I felt obliged to become what I myself am.'

Although his sister Trudi went on for years doing secretarial work and bookkeeping for him, almost nothing is said about her. In the German edition a footnote is devoted to her, and this has been incorporated into the English text. There is nothing about Toni Wolff, and readers have inferred that he set little value on any of these relationships. In 1963, some reviewers wrote scathingly about his egotism. But in the material he dictated, he had a lot to say about Toni, Emma and other members of his family.

In the published book, most of the references to his mother are negative. The auntifiers wanted to soften his criticism of her – 'neurotic' is substituted for 'hysterical' and 'stout' for 'very fat' – but the conjuring tricks make the love vanish, and the ambivalence looks more like hostility. Though he criticised her for being uncouth, unable to stand on her own feet, to run a household or to deal with money, and though he sometimes had anxiety dreams about her, he felt deeply guilty about abandoning her in Basel when he went to work in Zurich.

He felt compassion for both parents – both victims of a bad marriage. Jung was still very young when he realised how bad it was. Disappointed with Paul, Emilie was pushing him aside. She lived in a world of fantasy and made herself into a hypochondriac, but after Paul died, she became healthier and less unstable. Jung's compassion for his father is evident from the book, but most of what he dictated about his mother was suppressed.

The auntifiers also felt entitled to tamper – damagingly – with his language. Since his experiences are available to us only through the words he chose to describe them, changing the words amounts to changing the experience. One of the turning points in his life – he calls it the key to everything – occurred when he was eleven. In the dictated material, he returns at least seven times to the dream or vision of the shitting God, most often referring to it as a dream, but his most detailed account of it is as a daytime vision. In either case, he gave it the status of an objective event he had witnessed – he describes it as 'something tangible'. Talking about it to Jaffé in March 1957, when he had not yet decided to write the first three chapters of the book, he said God shat on the cathedral and the turd was so enormous that the roof collapsed under its weight. That was how he worded it. This episode comes in the second chapter, but the wording was changed when she and members of the family joined forces to eliminate the most offensive of his indiscretions. But it would have been out of character for him to sidestep into such circumlocutions as 'God sits on his golden throne, high above the world, and under the throne falls a massive piece of excrement on the new, brightly coloured dome of the the church, shatters it and the walls of the building collapse.'

It seemed to him afterwards that at the age of eleven, he had been given solid proof of God's existence, and that all his subsequent thinking was rooted in the answers he gave himself to the question of why such a disgusting thought had come into his mind. The answer was that God had wanted this to happen. God *wanted* him to do something wrong. *Wanted* is changed in red to *forced*, which changes the emphasis. Jung's point was that God *wanted* him to believe in a God who was not entirely good.

Nothing was more central to his thinking than the idea that we cannot fully experience goodness without accepting evil. The childish image of a God who shits is a pictorial rejection of purity. The young Carl Jung was facing a dilemma. Either he had to discuss the problem with other people or to remain silent, adding a weighty new secret to his collection. Turning towards other people would have meant turning away from God; turning towards God meant turning away from other people.

His silence about the shitting God may have made it easier for him to live with the secret of the homosexual episode, but the problem of secretiveness was to become more complicated in adult life, and in his eighties, writing about eighty secretive years, how much of the truth should he try to tell? In his doctoral thesis, describing the seances, he had revealed neither that Helly was his cousin nor that she was only thirteen and a half when the seances started. In the dictated material, he revealed that she was his cousin – this revelation was suppressed – but not that he had known her all her life or that he had taken the initiative in starting the seances. He says she had already held seances with her sisters, and that he did not meet her until 1897. He may have wanted to avoid contradicting the thesis, which had been published in his collected works.

One of Jaffé's problems was that she had to fortify the book as well as she could against challenges that might be thrown down by readers who compared the new account of an event or a dream with other accounts in writings, interviews and seminars. Nor could she know how much of the material that was still unpublished in 1963 would come out subsequently. Transcripts of seminars had been circulated, with Jung's permission, among students, but he had never revised them or allowed them to be published.

She did not know whether his correspondence with Freud would ever come out in book form. A secret cache had been built into one of the walls in Jung's study. He kept it locked, and carried the key around in his pocket. The cache contained his letters from Freud in a linen portfolio; he did not want their correspondence to be published, and it did not appear until 1974 – thirteen years after his death, and eleven years after the appearance of *Memories, Dreams, Reflections*, which of course said nothing about the homosexual undertow in the relationship between the two men. It also understated the deference Jung showed before they started to quarrel. To read the letters they exchanged is to realise how grandiloquently Jung was distorting the facts when he said:

> My scientific conscience did not allow me, on the one hand, to let what is good in Freud go by the board, and on the other to countenance the absurd position which the human psyche occupies in his theory. I suspected at once that this partly diabolical sexual theory would turn people's heads and I have sacrificed my scientific career in doing all I can to combat this absolute devaluation of the psyche.

Nor did Jaffé know which of Jung's other letters would be published. At the beginning of the sixties she could not foresee that she would edit his letters for the three-volume German selection and co-edit them for the two-volume English version. As she was aware, he had never felt obliged to tell the truth, the whole truth and nothing but the truth. When she was his secretary, one of her duties had been to help him cover up anything he wanted to cover up. But after his death, she may have felt ambivalent. Though she was not so much a biographer as a collaborator on an autobiography, she may have felt qualms about falsification.

If she and the other auntifiers made him out to have been more heroic than he actually was, they were only doing what he often did himself. If he wanted his story to seem like a myth, it was partly because he wanted to appear as a hero, and never as a victim. The book must not merely show him fighting courageously against the psychosis that was unbalancing him in 1913–17. He must seem to be entering an underworld voluntarily, like Orpheus or Ulysses: choosing 'Confrontation with the Unconscious', as the title for the sixth chapter implies this. Jung also liked to make out that he was taking enormous risks for the sake of humanity, which would benefit if he came back with new information about the uncharted depths of the unconscious.

Reviewing *Memories, Dreams, Reflections*, the poet Kathleen Raine wrote: 'Jung's life, even so fragmentarily revealed, invites comparison not with profane autobiography, but with the lives of Plotinus or Swedenborg, the lives of the saints and sages, interwoven with miracles.' If Jung had been the sole author, the narrative could be described as an autohagiography.

To say that his behaviour was less exemplary is not to say that he was incapable of acting with great courage, as he did in the Sudanese village on the way back from the expedition to Africa in 1925. Cracking his whip and swearing loudly in Swiss German, he had taken command of the situation, but is was characteristic of him that when he told the story to Jaffé, he said it was the first time in his life he had known exactly what to do. It was characteristic of her to cut this remark.

He may have dictated more detail about his breakdown than appears in the book, but it is clear that she and the family were anxious not to let him come across as unbalanced or eccentric or superstitious. Generally the tendency is to exclude anything that might seem provocative, though he was at his best when being provocative, as when he said Buddha was a more complete personality than Jesus. Jesus had the mentality of an illegitimate child – a strong auto-erotism he needed to compensate. In the absence of the father, the son has to fill his place, and may be driven to extremes in his dealings with the mother, as Jesus was with Mary: 'Woman, what have I to do with thee? Mine hour is not yet come.' Ignorant of his inner dependence on her, he deals with her as a mere woman, and from then on goes through the world as uncommitted as any priest to a relationship with a woman. He does not find women attractive. He is the *puer eternus* who lives in the world of the mother, which for him is the world of the spirit. This qualified him to be the god of a male world from which women were virtually excluded.

Many of the best passages Jung dictated were left unused, sometimes because they imply premises that might strike some readers as far-fetched. The auntifiers were nervous of his views on reincarnation. Talking to Jaffé in 1958 about a visit to India in 1937, he said he had often wondered whether he had been Indian in a former life. If so, he would certainly have been a

Buddhist. Looking at the stupas of Sanchi – hemispherical tombs on a rocky hill where Buddha delivered his fire sermon – Jung had felt overwhelmed with emotion, and he remembered that Richard Wilhelm had marvelled at his understanding of Eastern wisdom and had asked: 'How do you know all that?' Jung said he had not read much about it. His knowledge came from inside himself, perhaps from a former existence, and if he had once lived in India, it would explain why he took an outsider's view of European materialism. Perhaps it was his life-task to effect a spiritual reconciliation between East and West.

In the last years of his life, he sometimes had the impression that people he had loved and lost were returning as animals. One year, on the anniversary of Toni Wolff's death, he was at Bollingen with Hans Kuhn. Late in the afternoon, after bringing a load of dry wood down to the house, Hans was puzzled by the behaviour of a bird, a robin sitting on a branch. He seemed slightly embarrassed when he told Jung it would not fly away. Even when the two men went close, the bird stayed there, unafraid. An hour later, it was still there, and as the sky was darkening, it flew onto the dry wood in the yard. When Hans, who knew it was the anniversary of Toni's death, asked whether the bird was her soul, he was giving voice to a feeling Jung already had.

He also dictated his memories of a dog called Pasha. Its behaviour was never as unusual as the robin's but one day, in the garden, when it was staring expectantly at Jung, the expression in its eyes reminded him forcibly of his father and the way his father had looked at him. Primitive man had believed the dead returned to the world in the form of animals. Could the pastor have been reincarnated as a dog?

In 'Late Thoughts', a chapter he started in January 1959 for the book, he resumed the argument he had advanced in *Answer to Job* about changes in God's character and the possibility that he had not been conscious when he created the world. Though most Christians take God's stability for granted, it seemed to Jung that Christianity had predicated the possibility of development. He was no longer the same after the incarnation, 'which was also a decisive event for the Creator himself. In the eyes of those who had been delivered from darkness, he cast off his dark qualities and became the *summum bonum*.'

For a thousand years after the Crucifixion, humanity had been able to ignore God's dark side, but this had gradually become more visible, and now, in the twentieth century, the Christian world was undeniably

confronted with the principle of evil, with open injustice, tyranny, lies, slavery and enslavement of conscience. This manifestation of undisguised

evil has taken on an apparently permanent form in the Russian people, but
the first violent outpouring was in the Germans . . . Evil has become the
decisive reality . . . The criterion of ethical behaviour can no longer consist
in the assumption that what is recognised as 'good' has the force of a
categorical imperative, and that so-called evil must at all costs be avoided.

The keynote for the second millennium had been struck when the belief
emerged that the devil had created the world. Here Jung reiterated a lot of
the ideas he had already put forward about mandalas and flying saucers as
symbols of unity. If all energy, as he believed, proceeded from opposition,
the energy underlying psychic life must have pre-existed it, and must
therefore have been unconscious.

The idea of an unconscious God came partly from Gnosticism and partly
from Schopenhauer, a nonbeliever who had taken everything outside the
world of our experience to be undifferentiated. What he called *Will* was an
ultimate force or energy striving blindly to assert itself in life. Anticipating
twentieth-century ideas of the unconscious, he represented *Will* as a blind
man carrying a lame man, intellect, on his back.

It seemed to Jung that God had not created the universe according to any
preconceived plan, but had allowed it to evolve over billions of chaotic years
in which creatures and galaxies had destroyed each other. Until consciousness came into existence, the universe had no meaning, though perhaps –
Jung is vague about this – it had somehow been latent or concealed in the
turbulence before warm-blooded vertebrates developed a differentiated
brain. God was conscious neither of himself nor of his creation. If he
had been, he would not have needed man. What point could there have
been in devising a new consciousness that would be inferior to the one he
had already? Jung offered this theory as 'an explanatory myth which has
slowly formed within me over the decades'.

He sent a draft of the chapter to Erich Neumann, who wrote back at
length in February 1959, objecting to what he called 'Darwinistic residue' in
Jung's account of 'haphazard and casual transformation'. Neumann suggested that archetypes could already have been at work during the Creation,
but Jung insisted they too had come into existence 'almost by accident and
casually . . . The initial event was the arrangement of indistinct masses in
spherical form. Hence the primordial archetype (mandala) appears as the first
form of amorphous gases, for anything amorphous can manifest itself only in
some specific form or order.'

Jung had enough faith in the mandala to base his creation myth on it. 'In
this chaos of chance, synchronistic phenomena were probably at work,
operating both with and against the known laws of nature to produce, in

archetypal moments, syntheses which appear to us miraculous.' In the letter, as in the chapter, Jung was speculating about the beginnings of consciousness, but less like a psychologist than a theologian, and less like a theologian than a prophet relaying what has been revealed to him.

Thirty-Eight

When You Come to the Other Side

Hearing in the winter of 1959 that Victor White had cancer, Jung broke his long silence with a letter explaining: 'You expressed yourself publicly in such a negative way about my work that I really did not know what your real attitude would be.' In February 1960 he learned from the Mother Superior of a contemplative order that his old friend had undergone 'a serious operation to the intestines for a malignant growth'. Jung replied that his dreams had warned him 'of this unexpected development . . . As there are so few men capable of understanding the deeper implications of our psychology, I had nursed the apparently vain hope that Father Victor would carry on the *opus magnum*.' This was a term alchemists used to describe their work.

Six weeks later, Jung wrote to the invalid, suggesting that since he was 'very much in the situation of the suffering Job', he should apply his 'personalistic viewpoint' to himself. In his review of Jung's book, he had explained Job's complaint against God as a neurotic outburst, not an objective criticism, and he had written an article titled 'Theological Reflections', which appeared in the April 1960 issue of the *Journal of Analytical Psychology*, saying the task of theology 'is not the same as that of analytical psychology, however closely related. And I am rather seriously afraid that if one tries to be any substitute for the other they can only clash and quarrel.'

Hearing that White was dying, Jung wrote again at the end of April, saying he would have liked to come and see him in England, but having had another embolism in February, he was too ill to travel. 'I want to assure you of my loyal friendship. I shall not forget all the useful things I have learnt through our many talks and through your forbearance with me.'

On 8 May the priest dictated a message thanking him for his 'wonderful and comforting letter'. He ended: 'May I add that I pray with all my heart for your well-being whatever that may be in the eyes of God. Ever yours cordially and affectionately, Victor White.' Two weeks later he died.

With his death, Toni's and Emma's, Jung had lost the three people who had been closest to him. He had always been a solitary man, and from now on, he would be a lonely one. It was harder to make the effort involved in writing, dictating and talking to patients or visitors when there was no possibility of intimacy and no desire for it.

He grieved for both Emma and Toni, but in different ways. Once he dreamed Toni was alive again, that some kind of misunderstanding had been involved in her death and that she had come back to resume her life. But he never entertained the idea that Emma might return. Having risen to a level Toni had never achieved, she was further away from earthly life – less likely to make her presence felt.

There was pleasure to be had from contact with his family and from the companionship of warm, simple people like Ruth Bailey and Hans Kuhn. Unlike patients, they never tried to impress, made no demands and their only questions were practical ones about his needs. With either of them he could say whatever came into his head, and to Ruth he sometimes recited verse:

> Wherever there are two they are not without God,
> And wherever there is one alone, I say I am with him.
> Raise the stone and there thou shalt find me,
> Cleave the wood, and there am I.

He was also fond of quoting Jesus. 'The greatest of all lessons is to know oneself. Let not him who seeks cease until he finds. And when he finds he shall be astonished.'

Sometimes he let Ruth do the cooking, but lost his temper one night when she put two tomatoes into a stew without being told to. When he refused to eat any dinner, she said he had better find someone else to look after him. In the morning he was cold and taciturn at breakfast, but then invited her to go for a walk with him by the lake. 'You must never forget that I once had red hair, and I've got a frightful temper. You must never rouse my temper, Ruth.' He went on to say: 'What I want you to do is to see me out, will you? Will you stay with me and see me out?'

She answered: 'Yes, I think I could do that.'

Though he was never again to travel abroad, he enjoyed being driven around Switzerland with her in Fowler McCormick's car. Wanting to revisit places he expected not to see again, Jung sat in the front seat, next to Fowler, holding the map he had studied the previous evening to plan a route involving a minimum of main roads. The acronym they devised was ITCRA – International Touring and Culinary Research Association. Their motto was: 'When we don't eat, we drive. When we don't drive, we eat.'

A former patient who visited Jung found he had not lost the 'kindly twinkle behind those penetrating eyes'. When he said: 'Pull up your chair, for I am getting deaf and old and stupid,' she reminded him he had used the same words eleven years earlier. He chuckled. 'Well, it doesn't seem to get any better.'

His redefinitions of the unconscious brought it steadily closer to being synonymous with God:

> The unconscious is surely the *Pammeter*, the Mother of All (i.e. of all psychical life). Being the matrix, the background, and foundation of all the differentiated phenomena we call psychical: religion, science, philosophy and art. Its experience − in whatever form it may be − is an approach to wholeness, the one experience absent in our modern civilisation. It is the avenue and via regia to the Unus Mundus.

Nietzsche on the threshold of madness saw himself as the man whose mission it was to revalue all values. 'Only the day after tomorrow belongs to me,' he wrote in September 1888, drafting a preface for the book he intended to call *Revaluation of All Values*. He thought his book *The Antichrist* contained the greatest criticism ever written of Christianity. 'The work cuts clean through the centuries. I swear that everything that has been said and thought about Christianity is pure childishness in comparison.'

Jung had thought of himself as the man who could shoulder the same strain as Nietzsche without going crazy. 'Others have gone to pieces. Nietzsche, and Hölderlin too, and many others. But there was a demonic strength in me, and from the start, it held firm.' But it was a grandiose delusion to think he could make radical changes to Christianity. In 1953 he had told Victor White: 'Somebody is entrusted with the task of looking ahead and talking of the things to be.' A letter written seven years later expresses the same idea of himself as a guardian of wisdom. 'In each aeon there are at least a few individuals who understand what Man's real task consists of, and keep its tradition for future generations and a time when insight has reached a deeper and more general level.'

After interviewing him for the BBC in 1959, John Freeman became a friend, and Jung involved him in working on the book *Man and His Symbols*. Freeman described him as 'a highly sociable person . . . He couldn't have been easier to get on with once you'd broken the ice and been accepted into his circle . . . He enjoyed drinking wine, and he enjoyed going and fetching a special bottle and saying "Try this." . . . He was the most unsolemn shrink that you could ever expect to meet anywhere, irreverent to the end.'

Freeman visited him several times in Küsnacht. At eighty-five,

> he was a very handsome man . . . He had great physical strength, and constantly in his conversation he made references or allusions back to his physical strength . . . I imagine that when Jung was in his prime he would have been about six foot four or five, and hugely broad, a very striking physical specimen . . . You couldn't help but noticing the enormous pleasure he took in women and in their company.

Invited to a dinner party in Zurich, Freeman took the lady Jung had asked him to bring. 'He very properly sat her at his right hand side at the table, and I doubt if his hand was off her knee for the whole period of the dinner.'

Generally he was 'preoccupied' with the thought that 'this is the Marian age in which the female is going to dominate . . . He did again and again harp back to this thought.'

The other subject that kept recurring in conversations with Freeman was Freud, 'to whom he clearly owed an enormous lot, and whom he clearly loved in a way and up to a point . . . It was like a sore. He would constantly come back and scratch it.'

In September 1960, Jung made the last of his motoring expeditions with Fowler and Ruth. While they were in Onnens in the west of Switzerland, Jung suffered a bout of severe pain. He was driven home in an ambulance, and the trouble was found to centre on his gall bladder. One night he seemed to be in a state of coma, but he recovered and told Aniela Jaffé how wonderful that state of unconsciousness had been.

Though he never recovered his stamina, and knew he had little time left, he was determined to finish the essay he was writing for *Man and His Symbols*. This was apparent whenever he asked 'What have I still to do?' or said 'I cannot go to Bollingen before I've finished all that has to be done.'

When spring brought warmer weather, he stayed there again after an unprecedented absence of eight months. It gave him great pleasure to be there, but he always seemed exhausted and his interest in external reality was dwindling. 'He sometimes forgot, sometimes even confused things . . . His appetite was poor and he looked more and more thin and frail. Mentally he was very quiet and cheerful. The last book he read with greatest interest was by Charles Luk on CH'AN and ZEN teaching.'

After reading a depressed letter Jung had written, Michael Fordham decided to visit him. Written in a shaky hand, the letter said nobody understood him and his work had been a failure. When Fordham arrived in

Zurich, Ruth Bailey answered the telephone and said that though Jung was ill, it would do him good to have a visitor.

Fordham found him wearing a dressing gown and a skullcap. Wanting to cheer him up, Fordham talked about the interest English people were taking in his work. 'He looked at me as though I were a poor fool and did not know a thing. Then he started to talk about L.S.D. and the *abaissement du niveau mental* that it produced, so that archetypes could come into the field of consciousness. I had heard this dissertation more than once and it had always been a bad sign.'

He did not look like his usual self, and it was clear he was dying. 'He eventually became confused and distressed, and I asked him what the matter was. He did not speak for a minute or two, and then he said "You had better go", and regretfully I did so.'

There was no sign now of the euphoria he had felt when he thought he was going to die after his heart attack. It looked as if he no longer believed either in his special relationship with God or in his mission to preserve peace by presenting the world with a new combination of Christianity and depth psychology. The drift of the ethos was away from religion, and though he had once believed Victor White would do for him what he had been expected to do for Freud, the priest was dead, and no one else could perform the same service.

When Jung said he knew from his dreams that he would die soon, Ruth asked: 'Whatever shall I do when you go and leave me?'

'Well,' he said, 'I'll do my very best to welcome you when you come to the other side.'

Another bout of illness began with a gall-bladder attack. He appeared to recover, but, as Aniela Jaffé put it, 'his forces were less and less at his disposition. Nearly no visitors, no dictating letters. Only rereading his article which had been gone through by Barbara Hannah. Sometimes he sat in the garden, and even made a drive from time to time.'

He had a peaceful day on 16 May, but during breakfast the next morning, he had an embolism which affected his speech. Though he could still think clearly, the words that came out were not the ones he wanted to say. After a few days, he began to recover, but he could not read so easily, and Ruth spent a lot of time reading to him. When he talked, it might be in German, Swiss German, English or French. He seemed unaware of which language he was speaking, and often failed to find the words he wanted. 'It was heartbreaking,' wrote Aniela Jaffé,

to see him in pain to formulate. Even at that stage, he asked for the letters, and we found out a way of understanding. This *sacrificium* intellectus was nearly too much. I suppose that it led him to the strong wish to go away definitely, though the doctor said that he might recover just as well. He did not want anymore. It was at that time that he went into bed because his forces completely failed. He slept most time.

On 30 May they were having tea together at the window of the library when he collapsed.

He was taken to his room. Barely able to speak, he grew gradually weaker, but he often smiled. The last time he sat on the terrace with Ruth, he told her about a dream: 'Now I know the truth, but there is still a small piece not filled in, and when I know that, I shall be dead.' He had another dream, which he told her during the night. On a high plateau was a huge block of stone inscribed 'And this shall be a sign to you of wholeness and oneness'.

His daughter Marianne came to stay in the house and helped Ruth to look after him. Finally a nurse was called in, but only for the last few days of his life, when he was mostly sleeping. He seemed to be dreaming and sometimes, when he briefly recovered consciousness, he tried to talk but could say almost nothing coherent.

On the last evening of his life, Franz and Ruth were in his room with him while he sat watching the sun set. He told Ruth to take his keys and fetch a bottle of very good wine from the cellar. The three of them drank it together.

They were both with him during the afternoon of the next day when he was in bed, trying to talk, but they could not understand him. His mouth was very dry, and, after fetching a piece of flannel and some camomile, she tried to moisten it for him, which seemed to please him. But suddenly Franz was saying: 'Don't bother, Ruth. It's too late.'

There was a thunderstorm in the night, and another one during the funeral service. Agathe, who was sitting next to Ruth, said: 'That's Father grumbling.'

Notes

When abbreviated titles are given for books or articles, see Bibliography. Because translations of Jung are so unreliable, I have either made a new translation of everything I quote or revised an existing one. Translations from *MDR* are all new, but for this book I give page references to both the published English text and the German.

Chapter One: Bursting Out

3	have ever met.' Barbara Hannah 'Glimpses'
3	very much themselves.' Joseph Henderson in Begg 1975
3	I ever met'. Fordham *Contact with Jung* p 221
3	I could imagine.' Una Thomas FCL
3	found it indispensable.' Jutta von Graevenitz in Jensen p 29
4	really sink in. Henderson 'Picture'
4	happen to him. Margaret Gildea in Jensen pp 24–5
4	ultimately identical or not.' Letter to A. Vetter 8 Apr 1932
4	calls the collective unconscious. Letter to Pastor Fritz Buri 10 Dec 1945
4	contradistinction to "human" '. Letter to Pastor Max Frischknecht 8 Feb 1946
4	I am talking.' Letter to Father Victor White 5 Oct 1945
4	the necessary proofs.' Letter to M. Patzelt 29 Nov 1935
4	theology and science".' Letter to Paul Maag 12 Jun 1933
5	of the God-image.' Letter to J. Goldbrunner 8 Feb 1941
5	the nature of God.' Letter to V. White 5 Oct 1945
5	the Christian truth.' Letter to H. Irminger 22 Sep 1944
5	the Turin Shroud. Donn p 26 and pp 131–2
5	formerly vague expectations.' Letter to Upton Sinclair 24 Nov 1952
5	of his multitudinous nature.' CW15 p 13

Chapter Two: A Cannibal Jesus

6	gods as Venus and Baldur. *Speaking* p 178
6	incantations about witches. Bennet *Meetings* pp 45–54
6	archaic customs were preserved. CGJ interview on 14 Apr 1951 with Anthony Storr, and Storr interview with the author on 14 Oct 1998

6   them with blood?' *Speaking* p 142
6   usually lost for words'. *MDR* p 66/55
7   Jung grew up.' Ryce Menuhin pp 233–40
7   records and statistics. Brockway p 62
8   in the ground.' pp 24–5/16–17
8   silence of the night.' *MDR* p 22/14
8   or seven times. *MDR* pp 33–4/24–5
8   wise and courageous. Ellenberger pp 661–2 and Oeri
9   him very well.' Hannah pp 21–2
9   still standing there.' CW18 pp 171–2
10   Goethe's great-grandson. Steiner
10   fields and rivulets. Adolf Portmann in *Spring* 1976
11   as neurotic hysteria. Elms p 63
11   after his death. TS of *MDR* in FCL
11   I started with.' *MDR* p 23/15
11   anti-social monster.' Albert Oeri in *Die kulturelle Bedeutung der komplexen Psychologie* Zurich Psychological Club, Berlin 1935
11   observed or criticised.' *MDR* p 33/24
11   the man-eater.' *MDR* p 27/19
12   spoke about 'heathens'. *MDR* p 33/24
12   the individual himself. *MDR* p 376/346
13   cursed or blessed'. *MDR* pp 57–8
13   of three of four. *Wandlungen und Symbole der Libido* (*Transformations and Symbols of the Unconscious*) was the title of the 1912 book translated into English as *Psychology of the Unconscious* (New York 1916 and London 1917). Substantially rewritten, this reappeared as *Symbols of Transformation* CW6.
13   modes of adaptation.' CW Supp vol B pp 395–6
13   variance with himself.' *Soul* p 115
14   my blunt statement.' Fordham *Fenceless* p 114
14   as more disturbed. Interview with Michael Fordham 31 January 1995
14   be more explicit. *MDR* p 66/55
14   suffering and anger. *Kundalini* p 35 and p 45
14   in my self.' *MDR* pp 34–5/25–6
14   flavour of sanctity'. *MDR* 35/26
14   my favourite game.' *MDR* German p 26; missing in English edn
14   will devastate him.' R. D. Laing *The Divided Self* London 1960 p 47
15   he destroyed with earthquakes. *MDR* p 33/24
15   in his trouser pocket. *MDR* pp 35–6/26–7
15   was becoming unbreathable.' *MDR* p 34/25
15   about my manikin.' *MDR* pp 36–7/27–8
16   a transitional object. Fordham *Fenceless* p 74
16   into a monkey?' *MDR* 41/32
16   with the birth.' Ibid

Chapter Three: Such a Wicked Thought

17   wipe your nose.' *MDR* pp 41–2/32–3

18 ∙ how to move. *MDR* p 45/35–6

18   English friend Edward Bennet. E. A. Bennet *C. G. Jung* p 16

18   not be seen.' I am indebted to Catherine Peters for this point.

19   of his unconscious. AJ UM

20   was running away. *MDR* p 47/36–7

20   want to know.' *MDR* 54–8/43–8

20   than Jung tells us. Mumford 'Demons'

20   is, I submitted'. Erik H. Erikson 'Themes of Adulthood in the Freud–Jung
      Correspondence' in *Themes of Work and Love in Adulthood* Cambridge, Mass.,
      1980 p 55

20   he was eighteen. Jolande Jacobi FCL

20   out His will. Hofer p 110

21   what you say.' CW18 p 204

21   earn a living?' *MDR* p 47/37

21   morning till seven.' *MDR* p 48/38

21   those buckled shoes. *MDR* pp 51/40–1

22   of the parents. CW vol B p 28

22   without medical treatment. CW vol 4 p 137

22   in a coach. *MDR* p 50/40

22   not from nature. *MDR* p 62/50

22   this was unfair. *MDR* p 61/49–50

23   the "natural mind".' *MDR* pp 67–9/56–7

23   made me do?' *MDR* p 63–4/51–2

24   beautifully arched eyebrows. Zumstein-Preiswerk p 122

24   as his first love. Letter to Andreas Vischer cited in Micale p 302

24   love with her. AJ UM

24   to the paths. *MDR* pp 97/81–2

25   anything about it.' *MDR* p 70/58

25   of his trousers. *MDR* pp 70–2/58–60

25   evil seem innocuous. *MDR* pp 78–9/65–6

25   somehow suited me'. *MDR* pp 85/71

26   and living matter. *MDR* pp 85–86/72–3

26   but somewhat remote'. *MDR* p 87/74

26   I had before.' *MDR* p 89/75–6

28   part of himself. *MDR* pp 104–9/89–92

29   things to go on.' *MDR* pp 113–14/98–9

29   find nothing wrong. *MDR* p 114–15/99–100

29   is usually acknowledged'. CW10 pp 104–5

Chapter Four: The Geology of the Person

30 the evolutionary ladder. Adolf Portmann 'Recollections of Jung's Biology Professor' in *Spring* 1976 pp 149–54

30 of God's world, *MDR* pp 85–6

31 our nervous system.' Ibid

31 its widest sense". *MDR* pp 121/107–8

31 his own problems. Steiner pp 130–7

32 1896 or 1897. Bennet *Jung* pp 19–20

32 a higher world.' David Straus *Charakteristiken und Kritiken* Leipzig 1839

33 textbook, *Suggestive Therapeutics. De la suggestion et de ses applications à la thérapeutique* Paris 1886

33 hypnotists in action. Ellenberger pp 85–8 and Shamdasani 'Psychoanalysis Inc'

33 to move them. Bennet *Meetings* p 41

33 cursed or blessed'. *MDR* pp 57–8

33 No Two personality. *MDR* German edn p 107

35 on his conquest. Zumstein-Preiswerk p 71 and Micale pp 294–5

36 thoughtful, faraway look'. CW Fifth Zofingia lecture, intro

36 weekly housekeeping money. *MDR* p 116/101

37 for a year. *MDR* p 117/102

37 the wild garden. Zumstein-Preiswerk pp 59–64

37 friend, who laughed. Appendix in German edn *MDR* p 406

37 you are gone.' *Speaking* p 294

37 the trip back.' Oeri 'Die kulturelle Bedeutung der komplexen Psychologie', op. cit.

38 drenched in sweat.' Ibid

38 what matter is. Nagy p 13

39 shall not know.)' *The Zofingia Lectures* paras 71–2

39 the Holy Ghost. *MDR* p 118/104

Chapter Five: Magnetic Passes

40 Jung so seriously. Zumstein-Preiswerk pp 50–1

41 medium's own disposition.' CW1 p 53

41 a psychological viewpoint'. p 128/114

41 between cosmic forces. Goodheart pp 6–7 and 27–30

43 plan was abandoned. Micale p 295

44 always this girl!' Letter from Sabina Spielrein to Sigmund Freud 20 Jun 1909 in Caretenuto p 105

44 but as ignorant.' Schopenhauer *Parerga und Palipomena* Berlin 1862 p 243, quoted in 2nd Zofingia lecture

44 of a body.' Schopenhauer *Parerga und Palipomena* trans E. J. Payne Oxford 1974 pp 298–9

45   the mechanical advantage'. Kant *Träume eines Geistersehers* Leipzig 1899
45   he underestimated it. Steiner pp 141–2
45   declared the winner. Ibid p 155
45   only to him'. Ibid p 137
45   and showed it. Steiner pp 144–7
46   of the soul'. *MDR* pp 119–20/105–6
46   were at work.' Oeri p 188
46   I have seen. Letter to Father Norbert Drewitt 25 Sep 1937
46   through every illusion.' Johannes Hemleben *Rudolf Steiner* East Grinstead
      1975. Jung and Steiner are compared by Anthony Storr in his book on gurus,
      Feet of Clay, pp 69–70.
47   them from within.' Letter to Oskar Schmitz 26 May 1923
49   Stefanie Zumstein-Preiswerk. p 87
49   a white robe. Kerr p 50
49   may have been". Elms p 64
49   table had split. Letter to B. Rhine 27 Nov 1934
50   as a medium. Zumstein-Preiswerk. pp 80–1
50   in the blade. Letter to J. B. Rhine 27 Nov 1934. The photograph is
      reproduced in *Letters* vol 1 p 181.
50   fire with suspense.' quoted in Sabina Spielrein's diary 26 Nov 1910 cited in
      Carotenuto p 347
50   collide with spirit.' *MDR* p 130/116
51   are much worse." ' CW18 p 85

Chapter Six: Lunatic Asylum

52   after 340 inmates. *Kantonale Psychiatrische Universitätsklinik Burghölzli Zürich*
      privately printed, undated
52   some for me.' Letter to V. White 8 Jan 1948
52   inspired suicidal ideas. Manfred Bleuler FCL
52   come in later. Ellenberger pp 666–7
53   in the morning. A. A. Brill *Freud's Contribution to Psychiatry* New York 1944
      p 30
53   at his age.' Letter to Freud 20 Feb 1908
53   with other people. C. A. Meier FCL
53   for low wages.' Alphonse Maeder in Ellenberger pp 667–9
54   abreast of it. Prof. Jakob Wyrsch cited in Ellenberger p 667
54   please you so?' CW B pp 184–5
54   dance with doctors. Franz Jung in interview with Linda Donn in Donn p 60
54   compensated by megalomania. Letters to Freud 17 Apr and 13 May 1907
54   world with noodles.' CW3, pp 76–7, p 101, p 114, p 103 and AJ UM
54   the chronic cases. CW3 pp 160–2
54   he's messiah.' CW3 p 91
55   their classical purity.' CW7 pp 143–4

55   spoken for years. CW7 p 171
55   to reflex action". CW7p 96
55   came too close. Oeri p 10
55   or pathological psychology.' Freud *Letters to Fliess* p 461 n 3
55   impact on Jung. CW10 p 1034a
56   my own ideas.' *MDR* 169–70/151–2
56   was just beginning.' *Speaking* pp 277–8
56   a serial publication. *Grenzfragen des Nerven- und Seelenlebens* ed. L. Löwenfeld and H. Kurella, Wiesbaden 1901
56   his posthumous writings. CW18 pp 361–8
56   to sell them. Mumford 'Demons'
57   *to Planet Mars.* Théodore Flournoy *Des Indes à la planète Mars* Paris and Geneva 1900
57   young girl somnambulist'. CW7 p 123
58   literature and philosophy. Ellenberger pp 112–13, 122–3
58   for Jung's thesis. Shamdasani 'Geneva'
58   her normal consciousness.' Ibid
58   to conscious lying.' CW1 pp 78–9
59   been a fake. *Volksrecht* Zurich 22 Sep 1905
59   onset of sleep.' Freud *The Interpretation of Dreams* p 593
59   consciousness only briefly. CW1 pp 68–9
59   as autonomous personalities. CW1 pp 77–8
59   difference of degree.' CW1 p 67
60   of the automatisms.' CW1 pp 53–4
60   as "thought insertion".' Anthony Storr letter to the author 21 Mar 1999
60   and a visionary'. CW1 pp 17–18
61   act of 'revenge'. Carotenuto p 105
61   the same way. Micale pp 303–4

Chapter Seven: Wearing a Cardboard Collar

62   wore green livery. Donn pp 46 and 173
62   she said yes. Testimony of Franz Jung. In Linda Donn pp 61–2 and Ruth Bailey interview with Glin Bennet
63   a psychiatric review. Sigbert Ganser 'Über einen eigenartigen hysterischen Dämmerungzustand' *Archiv für die gesamte Psychologie* Leipzig XXX 1898
63   in the hospital. AJ UM
64   approaching the unconscious. Ellenberger p 692 and James Donat 'Depth Psychology'
65   on a lie." ' *MDR* pp 171/152–3
65   the Freud-Breuer sense', Lecture to the Society of Swiss Physicians reported in the *Psychiatrisch-neurologische Wochenzeitung* Kerr p 60
65   before the end. CW2 p 192
65   all of hysteria.' Jung 1945 letter cited in Shamdasani 'Geneva'

65   propensity for 'dissociation'. John Haule *Spring* 53

65   reversed, he said. Letter to Andreas Vischer 22 Aug 1904 cited by Ellenberger in Micale p 304

66   unaffected by it. Letter to A. Vischer 14 Feb 1902 in Micale pp 303–4

66   the Berlitz School. Ellenberger p 303

66   by a street vendor. Ruth Bailey FCL

66   to the theatre. Zumstein-Preiswerk pp 100–2

67   for his wedding. Letter to Helene Preiswerk 2 Jan 1903 published as appendix to Zumstein-Preiswerk

67   American Trigant Burrow. McGuire 'Affinities'

67   the Canary Islands, Ibid

67   gone another way.' Letter to Victor White 2 Apr 1955

68   to Emma's wealth'. Anthony Storr letter to the author 21 Mar 1999

68   was still unfinished. Letters to Freud 28 Jun and 6 Jul 1907

68   have been revealed.' Eugen Bleuler's review of *Die psychischen Zwangserscheinungen* by L. Löwenfeld in the *Münchener medizinische Wochenschrift* 51 (1904) p 718

68   slightly jealous fears'. 'The Reaction-Time Ratio in the Association Experiment' CW2 pp 221–70

69   was gradually overcome. Letter from Medill McCormick to his wife 10 Mar 1909, Kristie Miller (ed.) 'The Letters of C. G. Jung, Medill and Ruth McCormick' *Spring* 50 (1990).

69   a natural product. *Notes to Seminars* vol 1 p 14

69   question of competition. CW17 p 191

69   of their own.' CW10 p 104

70   kind of sexuality.' CW10 pp 105–6

70   a spiritual sense. Letter to Carol Jeffrey 18 Jun 1958

70   to partial identity'. CW6 pp 456–7; Lucien Lévy-Bruhl trans L. A. Clare *How Natives Think* London 1926

71   like Till Eulenspiegel.' *Kundalini* p 7

71   relation is impossible.' *Dream Analysis* Part 1 p 63

71   the number Three.' Serrano p 58

71   absolutely no foundation.' CW18 p 77

71   to give birth.' *Letters* vol 2 p 15

71   dangers of overpopulation. Letter to B. Aschner 28 Mar 1951

Chapter Eight: Moon People

72   her as cured. CW3 pp 264–5

72   is most contagious'. Letter to F. Bertine 9 Jan 1939

73   sign of hatred.' Her summary of what Jung said in her draft of a letter to Freud 13 Jun 1909, in Carotenuto p 101.

73   since his youth. Jung in a report written for Freud but never sent, *International Forum for Psychoanalysis* vol 5, 1996

Chapter Nine: Lusty Stallion

84   broad as daylight.' CW3 pp 24–5

84   are chaotically liberated. CW3 p 34

84   among my followers'. Letter from Freud 7 Oct 1906

84   of the case. Letter to Freud 23 Oct 1906

84   difficult for them.' Letter from Freud 4 Dec 1906

84   to the theory.' Letter to Freud 4 Dec 1906

84   of his fallibility. Letter from Freud 6 Dec 1906

84   would welcome criticism. Letter to Freud 29 Dec 1906

84   thinking about him. Letter drafts in Carotenuto pp 107–8

84   anything she liked. Carotenuto pp 12–13

85   filled with tears. Carotenuto p 100

85   have seen it. Carotenuto pp 6 and 101–5

85   speaking to her. Draft of letter from Salina Spielrein to Freud c. 1909 in
      Carotenuto p 108

85   must remain pure. Carotenuto p 108

85   has Jewish blood.' Jolande Jacobi FCL

86   and still are.' Ludwig Binswanger 'On the Psychogalvanic Phenomenon in
      Association Experiments' in C. G. Jung (ed.) *Studies in Word Association*
      London 1918, William McGuire 'Jung's Complex Reaction' in *Spring* 1984
      and Kerr pp 124–6

86   feet in the second. Ibid

86   of new "sensations" '. *Spring* 1984 p 17

86   to the experimenter'. Ibid p 23

86   "will to power" ' Ibid p 17

87   too committed to it.' Letter to Freud 8 Jan 1908

87   to the meeting Letter from Freud 21 Feb 1907

87   her embarrassed Emma. Unpublished notes by John Billinsky on 1957
      interview, cited by Kerr p 136

87   thin close-cropped hair. Martin Freud *Glory Reflected: Sigmund Freud Man and
      Father* London 1957 pp 108–9

87   even my thinking.' Eva Brabant, Ernst Falzedar and Patrizia Giampieri-
      Deutsch (eds.) *The Correspondence of Sigmund Freud and Sándor Ferenczi Vol 1
      1908–24* Harvard 1994

88   give and take.' Ernest Jones *The Life and Work of Sigmund Freud* vol 2 p 32

88   shrewd, altogether remarkable.' *MDR* p 148/134

88   of his life. Richard Evans FCL

88   around the ears. Carotenuto p 100

88   take his place. Ludwig Binswanger *Sigmund Freud: Reminiscences of a Friendship*
      London 1957 pp 10–11

88   and religious rituals. SE vol 9

88   seen the gang.' Binswanger p 4

89   introduced into it.' Wittels *Sigmund Freud: His Personality, His Teaching and
      His School* London 1924 p 134, cited by Shamdasani in 'Psychoanalysis Inc'

89   through their room. Evidence of the maid Paula Fichtl in Donn p 12

89   indeed very intimate.' John Billinsky 'Jung and Freud' *Andover Newton Quarterly* 1969 p 42

89   advances to her. Alan C. Elms *Psychology Today* Dec 1982

89   when examining Freud, Gay p 60

89   his 'closest confidante', Letter to W. Fliess 21 May 1894

89   my death deliria'. Letters to Wilhelm Fliess 19 and 25 Apr 1894

89   of her husband. Letter to Freud 11 Sep 1907

89   he later called it. Letter to Freud 4 Jun 1909

89   in an uproar.' Letter to Freud 31 Mar 1904

90   all too fleeting.' Letter to Freud 31 Mar 1907

90   it in him.' *Seminars* vol 3 pp 20–1

90   belongs to us'. Letter from Freud 1 Jan 1907

90   always been necessities.' SE vol 5 p 483

90   something of myself.' Letter from Freud to Fliess 1 Aug 1890

91   than I am', Letter from Freud to Fliess 31 Oct 1895

91   just for you.' Letter from Freud to Fliess 18 May 1898

91   longer making love. Letter from Freud to Fliess 20 Aug 1893

91   in the friendship, Letter from Freud to Sándor Ferenczi 6 Oct 1910

91   on my character.' Letter from Freud 19 Apr 1908

91   voice was yours.' Letter from Freud 2 Sep 1907

91   rich man's table'. Letter to Freud 4 Jun 1907

91   achievement and mine. Letter from Freud 18 Aug 1907

92   writer Wilhelm Jensen, 'Delusions and Dreams in Jensen's *Gradiva*'

92   dishonesty towards myself. Letter to Freud 24 May 1907

92   and become clairvoyant.' Letter to Freud 30 May 1907

92   tree of knowledge.' Letter to Freud 4 Jun 1907

92   as a director.' Letter from Freud 6 Jun 1907

92   to be expected.' Letter to Freud 28 Jun 1907

93   five hundred men. Letter to Freud 4 Oct 1911

93   conference in Amsterdam. Letters to Freud 6 Jul and 12 Aug 1907

93   of the complexes'. CW4 p 15

93   as clinical groups'. CW4 pp 22–3

93   were not sexual. Letter to Freud 19 Aug 1907

93   already prejudiced audience.' Jones vol 2 p 126

93   to know you.' Letters to Freud 4 and 11 Sep 1907

94   about twelve members. Letter to Freud 25 Sep 1907

94   is sexual immorality.' Letter to Freud 25 Sep 1907

94   Jung in return. Ibid

94   cases like this? Letter to Freud 10 Oct 1907

94   banal or exhibitionistic.' Letter to Freud 28 Oct 1907

94   to be embraced.' Jolande Jacobi FCL

95   fantasies about seduction. Freud–Fliess correspondence pp 230–1 and 264–5

95   only sensible reaction, Letter to Freud 8 Nov 1907

95   sanctity of monks.' Letter to Freud 20 Feb 1910

Chapter Ten: Ardent Freudian

96   him and Emma. Letter to Freud 2 Nov 1907

96   it with this.' Letter to Freud 8 Nov 1907

96   object of worship. Letter from Freud 15 Nov 1907

97   test Freud's theories.' A. A. Brill 'The Development of Freud's Work in the United States' *American Journal of Sociology* vol 45 no. 3 Nov 1939

97   disseminating Freud's theories.' A. A. Brill *Lectures on Psychonalytic Psychiatry* New York 1946 pp 26–7

97   mince his words.' Vincent Brome *Ernest Jones* pp 48–9 and *Jung* p 100

97   Salzburg or Innsbruck, Letter to Freud 30 Nov 1907

97   an international journal, Letter to Freud 16 Dec 1907

97   for our ideas.' Letter from Freud 21 Dec 1907

98   glad of it.' Letter to Freud 2 Jan 1908

98   by mid-February. Letter to Freud 15 Feb 1908

98   his own work. Letter to Freud 11 Apr 1908

98   at a standstill.' Letter to Freud 30 Apr 1908

98   and unstrained relationship.' Letter to Freud 20 Feb 1908

98   up if necessary. Draft of a letter from Sabina Spielrein to Freud 9 Jun 1909 in Carotenuto pp 96–7

99   birth to the son. Journal p 166

99   your western contingent,' Letter from Freud 31 Jan 1908

99   Freud little credit'. Clark pp 249–50

99   accustomed to in London.' Ernest Jones *Free Associations* p 167

99   laid against him. RH *K: A Biography of Kafka* London 1981 p 50

99   for us today.' Martin Green *The von Ricathofen Sisters: The Triumphant and the Tragic Modes of Love* London 1974

100   to see again.' Jones *Free Associations* p 172

100   after the congress. Letter to Freud 24 Apr 1908

100   fruit of their relationship. Martin Green op. cit. p 45

100   who are feeble.' Letter to Freud 25 Sep 1907

101   the passage of time.' Ernest Jones *Free Associations* London 1959 p 166

101   his obsessional idea'. Freud SE vol 2 p 216, cited by Kerr pp 184–5

101   a faithful follower.' Letter to Freud 30 Apr 1908

101   while besieging Troy.' Letter from Freud 3 May 1908

101   charge of him.' Letter from Freud 6 May 1908

101   him every day. Letter to Freud 25 May 1908

101   analysing each other. Jones p 174

101   of minor obsessions.' Letter to Freud 25 May 1908

102   my twin brother'. Letter to Freud 19 Jun 1908

102   in her heart'. CW4 p 323

102   of our sexuality.' CW4 pp 317–20

102   his dearest friend. Carotenuto pp 30 and 107

102   to that fate.' Letter to Sabina 30 Jun 1909

102   into her hands. Letter to Sabina 30 Jun 1908 and Carotenuto pp 32 and 106

102   to Professor Freud.' Sabina's diary 19 Oct 1910 in Carotenuto p 30

103   free and independent. Carotenuto German edn p 189

103   in his life, Sabina's diary 19 Oct 1910 in Carotenuto p 30

103   become so pretty?' Letter to Sabina 12 Aug 1909, Carotenuto German edn
       pp 190–2

103   in the month. Letter to Sabina 2 Sep 1908

103   for this mission.' Letter from Freud 13 Aug 1908

103   someone so ugly. *MDR* p 149/134

103   a common core.' Letter from Freud 13 Aug 1908

103   into genuine fondness, Letter to Sabina 28 Sep 1908

103   following our approach'. Letter from Freud to Abraham 24 Sep 1908

103   in high spirits.' Letter from Freud 15 Oct 1908

104   Honoured Herr Professor') Letter to Freud 21 Oct 1908

104   would fall down. CW17 pp 16–17

104   her mother's insecurity. Rosenzweig pp 136–44 and 147–9

104   baby is born. CW17 pp 28–9

104   was not funny. CW17 pp 18–25

105   9.15 and midday? Letter to Sabina 4 Dec 1908

105   on a boss. Letter to Freud 21 Dec 1908 and unpublished letter to the
       management of the Burghölzli 3 Mar 1909 Burghölzli archive

105   only from afar.' Letter from Freud 17 Jan 1909

105   who is ill. Letter to Sabina 4 Dec 1908 in Carotenuto pp 102 and 168–9

106   'the prosaic solution'. Letter to Sabina in Carotenuto p 94

106   liberate her inwardly.' Carotenuto p 95

106   over the knife. Carotenuto p 97

107   into the theological style'. Letter from Freud 9 Mar 1909

107   blame for them.' Friedrich Nietzsche *Menschliches, Allzumenschliches* Part 1,
       section 142

107   an autonomous personality.' Samuels (ed.) *The Father* p 239

107   on their account.' Letter from Freud 9 Mar 1909

108   at me aghast. *MDR* pp 178–9/159–60

108   of your person.' Letter from Freud 16 Apr 1909

109   sacrifices to understanding.' Letter from Freud 16 Apr 1909

109   your paternal authority.' Letter to Freud 2 Apr 1909

109   the same laws.' Letter to Freud 12 Apr continuation of letter dated 2 Apr
       1909

109   by our psychology.' *Notes to Seminars* vol 3 p 493 n 17

109   of the patient'. Bishop 'Jung's Use of Kant'

Chapter Eleven: Lakeside House

110   he bought the site. Letter to Freud 22 Jun 1909

110   D.p. is worse.' Letter to Dr Louis S. London 24 Sep 1926

110   of skirmishing dogs.' Elizabeth Sergeant 'Dr Jung: A Portrait' *Harper's* May
       1931 reprinted in *Speaking* pp 50–7
111   desk, eyeing me . . . Jane Wheelwright in Jensen p 102
111   going outside Switzerland. Ruth Bailey and Marie-Jeanne Schmid FCL
111   for her brother, *Freud–Jung Letters* p 389 n 3
111   watch him carefully. Draft of letter to Freud 10 Jun 1909 in Carotenuto p 93
111   would see her. Letter from Sabina to Freud end May 1909
111   you know nothing.' Letter from Freud 3 Jun 1909
112   in my head. Letter to Freud 4 Jun 1909
112   good-for-nothing lot.' Ibid
112   nature's greatest spectacles.' Letter from Freud 7 Jun 1909
112   from his mistakes. Letter to Freud 12 Jun 1909
112   he had expected. Letter to Freud 2 Jun 1909
112   transferred to Sabina. Sabina's diary 11 Sep 1910 in Carotenuto pp 11–12
113   the whole truth. Letter to Freud 21 Jun 1909
113   in high esteem.' Letter from Freud to Sabina 24 Jun 1909
113   possibly be angry.' Letter from Freud 30 Jun 1909
113   makes it important.' Letter from Freud to Oskar Pfister 13 Jun 1909
113   wish against him. *MDR* p 179/160
114   from full-scale psychoanalysis. Kerr's interview with John Billinsky p 267 and
       MDR pp 181–2/162–3
114   can be seen'. Letter to Emma 6 Sep 1909
114   smothered in earthworms'. Jaffé *Word and Image* p 48
114   big, beautiful trees.' Letter to Emma 6 Sep 1909
114   fortunately private, commentary'. AJ UM
114   of the town. Ibid
114   the word-association test. SE *Five Lectures on Psychoanalysis*
114   was his daughter. Rosenzweig pp 136–44 and 147–9
114   fire and life'. J Putnam 'Personal Impressions of Sigmund Freud' *Journal of
       Abnormal Psychology* vol 4 pp 293–310 and vol 5 pp 372–9
115   overcome the father.' *Freud–Jung Letters* p 348
115   desire for objectivity', Taylor 'William James'
115   the other pocket. Letter to Virginia Payne 23 Jul 1948
115   with fixed ideas'. Letter from W. James to T. Flournoy in Taylor 'James'
115   slowly but surely.' Letter to Emma 8 Sep 1909
115   glass, of course.' Letter to Emma 22 Sep 1909
115   big newspapers etc.)' Letter to Freud 7 Mar 1909
116   former immoral tendencies'. McGuire 'Affinities'
116   in this country'. Letter from Medill McCormick to his wife 21 Sep 1909
       Spring 50 (1990)
116   in his work.' Letter from Medill McCormick to his wife 10 Mar 1909 in
       McGuire 'Affinities'
116   and enjoyed it.' Ibid
116   enjoyed the games. Clark *Freud*

116   a great discovery. *Notes to Seminars* vol 3 pp 22–3
117   the personal psyche'. *MDR* pp 182–5/163–4

Chapter Twelve: Our Psychoanalytical Flag

118   mine of wonderful material.' Letter to Freud 14 Oct 1909
118   back into life.' *Notes to Seminars* vol 3 p 23 and Letter to Freud 8 Nov 1909
118   financially a little?' Letter to Freud 14 Oct 1909
118   a reasonable fee?' Letter from Freud 17 Oct 1909
118   three-week course, Unpublished letter to Ferenczi 4 Nov 1909 in *Freud–Jung Letters* p 161 footnote
118   *Especially the Greeks Symbolik und Mythologie bei den alten Völker, besonders bei den Griechen* Leipzig 1810–12; *MDR* pp 185–6/166
118   for the yearbook.' Letter to Freud 8 Nov 1909
119   the original edition. Noll *Cult* pp 179–80
119   read these signs! Letter to Freud 30 Nov and 2 Dec 1909
119   other way round?)' Postscript added on New Year's Eve to Letter to Freud 25 Dec 1909
120   their spiritual ancestry'. G. R. S. Mead *A Mithraic Ritual* 1907 p 6; Noll *Cult* pp 67–9 and 327
120   but revelatory experience. Gilles Quispel, cited by Ean Begg; Tuby p 164; Clark Emery *William Blake: The Book of Urizen* Coral Gables, Florida, 1966 pp 13–14 cited by Stephan A. Hoeller in *Gnosis* no. 23 Spring 1992; and Nicholas Goodrick-Clarke *The Occult Roots of Nazism: Secret Aryan Cults and Their Influence on Nazi Ideology* London 1985 p 17
120   onto Miss Miller's'. *Notes to Seminars* vol 3 p 27
120   her own poems. Sonu Shamdasani 'A Woman Called Frank'
121   thoroughly impersonal character'. *Seminars* vol 3 p 24
121   Jung had predicted. Shamdasani op. cit.
121   of Dem. pr.' Letter to Freud 21 Jun 1909
122   discussed their dreams. Letter to Freud 15 Nov 1909 and 30 Jan 1910
122   the collective unconscious. *Speaking* p 434
122   with a patient, CW8 p 139
122   a schizophrenic patient . . .' CW5 p 101
122   with my patient.' *Speaking* p 435
122   actually the second'. CW8 p 150
122   consists of *archetypes*'. CW9 part 1 p 42
122   familiar mythological motifs. CW6 p 443
123   to and fro. CW9 part 1 pp 42–52
123   it to Jung. Meier *Soul* p 78
123   himself, not Schwyzer. Herman Nunberg *Memoirs* New York 1969 p 116
123   of the libido.' Abstract of report by Honegger reprinted by Walser in 'Honegger'
123   a suitable object'. Letter to Freud 6 Apr 1910, and Hans Walser 'Honegger'

123   as his secretary. Letter to Freud 24 May 1910

124   his own nature', Letter to Freud 9 Jun 1910

124   the pleasure principle.' Letter to Freud 31 Mar 1911

124   that can be saved'. Letter to Freud 19 Apr 1911

124   publication in preparation.' *Psychology of the Unconscious* part 2 ch 2 n 33

124   appeared in print. Walser p 245

124   of *ihnen* (them). Letter from Freud 11 Nov 1909

124   neurosis', Jung wrote. Letter to Freud 15 Nov 1909

124   society is ours.' Letter to Freud 22 Nov 1909

124   of detailed studies.' Letter from Freud 2 Jan 1910

125   could have perpetrated.' Ibid

125   or mythologically typical.' Letter to Freud 30 Jan 1910

125   with the individual. Forrester p 105

125   to the yearbook.' Letter to Freud 13 Jan 1910

125   of pruning and rewriting. Letter to Freud 11 Feb 1910

125   almost autoerotic pleasure'. Letter to Freud 17 Apr 1910

126   but in Jung. Jolande Jacobi FCL

126   she responded well Letter to Freud 1 Oct 1909

126   to be unfaithful.' Letter to Freud 30 Jan 1910

126   connoisseur of men.' *Free Associations* p 215

126   all noble souls.' Letter to Freud 11 Feb 1910

127   to be disciplined.' Letter from Freud 11 Nov 1909

127   chemist, Alfred Knapp. Letter from Freud 2 Jan 1910

128   of an animal.' Letter to Freud 11 Feb 1910

128   with another group. Letter from Freud 13 Feb 1910

128   like a monarch.' Ernest Jones *Free Associations* p 214

128   his mental health. Letter to Freud 9 Mar 1910

128   *certainly* be there.' McGuire 'Affinities'

128   a relief map. Ibid

129   to social disorder. SE vol 2 p 145

129   being dragged down. McGuire 'Affinities'

129   treating a rich patient'. Ibid

129   than to Switzerland.' SE vol 14 p 27

130   you as well. Fritz Wittels *Sigmund Freud: His Personality, His Teaching and His School* London 1924 p 140

130   had anything fresh.' Alphonse Maeder FCL

130   of my statesmanship.' Letter to Jung 12 Apr 1910

130   power of veto. Letter from Freud 2 May 1910

Chapter Thirteen: Sleepless Nights

131   of winning people. Letter from Freud 10 Aug 1910

131   Cook & Co.' Letter to Freud 11 Aug 1910

131   mechanisms of theirs.' CW B p 6

132   in Part Two. Bishop *Dionysian Self* p 91

132   out of *fear*'. Friedrich Nietzsche *On the Genealogy of Morals* Second Essay, Sections 16–19

132   our ancestors originated. Bishop op. cit. p 94

132   of his teachings'. Letter to the Rev Arthur Rudolph 5 Jan 1961

132   a significant humanity', Nietzsche *Nachgelassene Fragmente* Sep 1870 to Jan 1871

133   will be Dionysus.' Ibid

133   which we honour.' *Notes to Seminars* vol 2 p 83

133   every good man.' Ibid p 75

133   inferior to Mithraism. Ibid p 72

133   proved especially efficacious.' Ibid p 74

133   son and fire. Ibid p 86

133   calls the Devil'. Ibid p 60

133   won great applause'. Letter to Freud 24 May 1910

133   its vigorous drives'. Undated notes posted by Freud c. 22 Jun 1910, quoted in *Freud–Jung Letters* pp 332–5

134   subjugating the instinct.' Letter to Freud 26 Jun 1910

134   do with dreams.' Letter from Freud 5 Jul 1910

134   in the yearbook. Sabina's diary 9 Sep 1910 in Carotenuto p 10

134   a new era. Sabina's diary undated (September 1910) Carotenuto p 8. He prints the diary extracts in the wrong order.

135   the psychoanalytical association. Sabina's diary 14 Sep 1910 in Carotenuto p 14

135   and sleepless nights . . . Sabina's diary? Sep 1910 in Carotenuto p 16

135   want, after all?' Ibid pp 15–16

135   this to herself. Ibid p 17

135   the two ladies.' Letter to Freud 8 Sep 1910

136   in the depths.' Sabina's diary Sep 1910 in Carotenuto p 19

136   work unites us. Ibid p 20

137   because it was sexual. Appignanesi and Forrester pp 213–18

137   the death wish. Carotenuto pp 19–20

137   front of Jung. Sabina's diary 9 Oct 1910 in Carotenuto p 21

138   he had sent. Letter to Freud 20 Oct 1910

138   the Christmas holidays. Letter from Freud 23 Oct 1910

138   *for the Tailoring Trade.* Ellenberger pp 582–3 and 599–602

138   over their *Zentralblatt.* Letters to Freud 29 Oct and 7 Nov 1910

138   a new meaning. *MDR* pp 161–2/144

139   achieve worldly recognition. Sabina's diary 9 Nov 1910 pp 33–4

139   love for him. Letter to Freud 13 Nov 1910

139   his own idea? Sabina's diary 26 Nov 1910 in Carotenuto p 35

139   what she was. Ibid 21 Dec 1910 in Carotenuto p 38

139   with the devil. Ibid 8 Dec 1910 in Carotenuto p 37

139   mother of his children. Ibid

139 on 11 February. Kerr pp 313–14
140 receive some message.' Sabina's diary Feb 1911 in Carotenuto p 39

Chapter Fourteen: Enough Women

141 to you willingly.' Letter from Freud 3 Dec 1910
141 heard from me'. Letter to Freud 13 Dec 1910
141 see Jung afterwards. Letter from Freud 22 Dec 1910
141 attitude' towards him. Letter from Freud to Binswanger 1 Jan 1911
141 had this conversation, *MDR* pp 173–4/156–7
142 projected onto Freud. Barry Silverstein 'Freud's Lost Metapsychological Papers' in Stepansky
142 thanks for Munich,' Letter to Freud 18 Jan 1911
142 of the future.' Letter from Freud to Ferenczi 29 Dec 1910
142 little great-grandfather'. Letter from Freud 22 Jan 1911
142 our medical motherland.' Letter from Freud 22 Jan 1911
142 should come of it.' Letter to Freud 28 Feb 1911
142 against his father. 'Formulations on the Two Principles of Mental Functioning' SE vol 12 pp 255–6
143 ask your advice.' Letter to Freud 19 Mar 1911
143 everything here collapses'. Letter from Freud 30 Mar 1911
143 of the unconscious. Letter to Freud 8 May 1911
143 their natural witchery.' Letter to Freud 14 Dec 1909
143 discover something big.' Letter from Freud to Ferenczi 6 Oct 1909
143 cannot accompany you.' Letter from Freud to Ferenczi in Jones vol 3
144 in the homeland.' Letter from Freud 12 May 1911
144 has been shattered.' Letter from Freud 15 Jun 1911
144 to the next.' Letter to Freud 18 May 1911
144 save his life. Letter to Freud 12 Jun 1911
144 by real life'. Letter from Freud 15 Jun 1911
144 a given moment. Letter to Freud 12 Jun 1911
144 of money making'. Letter from Freud 21 Jul 1911
145 by increased emulation.' Letter to Freud 26 Jul 1911
145 little son, Siegfried.' Letter from Sabina undated, in Carotenuto p 48
145 on its own. Letter to Sabina 8 Aug 1911 *Tagebuch* pp 199–200
145 nearly an hour. CW4 pp 85–216
145 of the Lib'.'' Letter from Freud 20 Aug 1911
146 what you say.' Letter to Freud 29 Aug 1911
146 *Totemism and Exogamy* James Frazer *Totemism and Exogamy* London 1910
146 must be imminent. Letter from Emma to Freud 6 Nov 1911
146 someone like me.' Letter from Freud to Wilhelm Fliess 31 Oct 1897
146 he is resisting'. Letter from Emma to Freud 6 Nov 1911
146 'broken inwardly'. Maeder FCL
146 in San Francisco. Anthony p 52

147   until about 1913. Anthony p 28
147   able to cure. Donn p 179
147   end of 1912, Letter from Freud to Ferenczi 23 Dec 1912 in *Freud–Ferenczi Correspondence* p 446
147   was the one. Letter from Freud to Ferenczi 30 Dec 1912, Freud Collection Accession 19042
147   bringing from Zurich.' Letter from Freud to Jung 1 Sep 1911
147   attend the congress.' Letter to Sabina Sep 1911
147   in your life.' AJ UM and Henry Murray FCL
147   other such 'feats' ". International Forum for Psychoanalysis 5:203–17 1996
148   from primitive man'. Jones vol 2 p 86
148   are not extinct'. Freud SE vol 12 p 82
148   the Great Mother. CW 18 p 446
148   a healthy coarseness. Jones vol 2 p 85
148   things were moving.' Letter from Jones to Freud 25 Mar 1926
148   in the individual'. Letter to Jung 13 Oct 1911
148   stuff also occurs'. Letter to Freud 17 Oct 1911
148   confrontation with Jung. Letter from Emma to Freud 30 Oct 1911
148   keep a lot?' Letter from Emma to Freud 6 Nov 1911
148   shot without remorse.' Letter from Freud 2 Nov 1911
149   potential to fulfil.' Letter from Emma to Freud 6 Nov 1911
149   into this field?' Letter from Freud 12 Nov 1911
149   to Dem. Praec.' Letter to Freud 14 Nov 1911
149   work really involves'. Letter from Emma to Freud 14 Nov 1911
150   are with people. Letter from Emma to Freud 24 Nov 1911
150   about their contents. Ibid
150   of the society. Letter from Freud 12 Oct 1911
150   material at random.' Minutes 3 332–5
150   latent original forms . . .' Letter from Freud 17 Dec 1911
150   can be termed libido'. Letter from Freud 30 Nov 1911
150   read in Amsterdam. 'The Freudian Theory of Hysteria' CW4 pp 10–24
151   was inevitable here.' Letter to Freud 11 Dec 1911
151   her was unemotional. Letter to Sabina 11 Dec 1911
151   for the yearbook. Letter to Sabina 23 Dec 1911
151   of mythological fantasies.' Letter to Freud 23 Jan 1912
151   the incomprehensible Jehovah'. *Psychology of the Unconscious* pp 252 and 453–5
152   to a higher purpose.' Ibid p 478
152   Coming into Being.' Letter to Sabina 18 Mar 1912 Carotenuto Ger edn p 206
152   penetration of thoughts'. Letter to Sabina 25 Mar 1912 Carotenuto Ger edn p 208
152   conflict through suffering". CW B p 290
153   making him *dangerous*.' Letter from Ferenczi to Freud 20 Jan 1912
153   a 'sentimental donkey', Letter from Freud to Ferenczi 23 Jan 1912

153   would remain intact. Letter from Freud to Ferenczi 2 Feb 1912

153   deal' of himself. Letter from Freud 31 Dec 1911

153   disagreement in principle.' Letter to Freud 9 Jan 1912

153   articles to patients. 'Recommendations to Physicians Practising
      Psychoanalysis' *Zentralblatt* 11

153   in psychotic fantasies. 'Über einige Übereinstimmungen im Seelenleben der
      Wilden und der Neurotiker, I Der Inzestscheu' in *Imago* 1, March 1912

153   have phylogenetic roots. 24 Jan 1912 Minutes 4, 25–6

153   to hear John. Freud 'Gross ist die Diana der Epheser' *Zentralblatt für
      Psychoanalyse* SE vol 12 pp 342–4

153   and mother goddesses. Ellenberger p 816

153   religious-libidinal cloud.' Letter from Freud 18 Feb 1912

154   psychoanalysis on education.' Letter to Freud 25 Feb 1912

154   the dog's health. Letter from Freud 10 Jan 1912

154   remissness as a correspondent, Letter to Freud 25 Feb 1912

154   my excess libido.' Letter from Freud 29 Feb 1912

154   who remain pupils.' Nietzsche *Also sprach Zarathustra* Part One section 3

154   tolerate greater intimacy?' Letter from Freud 5 Mar 1912

154   half a fish.' Letter to Freud 1 Apr 1912

154   out the tyrant'. Letter from Freud to Sabina Aug 1912 in Carotenuto
      p 117

Chapter Fifteen: Giving His Throne Away

155   the social structure).' Letter to Freud 8 May 1912

155   recognised Jung's source, Letter from Freud 14 May 1912

155   to do more.' Letter from Freud 23 May 1912

156   we Swiss are.' Letter to Freud 8 Jun 1912

156   of it yourself.' Letter from Freud 13 Jun 1912

156   of Adler's disloyalty.' Letter to Freud 13 Jul 1912

156   previously friendly relations', Letter from Freud to E. Jones 23 Jul 1912

156   oil and water.' Letter from Freud to Ferenczi 29 Jul 1912

156   superior Jewish race.' Letter from Freud to Sabina Aug 1912 in Carotenuto
      p 117

156   into a breach'. Letter from Freud to Sabina 14 Jun 1912 in Carotenuto p 16

156   continue as president. Letter to Freud 2 Aug 1912

157   was in it. 'America Facing Its Most Tragic Moment' *New York Times* 29
      Sep 1912, *Speaking* pp 11–24

157   of someone else.' CW4 p 199–200

157   are still active. CW4 pp 84–224

158   adjustment to life.' *Speaking* pp 18–21

158   much too narrow'. Quoted by Kerr p 419

158   in your mind.' Letter from J. J. Putnam to Fanny Bowditch 12 Oct 1912 in
      Noll *Aryan* p 169

159   followed too implicitly. Letter from J. J. Putnam to Fanny Katz 1 Dec 1912 in Noll *Aryan* p 169

159   than of physician'. William McGuire in correspondence with Laurie Lathrop, see Lathrop 'What Happened at St Elizabeth's' *Spring* 1984

159   Negroes, with demonstrations', Letter to Freud 11 Nov 1912

159   categories of imagination'. E.g. CW18 p 38 and letter to Mircea Eliade 19 Jan 1955

159   mentally deranged Negroes'. CW5 p 102

159   a *collective* nature.' CW18 p 37

159   fertility of the earth.' CW18 p 39

159   from mental disorders'. CW6 p 443

160   he is awake.' Sir Walter Spencer and Francis Gillen *The Northern Tribes of Central Australia* London 1904 and CW6 p 30

160   in this perspective. *Notes to Seminars* vol 3 p 30

160   we resent it.' Ibid pp 59 and 105

160   to partial identity'. CW6 p 456

160   God by work.' *Notes to Seminars* vol 3 pp 30–1

161   of our common efforts.' Letter to Freud 11 Nov 1912

161   version of them.' CW4 p 86

161   for the interim, Letter from Freud 14 Nov 1912

161   off these impressions.' Letter from Freud to Ferenczi 26 Nov 1912, Freud Collection Accession no. 19042

161   of this occasion.' Leonhard Seif to E. Jones 26 Dec 1912, Ernest Jones Archive, London

162   I were his father.' *MDR* p 157/161

162   be to die.' Jones vol 1 p 317

162   of the cause.' Letter from Freud to Ferenczi 26 Nov 1912

162   unruly homosexual component', Ibid

162   predecessor of his'. Ludwig Binswanger *Sigmund Freud: Reminiscences of a Friendship* New York 1957 p 49

162   further successful co-operation.' Letter from Freud to Putnam 28 Nov 1912 in Hale (ed.) Putnam Letters p 150

162   separation or defection.' Letter from Freud to Ferenczi 26 Nov 1912

162   sounded on Wednesday?' Lou Andreas-Salomé *The Freud Journal* trans Stanley Leavey New York 1964 p 58

162   so many disappointments.' Letter to Freud 26 Nov. 1912

162   this letter condescending. Letter from Freud to Karl Abraham 3 Dec 1912 in Hilde Abraham and Ernst Freud (eds.) *A Psycho-Analytic Dialogue: The Letters of Sigmund Freud and Karl Abraham 1907–26* New York 1965 p 128

162   'Your untransformed Freud'. Letter from Freud 29 Nov 1912

162   So watch out!' Letter to Freud 3 Dec 1912

162   of my authority.' Letter from Freud to Ernest Jones 8 Dec 1912, Freud Collection Box D2

163   without getting angry? Letter from Freud 5 Dec 1912

163 Freud in public. Letter to Freud 18 Dec 1912

163 he certainly is'. Letter from Freud to Ferenczi 23 Dec 1912, Freud Collection Accession 19042

163 the utter insolence.' Letter from Freud to Jones 26 Dec 1912, Freud Collection D2 LC

163 delusions of grandeur. Letter from Jones to Freud 29 Dec 1912 in Paskauskas *Freud–Jones Correspondence* p 189

163 worth the ink'. Letter from Freud to Jones 1 Jan 1913 ibid

163 a colossal narcissism'. The article was published in *Internationale Zeitschrift für ärtzliche Psychoanalyse* 1 (1913) pp 313–29. An English translation appears in Jones *Essays in Applied Psychoanalysis* vol 2 New York 1964 pp 255 and 247

164 personal relationship entirely.' Letter from Freud 3 Jan 1913

164 rest is silence." ' Letter to Freud 6 Jan 1913

164 be his son', *Notes to Seminars* vol 3 p 22

164 never deceives people.' Muser, second page of unpaginated text

164 interpretation is possible.' Letter to Freud 29 Jul 1913

165 of their master'. Letter from Jones to Freud 7 Aug 1912 Colchester

165 most reliable men.' Letter from Freud to E. Jones 1 Aug 1912, Freud Collection Box D2

165 my position was.' *MDR* p 194/174

165 my father's house.' Joseph Henderson cited in Stein p 94

165 that come from?" ' *MDR* p 194/174

165 is a paradox.' Tina Keller *Spring*

165 through yoga practices". *MDR* p. 201/180

165 blew over one'. Fowler McComicle quoted by Shamdasani *Kundalini* intro p xxv and McCormick FCL

165 a 'psychic disturbance'. *MDR* p 197/177

166 consultant, he refused. McGuire 'Affinities'

166 settle in Zurich. Ammann p 10

166 on Ward's Island.' Letter from Jones to Freud 25 Apr 1913

166 of her suite. Noll *Aryan* p 212

166 to the surface.' Letter from Freud to Sabina 8 May 1913, in Carotenuto pp 119–20

167 asserted in this respect!' Letter from J. J. Putnam to E. Jones 2 Sep 1913 in Noll *Aryan* p 172

167 his own satisfaction.' Letter from J. J. Putnam to E. Jones 24 Oct 1913 in Nathan G. Hale (ed.) *James Jackson Putnam and Psychoanalysis: Letters between Putnam and Sigmund Freud, Ernest Jones, Sándor Ferenczi and Morton Prince* Cambridge, Mass., pp 276–7

167 overrating the danger.' Letter from Freud to Ferenczi 5 Aug 1913

167 or appreciate us.' Letter from Freud to Sabina 28 Aug 1913

167 an *energic viewpoint*.' CW4 para 566

168 the subliminal door.' William James cited by Sonu Shamdasani in 'Religion'

168 counterweight to Freud. *MDR* German edn pp 378–9

169   and intellectual brutality.' Stanley A. Leavy *The Freud Journals of Lou Andreas Salomé* New York 1964 p 168

169   role to sensation.' CW6 p 508

169   each other again'. Freud SE vol 14 p 45

170   of his doctrine.' Sabina's *Tagebuch* p 209 and Carotenuto p 184

Chapter Sixteen: Creative Illness

173   of my weakness.' Typescript of *MDR* FCL and *Notes to Seminars* vol 3 pp 41–2

173   *Memories, Dreams, Reflections MDR* pp 199/178–9

173   arrived at Schaffhausen. *Speaking* p 232

173   neurasthenia and hysteria. Ellenberger pp 672–3

173   from its grip.' *MDR* p 199/179. The final sentence is omitted from the English translation.

173   a *God figure*.' Fowler McCormick FCL

173   of the yearbook, Letter to Freud 29 Oct 1913

174   cease to exist.' Letter to A. Maeder 29 Oct 1913

175   views and activities. CW7 p 282

175   a schizophrenic episode'. C. A. Meier FCL

175   sense and nonsense.' From Jung's 'Red Book' – Jaffé *Spring* 1972 pp 174–6

175   not understand him.' Ibid

176   of the unconscious observed.' *Notes to Seminars* vol 3 pp 33–5

176   my superior function.' Ibid pp 56–7 and *MDR* p 205/184

176   hero-like must happen. Ibid pp 88–9

176   the collective unconscious.' Ibid p 63

177   out, other fantasies.' Ibid p 47

177   full of blood.' Ibid p 93

177   the Mithraic mysteries. Ibid pp 97–8

178   *of the soul. MDR* pp 207–8/186

178   so lonely and isolated.' Hannah 'Glimpses'

179   me illuminating insights'. *MDR* p 208/187

179   Philemon no horns. Jaffé *Image* p 67

179   strength in me.' *MDR* p 201/180

180   into dark depths.' *MDR* pp 203/182–3

180   circles all day? Franz Jung in Donn p 172

180   not to speak. Ibid pp 172–3

180   crawled into them. Ibid p 173

181   villages all disappeared.' Donn p 160

Chapter Seventeen: The Woman Inside Me

182   love for him'. Letter from Fanny Bowditch to J. J. Putnam 18–23 Nov 1913 in Noll pp 174–8

183   to criticise you.' Letter from J. J. Putnam to Fanny Bowditch 10 Dec 1913 in Noll pp 178–9

183   his own satisfaction'. Letter from J. J. Putnam to E. Jones 24 Oct 1913 in Nathan G. Hale (ed.) *James Jackson Putnam and Psychoanalysis: Letters between Putnam and Sigmund Freud, Ernest Jones, Sándor Ferenczi and Morton Prince* Cambridge, Mass., pp 276–7

183   it the *anima*. *MDR* pp 210/188–9

184   that of others.' *MDR* Ger edn p 190, passage omitted in Eng trans

184   the big office.' H. Steiger FCL cited by Sonu Shamdasani *Fictions* p 16

184   it in life.' *MDR* p 217/196

184   Earth with heaven. *MDR* pp 213/192–3

184   in every age.' Jaffé *Image* p 67

185   and reintegrated personality.' van der Post p 172

185   of my anima'. AJ UM and *MDR* p 23/15

185   for his soul.' CW18 pp 453–4

185   by the ear.' Fordham in *Matters of Heart*

185   back to reality.' Liliane Frey-Rohn in *Matters of Heart*

186   gripping the table. AJ UM and Sonu Shamdasani 'Memories'

186   pressure became images.' Tina Keller *Spring* p 285

186   talk with them'. Ibid p 288

186   from the unconscious.' Irene Champernowne pp 5–8

186   were always expressive.' Helena Henderson in Jensen p 31

186   haughty and forbidding'. Peter C. Lynn in Jensen p 42

186   Jung to bear.' Donn p 180

186   had no body.' Donn pp 178–81

186   them accept it.' Anthony p 31

187   stronger than before! Jensen p 48

187   of divorcing Emma, C. A. Meier FCL

187   narrowly escaped disaster. Susanne Trüb FCL

187   touch with them.' *MDR* p 211/190

188   with a female ghost'. *MDR* p 210/189

188   about their contents. *MDR* p 212/191

188   father and daughter.' Toni Wolff *Spring* 41 pp 96–103

189   of the soul. *MDR* pp 217/195–6

189   our rational age'. *MDR* p 213/192

189   than Dr Jung.' Letter from H. F. McCormick to John D. Rockefeller 28 Dec 1913 in Noll *Aryan* p 209

189   must suffer much.' Letter to Sabina 15 Apr 1914 in Carotenuto p 185

189   large crowd. *MDR* p 200/179

Chapter Eighteen: Preaching to the Dead

190   out our intentions.' Letter from Freud to Abraham 24 Apr 1914 in Abraham *Letters* p 173

190   the intellectual world.' *MDR* p 218/197

190   interchange of ideas.' *Letters* vol 2 p 30

190   no real friends.' Marie-Jeanne Schmid FCL

191   by the mob'. Letter from Freud to Sabina 12 Jun 1914 in Carotenuto p 122

191   to 'this phantom'. Letter from Freud to Sabina 12 Jun 1914 in Carotenuto p 122

191   as the old one.' SE p 66, cited by Sonu Shamdasani in 'Psychoanalysis Inc.'

191   importance of dreams.' CW3 p 206

191   do things wrong.' Letter from Edith McCormick to John D. Rockefeller 26 Jun 1914 in Noll p 219

191   a 'latent schizophrenic'. McGuire 'Affinities'

192   to say next. Ellenberger pp 70–4 and 113

192   heard or read.' William James *Principles of Psychology* London 1918 p 601

192   nine years later. Herbert Silberer *Problems of Mysticism and Its Symbolism* (*Probleme der Mystik and ihrer Symbolik*) Vienna 1914

193   before been conscious.' Dan Merkur *Gnosis: An Esoteric Tradition of Mystical Visions and Unions* Albany, New York, 1993 pp 50–3

193   of one's soul.' F. Katz a note of 15 Feb 1915 in Noll *Aryan* pp 180–1

193   as her analyst. Tina Keller 'Beginnings of Active Imagination' *Spring* 1982

194   Idea in Plato's sense.' Letter from E. Jones to Freud 27 Jul 1914

194   a *spiritual child*. Tina Keller FCL

194   in another's belief.' Isherwood *Diaries* vol 1 ed. Katherine Bucknell London 1996, entry for 28 Apr 1958

194   of free research'. Muser

195   August 1st 1914.' *Notes to Seminars* vol 3 p 44

195   gods and ghosts. Ibid pp 44–5

196   inner world unfolding.' Tina Keller FCL

196   me all the time.' Letter from H. McCormick to his mother 28 Nov 1914 in Noll *Aryan* p 212

196   to the army. Ammann p 13

196   on and developing.' Letter from Edith McCormick to John D. Rockefeller 14 Apr 1915 in Noll *Aryan* p 214

196   man can be', Note by H. McCormick 31 Aug 1915

196   to feel more. Letter from H. McCormick to John D. Rockefeller 31 Aug 1915

197   is the body. Ljunggren pp 89–106

197   of his books. Ljunggren pp 110–30. The letter to Anna was sent in January 1923

197   a bigger loan.' Letter from Edith McCormick to John D. Rockefeller 20 Jul 1916 in Noll p 225

198   as club librarian. Ammann p 15 and Ljunggren

198   most of them, Hannah p 130

198   during their hours'. Ibid

198 and its conditions.' Prefatory note to 'Individuation and Collectivity' talk given at Psychological Club in Oct 1916, cited in Shamdasani *Fictions* p 24

198 and too light.' Fowler McCormick FCL cited in Shamdasani *Fictions* p 22

198 will be accepted.' Maeder FCL

199 will be kept.' Circular letter 20 Apr 1916 to analysts of the Association for Analytical Psychology, cited in Shamdasani *Fictions* p 39

199 into the light. Letter to Hans Schmid 6 Nov 1915

200 he started writing. *MDR* pp.215–16/194–5

200 opportunity to appear.' *MDR* p 217/194

200 which Christianity obliterated'. Letter to Alphonse Maeder 19 Jan 1917

201 a priest there. Quispel reprinted in Segal p 222

201 not answer it.' *MDR* p 318/281

201 the social gatherings'. Tina Keller FCL

202 to be independent.' Alphonse Maeder FCL

202 about the quarrel. Alphonse Maeder FCL

202 onlookers as unimportant. Noll *Aryan* p 229

202 efficiently', Jung said. Letter to S. E. Jelliffe Jul 1915 in Burnham and McGuire p 198

202 and seemingly lost!' Letter from Edith McCormick to John D. Rockefeller 27 Mar 1919 in Noll pp 231–2

202 feel any guilt.' Ammann pp 15–19

Chapter Nineteen: The Importance of Going Astray

203 pertain to me.' *Notes to Seminars* vol 3 p 45

203 them of power.' Ibid

203 own personal experience.' Ellenberger p 673

204 *oppositorum*, psychological theories). Stein p 75

204 which they reflect'. Ibid

205 unconscious, instinctive way.' Jung *The Transcendent Function* trans A. R. Pope Zurich 1957

205 in his work. CW8 p 80

205 will be produced'. CW8 p 83

205 is analysed intellectually. CW8 pp 84–5

205 and moral considerations.' CW8 pp 86–7

206 the temple rebuilt. *Notes to Seminars* vol 3 pp 3–5

206 the original event.' Letter to M. Lasky 10 Oct 1960

206 for the individual,' CW7 p 186

207 personal and impersonal. CW7 p 280

207 "universal" collective psyche'. CW7 p 275

207 collective psyche speaks.' CW7 pp 277–81

207 psychology of primitives'. CW7 pp 283–4

208 reparation of the collective.' CW18 p 453

208 are being ignored. CW10 pp 14–15

208   not think it.' CW10 p 12

208   only two years. Letter to A. Maeder, undated, but written after 1918, cited in
        Shamdasani *Fictions* p 25

208   resigned her membership. Shamdasani *Fictions* pp 66–72

208   Club in Zurich.' Jung Introduction to Antonia Wolff *Studies in Jungian
        Thought* 1959

209   *Symbols of the Libido*. Joseph Mileck *Hermann Hesse: Life and Art* Los Angeles
        1978 pp 101–2

209   is to come.' Ralph Freedman *Hermann Hesse: Pilgrim of Crisis* London 1979
        pp 187–8 and Noll *Cult* pp 233–4

210   Hesse's poetic nature'. Stefan Zweig 'Der Weg Hermann Hesses' in Volker
        Michels (ed.) *Materialen zu Hermann Hesses Siddhartha* Frankfurt 1974 pp 26–32

210   honestly and impartially. 'Künstler und Psychoanalyse' ('Artists and
        Psychoanalysis') in *Gesammelte Schriften* vol 7 p 139 Frankfurt 1957

210   him to himself.' Hesse *Demian* Zurich 1949 pp 8–9 and p 64

211   is called Abraxas.' Ibid p 125

211   and the diabolical.' Ibid p 127

211   Hesse to Abraxas. Mark Boulby *Hermann Hesse: His Mind and Art* Ithaca, New
        York, 1967 p 111

211   are in us.' Hesse *Demian* pp 154–5

211   constant hammer-blow". Ibid p 146

211   desires, as outlets.' Ibid pp 144–5

211   active inside him. Ibid pp 147–8

211   happens without death'. Ibid p 212

212   mystery of individuality. Letter to Hesse 3 Dec 1919

212   at a stretch. Letter to Fanny Bowditch 22 Oct 1916

212   among the prisoners. Letter to Gret summer 1917 in Jaffé *Word and Image*
        pp 142–3

212   possible for me.' *MDR* p 222/200

213   through this process. Letter from Sabina probably 27–8 Jan 1918 in
        Carotenuto p 85

213   repaired the damage.' Michael Fordham obituary of Jung in the *British Journal
        of Medical Psychology* vol 34 nos. 3–4 p 167

213   the Siegfried dream.' Letter from Sabina 6 Jan 1918 in Carotenuto p 77

213   is that spark.' Letter to Sabina 3 Apr 1919 in *Tagebuch* p 222

214   order to survive. Letter to Sabina 1 Sep 1919

214   it is suitably camouflaged. Appignanesi and Forrester p 223

Chapter Twenty: Cooking in the Rain

217   its preordained shape. *Speaking* p 210

218   the wilful guests.' Katherine Mansfield note on a loose sheet of paper c. 1920
        in Margaret Scott (ed.) *The Katherine Mansfield Notebooks* 2 vols Lincoln, New
        Zealand, 1977

218 narrow materialistic outlook'. CW10 pp 167–70

219 a hard taskmaster.' C. A. Meier FCL

219 stand on Kant,' Letter to Josef Goldbrunner 8 Feb 1941

219 everyday psychological language.' Letters to B Lang 14 Jun 1957 and later in the month (not date given)

219 of doctrinal oppressiveness'. *Transformations* p 262 and Bishop 'Kant' p 114

219 highest psychic value.' CW6 pp 45–6

220 kinds of truth', E.g. *Psychology of the Unconscious* p 529

220 other, 'only psychic'. de Voogd in Papadopoulos and Saayman pp 204–22

220 conclusions of scientists'. Nagy p 265

220 no longer space'. Letter to E. Whitmont 4 Mar 1950

220 surrounded and led.' *Spring* 1972 p 184

220 could be demonstrated'. *MDR* p 13/7

221 and miniature cities. Jaffé *Word and Image* pp 140–1

221 seeping into it. Agathe, Gret and Lutz Baumann in video film by Werner Weick

221 also her father. Franz Jung to Linda Donn in Donn pp 15, 27 and 173

222 a religious man. Gret in Begg

222 in his kitchen.' Elizabeth Howes in Jensen p 20

222 with iron plates.' Letter to Marianne Jung 1 Jul 1919

222 the primitive does.' CW3 p 211 and CW8 pp 303 and 318

223 chance to develop.' Letter to Oskar Schmitz 25 May 1923

223 have been uttered. Cazeneuve pp 2–17. I am indebted to Mr Andrew Burniston for alerting me to the depth of Lévy-Bruhl's influence on Jung.

224 only an instrument. Lucien Lévy-Bruhl *La Mentalité primitive* Paris 1922 pp 510–12

224 sacrifice a bull. CW10 pp 50–7

225 the digestive tracts.' T. S. Eliot *Selected Essays* London 1932 pp 287–90

225 Jung in Küsnacht, *Speaking* p 214

225 Berlin from 1932, CW15 p 33 n

225 every human mind.' Lucien Lévy-Bruhl *Les Carnets* Paris 1949 pp 131–2

225 intimidated by critics. *Speaking* p 214

226 confusion and participation.' Claude Lévi-Strauss *The Savage Mind* London 1966 p 268

227 of archetypal images.' CW8 pp 135–7

227 they were awake.' Nietzsche *Human All Too Human* part 1 sections 12–13

227 dreams and fantasies.' CW5 pp 27–8

227 into a torrent'. CW15 pp 80–1

227 categories of understanding. CW15 pp 135–8

228 counterpart in experience'. CW6 pp 438–5

228 these same experiences.' CW7 pp 66–70

228 of our ancestors'. CW8 p 99

228 of archetypal ideas. CW8 p 158

229 the old paths. CW8 p 112
229 in an armchair. Jung's contribution to Liselotte Moser *Spuk: Irrglaube oder Wahrglaube?* Zurich 1935 pp 321–5
229 summer of 1920, CW18 p 320
229 of Maurice Nicoll. Ean Begg 'Lieutenant'
229 of psycho-transformism.' Letter from M. Nicholl to Jung 4 May 1950, quoted by Begg 'Lieutenant'
229 yet unknown ideas'. CW8 p 315
229 potentiality for divinity.' p 63 quoted in CW6 p 91
230 immersion in reality'. CW6 p 91
230 Miss M. Moltzer.' CW6 n to para 773
230 an unconscious content.' CW6 pp 247–8
230 the conscious mind. CW6 pp 250–1
231 described as "personality".' CW6 p 463
231 conclusions and judgements.' CW6 304
231 of all experience. CW6 p 445
231 of the experiencable'. CW6 pp 437–8
231 their empty forms. CW6 p 305
231 as religious experiences. CW6 p 348
231 painful or unpleasant. CW6 pp 356–61
232 absurd bodily sensations. CW6 pp 367–71
232 brutalised and plagiarised. CW6 pp 373–85
232 bordering on caricature. CW6 pp 373–93
232 processes of consciousness. CW6 p 401

Chapter Twenty-One: There Is Greatness in You

233 discussed their dreams. Donn p 180
233 from the unconscious'. Hannah p 201 n
233 pompous or self-indulgent. Michael Fordham in Anthony p 17
234 own against him'. Fordham in 'Memories'
234 to be honest.' C. A. Meier FCL
234 look after them. Kurt and Agathe Niehus FCL
234 home with them. Ibid
234 touch with insanity. Gret Baumann in Werner Weich
234 most easily loses'. Wolff pp 100–1
235 European from outside'. *MDR* p 266/242
235 I could not understand.' Ibid
235 with a handshake. Letter to Emma Mar 1920 in Jaffé *Word and Image* pp 150–1
235 aeroplanes and rockets.' *MDR* pp 268/243–4
236 an underground existence.' *MDR* pp 273/248
236 accept woman interns. Anthony p 44
236 blue at university. Hannah p 140

236 *of Peter Blobbs, Authentic Dreams of Peter Blobbs and of Certain of His Relatives. Told by Himself with the Assistance of Mrs Blobbs, Hubbard, A. J and Mrs Hubbard* London 1916

236 material from myth. Esther Harding in Fordham *Contact* pp 180–1

236 they played games. Charet p 262

236 winning word games. Harding p 182

236 'This is difficult.' Harding p 181

236 absence in England. Letter to A. Oeri 3 Dec 1920

236 him their uniqueness.' Jane Wheelwright in Jensen p 105

237 must serve this." ' Lilian Frey-Rohn in Begg 1975

237 century would have.' Vera von der Heydt ibid

237 and then disturbing'. Jolande Jacobi FCL

237 is a woman.' Anthony p 5

237 judgements or opinions.' CW13 p 41

237 library, perfectly dry.' *Notes to Seminars* vol 1 p 14

237 nebulous, and morbid.' CW10 p 125

237 had no soul. Liliane Frey-Rohn in Anthony p 3

237 injuring their femininity. 'Women in Europe' CW10 pp 113–33

238 live it now".' Isabelle Hamilton Rey, letters to her husband 17 Jan and 21 Jun 1933 in Jensen p 70

238 and more human. Margaret Gildea in Jensen p 23

239 trickery and psychosis'. Storr *Feet of Clay* p 11

239 and wondrous mystery. Letter to B. Baur-Celio 30 Jan 1934

240 on his *anima*. Jane Wheelwright cited in Douglas *Mirror* pp 44–7

240 a lamentable state'. Segaller and Berger p 100

240 dreams and fantasies. CW16 pp 134–7

241 this extra time.' Jane Wheelwright in Fordham *Contact* p 226

241 stopped seeing them. Jane and Joseph Wheelwright FCL

241 to San Francisco. Jane and Joseph Wheelwright FCL

241 of imagined neglect.' Jensen p 98

241 her to sleep. Segaller and Berger p 56

242 of his science. Mileck p 102

242 me very much.' Freedman p 224

242 scarcely yet confront.' *Materialen zu Siddhartha* vol 1 pp 130–1

242 to transcendental vision. Freedman pp 224–5

242 are simply beautiful.' Letter to Hesse 28 Jan 1922

243 wherewithal for this.' Hesse undated letter to Emanuel Maier 1950 in *Psychoanalytical Review* 50 Fall 1963 p 16

243 herself to it. Entry for 3 Jul 1922 in Esther Harding's notebooks, cited in *Speaking* p 25

243 of a row.' entries for 4 and 5 Jul, ibid pp 26–7

243 to run away.' Ibid p 27

244 in a trap.' Ibid

244 cuts that out.' Ibid p 28

244   our own way.' entry for 5 Jul 1922, ibid pp 28–9

244   be with itself. Bishop 'Trüb'

245   of December 1923. Bishop 'Trüb'

245   than physical events. Hermann Graf Keyserling *The Travel Diary of a Philosopher* New York 1925 p 255 and 124–5

245   made by Jung. CW11 p 481

245   letter in support. Hayman *Mann* p 320

245   development of man.' Oskar Schmitz *Psychoanalyse und Yoga* Darmstadt 1923 p 65

245   of his psychology'. Jensen p 39

246   them from inside.' Letter to Oskar Schmitz 26 May 1923

246   into old bottles'. Ibid

246   a single Chinese'. *MDR* pp 405–6/382–3

246   live in Germany.' Hermann Graf Keyserling *Reise durch die Zeit* vol 1 Vaduz 1948 p 290

246   recently been civilised.' CW13 pp 46–7

246   high cultural achievement.' CW13 p 11

246   as it moves'. Stephen Karcher in *I Ching: The Classic Chinese Oracle of Change* trans Rudolf Ritsema and Steven Karcher, Shaftesbury 1994

247   any other man.' CW15 pp 52–63

247   the Roman Empire.' CW15 p 60

247   found the truth. Richard Wilhelm 'My Encounter with C. G. Jung in China' *Neue Zürcher Zeitung* 29 Jan 1929

247   wills' of everybody. Quoted from the ten 'Wings' of commentary added to the *I Ching* between 200 BC and AD 200 in Stephen Karcher 'Oracle's Contexts: Gods, Dreams, Shadow, Language' *Spring* no. 53 (1992)

247   out in 1882, *The Yi King* trans James Legge, Sacred Books of the East vol 16, 1882

247   stay with him. Jaffé 1972 p 27

247   obsolete magic spells, CW11 p 597

247   to superstitious use', CW11 p 602

247   thousands of years'. CW15 p 55

248   such a maiden.' *MDR* pp 405–7/380–1

248   off its foundations'. CW15 p 55

248   moment of observation.' CW11 p 591

248   can be determined'. CW11 p 593

248   a given situation.' CW11 p 593

Chapter Twenty-Two: Tangible Silence

249   train from Lugano, AJ UM

249   over to grief.' *MDR* pp 345/316–17

249   kind of "togetherness".' Letter to Hermann Keyserling 2 Jan 1928

249   as the crypt. AJ UM

249 idea of wholeness.' *MDR* p 250/227
250 they were finished. AJ UM
250 intellectual or physical. Donn p 16 and Elizabeth Shepley Sergeant in *Speaking* pp 50–1
250 what to do.' *MDR* pp 264–5/241
250 too much modernity. Letter to G. Farner 29 Jun 1934
250 chat with them. Serrano p 98
250 visitors: 'It's human.' *Speaking* p 147
251 hear the squeals. Lucien Lévy-Bruhl *La Mentalité primitive* pp 452–3
251 where it belonged. C. A. Meier and Mr and Mrs Walther Willi-Niehus FCL
251 banks of rivulets. Agathe in Weick, and Donn p 17
251 for ten minutes. Dieter Baumann in Weick
252 solidly three-dimensional. Weick
252 of his first carvings, C. A. Meier FCL
252 indeed been bedevilled'. Letter to R. F. C. Hull 3 Aug 1953
252 the ball rolling. Letter to I. Tauber 13 Dec 1960
252 form in it.' Letter to D. Stacy 1 Sep 1952
253 unconcern for the beholder.' CW15 pp 135–7
253 with psychic torture.' Letter to Meinrad Inglin 2 Aug 1928
253 on his brow. Letter to Aniela Jaffé 12 Oct 1954
253 modes of creation.) CW15 p 89
253 life's deepest springs.' CW15 pp 74–82
254 with something worse. *MDR* pp 263/239–40
254 till the spring. McLynn p 272
254 Philemon and Baucis' Letter to P Schmitt 5 Jan 1942
254 through the gods. Wolfgang Giegerich 'Betrayal'
254 the open air. Lutz and Agathe Niehus FCL
255 ideological changes. Harding in Fordham *Contact* pp 182–3
255 respect the unconscious. *Notes to Seminars* vol 3 p 113

Chapter Twenty-Three: Dark-faced Men

256 not yet religion. D. H. Lawrence 'New Mexico' in *Phoenix* London 1936 pp 141–5
256 proposal Jung accepted. William McGuire in 'Jung in America' *Spring* 1978 pp 49–50
257 nothing about it.' Letter to Frances Wickes 1 Jan 1925 quoted in William McGuire pp 39–40
257 into a cathedral. 1925 Seminar p 47
257 study with Jung. Ibid pp 41–2
257 the Taos Pueblos'. *MDR* p 275/251 and *passim*
257 felt at home.' *MDR* pp 276–81/250–5 and *Wisdom of the Dream* pp 132–4
258 Biano had said. Letter to M. Serrano 14 Sep 1960

258 above his fireplace. Letter from Frances Wickes 3 Jul 1935 quoted by William McGuire in 'Jung in America' *Spring* 1978 p 43

258 on the ceiling. Fowler McCormick FCL

258 impossible for Europeans. Notes by Esther Harding in *Speaking* pp 30–1

258 worth almost nothing. McGuire 'Affinities'

259 of poltergeist manifestations. Letter to W. Schaffner 16 Feb 1961

259 with materialisation mediums'. Letter to L. M. Boyers 30 Sep 1932

259 greyish-whitish quasi-gaseous masses'. Anita Gregory *The Strange Case of Rudi Schneider* Metuchen, New Jersey, 1985 pp 408–10

259 spirit and heaven. Esther Harding's notes for 13 May 1925 in *Speaking* p 31

259 be a physician.' Smith Ely Jelliffe to Freud 8 Jun 1926; W. McGuire in 'Jung in America' *Spring* 1978 p 46

260 treatment for neurosis.' Anthony Storr 'Is Analytical Psychology a Religion?' Address at a Feb 1999 conference held by the Society of Analytical Psychology.

260 in older patients, CW13 p 45

260 of the soul'. CW13 p 47

260 significant change thereafter'. Homans p 21

260 a birthday cigar.' Letter to Jolande Jacobi 20 Nov 1928

260 on the canvas. Harding in Fordham *Contact* pp 181–3

261 to have deep dreams.' Harding pp 183–4

261 New Education Fellowship. *Letters* vol 1 p 50

261 was an Englishman.' Hannah p 234

261 *Christina Alberta's Father*, Bennet *Meetings* pp 50–1

261 happens to him.' CW7 p 181

262 had behaved well. Interview with H. Murray in June 1970, in Robinson p 124

262 out of books'. Robinson pp 121–7

262 in her diary. Douglas pp 132–7

263 her personality type. Robinson p 206

263 waste your time.' Aniela Jaffé in Wagner *Matters of Heart*

264 once or twice. Joseph Wheelwright FCL

264 vestige of childhood.' Letter to anon correspondent 27 Oct 1930

264 social distance interpersonally. Homans p 111

264 thinking is creative.' Christiana Morgan 'Analysis' FCL

265 the present time.' Letter from C. Morgan to H. Murray Sep 1925 in Douglas pp 139–40

266 birth and death. Hannah p 167

266 you go out.' Ruth Bailey FCL

266 concealing his irritation. Hannah p 166

266 music-hall song. Hannah p 167

266 and amoebic dysentery. *MDR* p 282/257

266 Tall coconut palms.' Letter to Hans Kuhn 1 Jan 1926

266 raced the train. Ibid

266 and a cook. Ibid
267 chatted with Ruth. Ruth Bailey FCL
267 was against it. Ibid
267 and don't worry.' *MDR* p 285/260
268 millions of fleas. Francis Daniel Hislop 'Dr Jung, I Presume' *Speaking* pp 32–7
268 lost its meaning.' *MDR* p 291/265
268 between the sexes. *MDR* pp 292–3/267
269 into primeval expanses.' *MDR* pp 293/267–8
269 fighting and killing.' *Kundalini* pp 40–1
269 English knew everything. *MDR* pp 294–5/269
269 did no harm. *MDR* pp 296–7/270–1
270 by the tribe. *MDR* 299–301/274–5

Chapter Twenty-Four: Negotiating with Heaven

271 I ought to.' Letter to Frances Wickes 9 Aug 1926
271 I can do.' Letter to Frances Wickes 6 Nov 1926
271 once a month. Cornelia Brunner FCL
272 in my estimation.' Anthony p 33
272 like a pigeon.' Regula Rohland-Oeri FCL
272 into it herself.' Hannah p 168
272 imagination at all.' Marie-Louise von Franz in Ian F. Baker (ed.) *Methods of Treatment* p 91
272 powerful therapeutic agent.' Letter to R. Pfahler 12 Dec 1932
273 far beyond them. Jane Wheelwright in Jensen pp 102–3
273 at that moment.' Ibid p 104
273 fury and feeling.' Ibid p 70
273 acknowledge spiritual truths.' Letter to Pastor J. Schattauer 20 Feb 1933
273 are ultimately grounded.' Letter to G. Meyer 20 May 1933
274 a human being?"' Jane Wheelwright in Jensen p 103
274 King of Switzerland.' Hermann Graf Keyserling *Reise durch die Zeit* vol 2 Darmstadt 1958 pp 197–8
274 the human psyche.' Jensen p 96
274 case to Jung. Dana Sue McDermott 'Creativity in the Theatre: Robert Edmond Jones and C. G. Jung' *Theatre Journal* May 1984
274 with the demons.' Robert Edmond Jones, undated letter to Mary Foote, quoted in Edward Foote 'Who was Mary Foote?' *Spring* 1974 p 258
274 believe their eyes.' Letter written in Oct 1927, *Spring* 1974
275 up to today?"' Douglas pp 153–5
275 continue psychological discussions. Jane Wheelwright in Jensen p 101
275 on them *afterwards*. Letter to Hermann Keyserling 23 Apr 1931
276 of definite people.' Tavistock Lectures
276 characters he creates.' Ibid pp 80–1
276 sculpting in stone. Douglas pp 103–4

277   is your soul.' Her note for 8 Jul 26 in C. Morgan 'Notebook. Dreams, Analysis, 8 Jun – 20 Oct 26' FCL

277   given up nature.' Note for 11 Jun 1926

277   out of them. Note for 12 Oct 1926

277   if playing football. C. Morgan diary FCL

277   or personal involvement. *Spring* 1961 pp 268–71

278   from his patients.' Mikkel Borch-Jacobsen cited by Sonu Shamdasani in 'Psychoanalysis Inc.'

278   produced the visions, Henry Murray FCL

278   search for truth'. *Visions Seminars* p 517

279   powerful he is. *Spring* 1960 pp 12–13

279   should be having. Diary 21 and 24 Oct 1926 FCL

279   saying something evil. *Spring* 1960 p 13

279   of female opinionating. Douglas *Mirror* pp 83–5

279   the law-giver'. Robinson pp 206–7

279   *non* of spirituality'. Robinson p 159

280   completion of the self.' Letter to H. Murray 11 Jan 1929 in Robinson p 152

280   became a nuisance.' Letter to H. Murray 21 Sep 1931 in Robinson p 206

280   was his Olympus. Robinson p 162

280   and enfold her.' CW17 p 199

280   have had ours.' Letter from C. Morgan to Lewis Mumford 3 Aug 1963

280   is spirit now? Christiana note for 26 Oct 1926 FCL

281   Yours affectionately, C. G. Letter to C. Morgan 28 Dec 1927

281   on 'libidinous affection'. Robinson p 207

Chapter Twenty-Five: His Magic Wand

282   is simply fabulous.' CW18 p 67

282   of Chinese science.' CW10 p 90

282   E. von Hartmann.' Letter to A. Vetter 25 Jan 1932

282   again and again.' CW13 p 50

282   to outgrow them. CW13 p 15

282   India and Buddhism. Clarke pp 78–89

283   call a dream.' CW11 pp 559–60

283   brands of Christianity.' CW19 p 698

283   the Oriental spirit'. CW18 p 554

283   by Christianity's oppositions.' CW12 p 23

283   decidedly masculine deity.' CW12 p 22

284   of real insight.' CW13 pp 16–17

284   only be psychological.' CW18 p 747

284   whom is Chinese'. CW13 p 11

284   and his spirit.' Mircea Eliade interview in *Encounter* Mar 1980

284   Hermeticism and mysticism. Mircea Eliade 'Alchemy: An Overview' in Mircea Eliade (ed.) *The Encyclopedia of Religion* vol 1 New York 1987

284   his own ideas'. Gopi Krishna *Kundalini for the New Age* ed. Gene Kieffer New York 1988 p 43, cited in *Kundalini* p xlv

285   exactly right either.' Joseph Needham *Science and Civilisation in China* Cambridge 1956

285   they may be'. CW13 p 25

285   consciousness and life. CW13 p 24

285   of the personality.' CW13 p 34

285   somewhere outside ourselves.' CW13 p 36

286   from joyful happenings.' CW13 pp 45–6

286   that was alchemy.' Marie-Louise von Franz 'Library'

286   continuity with Gnosticism.' *MDR* p 231/209

286   call active imagination' CW12 p 346

286   in psychological treatment'. CW9 part 2 pp 184–221

286   doctoral thesis (1901–2). *Merkur* p 49

287   of his time'. Marie-Louise von Franz intro to Barbara Hannah *Encounters with the Soul: Active Imagination as Developed by C. G. Jung* Boston 1991 pp 1–2, and *Merkur* pp 37–8 and 49–52

287   existence of archetypes, Letter to H. Flournoy 29 Mar 1949

288   an extraordinary extent.' Letter to M. Serrano 31 Mar 1960

288   time on alchemy, Ruth Bailey in Glin Bennet interview

288   of the psyche. Toni Wolff 'A Few Words on the Psychological Club Zurich and on Professor Jung's Work since 1939' reprinted in *Harvest* vol 36 (1990)

288   real spiritual longing.' Letter to M. Lasky 19 Oct 1960

288   the external world. CW8 pp 319–37

288   being without soul' p 51

288   of the Church. CW18 p 166

289   completion of the self.' Letter to H. Murray 11 Jan 1929 in Robinson p 152

289   of everyone present.' Elizabeth Sergeant *Speaking* pp 53–4

289   by the dreamer. *Dream Analysis* part 1 p 3

289   understand its language.' CW18 p 82

290   out their dreams. *Speaking* p 89

290   success of marriage'. Elizabeth Sergeant *Speaking* p 54

290   come to life.' Fordham in 'Memories'

290   a sympathetic audience. Hannah pp 194–8

291   his magic wand. CW9 part 1 pp 291–2

291   such different epochs. Champernowne p 33

291   in her life. Ibid pp 33–4

292   edited by Keyserling, Hermann Keyserling (ed.) *Mensch und Erde* Darmstadt 1927

292   of the amoeba'. Ibid p 152

292   product without history'. CW18 p 227

292   hexagrams from memory. Anthony pp 55–6

292   Freud and Janet', *Speaking* p 39

292   Protestants and Jews. Ibid pp 40 and 45

292   time, the neuroses'. Ibid pp 43–4
293   disturbances is removed'. Ibid pp 43–5
293   can do now.' Letter to W. Conti 12 Sep 1929
293   from inside me! Brome p 201
294   all too familiar.' Emma Jung 'How Does One's Psychological Type Affect
      Relations with Other People?' Lecture to Psychology Club translated by
      Winifred Neie. Typescript. Kristine Mann Library
294   enormous psychic loss.' CW10 p 126
294   were very decided. Hannah p 191
295   dog or me?' Ibid p 192
295   after the cars. Hannah Ibid p 198
295   is not meat.' Linda Donn, drawing on interviews with Franz Jung, Donn
      p 16
296   to teach you!' Hannah p 199
296   another medieval gesture. Helena Henderson in Jensen p 117
297   of the East'. CW16 pp 53–75

Chapter Twenty-Six: The Purity of Divine Dirt

298   own lost wholeness'. Hannah p 196
298   be so stupid.' Hannah 'Glimpses'
299   maintaining its vitality. CW15 pp 98–103
299   and reproductive consciousness! CW15 pp 111–23
299   woman, I didn't.' Letter to James Joyce quoted in Ellmann p 629
299   of the Antichrist. CW14 p 324
299   he was doing'. CW14 p 324
300   hatred of hysterics.' quoted in CGJ's *Letters* vol 1 p 75
300   decided moral improvement.' Letter to H. Walpole 15 Aug 1930
300   in the room. *Speaking* pp 50–6
300   denied themselves before'. *Visions: Notes of the Seminars Given in 1930–34* p 413
300   of primitive psychology.' *Spring* 1960 pp 107–8
301   and Christian mysteries. Douglas *Mirror* pp 78–9
301   of the problem'. *Spring* 1960 p 10
301   the real thing.' *Visions Seminars* p 2
301   higher suprapersonal consciousness.' Jung's lecture on 'Indian Parallels' 7 Oct
      1931 cited by Sonu Shamdasani in intro to *Kundalini* p xxiii
301   of inner experience'. Ibid p xxix
301   down by Christianity'. CW11 pp 529–37
301   of personality changes'. Ibid pp 529–37
301   contains extensive annotations. Shamdasani p xxvi
302   opposites are joined. Coward p 113, and Heinrich Zimmer (ed.) Joseph
      Campbell *Philosophies of India* Princeton, New Jersey, 1951 pp 584–5
302   very nice chap' both cited in Shamdasani intro pp xxxii–xxxiii
302   no general confusion. Meier interview with Shamdasani, intro p xxxiv

302 you are pointing'; Letter to W. Hauer 20 Nov 1931 cited in Shamdasani
     p xxxv
302 view and yoga', Letter to W. Hauer 30 Nov 1931 cited in Shamdasani
     p xxxvi
302 on permanent display. Shamdasani p xxxviii
302 point of view.' Shamdasani p xxxix
303 of Zen initiations'. Margaret H. Case (ed.) *Heinrich Zimmer: Coming into His
     Own* Princeton 1994 pp 43–7
303 energy in them. Coward p 110
303 but canalised current.' H. Zimmer *Philosophies of India* p 579
303 mystery of woman'. Mircea Eliade *Yoga: Immortality and Freedom* London
     1989 p 202
304 and sexual intercourse. H. Zimmer *Philosophies of India* p 572
304 in either way. Sonu Shamdasani intro p xliii
304 the suprapersonal processes.' *Kundalini* p 70
304 psyche from above.' Ibid p 67
305 of divine dirt. Letter from John Layard to Anthony Stadlen 17 Oct 1968 cited
     in Shamdasani p xxix
305 the only reality. *Kundalini* pp 67–8
305 of religious experiences.' Ibid pp 26–7
305 from psychical reasons.' Ibid p 46
305 affairs of state'. Letter to F. Kunkel 10 Jul 1946
306 of one person.' *Visions Seminars* vol 7 p 7
306 and killed himself. Douglas *Translate* pp 209–11
306 very peculiar way.' *Visions Seminars* p 438
306 couldn't touch them.' *Visions Seminars* p 1258
306 her dreams and visions. Douglas intro to *Visions Seminars*
306 this into account. Robinson p 207
307 the book beforehand'. CW7 pp 111–12, CW16 pp 330–7, CW18 pp 145–6

Chapter Twenty-Seven: Hitler Is a Medicine Man

308 of natural justice. Isaiah Berlin *The Proper Study of Mankind* ed. Henry Hardy
     and Roger Hausheer London 1998 pp 243–5
309 the natural environment'. CW10 pp 67–70
309 kept no copies, *Letters* vol 2 p 10
309 in my favour!' Hannah p 205
309 into an office. Marie-Jeanne Schmid FCL
309 is just sickening.' Marie-Jeanne Schmid FCL
310 to inanimate objects. Ibid
310 is a fool.' Henry Fierz in Jensen p 17
310 of my tower.' Ibid pp 15–18
310 mystical, otherworldly, untroubled.' Margaret Gildea in Jensen p 23
311 tries to interpret. Ljunggren

311 its subterranean prison". CW10 pp 13–14

311 or medicine man. CW18 pp 569–71

312 aligned German edition. Martine Gallard

312 not be 'corroded'. Matthias von der Tann 'A Jungian Perspective on the Berlin Institute for Psychotherapy; A Basis for Mourning' in the *San Francisco Jung Institute Library Journal* vol 8 no. 4

312 'in the Führer'. Ibid

312 of the race'. *Speaking* pp 60–5

313 all intelligent people'. CW10 p 1014

313 "a fair trial".' *Essays on Contemporary Events* pp 83–4

313 the significant whole. *Zentralblatt* vol 7 nos 1–2

313 found its leader.' *Wirklichkeit der Seele* Zurich 1934 p 180 cited by Stanley Grossman in *Jung in Contexts: A Reader* ed. Paul Bishop London 1999

314 if you prefer.' 'Psychology of Dictatorship' interview with Jung in *Living Age* cccli Sep 1936–Feb 1937 cited by Grossman

314 a friendly chat. Fordham 'Memories' in *JAP*, and Samuels *Political* p 303

314 of the Jews'. Letters to R. J. Z. Werblowsky 28 Mar 1951

314 classmates to Bollingen. Hannah p 215

315 home completely happy.' *Matters of Heart*, Begg, and Anthony p 65

316 course I'll come.' Anthony p 71

316 middle of each. John Layard FCL

316 hands on her. Jolande Jacobi FCL

316 off the ground. McGuire *Bollingen* pp 27–8

Chapter Twenty-Eight: This Jewish Gospel

317 the Oxford Movement'. Letter to van der Hoop 2 March 1934

317 the situation in Germany', mentioned in Jung's letter to A. Maeder 22 Jan 1934

317 knowledge or permission. Letter to Oluf Bruel 19 Mar 1934

317 the racial psychologists'. *Neue Zürcher Zeitung* 27 Feb 1934

317 Jews at all?' CW10 p 541

318 from other people". Letter to A. Pupato 2 Mar 1934

318 but only once. AJ UM

318 his 'affiliation' openly.' Thomas Mann entry for 14 Mar 1934 in *Diaries 1918–1939* London 1983 p 201

318 a limited extent. CW10 pp 165–6

318 of the psyche.' Letter to C. Jensen 29 May 1933

319 stuff also occurs', Letter to Freud 17 Oct 1911

319 as his host'. CW10 pp 165–6

319 intellectually and morally. Mann *Diaries* p 235

319 always a half-Nazi'. Letter from Mann to Rudolf Humm 24 Sept 1942, quoted by Paul Bishop in ' "Literarische Beziehungen haben nie bestanden"? Thomas Mann and C. G. Jung' in *Oxford German Studies* no. 23 (1994)

319   against the Chinese.' CW7 p 152
320   to the government. Letter to W. M. Kränefeldt 9 Feb 1934 in Maidenbaum
        and Martin p 108
320   than all science.' Samuels *Political* p 300
320   in any soil.' Letter to E. Neumann 22 Dec 1935
320   *in Modern Thought*, 1929
320   sins to people.' Letter to A. Roback 19 Dec 1936
320   to their religion'. Letter to W. Hauer 7 Jun 1937
320   and 'Jewish psychology'. Jeffrey Masson *Against Therapy: Emotional Tyrrany
        and the Myth of Psychological Healing* New York 1989
321   a higher humanity.' Letters to J. Kirsch 26 May 1934
321   their own nature. Letter to G. Adler 9 Jun 1934
321   statement as anti-Semitic. Ronald Hayman *Writing Against: A Biography of
        Sartre* London 1986 pp 212 and 427
322   person was absent. Hildegard Kirsch 'Crossing the Ocean: Memoirs of Jung'
        Psychological Perspectives 6 (1975)
322   to the visions. *Notes to Seminars* vol 2 p 3
322   mad – *Ecce Homo* – CW1 pp 82–103
323   have unburdened myself'. Nietzsche letter to Franz Overbeck 9 Feb 1883
        Ronald Hayman *Nietzsche* London 1980 p 256
323   I am lost.' Letter to Franz Overbeck 25 Dec 1882 Hayman p 254
323   lethal,' says Zarathustra. Part One 'On Reading and Writing'
323   work of art.' CW15 p 55
324   what is creative.' Part Two 'On Self-Conquest'
324   and above humanity.' p 1090
324   at mildest – exploiting.' *Beyond Good and Evil* section 259
324   a higher order. Ibid section 269
324   what they do.' *On the Genealogy of Morals* section 10
324   a 'new faith'. *Kommende Gemeinde* vol 5 nos. 2–3 Jul 1933
325   invited to Eranos. McGuire *Bollingen* p 26
325   the other diving'. Jung in 1953 interview, Ellmann p 680
325   of my soul.' 1953 interview
325   of her disease. Letter to Patricia Graecen (Patricia Hutchins, author of *James
        Joyce's World* London 1957) 29 Jun 1955
325   the nineteenth century.' CW15 p 37
326   quantity of energy'. Ibid
326   of the review. Book review in *Die Neue Rundschau* vol 45 no. 2
326   repression for sublimation. Letter to Hesse 18 Sep 1934
326   but by grace.' Hesse *Briefe* Frankfurt 1965 p 126ff
326   are in abeyance.' Letter to Hesse 1 Oct 1934
326   and beaten up'. CW18 pp 173–4
327   about archetypal material'. CW18 pp 174–5
327   was analysing Pauli, Layard FCL
327   of the unconscious. Erkelens

327 to the dreamer.' CW12 p 42
327 of personal relationships.' Layard FCL
327 his only guidance.' CW18 p 285
327 with Erna Rosenbaum. Marie-Louise von Franz interview in *Psychological Perspectives* no. 24 (1991)
328 of the East.' *Notes to Seminars* vol 1 p 44
328 same time content'. Ibid p 103
328 or psychic states. CW15 p 56
328 the soul's needs.' CW11 p 42
328 and trans-temporal character'. CW8 p 413
328 as Erna Rosenbaum. Statement made by Franca Pauli to D. Lindorff cited in Lindorff *JAP*
329 experience in life. *Briefwechsel* p 10
329 a single person'. Letter to W. Pauli 29 Oct 1934
329 and strive for. CW8 p 405
329 in its end'. CW8 p 408
329 unconscious psychic activity.' CW8 p 409
330 space and time. CW8 p 413
330 states of possession.' Letter to F. Pfafflin 10 Jan 1939

Chapter Twenty-Nine: The Thieves Were Redeemers

331 on its own.' CW10 p 547
331 an Austrian group.' CW10 p 558
331 tolerable existence possible.' Letter to Pastor Ernst Jahn 7 Sept 1935
332 of the Church.' Letter to Jolande Jacobi 24 Jun 1935
332 not need him. CW18 p 162
332 shared religious confession'. Letter to anon recipient 7 Sep 1935
332 prognosis to match'. Letter to Pastor Walter Uhsadel 18 Aug 1936
332 'represent' Toni Wolff. AJ UM
332 hear a poltergeist. Hannah pp 232–3 and Hans Kuhn FCL
332 *Psychology and Alchemy*, Reprinted as CW12
332 words the "unconscious" ', CW12 p 43
333 blocks their view. CW12 p 48
333 of the unconscious', CW12 p 52
333 of the unconscious.' CW12 p 54
333 *vom philosophischen Stein. Geheime Figuren der Rosenkreuzer, aus dem 16 und 17. Jahrhundert* Altona 1785–8 2 vols
333 such an employee. CW12 pp 67–92
333 Christian spiritual tradition. Charles Rycroft *Psychoanalysis and Beyond* London 1985 p 113
334 must exclude thinking.' CW18 p 17
334 is the *hunch*.' CW18 p 18
334 anything might enter.' CW18 pp 20–1

334 new about ourselves'. CW18 p 21
334 instance, tax-collectors.' CW18 p 24
334 all the same.' CW18 p 42
335 control by willpower. CW18 pp 43–5
335 function is inferior', CW18 p 48
335 is functionally moving'. CW18 pp 57–62
335 innervation of the skin. CW18 p 71
336 of the complexes?' CW18 p 72
336 characters he creates.' CW18 p 73
336 in these manifestations.' Ibid
336 mere anthropomorphic idea. CW18 pp 82–3
336 redeemers of mankind . . . CW18 p 97
336 to be independent.' CW18 p 98
337 his particular situation.' CW18 p 103
337 would be higher. CW18 p 104
337 centre of it. CW18 pp 122–3
337 think about desires. CW18 pp 125–6
337 is not myself.' CW18 p 126
337 vast historical storehouse". CW18 p 127
338 taboo to them.' CW18 p 128
338 through mutual unconsciousness'. CW18 pp 141 and 168
338 is no resisting it.' CW18 p 164
338 a new analyst. Fordham 'Memories' and FCL
338 had on arrival. Hannah p 236

Chapter Thirty: The Incompetent Mind of the Masses

339 with mythological motifs. CW9 part 1 p 58
339 lies to hand.' Ibid p 63
340 is inspired, really.' Letter from Eleanor Du Vivier to Mary Foote 24 Feb 1936
340 do with him.' Ibid
340 rage and frenzy. CW10 pp 185–9
340 a new world.' FCL
341 in a pogrom.' FCL
341 won the argument. Jaffé 'Eranos'
341 archive at Eranos. Jaffé 'Eranos'
342 to have visions.' Anthony p 73
342 Murray defended him. Andrew Samuels Political p 295
342 for some time'. Gershon Scholem (ed.) The Correspondence of Walter Benjamin and Gershon Scholem 1932–40 pp 197–203, cited in Samuels Political pp 295–6
342 of the mind. CW18 p 564
342 is really great'. Speaking p 88
342 the Delphic oracle.' Ibid pp 92–3
342 if never before.' Speaking pp 94–5

343 fallen autumn leaves'. CW18 p 575
344 disadvantage of others.' Ibid p 580
344 General Franco's army.' CW18 p 567–79
344 withdrew to Figueras. Statement of 15 Feb 1939 *Notes to Seminars* vol 2 part 2 p 1542
345 of being hanged. Carpenter pp 85–101
345 themselves and others'. Alfons Paquet *An der Schwelle: Bericht über die Arbeitswoche des Kongener Kreises in Königsfeld vom 1. bis 7. Januar 1937* ed. Rudi Daur Heilbronn 1937 p 47
346 these crazy people. Ibid
346 them a chance.' C. A. Meier FCL and interview with Linda Donn in Donn p 22
346 and to society.' Interview with H. R. Knickerbocker in *Speaking* p 132
346 to be called. AJ UM
346 alteration of consciousness'. CW11 pp 6–8
347 curse of pathology.' Letter to P. W. Martin 20 Aug 1945
347 God and man'. CW11 pp 58–61
347 of individual revelation'. CW11 pp 15–21
347 excess of tension'. CW11 p 49
347 also by heredity'. CW11 p 50
347 in the individual.' CW11 pp 50–1 and Nietzsche *Human All Too Human* Part I
348 brothers of Christ. *Speaking* pp 95–8, but dated wrongly here
348 'ever-repeated typical experiences'. CW7 pp 66–70
348 to the archetypes.' CW8 p 158
348 of our ancestors'. CW8 p 99
348 the old paths'. CW8 p 112
348 of 'inborn images'. CW7 p 188
348 in form only.' CW9 Part 1 p 155
348 and his shirt. Robert Grimell 'Jung at Yale' in *Spring* 1976
349 of Dr Jung?' Fowler McCormick FCL
349 not the last.' CW10 pp 516–17
349 himself is nature'. CW11 p 534
350 blankness and emptiness'. *MDR* p 306/280
350 call a dream'. CW11 pp 560–1
350 never seriously disputed.' CW11 p 499
350 of mysterious truths. CW10 pp 528–9
350 a white surface.' CW11 p 577
350 its own abolition.' CW11 pp 577–8
351 as 'this clod'. CW10 pp 578–83
351 nature brings me.' *MDR* pp 305/278–9
351 before each one. *MDR* pp 308–9/282
351 to bony coarseness.' CW10 pp 520–1
352 floors in temples. Fowler McCormick FCL

352 the determining principle. CW10 pp 316–20

352 figure of Christ. Walther Uhsadel *Evangelische Seelsorge* 1936. Jung *Letters* vol 1 p 236 n 1

352 to endure misery.' Letter to V. Subramanya Iyer 16 Sep 1937

352 his later years.' Fowler McCormick FCL

353 Jung until 1934. Liliane Frey FCL

353 do with you?' John Layard FCL

354 of the Transference'. CW16 pp 223–40

Chapter Thirty-One: The German Psychosis

357 centuries have built.' *MDR* pp 311–13/284–6

358 the old commandments. CW11 pp 179–89

358 he had inherited. Stein p 108

359 to him again. Vladimir Rosenbaum FCL

359 of psychological analysis'. CW10 p 565

359 guests were invited. Letter to J. H. van der Hoop 14 Jan 1946

360 of the day', Samuels 'National Psychology'

360 interpolate Nazi propaganda. Fordham 'Memories'

360 in the *Zentralblatt*. *Zentralblatt* vol XI (1939) 1–2 p 2

360 disrespect for ceremony.' Fordham 'Memories'

360 a cool answer'. Michael Molnar (ed.) *Freud's Diary* London 1992 p 245

361 war comes, wait.' *Speaking* pp 117–34

361 a hundred francs. Hannah pp 235 and 258

362 that last night.' Ibid p 259

362 for some days.' Ibid p 260

363 do with it?' McGuire 'Affinities'

363 of mystical learning', Mellon p 163

363 opposed this idea, Erlo van Waveren FCL

363 to kick out.' Mellon p 164

363 and absolutely unapproachable.' Hannah pp 262–4

363 was 'God's instrument'. Ibid pp 262–5

363 the German Psychosis.' Letter to H. Crichton-Miller 2 Sep 1939

364 to be analysts. Mellon p 158

364 sense of humour.' Ibid p 165

364 provisionally,' Jung wrote. Letter to E. Harding 28 Sep 1939

364 Jung and Emma. Jaffé 'Details'

365 of the way'. CW15 pp 41–8

365 of being insulted.' Letter to Robert Loeb 26 Aug 1941

365 risk their lives. Letter to Gottlieb Duttweiler 4 Dec 1939

365 to fight others'. Letter to Erdo van Waveren 25 Sep 1946

Chapter Thirty-Two: Trinity + Devil = Quaternity

374 men, twin Jungs', Schoenl p 11

374 to you, Mary.' Letter from M. Mellon to Jung 26 Jul 1941 in Schoenl pp 14–15

375 Dr Jung, Mary'. Letter from M. Mellon 26 Nov 1941

375 be wound again. Letter to M. Mellon 31 Jan 1942

375 'from above downwards'. CW13 pp 111–64

376 intends towards man.' CW15 pp 6–30

376 for a woman.' Jolande Jacobi FCL

377 feel human again.' Letter to Mrs A. Crowley 20 Dec 1941

377 with enemy aliens. Letter from M. Mellon 25 May 1942

377 without Hitler's consent? Joachim C. Fest *Hitler* London 1971 p 701

377 stayed in Switzerland. Marie-Louise von Franz p 64

378 of empirical science? Letter to Arnold Künzli 4 Feb 1943

378 odds with himself.' Letter to Arnold Künzli 28 Feb 1943

378 ready for use. Letter to Arnold Künzli 16 Mar 1943

Chapter Thirty-Three: What Happens After Death

379 and never reached.' Letter to Kristine Mann 1 Feb 1945

379 coast of Africa. Letter to M. Fierz 12 Jan 1949

379 for his return. Lilian Frey-Rohn quoted in Brome p 143

380 at that moment. Hannah p 278

380 about his condition. Ibid p 279

380 by his illness. Ibid

380 loss of meaning.' Letter to anon correspondent 11 Jul 1944

381 absent from it. *MDR* 330–3/302–4

381 also by Jung. Molly Tuby interview with the author Apr 1995

381 of the Allies. Hannah p 284

381 the putsch failed'. Bancroft 'Jung and His Circle' pp 122–5

382 of Church doctrine'. Letter to H. Irminger 22 Sep 1944

382 in the club. Aryeh Maidenbaum 'Lingering Shadows: A Personal Perspective' in Maidenbaum and Martin pp 296–7

382 on all sides'. Letter to Kristine Mann 1 Feb 1945

382 two or three. Liliane Frey FCL

383 are hopeless psychopaths.' *Speaking* pp 149–55

383 by evil spirits. CW10 pp 194–217

383 throughout the world.' Mellon p 170

384 at least civilisation.' Letter to Pastor H. Wegmann 12 Dec 1945

384 in the head.' Letter to P. Bachler 8 Mar 1948

384 may have meant.' Baldwin Sawyer in Jensen p 77

384 or unfavourable form. Letter to Hans Meyer 30 Jan 1946

385 truths of philosophy. Lammers pp 35 and 278–9, and Charet 'Dialogue'

385 is gigantic indeed.' quoted in Jung's Letter to Victor White 5 Oct 1945

385 boredom and loathing.' Note by White cited by Cunningham

Chapter Thirty-Four: Call Me C.G.

395   or a god.' Letter from V. White 3 Jan 1948
395   fundamental Taoist ideas.' Letter to V. White 21 May 1948
396   objective as well.' Letter to Jolande Jacobi 8 Jul 1947
396   to your estates.' Hannah pp 295–6
396   training and research. Paul Bishop 'Rascher'
396   analyst Ludwig Binswanger. Anthony pp 1–3
396   Franz and others. CW18 pp 471–6
397   own serpent side.' Sheila Moon in Jensen pp 121–2
397   in my own.' Jensen pp 36–8
397   central since then.' Ibid p 124
398   the dreaming area. van der Post pp 55–6
398   similar to mine.' Letter to Esther Harding 8 Jul 1947
398   won't cut it." ' Speaking p 180
398   in his presence.' Dorothy Sawyer in Jensen pp 79–81
398   softly but tightly.' Letter to V. White 16 Dec 1948
398   inferior function behaves.' Letter to V. White 8 Jan 1949
399   its 20 horsepower.' Letter to Alwine von Keller 2 Jan 1949
399   honour it deserved. CW18 pp 591–9
399   of the sages.' Letter to anon correspondent 25 Oct 1935
399   right,' he said. Letter to Hugo Charteris 9 Jan 1960
399   decided not to, letter to W. Lay 20 Apr 1946
399   of our sexuality.' CW4 pp 319–20
399   simple, too naive.' CW4 p 301
400   development of consciousness'. CW4 pp 319–20
400   long ancestral history.' CW4 p 302
400   way? That's awful!' Max Zeller in Jensen p 108
400   robust and energetic, Charles Baudouin in Speaking pp 190–1
400   asked the question.' Peter Lynn in Jensen p 42
401   the analytic community.' Joseph Wheelwright in Jensen pp 106–7
401   'a new authoritarianism'. Saturday Review of Literature 11 and 18 Jun 1949
401   man's metaphysical foundation'. Letter to Dorothy Thompson 23 Sep 1949
401   will register there.' Letter to H. Murray 2 and 18 Jul 1948

Chapter Thirty-Five: Jesus and Satan Are Brothers

402   come out right.' Jaffé Last Years
403   liable to argue. Ruth Bailey in Spring 1986
403   of the opposites.' White manuscript cited by Cunningham
404   the mystic Adam', CW9 part 2 p 36
404   of the Antichrist. CW9 part 2 pp 45–50
405   of the doctrine. Letter from W. Pauli to Markus Fierz 11 Oct 1953 cited in
        Laurikainen pp 110–11
405   calls for cure.' V. White in Dominican Studies vol 2 Oct 1949
405   am a heretic,' Letter to V. White 31 Dec 1949

405   experiences in Africa. Buffie Johnson in Jensen pp 35–6
405   that did it.' Mircea Eliade FCL
406   the room above. King p 261
406   and unrecognisable urges. Letter to Herbert Read 2 Sep 1960 in King p 294
406   time and space'. Letter to Pastor W. Arz 17 Feb 1933
406   in human life'. Letter to W. Arz 10 Apr 1933
406   synchronicity but collaborated. Letter to W. Pauli Jun 1949
407   been seriously misunderstood. Atmanspacher and Primas p 118
407   archetypal, acausal ordering'. Atmanspacher and Primas p 120
407   the synchronicity disappears. Letter from W. Pauli *Briefwechsel* pp 44–5
407   fields of associations'. V. White p xviii
407   of the archetype'. Letter to Z. Werblowsky 17 Jun 1952
408   not quantitative – relationships. Letter to 'Dr H' 30 Aug 1951
408   most primitive superstition'. Letter from W. Pauli to Markus Fierz in
      Laurikainen pp 144ff and 225ff
408   sometimes teaches them.' Letter to Emma Jung from W. Pauli 16 Nov 1950
408   a common rose-chafer. CW18 pp 525–6
408   of radioactive substances. Lindorff
409   framework for therapy'. Marie-Louise von Franz 'Love, War and
      Transformation'
409   Faculty of Philosophy.' Letter from W. Pauli to von Franz 18 Apr 1951 in
      Erkelens
409   give his associations. Erkelens and von Franz 'Love, War and Transformation'
      in *Psychological Perspectives*
409   of a psychic statistic.' Letter from W. Pauli to M. Fierz 25 Dec 1950
409   the psycho-physical problem.' Leter from W. Pauli 17 May 1952
410   no real ideas.' Letter to A. Jaffé 29 May 1951
410   under certain conditions'. Letter to S. Wieser 6 Jul 1951
410   even an evildoer.' *Speaking* pp 225–6
410   New Testament one?' Letter to Pastor H. Wegmann 6 Dec 1945
410   Frend and psychoanalysis.' Stein p 163
410   and the floor. *MDR* pp 244–6/221–4
410   a liver disorder. Letter to Dr H 30 Aug 1951
410   like an earthquake.' Ibid
411   came into existence.' Letter to A. Jaffé 18 Jul 1951
411   story of Job? CW11 pp 365–6
411   "Sons of God".' CW11 p 357
411   Garden of Eden. CW11 pp 392–3
411   Neck, New York. *Pastoral Psychology* vol VI no. 60 Jan 1956
411   the left Satan'. CW11 pp 357–8
411   Christ the younger.' CW11 p 313
412   his Ten Commandments, CW11 p 376
412   not *compos mentis*. CW11 p 404
412   lack of reflection. CW11 p 383 and n

413 become human himself.' CW11 p 405
413 a master workman'. CW11 p 391
413 to become man.' CW11 p 397
413 fits of rage'. CW11 pp 408–11
414 paragon of goodness. CW11 pp 418–9
414 the evil angel.' CW11 p 434
414 apprehends his being.' Letter to Pastor J. Amstutz 28 Mar 1953
414 for becoming conscious'. Letter to anon correspondent 3 Aug 1953
414 vials of wrath.' CW11 p 461
414 of the kind.' Letter to J. Vontobel-Ruosch 28 Apr 1959
414 of "my people" '. Anthony Storr, interview with Jung on 14 April 1951 in
        Storr *Feet* p 96
415 chance is involved'. CW8 p 520
415 and extrasensory perception. Wilson pp 113–14
416 facts in time'. CW8 pp 530–1 and letter to J. R. Smythies 29 Feb 1952
416 of the universe.' CW15 p 9
416 fields of knowledge'. Letter to Olga Fröbe-Kapteyn Aug 1951 in Jaffé 'Eranos'
416 the seminar room.' Besse Bolton in Jensen pp 113–14
417 through the window. Camille Flammarion *The Unknown* London 1920
        pp 191–202 and CW8 p 430
417 the appropriate things. Albertus Magnus *De mirabilis mundi* and CW8 p 448
417 Nazism, Communism, etc.' Letter to Horst Scharschuck 1 Sep 1952
417 made some miscalculations. CW8 p 475
418 without a brain.' CW8 p 505
418 outside the body. CW12 pp 279–82
418 from a brain.' Letter to Alice Eckstein 16 Sep 1930

Chapter Thirty-Six: She Was a Queen

419 really Israel too.' Letter from E. Neumann 5 Dec 1951 in *Letters* vol 2 p 33
419 deny him admission.' Letter to E. Neumann 5 Jan 1952
419 about the *facts*'. Letter from V. White 5 Apr 1952 in *Letters* vol 2 p 51
420 even a nonsense'. Letter to V. White 9 Apr 1952
420 different philosophical climates.' Letter from V. White 20 Apr 1952 in *Letters*
        vol 2 p 58
420 a necessary opposite'. Letter to V. White 30 Apr 1952
420 such an undertaking.' Letter to Dorothee Hoch 3 Jul 1952
421 the psychical hinterland'. CW9 part 2 p 154
421 are therefore psychological', CW11 p 511
421 archetypal God image', CW11 p 160
421 semi-satanic demiurge. Martin Buber 'Religion and Modern Thinking'
        Merkur Feb 1952, Maurice Friedman *Encounter on the Narrow Ridge: A Life of
        Martin Buber* New York 1993 pp 354–6 and Edward Whitmont 'Prefatory
        Remarks to Jung's "Reply to Buber" ' *Spring* 1973

421 by the Pope'. CW18 pp 663–6
422 them in faith'. Friedman p 358
422 God has appeared.' Letter to B. Lang 14 Jun 1957
422 must answer "no".' Ibid
422 get along with.' Letter to Aniela Jaffé 9 Jul 57
422 believe. I know.' *Speaking* p 428
422 that he exists.' Interview with F. Sands in the *Daily Mail* 29 Apr 1955
422 a decent tool.' Letter to V. White 30 Jan 1948
423 this compelling force.' Letter to Lucas Menz 28 Mar 1955
423 very much so!' Letter to P. Hilty 25 Oct 1955
423 with his grandfather. Andreas and Lorenz Jung FCL
423 narrowly missed Andreas. Ibid
423 spirits would cooperate. Wolfgang Baumann FCL
423 work from me.' Letter to Valerie Reh 28 Jul 1952
423 suffered from tachycardia. Letter to J. Perry 24 Feb 1953
424 writing a week. Letter to Aniela Jaffé 9 Sep 1953
424 smoking as mine.' Hannah p 312
424 to the candidates.' speech by C. Meier at her funeral
424 he resumed working. Una Thomas FCL
424 of his study, Bennet *Meetings* p 67
424 any other man. Lilian Frey FCL
424 of a broken heart, Molly Tuby interview with the author April 1995
425 brink of eternity.' Letter to Aniela Jaffé 9 Sep 1953
425 of the self? Letter from V. White 8 Nov 1953
425 invalidation of Christ. Letter to V. White 24 Nov 1953
425 good/evil as such.' White 'Good and Evil' *Harvest* 1966
425 transcends everyday contradictions. Cp Cunningham 'Victor White, John Layard and C. G. Jung'
426 for all things.' Letter from V. White 10 May 1955
426 it so badly.' Letter from V. White 17 Mar 1955 in *Letters* vol 2 p 238
426 should be suspended. Heisig 'Theology'
426 without his clothes.' Victor White 'Jung on Job' in *Blackfriars* vol 36 Mar 1955. These passages were cut when the review was reprinted in White's book *Soul and Psyche*, but Adrian Cunningham quotes them in 'Victor White, John Layard and C. G. Jung'.
426 us in Küsnacht'. Letter to V. White 2 Apr 1955
427 under any obligation.' Letter to V. White 6 May 1955
427 work and friendship.' *Letters* vol 2 p 251
428 a latent psyche'. CW8 pp 226–34
429 the other rubbish. Jaffé *Life and Work* pp 99–104 and Bennet *Meetings* p 109
429 *in the Skies*. CW10 pp 309–433
429 note of warning'. CW10 p 311
429 a *living myth*', CW10 p 322
429 a widespread myth'. CW10 p 320

429   therefore a symbol'. CW10 pp 324 and 328–9
429   epiphany from heaven'. CW10 pp 406–7
430   or the Buddha'. CW10 p 410
430   and living mediator.' CW10 p 414
430   man's higher development'. CW10 pp 344–5
430   this any longer.' CW10 p 415
430   the right of Emma. Bennet *Meetings* pp 53–6
431   off at Rapperswil.' Mary Crile in Jensen p 114
431   with the music. Bennet pp 53–6
431   by five runs. *British Medical Journal* 27 Aug 1955
431   in the air.' Bennet pp 59–60
431   she was dead. Adrian Baumann FCL
432   little old man.' Frieda Fordham FCL
432   in a hut. Frieda Fordham FCL
432   on the family. Ruth Bailey FCL
432   *anything* about it'. Hannah p 325
432   was all right.' Aniela Jaffé FCL. She gave an interview in December 1969, but
       withdrew it and substituted a written statement, from which she had cut
       many of her more personal remarks.
432   devotion and obedience.' Mr and Mrs Walther Willi-Niehus FCL
432   contained 'archaic vestiges'. CW10 pp 439–40
432   the animal psyche'. CW10 p 448
432   evil spirit, etc.' CW10 p 447
433   and some kirsch. Bennet *Meetings* pp 99–100
433   way of life.' Elizabeth Osterman in *Speaking* pp 162–3
433   in the earth.' Ibid pp 202–4 interview with Hans Carol 1950
433   were penetratingly observant.' Serrano pp 48–9
433   to the chemist. Ruth Bailey FCL

Chapter Thirty-Seven: Mythification and Auntification

434   in persuading him. Elms pp 55–6 and Jacobi interview FCL
434   the *Basler Stadtbuch*. Steiner pp 126–8
434   fable, *my* truth.' MDR p 17/10
435   was 'the Jaffé enterprise'. Steiner p 117
436   credited with authorship. Shamdasani 'Omissions'
436   adolescent religious preoccupations. Letter from R. Hull to A. Jaffé 9
       Sep 1961 Elms p 61
437   typed but composed. A. Jaffé FCL and Shamdasani 'Omissions'
437   a honey pot'. A. Jaffé 1972
438   truck with convention. AJ UM
438   the English text. MDR p 133/119
438   and less unstable. AJ UM
439   the building collapse.' MDR p 45/56

440 her until 1897. AJ UM
441 interwoven with miracles.' Kathleen Raine in the *Listener* 22 Aug 1963 cited in Shamdasani 'Omissions'
441 what to do. AJ UM
441 were virtually excluded. AJ UM
442 Jung already had. AJ UM
443 costs be avoided. *MDR* pp 360–1/331–2
443 created the world. *MDR* p 365/336
443 over the decades'. *MDR* p 371/341
443 and casual transformation'. *Letters* vol 1 p 494
444 to us miraculous. Letter to E. Neumann 10 Mar 1959

Chapter Thirty-Eight: When You Come to the Other Side

445 attitude would be.' Letter to V. White 21 Oct 1959
445 the *opus magnum*.' Letter to a Mother Superior 6 Feb 1960
445 clash and quarrel.' Victor White 'Theological Reflections' *Journal of Analytical Psychology* vol 5 no. 2 Apr 1960
445 later he died. *Letters* vol 2 p 555
446 her presence felt. AJ UM
446 could do that.' Ruth Bailey in *Spring* 1986
446 drive, we eat.' Fowler McCormick FCL
447 get any better.' Mary Crile in Jensen p 114
447 the Unus Mundus. Letter to M. Serrano 14 Jan 1960 in Serrano p 68
447 childishness in comparison.' Letter from Nietzsche to Franz Overbeck Sep 1888 in Hayman *Nietzsche* p 326
447 it held firm.' *MDR* p 201/180
447 more general level.' Letter to M. Serrano 14 Sep 1960
448 and scratch it.' John Boe in interview with John Freeman in the *San Francisco Jung Institute Library Journal* vol 8 no. 4
448 to be done.' Fowler McCormick FCL and letter from A. Jaffé to Vaun Gillmor 14 Jun 1961 Kristine Mann Library
448 and ZEN teaching.' Letter from A. Jaffé to Vaun Gillmor 14 Jun 1961
449 I did so.' Fordham 'Memories'
449 the other side.' Ruth Bailey in *Spring* 1986
449 time to time.' Letter from A. Jaffé to Vaun Gillmor 1961
449 wanted to say. Adrian Baumann FCL
450 slept most time. Letter from A. Jaffé to Vaun Gillmor 1961
450 wholeness and oneness'. Serrano p 104
450 'That's Father grumbling.' Ruth Bailey in *Spring* 1986

Bibliography

Abbreviations

AJ   Aniela Jaffé

CW   Collected Works

FCL   The Francis A. Countway Library. The Jung Collection in its Rare Books Department at the Harvard Medical Library contains about 140 transcriptions of unpublished interviews by Gene Nameche with people who knew Jung. Most of the interviews were recorded on tape in 1969–70, and some of the transcriptions are not yet available for consultation, but most of them are.

JAP   *Journal of Analytical Psychology*

MDR   *Memories, Dreams, Reflections*

SE   *Standard Edition* (of Freud's collected works)

Speaking   *C.G. Jung Speaking*

UM   unused material

Works by Jung

The Collected Works ed. Herbert Read, Michael Fordham and Gerald Adler trans R.F.C. Hull. 20 vols London and Princeton 1957–79

vol A. *The Zofingia Lectures*

Modern Man in Search of a Soul trans W.S. Dell and Cary Baynes London 1933

Notes to Seminars ed. William McGuire 3 vols (vol 2 is in 2 parts) London and Princeton 1984–90

1 *Dream Analysis (1928–30)*

2 *Nietzsche's Zarathustra*

3 *Analytical Psychology (1925)*

The Psychology of the Unconscious: A Study of Transformations and Symbols of the Libido trans Beatrice Hinkle London 1916

The Psychology of Kundalini Yoga: Notes of the Seminar Given in 1932 ed. Sonu Shamdasani London 1996

Visions: Notes of the Seminars Given in 1930–34 ed. Claire Douglas London 1998

Letters ed. Gerhard Adler in collaboration with Aniela Jaffé 2 vols London and Princeton 1973–6

The Freud/Jung Letters ed. William McGuire trans Ralph Manheim and R. F. C. Hull London and Princeton

C. G. Jung/Aniela Jaffé *Memories, Dreams, Reflections* trans Ralph and Clara Winston London 1963

Other Works

H. C. Abraham and E. L. Freud (eds.) *The Freud-Abraham Letters 1907–26* London 1965

Emile Ammann 'Driving Miss Edith' *Spring* 1992

Maggy Anthony *The Valkyries: The Women around Jung* Shaftesbury 1990

Lisa Appignanesi and John Forrester *Freud's Women* London 1982

Harald Atmanspacher and Hans Primas 'The Hidden Side of Wolfgang Pauli: An Eminent Physicist's Extraordinary Encounter with Depth Psychology' *Journal of Consciousness Studies* vol 3 no 2 1996

Ruth Bailey 'Domestic Life with C.G. Jung' Interview with Glin Bennet in *Spring* 1986

Mary Bancroft, *Autobiography of a Spy* New York 1983

Ean Begg *C.G. Jung 1875–1962* A radio programme compiled and presented by Ean Begg BBC Radio 3, 27 Jul 75

—'Jung's Lost Lieutenant: Jung's Friendship with Maurice Nicoll' *Harvest* 1976

E. A. Bennet *C.G Jung* London 1961

—*Meetings with Jung: Conversations Recorded during the Years 1946–61* Zurich 1982

Paul Bishop *The Dionysian Self: C.G. Jung's Reception of Friedrich Nietzsche* Berlin and New York 1995

—'Jung's Use of Kant' in *Journal of European Studies* (1996) vol xxvi

—'C.G. Jung, Hans Trüb und die "Psychosynthese" ' *Analytische Psychologie* 1996 vol 27

—'On the History of Analytical Psychology: C.G. Jung and the Rascher Verlag' 2 parts *Seminar* Oct and Nov 98

Robert W. Brockway *Young Carl Jung* Wilmette, Illinois, 1996

Vincent Brome *Jung* London 1978

—*Ernest Jones: Freud's Alter Ego* London 1982

Ian F. Brown (ed.) *Methods of Treatment in Analytical Psychology* Fellback 1980

John C. Burnham and William McGuire (eds.) *Jelliffe: American Psychoanalyst and Physician and His Correspondence with Sigmund Freud and C.G. Jung* Chicago 1983

Aldo Carotenuto *A Secret Symmetry: Sabina Spielrein between Jung and Freud 1984*

—*Sabina Spielrein: Tagebuch einer heimlichen Symmetrie: Sabina Spielrein zwischen Jung und Freud* Freiburg 1986

Humphrey Carpenter *W.H. Auden: A Biography* London 1981

Jean Cazeneuve *Lucien Lévy-Bruhl* Oxford 1970

Irene Champernowne *A Memoir of Toni Wolff* San Francisco (CGJ Inst) 1980

F. X. Charet *Spiritualism and the Foundations of C.G. Jung's Psychology* Albany, New York, 1993

—'A Dialogue between Psychology and Theology: The Correspondence of C.G. Jung and Victor White' *JAP* vol 35 no 4 Oct 90

Ronald W. Clark *Freud: The Man and the Cause* London 1980

J. J. Clarke *In Search of Jung* London 1992

Harold Coward *Jung and Eastern Thought* New York 1985

Adrian Cunningham 'Victor White, John Layard and C.G. Jung' *Harvest* 1992 vol 38

James Donat 'Is Depth Psychology Really Deep? Reflections of the History of Jungian Psychology' *Harvest* 1994 vol 40

Linda Donn *Freud and Jung: Years of Friendship, Years of Loss* New York 1988

Claire Douglas *The Woman in the Mirror: Analytical Psychology and the Feminine* Boston 1990

—*Translate This Darkness: The Life of Christiana Morgan* New York 1993

Henri F. Ellenberger *The Discovery of Consciousness: The History and Evolution of Dynamic Psychiatry* London 1970

Alan C. Elms *Uncovered Lives: The Uneasy Alliance of Biography and Psychology* New York 1994

Herbert van Erkelens 'Wolfgang Pauli's Dialogue with the Spirit of Matter' *Psychological Perspectives* no 24, 1991

Joachim C. Fest *Hitler* London 1974

Michael Fordham *The Fenceless Field* London 1977

(ed.) *Contact with Jung: Essays on the Influence of His Work and Personality* London 1963

—'Memories and Thoughts about C.G. Jung' *JAP* vol 20 no 2 Jul 75

John Forrester *Language and the Origins of Psychoanalysis* London 1980

Marie-Louise von Franz *C.G. Jung: His Myth in Our Time* New York 1975

—'C.G. Jung's Library' *Spring* 1970

—'Love, War and Transformation' An Interview. *Psychological Perspectives* 24, Spring–Summer 1991

Sigmund Freud and Wilhelm Fliess *The Complete Letters of Sigmund Freud and Wilhelm Fliess 1887–1904* ed. Jeffrey Moussaieff Masson London 1985

Martine Gallard 'Jung's Attitude During the Second World War in the Light of the Historical and Professional Context' *JAP* vol 39 no 2 Apr 94

Peter Gay *Freud: A Life for Our Time* London 1988

Wolfgang Giegerich 'Jung's Betrayal of His Truth' *Harvest* vol 44 no 1 1998

Naomi R. Goldenberg *Returning Words to Flesh: Feminism, Psychoanalysis and the Resurrection of the Body* Boston 1996

William B. Goodheart: 'C.G. Jung's First "Patient": On the Seminal Emergence of Jung's Thought' *JAP* vol 29 no 1

Nathan G. Hale (ed.) *James Jackson Putnam and Psychoanalysis: Letters between Putnam, Sigmund Freud, Ernest Jones, Sándor Ferenczi and Morton Prince* Cambridge, Mass.

Barbara Hannah *Jung: His Life and Work* London 1977

—'Some Glimpses of the Individuation Process in Jung Himself *Quadrant* no 16 Spring 1974

John Haule 'Jung's "Amfortas Wound": *Psychological Types* Revisited' *Spring* 53

Ronald Hayman *Nietzsche: A Critical Life* London 1980

—*Thomas Mann: A Biography* London 1996

James Heisig *Imago Dei: A Study of C.G. Jung's Psychology of Religion* Cranbury, New Jersey 1979

—'Jung and Theology: A Bibliographical Essay' *Spring* 1973

Joseph Henderson 'C.G. Jung: A Reminiscent Picture of His Method' *JAP* Jul 75 vol 20 no 2

James Hillman *Revisioning Psychology* New York 1975

Renate Hofer *Die Hiobsbotschaft C. G. Jungs: Folgen sexuellen Misbrauchs* Lüneburg 1993

Jolanda Jacobi *The Psychology of C.G. Jung* New Haven, 1973

Aniela Jaffé trans R. F. C. Hull *From the Life and Work of C.G. Jung* London 1972

—*C.G. Jung: Word and Image* Princeton 1979

—*Jung's Last Years and Other Essays* Dallas 1984

—'C.G. Jung and the Eranos Conference' *Spring* 1977

—(ed.) trans Krishna Winston *C.G. Jung: Word and Image* Princeton 1979

—'Creative Phases in Jung's Life' *Spring* 1972

—'Details about C.G. Jung's Family' *Spring* 1983

Ferne Jensen (ed.) *C.G. Jung, Emma Jung, Toni Wolff: A Collection of Remembrances* San Francisco 1982

Ernest Jones *Free Associations* London 1959

Walter Kaufmann *Discovering the Mind* vol 3 New York 1980

Tina Keller 'Beginnings of Active Imagination: Analysis with C. G. Jung and Toni Wolff 1915–1928' *Spring* 1982

John Kerr *A Most Dangerous Method: The Story of Jung, Freud and Sabina Spielrein.* London 1994

James King: *The Last Modern: A Life of Herbert Read* New York 1990

Hildegard Kirsch 'Crossing the Ocean: Memoirs of Jung' *Psychological Perspectives* 6 (1975)

Arthur Koestler *The Act of Creation* London 1964

Ann Conrad Lammers *In God's Shadow: The Collaboration of Victor White and C.G. Jung* New York 1994

K. V. Laurikainen *Beyond the Atom: The Philosophical Thought of Wolfgang Pauli* trans Eugene Holman New York 1988

John Layard Autobiography 1967 version unpublished. Mandeville Department of Special Collections, San Diego Library, University of California

D. Lindorff 'One Thousand Dreams: The Spiritual Awakening of Wolfgang Pauli' and 'Psyche, Matter and Synchronicity: A Collaboration between C.G. Jung and Wolfgang Pauli' *JAP* vol 40 no 4 Oct 95

Magnus Ljunggren *The Russian Mephisto: A Study of the Life and Work of Emilii Medtner* Stockholm 1994

William McGuire *Bollingen: An Adventure in Collecting the Past* 1982

—'The Arcane Summer School' *Spring* 1980

—'How Jung Counselled a Distressed Parent' *Spring* 1981

—'Firm Afinities: Jung's Relations with Britain and the United States' JAP vol 40 no 5 Jul 95

William McGuire and R. F. C. Hull eds. *C.G. Jung Speaking: Interviews and Encounters* Princeton 1977

Frank McLynn *Carl Gustav Jung* London 1996

Aryeh Maidenbaum and Stephen A. Martin (ed.) *Lingering Shadows: Jungians, Freudians and Anti-Semitism* Boston 1991

C. A. Meier *Soul and Body: Essays on the Theories of C.G. Jung* Santa Monica, San Francisco 1986

—(ed.) *Wolfgang Pauli und C.G. Jung: ein Briefwechsel* Berlin 1992

Paul Mellon *Reflections in a Silver Spoon* New York 1992

Dan Merkur *Gnosis: An Esoteric Tradition of Mystical Visions and Unions* Albany, New York 1993

Mark Micale (ed.) *Beyond the Unconscious* Princeton 1993

Joseph Mileck *Hermann Hesse: Life and Art* Los Angeles 1978

Lewis Mumford 'The Revolt of the Demons' *New Yorker* 23 May 1965

Friedel Elisabeth Muser *Zur Geschichte des Psychologischen Clubs Zurich bis 1928* Zurich 1984, privately reprinted from the annual report of the Psychology Club

Marilyn Nagy *Philosophical Issues in the Work of C.G. Jung* New York 1991

Richard Noll *The Jung Cult: Origins of a Charismatic Movement* Princeton 1994

—*The Aryan Christ: The Secret Life of Carl Jung* New York 1997

Albert Oeri 'Some Youthful Memories of C.G. Jung' *Spring* 1970

Renos K. Papadopoulos and Graham S. Saayman (eds.) *Jung in Modern Perspective: The Master and His Legacy* Bridport, Dorset, 1961

Andrew Paskauskas (ed.) *The Correspondence of Sigmund Freud and Ernest Jones* London 1993

Wolfgang Pauli und C.G. Jung: ein Briefwechsel ed. C. A. Meier Berlin 1992

Laurens van der Post *Jung and the Story of Our Time* London 1977

James Jackson Putnam *Letters* Cambridge, Mass. 1971

Forrest G. Robinson *Love's Story Told: A Life of Henry A. Murray* Cambridge, Mass. 1992

S. Rosenzweig *The Historical Expedition to America (1909): Freud, Jung and Hall the King-maker* St Louis 1994

Joel Ryce-Menuhin (ed.) *Jung and the Monotheisms; Judaism, Christianity and Islam* London 1994

Andrew Samuels *Jung and the Post-Jungians* London 1985

—*The Political Psyche* London 1993

—'National Psychology, National Socialism and Analytical Psychology' *JAP* Apr 1992 vol 37 no 2

—with Bani Shorter and Fred Plaut *A Critical Dictionary of Jungian Analysis* London 1986

—(ed.) *The Father: Contemporary Jungian Perspectives* London 1985

Leon Schlamm 'C.G. Jung's Ambivalent Relationship to the Hindu Religious

Tradition: A Depth-Psychologist's Encounter with 'The Dreamlike World of India' *Harvest* 1948 vol 44 no 2

William Schoenl *C.G. Jung: His Friendships with Mary Mellon and J.B. Priestley* Wilmette, Illinois, 1998

Stephen Segaller and Merrill Berger *The Wisdom of the Dream: The Word of C.G. Jung* Boston 1989

Miguel Serrano trans Frank MacShane *C.G. Jung and Hermann Hesse: A Record of Two Friendships* London 1966

Sonu Shamdasani *Cult Fictions: C.G. Jung and the Founding of Analytical Psychology*. London 1998

—'A Woman Called Frank' in *Spring* no 50 1990

—'Memories, Dreams, Omissions' in *Spring* 1995

—'From Geneva to Zurich: Jung and French Switzerland' *JAP* vol 43 no 1 Jan 1998

—'Is Analytical Psychology a Religion?' paper read to Society of Analytical Psychology, London at conference on 'Is Analytical Psychology a Religion?' February 1999

—'Psychoanalysis Inc.' in Roger Cooter and John Pickstone (eds.) *Medicine in the Twentieth Century* forthcoming

Iulian K. Shchutskii *Researches on the I Ching* New Jersey 1979

Robert C. Smith *The Wounded Jung: Effects of Jung's Relationships on his Life and Work* Evanston, Illinois, 1996

Murray Stein *Jung's Treatment of Christianity: The Psychotherapy of a Religious Tradition* Wilmette, Illinois 1985

Gustav Steiner 'Erinnerungen an Carl Gustav Jung' *Basler Stadtbuch* 1965 ed. Fritz Grieder, Valentin Lötscher and Adolf Portman, Basel 1965

Paul Stepansky *Freud: Appraisals and Reappraisals* New Jersey 1988

Anthony Storr *Feet of Clay: A Study of Gurus* London 1996

—'Is Analytical Psychology a Religion?' paper read to Society of Analytical Psychology, London at conference on 'Is Analytical Psychology a Religion?' February 1999

Eugene Taylor 'William James and C.G. Jung' *Spring* 1980

Stephanie de Voogd 'C.G. Jung: Psychologist of the Future, "Philosopher' of the Past' *Spring* 1977

Hans H. Walser 'An Early Psychoanalytic Tragedy – J.J. Honegger and the Beginnings of Training Analysis' *Spring* 1974

Gerhard Wehr *Jung: A Biography* trans David M Weeks Boston 1988

Joseph B Wheelwright Interview with D. Serbin *Psychological Perspectives* vol 15, no 2

Victor White *God and the Unconscious* London 1952

Colin Wilson *Lord of the Underworld: Jung and the Twentieth Century* Wellingborough, 1984

Toni Wolff 'A Few Thoughts on the Process of Individuation in Women' *Spring* 1941

B. Zabriskie 'Jung and Pauli: A Subtle Asymmetry' *JAP* vol 40 no 4 Oct 1995

Stefanie Zumstein-Preiswerk *C.G. Jungs Medium* Munich 1975

Material on Film and Video

Interview with Richard I. Evans 1957. Segaller Films 1990. Selection by Merrill Berger

Jonas Mekas *Dr Carl C. Jung or Lapis Philosophorum*. Arthouse Inc. 1996 Produced from an unfinished film made in 1950 by Jerome Hill

Suzanne Wagner *Matters of Heart*. A film conceived and written by Suzanne Wagner, directed and edited by Mara Whitney. Produced by Michael Whitney. Executive producer George Wagner

Werner Weick *Carl Gustav Jung: Artist of the Soul* Mystic Fire Video. 1997 English-language version of the Italian video produced in 1991

Index